RECREATION ECONOMIC DECISIONS:

COMPARING BENEFITS AND COSTS

Richard G. Walsh
Colorado State University

Venture Publishing, Inc.
State College, Pennsylvania

Cover Design by Sandra Sikorski

Production Assistance by Bonnie Godbey

Library of Congress Catalogue Card Number 86-50932

ISBN 0-910251-15-0

Distributed outside North America
by E & F N Spon Ltd.
11 New Fetter Lane
London, England EC4P 4EE

Contents

Preface

This book is a definitive and indispensable money-saving guide for managers of public and private recreation resources serving consumers taking day outings, overnight trips, and vacations. It summarizes and makes accessible in one place the principal lessons learned in 25 years of applied recreation economics. Based on the latest and most reliable research, this book shows how to make recreation programs as beneficial as possible at the lowest possible cost.

There are two key features of the book that I believe make it different and better than other recreation economic books and in combination will make it useful in training planners and managers.

First, throughout the book there is continuing discussion of decision making as the process of comparing the benefits and costs of alternatives. This emphasis will help managers make better economic decisions — to organize their thoughts, think things through, and form plans having the best possible results.

Today's managers are part of the first generation with ready access to desktop computers and software packages. In an information age, it is important to devote some time and effort in deciding what to compute. It is now possible for managers to analyze their own programs' unique conditions of supply and demand. Managers will be able to see where they are going or, if their direction is unplanned, where they will end up.

Second, the topics considered include the economics of consumption, with emphasis on how consumer demand affects management. The book explores the fact that park and recreation programs have both direct and indirect output. This means that there are private benefits from recreation use and public benefits from knowing that the resources are protected. Understanding the implications of these two types of demand should help managers of park and recreation programs serve the dual purpose of protecting environmental resources and making them available for the enjoyment of people.

The subject of recreation economics has undergone extensive change in the last few decades. Before 1960, the principal topics for study included the trends in participation and growth of the tourist industry, private and public recreation expenditures, and their impact on regional employment and economic development. The chief concern was to meet the need for development of access roads and recreation facilities such as campgrounds and boat-ramps at new reservoirs and parks. We were all growth oriented then. Since that time we have become aware of the complexity of growth in the tourist industry. With the renewed emphasis on accountability, a special concern about the benefits of expenditures on recreation programs has developed. Recreation planners and managers are faced with the problem of allocating increasingly scarce resources among competing uses. As a result, they are interested in improving the application of economics to assist in the decision making process.

In recent years, the two major themes that have emerged in the professional literature on recreation economics have been a growing understanding of the nature of consumer demand and the comparison of benefits and costs in resource allocation decisions. Application of the economic concept of demand, with an intellectual history dating at least from Marshall's writings in 1890, was applied to recreation by Clawson and Knetsch in 1966, and has since been extended by many others. The work has established an empirical basis for the concept of willingness to pay and established it as an acceptable economic measure of individual benefits (i.e., consumer surplus) from recreation activities. The application of economics to government and business expenditure decisions has an equally long history, but entered a new era with comparison of the benefits and costs of recreation programs during the 1970s.

I have included the new emphasis in this book. Much of the material on the economics of consumption and the methods of measuring benefits and costs cannot be found elsewhere outside of the professional economic literature. I believe that emphasizing these topics, which reflect recent developments, will contribute to the discussion of current policy issues. It illustrates the role of economics in recreation resource decisions. Throughout, I have illustrated the concepts and methods of economics with examples drawn from existing parks and recreation programs.

This book consists of three major sections. In the first, we establish an appropriate framework for consumer decision making and present the unique definitions of quantity and price appropriate to recreation. A distinguishing characteristic of recreation presented in Chapter 2 is that, for the most part, the consumer is the producer, providing inputs of time and effort as well as dollars. The general problem is to combine these resources along with the natural environment in proportions that result in the most benefits. Chapter 3 presents two additional features of recreation. First, it is a human activity, and thus, the quantity consumed is measured in terms of the number of occasions or amount of time that individuals choose to participate. Second, recreation programs have both direct and indirect output. The latter refers to the fact that the general public benefits from knowing that the resources are protected. In Chapter 4, a realistic proxy for the price of recreation is defined as direct travel and time costs.

The second section focuses on the demand for recreation. Chapter 5 describes in simple and direct terms the nature of a demand curve.

One of the most important applications of empirical demand studies is to estimate economic benefits. Learning how to calculate benefits from a demand curve will enable you to provide useful information for recreation economic decisions. Chapter 6 illustrates how to derive a demand curve from a demand function, and demonstrates how statistical demand functions provide estimates of the shifts in demand curves with changes in nonprice variables. Chapter 7 includes a discussion of the present state of knowledge about the determinants of demand: characteristics of users, attractiveness of sites, availability of substitutes, travel time, and congestion. While this list may change with advances in knowledge, most observers today believe that without information on these variables, it is impossible to accurately estimate demand for a recreation site. Chapter 8 describes the three methods used to measure the benefits of recreation activities and resources authorized by the federal guidelines. These are the travel cost, contingent valuation, and unit day value methods. While any one of these may provide a satisfactory measure of the benefits of a recreation project, it is important to understand when each method should be used and how to improve the accuracy of results.

Chapters 9-12 illustrate a toolbox of economic methods, starting with fairly simple elasticities of demand, adding such complexities as how to treat outcomes that are uncertain or that have consequences over future time periods, and regional economic impacts on income and employment. Elasticities are widely used in recreation economic decisions because of their simplicity and convenience. When an elasticity is multiplied by an expected percentage change in a variable, it gives an estimate of the expected change in demand. Consumption of recreation may be particularly risky because the experience cannot be examined before its purchase and consumers searching for variety tend to try new destinations.

The regional economic activity generated by recreation use is not the same thing as the value that people place on the resource. The concepts of economic impact and economic value ask two distinct questions. Recreation programs redistribute income to the regional economy of parks from other regions of the country. These changes in distribution represent transfers of income and are placed in a separate account. They are not benefits to the nation unless the region has long-run unemployment, which is sometimes the case in economically depressed recreation areas.

The third section shows how to compare the benefits and costs of recreation projects and programs. We begin with resource supply and costs of recreation development in Chapter 13 and put demand and supply curves together in Chapter 14, to show how the price and the output of recreation is determined by public and private enterprise. We describe the three methods used to estimate costs: engineering economic, cross-sectional, and time-series. In Chapter 15, we introduce the concepts of discounting and net present value, which enable us to make systematic comparisons between benefits and costs occurring at different times in the future.

Here we address the fundamental economic problem of governments throughout the world, i.e., how large the recreation program should be. How much should government tax and spend for recreation and parks? The comparison is between the value to the private sector of what it gives up to support a government recreation program (represented by taxes, user fees, and opportunity costs) and the value of the output that the government provides with the resources (represented by the willingness of citizens to pay for the government-produced opportunity, if they had to). A public recreation program can increase the welfare of society if the resources given up by the private sector are used to produce greater benefits than they would produce in the absence of the government programs. Comparing benefits and costs helps responsible public officials choose among alternative recreation programs and projects that vary in size, design, and purpose.

Readers will observe that although the chapters uniformly present the same basic approach, they vary somewhat in scope and level of treatment. These variations occur for several reasons, particularly the varying interests of the researchers involved in the subject matter, and the limited nature of economics. The latter is a result of the inability of social scientists to control the environment of their subjects, and the variation in training and perspective of researchers working on a particular topic.

The level of verbal and graphic exposition in this book is appropriate for introducing recreation economics to intelligent readers with a minimum of economic training. I have used simple algebra and multiple regression statistics to illustrate how to derive the empirical relationships expressed in a demand function. These sections of the book are optional and not essential to understanding the key ideas. The emphasis is on economic concepts, especially on the integration of consumer economics with the economics of decision making by private and public recreation resource managers. This emphasis carries over into the sections on demand and supply, where I have concentrated on the applied economic aspects of benefits and costs rather than on either theory or statistics. Overall, I hope the result is a book that challenges readers intellectually and focuses their attention on timely issues.

The work upon which this book is based was supported, in part, by Colorado State University and by the National Park Service, which provided a part-time appointment in its Science Branch, Planning Division, where many of the ideas were developed and tested in the parks planning process. I am indebted to many managers and researchers throughout the United States and around the world for their insights into aspects of recreation economic decisions. I would like to express my thanks to Becky Johnson, John Loomis, Bill Hansen, George Nez, John Hof, Dan Williams, and Jack Knetsch for commenting on preliminary versions of the manuscript, and to my colleagues, Ken Nobe, John McKean, Bob Young, Dave Seckler, and Donn Johnson, who offered many valuable suggestions for improvement.

Greatest of all, however, are the thanks due Jan Schweitzer, who edited the entire manuscript with skill, care, and remarkably good humor. The manuscript was typed efficiently by Denise Davis. To all of these individuals I express my thanks, as also to my wife, with whom I have discussed many of the problems and from whom I have had loyal support. Insofar as the work is still deficient, the fault is mine. As an applied economist, I do not deny that someone in economic theory could have written a more advanced book from the same material. However, like Parkinson, I maintain that a book on applied recreation economics had to be written sometime by somebody. The results should be considered tentative, of course, subject to improvement with further work.

Fort Collins, Colorado   Richard G. Walsh
July 1986

Chapter One

Introduction

This chapter defines the problem of managing recreation resources in a modern industrial economy that is becoming more information and service-oriented; introduces the basic approach to recreation economic decision making used throughout this book; and illustrates the subject matter to which it is applied.

Recreation is one of the largest industries in the United States. Expenditures on recreation goods and services account for more than 14 percent of personal consumption and 8 percent of the gross national product, according to estimates prepared by Bever for the Third Nationwide Outdoor Recreation Plan. Consumer recreation expenditures were more than $250 billion in 1982, exceeding spending on national defense and home construction. Recreation was the third largest retail industry in terms of sales and the second largest private employer.

There is a continuing debate over how to define the recreation industry and measure its output. We do not know what proportion of consumer spending is for the recreation use of parks and other recreation resources. Recreation activities include the various forms of entertainment and sports, indoors as well as outdoors. Recreation travel involves the payment for transportation services, recreation opportunities, food and beverages, lodging, and a variety of other products and services. It is clear that private recreation expenditures are much larger than those of government. All levels of government spend around $8 billion on parks and recreation programs, according to the 1982 Census of Government. This represents less than three-tenths of 1 percent of total government spending. Yet, government provides nearly half of the total outdoor recreation opportunities in the United States, an estimated 3.1 billion of a total 6.6 billion recreation visitor days.

The dollar amounts have changed substantially owing to changes in the purchasing power of the dollar. However, the relative importance of recreation spending has not changed appreciably. Most states rank tourism as one of their major industries, in particular such states as Florida, Hawaii, and Colorado. Consumer demand for recreation services offers many individuals the opportunity to operate their own small business. Ninety percent of private recreation companies are classified as small business, according to Owen, and they provide nearly 7 percent of total employment in the United States, a relatively high proportion of which represent seasonal part-time and less-skilled jobs suitable for the underemployed and hard-to-employ workers. Also, recreation contributes to solution of the nation's balance of trade problem, as spending by foreign tourists in the U.S. accounts for about 4 percent of our total exports of goods and services.

Every society is vitally concerned with the role of recreation and tourism. That concern is heightened by the 20th century industrial revolution. The forces of economic development have radically shifted the demand and supply of recreation resources in this century. On the demand side, the growth in population and per-capita income, the shorter work week, and improved transportation facilities have dramatically increased participation in recreation activities. From 1900 to 1980, population increased nearly three times and individual income, about 1.5 times. Leisure time increased as the average work week declined from nearly 60 hours at the turn of the century to less than 40 hours today. Improved auto transportation and air travel have made even remote recreation sites accessible to more and more consumers. Nesbit characterizes the 20th century as the "Age of Leisure," with reduced work weeks, expanded holidays and vacations, earlier retirement age, greater longevity, unemployed youth, growing social welfare rolls, and an increase in the number of affluent who live in resort communities during much of the year. As a result, Nesbit concludes that a larger number of people have "much more leisure than any population in history has ever had prior to our century."

On the supply side, private companies have responded to increased demand by providing more recreation goods and services at prices that reflect the conditions of demand and supply. However, increasing residential development and industrial exploitation of the natural environment have eliminated a large amount of land formerly available for recreation use. Environmental pollution also has contributed to the reduction in the quantity and quality of natural environment available for recreation. For example, McConnell and Sutinen report that some waterways, such as Long Island Sound and the Delaware Bay, once major water recreation areas, are no longer available for certain water sports because of pollution. In the western states, strip mining eliminates entire mountains, and mine tailings fill in the river valleys. The dwindling availability of land and water suitable for recreation use presents a challenge to the public interest in providing access to natural environments for recreation in the future.

Historically, governments (and many private landowners) have provided recreation resources free, with little or no formal consideration of benefits and costs. When demand was low, the cost of granting access for recreation was also low. However, as increased demand began to exceed supply, free access led to increased costs, including congestion and deterioration in the quality of the natural environment. Initially the response was to meet the need by developing more access roads and recreation facilities, such as campgrounds and boat-launching ramps at new reservoirs and parks. More recently, managers of both public and private recreation resources have become aware of the complexity of growth in recreation demand. With the renewed emphasis on efficiency in government, managers have become more concerned with the benefits of expenditures on recreation programs. As a result, increased attention has focused on comparing the benefits of proposed recreation programs to their costs and deciding which alternatives are most beneficial, given a limited budget for parks and recreation programs.

MANAGERIAL DECISION MAKING

The approach to decision making throughout this book is that of the decision maker who considers the benefits and costs of alternative recreation activities and programs, then chooses the most beneficial one possible at the lowest possible cost. This approach has been described by Stokey and Zeckhauser in their excellent book, *A Primer for Policy Analysis.* The authors begin by showing that the individual consumer or manager may perform the analysis or commission others to do parts or all of it. The decision maker may be an individual or a group, such as a family or division of a private company or public agency that acts essentially as a unit. Also, we will consider the situation in which several decision makers with conflicting objectives participate in a decision. The approach presented here should prove helpful to individuals who takes part in such a process of shared decision making, whether as members of a group deciding how to vote, or as managers trying to line up support for a proposal.

For example, what do you do when a complicated recreation policy issue lands on your desk? Suppose you are a manager in a California state park and recreation agency. You are directed to investigate the benefits and costs of alternative forest management programs in state recreation areas. Questions are raised about planting native or exotic species of trees, the use of controlled and natural fire, the eradication of forest insects, and the selective harvest of firewood in over-stocked stands. The problem has so many ramifications you wonder how you will ever sort them out — and even where to begin. You can always muddle along, hoping eventually to develop a feel for the situation, but such a hit-or-miss approach rather goes against the grain. Chances are that you would prefer to have a standard procedure that will at least help you make a start on digging into a complex policy issue.

Economists have experimented with several ways to structure problems like this one. They usually suggest the following five-part framework as a starting point. However, as you gain experience in thinking about the benefits and costs of recreation activities and programs, you

3

may wish to revise it to suit your own needs. The framework for decision making is as follows:

(1) Define the problem and objectives;
(2) Identify the alternative courses of action;
(3) Estimate the consequences of each alternative;
(4) Value their benefits and costs;
(5) Choose the most beneficial alternative relative to costs.

You will find this outline useful as a background for reading this book, to help you tie together the many concepts and methods that are considered. The concepts described in the following chapters should enable you to provide better answers to one or another of the questions that come up as you follow the five-step decision making approach. At every point as you work your way through the following chapters, ask yourself, "How does this concept fit into the overall picture?" You are beginning a steplike process analogous to the work of craftsmen who first make the legs, arms, backs, and seats of a chair. They experience satisfaction from seeing the chair take form step-by-step, and finally producing the finished chair.

Recreation Economic Decisions is meant to be an essentially practical work, emphasizing all aspects of benefits and costs in policy analysis. I want to get you thinking right away in terms of the benefit cost framework, especially if this is a way of thinking you find a bit unfamiliar. Therefore my perennial advise is "Practice!" Practice on all kinds of problems, large and small, public and private. Practice on your own recreation problems and decisions, using benefits and costs to get your thinking straight or to illuminate commonplace events. For example, when a friend or relative proposes a weekend trip to a resort area, think about the travel costs that will be shared and about the opportunity costs of foregone alternative leisure activities. Will your benefits offset your costs? When you find yourself waiting in line to enter a recreation event, ask yourself what it would cost to provide additional service capacity, and what the benefits of such a move would be.

Stokey and Zeckhauser suggest that we look regularly at the local newspaper and think about one of the policy problems featured. Perhaps a proposed plan to build a dam on a local river is under discussion. See if you can define the immediate objectives of the plan and their relationship to the underlying problem. Who would benefit and who would pay the costs, including the costs of foregone river recreation? What further information would you want? What benefits and costs would you include in an evaluation of the success of the proposed policy? On what basis should the decision be made? Should the plan be delayed or implemented sequentially?

Practice thinking informally in terms of benefits and costs in your day-to-day work. Imagine that you are taking part in the budgeting

4

process for an organization with which you are familiar. Consider what the organization's objectives are and what various expenditures would accomplish in terms of benefits. How should the budget available be allocated so as to provide the most benefits relative to costs?

PURPOSE

The purpose of economics is to increase the welfare or well-being of individuals in society, and each person is considered the best judge of how well off he or she is in a given situation. Both of these propositions follow the predominant Western moral tradition of recent centuries, which regards the individual as the ultimate objective of public policy. To economists, recreation is a part of the overall economic problem of how to manage our activities so as to best meet our needs and wants with scarce resources. This means that recreation managers who succeed will be those who stay in touch with consumer demand for their services. They will, in short, engage in a continuing effort to improve their recreation economic decisions.

The purpose of this book is to provide intelligent managers and prospective managers with an introductory guide to recreation economic decisions. The goal is to show how to make recreation as beneficial as possible at the lowest possible cost. Based on the latest and most reliable research, the book is a money-saving guide for managers of public and private recreation resources serving consumers taking day outings, overnight trips, or vacations. The focus is on individual users of recreation resources, and how their decisions affect management. This will help you make better managerial economic decisions — to organize your thoughts and think things through, to compare the benefits and costs of alternatives, and to formulate plans with the most satisfactory results.

The subject matter treated in this book includes:

(1) Consumer choice of recreation activities, such as picnicking, swimming, hiking, running, bicycling, camping, hunting, fishing, skiing, traveling, sightseeing, vacation home living, playing golf, tennis, and the like.

(2) Managerial decisions by private businesses to provide recreation goods and services. Services include lodging, food, beverage, air travel, tour packages, guides, ski lifts, campgrounds, tennis courts, and golf courses. Consumer goods include a great variety of equipment such as skis, hiking boots, backpacks, sleeping bags, tents, campers, cameras, boats, guns, fishing tackle, special clothing, bicycles, trail bikes, four-wheel-drive vehicles, golf clubs, tennis rackets, condominiums, and other retirement-vacation homes.

(3) Public agency planning to develop parks, beaches, access roads, and trails; to manage fish and wildlife; to protect natural and scenic resources; and to preserve the nation's cultural heritage of historic sites.

The people involved in decision making at these three levels of the recreation industry are interested in what can be learned from recent experience to improve recreation economic decisions. For example, how do choices of recreation activities differ from decisions to purchase recreation equipment? How much can a camper afford to pay for a travel trailer? How can economics help a tourist choose between a trip to Acapulco and a Caribbean cruise? Should a business executive in New York purchase a condominium in Florida, Hawaii, the French Alps, or the Rocky Mountains? How much do costs of resort development increase at high elevations or on seashores subject to extreme climatic conditions? Can standard building methods be used effectively? How does the seasonal nature of recreation activities affect the feasibility of investment by Hilton, Disney, Vail, and similar corporations? What is the difference between decision making by private and public agencies supplying recreation resources and facilities? What is the carrying capacity of a wilderness trail or a trout stream? What is the regional economic impact of alternative park development plans? How can public agencies measure the cost-effectiveness of historic and environmental preservation programs? What proportion of operating costs should be attributed to recreation use compared to environmental protection? What are the implications of these two objectives for user fee policies?

In presenting the proposed decision making framework, we will rely on economics as the basic approach. In this regard, we follow the lead of Becker whose book, *The Economic Approach to Human Behavior,* demonstrates that economics provides an effective way to organize the contribution of other subject matter to decision making. Studies of benefits and costs draw on a variety of disciplines, including the social sciences of psychology, sociology, and political science, on the one hand, and the physical and biological sciences of forestry, fishery, landscape architecture, and engineering, on the other. Indeed, this book is written for specialists in the technical aspects of managing parks and recreation, forests, wildlife, and related natural resources. While specialization in understanding the technical aspects of recreation resources and programs is of primary importance, managers also need to consider the economic principles of decision making. Thus, the emphasis in this book is on how decisions ought to be made, rather than on the details of information that should serve as inputs to the decisions. We will have little to say about the complementary disciplines, although we recognize their relevance to managing recreation resources.

6

Our concern here is with how decision makers should structure their thinking about recreation choices and with the economic concepts that will aid understanding and prediction. We emphasize the need to develop managerial skills to cope with the high risk economic environment in which the recreation industry is now operating and will continue to face in the future. Achieving a viable balance in response to both technical and managerial needs will be a major issue confronting public and private organizations for some time to come.

It is useful, for example, to think of recreation economics as a part of environmental economics. The natural environment is a resource that yields a variety of valuable services to individuals in their roles as consumers and producers, as outlined by Freeman. The environment can be used for recreation. It is the source of the basic means of life support — clean air and clean water — and provides the means for growing food. It is a source of energy, minerals and other raw materials, such as timber. It is the source of visual amenities, the habitat for fish and wildlife, and it can be used as a place to deposit wastes from production and consumption activities. The economic problem of the environment is that it is a scarce resource. It cannot provide all of the desired quantities of all of the services at the same time. Greater use of one type of environmental service usually means less of some others. Thus the use of the environment involves trade-offs, and it should be managed as an economic resource.

Consider, for example, the question of how much wilderness to protect as illustrated in Figure 1-1. The upper panel shows the total bene-

ubiquitous -
free to all
unlimited
unique - one -of -a-kind

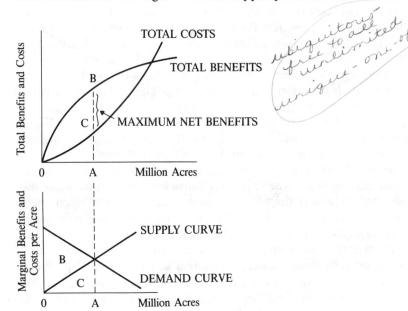

Figure 1-1. Optimum Amount of Wilderness Protection, United States

fits of wilderness compared to the total costs of wilderness protection including management and opportunity costs. The lower panel on the same figure shows the marginal benefits and costs derived from the totals in the upper panel. The marginal curves are simply the changes in value of the total curves resulting from changes in the amount of wilderness protected. They may be more familiar to you as demand and supply curves, with the best solution occurring where the two intersect, i.e., where supply equals demand. If the relationship between total and marginal benefits and costs is not familiar to you read the first section of chapter 5 on the demand for recreation trips.

For the first million acres, individual willingness to pay is likely to be high because of scarcity value, and the cost is likely to be low because of few alternative uses such as timber harvest or mineral and energy extraction. With further increases in wilderness protected, the willingness to pay for an additional million acres decreases, and the additional opportunity costs of alternative uses rise. As individual demands for wilderness are fully satisfied, the shape of the total benefits curve flattens out. Less suitable sites are protected, and the opportunity costs of alternative uses rise. The net benefits of wilderness protection are at a maximum where marginal willingness to pay equals marginal cost. This is the point at which wilderness designation should be set, from the viewpoint of economic efficiency. If wilderness protection is less than this amount, some potential benefits would not be realized. Designations of wilderness beyond this point would result in larger costs than the benefits they produce.

There are two points that should be made about this approach to the allocation of environmental resources. First, the amount of wilderness designated by this rule will almost never equal all of the potential wilderness areas. As the best areas are protected, the willingness to pay for additional wilderness designation will decrease, while the extra cost of further designation will be increasing. The extra cost of going from designation of 95 percent to 100 percent of potential wilderness areas may often be several times larger than the total cost of obtaining the first 95 percent. It will seldom be worth it in terms of willingness to pay, as our studies show (Walsh, Loomis, and Gillman).

The second point is that comparing benefits and costs does not require that citizens who benefit pay for those benefits or that individuals who ultimately bear the cost of wilderness designation be compensated for those costs. It is true that if the amount of wilderness designation is set so as to maximize net benefits, then the gainers could fully compensate the losers and still come out ahead. But when beneficiaries do not compensate losers, there is a serious political problem. Those who benefit call for evermore wilderness designation, because they obtain the benefits and bear few if any of the costs. Meanwhile, those who bear the costs in the form of foregone profits from timber harvest or mineral and energy development call for less wilderness designation.

In environmental economics, wilderness is considered a public good, as distinguished from private goods where individuals have effective property rights in land, labor, and capital, with markets to allocate resources to their highest valued uses. In private business, we rely upon profits and competition to furnish the necessary incentives and to make the necessary tradeoffs. While the system is basically sound in the case of private goods, it is virtually nonexistent for public goods. In government, we compare benefits and costs to help make choices among competing claims on scarce resources in a nonmarket context. From among the competing claims on our resources, we should choose those which contribute the most to our national objectives, and choose efficiently in order to free some of our scarce resources for other useful purposes.

The comparison of benefits and costs is often sufficient for use in decision making even though, for a number of reasons, measures may not be complete. For example, there may be long-run ecological values that are not included. It is difficult for biologists to predict what these might be let alone measure and incorporate them into economic estimates of value. In addition, there may be psychological values associated with recreation resources that exceed economic measures. Economic values are constrained by consumer income, availability of leisure time, and other variables. However, psychological values may not be so constrained. For these and related reasons, economic values represent conservative estimates of the total values to society. These limitations should be considered in applying economics to important decisions about future recreation resource use.

This wilderness example illustrates the basic economic approach to decision making at other levels of park and recreation management. You should read this section again and substitute some current problem familiar to you. Repeating this exercise should provide a personal basis for understanding the usefulness of economics in managing parks and other recreation resources.

SOURCE

The content of this book draws on previous work by others in economic decision making and in the economics of recreation. Its contribution is in organizing and relating the ideas presented. In 1959, Clawson published a pioneering work on the travel cost approach to the demand for recreation. He outlined the basic framework for a meaningful study of the demand for recreation, albeit based on the ideas of earlier economists, notably Hotelling. Applications that appeared fruitful to farsighted observers more than two decades ago are

9

well underway, enough so that this work on recreation economic decisions is possible. Much more research is needed, however, on the demand and supply of recreation before we will understand all of the pertinent relationships between benefits and costs. Thus, the material presented in this book should be viewed as a first approximation to be improved by further study.

The impetus for empirical work on the benefits and costs of recreation, like many other topics in environmental economics, stems from a small band of scholars at Resources for the Future, Washington, D.C., a nonprofit organization initially supported by the Ford Foundation. A pathbreaking book by Clawson and Knetsch, *Economics of Outdoor Recreation,* came out of Resources for the Future in 1966 and provides an excellent review of the history of economic thought and empirical research on outdoor recreation up to that time. It was supplemented by collections of case studies edited by Kneese and Smith, *Water Research,* and Krutilla, *Natural Environments.* These books were followed by Hammack and Brown, *Waterfowl and Wetlands: Toward Bioeconomic Analysis,* Krutilla and Fisher, *The Economics of Natural Environments,* Freeman, *The Benefits of Environmental Improvement,* Vaughan and Russell, *Freshwater Recreation Fishing; The National Benefits of Pollution Control,* Kneese, *Measuring the Benefits of Clean Air and Water,* and many other related works.

Each of these Resources for the Future books contains significant developments in the theoretical basis and empirical procedure appropriate for work on the benefits and costs of recreation. The theoretical and methodological contributions at Resources for the Future became the basis for a great deal of empirical work at universities and in government agencies, which has resulted in further advances in theory and method. Professional researchers from around the world also have contributed to our understanding of recreation economics.

National interest in recreation economics was stimulated by the 27 study reports of the Outdoor Recreation Resources Review Commission published in 1962. As a result of this work, Congress passed the Land and Water Conservation Fund Act in 1964, under which the federal government provides grants to the states for acquiring and improving parks and other recreation areas. The act requires that, to qualify, each state prepare a recreation plan based on studies of the demand and supply of recreation resources. This provision has stimulated research on recreation economics.

Also, in 1962, the federal government adopted uniform procedures to value the multiple output of resource development projects. Correctly based in welfare economics, Senate Document 97 stimulated the economic measurement of benefits and costs in planning water and related land resource development by federal agencies. In 1964, Supplement No. 1 to the senate document established the unit-day

10

value method for estimating the benefits of recreation. The Water Resources Council, an interagency committee of the U.S. government, authorized use of the travel cost method when the guidelines were revised in 1973, and again in 1979 when use of the contingent valuation method was approved. These methods were reauthorized in essentially the same form in 1983. They are expected to be reviewed and updated in future years. Throughout this book, we use the term federal guidelines to refer to the manuals of the Water Resources Council. They are listed at the end of this chapter.

The guidelines stimulated recreation economic research in several of the federal agencies. These include the water development agencies such as the Corps of Engineers, Bureau of Reclamation, and Soil Conservation Service. In addition, other agencies have relied on the guidelines in water and related land use planning. Those with limited application include the National Park Service, U.S. Forest Service, Environmental Protection Agency, and other federal agencies. Several of these agencies have prepared similar guidelines that apply to their particular resources. Also, some cities and states have used the federal guidelines in their recreation studies with comparable results.

We recommend that the federal guidelines be applied in the recreation and park programs of federal agencies, as they were intended. We also suggest that they be used in future recreation, wildlife, and environmental resource studies at all levels. It is especially important that state and local government and private companies adopt similar procedures. Recreation economic studies can be cheaply done by anyone with a desk-top computer. There is a need for use of uniform methods in order to compare the results of any two studies, as shown by Sorg and Loomis. The guidelines are not meant to be restrictive or constraining; rather, they encourage individual innovation with full explanation. They are periodically revised to include the best available economic research procedures. If the Water Resources Council were to be abolished, it would be essential that some other organization prepare acceptable guidelines for recreation economic research.

Recreation economics also has been encouraged by other legislation. In 1976, the Congress provided for comparing recreation benefits and costs in planning by the U.S. Forest Service and the National Park Service. In 1982, Congress provided a similar approach to valuing recreation and other output of the Bureau of Land Management. The economic value of the output of each agency is defined uniformly as net willingness to pay. This is the value of recreation to users, wildlife to hunters, forage to ranchers, irrigation water to farmers, timber to loggers, and minerals to miners. Congress wanted the economic value of alternative uses to be commensurate, meaning that they measure the same thing. The recreation economic values described in this book are intended to represent net willingness to pay and to be commensurate with the values of other resource uses.

11

SUMMARY

In this chapter, we introduced the framework for decision making that will be used throughout the book. The decision maker simply considers the benefits and costs of alternatives, then chooses the most beneficial one possible at the lowest possible cost. The essential steps are: (1) define the problem and objectives; (2) identify the alternative courses of action; (3) estimate the consequences of each alternative; (4) value their benefits and costs; and (5) choose the most beneficial alternative relative to costs.

Next we illustrated the subject matter to which this concept of decision making will be applied. Included are the: consumer choices of recreation activities; decisions by private businesses to provide recreation goods and services; and decisions by public agencies to develop recreation sites, manage fish and wildlife, protect natural and scenic resources, and to preserve the nation's cultural heritage of historic sites. The people involved in decision making at these three levels of the recreation industry are interested in what can be learned from recent experience to improve recreation economic decisions.

The content of this book draws on previous work by others in economic decision making and in the economics of recreation. Its contribution is in organizing and relating the ideas presented. Applications that appeared fruitful to farsighted observers more than two decades ago are well underway, enough so that this work on recreation economic decisions is possible. The comparison of benefits and costs is often sufficient for use in decision making even though, for a number of reasons, the measures may not be complete. The wilderness example illustrated the basic economic approach to decision making at other levels of park and recreation management.

Finally, we reviewed the legal basis for the recreation economic values described in this book. The Congress of the United States has established net willingness to pay as the basis for valuing recreation and other resource uses. We recommend that the federal guidelines be applied in future recreation economic studies by all levels of government — federal, state, and local — and by private companies. Use of uniform methods would provide comparable results.

The framework for decision making introduced in this chapter will help us tie together the many concepts and methods presented in each of the subsequent chapters. We shall refer to the framework when we look at each of its parts.

READINGS

Becker, Gary S. *The Economic Approach to Human Behavior.* University of Chicago Press, Chicago. 1976.

Bever, Thomas D. "The Importance of Recreation to the Economy." The Third Nationwide Outdoor Recreation Plan. Appendix IV, Private Sector Outdoor Recreation. Heritage Conservation and Recreation Service, U.S. Department of the Interior, Washington, D.C. 1979. 261-336.

Clawson, Marion, and Jack L. Knetsch. *Economics of Outdoor Recreation.* Johns Hopkins University Press, Baltimore. 1966.

Driver, B. L. (ed.). *Elements of Outdoor Recreation Planning.* University of Michigan Press, Ann Arbor. 1970.

Fisher, Anthony C. *Resource and Environmental Economics.* Cambridge University Press, Cambridge, England. 1981.

Freeman, A. Myrick, III. *The Benefits of Environmental Improvement.* Johns Hopkins University Press, Baltimore. 1979.

Freeman, A. Myrick, III. "The Ethical Basis of the Economic View of the Environment." The Morris Colloquium on Environmental Policy: Ethics and Economics. Dept. of Philosophy, University of Colorado, Boulder. 1982.

Hammack, Judd, and Gardner M. Brown, Jr. *Waterfowl and Wetlands: Toward Bioeconomic Analysis.* Johns Hopkins University Press, Baltimore. 1974.

Hicks, John R. *A Revision of Demand Theory.* Oxford University Press, London. 1956.

Hotelling, Harold. "The Economics of Public Recreation." *The Prewitt Report.* Land and Recreation Planning Division, National Park Service. U.S. Dept. of the Interior, Washington, D.C. 1949.

Irland, Lloyd C. *Wilderness Economics and Policy.* D. C. Heath and Company, Lexington, Mass. 1979.

Johnson, George M., and Peter M. Emerson, (eds.). *Public Lands in the U.S. Economy: Balancing Conservation and Development.* Westview Press, Boulder, Colo. 1984.

Jubenville, Allan, Scott C. Matulich and William G. Workman. "Toward Integration of Economics and Outdoor Recreation Management." Bulletin 68, Agricultural and Forestry Experiment Station, University of Alaska, Fairbanks. 1986.

Kneese, Allen V., and Stephen C. Smith, (eds.). *Water Research.* Johns Hopkins University Press, Baltimore. 1966.

Kneese, Allen V. *Measuring the Benefits of Clean Air and Water.* Resources for the Future, Inc., Washington, D.C. 1984.

Knudson, Douglas M. *Outdoor Recreation.* Macmillan Publishing Co. New York. 1980.

Krutilla, John V. (ed.). *Natural Environments: Studies in Theoretical and Applied Analysis.* Johns Hopkins University Press, Baltimore. 1974.

Krutilla, John V., and Anthony C. Fisher. *The Economics of Natural Environments.* 2nd Edition. Johns Hopkins University Press, Baltimore. 1985.

Loomis, John B., George Peterson, and Cindy F. Sorg. "A Field Guide to Wildlife Economic Analysis." *Transactions.* 49th North American Wildlife and Natural Resources Conference. Wildlife Management Institute, Washington, D.C. 1984. 382-92.

McConnell, Kenneth E., and John G. Sutinen. "A Conceptual Analysis of Congested Recreation Sites." Vol. 3, *Advances in Applied Micro-Economics.* V. Kerry Smith and A. D. Witte (eds.). JAI Press, Greenwich, Conn. 1984. 9-36.

McIntosh, Robert W, and Charles R. Goeldner. *Tourism: Principles, Practices, and Philosophies.* Fourth Edition. Grid Publishing Co., Columbus, Ohio. 1984.

Nesbit, Robert. *History of the Idea of Progress.* Basic Books, New York. 1980.

Owen, John D. *The Price of Leisure.* Rotterdam University Press, Rotterdam. 1969.

Sorg, Cindy F., and John B. Loomis. "Empirical Estimates of Amenity Forest Values: A Comparative Review." General Technical Report RM-107, Rocky Mountain Forest and Range Experiment Station, Forest Service, U.S. Dept. of Agriculture, Fort Collins, Colo. 1984.

Stokey, Edith, and Richard Zeckhauser. *A Primer for Policy Analysis.* W. W. Norton & Co., New York. 1978.

Thompson, Mark S. *Benefit Cost Analysis for Program Evaluation.* Sage Publications, Beverly Hills, Calif. 1980.

U.S. Dept. of the Interior. "The Third Nationwide Outdoor Recreation Plan, Appendix II." Survey Technical Report 4. Heritage Conservation and Recreation Service. Washington, D.C. 1979.

U.S. Water Resources Council. "Policies, Standards, and Procedures in the Formulation, Evaluation, and Review of Plans for Use and Development of Water and Related Land Resources." 87th Congress, Second Session, Senate Document 97. Washington, D.C. May 1962.

U.S. Water Resources Council. "Evaluation Standards for Primary Outdoor Recreation Benefits." Supplement No. 1 to Senate Document 97. Washington, D.C. June 1964.

U.S. Water Resources Council. "Principles, Standards, and Procedures for Water and Related Land Resource Planning." *Federal Register* 38(Sept. 10, 1973):174, Part III.

U.S. Water Resources Council. "Procedures for Evaluation of National Economic Development (NED) Benefits and Costs in Water Resources Planning." *Federal Register* 44:242(Dec. 14, 1979):72,950-65.

U.S. Water Resources Council. "Economic and Environmental Principles and Guidelines for Water and Related Land Resource Implementation Studies." Sup. of Doc., U.S. Govt. Print. Off., Washington, D.C. 1983.

Van Doren, Carlton S., George B. Priddle and John E. Lewis, (eds.) *Land and Leisure: Concepts and Methods in Outdoor Recreation.* 2nd Edition. Maaroufa Press, Inc., Chicago. 1979.

Vaughan, William J., and Clifford S. Russell. *Freshwater Recreation Fishing: The National Benefits of Water Pollution Control.* Resources for the Future, Washington, D.C. 1982.

Walsh, Richard G., John B. Loomis, and Richard S. Gillman. "Valuing Option, Existence and Bequest Demand for Wilderness." *Land Economics* 60(Febr. 1984):14-29.

Chapter Two
Household Production Process

This chapter describes household production in which recreation is produced by consumers with purchased goods and services, self-sufficiency, leisure time, and other inputs that are publicly provided such as park facilities and a natural environment. Consumers learn through experience what combination of money, effort, and time provides the most benefits relative to costs.

Two questions are basic to the recreation economic decisions of individual consumers such as yourself. What do you want and what can you get? It is part of human nature to try to make the most of all life's activities, including recreation. How much you enjoy a particular activity determines how much you would be willing to pay rather than forego it. Many economists believe that your willingness to pay provides a straightforward measure of the economic value of your individual benefits. What you want is based on your assessment of the relative benefits of alternative activities available to you.

What you get depends, in part, on your ability to pay the costs. Economists observe that consumers such as yourself do not measure costs in the same way that accountants do, as simply the price of goods and services purchased from others. A distinguishing characteristic of recreation is that for the most part, you are the producer, providing inputs of time and effort as well as dollars. Your choices are constrained by how much of these three types of resources are available and their opportunity costs. The economic decision rule is: you should choose to participate in those activities that have the highest benefits relative to costs until your available resources run out.

In this chapter, we explore the meaning of these concepts and apply them to the recreation economic decisions of consumers. The general problem of household production is to combine the resources available in proportions that result in the most benefits. For example, it is possible that with more time and effort, an individual consumer could produce more benefits with relatively fewer dollars. The correct proportion of dollar, effort, and time resources to put into recreation trip depends on differences in personality, lifestyle, and skill as a manager of the resources available.

The purpose of this chapter is to help you, a prospective manager or manager of recreation resources, understand how the economics of consumer decision making applies in your own life. Hopefully, this insight will provide a personal basis for understanding the usefulness of economics in managing parks and other recreation resources.

COMPREHENSIVE INCOME

Recreation economic decisions contribute to individual consumer welfare because they determine, in part, the level of comprehensive income achieved. Comprehensive income is an economic measure of the total benefits from all life's activities, including recreation. It is simply the sum of how much consumers would be willing to pay for each of life's activities, one by one, rather than give them up. As such, it is likely to exceed the regular income of most individuals. Comprehensive income includes the sum of: (1) the market value of goods and services that consumers purchase with dollars from regular income; (2) the willingness to pay for self-sufficiency goods and services that consumers produce for themselves; (3) the opportunity cost of leisure time that consumers commit to the activities; and (4) the consumer surplus and producer surplus of individuals, an economic approximation of benefits net of costs (items 1-3).

For example, consider a household with regular income of $30,000 per year. The household's comprehensive income rises to $50,000 per year when the values of self-sufficiency, leisure time, and consumer surplus are added to regular income. This is illustrated below for all life's activities and separately for recreation, assuming 100 household days per year for a family of 2.6 persons.

| | | Recreation | |
Comprehensive Income	Total	Total	Per Day
Regular Income	$30,000	$3,000	$30
Self Sufficiency	5,000	3,000	30
Leisure Time	5,000	2,000	20
Consumer Surplus	10,000	7,000	70
Total	50,000	15,000	150

The household is shown to be willing to pay $15,000 per year for recreation. This greatly exceeds expenditures of $3,000 from regular income because it includes an additional $3,000 worth of self-sufficiency, $2,000 of leisure time, and $7,000 of consumer surplus.

Figure 2-1 shows typical demand and supply curves for the household production of recreation. The demand curve represents the willingness to pay for each additional hour of recreation. It slopes downward from left to right as illustrated. The declining curve indicates that successive amounts of recreation are likely to be less and less important for most households. Willingness to pay falls with increases in

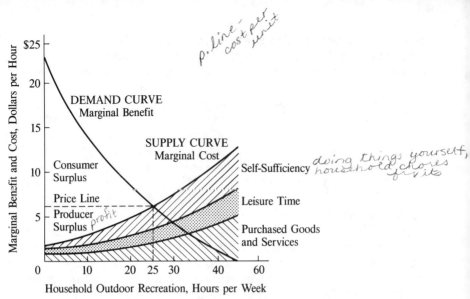

Figure 2-1. Household Demand and Supply of Recreation

the number of hours until at 45 hours per week, no benefits are received from an additional hour of recreation.

The supply curve represents the cost of each additional hour of recreation. It slopes upward from left to right as illustrated. The rising supply curve indicates that for most households, successive amounts of recreation are likely to be more and more costly. There are added expenditures from regular income for travel and for goods and services such as lodging (McConnell). Leisure time costs rise because of the increasing opportunity cost of foregone alternatives (Wilman). Self-sufficiency costs increase as more productive time is devoted to recreation (Quah). The supply curves for these three resources are illustrated in Figure 2-1. The household supply curve for recreation is the sum of the three, shown as the shaded area.

Economists suggest that there is an implicit market within each household. The most beneficial amount of recreation to produce is determined by the intersection of the household demand (marginal benefit) and supply (marginal cost) curves. This means that households facing the demand and supply curves shown in Figure 2-1 would devote 25 hours per week to household production of recreation (or about 9 hours per person). At this level, the welfare of the household is maximized. This is equivalent to 2.6 persons participating an average of 5 hours per day for about 100 days per year, which is a close approximation of the average for participating households in the United States.

We can identify the various measures of the economic value of household time devoted to recreation. When the purpose of measurement is to estimate the welfare of participants, then the appropriate concepts are total benefit and net benefit. In Figure 2-1, total benefit is the sum of the area under the demand curve for 25 hours of recreation. Also, there is a residual value or net benefit, which economists commonly refer to as consumer surplus and producer surplus of recreation.

Consumer surplus is the area of a right triangle under the demand curve and above the price line of $6 per hour for 25 hours. The household would have been willing to pay much more for the 1st through 24th hour as indicated by all points on the demand curve above $6. For the 25th hour, the household gained no consumer surplus as benefit was just $6, which is what it cost. The relevance of consumer surplus to the problem of estimating the benefits of recreation has been demonstrated by numerous empirical studies which will be reviewed in subsequent chapters. Producer surplus also is likely to be an important part of the individual benefits of recreation, although it has been neglected thus far.

Producer surplus is the area below the price line and above the supply curve. It is useful to think of producer surplus as the mirror image of consumer surplus. The symmetrical relationship between the two concepts can be easily seen by considering the two unshaded areas of Figure 2-1. Producer surplus results when households produce recreation goods and services for themselves, as discussed in the section of this chapter dealing with self-sufficiency. The net benefit of recreation is the sum of consumer and producer surplus. It is the total area below the demand curve and above the supply curve for 25 hours per week.

When the purpose of measurement is to estimate a price proxy consistent with the price for marketed outputs, then the appropriate concept is marginal benefit. This is the value that households place on the last hour of recreation. In Figure 2-1, the marginal value is $6 for the 25th hour of recreation per week. This point where marginal benefit equals marginal cost is equivalent to market price even though it includes nonmonetary values for leisure time and self-sufficiency.

Note that the demand and supply curves shown here are for households rather than for particular recreation activities, sites, or industries. This is simply a matter of convenience for purposes of illustration. The identical principles apply at the higher levels of aggregation because sites and industries are simply horizontal sums of their parts. In subsequent chapters, we will discuss the nature of demand and supply for particular activities at recreation sites. It will be shown that the shape of demand and supply curves vary depending on site-specific conditions. For convenience, they are shown here as hypothetical curves.

REGULAR INCOME

The quantity of recreation consumed is determined, in part, by income, as it affects how much individual consumers are willing and able to pay. Regular income is defined as the dollar amount of wages and salaries, interest and dividends on investments, and miscellaneous receipts such as transfer payments and payments in kind. Income is the most clearly understood individual resource available for allocation to participation in recreation. Personal income levels determine ability to pay. Income provides the dollars necessary to purchase recreation goods and services which are produced by others. These expenditures may include: user fees, transportation costs, lodging, added food, consumable supplies, and recreation equipment such as special clothing, tents, fishing tackle, recreation vehicles, etc.

Participation and Expenditure

Income is positively related to participation in recreation. Overall, more higher income households participate more days per year. In this chapter, "household" and "family" are used interchangeably. Table 2-1 illustrates the effect of income on the probability of participating and the average number of days per participant. An average of 76 percent of the U.S. population 9 years of age and older participate in outdoor recreation an average of 95 days per year. However, when income is considered, 90 percent of high income families participate an average of 132 days per year, compared with only 57 percent of low income families who participate an average of 80 days per year. Note that there is considerable variation among recreation activities in this regard.

While higher income may enable more households to participate in a particular type of recreation, their days per year may not be affected. Once the decision to participate in an activity is made, income is not uniformly related to number of days per year engaged in walking for pleasure, attending outdoor sports events, theatre, concerts and fairs, fishing, bicycling, camping, nature walks, hunting, bird watching, and wildlife photography. However, income is positively related to the number of days per year of swimming, boating, horseback riding, and playing outdoor games and sports. Middle income households are more likely to participate in picnicking, camping, fishing, and hunting than either higher or lower income groups.

Income is positively related to level of expenditures on recreation. While information on the total expenditures on recreation is not available for income groups, it is indicative that higher income households spend more for recreation travel. Table 2-2 illustrates the effect of average annual income on household expenditures for overnight recre-

Table 2-1. Effect of Family Income on Participation in Outdoor Recreation Activity, United States[a]

Recreation Activity	Family Income Before Taxes					
	All Families	Low	Lower Middle	Middle	Upper Middle	High
Total Participation, U.S.						
Average Annual Days[b]	94.8	79.9	86.3	103.5	116.2	132.0
Percent Reporting	76.2	56.8	78.2	87.7	89.2	89.8
Swimming						
Average Annual Days	22.3	18.7	19.1	23.1	27.1	36.7
Percent Reporting	46.0	24.4	46.4	59.3	65.4	68.6
Picnicking						
Average Annual Days	6.6	6.1	6.4	6.7	7.5	7.5
Percent Reporting	48.9	32.1	52.4	60.9	56.6	48.5
Playing Outdoor Sports						
Average Annual Days	44.6	39.4	41.6	47.7	50.7	53.8
Percent Reporting	35.7	21.2	36.6	45.4	47.6	50.7
Walking for Pleasure						
Average Annual Days	37.0	54.2	33.4	32.6	31.6	37.8
Percent Reporting	29.9	23.2	29.2	34.0	39.3	35.7
Attending Outdoor Sports Events and Concerts						
Average Annual Days	10.6	10.3	10.6	10.9	10.5	9.9
Percent Reporting	35.4	18.7	34.8	46.0	52.2	57.7
Fishing						
Average Annual Days	11.4	12.4	11.7	11.1	10.0	9.1
Percent Reporting	29.4	21.5	31.5	34.3	33.3	30.4
Boating						
Average Annual Days	10.2	9.0	9.3	10.6	11.4	13.4
Percent Reporting	24.5	10.9	22.7	33.4	38.5	48.4
Bicycling						
Average Annual Days	46.8	42.4	46.4	49.4	45.9	52.5
Percent Reporting	22.1	13.8	22.1	27.8	31.4	29.9
Camping						
Average Annual Days	11.3	10.1	10.6	12.4	12.1	10.6
Percent Reporting	21.0	10.8	22.8	27.9	27.4	20.4
Nature Walks						
Average Annual Days	12.3	16.9	11.3	11.4	11.5	17.9
Percent Reporting	18.2	11.0	17.8	23.5	26.1	21.7
Hunting						
Average Annual Days	10.4	9.9	11.2	10.2	8.5	6.8
Percent Reporting	12.4	9.4	14.4	14.0	11.6	9.6
Horseback Riding						
Average Annual Days	12.9	10.6	12.5	13.1	13.8	18.8
Percent Reporting	9.6	5.9	9.5	11.6	12.9	17.0
Bird Watching						
Average Annual Days	58.0	69.9	54.4	53.2	60.8	56.2
Percent Reporting	4.4	3.2	3.6	5.2	7.9	7.0
Wildlife Photography						
Average Annual Days	8.2	7.8	7.7	9.0	8.7	6.5
Percent Reporting	2.9	1.9	2.5	3.6	4.9	5.2

[a]Participation by persons 9 years of age and older in U.S. households, of which 27.4 percent had income before taxes of under $5,000; 30.3 percent, $5,000 to $9,999; 23.2 percent, $10,000 to $14,999; 15.1 percent, $15,000 to $24,999; and 4.0 percent, $25,000 and over. Total U.S. population 9 years of age and older was 167,943,000 in 1970.
[b]To convert average annual days per participant to days per capita, multiply by percent reporting.
Source: Bureau of Outdoor Recreation, 1972.

Table 2-2. Effect of Income on Household Expenditures for Overnight Recreation Trips and Equipment, United States

Recreation Expenditures	All Families	Low	Lower Middle	Middle	Upper Middle	Lower High	High
Recreation Overnight Trips, Total[a]							
Average Annual Expenditure	$400	$196	$243	$317	$421	$572	$951
Percent Reporting	62.5	35.4	56.9	72.1	81.1	86.1	87.9
Food							
Average Annual Expenditure	$106	$ 54	$ 65	$ 85	$117	$146	$222
Percent Reporting	53.9	26.0	46.2	64.3	73.9	80.5	82.4
Alcoholic Beverages							
Average Annual Expenditure	$ 28	$ 23	$ 24	$ 24	$ 29	$ 28	$ 40
Percent Reporting	24.7	8.2	17.0	28.0	37.0	43.6	56.7
Lodging							
Average Annual Expenditure	$115	$ 80	$ 70	$ 88	$106	$142	$212
Percent Reporting	35.7	11.4	26.6	42.0	53.6	63.7	69.3
Transportation, Total							
Average Annual Expenditure	$144	$ 93	$100	$116	$146	$175	$313
Percent Reporting	60.0	32.4	54.3	69.9	78.3	84.3	86.9
Gasoline							
Average Annual Expenditure	$ 60	$ 35	$ 50	$ 58	$ 66	$ 76	$ 82
Percent Reporting	53.1	24.1	46.7	64.4	73.3	79.3	79.2
Other Transportation							
Average Annual Expenditure	$140	$112	$103	$102	$126	$140	$287
Percent Reporting	39.0	19.5	30.4	43.3	52.0	62.7	72.1
All Expense Tours							
Average Annual Expenditure	$456	$309	$399	$387	$401	$509	$640
Percent Reporting	7.7	2.9	5.0	7.1	9.9	15.5	20.6
Other Vacation Expenditures[b]							
Average Annual Expenditure	$ 59	$ 40	$ 39	$ 45	$ 59	$ 68	$111
Percent Reporting	38.9	14.5	29.1	47.2	56.7	67.0	71.2
Recreation Equipment[c]							
Average Annual Expenditure	$546	$268	$362	$420	$604	$749	$825
Percent Reporting	15.3	4.3	10.2	20.3	23.6	26.6	29.2

[a]Recreation overnight trips include trips of two or more days for recreation purposes, both domestic and foreign.
[b]Other vacation expenses include admission fees to recreation areas, participation fees, and equipment rental.
[c]Recreation equipment includes the purchase, repair, storage, maintenance, and lease of new and used boats, pleasure aircraft, motorcycles, detachable trailers, and other recreation vehicles.
Source: Bureau of Labor Statistics, 1977.

ation trips and recreation equipment. Families with high income who take overnight recreation trips spend more than twice as much as those with middle income. Low income families spend less than half as much as those with middle income. The expenditures shown are in 1972-73 dollars and have more than doubled in the 1980s. Expenditures in any given year can be estimated by applying an appropriate index of changes in consumer prices for travel and recreation equipment.

Recreation expenditures are equal to about 15 percent of personal income in the United States, although official estimates vary with incomplete coverage. Whether a household budgets 10, 15, or even 20 percent of regular income for recreation is limited by the proportion of discretionary income available for leisure time spending. Few families would budget 25 percent of income for recreation because they must spend more than 75 percent of income on such necessities as food, lodging, clothing, transportation, and medical care. Of course, the proportion of regular income that consumers budget for recreation varies because it also depends on individual personality and preferences as to lifestyle.

Table 2-2 shows that only 35 percent of low income families allocated income for overnight recreation trips. By comparison, 70-80 percent of middle income families and 90 percent of high income families choose to allocate discretionary income to overnight recreation trips. The proportion of households reporting overnight lodging expenses is particularly revealing. Of those families taking overnight trips only 11 percent of low income families reported expenditures on overnight lodging compared with nearly 25-50 percent of middle income families and two-thirds of high income families. With higher income, an individual can afford to travel by air, sleep in a condominium or first-class motel adjacent to the recreation site, eat in restaurants, rent equipment, and pay for the services of a guide. Less than 5 percent of low income families participate in all-expense-paid tours compared with nearly 10 percent of the middle income families and 20 percent of those with high income.

According to Table 2-2, only about one-fourth as many households report expenditures on recreation equipment as on overnight recreation trips. Recreation equipment expenses include the purchase, repair, storage, maintenance, and lease of new and used recreation equipment such as boats, aircraft, motorcycles, trailers, and other recreation vehicles. The probability of household spending on recreation equipment was positively related to income, as expected. Moreover, families reporting recreation equipment expenditures spent more money for that purpose than for recreation trips in all income categories except the highest. A minimum of recreation equipment is essential to some types of overnight recreation trips, and equipment may substitute for trip expenses, such as a travel trailer providing overnight lodging instead of commercial accommodations.

This cross-sectional data shows a positive total relationship; that is, higher participation and expenditure on outdoor recreation are associated with higher income where no other variables are held constant. In Chapter 7 we will show several studies of the partial effect of income with all else held constant, which is the short-run effect of a change in income not affecting people in a basic way. The cross-sectional data presented here shows the total effect of being in particular income categories which includes a number of related variables such as education, patterns of preference, and position in society, as noted by Simon.

Savings, Investment, and Payment in Kind

Households can vary their total consumption of recreation from year to year by saving a larger portion of regular income in some years and spending the savings in other years. For example, assume that a household spends 15 per cent of regular income on recreation during the average year. The decision may be made to save half of this during years 1 and 2, then spend twice as much as usual (30 percent) in year 3. In this manner, some households accumulate sufficient dollars to pay for the goods and services necessary to take an occasional trip to Europe or an extended visit to several National Parks in the western United States. As a result, annual expenditures on recreation by some households do not equal 15 percent of regular income, but are minus recreation savings and plus withdrawals from savings.

Similarly, consumers may reach a preferred pattern of consumption by borrowing for recreation expenditures in the present and paying back in future years. In both of these ways, consumers can vary their recreation consumption patterns in one year while varying hardly at all the proportion of their regular income spent on recreation from year to year. This reflects the fact that, for most people, regular income is reported to vary more than annual consumption. Of course, consumption of necessities such as food, clothing, and housing varies less from year to year than discretionary spending on recreation.

Individuals have varying preferences about the allocation of their expenditures over time, meaning the allocation between present and future consumption. If they postpone consumption, they earn interest on the resultant saving; if they pay off outstanding debts, they reduce their interest payments accordingly. Rational consumers will allocate their expenditures over time in such a manner that the rate at which they are willing to give up present consumption for the interest income made possible by an increase of saving will be equal to the interest rate received. Thus, savers will push their consumption to the point where the satisfaction from the future interest rate earned on savings is exactly equal to the satisfaction they derive from the marginal dollar of consumption. Similarly, borrowers will derive satisfaction from their marginal dollar of consumption equal to the stream of interest they must pay on the marginal expenditure dollar which they have borrowed.

Much of consumer borrowing is for the purpose of purchasing durables before sufficient cash can be set aside to pay for them. Mortgages on second homes and condominiums in resort areas and most installment debt fall into this category. Such borrowing is for consumer investment rather than consumption, since the assets yield a return to the purchaser. This return may be monetary; owning a resort condominium reduces rental payments. It may be a saving of labor, as in the case of a mobile home or a travel trailer for camping. The rest of the return may be in the form of satisfaction enjoyed directly, sometimes as extra convenience and enjoyment of consumption through use of the durable equipment. But whatever the form of the benefit, rational consumers will borrow at a given interest rate only if their benefits from enjoyment of the durables purchased are at least equal to their interest payments.

This depends on the phase of the consumer's life cycle of earnings and of expenditure needs. Young married persons — with an expectation of rising income, with dependent children, and with the need to equip a household with standard durables — have a high preference for current consumption expenditures. Older persons, expecting a falling income and retirement, save to increase their consumption later on. Individual attitudes toward satisfaction enjoyed at different points of times vary substantially. Those with a very short time horizon will have strong preferences for present consumption, while misers will have the reverse. Of course, individual needs and desires to provide for financial contingencies will determine these preferences in part, as will many other factors.

In an inflationary era, some individuals sought protection against inflation by transferring savings out of fixed capital accounts into real property. Some people invested in recreation land and equipment as a means of protection against inflation. For example, the ownership of rare firearms, boats, recreation vehicles, and recreation real estate has provided protection against inflation because it is the prices of these goods and services that are rising. While these investments are not essential to participation in recreation, they often enhance benefits. In some cases, increases in the market value of recreation assets have been sufficient to offset the costs of ownership and use; thus the recreation services flowing to the owner have been provided free. Our studies suggest that capital gains on condominiums have provided their owners with free lodging at some resorts.

Some income is received as "payment in kind," meaning income is in the form of goods and services rather than ordinary dollar income which the consumer would use to purchase goods and services. For example, some employers furnish employees on a periodic basis such recreation facilities and equipment as lodging facilities and boats on a lakeshore, river, or estuary. If such fringe benefits reduce the direct cost or price of recreation to individual consumers by, say, $100, this is equivalent to tax-free income. Individuals in a 30 per cent tax bracket would have to earn $142 to have $100 left after taxes. Notice this means that employers who provide recreation goods and services as payment in kind can be a little less skillful than commercial resort operators who might be hired instead. In this case, up to $42 less skillful! Individuals who receive the services would have to earn enough above what commercial resorts charge to pay them and the tax on what they pay them. Thus, employers can afford a few lapses in the quality of goods and services provided as payments in kind.

Tax Payments and Income

The information on income distribution presented in Tables 2-1 and 2-2 is based on annual household income before the payment of taxes, which is the usual form in which income statistics are available. The U.S. Census collects income information in this form and numerous recreation surveys ask respondents to check the income category that represents their best estimate of annual household income before taxes. Thus, we can conclude that annual household income before taxes is considered a reasonable proxy of ability to pay for outdoor recreation. Still, it should be noted that the actual dollars of income available for expenditure on goods and services are after taxes have been paid. It is simply that this statistic is not as readily available because people are not generally aware of their total tax bill.

It is possible to estimate total taxes paid from Internal Revenue Service summaries. Table 2-3 is based on the available information suggesting that low income households pay an average of about 25 percent of their income as taxes compared with 30 percent for middle income and 38 percent for high income households. This indicates that total tax rates are not as progressive as is often assumed. The term "progressive" refers to a tax rate schedule in which higher income households pay a higher percentage of their income in taxes than do lower income households. Federal income tax rates are considerably more progressive than these total tax rates. However, federal payroll, excise, and highway user taxes are regressive. Distribution of the state and local tax burden among income groups tends to be prac-

Table 2-3. Distribution of Households, Outdoor Recreation, Income and Tax Payments by Income Groups, United States

| Category | Income Group | | | | | |
	Low	Lower Middle	Middle	Upper Middle	High	Total
Proportion of	-------- Percent Distribution --------					
Households	•27.4	•30.3	23.3	15.1	4.0	100.0
Income	10.7	26.0	27.1	21.6	14.6	100.0
Tax Payment[a]	8.8	22.8	•26.5	23.9	18.1	100.0
Outdoor Recreation Days	11.3	23.5	31.0	25.9	8.3	100.0
Gain or Loss[b]	2.5	0.7	• 4.5	2.0	• -9.8	

[a]Taxes as a percent of income for income groups: low, 25.3; lower middle, 27.0; middle, 30.1; upper middle, 34.0; high, 38.2; and total, 31.4 percent. Taxes include: federal income payroll, highway use, and other excise; state and local income, property, sales, highway use, and excise.
[b]The percent of tax payment by an income group less the percent of outdoor recreation days by the same group.
Source: Bureau of Outdoor Recreation, Bureau of the Census, and State tax reports.

tically the same as the distribution of income. State income taxes are usually somewhat progressive, although not nearly so progressive as the federal income tax. Other state and local taxes tend to be regressive, with lower income households paying a disproportionately higher percentage of their income in taxes. Regressive state and local taxes include: property tax, sales tax, highway user tax, and excise tax primarily on cigarettes and alcoholic beverages.

The policy of using tax revenues to provide free or nominal cost public recreation resources has been attacked by a number of critics. They have suggested that this policy constitutes a subsidy to upper middle and high income households at the expense of low income households. It is possible to provide a tentative test of the validity of this proposition. If the distribution of recreation use among income groups is substantially different from the distribution of tax payments, this would suggest that there is a subsidy. It becomes an empirical question as to which income groups receive a recreation subsidy if any.

The proposition that lower income households subsidize the public recreation opportunities of those with higher incomes is not supported by the information presented in Table 2-3. The tentative evidence suggests that high income households subsidize those with low incomes and, in particular, middle incomes. Those less able to pay appear to be subsidized by those most able to pay because of their higher absolute income and the progressive aspects of the tax system. Low and lower middle income households have fewer days of recreation per year than upper middle and high income households. However, the share of tax payments by low and lower middle income households is even less than their share of participation in recreation.

On the basis of this information, it is concluded that lower income households receive a subsidy in kind from the use of public recreation resources, albeit a small one. Apparently, middle income households receive the largest subsidy, as measured by how much their share of participation in recreation exceeds their share of tax payments. Upper middle income households also receive a small subsidy. The proportion of tax payments by high income households substantially exceeds their participation in recreation (even though their participation per household is the highest of any income group, as was shown in Table 2-1).

Table 2-4 shows the proportion of total tax payment by households for the recreation programs of federal, state, and local government in the United States. The expenditure of tax revenues for recreation programs represents only 0.4 percent of average household income, or 1.3 percent of average total tax payments. The share of tax revenues spent for recreation programs was estimated as $60 for the average household with an income of $14,000 in 1975. This is equivalent to $0.27

Table 2-4. Outdoor Recreation Expenditures by Federal, State, and Local Government, United States, 1975

| Agency | Million Dollars | Per Household[a] | |
		Dollars	Percent
Federal Departments	$2,093	$28.72	47.6%
Agriculture	126	1.73	2.9
Commerce	43	0.59	1.0
Defense	19	0.26	0.4
Housing and Urban Development	117	1.63	2.7
Interior	610	8.37	13.9
Labor	600	8.23	13.6
Transportation	169	2.31	3.8
Treasury	375	5.15	8.5
Other[b]	36	0.49	0.8
Less Grants	(1,422)	(19.52)	(32.3)
Less Fee Revenues	(50)	(0.69)	(1.1)
Adjusted Total	621	8.52	14.1
State and Local	4,179	57.35	95.0
States	1,164	15.97	26.4
Counties	741	10.17	16.8
Cities	2,274	31.20	51.7
Less Grants	(1,422)	(19.52)	(32.3)
Less Fee Revenues	(400)	(5.49)	(9.1)
Adjusted Total	2,357	32.35	53.6
Total Tax Revenues	4,400	60.38	100.00

[a]Households = 72,867,000.
[b]Includes the Small Business Administration and Tennessee Valley Authority.
Source: Bureau of Outdoor Recreation; Heritage, Conservation and Recreation Service; and Bureau of the Census.

per day for the 220 recreation days per year by the average household of 2.9 persons.

Payment of taxes for recreation programs varied with level of household income. Low income households with $5,000 annual income paid $16 per year in taxes for recreation programs, which equaled $0.18 per day for the 91 recreation days per year by the average household of 2.0 persons. Upper middle income households with $25,000 annual income paid $110 per year in taxes for recreation programs, equivalent to $0.29 per day for 373 recreation days per year by the average household of 3.6 persons. High income households with $50,000 annual income paid $248 per year in taxes for recreation programs, which equaled $0.55 per day for 450 recreation days per year by the average household of 3.8 persons. All of these estimates are in 1975 dollars and would be higher in current dollars.

Direct federal expenditures from tax revenues were estimated as $621 million per year, which was equivalent to only $8.50 per household in the United States. These federal expenditures included: 46.7 percent for operation, maintenance, and management; 24.4 percent for construction and development; 15.6 percent for land acquisition;

27

and 13.3 percent for other costs of recreation programs. Agencies include the National Park Service, Forest Service, Fish and Wildlife Service, Bureau of Reclamation, Army Corps of Engineers, and Tennessee Valley Authority. Transportation Department expenditures are for road construction in public recreation areas.

Most tax payments for recreation programs were made directly to state and local units of government and to the federal government for grants to state and local government. Nearly $2.4 billion of tax revenues for recreation programs were paid directly to state and local government and an additional $1.4 billion was paid to the federal government for grants to state and local government. Combined, the $3.8 billion recreation expenditures from tax revenues averaged nearly $52 per household or 86 percent of total public spending on recreation programs from tax revenues.

Expenditures by city government, nearly $2.3 billion per year, were larger than direct expenditures by either state or federal government, although a substantial portion represented grant monies from the federal government and some user fee revenues are included in total expenditures. Local park and recreation expenditures represented 4.7 percent of the total budget of city governments in the United States.

It should be noted that some unknown portion of the expenditures by state and local government are for indoor recreation and for related forestry and natural resources. The federal expenditures are specifically designated for outdoor recreation, while state spending is for forestry and parks, and county and city spending is for parks and recreation. Analysis and comparison of expenditure levels would be facilitated if all levels of government defined "outdoor recreation" and "indoor recreation" consistently. However, the estimates presented here are sufficient to indicate overall trends.

Income and Satisfaction

Finally, as a general economic principle the higher your income, the more you can spend; and the more you can spend, the more satisfaction you should receive from all life's activities, including recreation. Table 2-5 presents the results of a study relating income to how people rate their own happiness. Gurin, et al. asked a representative sample of 2,390 people in the United States this question: "Taking all things together, how would you say things are these days — would you say you're very happy, pretty happy or not too happy?" Expressed happiness was positively related to income level. For example, over half of the high income group reported they were happy compared with only one-fourth of the low income group. Nearly one-fourth of the low income group reported they were not very happy compared with only about one-twentieth of the high income group. Numerous

Table 2-5. Effect of Income on How People Rate Their Own Happiness, United States

Category	Income Group					
	Low	Lower Middle	Middle	Upper Middle	High	Total
Proportion of Income Groups	Percent Distribution of Income Groups					
Very Happy	22	34	42	46	52	
Fairly Happy	55	56	54	49	42	
Not Very Happy	23	10	4	5	6	
Total	100	100	100	100	100	
Proportion of Total U.S.	Percent Distribution of Total U.S. Population					
Households	27	30	23	15	4	100
Income	11	26	27	21	15	100
Very Happy	17	29	28	20	6	100
Fairly Happy	28	32	23	14	3	100
Not Very Happy	56	27	8	7	2	100

Source: Gurin, et al. combined data for 11 income categories; and Table 2-3.

studies reviewed by Simon and Scitovsky have supported these general findings, and suggest that the general relationship has remained relatively unchanged since 1947.

Indications are that income is positively related to gaining satisfaction and avoidance of dissatisfaction from all life's activities including recreation. However, this does not mean that income buys happiness, or satisfaction from recreation activities. Higher incomes enable consumers to spend more money, but later sections of this chapter will show that some individuals are more skillful than others in substituting self-sufficiency for income, and that individual effort is related to the amount of pleasure from recreation activities. As a result, the effectiveness of a dollar of income in providing satisfaction appears to be less for high income groups than for those with low incomes. For example, the low income groups included 17 percent of the very happy people in the United States but they received only 11 percent of total income. The high income group included 6 percent of the very happy people, while accounting for 15 percent of total income. On the other hand, the effectiveness of a dollar of income in avoiding dissatisfaction appears to be much greater for high income groups than for those with low incomes. For example, the low income group included 56 percent of the not very happy people in the United States compared with only 2 percent in the high income group.

The question of the effectiveness of a dollar of income in providing satisfaction, happiness, or benefits to income groups remains an unsettled area of economics, i.e., "What is the marginal utility of income?" Some observers suggest that individual wants are a function of means and that the utility of a dollar to any person, rich or poor, is likely to be the same. However, the more accepted view in the United States seems to be that the rich do not value an additional dollar as highly as the poor. Indeed, Congress acted on this principle in setting up the progressive income tax structure and a number of social welfare programs. Shabman and Kalter used the income tax structure to weight the relative utility of recreation benefits to income groups in New York State. Benefits reported by low income households were multiplied by 1.8, lower middle income, 1.1; middle income, 1.0; upper middle income, 0.7; and high income, 0.4. The overall effect was to increase the measured recreation benefits by 14 percent owing to a disproportionately large number of lower income users from large metropolitan areas.

SELF-SUFFICIENCY

A distinguishing characteristic of recreation is that individuals are producers as well as consumers of recreation activities. Yet, this is the least understood aspect. Self-sufficiency is defined as the production of goods and services for oneself rather than for the market. It is freely chosen nonmarket work during leisure time, not including personal care such as eating, bathing, and sleeping. The individual consumer, or household made up of two or more individuals, produces recreation days with a desired set of characteristics by combining: (1) its own inputs of knowledge, skill as a manager, and effort with nonmarket work time; (2) purchased goods and services produced by others; and (3) other inputs that are publicly provided such as a state park or reservoir. Individual or household production is constrained by nature (weather, terrain, insects, and availability of fish and wildlife) over which the household has no control, and by the level of technology available to the household at a given time. The concept of household production is a useful approach to understanding decision making in the activity of producing and consuming non-market recreation. The approach builds on the general theory of household production developed by Becker, Lancaster, and others.

Alternative Measures

Several approaches have been used to measure the economic value of self-sufficiency. These include the market prices of outputs, opportunity costs of input time, and willingness to pay for the outputs less purchased inputs. According to the first approach, time devoted to household production is assigned the price the households would have to pay had they purchased the goods and services in the market. From the estimated market value of total output, we have to subtract the value of market goods and services purchased as inputs combined with household time. Problems arise in application of the market prices approach as it assigns prices to household production that have been explicitly rejected by the household. The family could have purchased the home services in the market but preferred not to do so, either because it found their prices too high, or because it found their quality wanting.

According to the second approach, the time input in household production is valued at its opportunity cost, which is assumed to be the price at which individuals can sell additional work on the labor market or the current hourly wage rate for level of ability and occupation. The opportunity cost approach assigns to household production time the wage rates that have been explicitly rejected by households as a true measure of their productivity. Members of the family could have offered more work time to the labor market but preferred not to do so, either because they found the wages too low, or because they found satisfaction on the job less than desired. The approach also ignores the fact that persons working at home are self-employed, contributing to the production process both their labor services and their managerial skills. The producer surplus generated by self-directed family members is ignored in the conventional opportunity cost approach.

Moreover, if employment opportunities are not available during the hours when leisure time occurs, the opportunity cost becomes zero. In this case, the market price measure of the output of self-sufficiency projects during these hours of leisure time would become the preferred approach of the two discussed thus far. Another fundamental objection to using the wage rate as an opportunity cost of household production time can be raised on conceptual grounds. The real cost of foregone work time outside the home is not wages, but the benefits of goods and services purchased with the income received minus the disbenefits of work. Disbenefits of work will be less to those who enjoy their work than to those who do not. Thus, gross wage receipts are not likely to be a good proxy of the net benefits of employment.

A survey of the studies of aggregate household production by Hawrylyshyn found that both the market price and opportunity cost approaches have yielded measures that are not significantly different. Estimates of total self-sufficiency income of households in the United States average approximately 60 percent of regular income. This has been interpreted by Becker, Nordhaus, Tobin, and others as resulting in so-called full income or real income of 1.6 times dollar income. These estimates should be considered as very tentative. Gronau has suggested that both the market price and opportunity cost approaches provide equally unsatisfactory results. The basic fallacy in considering the final figure as real income comes from assuming that household members would actually have spent or worked that much if household production had been impossible.

A third possible approach to measure the economic value of self-sufficiency income is the expressed willingness to pay for the goods and services produced by the household less the price of market goods and services purchased to use as inputs in the household's production process and the cost of time used in production. In direct interviews we could consider the full range of important household production activities such as housework, child care, shopping, yard care, equipment maintenance, gardening, recreation travel, etc. Willingness to pay to gain or avoid these self-sufficiency activities would provide the best available measure of their contribution to the real income of consumers. The approach is superior on conceptual grounds, as not all self-sufficiency time is of equal value and it allows individuals to judge the consumer and producer surplus benefits of goods and services produced by the household. Net willingness to pay information can be obtained, by asking consumers to subtract from total willingness to pay the disbenefits of household production time and the market prices of goods and services used in the production process.

It seems likely that the willingness to pay approach would yield results significantly different from the market price and opportunity cost approaches. For example, in Chapter 4 we will present the results of a household survey that suggests willingness to pay for self-sufficiency time driving to river-based recreation sites may be a declining function of distance traveled in the Rocky Mountains of the United States. Apparently, net willingness to pay is positive for one-way travel time of 1-2 hours on single-day trips. However, for longer trips it declines with distance. For 2-day trips, with one-way travel time of 2-4 hours, net willingness to pay is positive up to about 90 miles and thereafter becomes negative. For vacation trips of 3 days or more, with one-way travel time of 4-8 hours, net willingness to pay is positive up to about 250 miles and thereafter becomes negative. These are trips to engage in fishing, boating, swimming, camping, and related activities at study rivers. Willingness to pay to avoid travel time may be significantly different for trips where the destination is the primary goal, for travelers who do not consider enjoyment of scenery an important part of the recreation experience, and for trips in regions with little or no scenic value. There is a need for further research on the willingness to pay for travel time.

Household Characteristics

Self-sufficiency income can explain a good deal about personal welfare and behavior that cannot be explained in terms of regular income alone. Such comments as "How do they live so well on what they make?" or "I don't see why he is always broke — he makes good money" obviously miss the point by equating human welfare with money income. People who live well on modest money incomes may have high self-sufficiency incomes. People can supplement a low money income by such things as repairing their own car, appliances, and plumbing and by doing their own painting, refinishing of furniture, or even remodeling of their vacation homes. High income households could better afford to purchase these services, expending dollars from their regular income, and therefore would have little or no self-sufficiency income.

Total self-sufficiency income varies with the level of regular income, education, age, and number of children in the households. Gronau reported that the relationship between self-sufficiency income and regular income is inverted U-shaped, as is the relationship with age. The age-household production profiles are flatter the lower the husband's education, and they tend to funnel out with age. Still there are some important differences between the effects of regular income and age. The value of self-sufficiency income increases up to ages 35-39 and declines thereafter. It tends to increase with age at a faster rate than with regular income during the early phases of life, peaks earlier and usually drops more sharply. Households with young children have more self-sufficiency income than other households.

Lazear and Michael show that household size affects the efficiency of household production of goods and services. Larger households tend to be more efficient in transforming dollars into services, with the result that real income rises substantially with increases in number of persons per household. Actually, Lazear and Michael show that the average price of goods and services consumed falls. They suggest that this is the result of specialization of labor, economies of scale, rate of utilization of indivisible equipment, and public goods whose consumption by one member of a household does not diminish their availability to other members. For example, if the direct out-of-pocket cost and disbenefit of driving an automobile on a short recreation trip is $5 by the man traveling singly, and $5 by the woman taking the same trip separately, then traveling together the price is to each $2.50, a reduction in the price of the recreation experience resulting from the change in household size. In the same way, other benefits are affected. A TV set may yield either more or less entertainment benefits if two or more individuals share the experience of viewing. Benefits may be more if they both enjoy and discuss the show and less if the second member interferes with the viewing by the first. Benefits of a shared recreation trip may be less than to individual traveling alone, if travel distances are increased to meet desires of a second family member.

Self-sufficiency income of the middle class in the U.S. appears to be higher than for those with high income, who pay for the services of others, or for those with low income, who may often lack the necessary skill and motivation. The following serve as examples. Renters generally are not rewarded by their landlords for house maintenance, while a majority of middle class families own their home and have maintenance skills. The wealthy find it economical to have the poor do their household chores that they could just as competently do for themselves, because this frees their time for more pleasant or more lucrative use of their time. Domestic servants are particularly numerous in well-to-do households of a poor country. Many upper middle class households in the United States have cleaning women in one day a week to perform routine household cleaning. Households at all income levels purchase precooked dinners, which reduces the self-sufficiency income from food preparation.

Clawson and Knetsch present time budget data which suggest that household time spent on chores are declining as a long-run trend in the United States. This has definite implications for recreation activities, because household chores account for sizeable amounts of time. Time budgets in 1966 for housework, gardening, and running errands showed housewives averaged 6 hours, 23 minutes per weekday; employed women, 2 hours, 44 minutes; and employed men, 43 minutes. There are important trade-offs between self-sufficiency income derived from home maintenance and recreation activities. With a minimum of self-sufficiency work around the home, there is more time available for weekend and vacation trips. There is often a trade-off at the end of a workday between lawn care and golf, tennis, or a swim in a nearby pool. Nonwork time can be spent on either recreation and leisure or self-sufficiency household work.

Self-sufficiency in recreation activities seems to vary in a pattern similar to total self-sufficiency income. Middle class families often have both the incentive and the skills to devote large amount of self-sufficiency efforts and time to providing a substantial part of recreation products and services for themselves. Low income households may lack the necessary skills or motivation required to devote large amounts of self-sufficiency income to most recreation activities. High income households may put low self-sufficiency resources into recreation activities because they purchase most of their required goods and services.

Recreation Examples

The purpose of this section is to illustrate the many ways in which individual consumers participate in the process of producing a recreation experience. The most obvious is the actual on-site recreation activity. To a considerable extent, self-sufficiency and recreation activities are indistinguishable; without a minimum of effort and skill it is impossible to participate in recreation. Scitovsky observes that there are some recreation activities such as walking near home, that can be participated in without the expenditure of additional dollars from regular income, but there are none that do not require at least a minimum commitment of individual effort and skill. Even a walk near home requires the effort to leave the comfort of home and a minimum of skill to appreciate and identify the flowers, trees and shrubs of the passing scene.

In backpacking and camping in a wilderness area self-sufficiency reaches its zenith. For example, on-site self-sufficiency includes camping effort, skill, and time to set up camp including putting up the tent, gathering wood, building a campfire, and preparing food. In particular, self-sufficiency with respect to food preparation is a vital part of the camping experience, which often would not be complete without weiners or hamburgers and marshmallows roasted over an open fire. The same may be said for picnicking. Special freeze-dried food may be an essential convenience to backpacking on long trips because of weight considerations; however, simple, even gourmet, dishes prepared from ordinary basic foods are often tastier and provide the backpacker an opportunity to demonstrate his cooking skills under adverse conditions on the trail.

Restaurant meals may substitute for self-sufficiency in food preparation and are a treat to most people when spaced between several meals eaten at home or around a campfire. However, a solid weekend or vacation of restaurant meals in a resort area can be monotonous and too much of a good thing for most pallets. Moreover, fast food restaurant eating on the run may provide much less pleasure and even contribute to indigestion. As a result, commercial overnight accommodations in resort areas often include cooking facilities and utensils so that a majority of meals can be prepared rather than eaten out.

Other examples of on-site self-sufficiency abound. Self-sufficiency in water-based recreation activities includes boat launching, docking, navigating, and operating of sailboats, motorboats, and canoes. For most people, self-sufficiency is preferred to renting dock facilities, hiring a skipper to operate the boat, or fishing in a charter boat. Self-sufficiency in fishing includes providing one's own fishing tackle and lures, baiting hooks, removing fish caught, and cleaning and icing the catch. Self-sufficiency in water skiing and swimming includes providing a motorboat of sufficient horsepower and an operator with sufficient skill to keep the tow rope taut. Swimming self-sufficiency includes diving from the boat in any protected cove or along any likely beach far from the crowds of public or commercial swimming beaches and incidentally without the protection of lifeguards.

On-site self-sufficiency in hunting may include the skill and effort to train and keep a good retriever dog for waterfowl, upland bird, and small game hunting. In the United States legal hunting of big game, such as deer, antelope, and elk, requires that flushing and retrieving be accomplished by members of the hunting party rather than by trained dogs. Private hunting preserves may hire beaters, flushers and even shooters, similar to the experience of hunting tiger or elephant elsewhere in the world. Self-sufficiency in gutting, butchering, wrapping, and cooling of game meat substitutes for the services of a meat locker.

In addition to on-site activities, consumers participate in other ways to produce recreation. Clawson and Knetsch define the recreation experience to include five parts: anticipation, travel to the site, on-site recreation activity, return travel, and recollection. On-site recreation activity may be the basic reason for the whole recreation experience, and the remaining parts of the total experience may be built around it. It is the part which is usually discussed and studied in most detail, and many seem to think of it as the total recreation experience. But it is only a part. Clawson and Knetsch suggest that the on-site recreation activity may be less than half of the total experience, whether measured by time involved, expense incurred, or total satisfactions gained.

Driving a private automobile to and from a recreation site is probably the largest single example of self-sufficiency by individuals taking recreation trips of over 100 miles. Our studies in the Rocky Mountains suggest that driving time averages roughly 20-30 percent of total time on trips for such recreation activities as fishing, boating, camping, picnicking, backpacking, and hiking. Auto travel time often has an implicit cost because it requires special skill and effort on the part of the driver and results in fatigue of both driver and passengers. As much as 95 percent of total access to state and federal parks is by private auto. Individual effort is also required to walk or ride a bicycle to city and county parks.

Public transit has not provided a viable alternative means of access to most recreation sites in the past. Now this is changing, as more people discover that driving a car is not an inherent part of most recreation activities. The major exception is pleasure driving for the purpose of sightseeing, which remains the most popular recreation activity in both the United States and Europe. Even in this case, tour buses are becoming more popular. When recreation travel is by public transit (plane, boat, train, bus), self-sufficiency is involved in preparation for the trip, including learning the scheduled times of departure, arranging to arrive at the departure station in sufficient time, arranging for food while in transit, bringing reading materials, etc.

Self-sufficiency is important in the anticipation or planning phase of recreation. Most households put considerable time and effort into planning a recreation trip for themselves rather than purchasing the services of a travel agent, who may provide a package plan complete with reservations for transportation, lodging, and recreation activities. The longer the trip and/or the more specialized the recreation activity, the more time and effort is likely to go into preparations. Participants learn the importance of self-sufficiency in preparation by doing it repeatedly, and this experience builds into knowledge.

Effectiveness of individuals or households in producing desired characteristics of a recreation experience depends in large part on their skill and effort in making preparations. Shopping for goods and services is a necessary part of preparation for a recreation trip. Preparing food before departure is necessary when food services are not available at recreation sites. Often sufficient food is purchased for the entire trip. Recreation equipment must be checked — for example, a deer rifle re-sighted, fishing tackle tested for function and strength of line. Packing suitcases and loading the car is often no small under taking.

Linder reminds us that the necessary maintenance of consumption equipment of all kinds is taking an increasing share of our discretionary leisure time. As we accumulate more recreation equipment, the time required for necessary maintenance and repairs rises at an alarming rate. Even if owners of recreation equipment choose to hire the service done by others, a considerable amount of their own time must be spent arranging for the work. There is the minor repair and cleaning of special clothing used in recreation. It may be necessary to apply waterproofing and sew a patch on a tent or poncho. Small equipment such as a fishing reel, a hunting firearm, or a ski binding must occasionally be taken apart, cleaned, and oiled. Snowmobiles, trail bikes, and other off-road vehicles must be serviced including changing the oil and filters, grease jobs, and tuneups. Similar maintenance and minor repairs must be made to the family car, as about 40 percent of its use is attributed to recreation travel in the United States. Ownership of such large recreation equipment as motor homes and travel trailers requires periodic cleaning and maintenance of the stove, water system, toilet, furniture, floor, tires, roof, and hitch. Boat motors require periodic service and repair. Sails must be patched and the hull, oars, tiller, and deck of wooden boats revarnished.

Both short-run and long-run decisions are made in the anticipation and recollection phases of the outdoor recreation experience. Long-run decisions include whether to begin participating in a new form of recreation activity or whether to continue participating in an established activity. These are occasions to check whether new durable recreation equipment might improve the input/output relationship in the production of the recreation activity. The level of technology available to the household or individual determines, in part, the efficiency of household production. An improvement in technology, such as the addition of a scope to a high-powered rifle may permit a big-game hunter to bag a deer in less time and thus, less direct cost of time, effort and materials. A hunter training program may increase the efficiency of young hunters in the field, resulting in lower cost production of the hunting experience.

Long-run durable recreation equipment decisions involve comparative price shopping and decisions on whether to buy or to make. These types of self-sufficiency can increase the household's access to necessary recreation equipment by lowering its direct cost. This may include do-it-yourself projects such as fly tying, sewing special clothing and tents, building boats, etc.

LEISURE TIME

Time is one resource that every person has in equal amount — 24 hours a day 365 days a year. This is related to the fact that time, unlike other economic resources, cannot be accumulated. Individuals and households cannot build up a stock of time as they would a stock of capital. Each person has around 16 waking hours a day to use in working, routine living, and enjoying life. For most persons, leisure time is the residual that is left after necessary obligations are met to work, sleep, eat, and maintain personal hygiene. Leisure is defined as discretionary time to be used as one chooses. As such, it is analogous to the concept of discretionary income which is available for spending on recreation goods and services after the necessary costs of living have been paid.

Measures of Time

Availability of leisure time varies with relatively more for some individuals than others and at different times for the same individual. Clawson and Knetsch observe that leisure time for most persons ages 6-65 comes in three forms: (1) weekdays, for approximately 180 school days or 240 workdays, in amounts of 3-6 hours each day, not necessarily continuous, after demands for school or work, sleep, and personal chores have been met; (2) on weekends, for about 114 days per year, including 10 3-day holiday weekends when work is typically absent and leisure time may run as much as 12 hours per day; and (3) on vacations extending over a period of 75-90 days for school children and 7-30 days for employed persons. Preschool and retired persons have different patterns, less regular and less geared to weekly, seasonal, and annual cycles; to a lesser extent, so do housewives who do not work outside the home. The use of leisure time by all households is affected by the schedules of the members in school and working.

Table 2-6 illustrates the distribution of leisure time per week for income groups of working adults and for college students in the United States. The table shows that all individuals, regardless of income, have roughly 108 waking hours per week. College students have the most average weekly leisure time, particularly summer vacation expressed

Table 2-6. Estimated Distribution of Weekly Time by Income Groups, United States

Category	College Student	Low Income	Low Middle Income	Middle Income	Upper Middle Income	High Income
	----------- Percent -----------					
Households, U.S.	4%	23%	30%	23%	15%	4%
	---------- Hours per Week ----------					
Total Non-sleep Time	108	108	108	108	108	108
Leisure Time	55	53	51	48	47	45
Weekday	13	27	24	20	18	15
Weekend	25	25	25	25	25	25
Vacation	17	1	2	3	4	5
Work Time	27	30	35	40	48	55
Other Time[a]	26	25	22	20	13	8
Outdoor Recreation Time	16	7	8	10	11	12
	-------- Percent of Leisure Time --------					
Outdoor Recreation	29%	13%	16%	21%	23%	27%

[a]Includes personal care, idle time and nonmarket work time averaging 18 hours per week according to Owen.
Source: Bureau of the Census; Bureau of Outdoor Recreation.

on a weekly basis. For employed adults, the lowest income group has the most leisure time. Total leisure time per week declines as income increases, despite the fact that annual vacation time expressed on a weekly basis rises with added income. Some nonwork time of the low income group is the result of inability to obtain full-time jobs. Forced idleness is not considered leisure time in the usual sense.

Higher income groups tend to work more hours per week and have less leisure time on weekdays than lower income groups. Individual business proprietors in the United States typically work 55 hours per week compared with 40 hours by their employees. There is a similar pattern in West Germany where managers of overnight lodging accommodations and restaurants worked an average of 67 hours weekly compared with 45 hours by their employees in 1970. In the 1960s, medical doctors in the United States worked 57 hours per week and college professors, 60 hours. Finally, it is interesting to note that leisure time during weekends and holidays tends to be the same for all income groups.

Outdoor recreation activities are a substantial part of leisure time in the United States. The proportion of leisure time used for outdoor recreation is positively related to income. For middle income groups, approximately 21 percent of average weekly leisure time is used for outdoor recreation, compared with 13 percent for low income and 27 percent for high income households. College students use a larger proportion of their leisure time for outdoor recreation than employed persons, in particular, bicycling and playing organized games and sports.

The proportion of leisure time used for indoor recreation activities, such as watching television, reading, and playing table games is presumably the balance of leisure time after outdoor recreation has been subtracted from the total. Based on this measure, middle income groups used approximately 79 percent of their leisure time indoors. Low income groups tend to do physical labor at work and prefer less active indoor leisure pursuits. High income groups are less likely to be physically active at work and favor more outdoor recreation activities.

Leisure vs. Work

Economic analysis of leisure vs. work is based on the following observations. Given the fixed amount of 108 waking hours in a week, an individual's decision to spend 60 of those hours working is simultaneously a decision to demand 48 of them for other purposes, including approximately 30 hours of leisure time. Another person's decision to spend 40 hours working is simultaneously a decision to demand 68 of them for other purposes, with 50 hours of leisure time, as 18 hours of personal care and other daily chores remains unchanged.

Wage rates have both income and substitution effects on the demand for leisure time activities, including recreation. An increase in the wage rate raises the opportunity cost of earnings lost by taking leisure time. Thus, the substitution effect of an increase in wages is to encourage individuals to demand less leisure time. At the same time, the wage increase also raises income making people more able to afford to buy more goods and services, including recreation and other leisure activities. Thus, the income effect of an increase in wages is to encourage individuals to demand more leisure time. A rise in income also increases ability to pay for time-saving household appliances and services which increase leisure time by reducing the hours of personal care and other daily household chores. The actual change in an individual's demand for leisure is the net balance of the two opposing influences.

Throughout the 20th century, the income effect of increased wages apparently has prevailed, causing the demand for leisure to increase and the length of the workweek to decline. Owen found that about 75 percent of the increased demand for leisure since 1900 is explained by increases in the real hourly wage rate. About 25 percent is explained by declines in the relative price of recreation goods and services. Real wage rates (measured in dollars of 1967 purchasing power in the United States) had been rising until recently. At the beginning of the century, the real wage rate averaged $0.70 per hour. By 1970, it averaged $3.00, and then declining to about $2.70 in 1980. Over the 80-year period, the real wage rate increased by nearly three times in terms of the quantity of goods and services those dollars can buy.

During the same time period, hours of work have generally declined and leisure time has increased. Organized labor has asked for and received reductions in the length of the workday and workweek. At the beginning of the century, a workweek of 5-6 days and a workday of 10 or more hours was standard, making a workweek of 50-60 hours. Since then, hours of work have generally declined, until today the standard workweek is down to 35-40 hours. This means that demand for other time, including leisure, increased by one-third, from an average of 53 hours per week at the beginning of the century to 70 hours today. The trend has been much the same in most other developed countries. An even shorter workweek seems possible in the future as part of a standard of living that is partly in the form of leisure.

Opportunity Cost of Leisure

Several approaches have been used to estimate the opportunity cost of leisure time. These include: (1) theoretical, assumed equal to the average wage rate; (2) empirical measurement of the value of work actually foregone; and (3) loss in benefits from foregoing alternative leisure activities. There are other approaches to the economic value of leisure time. However, these have already been discussed in the section of this chapter on self-sufficiency.

According to the first approach, individual time used in leisure activities is valued at its opportunity cost, which theoretically is the price at which the individual can sell additional work on the labor market. Otherwise individuals would work more and take less leisure. This is usually interpreted to be the current hourly wage rate for their level of ability and occupation. For example, the cost of a college education includes the income foregone from work that could have been performed while attending college. Until recently, no empirical studies were available on the opportunity cost of leisure time in total or that portion used for recreation. The lack of evidence did not deter a theoretical approach to the subject by a number of economists most notably Becker, but also Owen, Kurtz, McConnell and Strand, Wilman and others.

General application of the opportunity cost principle has resulted in large estimates of the value of leisure time, ranging from 60 to 160 percent of regular income. The usual procedure has been simply to multiply hours of leisure time by the average wage rate. On this basis, Nordhaus and Tobin calculated the total value of leisure time as a proportion of the value of national income in the United States in 1965. Using this procedure, the value of leisure time is equivalent to 120 percent of the regular income of middle income households in Table 2-6.

Application of the opportunity cost principle also results in some very large estimates of the value of leisure time devoted to recreation activities. With on-site recreation time equal to the national average of 5 hours per day and average wage of $12 per hour (equal to $24,000 per year), then the opportunity cost of time is $60 per recreation day. With on-site recreation time equal to a standard recreation visitor day of 12 hours, then time cost is an unbelievable $144 per recreation visitor day. Using lower wage rates of around $3 per hour, a Louisiana study of the Atchafolaya Basin by Soileau, et al, estimates the opportunity cost of time as about $38 per 12-hour fishing day, somewhat more than their estimate of $27.50 cost for boating, water skiing, and swimming because of the larger numbers of youth participating with lower wage rates. McConnell and Strand estimate that sport fishermen on Chesapeake Bay value travel time as about 60 percent of their hourly household income. In this application, the regression coefficient for hourly income multiplied by roundtrip travel time is divided by the coefficient for trip transportation costs. This results in an estimate of the marginal rate of substitution between travel time and travel cost inputs in the production of recreation trips.

These estimates are subject to a number of important qualifications. Not all leisure time has the same opportunity cost. For a typical individual who is already working an 8 to 5 40-hour week, employment opportunities during weekday evenings, weekends, and vacations may be at a much lower rate of pay than regular employment on the first job. Moreover, if employment opportunities are unavailable during the hours when leisure time occurs, opportunity cost of wages foregone becomes zero. Perhaps self-sufficiency projects could be pursued during leisure time, in which case the opportunity cost of other leisure activities would become the willingness to pay for the goods and services that would have been produced less the price of purchased inputs.

The federal guidelines recommend that on-site recreation time costs for individuals whose work time is variable should be measured as the income foregone. Worktime is variable for most professionals, such as doctors and lawyers, and other individuals who operate their own business. Their income is a direct function of the number of patients, clients, and customers served which varies with work time. However, professionals and business managers who take a work day off for a preferred leisure activity usually do not sacrifice income by doing so. Doctors, for example, trade worktime or cover for each other during these times. And, assistant managers fill in while the manager of a business is absent.

Others observe that the opportunity cost approach assigns to leisure time the wage rates that have been explicitly rejected by the household as a true measure. Those individuals who could have offered more work time to the labor market preferred not to do so, either because they found the wages too low or job satisfaction less than desired. The real opportunity cost of for⸴ ⸴ne work time outside the home is not the wage lost but the consumer surplus benefits of the goods and services that could have been purchased with the income foregone plus the producer surplus benefits of work.

Review of recent psychological studies led Scitovsky to the conclusion that apparently, there is some optimum proportion of work and leisure time for each individual. The principle of diminishing marginal returns would apply in both cases. Thus, the physical and mental abuse of working overtime or at a second job rather than enjoying recreation during usual leisure time may reduce individual productivity. The labor market places a very low value on an exhausted worker asleep on his feet. Pushed to this biological limit, the opportunity cost of leisure time becomes negative. This is the familiar proposition, as yet unverified by empirical research, that worker productivity and thus regular income is actually increased because of the physical and psychological renewal provided by leisure time activities.

According to the second approach, only the value of work time actually foregone would be considered a cost of leisure time activities. The direct interview approach would enable the observer to question those household members who report they would have worked if they had not been engaged in the leisure time activity. Questions could be asked about the amount of time and the amount of wages foregone; the loss of benefits from the goods and services which would have been purchased with the income foregone; the producer surplus from enjoyment of work foregone; and the expected benefits foregone from work as a form of investment expected to provide higher income in the future. For households where several members would have earned income, opportunity cost should be estimated for each member. Those who report no work time foregone would be assigned a zero opportunity cost and questioned about possible benefits foregone from alternative leisure time activities.

It seems likely that the direct interview approach would yield results significantly different from those obtained using a constant opportunity cost of time equal to (or a proportion of) the average wage rate. Our studies of the opportunity cost of recreation time in the Rocky Mountains of the United States indicate that less than 30 percent of user households report any members would have worked during on-site recreation time spent fishing, hiking, backpacking, camping, and picnicking. For households reporting opportunity cost, foregone wages were equivalent to $1.54 per hour of individual on-site recreation time in 1979 dollars. Averaged over the entire sample, the opportunity cost of wages foregone was equal to about $0.40 per hour of individual recreation time. Thus, the opportunity costs of wages foregone averaged $2.00 for the typical 5-hour recreation day. This suggests that the opportunity cost of recreation time may be a very small and insignificant part of the total direct cost of recreation in the United States.

According to the third approach, individuals with no working time cost may nonetheless have opportunity costs represented by the loss in benefits from the most valuable alternative leisure activities foregone. The federal guidelines recommend that the cost of time used for recreation include the opportunity cost of leisure activities foregone. According to the guidelines, this leisure time cost may range between zero and the individual's value of work. It is zero if the individuals would not have engaged in any other leisure activity had they not taken recreation trips. Leisure time cost would equal the individuals' value of work if the alternative leisure activity is valuable enough to forego work, given the opportunity.

In between these two extremes, the opportunity cost of alternative leisure activity may be estimated by comparing willingness to pay for the two activities. For example, assume that individuals forego an alternative leisure activity such as lawn mowing for which they would be willing to pay $10 per day in order to go fishing. Their opportunity cost of fishing time is $10 per day. This represents their leisure time benefits foregone in order to go fishing and would be added to other direct costs to determine their price of fishing. However, few consumers would knowingly choose the lesser valued leisure activity, so the direct leisure time cost of recreation usually will be zero.

There is another important application of the opportunity cost principle in recreation economic decisions by individual consumers. The benefits from work or alternative leisure activities actually foregone provide a minimum estimate of the benefits from recreation. If recreation benefits do not at least equal the benefits from work or the most valuable alternative leisure time activity, whichever is higher, the consumer should probably reexamine the decision to participate in recreation. Benefits of the activity chosen should exceed the benefits of the activity foregone. The next section will explain more fully the concept of recreation benefits, followed by a section on the problem of choice among alternative inputs available.

NET BENEFITS

Throughout this book we will use the word "benefit" as a proxy for the economic value of all the psychological satisfactions from outdoor recreation activities. This is consistent with the definition of benefits in the federal guidelines. Readers also may recall that this is similar to the concept of utility which has been an important part of the economic literature for more than a century. There has been some confusion related to the meaning of utility in the writings of economists. So we shall employ the term "satisfactions" to mean any type of psychological stimulation or pleasure from recreation. This is identical to a widely accepted meaning of the term "utility."

Willingness to pay is a dollar measure of benefits, meaning how much individuals enjoy recreation activities. The psychological content of benefits includes all of the feelings of pleasure which lead participants to exclaim "what a good time they had" or "what a good buy" or possibly "it wasn't worth it." The latter possibility reflects the fact that recreation economic decisions are made before the fact and actual benefits may not come up to expectations. In Chapter 10, we will discuss decision-making under conditions of risk and uncertainty.

Consumer Surplus and Producer Surplus

Economists do not measure the value of recreation activities in the same way that accountants do as simply the price of recreation goods and services purchased. Since the work of Alfred Marshall nearly a century ago, economists have known that the use value of what we consume is higher than its exchange value, except at the margin where the use value of the last unit consumed equals its exchange value, otherwise we would consume more. Today, economists substitute the term "total benefit" for use value and the terms "direct cost" or "price" for exchange value but the concepts remain about the same. Total benefit is defined as the maximum amount that individuals would be willing to pay for a recreation activity rather than forego it. Net benefit is defined as total benefit less all direct costs in dollars, effort, and time. Some confusion may result from the fact that net benefit is not paid to anyone, thus does not appear in national accounts. Rather, net benefit represents the real savings to consumers from managing the resources they control in ways that result in consumer surplus for themselves after all costs are paid. As such, net benefit to consumers is analogous to net profit to business firms. In both cases of consumer and producer surplus, the value of the activity is determined by what is left over after all costs are met.

The federal guidelines recommend willingness to pay as the appropriate economic measure of the benefits of recreation. Net benefits are equal to what users would be willing to pay above what they now pay rather than forego a recreation activity. For example, if individual anglers now pay $20 per trip (in money, effort, and time) and takes 10 trips to a lake each year, they spend a total of $200 per year. If they would be willing to pay an average of $30 per trip rather than do without the satisfaction of taking the same 10 trips to the same site, they would be willing to spend a total of $300 per year. The difference of $10 per trip, or $100 per year represents the added amount they would be willing to pay. When individuals spend $200 per year and would be willing to pay $300 per year for the same recreation, they are receiving net benefits or consumer surplus of $100 per year over what they are paying.

Fisher and Krutilla compare the willingness to pay measure of benefits to nonmonetary alternatives such as consumer preference studies. Measuring intensity of preferences on a 5-, 10-, or 100-point scale with the highest number defined as complete satisfaction from a recreation experience, provides useful information to resource managers about some of the specific psychological characteristics of individual users. Also, information on consumer preferences is an important feature of demand functions for recreation, discussed in chapter 7. Recently, social psychologists have made considerable progress in understanding user preferences for recreation resources. There is a need for further research to overcome possible problems. First, Fisher and Krutilla caution that there is a problem in aggregating intensities of preferences across individuals. To appreciate this point, consider two individuals, each reporting 80 percent of complete satisfaction. One individual has a keen interest in the outing with high expectations associated with it, and the second is only mildly enthusiastic. Both may have their expectations realized to the same degree, indicated by the same 80 percentage of complete satisfaction, yet the amount of pleasure each would derive from the experience would differ. This difference should be reflected in the willingness to pay measure.

Second, consumer preferences are variable, influenced by example, custom, and suggestion; changed by the accumulation of experience; modified by changes in price and income; and subject to the availability of some satisfactions and absence of others. It would be difficult for consumer preference studies to account for these relevant dimensions of the psychology of a recreation experience in a single study. Users would have to be asked a very large number of questions. The willingness to pay approach aggregates the intensities of preferences into a single question. Also, income effects on willingness to pay can be controlled by applying conventional statistical techniques.

Third, there may be a problem when asking individuals what they like or desire. It would be of little use to provide mere "wish lists" unconstrained by reality. The eminent American philosopher, John Dewey, suggested that what people report they like may provide a weak basis for understanding human values. Because values emerge from the process of solving day-to-day recreation problems, individual experience determines what recreation activities prove most desirable in fact. Some observers have suggested that the willingness to pay approach may be consistent with Dewey's theory of valuation. The intensity of values is reflected in willingness to pay based on the outcome of recreation experiences constrained by the actual dollar, effort, and time costs of individual participants.

Psychology of Recreation

Review of recent psychological studies led Scitovsky to conclude that, apparently, the components of individual satisfaction from recreation include: the stimulation of exciting activities, the novelty of new experiences, the difficulty of physical and mental effort, and the threat of dangerous situations. People prefer alternating high and low levels of excitement to an even level of serenity. After experiencing a high level of excitement, they welcome a period of quiet; then they get bored and seek a more exciting activity again.

Perhaps the most important psychological motive of consumer behavior is a yearning for novelty, that is, the desire to know the unknown. It has been suggested that the search for new experiences and ideas is the source of all progress of civilization. Repeated visits to a recreation site render the experience less new and surprising; thus it becomes less exciting and gets less attention. This is the psychological basis for the familiar economic principle of diminishing marginal utility or benefit, which will be discussed in Chapter 5.

The difficulty of a recreation activity is probably a necessary component of individual satisfaction. For as Scitovsky points out, psychologists have found that discomfort often precedes pleasure. On a holiday we may feel averse to physical effort. But if we yield to the exhortations of some more energetic companion and start an expedition, after a little while we begin to enjoy the muscular exertion and may even express gratitude to the disturber of our rest, saying, "I'm glad you dragged me out."

The threat of dangerous situations increases the pleasure of many recreation activities. Our attention is automatically caught by the most striking, potentially most threatening feature of the environment. This is most obvious in such dangerous sports as technical mountain climbing, where a false step can lead to serious injury or death. The chance of failure is slight if we are careful, but the consequences of failure are great. Most people enjoy watching the flames of a campfire from a safe distance, the beauty of a thunderstorm from under a shelter, and the waves of the sea from shore or from on board a sturdy ship. Even children are thrilled by being thrown into the air and caught again, as Scitovsky notes.

Lancaster believes that demand is related to the characteristics of what we consume. Activities with different characteristics vary in their capacity to satisfy our basic psychological needs and desires. The psychology of recreation benefits has been studied by a number of social scientists, most notably Driver, Brown, and Hendee. Such investigations provide evidence for the classification of outdoor recreation activities according to differences in the psychological motivation of individual participants. These include active, passive, extractive, ap-

Table 2-7. Effect of Psychological Motivation on Characteristics of Demand and Supply of Outdoor Recreation

Variables	Basic Psychological Motivation					
	Active	Passive	Extractive	Appreciative	Social	Learning
Source of Psychological Benefits	Physical exercise heightens excitement, and benefits rise	Emphasis on comfort and relaxation, for balanced living	Consumptive benefits relate to number and size of catch	Nonconsumptive benefits relate to unique-ness and beauty	Stimulating conversation while participating	Develop recreation skills, and knowledge about nature and history
Examples of Outdoor Recreation Activities	Outdoor games and sports, swimming, running, skiing, backpacking[a], mountain climbing[a], hiking[a]	Developed camping, attending outdoor events, sightseeing[a], sunbathing	Hunting, fishing, gathering rocks, driftwood, and firewood	Birdwatching, nature walks, visiting zoos, photography	Picnicking, playing shuffleboard, horseshoes, walking with friends, lawn parties	Visiting museums, attending interpretive programs, taking lessons, reading, going to summer camps
Users' Costs: Equipment	Usually can be rented or provided free. Low to medium cost	Low to high	Medium to high, cost for guns, 4-wheel-drive vehicles, etc.	Low to medium cost for cameras, binoculars, etc.	Usually provided at site at no cost	Usually none required, or provided at site
User Fees	Low to high	Low to high	Medium to high license fees	Usually no entrance fees	Usually none	Low to high
Travel	Low to high	Low to high	Usually high	Usually low to medium cost	Low	Usually low
User Benefits	$14/day	$12.50/day	$12.75/day	$12/day	$11.75/day	$11.75/day
Natural Environment Required for Activity	Usually none. Can be high	Usually low	High	Highest	Little or none	Little or none
Management Costs: Investment in Facilities and Equipment	Usually low to medium. Skiing is high	High cost of convenient facilities	Little or none	Usually low; zoos are high	Medium	Low to high
Operation and Maintenance	Medium to high	Medium to high	Usually very high	Medium to high, to protect natural environment	Medium	Medium to high
Carrying Capacity, Number of Users	Limited by capacity of facilities	High, crowding expected	Low, must be limited	Usually low to medium	High, crowding appreciated	Limited by capacity of facilities

[a]Also appreciative.

preciative, social, and learning motives. Each of these motivations is probably shared by all participants, but some are relatively more important for particular activities than are others. Table 2-7 illustrates the effects of psychological motivation on the characteristics of demand and supply of recreation resources.

Active recreation involves physically strenuous exercise, which heightens psychological stimulation, excitement, and benefits, according to studies reviewed by Scitovsky. Active recreation includes jogging, bicycling, playing outdoor games, tennis, golf, driving off-road vehicles, snow skiing, swimming, waterskiing, boat racing, and snowmobiling. Individuals usually pay entrance fees and travel costs and purchase special recreation equipment such as running shoes, 10-speed bicycles, balls and bats, off-road vehicles, boats, and snowmobiles. Owners and operators of ski areas, golf courses, tennis courts, ball fields, swimming pools, and marinas often invest a substantial amount of capital to develop these recreation facilities. Usually all that is necessary to participate in the other activities listed is a natural environment with an access road. The number of users is limited by the capacity of facilities.

Passive recreation requires relatively little physical effort, and the emphasis is on individual comfort. Psychological stimulation, excitement, and benefits are expected to be lower than for other types of recreation. Still, relaxation after overstimulation from work is an important part of balanced living. Thus, willingness to pay for the opportunity to relax out of doors may be substantial. Passive activities include attending outdoor sports events, concerts, and plays; relaxing and reading outdoors; sunbathing; trailer and motor-home camping; sightseeing by car or tour bus; and quiet boating and canoeing. Individuals usually pay for entrance fees, travel costs, and special recreation equipment such as trailers, motor homes, and boats. No special equipment is required to attend outdoor sports events, concerts, and plays or to go sightseeing by bus. Participants also are likely to attend interpretive programs. Managers providing opportunities for these types of recreation experience should develop convenient facilities to assure the comfort of participants. A natural environment may contribute, but it is usually not required. Daily use of facilities can be high, as participants expect to be part of a crowd.

Extractive recreation involves harvesting the bounty of nature. Psychological satisfaction from consumptive activities is related to the number and size or uniqueness of the trophy, which is symbolic of the skill of the individual participant. Extractive activities include fishing, hunting, and collecting rocks, shells, edible plants, driftwood, firewood, etc. Individuals may pay for hunting and fishing licenses, travel, and equipment such as fishing tackle, guns, chainsaws, guide books, and special clothing. A sizable state fish and game management program is required, as is an extensive natural or semi-natural environment. The development of recreation facilities can be minimal. Even with fish and game stocking programs, biological carrying capacity is limited, requiring that the number of users be limited.

Appreciative recreation involves viewing the natural beauty of the environment. Psychological satisfaction from non-consumptive activities is related to individual knowledge and sensitivity to wildlife, geology, plants, color, and natural form. Appreciative activities include hiking, backpacking, horseback riding in natural areas, mountain climbing, bird-watching, nature study, and photography. Some of these activities also involve physically strenuous exercise. Individual participants may pay substantial direct costs for travel to suitable sites and for special equipment such as hiking boots, packs, tents, sleeping bags, horses, saddles, trailers, binoculars, and cameras. Development of recreation facilities should be limited to trails and toilets, as appreciative users prefer to experience nature on foot or horseback rather than through the window of a restaurant, lodge, car, bus, or train. Resource managers may provide interpretive programs. The manager's primary role should be preserving the natural environment by protecting air and water quality, controlling forest fires, restricting hunting, and maintaining relatively low user density.

Social interaction and learning includes visiting with family and friends; learning about nature and history; and acquiring special recreation skills by attending lectures, demonstrations, and exhibits. Social interaction is a part of virtually all recreation activity in some degree. A stimulating conversation is the principal source of pleasure for some individuals. Social interaction includes visiting with family and friends while engaged in: picnicking, camping, nature walks, and playing outdoor games such as volleyball, shuffle board, and horseshoes. Some recreation equipment is required, but, with the exception of camping, it may be provided on-site by park and recreation departments. Social interaction usually is not limited by the ownership of equipment, the elaborate development of recreation facilities, or their level of use. A natural environment is not required.

HOUSEHOLD PRODUCTION PROCESS

Thus far in this chapter we have described the four types of comprehensive income: money, effort, time, and net benefits. The recreation economic decision of consumers is to combine the resources available to them in proportions that result in the most net benefits. The correct proportion of dollar, effort, and time resources to put into a recreation trip depends on differences in individual personality, lifestyle, and skill as a manager of the resources available. The purpose of this section is to describe the process that households and individuals use to choose among various inputs, such as purchased goods and services, self-sufficiency time, leisure time, and recreation equipment, to determine the least costly way to produce whatever quantity of recreation they choose to consume. The process is equally applicable to private and public managers of recreation resources.

Consumer Decision Making

In principle, the process of decision making by the household or individual consumer of recreation is identical to that of managers of public and private recreation resources. H. A. Simon, winner of the 1978 Nobel Prize in economics, believes that economic decision making comprises three principal phases, which are closely related to the stages in problem-solving first described by John Dewey as: What is the problem? What are the alternatives? Which alternative is best? These three activities together account for most of what business executives do, according to investigations by Simon. The same is true for recreation economic decisions by individual consumers and managers.

The recreation economic problem of individual consumers is to choose among a few alternative activities that are realistically available to them at the time of choice. The short-run decision of what to do next is usually constrained by the amount of time available and the season of the year. For example, the choice of what recreation activity to choose after work on a fall weekday is limited to a few alternatives close to home such as playing tennis, handball, or golf. Making the most of it under the circumstances, individual consumers chooses the best from a few available activities, all of which may have lower net benefits than activities on overnight and vacation trips which require larger blocks of leisure time. Thus, rational consumers do not always choose the recreation activity with the highest benefits relative to costs. Rather, they choose the activity that will do, that is good enough under the circumstances, which economists define as the "satisficing goal" in economic decision making.

Simon says that a rational economic choice is whatever reasonably intelligent human beings do. Consumers engage in both long-run and short-run planning of their recreation activities. An individual consumer may decide, as a New Year's resolution, that he or she intends to do more jogging, skiing, or fishing, or perhaps this will be a very special year for a sightseeing vacation in the West. Long-run planning may be illustrated by the problem of whether to take a trip to western national parks next summer. During the winter months, the individual may collect information on the alternatives, lay out the best itinerary, get together the necessary durable equipment, and make reservations.

Some economists have misinterpreted consumer decision making as the process of ranking an array of all leisure activities that can be consumed in any given year from the most preferred to the least preferred. However, planning by the typical individual does not involve deciding at the beginning of the year to engage in 95 recreation days, then starting with the activity providing the highest net benefits and proceeding to the lowest by the end of the year. Simon advises young economists to try to get closer to human behavior, in a sense to become naturalists again, to grow more empirical and not so contemplative. One of my teachers, T. W. Schultz, winner of the 1980 Nobel Prize in economics, shares this view of his own career, regretting that he did not do more empirical studies of human behavior.

When a problem arises about what to do next, individual consumers consider the alternatives available and decide which alternative they expect to be best. Alternatives can be ranked according to their total benefits when direct cost or price is no object or when the alternatives have identical costs. Perhaps one alternative has very high benefits; another fairly high; a third, medium, and a fourth, low. The rational individual would probably choose the alternative with the highest benefits. However, for most individuals, recreation economic decisions involve two things: what they want and what they can get. After estimating the rough dollar amount of benefits expected from each alternative, consumers must consider each alternative's direct cost in terms of dollars, effort, and time. What individuals can get is limited by the amount of these resources at their disposal. Activities with the highest benefits relative to costs will be chosen first, and choices will continue until available resources run out.

For the most part, recreation economic decisions by individual consumers can be casual and made with little or no effort or time. Experience gained from repeated decisions provides sufficient knowledge of benefits and costs when conditions remain unchanged. In this case, occasional checking to see whether conditions have changed is recommended. In other cases, careful analysis of alternatives is not worth the effort. For example, the decision whether to have hot dogs or hamburgers at a picnic is trivial when the expenditure is small and the benefits relative to costs are very close. In cases where expenditures are large and alternatives have substantially different benefits relative to costs, careful decision-making is worth the extra effort required. According to psychologist, Abraham Maslow:

> ... the better, more realistic, higher consumer ... must be assumed to be rational, that is, he will want the best product for his purposes. This means also ... that he will look for factual information, examine specifications, read the labels ... will choose the lesser price if quality is equal, will not be seduced by irrelevancies ... get indignant over being swindled instead of taking it for granted ... all these qualities are characteristics of higher psychological health, growth toward self-actualization.

Decisions by individual consumers may have external benefits for which they do not pay and costs for which no compensation is received. Third-party effects are an important by-product of economic activity, and they ought to be taken into account when economic decisions are made. Measuring external effects is one of the contemporary problems of economics. The sight of a tent may not please every neighbor and passerby who sees it. The increased motorization of recreation may have unpleasant side effects, such as noise and air pollution. Mineral and energy development may increase air and water pollution and decrease the water level in streams and reservoirs, all of which represent external costs to recreation.

The choice of where to live and work affects the external benefits and costs of individuals and households. Those who live near recreation resources receive an external benefit in the form of reduced travel cost. They may make some concession as to ordinary income to enjoy other things that they value. Those who live in a large city with polluted air and congested traffic may receive higher incomes, but they bear external costs. Maslow reports that:

> ... when anybody offered me a job I tried to put some rough money value on all sorts of intangibles, like for instance, giving up a friend, or beautiful surroundings. Is my best friend worth $1,000 a year or $500 a year or $5,000 or what? Anyway, it's quite clear that he is worth something which I had better take into account. If, for instance, I arbitrarily assign a value of $1,000 a year to having an intimate friend (which is certainly a modest figure), then this new job which has been offered at a raise, let's say $2,000 or $3,000 or $4,000 a year is simply not what it looked like at first. I may actually be losing value, or dollar value, if I take into account all these other higher need intangibles which nobody puts into the contract nor on the balance sheet, but which are nonetheless very, very real to any sensible person.

Bayless reported that air pollution is directly associated with salaries paid to university professors in the United States. Payments must be higher in cities with higher air pollution, other things being equal, to compensate for the external cost.

Learning by Doing

Casual observation of recreation behavior may suggest that the household or individual really has very little discretion in choosing inputs. Physical necessity alone, it would appear, dictates such choices. A particular type of recreation may require driving 200 miles, the purchase of certain goods and services, leisure time, and a certain amount of equipment — no more, no less. But this is an overly narrow view of the matter. Joseph Sax, who teaches environmental law and public land management at the University of Michigan, has described how consumers learn through experience what combination of their money, effort, and time will provide the least costly way to produce a recreation experience. In his work on recreation policy for the public lands, Sax presents the following case study of backpacking:

Perhaps I can give some concrete content to these reflections by describing what I have called an authentic encounter with nature. Hiking with a pack on one's back appears superficially to be a strangely unappealing activity. The hiker, vulnerable to insects and bad weather, carried a heavy load over rough terrain, only to end up in the most primitive sort of shelter, where he or she eats basic foods prepared in the simplest fashion. Certainly there are often attractive rewards, such as a beautiful alpine lake with especially good fishing. But these are not sufficient explanations for such extraordinary exertions, for there are few places indeed that could not be easily accessible, and by much more comfortable means.

To the uninitiated backpacker a day in the woods can be, and often is, an experience of unrelieved misery. The pack is overloaded; tender feet stumble and are blistered. It is alternately too hot or too cold. The backpacker has the wrong gear for the weather or has packed it in the wrong place, the tent attracts every gust of wind and rivulet of water. The fire won't start, or the stove fails just when it's needed. And the turns that seemed so clear on the map have now become utterly confusing.

Such experiences, familiar in one form or another to all beginners, are truly unforgiving; and when things go wrong, they do so in cascading fashion. Yet others camping nearby suffer no such miseries. Though their packs are lighter, they have an endless supply of exactly the things that are needed. Their tents go up quickly; they have solved the mystery of wet wood, and they sit, dry under a deceptively simple rain shelter, eating their dinner in serene comfort. What is more, they are having a good time. The woods, for the beginner an endless succession of indistinguishable trees apparently designed to bewilder the hapless walker, conceal a patch of berries or an edible mushroom; nearby, but unseen, are beautiful grazing deer or, overhead, a soaring eagle.

With time, patience and effort one recognizes that these things are available to everyone; that one can get in control of the experience. The pack lightens as tricks are learned; how to substitute and how to improvise quickly, out of available materials, the things previously lugged. The more known, the less needed. Everything put in the head lessens what has to be carried on the shoulders. The sense of frustration falls away, and with it, the fear that things will break down. One knows how to adapt. The pleasure of adaption is considerable in itself because it is liberating; one is able to take advantage of conveniences, but is not a captive of them. It isn't only a lifting of burdens. The backpacker discovers that the positive quality of the voyage is directly related to one's own knowledge and resources.

Backpacking provides an interesting illustration of how the consumer learns through experience. The beginner overinvests in durable backpacking equipment. As a result, the pack is overweight, perhaps weighing 40-60 pounds, and the effort required to carry it up the trail reduces the backpacker's pleasure below an acceptable level. Willingness to pay for backpacking is exceeded by its opportunity cost in money, effort, and time. Through repeated experience, the individual learns to reduce the amount of equipment in the pack to bare essentials. For example, a tube tent also doubles as a rain fly for cooking. As a result of these kinds of adjustments, the pack's weight falls to under 30 pounds, and individual effort is reduced to pleasurable levels. No doubt, this person would devote more leisure time to backpacking in the future.

The case study of backpacking is repeated over and over again in recreation. Some consumers are lured by advertising to put too many of their hard-earned dollars into recreation equipment, on the assumption that this will solve their recreation problem. Whether the purchase of durable recreation equipment is a good investment depends on how much it is used and its opportunity cost. The purchase of a snowmobile, for example, may provide added comfort during winter outdoor recreation, but an opportunity cost of comfort is reduced effort, excitement, and pleasure and thus lower benefits. Also, a $2,000 investment in a snowmobile in a single year may deplete the household's regular income available to purchase alternative recreation goods and services. This may result in less varied recreation and declining benefits from novelty.

Perhaps as a result, the consumer cannot afford to invest a mere $100 in cross-country ski equipment. Thus, the individual misses out on skiing's pleasurable physical exertion. The consumer is forced to choose lower valued recreation days of snowmobiling rather than higher valued cross-country skiing days during the winter months. The total leisure time of the individual cannot be allocated in the best way possible. It would have been possible to take more days of the higher valued cross-country skiing at a lower price per day because there are not added cost of gasoline, maintenance, repairs, and license fees for the snowmobile. Lowering the price per day of recreation results in increased net benefits from the activity. Lowering the price of one activity also means that consumers have more dollars left in their recreation budgets. This gives them the choice of either more total days of recreation or more high-priced days, such as a week at a ski resort, which may enlarge the total benefits of recreation.

The four types of comprehensive income are separate accounts, and the necessity of considering each separately in decision-making cannot be overemphasized. However, money, effort, and time resources can be substituted one for another within limits. And it is not an oversimplification to state that individual skill in combining the right amount of each in the production of recreation activity determines its contribution to comprehensive income. Individuals and households will exchange one resource for another when the benefits received from the one are greater than the opportunity costs of the other.

When the benefits from self-sufficiency exceed the opportunity cost of leisure time activities foregone, the consumer will choose more self-sufficiency and will continue to do so until no more additional net benefit can be gained. For example, driving an automobile on a recreation trip takes more time than flying, leaving less time for alternative leisure activities such as on-site recreation. Self-sufficiency time used in driving to a recreation site also substitutes for the direct out-of-pocket cost of commercial airline travel.

This is the same logic that managers of private recreation resources would follow when the gains from self-sufficiency exceed those from the purchase of production inputs on the market. Businessmen will choose more self-sufficiency and will continue to do so until no more additional profits can be gained by the substitution of one for the other. It is the same logic that the manager of public recreation resources would follow when the public benefits from self-sufficiency exceed those from the purchase of production inputs on the market. Public officials will choose more self-sufficiency and will continue to do so until no more additional public benefits can be gained by the substitution of one for the other. Still, the prevailing view in the United States seems to be that while businessmen do so as a matter of good management practices, government officials and consumers are expected to refrain from so crass a calculation. For managers of recreation resources, the right decision is expected to be determined by law or regulation. Individual consumers are expected to acquire marketable job skills, but consumption and household production skills are not valued as highly, according to a review of recent experience in the United States by Scitovsky.

Consumers and managers of public agencies could use some help in selecting the combination of inputs that can produce the desired output most cheaply. An appendix to this chapter contains some useful information in this regard. It explains the formal concept of the production function, which economists invented to indicate the maximum amount of output that can be produced from any specified combination of inputs, given the current physical and technical constraints.

SUMMARY

The subject of this chapter, household production, is perhaps the least understood aspect of recreation economics. Household production refers to the fact that consumers provide inputs of time and efforts as well as dollars. Recreation activity is produced by consumers with purchased goods and services, their own self-sufficiency, leisure time, and other inputs that are publicly provided such as park facilities and a natural environment. The general problem of consumers is similar to any other production process, to combine the resources available in proportions that result in the most benefits. Economists refer to comprehensive income as the total output of household production.

Comprehensive income is an economic measure of the total benefits from all life's activities, including recreation. It was defined as simply the sum of how much consumers would be willing to pay for each of life's activities rather than forego them. We examined four types of comprehensive income: (1) the market value of goods and services that consumers purchase with dollars from regular income or savings; (2) the willingness to pay for self-sufficiency goods and services that consumers produce for themselves; (3) the opportunity cost of leisure time that consumers commit to the activities; and (4) the consumer and producer surplus to individuals, representing the net benefits of all life's activities over and above consumer costs in dollars, effort, and time.

Regular income was defined as the dollar amount of wages and salaries, interest and dividends on investments, and miscellaneous receipts such as transfer payments and payments in kind. Personal income levels determine ability to pay for recreation goods and services that are produced by others. However, it does not constrain comprehensive income, which is likely to exceed the regular income of most individuals. We demonstrated that higher income groups are more able to pay direct out-of-pocket costs and thus are more likely to participate in recreation and to participate more days per year, although there is considerable variation among recreation activities.

Although information on total recreation expenditures was not available for income groups, higher income households do spend more for recreation travel and equipment. Also, we demonstrated that the share of tax payments by high income groups exceeds their share of participation in recreation. On the basis of this information, it was tentatively concluded that low and middle income groups receive a subsidy in kind from the use of public recreation resources that are provided free or for a nominal entrance fee. Most tax payments for recreation programs are made directly to state and local units of government, and to the federal government for grants to states, counties, and cities. Finally, it was shown that income is positively related to gaining satisfaction and avoiding dissatisfaction from all life's activities, including recreation.

Self-sufficiency was defined as the production of goods and services for oneself rather than for the market. It is freely chosen nonmarket work during leisure time, not including personal care such as eating, bathing and sleeping. It is a distinguishing characteristic of recreation that individuals are producers as well as consumers of recreation activities. The individual consumer or household of two or more individuals produces recreation days by combining its own inputs of knowledge and skill as a manager with non-market work time, purchased goods and services produced by others, and other inputs which are publicly provided, such as forests and parks. Household production is constrained by nature (weather, terrain, insects, and availability of fish and wildlife) over which the household has no control, and by the level of technology available to the household at a given point in time. The approach builds on the general theory of household production developed by Becker, Lancaster, and others. The concept of household production provides a useful approach to understanding decision making in the activity of producing and consuming nonmarket recreation.

We reviewed several approaches that have been used to measure the economic value of self-sufficiency. These include: the market prices of self-sufficiency outputs, the opportunity costs of input time, and the willingness to pay for self-sufficiency outputs less purchased inputs. According to the first approach, time devoted to household production is assigned the price the household would have to pay had it purchased the goods and services in the market. From the estimated market value of total output, one has to subtract the value of market goods and services purchased as inputs and combined with household time. According to the second approach, the time input in household production is valued at its opportunity cost, which is often assumed to be the average wage rate. The third approach to measure the economic value of self-sufficiency is the expressed willingness to pay for the goods and services produced by the household less the price of market goods and services purchased as inputs and combined with household time. Indications are that the best available measure of the contribution of self-sufficiency to the comprehensive income of consumers, is the willingness to pay to gain or to avoid activities such as child care, shopping, yard care, equipment maintenance, and recreation travel.

Self-sufficiency can increase any household's access to recreation activities and equipment by lowering their out-of-pocket cost. Self-sufficiency income of the middle class in the United States appears to be higher than for those with either high or low income. Middle class families often have both the incentive and the skills to devote large amounts of self-sufficiency effort and time to providing outdoor recreation products and services for themselves. Low income households tend to lack the necessary skills or motivation in most cases. High income households may have both the incentive and ability to purchase most of the required goods and services.

Leisure time was defined as discretionary time to be used as one chooses. For most persons, leisure time is the residual after necessary obligations are met to work, sleep, eat, and maintain personal hygiene. As such, it is analogous to the concept of discretionary income, which is available for spending on recreation goods and services after the necessary costs of living have been paid. While total time is one resource that every person has an equal amount of, the availability of leisure time varies, with relatively more for some individuals than others and at different times for the same individual.

We estimated that college students have the highest average weekly leisure time, particularly summer vacation expressed on a weekly basis. For employed adults, the lowest income group has the most leisure time, although some nonwork time is the result of inability to obtain full-time jobs; forced idleness is not considered leisure time in the usual sense. Total leisure time per week declines as income increases, despite the fact that annual vacation time, expressed on a weekly basis, rises with added income. Higher income groups tend to work more hours per week and have less leisure time on weekdays than do lower income groups. Leisure time during weekends and holidays tends to be the same for all income groups. The proportion of leisure time used for recreation is positively related to income. High income groups are less likely to be physically active at work and favor more physical recreation activities.

Total benefits were defined as the maximum amount that individuals would be willing to pay for a recreation activity rather than forego it. Net benefits were total benefits less direct costs. Thus, net benefits represent the consumer and producer surplus to individual participants above direct costs in dollars, effort and time. Consumer surplus was defined as the area below a demand curve above price, and producer surplus as the area above a supply curve below price. Net benefits represent the real savings to consumers from managing the resources they control in ways that result in consumer and producer surplus for themselves after all costs are paid. As such, net benefits to consumers are analogous to net profits to business firms. In both cases, the value of the activity is determined by what is left over after all costs are met. Yet, some confusion results from the fact that the net benefits to consumers are not paid to anyone and thus do not appear in national accounts.

Recreation activities are valued because they provide pleasure to individual participants. Review of recent psychological studies suggested that the components of individual satisfaction from recreation include: the stimulation of exciting activities, the novelty of new experiences, the difficulty of physical and mental effort, and the threat of dangerous situations. We noted that activities with different characteristics vary in their capacity to satisfy basic psychological needs and desires. Thus, recreation activities were classified according to differences in the psychological motivation of individual participants. These included: active, passive, extractive, appreciative, social, and learning motives.

We concluded with a discussion of the household production process. Consumers learn through experience what combination of their money, effort and time will provide the least costly way to produce a recreation day. It is possible to produce the same quantity of recreation in a variety of ways by substituting more of one input for less of another.

The measures of individual money, effort, and time resources introduced in this chapter are also used in empirical demand functions. We shall refer to this material in Chapters 4, 5, and 6.

READINGS

Allentuck, Andrew J., and Gordon E. Bivens. *Consumer Choice, The Economics of Personal Living.* Harcourt Brace Jovanovich, Inc., New York. 1977.

Bayless, Mark. "Measuring the Benefits of Air Quality Improvements: A Hedonic Salary Approach." *Journal of Environmental Economics and Management* 9(Mar. 1982):81-99.

Becker, Gary S. *The Economic Approach to Human Behavior.* University of Chicago Press, Chicago. 1976.

Behr, Michael R., and Dennis L. Nelson. *Economics: A Personal Consumer Approach.* Reston Publishing Co., Reston, Va. 1975.

Bockstael, Nancy E., and K. E. McConnell. "Theory and Estimation of the Household Production Function for Wildlife Recreation." *Journal of Environmental Economics and Management* 8(Sept. 1981):199-214.

Bureau of Labor Statistics. "Consumer Expenditure Survey: 1972-73." Report 455-4. U.S. Dept. of Labor, Washington, D.C. 1977.

Bureau of Outdoor Recreation. "Outdoor Recreation in America: Appendix A, An Economic Analysis." U.S. Gov. Print. Off., Washington, D.C. 1973.

Bruzelius, Nils. *The Value of Travel Time: Theory and Measurement.* Croom Helm, London. 1979.

Clawson, Marion, and Jack L. Knetsch. *Economics of Outdoor Recreation.* Johns Hopkins University Press, Baltimore. 1966.

Currie, John M., John A. Murphy, and Andrew Schmitz. "The Concept of Economic Surplus and its Use in Economic Analysis." *Economic Journal* 81(Dec. 1971):741-99.

Daumal, Rene. *Mount Analogue.* City Lights Books, San Francisco. 1967.

Dewey, John. *How We Think.* D. C. Heath and Co., New York. 1910.

Dewey, John. *Theory of Valuation.* University of Chicago Press, Chicago. 1939.

Deyak, Timothy A., and V. Kerry Smith. "Congestion and Participation in Outdoor Recreation: A Household Production Approach." *Journal of Environmental Economics and Management* 5(Mar. 1978):63-80.

Driver, Beverly L., and Perry J. Brown. "A Social-Psychological Definition of Recreation Demand, With Implications for Recreation Resource Planning." *Assessing Demand for Outdoor Recreation.* National Academy of Science, Washington, D.C. 1975. 1-88.

Gronau, Reuben. "Leisure, Home Production and Work — The Theory of the Allocation of Time Revised." *Journal of Political Economy* 85(Dec. 1977):1099-1123.

Gronau, Reuben. "Home Production — A Forgotten Industry." *Review of Economics and Statistics* 62(Aug. 1980):408-16.

Gurin, Gerald, Joseph Veroff, and Sheila Feld. *Americans View Their Mental Health.* Basic Books, New York. 1960.

Hawrylyshyn, Oli. "The Value of Household Services: A Survey of Empirical Estimates." *The Review of Income and Wealth* 22(June 1976):101-31.

Hendee, John C., Richard P. Gale, and William Catton, Jr. "A Typology of Outdoor Recreation Activity Preferences." *Journal of Environmental Education* 3(Fall 1971):28-34.

Hicks, John R. *A Revision of Demand Theory.* Oxford University Press, London. 1956.

Kalter, Robert J., and Thomas H. Stevens. "Resource Investments, Impact Distribution, and Evaluation Concepts." *American Journal of Agricultural Economics* 53(May 1971):206-15.

Kapteyn, Arie. "The Dynamics of Preference Formation." *Journal of Economic Behavior and Organization* 1(No. 1, 1980).123-57.

Krutilla, John V. "Is Public Intervention in Water Resources Development Conducive to Efficiency?" *Natural Resources Journal* 6(Jan. 1966):60-75.

Krutilla, John V., and Otto Eckstein. *Multiple Purpose River Development.* Johns Hopkins University Press, Baltimore. 1969.

Lancaster, Kelvin J. "A New Approach to Consumer Theory." *Journal of Political Economy* 74(Apr. 1966):132-57.

Latimer, Hugh. "Consumer and Producer Surplus in Tourism." *International Journal of Tourism Management* 2(Sept. 1981):141-61.

Lazear, Edward P., and Robert T. Michael. "Family Size and the Distribution of Real Per Capita Income." *American Economic Review* 70(Mar. 1980):91-107.

Linder, Staffan B. *The Harried Leisure Class.* Columbia University Press, New York. 1970.

Maslow, Abraham H. *Eupsychian Management.* Richard D. Irwin, Inc., Homewood, Ill. 1965.

McConnell, Kenneth E. "The Economics of Outdoor Recreation." in *Handbook of Natural Resource and Energy Economics,* Vol. II, A. V. Kneese and J. L. Sweeney (eds.). Elsevier Science Publishers, New York. 1985. 677-722.

Michael, Robert T. "Education in Nonmarket Production." *Journal of Political Economy* 83(Mar.-Apr. 1973):306-27.

Mitchell, Wesley. *The Backward Art of Spending Money and Other Essays.* McGraw Hill, Inc., New York. 1932.

Nordhaus, William D., and James Tobin. "Is Growth Obsolete?" *The Measurement of Economic and Social Performance.* Milton Moss, (ed.). National Bureau of Economic Research, New York. 1973. 509-31.

Owen, John D. "The Demand for Leisure." *Journal of Political Economy* 79(Jan.-Feb. 1971):56-76.

Quah, Euston. "Persistent Problems in Measuring Household Production: Definition, Quantifying Joint Activities and Valuation Issues Are Solvable." *American Journal of Economics and Sociology* 45(Apr. 1986):235-45.

Riesman, David. *The Lonely Crowd.* Yale University Press, New Haven. 1950.

Sax, Joseph L. *Mountains Without Handrails.* University of Michigan Press, Ann Arbor. 1980.

Scitovsky, Tibor. "Two Concepts of External Economics." *Journal of Political Economy* 62(Apr. 1954):143-51.

Scitovsky, Tibor. *The Joyless Economy: An Inquiry into Human Satisfaction and Consumer Dissatisfaction.* Oxford University Press, Oxford, England. 1976.

Scitovsky, Tibor. "The Desire for Excitement in Modern Society." *Kyklos* 34(No. 1, 1981):3-13.

Shabman, L.A., and Robert J. Kalter. "The Effects of New York State Administered Outdoor Recreation Expenditures on the Distribution of Personal Income." Agr. Econ. Res. Rep. No. 298, Cornell Univ., Ithaca, N.Y. 1969.

Simon, Herbert A. *The Science of Managerial Decision Making.* Harper, New York. 1960.

Simon, Herbert A. "The Decision-Making Process." *Managerial Economics and Operations Research.* Edwin Mansfield, (ed.). 4th Edition. W. W. Norton Co., N.Y. 1980. 8-10.

Simon, Julian L. "Interpersonal Welfare Comparisons Can be Made and Used for Redistribution Decisions." *Kyklos* 27(No. 1, 1974):63-98.

Sinden, John A., and Albert C. Worrell. *Unpriced Values: Decisions Without Market Prices.* John Wiley & Sons, New York, 1979.

Soileau, L. D., K. C. Smith, R. Hunter, C. E. Knight, D. K. Tabberer, and D. W. Hayne. "Atchafalaya Basin Usage Study." Interim Report by the Louisiana Wildlife and Fisheries Commission in Cooperation with the U.S. Army Corps of Engineers, New Orleans. 1973.

Szalai, Alexander, Ed. *The Use of Time.* Mouton, The Hague. 1972.

U.S. Dept. of Commerce. *Statistical Abstract of the United States.* Bureau of the Census. Washington, D.C. Published annually.

U.S. Dept. of Commerce. *Survey of Current Business.* Washington, D.C. Various years.

Walsh, Richard G. "Effects of Improved Research Methods on the Value of Recreation Benefits." *Outdoor Recreation: Advances in Applications of Economics.* Jay M. Hughes and R. Duane Lloyd, (eds.). General Technical Rpt. WO-2, Forest Service, U.S. Dept. of Agriculture, Washington, D.C. 1977. 145-53.

Weisskopf, Walter A. *The Psychology of Economics.* University of Chicago Press, Chicago. 1955.

Willig, Robert D. "Consumer's Surplus Without Apology." *American Economic Review* 66(Sept. 1976):589-97.

Wilman, Elizabeth A. "The Value of Time in Recreation Benefit Studies." *Journal of Environmental Economics and Management* 7(Sept. 1980):272-86.

Appendix
RESOURCE SUBSTITUTION

To help select the combination of inputs that can produce the desired output most cheaply, economists have invented the concept of a production function. The production function indicates the maximum amount of product that can be obtained from any specified combination of inputs, given the current physical and technical constraints. That is, it shows the largest quantity of recreation that any particular collection of household inputs is capable of producing. When only two inputs are considered, which are enough to indicate the basic principles involved, the production process can be represented graphically by means of an isoquant. The term "isoquant" is derived from iso, meaning equal, and quant, meaning quantity. It may be shown graphically as a straight line or curve that represents all the different combinations of two inputs which, when combined efficiently, produce a specified quantity of output in recreation activity days.

The shape of an isoquant reveals a great deal about the substitutability of resources available for household production; that is, the ability of consumers to substitute one input for another in the production process. This point is illustrated in panels 1, 2, and 3 of Figures 2-2 showing varying degrees of substitutability: (1) perfect substitutes, (2) complete nonsubstitutes, and (3) the more typical situation where inputs can be substituted for each other, but the substitutability is not perfect. The reader will note that the shape of isoquant lines indicate the degree of substitution between two inputs. The more they bend toward the origin near their middle, the more substitution decreases. As the curve approaches a straight line, substitution increases.

The slope of an isoquant is the change in the vertical axis (Y) divided by the change in the horizontal axis (X), or simply the change in input Y divided by the change in input X. This relationship is known

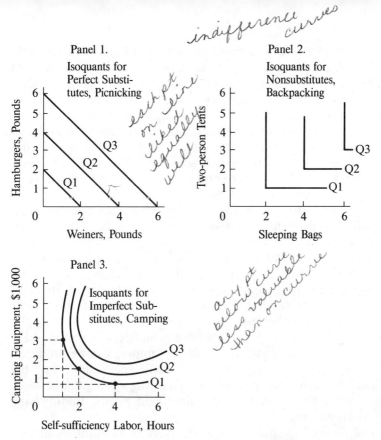

Figure 2-2. Substitution Among Resources in Household Production

as the marginal rate of substitution between two inputs in the production of any output, including recreation. It is a technical measure of the amount of one input (Y) that must be substituted for one unit of the other input (X) if output is to remain unchanged.

Some inputs are perfect substitutes, or nearly so, and the isoquants are straight lines as illustrated in panel 1 of Figure 2-2 for the meat portion of a picnic lunch. Assume that members of the household are prepared to accept either hamburgers or weiners as the meat portion of the meal. A satisfactory picnic experience, can be produced with 2 pounds of hamburger only, or 2 pounds of weiners only, or varying amounts of each. Two picnic meals would require 4 pounds of hamburger, or 4 pounds of weiners, or varying amounts of each. Three picnic meals would require 6 pounds of one or the other type of meat, and so on. Although the ratio of substitution between the two inputs is one-to-one in this illustration, it may vary for other resources. The important principle is that the ratio of substitution remains constant for resources that are perfect substitutes.

Some inputs in recreation are not substitutes at all, and the isoquants are right angles, as illustrated in panel 2 of Figure 2-2 for back-packing. A household of two persons requires exactly two sleeping bags and one 2-person tent to produce a night of camping on a wilderness trail. Physical limits of space available require that two pairs of backpackers have two tents and four sleeping bags. Three couples require three tents plus six sleeping bags, and so on. Other examples of recreation inputs that are not substitutes include: bicycle wheels and frames; ski boots and skis; turtleneck shirts and blue jeans. An individual attending an outdoor jazz concert requires exactly three hours of leisure time and one entrance ticket.

The more typical situation is one in which inputs can be substituted for each other but the substitution is not perfect. In this case, the isoquants are curves, as illustrated in panel 3 of Figure 2-2 for car camping. A household of two adults and a child can produce a night of car camping with a relatively small amount of self-sufficiency labor and a large investment in equipment such as a camper trailer. A night of camping can also be produced with less equipment if more self-sufficiency labor is used because members of the household set up the tent, blow air into the mattresses, build a campfire with wood available at the campsite, etc. Finally, a night of camping can be produced with still less equipment and more self-sufficiency labor, but the campers must be extremely innovative — hanging a tube tent between two trees, cutting firewood, picking edible wild plants, finding pine boughs to sleep on, etc.

Panel 3 of Figure 2-2 shows that a relatively small addition of self-sufficiency labor from 1 to 2 hours per day allows the input of recreation equipment to be reduced by half, from $3,000 to $1,500. A relatively large increase in self-sufficiency labor from 2 to 4 hours is required to obtain a reduction in equipment from $1,500 to $750. This illustrates the fact that as more and more self-sufficiency labor is substituted for camping equipment, the increment of labor necessary to replace equipment increases. Finally, at the extremes, the isoquant typically becomes positively sloped, indicating that there is a limit to the range over which the two inputs may be substituted for each other. In other words, it would be irrational for a household to put additional effort into self-sufficient camping beyond 4 hours per day when to do so also requires additional recreation equipment.

A production isoquant curve only describes what input combinations can produce a given output; it indicates the technological possibilities. Households or individuals cannot decide which of the available options suits their purposes best without the corresponding cost information; that is, the relative prices of the inputs. The problem of consumers is to produce a given quantity of output (say, a recreation day) with the smallest possible budget. A way to find the minimum budget capable of producing a recreation day is illustrated in Figure

2-3, which combines the production isoquant curve for one recreation day with a budget line (or isocost line) which is a representation of equally costly input combinations for households or individual consumers.

For example, if the leisure time of individuals has an average opportunity cost from foregone work of $1.25 per hour and the net willingness to pay to avoid self-sufficiency time used in driving is $2.50 per hour, then individuals who commit $10 worth of total time to a recreation trip can spend 8 hours of leisure time in on-site recreation but no time in driving (point A in panel 1 of Figure 2-3), or individuals can spend 4 hours driving and have no energy left to enjoy on-site recreation time (point B). But it is undoubtedly more sensible to pick some intermediate point on the budget line, dividing the $10 worth of total trip time between the two inputs.

A way to find the minimum time budget capable of producing a recreation day also is illustrated in panel 1 of Figure 2-3, which combines the production isoquant for one recreation day with several budget lines for time. The problem of individuals is to find the lowest time budget that will allow them to reach the one recreation day isoquant curve. Clearly, an expenditure of $7.50 worth of time is too little, because there is no point on the budget line that permits production of a recreation day. Similarly, an expenditure of $15 is too much because individuals can produce a recreation day more cheaply. The solution is at point C, where 2 hours of self-sufficiency driving time and 4 hours of on-site recreation time are used to produce a recreation day. The decision rule is: The least costly way to produce any given level of output is indicated by the point of tangency between a budget line and the production isoquant curve corresponding to that level of output.

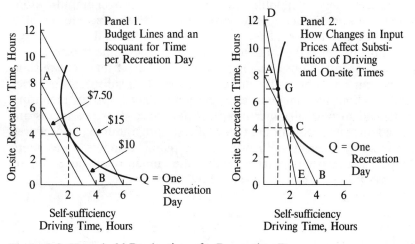

Figure 2-3. Household Production of a Recreation Day

Suppose now that the opportunity cost of on-site recreation time decreases because of fewer opportunities for overtime and part-time second jobs. At the same time, suppose the willingness to pay to reduce driving time rises because of heavier traffic or poorer road conditions. This means that the budget line will shift, and its slope will change. Specifically, with less costly on-site recreation time, any given time budget for outdoor recreation will buy more hours so the intercept of the budget line will shift upward. Conversely, with more costly self-sufficiency time used in driving, any given time budget will buy fewer hours of driving, so the intercept of the budget line will shift to the left.

Panel 2 of Figure 2-3 illustrates the effect of these changes. It combines budget line AB and tangency point C from panel 1 of the same figure and the new budget line, DE, resulting from the time price changes described in the previous paragraph. Notice that the new tangency point G lies above and to the left of point C, meaning that as the price of recreation time decreases and the price of self-sufficiency driving time increases, the individual consumer will devote more time to on-site recreation and less to travel. As common sense suggests, when the price of one input rises in comparison with that of another, it will pay the individual to employ less of this input and more of the other input to make up for reduced use of the more expensive input. In addition to this substitution of one input for another, a change in the price of an input may induce individuals to alter the level of output that they decide to produce. This will be discussed in Chapter 5 on the demand curve.

Households and individuals normally seek the least costly way to produce a recreation day, other things remaining the same. We have dealt with the choice between two inputs as if the tradeoff could be decided separately from other inputs. This is an oversimplification, for the choices between how much of two resources to employ depends on the amount of other resource available and their relative prices. For example, the amount of self-sufficiency time it pays an individual consumer to use depends on the amount of total leisure time available, and the prices of goods and services that substitute for time. Decisions about how much of each different input to use is, therefore, interdependent with all other inputs. When more than two inputs are involved in the production process, linear programming procedures are commonly used by both private and public planners. Consumers rely upon a similar computation within the human brain, according to recent psychological studies reviewed by Scitovsky.

Chapter Three
Nature of Consumption

This chapter defines several alternative measures of the quantity of recreation; shows how to convert the results of each measure to be comparable with other measures; explores the unique characteristics of direct and indirect recreation consumption; and discusses implications for recreation economic decisions.

The development and management of recreation resources provides an opportunity for people to take part in recreation activities. However, the production process always involves the participation of consumers, for a distinguishing characteristic of recreation is that it is a human activity, i.e. sightsee*ing*, hik*ing*, camp*ing*, ski*ing*, swimm*ing*, fish*ing*, hunt*ing*, and the like. Thus, the quantity of recreation consumed is measured in terms of the number of occasions or the amount of time that individuals choose to participate. The output of a recreation site is, therefore, the sum of the quantity of recreation activity demanded by individual consumers at the site.

Most recreation programs have a dual purpose, to protect the environmental resources and to make them available for the enjoyment of people. This complicates the problem of measuring total output because it means that recreation agencies produce both onsite and offsite services. Indirect consumption occurs offsite and appears to be of two broad types. One is the flow of information about recreation and environmental resources in books, magazines, and videos. The other is the preservation value to the general public from knowing that these resources are protected.

ALTERNATIVE MEASURES

Several approaches have been used to measure the quantity of recreation consumed. These include: (1) recreation days or activity days; (2) recreation visitor days, user days or hours; (3) trips, visits, or visitors; and (4) entrance permits, licenses, and tickets issued or units occupied. While each approach has provided a satisfactory measure of a particular type of recreation activity, a problem of comparability arises when two or more measures are combined. No standard unit of recreation use has been developed that is suitable for all purposes. Thus, it is important to understand when each measure should be used and how to convert the results of each approach to compare it with other measures. Accuracy of the alternative estimating procedures (car counters, campground and trail registration, licenses sold, spot checks, etc.) is a continuing problem.

Recreation Day

A recreation day is defined by the federal guidelines (Water Resources Council) as a visit by one individual to a recreation area for recreation purposes during any reasonable portion or all of a 24-hour period of time. This is virtually identical to an earlier definition by the Bureau of Outdoor Recreation of an activity day as one person participating in an activity for any part of one calendar day. The approach has provided satisfactory measures of the quantity of single or similar recreation activities demanded by individual consumers at recreation sites, where length of stay measured in hours per day does not vary appreciably among individual participants. Moreover, the approach is consistent with individual perception of a recreation day as an occasion or event with little or no regard for the amount of time involved.

Problems arise when the approach is used to measure individual participation in more than one recreation activity during a single recreation day. Application of the method can result in double counting of recreation days where one individual camping, swimming, boating, and fishing during a single 24-hour day may be counted as four recreation days, i.e., one in each of four categories. Also, problems can occur when this approach is used to compare the number of recreation days of 1-4 hours in length (i.e., picnicking and hiking) with days of 6-12 hours in length (i.e., backpacking and camping), where the effects on recreation resources vary according to the amount of time they are used.

Some observers have suggested that problems may arise when the approach is used to measure the quantity of recreation in applications of the travel cost approach to recreation demand analysis. For travel costs are more directly related to number of trips than to recreation days at the site. Nevertheless, recreation days have been used in a number of successful travel cost demand studies. Perhaps consumers find it more convenient to make decisions concerning how much recreation to consume in terms of recreation days rather than trips with varying lengths of stay.

Recreation Visitor Day

A recreation visitor day is defined by the U.S. Forest Service as 12 person-hours, which may be one person for 12 hours, 12 persons for

Table 3-1. Recreation Visitor Days in Six Recreation Opportunity Zones (ROS) of the National Forest, United States

Activity	Recreation Visitor Days	Percent of Recreation Visitor Days in ROS Zones					
		Primitive	Semi-primitive, Nonmotorized	Semi-primitive, Motorized	Roaded, Natural	Rural	Urban
Cold Water Fishing	12,402,300	11	12	19	48	9	1
Warm Water Fishing	4,096,400	1	3	15	69	11	2
Anadomous Fishing	3,208,227	11	12	19	48	9	1
Salt Water Fishing	316,700	16	0	62	20	1	0
Big Game Hunting	10,875,200	6	17	26	44	6	1
Small Game Hunting	2,884,700	1	8	19	62	9	0
Waterfowl Hunting	796,700	5	3	25	62	5	0
Upland Game Hunting	1,856,200	1	8	19	67	6	0
Motorized Boating	4,084,000	1	0	19	63	15	2
Non-motorized Boating	3,561,700	4	13	20	43	20	1
Motorized Travel	44,999,900	1	0	7	74	15	3
Camping	59,627,700	6	6	11	50	22	4
Picnicking	9,707,200	2	4	8	51	30	4
Hiking	12,458,600	17	22	22	32	7	2
Downhill Skiing	8,585,800	1	3	10	38	24	24
Water Sports	6,317,200	3	4	10	56	25	2
Total or Average	185,800,000	5	6	13	55	17	4

Source: U.S. Forest Service.

one hour each, or any equivalent combination of individual or group use, either continuous or intermittently. An earlier term, recreation user day, had the same definition. A recreation visitor hour has been defined as one or more users for continuous or intermittent periods of time aggregating 60 minutes. The approach has provided a satisfactory measure of the total quantity of recreation at sites where individuals participate in more than one recreation activity during a single recreation day. The method avoids double counting of recreation days at recreation sites administered by the U.S. Forest Service where an individual who hikes for 6 hours, picnics 2 hours, and fishes 4 hours would be counted as a single 12-hour visitor day. The approach also has provided satisfactory measures of total recreation resource use in a National Forest where recreation activities of varying lengths of time are combined into standard 12-hour visitor days. For example, Table 3-1 illustrates the number of recreation visitor days fishing, hunting, camping, hiking, skiing, and so forth, in six recreation opportunity zones ranging from primitive to urban.

Problems arise when studies of the quantity of recreation activity demanded by individual consumers are aggregated into visitor day statistics. Individual consumers perceive recreation activity as an occasion or event rather than as a standard 12-hour visitor day. Activities such as hiking, horseback riding, fishing, hunting, boating, and skiing are typically 4-6 hours per day rather than 12 hours. Beyond 4-6 hours, increasing fatigue results in diminishing satisfaction from additional hours engaged in the recreation activities. To extend an individual consumer's recreation day to 12 hours would result in a loss of satisfaction and benefit for most outdoor recreation activities. Exceptions are overnight stays in campgrounds, backcountry campsites, lodges, and seasonal homes.

The result is that it takes three 4-hour days of fishing to equal one 12-hour visitor day of camping. Moreover, the camper who stays an entire 24-hour day would be counted as two 12-hour visitor days, equal to six times the quantity of recreation attributed to a single 4-hour day of fishing. It is obvious that this approach vastly understates the quantity of most outdoor recreation activities as perceived by individual consumers. Thus, it is important to adjust the recreation visitor day statistics when considering individual consumers perception of recreation activity as an occasion of varying length.

There are two additional points that should be made about recreation visitor days. Reiling and Anderson describe the problems of measuring costs and charging user fees. As an example, 12 people who arrive at a site at the same time and use it for an hour would result in higher costs than one person using the facility for 12 hours. The authors also note that user fees usually are charged per party or person for a visit of varying duration or a calendar day. For example, a party of four using a campsite for 24 hours accounts for eight recreation visitor days. But the user fee is paid to occupy the campsite for one night. The authors conclude that alternative measures may be more suitable for purposes of costing and pricing recreation services.

Recreation Visit or Visitor

A recreation visit or visitor is defined by the National Park Service as the use by one individual of a recreation area for recreation purposes for any length of time. This is identical to the definition of a recreation trip when the sole purpose is visiting a particular recreation site. The approach has provided satisfactory measures of the quantity of recreation demanded by individual consumers on single day outings and/or overnight weekend trips to recreation sites within 150 miles of their place of residence. In this case, a recreation visit or trip is equivalent to one or, at most, two recreation days. When the length of stay by visitors to a recreation site is reasonably similar, the number of trips per capita has provided the most suitable measure of the quantity of recreation in applications of the travel cost approach to recreation demand analysis. For travel costs obviously are more directly related to trips than to either recreation days or recreation visitor days.

Problems arise when the approach is used to measure the quantity of recreation demanded by individuals on vacation trips with varying length of stay at a recreation site and/or with visits to more than one recreation site during a single trip. The annual summary of visits to recreation sites administered by the National Park Service includes a combination of users on single day outings, overnight weekend trips, and vacations with varying lengths of stay. As a result, comparisons of the quantity of recreation demanded at alternative recreation sites may be distorted unless adjusted for length of stay. Individuals usually visit more than one recreation site while on vacation trips and, to a lesser extent, on overnight weekend trips. In this event it is important to develop some reasonable basis for allocating total time on the trip among recreation sites visited. A number of approaches have been tried. Dividing by the total number of sites visited on the trip assumes an equal quantity of recreation at each site. Allocation on the basis of the proportion of recreation days at each site seems more reasonable, although it assumes that each day is of equal length.

A problem remains how to distinguish recreation travel time from on-site recreation time. In the past, it was assumed that the proportion of trip time devoted to necessary travel to and from a recreation site was nonrecreational, because of the dissatisfaction of driving, and thus travel time was not counted as part of the quantity of recreation. More recently, studies of consumer behavior report that a substantial proportion of recreation travel provides satisfaction associated with sightseeing as a recreation activity. From the point of view of consumers, a recreation trip is conceived as beginning when they leave home and ending when they arrive home at its end, i.e., portal to portal. In fact, national surveys of recreation show that sightseeing or driving for pleasure is a leading recreation activity in the United States. Since 1916, when the Forest Service started measuring recreation use, driving for pleasure within the national forests has ranked first or second to camping. To what extent this will continue in the future may depend in part on trends in travel cost.

Entrance Permits

The quantity of recreation activity also has been defined as the number of entrance permits or licenses issued and the number of recreation units occupied. Examples include: the number of fishing and

71

hunting licenses sold by state agencies, lift tickets issued by ski areas, overnight stays at resort lodges, and number of campsites occupied. When these sources are adjusted for known deficiencies, they provide the most accurate measures available of the quantity of recreation activity. For example, the number of fishing and hunting licenses sold provides the best available estimate of total fishermen and hunters in a state when adjusted for those over 65 and under 16, those who purchase a combination license, and estimated poaching. Wildlife management agencies supplement this information with that from game check stations or sample surveys to estimate number of days per hunter, amount of game bagged, and quantity of hunting in management units or resource areas.

Entrance permits to parks and historical monuments provide an accurate measure of the number of visits or visitors when adjusted for use of annual passes, size of parties, and periods of time when the entrance booth may not be occupied, such as at night and on special occasions when entrance is free. When individual recreation use is for less than one calendar day, as is frequently the case, a visit or trip is equivalent to a recreation day.

Problems arise when individuals enter a park for multiple-day visits and/or engage in more than one recreation activity while there. Entrance permits may provide little or no information about the quantity of sightseeing, hiking, picnicking, group games, fishing, and other recreation activities that occur in a particular park. Such information is essential to effective resource management. Thus, the statistical services branch of the National Park Service is making a concerted effort to overcome this deficiency in its park visitor statistics by using sample surveys to supplement the existing information on number of camping permits issued and number of concessioner lodging units occupied.

The following example illustrates the problem of measuring the quantity of recreation activity by this method. It shows that the number of lift tickets issued probably is not as accurate as the perception of individual consumers. If you ask a friend about a recent winter vacation, he may reply that he went skiing for a week. If you persist in your questioning, your friend will provide you with a day-to-day account of his trip. In fact he took an 8-day trip and purchased a 6-day ski permit which entitled him to ski from 9 A.M. to 4:30 P.M. daily. However, on Sunday he skied for 3 hours in the afternoon. Monday, a blizzard kept him in the ski lodge. Tuesday, Wednesday, and Thursday were sunny, and he skied 6 hours each day. Moreover, if your friend is a typical skier, he spent one-third of the time actually skiing, one-third in lift lines and riding ski lifts, and one-third in the base area. Friday he was sick and Saturday departed. Thus, skiing for a "week" really meant the opportunity to ski six days with only four days of actual skiing. Thus, to improve the accuracy of lift tickets issued as a measure of number of skiers, it is necessary to adjust multiple-day permits for actual days of use.

Methods of Conversion

The previous section defined the alternative measures of the quantity of recreation consumed which are currently applied by recreation resource managers. It should be clear to the reader that no standard unit of recreation consumption has been developed thus far that is suitable for all purposes of measurement. Thus, it is important to understand the methods of conversion from one approach to another.

To convert the number of recreation visitor days to recreation days, multiply by 12 and divide by the average number of hours per recreation day. Table 3-2 shows the standard number of hours per recreation day for National Forests in the Rocky Mountain Region and the range for all National Forests. For example, with four hours of fishing per recreation day, each 12-hour visitor day is equal to three recreation days. To convert recreation days to recreation visitor days, multi-

Table 3-2. Standard Hours per Day of Outdoor Recreation, Forest Service, United States

| Activity | Hours per Day in National Forests | |
	Rocky Mountain Region	Range, United States
Bicycling	3.0	0.9-3.0
Horseback Riding	4.0	1.0-4.6
Playing Outdoor Games or Sports	3.0	0.9-6.0
Fishing	3.5	1.9-4.5
Canoeing	2.0	2.0-4.1
Sailing	2.5	2.4-4.5
Other Boating	4.0	2.5-4.1
Swimming	1.5	0.8-2.9
Waterskiing	2.0	0.7-2.6
Camping	10.5	9.6-12.0
Mountain Climbing	6.0	3.5-7.4
Hiking	4.0	3.2-4.0
Walking for Pleasure	4.0	3.2-4.0
Bird Watching	4.0	1.8-4.0
Wildlife and Bird Photography	3.0	1.8-4.0
Nature Walks	3.0	0.3-4.7
Picnicking	2.0	2.0-4.0
Driving for Pleasure	2.5	1.5-3.2
Sightseeing	1.5	0.9-2.0
Attending Outdoor Sports Events	1.5	0.5-2.0
Hunting	4.0	2.3-7.8

Source: U.S. Forest Service.

ply the average number of hours per day by the number of recreation days and divide the result by 12.

To convert the number of recreation visits or trips to recreation days, multiply the former by the average number of recreation days per trip. For example, with 2.5 camping days per trip, 100 trips equal 250 recreation days of camping. To convert recreation days to trips, divide number of days by the average number of recreation days per trip.

To convert the number of visits or trips to recreation visitor days, multiply the former by the average number of recreation days per trip times the average number of hours per recreation day, then divide the result by 12 hours. For example, with 2.5 camping days per trip and 10 hours per camping day, 25 divided by 12 hours equals 2.08 visitor days of camping. To convert recreation visitor days to number of trips, multiply the number of visitor days by 12 and divide the result by average number of hours per recreation day. Then divide by the number of days per trip.

Entrance permits can be treated as equivalent to number of visits or trips when adjusted for number of persons per vehicle and for the estimated number of persons who enter without a permit. The number of fishing and hunting licenses sold can be treated as the number of participants when adjusted for the number of persons who are exempt from purchase of a license. To convert number of participants to other measures, it is necessary to conduct periodic sample surveys of the number of trips per participant, days per trip, and hours per day.

The number of ski lift tickets issued and the number of overnight stays at resort lodges can be treated as recreation days when adjusted for the estimated number of users who do not pay and those who pay but do not use the service. The number of camping permits issued can be treated as the equivalent of recreation days when adjusted for number of persons per party and the number of users who do not pay.

In the early 1980s, the President's Office of Management and Budget required all federal recreation agencies to report total visitor hours as well as their historic measures of recreation participation. This greatly facilitates the comparison of recreation output by the federal agencies. If a central clearing house would collect visitor hours for state, county, and city recreation facilities, we would have available information on total public output. Similar information on private facilities would allow us to estimate the trends in total outdoor recreation and compare the public and private sectors. Preliminary estimates are that all levels of government provided nearly one-half of total outdoor recreation activities, 3.1 of 6.6 billion recreation visitor days (12 hours each) in 1982.

CONSUMPTION PATTERNS

An understanding of the participation patterns of individual consumers is essential to effective recreation resource development and management decisions. Recent national surveys have established a number of distinguishing characteristics of recreation consumption. These include: (1) the proportion of the population participating in each recreation activity; (2) the number of recreation activities per participant; (3) the seasonal pattern of participation; (4) the frequency of partial-day or single-day outings, 2-3 day overnight stays, and vacation trips; (5) the proportion of recreation on weekends, and (6) the hours per day. Together, these characteristics of individual consumption constitute a substantial constraint on the output of recreation resources.

Recent studies have shown that approximately 80 percent of the people 12 years of age and over participate in outdoor recreation activities in the United States. Individual consumers exhibit consider-

Table 3-3. Participation in Outdoor Recreation Activities, United States

Activity	Percent of Population Participating
Camping in Developed Area	30%
Camping in Primitive Area	21
Canoeing, Kayaking, River Running	16
Sailing	11
Waterskiing	16
Fishing	53
Other Boating	34
Outdoor Pool Swimming and Sunbathing	63
Other Outdoor Swimming and Sunbathing	46
Nature Walk, Birdwatch, Photography	50
Hiking or Backpacking	28
Other Walking or Jogging	68
Bicycling	47
Horseback Riding	15
Driving Off-road Vehicles	26
Hunting	19
Picnicking	72
Golfing	16
Playing Tennis Outdoors	33
Cross-country Skiing	2
Downhill Skiing	7
Ice-skating Outdoors	16
Sledding	21
Snowmobiling	8
Playing Other Sports or Games	56
Sightseeing	62
Driving for Pleasure	69
Visiting Zoos, Aquariums, Carnivals, etc.	73
Attending Outdoor Sports Events	61
Attending Outdoor Dances, Concerts, Plays	41

Source: Heritage, Conservation, and Recreation Service, 1979.

able variation in preferences. Table 3-3 shows the proportion of the U.S. population that participates in each of 30 recreation activities. Over two-thirds of the people engage in picnicking, driving for pleasure, walking or jogging, and visiting zoos, aquariums, carnivals or amusement parks. Over one-half go fishing, swimming and sunbathing at outdoor pools, attend outdoor sports events, and play outdoor sports other than golf and tennis.

Individuals who participate average 11 recreation activities during a 12-month period of time. Fifteen percent participate in fewer than five activities; 26 percent, 5-9 activities; 40 percent, 10-15 activities; and 19 percent, 16 or more recreation activities per year.

There is a pronounced seasonal pattern of participation in most recreation activities. As a result, the use of recreation sites is concentrated into a peak season which seldom extends beyond 120 days in length. Table 3-4 shows the seasonal variation in the proportion of the people who participate in selected recreation activities in the United States. The summer season and, to a lesser extent, the spring and fall are preferred over winter. This is particularly true for the northern one-half of the United States. Areas with a year around temperate climate such as Florida, Texas, Arizona, and Southern California, experience much less seasonal variation in participation than does the rest of the nation.

Table 3-4. Seasonal Participation in Outdoor Recreation, United States

Activity	Percent of Annual Participation			
	Summer	Fall	Winter	Spring
Fishing	47%	18%	9%	26%
Canoeing	55	17	4	24
Sailing	56	36	4	4
Other Boating	62	18	7	13
Swimming	80	10	2	8
Water Skiing	75	14	2	9
Camping	52	24	8	16
Hunting	9	40	43	8
Bicycling	34	18	17	31
Horseback Riding	35	17	15	33
Playing Outdoor Games or Sports	29	22	20	29
Picnicking	60	18	6	16
Walking for Pleasure	24	24	27	25
Driving for Pleasure	32	21	23	24
Sightseeing	37	23	20	20
Attending Outdoor Sports	35	33	12	20
Attending Outdoor Concerts	54	22	7	17
Hiking	62	14	13	11
Nature Walks	27	25	23	25
Ice Skating	0	0	94	6
Snow Skiing	0	0	92	8
Sledding	0	0	85	15

Source: Outdoor Recreation Resources Review Commission.

Most participation occurs during the season when the weather is most suitable for the activity. Most hiking, swimming, and boating occurs in the summer; most skiing, sledding, and ice skating in the winter. Hunting is limited to the fall and winter seasons established by state wildlife management agencies. Some activities are year around — in particular, sightseeing, driving for pleasure, walking for pleasure, bicycling, and attending outdoor sports events. Fishing and water sports show some activity in the winter as weather allows.

The percent of total annual visits to the national parks occurring during each month of the year is:

January	3.1	July	18.6
February	4.0	August	16.0
March	5.2	September	8.8
April	7.6	October	6.9
May	9.5	November	4.2
June	13.0	December	3.1

Table 3-5. Type of Occasion for Outdoor Recreation, United States

	Percent of Annual Participation			
Activity	Vacation	2-3 day Overnight Trips	Single-day Outings	Few Available Hours
Total	13%	12%	52%	23%
Bicycling	10	6	14	70
Horseback Riding	15	9	28	48
Playing Outdoor Games or Sports	9	8	49	34
Golf	13	9	31	47
Tennis	8	9	32	51
Fishing	12	20	49	19
Canoeing	19	35	27	19
Sailing	19	19	46	16
Other Boating	14	22	50	14
Swimming	10	11	64	15
Ocean	11	8	72	9
Lake, Pond, Stream	10	15	62	13
Pool	13	5	48	34
Water-skiing	10	20	59	11
Camping	35	65	n.a.	n.a.
Remote Camping	21	79	n.a.	n.a.
Mountain Climbing	24	13	46	17
Hiking	20	18	42	20
Walking for Pleasure	16	12	46	26
Bird Watching	14	15	43	28
Wildlife and Bird Photography	32	6	43	19
Nature Walks	18	15	48	19
Picnicking	7	6	73	14
Driving for Pleasure	16	8	41	35
Sightseeing	25	10	47	18
Attending Outdoor Sporting Events	10	6	28	56
Attending Outdoor Concerts, Plays	17	5	28	50
Hunting	10	22	20	48

n.a. = not applicable.
Source: Bureau of Outdoor Recreation.

Numerous studies have pointed out that a unique characteristic of the consumption of recreation is that travel is necessary to participate. The information presented in Table 3-5 is important in this regard because it suggests that travel distance is not an important constraint for most recreation. Nonetheless, it is obvious that travel is crucial in consumer decisions to participate in recreation. Table 3-5 shows that most (75 percent) recreation activities of individual consumers occurs during a few available hours of a day within 1-5 miles from home, and on single-day outings within 50 miles. A much smaller proportion (25 percent) of recreation occurs on 2-3 day overnight trips within 100-200 miles and on vacation trips 500-1,000 miles or more from home.

This reflects the fact that most people are constrained by a fixed workday and workweek. They lack the leisure time to travel very far to engage in recreation activities during the few available evening hours of the workday. Moreover, the limited leisure time during the typical 2-3 day weekend limits travel to 1-3 hours one-way, whether it

Table 3-6. Hours per Day and Weekend Participation in Outdoor Recreation, United States

Activity	Percent of Total Activity Occurring on Weekends	Average Number of Hours of Participation per Activity Day
Picnicking	71	2.7
Sightseeing	62	3.1
Walking for Pleasure	64	1.9
Other Swimming Outdoors	69	2.6
Visiting Zoos, Fairs, Amusement Parks	55	4.5
Fishing	68	4.4
Playing Other Outdoor Games or Sports	65	2.6
Outdoor Pool Swimming	52	2.8
Nature Walks	70	2.0
Other Boating	74	2.8
Going to Outdoor Sports Events	57	4.2
Camping in Developed Campgrounds	62	12.0
Bicycling	69	2.0
Going to Outdoor Concerts, Plays, etc.	66	3.6
Horseback Riding	51	2.7
Hiking with a Pack and Rock Climbing	62	3.0
Tennis	79	2.1
Water-skiing	69	2.6
Golf	51	4.9
Camping in Remote or Wilderness Areas	80	12.0
Riding Motorcycles Off the Road	62	4.0
Bird Watching	75	2.1
Canoeing	72	2.3
Sailing	75	4.4
Hunting	64	4.4
Wildlife and Bird Photography	56	1.6
Driving 4-wheel Vehicles Off the Road	56	3.1

Source: Bureau of Outdoor Recreation.

be for single-day outings or overnight weekend trips. Thus, most recreation trips are short and transportation costs relatively minor, as will be shown in the following chapter.

Most recreation activities of individual consumers take place on weekends. Table 3-6 shows that in the case of every activity, more than one-half of total participation occurs on weekends. For some activities, weekend participation is 75 percent or more — tennis, bird watching, sailing, canoeing, and other boating. Weekends also account for 70 percent of the nature walks and 80 percent of the camping in remote or wilderness areas. This means that average daily use of recreation resources on Saturday or Sunday exceeds average daily use on Monday through Friday by more than 2.5 times.

For example, the number of households staying overnight at a National Forest in California during an average summer week can be expressed as a percent of the peak day:

Monday	41%	Friday	87
Tuesday	39	Saturday	100
Wednesday	41	Sunday	63
Thursday	53		

Weekend recreation behavior reflects the fact that most people are constrained by a fixed work week and receive paid vacations of 1-4 weeks per year. Most recreation occurs during periods when no working time is lost. The resulting peak-day demand on weekends and holidays requires that much more recreation resource capacity be developed than would be necessary if the consumption of recreation activities were more constant through time. As a result of existing consumption patterns, there is usually a large amount of excess capacity of recreation resources on weekdays.

With the exception of camping, no recreation activity averages more than 5.0 hours per recreation day. For example, Table 3-6 shows that picnicking averages 2.7 hours per recreation day. For the most part, picnicking trips would be combined with other activities such as: sightseeing, 3.1 hours per day; playing outdoor games or sports, 2.6 hours; and outdoor swimming, 2.6 hours. Thus, an individual consumer typically combines several activities while on a single trip. In the above example, the four activities total 11.0 hours which is nearly the equivalent of one recreation visitor day.

OTHER CONCEPTS OF CONSUMPTION

There are two additional points that should be made about the output of recreation and park programs. First, the production process is similar to that of a service industry. Managers of recreation sites supply the natural resources, facilities, and personal services that consumers combine with other resources to produce recreation experiences for themselves. Second, the multiple objectives of recreation agencies include programs to protect the natural environment as well as to provide for recreation use. As a result, a more nearly complete definition of the total consumption of service should include both direct and indirect output. Direct output refers to the onsite consumption of recreation activities by users. Indirect output refers to the offsite consumption of knowledge about the quality of the resource by the general public. The purpose of this section is to describe these two concepts which may some day improve the way we specify what is produced by recreation and park programs. Understanding output is especially important to improving the performance of service institutions, according to Peter Drucker, noted management expert.

Recreation as a Service Industry

Managers of recreation sites provide the services of natural resources, facilities, and personnel. The production of services differs from the production of physical products in several important ways. Kotler reviews the nature of service industries in our post-industrial society. Typically, services have four distinctive characteristics. Output is less tangible than for other industries, production cannot be separated from consumption, quality is more variable, and it is highly perishable. Each of these features will be described below.

First, services are less tangible than physical products. That is, they cannot be seen, tasted, felt, heard, or smelled before they are purchased. Thus, individuals going sightseeing in a national park cannot see the quality of the scenery before purchasing an entrance fee. The angler who purchases a fishing license cannot know the quality of fishing in advance. The same is true for tourists making reservations at resorts. Under the circumstances, consumer recreation economic decisions depend, in part, on information from the agencies providing the service. Managers can try to make the service more tangible. Visitor centers can provide clay models of the park, videotapes of the scenery, and illustrated maps. Managers can emphasize the benefits of the service in addition to describing its features. Thus, an interpretive program can describe the excitement of catching fish or the breathtaking beauty of rocky peaks, deep canyons, and waterfalls.

When managers produce recreation services, they usually do not provide a tangible physical product (fish and wildlife are notable exceptions). In fact, the usual provision of recreation services does not result in a transfer of ownership to the consumer. For most park visitors, the object is to have a recreation experience with their companions. The visit itself is simply a vehicle for obtaining a psychological and emotional experience. How should park managers treat these intangibles? They should define the bundle of goods and services provided consumers and the relative importance of each part to consumer benefits. This would help managers understand some of the elusive intangibles that affect consumer decisions. On this basis, they could improve the delivery of a total service package that emphasizes the most important parts.

Second, the production of services cannot be separated from consumption. They must occur simultaneously. The reason is that production is a process in which consumers participate. They travel to recreation sites at considerable cost to themselves. As a result, most sites are located relatively close to prospective users, and size is limited by local demand. Few recreation sites can take advantage of economies of scale by producing for multiple geographic markets, as is the case for manufacturers of physical products such as recreation equipment. Also, the manufacturing of physical products is of no interest to consumers of the products; consumers are interested only in the recreation equipment produced. In contrast, recreation consumers interact with service employees, facilities, and the physical environment that creates the service. This means that the production process itself is one dimension of the output of services. Consumers observe the service delivery system at the point of production. This affects their perception of the quality of service. For example, the appearance of ski lifts and the friendliness of operators are readily apparent to skiers.

Third, the quality of services is often more variable than physical products. In economic terms, recreational services tend to be heterogeneous or variable rather than homogeneous or identical. This means that the output of a single recreation site is variable as is that of a single service employee. For example, some anglers are successful while others are not. The services rendered by flight attendants vary from flight to flight and from person to person on the same flight. The output of tennis and ski instructors varies in the same manner. As a result, it is difficult for managers to establish standards for the output of services and even more difficult to ensure that standards are met each time the service is delivered to a recreation user. This inherent variability puts a large burden on quality control programs. Training of service employees is essential to reduce the possibility consumers will pay for a recreation service that is of lower quality than expected. Consumer demand studies and preference surveys can provide information for managers to develop service levels to maintain user satisfaction. For example, research by Driver, et al., suggests that standards of fishing services should be varied across the state of Wyoming to accommodate consumer preferences for wild trout fishing, put and take fishing, etc.

Fourth, services are highly perishable. They cannot be stored or stockpiled. While recreation equipment such as a fishing rod can be kept in inventory until it is sold, the potential revenue from an unoccupied campsite is lost forever. Many resort lodges charge individuals holding reservations but not showing up because the service value of rooms only exists at a point in time. Reservations preclude renting rooms to other potential users. The perishable nature of services is not a problem when demand is steady. But when demand fluctuates, service industries have problems. Because services are perishable, many service industries cannot operate at the same rate of output year round. Capacity is built to accommodate the peaks in use, and underuse occurs the rest of the year. For example, ski resorts have to use much more equipment because of peak demand during the Christmas holiday and on weekends than if demand were uniform throughout the winter. Also, it is difficult to staff the services with part-time workers in advance of the peaks.

There are two important problems that should be emphasized, one concerning the demand and the other the supply of recreation services. First, the "practical capacity" of parks and other recreation sites is much less than their physical or technical capacity, defined as the maximum number of persons who can occupy a site at one time. Practical capacity is defined as the maximum annual output of recreation services possible given the existing pattern of consumer recreation behavior which cannot usually be changed in the short run. Individuals prefer to engage in outdoor recreation during the season of the year when the weather is most favorable, on weekends rather than weekdays with their higher opportunity costs of work foregone, and during the most suitable hours of the day for the recreation activity. Practical capacity is expressed as a percent of maximum annual physical capacity of parks and other recreation facilities. For example, resorts operating one season have practical capacity of less than 50 percent of physical capacity in the United States, compared with 60 percent for two-season resorts and nearly 70 percent for resorts open year-round.

Attempts by managers to avoid inefficiency resulting from variations in the use of production capacity depend on the size of the site, the number of recreation activities available, and whether it is a destination vacation area. The size of public campgrounds can be limited to fewer campsites than peak demand, with private campgrounds filling in on peak demand days outside of parks. This is reported to be the situation at Yellowstone National Park, where private campground operators near the park favor restricted public campground capacity because it stimulates private campground use. However, as a result, private campgrounds near parks are expected to have greater variation in utilization and lower practical capacity. Recreation sites that offer a variety of recreation activities may experience less variation in use than those that specialize in one or a very few types of outdoor recreation. This depends on the ability of park workers to shift from one function to another, and the joint use of some equipment for diverse recreation activities. Finally, recreation sites such as ski areas that attract destination vacation users have lower variation in the use of facilities. Vacation skiers typically purchase a 7-day package from travel agencies which provide discounts on transportation as well as on ski lift and lodge room rates. The primary reason why price discounts are possible is that they enable business firms to even out the production cycle and achieve higher average levels of capacity utilization. This lowers production costs, and part of the savings is passed on to consumers as an incentive to engage in midweek recreation.

Barkley and Seckler suggest a long run solution to the problem of low practical capacity of recreation sites. They propose that the United States adopt a 3 1/2-day workweek with working time staggered throughout the seven days of the week. As a result, one-half of the population would be free to engage in recreation at all times, rather than nearly everyone participating on weekends and relatively few on Monday through Friday. Peak load problems of weekend congestion would be substantially relieved. Use would be averaged out over the days of the week. Practical capacity would tend to rise toward efficient carrying capacity of recreation sites.

Second, the physical capacity of recreation sites that typically offer multiple services is limited by the output rate of the service with the lowest capacity. Those with higher output capabilities simply operate at undercapacity. Managers attempt to install facilities and hire personnel at each stage of production with sufficient capacity that the natural resource can be used at close to its efficient carrying capacity on peak days. For example, in managing a swimming beach, each service is designed to have a capacity equal to or greater than that of the beach. Once the recreation production process is started, there must be a continuous movement of customers through the various stages until the recreation activity is complete. Variations in time between stages must be kept to a minimum. Sufficient parking space for peak utilization, for example, is crucial to adequately serve customers. From parking through the various stages of bathhouse, lunch stand, beach area for sunning, and water edge for swimming, there is little opportunity for adjustment in production time.

Attempts by managers to avoid inefficiency resulting from any significant disparity between capacity at each stage of production are limited by the process of piecemeal replacement of equipment in the normal course of events over a period of years. The useful life of capital investment at the various stages of the recreation production process varies from 3 to 10 years for most equipment, while buildings and other facilities typically last 20 to 30 years or more without excessive maintenance costs due to wear and tear. In the long run, technical advance that raises both output per man hour and capacity per hour of operation, does not occur simultaneously at all stages of production. Replacement equipment which is more advanced technically and of larger capacity results in what is called functional excess capacity. This means that some of the new facilities at recreation sites operate at less than physical capacity, even on days of peak demand.

Direct and Indirect Consumption

Most parks and other recreation sites were established for two reasons: first, to preserve their unique historic, scenic, natural, and wildlife resources; and second, to make them available for the enjoyment of people. This complicates the problem of measuring total consumption because it means that recreation agencies produce both onsite and offsite output. There are benefits to individuals in addition to the values they receive from visiting a site or to individuals who may never visit the site at all. In Chapter 14, we will illustrate the proportion of total consumption benefits that are attributable separately to recreation use and to the general public from protecting the quality of the resource.

As a result of the dual public policy in the enabling legislation, there remain some important unsolved problems in measuring the total consumption of the services of recreation and environmental protection programs. In a broad social context, total consumption includes both direct and indirect output. Direct consumption refers to the flow of services supporting the experience of onsite use of parks and other recreation sites. The flow of direct consumption was described earlier in this chapter. Indirect consumption appears to be of two broad types, one a flow and the other a stock. Indirect use refers to the flow of information about these resources and its consumption as indoor recreation. We will refer to the other type of indirect consumption as preservation value, defined as knowing that recreation and environmental resources are protected. Both occur offsite yet depend on the programs of recreation agencies.

First consider indirect use, which is the flow of information about these resources consumed as indoor recreation activities. Examples include reading, viewing pictures, watching television, attending lectures, and visiting with others about recreation activities and resources. Indirect use of recreation resources is not associated with direct contact. Many people never visit parks and other recreation sites, but they derive satisfaction from indirect use. In addition, onsite users may also participate in these offsite activities.

Boyle and Bishop discuss the measurement problems associated with indirect use. They conclude it is more difficult to characterize and measure than direct use. Indirect use may be measured in different units than direct use and appears to have different prices. Little or no travel is necessary to participate in indirect use since the information is usually consumed at home or very nearby. Indirect users can borrow, rent, or buy books, pictures, or audio and video cassettes, and produce an offsite recreation experience in the comfort of their own living rooms. Expenditures by indirect users may not be necessary since environmental groups and government agencies do considerable public education about outdoor recreation and environmental resources. One approach to measuring the output of indirect use might be to estimate the total time spent in all types of consumption. However, the durability of books, video tapes, photographs, and other necessary equipment requires further consideration. It is possible that some types of indirect use could continue to occur even when a recreation resource no longer exists. *TV scenery no longer there*

The same cannot be said for the second type of indirect output, preservation value. This refers to the fact that many individuals benefit from knowing that recreation and environmental resources are protected. Preservation values represent a stock of knowledge or psychic capital. The problem of measuring the output of preservation values is complicated by the fact that they are nonmarket public goods. This means that their consumption is both nonrival and nonexclusive. Once the resources are supplied, preservation values are equally available to all individuals. They are the benefits to individuals in addition to the values they receive from direct and indirect use of a recreation site or to individuals who may never use the site at all. The environmental economics literature identifies several possibilities of willingness to pay for the preservation value of resources in addition to direct and indirect recreation use. Here we will hypothesize that preservation values include option, existence, and bequest demands, as suggested by Weisbrod and Krutilla. Each of these motivations will be described below.

Option value is defined as the annual payment of a kind of insurance premium to guarantee the possibility of future recreation use (in addition to the expected benefits of direct and indirect use). Economists use the term, option price, to refer to the sum of option value and the expected consumer surplus from possible future recreation use (Bishop). It is an adjustment in the monetary measure of consumer welfare to account for the uncertainty faced when the future state of the world is not known. Uncertainty may arise as to whether a recreation site will be open or whether a recreation resource will be protected for possible recreation use. Also some individuals may not be certain that they will want to participate in a recreation activity, even if it is certain that the site will be open and that the resource will be protected. In addition, individuals may not be certain as to the prices of market inputs to be purchased in future recreation use. Option value may be positive, negative, or zero (Freeman).

Existence value is the willingness to pay for the individual satisfaction of knowing that a recreational or natural resource is protected. Bequest value is defined as the willingness to pay for the satisfaction derived from endowing future generations with these resources. It seems likely that existence and bequest values are based on altruistic motives, including benevolence toward the interests of friends, relatives, and other people; sympathy toward living plants and animals; a sense of responsibility to protect environmental quality; and an understanding of the interregional effects of environmental damages (Boyle and Bishop). Existence and bequest values may be positive, zero, or negative. Consider the case of coyotes in the western United States. Some people may or may not like coyotes even though they will never come in contact with them.

It seems likely that both stock and flow are involved in the total consumption of recreation. A comment by Boulding suggests that recreation activities represent a flow of services which restore a depleting stock of psychic capital. Individuals go to a concert because they enjoy the experience itself and in order to restore a desirable psychic condition which might be called, just having gone to a concert. Once established, this psychic condition tends to depreciate and beyond a certain point, individuals go to another concert in order to restore it. If it depreciates rapidly, they go to a lot of concerts; if it depreciates slowly, they go to a few. Similarly, individuals engage in recreation sports which they enjoy and to restore muscle tone, that is, to maintain a condition of being in good physical condition. While the direct observation of scenic beauty is an important benefit of sightseeing trips, individuals also enjoy the recollection of scenic beauty seen in the past. In the same way, individuals enjoy reading in the *National Geographic* about the scenic beauty of a recreation site and subsequently enjoy its recollection.

Thus, for individuals to hold preservation values, it appears to be necessary that they obtain information about the recreation activity or resource. Knowledge may be experience-based or education-based. This means that individuals either have visited the site (direct use) or that they have learned about it (indirect use). Based on this knowledge, individuals receive satisfaction from the preservation of recreation and environmental resources. Individuals report a willingness to pay an amount roughly equal to the dollar value of that satisfaction rather than forego it (Randall et al.; Greenley et al.; Brookshire et al.; Walsh et al.; Desvousges et al.). The studies thus far indicate that individuals who participate in recreation activities tend to be willing to pay more than those who do not. Presumably, individuals who engage in indirect use also develop knowledge of the resource and are likely to be willing to pay more than those who do not, although this has not been verified by empirical research.

The preservation value hypothesis appears to be related to an insight by Clawson and Knetsch that the total consumption of outdoor recreation is more than the onsite recreation activity. The authors define the recreation experience to include five phases: anticipation, travel to the site, onsite recreation activity, return travel, and recollection. The anticipation phase would include the option value of possible future recreation use. The recollection phase would include both the existence value of knowing that the recreation resource is protected and the bequest value of endowing future generations with the resource.

Attempts to measure the proportion of the population who consume preservation values of recreation resources find that a substantial number of citizens throughout the United States report they do so. This is the case for such unique resources as the Grand Canyon (Brookshire, et al.) and wilderness areas (Walsh, et al.). For less outstanding resources with regional rather than national significance, the proportion of the population who hold preservation values appears to be a declining function of the distance that they live from the resource (Sutherland and Walsh). In addition, there are important differences among the three types of preservation values. Option value appears to be positively related to income and the probability of direct use of recreation resources. It is negatively related to the availability of substitutes. Indications are that existence value is related to altruistic motivations of individuals to preserve natural scenery, ecosystems, and genetic strains. Also, it is related to the knowledge gained from direct use of recreation sites. Studies have shown that bequest values are higher for retired persons who, motivated by benevolence, receive satisfaction from the interpersonal transfer of recreation resources to future generations. Apparently, all income groups value existence and bequest values approximately equally.

SUMMARY

Thus far, no standard unit of recreation consumption has been developed that is suitable for all purposes of measurement. In this chapter we examined a variety of measures that are used including recreation days, visitor days, visits, and entrance permits. While each of these approaches has provided a satisfactory measure of the amount of outdoor recreation consumed under particular conditions, each also has its drawbacks. We discussed the problems of each approach and demonstrated under what conditions each measure should be used.

For example, the concept of a recreation day is consistent with the perception of individual consumers of recreation as an occasion or event, with little or no regard to the amount of time involved. As defined, the concept of a recreation visitor day has provided a satisfactory measure of the total quantity of recreation at sites where individuals participate in more than one activity during a single recreation day. A recreation visit or visitor provides a satisfactory measure of consumption when users are on single-day outings and/or overnight trips to recreation sites within 150 miles of their residence. The number of visits or trips per capita provides the most suitable measure in applications of the travel cost approach to recreation demand. The number of entrance permits is the most accurate measure available when it is adjusted for known deficiencies, such as users who do not pay.

Next we discussed the problem of comparability which arises when two or more measures are combined. We demonstrated how to convert the results of each measure to be comparable with other measures.

We presented several examples of recreation consumption patterns. Recent national surveys have established a number of distinguishing characteristics of recreation. Approximately 80 percent of the people 12 years of age and over participate in an average of 11 recreation activities per year. Most recreation activities occur during a peak season (seldom extending beyond 120 days in length) when the weather is most favorable. With the exception of camping, no recreation activity averages more than 5.0 hours per recreation day. Seventy-five percent of recreation occurs during a few available hours of a day within 1-5 miles from home and on single-day outings within 50 miles. This reflects the fact that most people are constrained by a fixed workday and workweek. In the case of every recreation activity, more than half of the total participation occurs on weekends.

Finally, we concluded with two additional points about the output of recreation and park programs. First, the production process is typical of a service industry. This means that the output is less tangible than for other industries, it is highly perishable, production cannot be separated from consumption, and quality is more variable. Second, we showed that the multiple objectives of recreation agencies include programs to protect the natural environment as well as to provide for recreation use. As a result, a more nearly complete definition of total consumption should include both direct and indirect output. Direct output refers to the onsite consumption of recreation by users. Indirect output refers to the offsite consumption of knowledge about the quality of the resources by the general public. Many people seldom visit parks and other recreation sites, but they get satisfaction from indirect use such as reading, viewing pictures, watching television, attending lectures, and visiting with others about recreation activities and resources. Preservation value is another type of indirect output defined as knowing that recreation and environmental resources are protected. Preservation values include option, existence, and bequest demands of the general public.

An understanding of the nature of consumption is essential to effective recreation resource development and management decisions. The measures introduced in this chapter are used in subsequent comparisons of benefits and costs.

READINGS

Barkley, Paul W., and David W. Seckler. *Economic Growth and Environmental Decay.* Harcourt Brace Jovanovich, Inc., New York. 1972.

Bishop, Richard C. "Option Value: An Exposition and Extension." *Land Economics* 58(Feb. 1982):1-15.

Boulding, Kenneth E. "The Economics of the Coming Spaceship Earth." *Environmental Quality in a Growing Economy.* Henry Jarrett (ed.). Johns Hopkins University Press, Baltimore. Md. 1966. 3-14.

Boyle, Kevin J., and Richard C. Bishop. "Economic Benefits Associated with Boating and Canoeing on the Lower Wisconsin River." *Economic Issues,* No. 84. Dept. of Agricultural Economics, University of Wisconsin, Madison. 1984.

Brookshire, David S., Larry S. Eubanks, and Alan B. Randall. "Valuing Wildlife Resources: An Experiment." *Transactions.* 38th North American Wildlife and Natural Resources Conference. Wildlife Management Institute, Washington, D.C. 1978. 310-20.

Brown, William G., and Farid Nawas. "Impact of Aggregation on the Estimation of Outdoor Recreation Demand Functions." *American Journal of Agricultural Economics* 55(May 1973):246-49.

Buist, L. J., and T. A. Hoots. "Recreation Opportunity Spectrum Approach to Resource Planning." *Journal of Forestry* 80(1982):84-86.

Clawson, Marion, and Jack L. Knetsch. *Economics of Outdoor Recreation.* Johns Hopkins University Press, Baltimore. 1966.

Desvousges, William H., V. Kerry Smith, and Matthew P. McGivney. "A Comparison of Alternative Approaches for Estimating Recreation and Related Benefits of Water Quality Improvement." Final Report to the Environmental Protection Agency by Research Triangle Institute, Research Triangle Park, N.C. 1983.

Driver, B. L., and Perry J. Brown. "A Social-Psychological Definition of Recreation Demand, With Implications for Recreation Resource Planning." *Assessing Demand for Outdoor Recreation.* National Academy of Sciences, Washington, D.C. 1975. 1-88.

Drucker, Peter F. *Management: Tasks, Responsibilities, Practices.* Harper Colophon Books, New York. 1985.

Freeman, A. Myrick III. "Supply Uncertainty, Option Price, and Option Value." *Land Economics* 61(May 1985):176-81.

Greenley, Douglas A., Richard G. Walsh, and Robert A. Young. *Economic Benefits of Improved Water Quality: Public Perceptions of Option and Preservation Values.* Westview Press, Boulder, Colo. 1982.

Heritage Conservation and Recreation Service. "Third Nationwide Outdoor Recreation Plan." Four Volumes based on the 1977 National Recreation Survey. U.S. Dept. of the Interior, Gov. Print. Off., Washington, D.C. 1980.

Jennings, Thomas A., and Kenneth C. Gibbs. "Some Issues Concerning Specification and Interpretation of Outdoor Recreation Demand Models." *Southern Journal of Agricultural Economics* 6(July 1974):165-69.

Kotler, Philip. *Marketing for Non-Profit Organizations.* 2nd Edition. Prentice Hall, Englewood Cliffs, N.J. 1982.

Krutilla, John V. "Conservation Reconsidered." *American Economic Review* 57(Sept. 1967):777-86.

National Park Service. "Public Use of the National Parks: Statistical Report." U.S. Dept. of the Interior, Washington, D.C. Published annually.

Outdoor Recreation Resources Review Commission. "National Recreation Survey." Report No. 19. U.S. Gov. Print. Off., Washington, D.C. 1962.

Randall, Alan, John P. Hoehn, and George S. Tolley. "The Structure of Contingent Markets: Some Results of a Recent Experiment." Paper presented at the Annual Meeting of the American Economic Association, Washington, D.C. 1981.

Randall, Alan, and John R. Stoll. "Existence Value in a Total Valuation Framework." in *Managing Air Quality and Scenic Resources at National Parks and Wilderness Areas.* Robert D. Rowe and Lauraine G. Chestnut (eds.). Westview Press, Boulder, Colo. 1983.

Recreation Advisory Council. "Federal Executive Policy Governing the Reporting of Recreation Use of Federal Recreation Areas." Circular No. 6. U.S. Gov. Print. Off., Washington, D.C. 1965.

Recreation Advisory Council. "Uniform Method for Measuring and Reporting Recreation Use on the Public Lands and Waters of the United States." Washington, D.C. 1965.

Shafer, Elwood L., Jr., and Roger C. Thompson. "Models that Describe Use of Adirondack Campgrounds." *Forest Science* 14(No. 4, 1968):383-91.

Sutherland, Ronald J., and Richard G. Walsh. "Effect of Distance on the Preservation Value of Water Quality." *Land Economics* 61(Aug. 1985):281-91.

Throsby, C. D., and G. A. Withers. "Measuring the Demand for the Arts As a Public Good: Theory and Empirical Results." *Economic Support for the Arts.* J. L. Shanahan, W. S. Hendon, Izaak Th. H. Hilhorst, and J. van Straalen (eds.). Center for Urban Studies, University of Akron, Ohio. 1983.

U.S. Bureau of Outdoor Recreation. "The 1965 Survey of Outdoor Recreation Activities." U.S. Gov. Print. Off., Washington, D.C. 1967.

U.S. Bureau of Outdoor Recreation. "The 1970 Survey of Outdoor Recreation Activities." U.S. Gov. Print. Off., Washington, D.C. 1973.

U.S. Bureau of Outdoor Recreation. "Outdoor Recreation in America: Appendix A, An Economic Analysis." U.S. Gov. Print. Off., Washington, D.C. 1973.

U.S. Dept. of Commerce. *Statistical Abstract of the United States.* Bureau of the Census. Washington, D.C. Published Annually.

U.S. Fish and Wildlife Service. "National Survey of Fishing and Hunting, 1970." Resources Publ. No. 95. U.S. Dept. of the Interior, Washington, D.C. 1972.

U.S. Fish and Wildlife Service. "National Survey of Hunting, Fishing and Wildlife Associated Recreation, 1975." U.S. Dept. of the Interior, Washington, D.C. 1977.

U.S. Forest Service. "The 1980 National Outdoor Recreation Trends Symposium." Vols. 1 and 2. General Technical Report NE-57, Northeastern Agricultural Experiment Station, U.S. Dept. of Agriculture, Broomall, Pa. Washington, D.C. 1980.

U.S. Forest Service. "1985 National Outdoor Recreation Trends Symposium II." Vols. 1 and 2. Technical Report NE-137, Northeastern Agricultural Experiment Station, Broomall, Pa. 1985.

U.S. Forest Service. "Recreation Information Management (RIM) Handbook." U.S. Dept. of Agriculture, Washington, D.C. Published annually.

U.S. Heritage Conservation and Recreation Service. "Third Nationwide Outdoor Recreation Plan." Vols. 1-4 based on the 1977 National Recreation Survey. U.S. Dept. of the Interior, Gov. Print. Off., Washington, D.C. 1980.

U.S. Water Resources Council. "Economic and Environmental Principles and Guidelines for Water and Related Land Resource Implementation Studies." U.S. Govt. Print. Off., Washington, D.C. 1983.

Walsh, Richard G., Larry D. Sanders, and John B. Loomis. *Wild and Scenic River Economics: Recreation Use and Preservation Values.* American Wilderness Alliance, Denver. 1985.

Weisbrod, Burton. "Collective-Consumption Services of Individual-Consumption Goods." *Quarterly Journal of Economics* 78(Aug. 1964):471-77.

Chapter Four

Direct Cost or Price

This chapter defines several alternative concepts of the price of recreation; describes when alternative measures of price can be used; illustrates recent pricing patterns for recreation goods and services; and discusses some important implications for recreation economic decisions.

Recreation poses a unique problem of defining a realistic proxy for price. Visits to recreation sites are not priced in any market. Most public recreation is a nonmarket service provided free of any appreciable entrance fee or price in the usual sense. However, this does not mean that recreation activities do not have a price or exchange value. Individual consumers incur expenses such as travel and time costs. The sum of direct monetary and nonmonetary costs is a reasonable proxy for the price of recreation. The fact that these expenses are not uniform and are paid to a number of different businesses should not distract from the fact that, together, they constitute the necessary costs or price of recreation. The direct cost or price of any good or service has several parts; the unique feature of recreation is that travel costs represent a larger part.

ALTERNATIVE MEASURES

Several approaches have been used in an attempt to develop a reasonably accurate proxy for the price of recreation. These include: (1) entrance fees and permits; (2) direct transportation costs, including fuel, tires, and repairs; (3) travel time costs, the dissatisfaction of driving; (4) opportunity cost of recreation time at the site; (5) total direct costs including lodging, added food and other consumable supplies; and (6) fixed costs of annual licenses and recreation equipment amortized over the expected period of use.

While any one of these approaches or a combination of approaches may provide a satisfactory measure of the price of a particular recreation activity, a problem arises when the results of two or more approaches are compared. Thus far, no standard proxy for the price of recreation has been developed that is suitable for all purposes of measurement. So, it is important to understand when each measure should be used and how to convert the results of each approach to compare it with other measures. Accuracy of the alternative estimating procedures is a continuing problem.

Entrance Fees

An entrance fee is defined as the price of admission to a recreation site or event, entitling the purchaser to participate in a recreation activity for a specified length of time on a particular date. This is the most clearly understood aspect of the price of outdoor recreation. For example, an individual consumer who contemplates attending a concert, play, or sports event asks about the availability of tickets and the price of admission. The same is true, to a somewhat lesser extent, for going swimming, playing tennis, or golfing, camping in developed campgrounds, downhill skiing, or visiting a zoo, zoological garden, amusement park, state or national park, and the like. Usually there are no entrance fees involved in individual decisions to go sightseeing, riding a bicycle or trail bike, camping in the backcountry or at undeveloped sites, walking for pleasure, hiking, picnicking or playing games in a city park, cross-country skiing, fishing, hunting, bird-watching, etc. If these recreation activities take place at a private recreation site, an entrance fee may be charged by the landowner or operator.

Entrance fees have provided a satisfactory measure of the price of recreation where participation requires little or no travel and other out-of-pocket costs. Examples are the recreation activities and events that take place in the neighborhood where individuals live. Other examples are recreation activities and events more distant from home where the entrance fee constitutes payment for a package of services which includes the provision of travel by bus to and from the site plus other on-site costs such as for food and incidental expenses.

By itself, the approach has not provided a satisfactory measure of the price of most recreation, because it does not include other expenditures required to participate in most recreation activities. Travel is nearly always necessary, as are other on-site expenditures. As a result, the out-of-pocket cost of recreation usually exceeds the entrance fee, in most cases substantially as will be shown in the following sections.

Problems arise when a basic entrance fee is uniformly assigned to all individual participants. Obviously, individuals who attend an amusement park that has a two-part tariff pay varying fees. While all individuals may pay a basic entrance fee, individuals would pay varying amounts for the rides and events within the amusement park. What is less well understood is that most entrance fees vary with the quantity and quality of service, the season of the year, and for other reasons. Basic camping fees may vary with the quality of service such as electrical hookups, location of the campsite (e.g., near a river or lake), number of persons, number of nights, etc.

Individual consumers of recreation are willing to pay higher entrance fees for an 18-hole golf course rather than for a 9-hole, an all day ski-lift ticket rather than a half-day ticket and so forth. Tickets to outdoor athletic contests vary in price with nearness to the playing area and quality of the view. Entrance fees are often discounted during off-seasons and on weekdays. In addition, persons over 65 and under 12 years of age may be admitted free or at reduced rates.

Direct Transportation Costs

Direct transportation costs are defined by the federal guidelines as a proxy for the money price of recreation. Generally they include the variable or out-of-pocket costs of operating an automobile. These are the average costs per mile of maintenance, accessories, parts, tires, gasoline, oil, and taxes. The federal guidelines suggest that these are the costs that potential users would be most aware of when making a decision about whether to visit a recreation site. Such fixed costs as depreciation, insurance, and registration are not included, as these would generally not affect the individual consumer's decision to travel additional miles to recreation sites. Because most individual consumers already own an automobile and intend to continue to own and operate it, the relevant question is "what do additional miles of recreation travel cost?" Although the individual consumer may consider gasoline the only short-run out-of-pocket expense for a particular recreation trip, it may well be true that increasing the number of miles driven will also increase expenditures for maintenance such as lubrication, oil changes, and tune-ups, for repairs, and for tires.

Distance traveled is converted to dollar values by multiplying round-trip miles to and from the recreation site by average direct cost per mile and dividing by the number of users per vehicle to determine per-capita travel cost.

The approach has provided satisfactory measures of a change in willingness to pay with increases in distance traveled when there is variation in travel distances by individual users (i.e., nonurban sites), and when trips are for the exclusive purpose of visiting a single recreation site. The travel cost approach has been applied successfully to the study of single purpose trips to state parks, lakes, and reservoirs where 95 percent of the users reside within 150 miles of the recreation sites, and where length of stay and primary recreation activities do not vary appreciably.

The approach is particularly well suited to demand studies where the only information available is number of visits from distance zones (i.e. license plate surveys, zip codes or counties of origin), secondary information on the socio-economic characteristics of zonal population, the number of substitute recreation sites located in zones, and annual use. Because the services provided by the typical public recreation site are not marketed, but are instead offered free of charge or at negligible prices, it is often necessary to impute demand curves on the basis of very limited price-quantity information. Limiting the concept of price to direct auto costs is justified on the basis of least effort and the belief that the slope of the demand curve is reasonably determined by the relationship between direct auto costs per mile and number of miles driven, not by other costs of individual users.

Problems arise when the approach is applied to urban or national parks. Variables other than distance traveled contribute to changes in the price of most urban recreation activities. Vacation trips to national parks tend to be multipurpose, with visits to several destinations on a single trip. Total direct travel costs of a vacation trip should not be attributed to a particular park. It is necessary to allocate trip costs according to the number of sites visited, the number of days at each site, net benefits per site, or some other reasonable basis.

Problems also arise when trips to urban and national parks include travel by cycle, bus, train or plane, in addition to private auto. Epperson estimates that roughly 20 percent of recreation travel is by means other than the private auto, with varying mileage costs. Moreover, auto travel costs tend to vary among individual users, depending on driving habits, the type and condition of the vehicle, and whether a trailer is being towed. When such information is available (typically, from survey samples), travel costs can be adjusted for these individual variations. Sample survey information also could enable travel costs to be allocated among recreation activities, such as sightseeing, fishing, and camping, by an individual on a single trip.

Travel and Recreation Time Costs

Travel and recreation time costs have been defined by the federal guidelines as the opportunity cost of work or leisure activities that are foregone for travel to and recreation at the site. For individuals whose work time is variable, the opportunity cost should be measured as income foregone. Most people, however, are constrained by a fixed workweek and receive paid vacation days. Individuals who travel and recreate during weekends and vacations when no working time is lost incur only leisure time costs. This value may range between zero and the individual's wage rate. Leisure time costs are zero if individuals would not have engaged in any other leisure activity had they not taken the trip. Leisure time costs would equal the individual's wage rate if the alternative leisure activity is valuable enough to forego earnings, given the opportunity. Both travel and on-site time costs can be added to direct travel costs to determine willingness to pay using the travel cost approach. Alternatively, they can be included as separate independent variables in the demand function.

This approach has improved our estimates of the price of recreation. Before 1970, the use of direct auto costs alone as a proxy for price ignored the effects of time on recreation decisions. Demand schedules were constructed under the hypothesis that increasing distance decreased use only because of higher monetary cost of travel. Exclusion of the opportunity cost of time could result in an underestimation of the price and value of recreation. The nonmonetary cost of additional time required to travel increased distances to recreation sites would seem to be, for some individuals, a deterrent equal to or greater than out-of-pocket auto costs.

Until recently, direct survey data on recreation travel time costs have not been available. Thus, the federal guidelines have relied on commuter studies to recommend that travel time be valued as 25 to 50 percent of the wage rate for adults and 25 percent of the adult value for children. For example, the average wage rate would be roughly $12 per hour for individuals receiving $24,000 for 240 eight-hour work days per year. With two adults and one child in a typical party, recreation travel time cost would be estimated as $3-6 per hour for each adult and $0.75-1.50 for the child, or an average individual travel time cost of $2.25-4.50 per hour. On this basis, a round trip of 180 miles at 45 miles per hour would have average travel time costs of $9-18 per person. This procedure is designed to estimate average travel time costs for users grouped by distance zones or counties in applications of the zonal travel cost method where limited information is available on individual users. Widespread adoption of the standard travel time cost has contributed to comparability among study results. This has been especially important because variation in time costs can account for a large proportion of estimated benefits as shown by Bishop and Heberlein. See Chapter 8 for a summary of their results.

Problems may arise in valuing travel time in terms of foregone earnings assumed constant per hour traveled. The procedure approved by the federal guidelines was derived from work by Cesario who reviewed several studies of the value of travel time to commuters on journeys to work in urban areas. Recreation travel usually involves distinctly different circumstances from work travel. Commuters are required to travel to a destination not of their own choosing, often during peak, rush-hour traffic. Recreation travel, on the other hand, is a discretionary leisure time activity. The route, time of departure and destination may be chosen to reduce time cost or provide a positive value of travel time.

It seems likely that when studies of recreation travel time become available, they will show that it is often less costly than travel time commuting to work. For example, an empirical study by Morrison and Winston estimated the value of auto travel time on vacation as 6 percent of the wage rate or $0.63 per hour. This represents the marginal rate of substitution of money for travel time. It is an estimate of the amount of money vacation travelers are willing to sacrifice for a reduction in the amount of time they spend driving on vacation trips. It is based on a sample of nearly 1,900 household vacation trips reported in the 1977 Census of Transportation. The results suggest that vacation travelers do not perceive the time spent driving to recreation sites as particularly unpleasant nor do they attach a high opportunity cost to the travel time.

The results of the Morrison and Winston study can be compared with those of the procedure recommended by the federal guidelines illustrated previously. The authors report the opportunity cost of travel time as 6 percent of the wage rate. Holding the wage rate constant at $12 per hour, the typical round trip of 180 miles at 45 miles per hour would have average individual time cost of $2.88. This is 16 to 32 percent of the estimated travel time cost of $9-18 for an identical trip following federal guidelines. Note that both estimates assume constant average travel time cost per mile. In reality, the value per hour of travel time may vary with travel distance and other variables as suggested below.

Wilman supports the federal guidelines with respect to valuing on-site recreation time in terms of the opportunity cost of time in its best alternative use. However, she proposes that travel time be valued as the difference between the beneficial value of time and its opportunity cost. This would be equivalent to valuing travel time on the basis of individual willingness to pay to reduce it. Direct surveys could determine what portion of individual travel time is in fact, beneficial sightseeing activity and what part represents a cost. That portion of travel time that is enjoyable because of roadside scenery would be attributed to sightseeing activity rather than a cost of access to on-site recreation activity at the destination.

Milam and Pasour studied the opportunity cost of on-site recreation time at 33 rural golf courses in the Piedmont region of North Carolina. The opportunity cost of on-site recreation time was assigned a value of zero for individuals playing golf on weekends or after 4 PM on weekdays. Opportunity cost was assigned a value of one (equal to the wage rate) for individuals playing golf during the week before 4 PM and employed full time. They found that opportunity cost was negatively related to the quantity demanded, and was significant at the 0.01 level. Opportunity cost of on-site time is expected to be an important consideration in the demand for recreation activities and the results of this study support the hypothesis. In future research, a continuous scale for the measurement of opportunity cost is needed to assess the effect more precisely.

Sanders studied household willingness to pay for travel time on river-based recreation trips in the Rocky Mountains of the United States. The pilot study suggests that future research on the demand for recreation travel is likely to show that it is a function of distance rather than a constant for each mile traveled. The demand curve is expected to shift with changes in the quality of scenery along the route and other variables. Apparently willingness to pay is often positive for short trips and when starting out on long trips. Sooner or later, willingness to pay reaches a breaking point and becomes negative. Willingness to pay becomes increasingly negative as distance traveled continues to increase.

The study found that net willingness to pay is positive for one-way travel time of 1-2 hours on single-day trips. However, for longer trips it declines with distance. For 2-day trips with one-way travel time of 2-4 hours, net willingness to pay is positive up to about 90 miles and thereafter becomes negative. For vacation trips of 3 days or more and one-way travel time of 4-8 hours, net willingness to pay is positive up to about 250 miles and thereafter becomes negative. The most relevant equations for overnight trips are:

Value of Travel Time
on 2-Day Trips = 0.23 - 0.0072 Miles
Value of Travel Time on
Trips of 3 Days or More = 0.23 - 0.0057 Miles

These equations represent inverse demand curves for travel time to rivers. The vertical intercept of 23 cents indicates that travel time at the beginning of recreation trips is very beneficial. Subsequently, the value of travel time declines by 0.72 of a cent per mile for 2-day trips, compared to a decline of 0.57 of a cent per mile for trips of 3 days or more. The sharper decline in the demand curve for travel time on 2-day trips is consistent with the observation that people are willing to travel less on weekends compared to vacations.

Norton presented empirical evidence to suggest that approximately half of total recreation travel in England is sightseeing or pleasure driving, with the views seen on the journey adding to the total satisfaction of the trip. My studies of recreation in the Rocky Mountains of the United States indicate that sightseeing is the primary purpose of nearly 40 percent of recreation travel, and a secondary purpose of 25 percent of travel to recreation sites for fishing, boating, hiking, backpacking, camping, and picnicking. Most households consider travel time either as a benefit or of zero value. Forty-two percent report they are willing to pay for additional travel time on trips to rivers. Fifty percent are not willing to pay either to gain or to avoid an increment in travel time. Only 8 percent indicate that travel time is a cost, reporting that they are willing to pay to avoid it. Average benefits of additional travel time are about $3 per hour for the entire sample.

A substantial amount of recreation travel is expected to remain destination-oriented, with travel time primarily a cost. Pearse reported that 95 percent of the travel of a sample of deer hunters in Canada is for the single purpose of hunting. The remaining hunters report other purposes such as sightseeing, visits with relatives and friends, and business activities. Horvath reports that Southeastern U.S. resident fishermen rate travel time as the most important factor in their choice of where to fish, followed by the abundance of fish, and low fisherman population densities at the site.

Total Direct Costs

Total direct costs are the added expenditures that the consumer must make in order to take part in recreation. The variable costs of transportation and admission are certainly important, but by no means the only direct costs involved. The economic concept of the monetary price of recreation is the total direct out-of-pocket cost to individual consumers of recreation. This price is analogous to the concept of transfer cost, which includes all of the direct money costs incurred by the consumer. In addition to the costs of transportation and admission, variable or direct transfer costs include: overnight lodging, food and beverage, equipment rental, guide service, other consumable supplies, and miscellaneous direct expenses. Together, these variable costs constitute the price per day of outdoor recreation. The fact that the price is paid to many suppliers — the resort lodge, gas station, grocery store, restaurant, drugstore, sporting-goods store, public park, and the like — should not detract from the essential nature of the monetary price paid.

The approach is particularly well suited to demand studies where sufficient resources are available to collect primary information from a sample of users. Direct costs should be obtained for households, families, or groups of individuals traveling in the same vehicle on a recreation trip. When direct costs are summed and divided by the number of users per vehicle and number of days at the site, the resulting cost per recreation day is the best available definition of the monetary price of outdoor recreation.

The approach has provided the most satisfactory measure of price when the costs of individual users vary with distance traveled. For example, users of a recreation site located over 100 miles from home are more likely to incur overnight lodging expenses and added expenses of eating in restaurants than are users closer to home, who are more likely to sleep in their own beds, prepare a picnic lunch, and take other meals at home before departing and after returning. In addition, users who travel greater distances to recreation sites are more likely to rent equipment on site and to employ personal services such as guides.

The approach facilitates the separation of travel costs from on-site costs. Once the travel costs have been incurred for getting to a site, some individual users may consider them as sunk, and their decision about how long to stay may depend solely upon the on-site costs of an additional day. However, most recreation trips are preplanned, and the length of stay is constrained by available leisure time. Generally the relevant concept of price includes all out-of-pocket costs of the trip combined into a single variable.

Ward describes a problem that may arise when the direct cost or price perceived by individual consumers differs from the economic definition of price. For example, some consumers may understate their cost of transportation on a recreation trip by considering their only out-of-pocket automobile cost to be for gasoline. However, increasing the number of miles driven on a recreation trip will also increase expenditures for lubrication, oil changes, tune-ups, repairs, and tires. Thus, the economic definition of direct cost or price includes these other auto costs. However, consumers have difficulty allocating such costs to short-run trips. The same is true for the allocation of the costs of fishing and hunting licenses that entitle the individual to multiple trips and/or days of use per year.

Along the same lines, some consumers of recreation may consider all out-of-pocket costs of food and beverage, in particular restaurant meals, as part of the direct cost or price of a trip to a recreation site. The economic definition of the price of a recreation trip would exclude that portion of food and beverage expenditures equivalent to what would have been spent for these items at home.

The U.S. Department of Agriculture reports that food and beverage expenditures equal 16 percent of annual household income. For example, for a household of 2.85 persons reporting annual income of $20,000, approximately $3 per person would be subtracted from daily expenditures of $10 for food and beverage on the recreation trip. Thus, only $7 of additional expenditure for groceries and restaurant meals should be included as part of the direct cost or price of outdoor recreation.

A problem also may arise when individual consumers substitute their investment in durable recreation equipment for rental costs. Fixed costs of depreciation and opportunity costs of the dollars invested in durable recreation equipment are excluded from the economic definition of short-run variable costs or price, while rental cost of recreation equipment is included. A real reduction in the direct cost or price of recreation may occur where the equipment rental cost is avoided by these individuals. However, Linder has pointed out that the ownership of recreation equipment entails the periodic expenditure of money and time for maintenance, repair, cleaning, and so forth. Increasing the number of days that equipment is used will increase these costs. Thus maintenance cost of recreation equipment should be included as part of price.

Problems arise when the approach is used to measure the price of a single recreation activity at a site when the trip is multipurpose or multidestination. A similar problem occurs in applying the travel cost approach where transportation costs must be allocated to each activity and site. It is necessary to allocate the costs of lodging, added food and beverage, entrance fees, and consumable supplies among the recreation activities and the sites visited. When sample survey information is available, all of these costs can be assigned to special recreation activities and sites, such as sightseeing while traveling to and from the recreation sites, fishing at site A and camping at site B, etc., based on the perception of individual consumers.

Fixed Costs

Fixed costs are defined as the amortized costs of consumer investment in durable recreation equipment and annual costs such as licenses over the period of use. Fixed costs include: (1) depreciation and opportunity cost of consumer investments in vehicles, boats, motors, fishing tackle, water skis, special clothing, tents, sleeping bags, camp stoves, travel trailers, skies, boots, backpacks, sporting equipment, binoculars, cameras, seasonal homes, recreation land, etc.; (2) annual costs of fishing, hunting, and other licenses, insurance, and taxes that are the same regardless of the number of recreation trips.

The concept of fixed cost applies to consumer decisions to purchase durable recreation equipment. Thus, it is applicable to decisions to begin participating in a recreation activity, where the purchase of durable equipment is often necessary in order to participate at all. It is also applicable to consumer decisions to continue participating in a recreation activity on those infrequent occasions when equipment owned wears out or becomes obsolete and the decision becomes whether to replace it with new or used equipment in order to continue participating. However, it is important to remember that the concept of fixed cost is not applicable to consumer decisions to take an additional trip to a recreation site. Thus, it would be unrealistic to consider fixed costs as part of the direct costs or price of outdoor recreation.

The measurement of fixed costs is always based on uncertain estimates of future events. The expectations of individual consumers vary with respect to the useful life of equipment, the opportunity cost of money invested, and anticipated future use. These differences lead some individuals to purchase more recreation equipment than others. An example will help to clarify these concepts. Table 4-1 illustrates the decision to purchase durable recreation equipment and whether to continue ownership after five years.

Table 4-1. Structure of a Decision to Purchase Durable Recreation Equipment

Fixed Costs	Initial Purchase	Continue To Use After Five Years
Investment (10 year life)	$2,000	$500
Annual Depreciation (10 percent)	200	100
Annual Interest (10 percent)	200	50
Annual Maintenance (5 percent)	100	100
Total Annual Fixed Costs	500	250
Fixed Costs Per Day of Annual Use		
50 Days	10	5
100 Days	5	2.50

Annual depreciation may be estimated simply by dividing initial investment less salvage value, if any, by the useful life of the equipment. For example, a $2,000 investment in recreation equipment with an average useful life of 10 years and no salvage value would have annual depreciation costs of $200. Opportunity cost of the investment may be estimated by multiplying the initial investment by the appropriate interest rate that the consumer could earn on the amount of money invested in recreation equipment. If the consumer could earn 10 percent, the opportunity cost of the investment of $2,000 is also $200 per year. If annual maintenance costs equal $100 (including insurance, taxes, and license), the total fixed costs of $2,000 worth of recreation equipment would be roughly $500 per year.

Fixed costs are allocated over the useful life of recreation equipment and apportioned between expected recreation use and other uses. If a consumer anticipates that the above equipment would be used 100 days per year, fixed costs would equal $5 per recreation day. If actual use fell to 50 days per year, fixed costs would rise to $10 per recreation day. It is apparent that average fixed costs of recreation equipment are quite sensitive to the level of use.

The consumer decision to continue to use recreation equipment once it is acquired is identical to ordinary business practice. Fixed costs of depreciation and opportunity costs are estimated on the basis of the salvage value on the used equipment market at that point in time, rather than on the initial investment value or some other basis. For example, a $2,000 initial investment in recreation equipment with an average useful life of 10 years may have a salvage value of only $500 after five years of normal use because of obsolescence. Annual depreciation on the remaining five years of useful life would fall to $100, and opportunity cost would equal $50 per year (= $500 × 10%). If annual maintenance costs remain the same at $100, and expected annual use is 100 days, fixed costs would equal $2.50 per recreation day rather than the $5 at the time of the initial investment. This explains why some consumers of outdoor recreation continue to use well-worn equipment.

Problems arise in applying the concept of fixed cost to individual investment decisions. For example, consumers do not typically accumulate a depreciation account over the life of recreation equipment, as is the ordinary accounting practice in business. Businesses estimate the opportunity cost of investment in equipment depreciated to the midyear of useful life, which is typically less than half of the initial investment value. However, consumers continue to incur opportunity cost on the full value of the initial investment in recreation equipment so long as they do not consider selling it. Thus, the opportunity cost of recreation equipment owned by individual consumers is typically more than twice the opportunity cost of the same equipment owned by businesses.

SHORT-RUN AND LONG-RUN COSTS

The price of recreation in the short run is defined as the direct or variable costs associated with taking an additional trip within a single year. These include: direct travel costs to and from the recreation site, expenditures on consumable services and supplies while at the site, the opportunity cost of recreation time, and the nonmonetary cost of travel time. Decisions to take an additional recreation trip are based on those direct costs that change as the number of trips is varied (and other variables such as income, age, sex, quality of the site, price and availability of substitutes, etc.). In the short-run, individual consumers will continue to visit a recreation site until their added benefits equal the additional short-run costs.

The price of recreation in the long-run is defined as the total costs associated with the decision to participate one or more additional years. Decision-making is distinguished by the fact that all costs become variable in the long-run. In addition to the direct costs associated with recreation trips, the long-run concept of price includes fixed costs of: (1) the vehicle and other recreation equipment annualized as depreciation and the opportunity costs of the investment, and (2) the annual expenditures such as for licenses, insurance, and taxes, that must be paid regardless of the number of trips.

The concept of long-run price applies to consumer decisions to begin participating in a recreation activity and whether to continue participating from year to year. In the long-run, consumers of outdoor recreation must decide whether to replace recreation equipment as it wears out or becomes obsolete. They must also decide at the beginning of each year whether to continue to incur the cost of licenses, insurance and taxes that must be paid if they are to use their equipment and continue to engage in particular outdoor recreation activities. Individual consumers will participate in outdoor recreation if their anticipated benefits equal or exceed total costs in the long-run.

Table 4-2. Short-run and Long-run Price of Resident Fishing and Big Game Hunting, Colorado

Category	Year	Price per Recreation Day of		
		Fishing	Deer Hunting	Elk Hunting
Short-run Price (Direct Cost)	1968	$ 9.60	$ 19.50	$ 18.00
	1973	10.20	20.50	20.90
	1981	20.80	30.60	22.90
Fixed Costs	1968	17.20	41.00	23.40
	1973	20.70	44.50	39.30
	1981	56.90	110.70	97.80
Long-run Price (Total Cost)	1968	26.80	60.50	41.40
	1973	30.90	65.00	60.20
	1981	77.70	141.30	120.70

Sources: Nobe and Gilbert; Ross, Blood and Nobe; McKean and Nobe.

Otherwise, consumers would not replace durable equipment when it wears out or becomes obsolete, and they would decide to discontinue the recreation activity.

As would be expected, long-run price is considerably higher than short-run price. Table 4-2 illustrates the trend in the short-run and the long-run price of fishing and big game hunting in Colorado. For example, the short-run price of resident fishing per day was $20.80 in 1981, with price defined as direct costs of transportation, lodging, added food, bait, and other consumable supplies. The long-run price was $77.70 per recreation day, with price defined as short-run direct costs plus such fixed costs as depreciation and opportunity cost related to recreation use of family vehicles, recreation vehicles, cabins and land, special clothing, sports equipment and licenses. The short run price was equal to only about one-third of the long-run price.

This means that the typical participant would anticipate average benefits equal to or in excess of average total costs of about $78 per day of fishing in the long-run. He or she would continue fishing during the year until the added benefits equaled the short-run direct costs of $21 per day.

A number of studies have illustrated the concept of the long-run price of recreation. For example, Brown et al. estimated the effect of fixed costs on the long-run price of salmon fishing and big-game hunting in Oregon. Generally, these and other studies show that the long-run price of these activities is more than double the short-run price, which is consistent with the Colorado study.

The long-run price of most recreation activities is a much lower multiple of short-run prices than that for fishing and big game hunting because of lower expenditures for equipment and licenses. For example, picnicking in a park requires no special equipment or license, nor does walking for pleasure or attending an outdoor sports event. Hiking may require special shoes and clothing, day pack, compass, sunglasses, etc., the fixed costs of which may represent a small fraction of the direct cost of an additional hiking trip. This seems to be typical of most recreation activities. However, the fixed costs of a motor home may exceed the direct costs of camping use by several times, depending on the number of days of annual use.

Table 4-3 illustrates the investment price range of selected durable recreation equipment. The Consumer Reports, "Buyers Guide," evaluates the quality of major brands of recreation equipment and recommends best buys. It is interesting to note the price dispersion of such recreation equipment such as ten-speed bikes. Price dispersion is defined as the percentage by which the highest priced brand exceeds the lowest priced brand of the same model. Price dispersion of very good ten-speed bikes is 48 percent, which means the individual consumer's investment price ranges from $149 to $220 for bicycles of virtually the same quality. In addition, the identical brand and model of most recreation equipment is priced at different levels in different stores, and the same is true for most food and articles of clothing. It would pay the consumer to comparison-shop for recreation equipment, because lower prices result in lower fixed costs.

The long-run price of recreation is similar to the concept of gross expenditures. However, the two concepts are not identical with respect to the treatment of fixed and variable costs. Gross expenditure studies are designed to measure the impact of outdoor recreation on the economy. Most states periodically survey the gross expenditures of fishermen, hunters, and other tourists.

Gross expenditure studies include the total investment value of recreation equipment purchased during the study year and omit any consideration of the fixed costs of equipment purchased in preceding years. In a stable market where recreation equipment has a useful life of 10 years, one-tenth of the inventory of equipment would be replaced each year. Thus current annual investment in equipment would be approximately equal to 10 percent depreciation on the total equipment inventory. However, expenditures for equipment by nonresident tourists outside of the state would be excluded. Even in a growing market, it would be a fortuitous circumstance if depreciation, opportunity cost on the investment, and maintenance costs equaled the investment value of recreation equipment purchased during the study year.

Gross expenditure studies include the direct cost of transportation, lodging, food and beverage, and other consumable supplies purchased within the state. The direct costs of nonresident tourists outside of the state are excluded, even though they are necessary to participate in outdoor recreation within the state. This tends to understate the long-run price of outdoor recreation. Finally, gross expenditure studies include the total cost of food and beverage purchased within the state.

Table 4-3. Price Dispersion and the Percent by Which the Highest Price Exceeds the Lowest Price for Durable Recreation Equipment, United States

Durable Recreation Equipment	List Price		Amount by Which the Highest Price Exceeds the Lowest Price	
	High	Low	Dollars	Percent
Sleeping Bags for Backpacking				
Thermal comfort zone of 60°F to 0°F	$180	$ 44	$136	309%
Thermal comfort zone of 70°F to 32°F	80	25	55	220
Camp Lanterns (1-2 mantles)				
Propane lanterns	30	13	17	131
Gasoline lanterns	29	20	9	45
Family Tents				
(9×12 foot cabin style)	275	100	175	175
Camp Stoves (2 burner)	46	26	20	77
Tennis Balls (can of 3 balls)	5	2.75	2.25	82
Small Outboard Boats (14 foot aluminum)				
Acceptable	592	480	112	23
Conditionally acceptable	481	459	22	5
Small Sailboats (11-14 foot)				
Small sailboats	752	525	227	43
Sailing dinghies	795	729	66	9
Fly-Fishing Reels				
Manual reels	69	13	56	431
Automatic reels	28	12	16	133
Ten-Speed Bikes				
Very good	220	149	71	48
Good to very good	200	135	65	48
Good	210	125	85	68
Fair to good	110	100	10	10

Source: Consumer Reports, Buying Guide 1978.

The long-run price of outdoor recreation includes only food and beverage costs above those that would have been incurred at home.

PRICE PATTERNS

An understanding of the variation in prices actually paid by individual consumers is essential to making effective recreation resource development and management decisions. Manthy and Tucker have reported that the costs of public and private suppliers of recreation facilities represent only a small portion of the total direct costs of consumption. What to include in price depends on the decision to be made. The general rule is to include all expenses that increase as a result of a decision to take a recreation trip.

When a family goes to the beach for a weekend, they spend money on gasoline and maintenance of their car, on additional food at restaurants and grocery stores, on entrance fees, on entertainment at the boardwalk, on suntan lotion, souvenirs, and the like. They also may pay for 1-2 nights lodging in a motel, hotel, resort lodge, or camp-ground.

The fact that these expenditures are paid to many different businesses should not detract from the conclusion that together they constitute the necessary direct costs or price of outdoor recreation. Combined, these expenditures are no less the price than expenditures paid in a lump sum to a travel agent for a package plan which may include transportation, lodging, food, entrance fees, etc. In addition, a nonmonetary cost may be incurred related to the dissatisfaction of driving, and there may be an opportunity cost of wages foregone to participate in outdoor recreation. Any individual time cost would be added to the monetary costs of the trip.

Type of Expenditure

National and regional surveys have established a number of distinguishing patterns of recreation expenditures. Table 4-4 shows the distribution of average total expenses of individuals per day on recreation trips of 100 miles or more for each state. For example, average total expenses were $41 per day in Colorado, including $6.60 for lodging, $11.60 for food, $14.50 for transportation, and $8.50 for other costs in 1977. Average total expenses varied substantially among the states from a low of $9.50 per day in Virginia to $93 in Alaska. Distribution of expenses among the four categories also varied substantially among the states. It seems likely that this is related to the proportion of single day outings, 2-3 day overnight trips, and vacations in each of the states. These estimates are updated periodically by the Business Research Division, University of Colorado, in cooperation with the Travel Research Association. Table 4-5 illustrates the overall pattern of recreation expenditures for the nation as a whole.

The price per day of recreation is more dependent on choice of lodging than any other single variable, according to Drake, et al. Overnight lodging is the largest single expense for nearly one-third of individual consumers who stay in commercial lodging accommodations. Wilman suggests that the decision to stay overnight in commercial accommodations at a resort area is based on the relative costs of the overnight lodging compared to the monetary and time costs of traveling home and back again in the morning. Nearly 20 percent stay overnight in campgrounds, hiking shelters, recreation vehicles, water craft, or personal vacation homes and condominiums. Approximately 47 percent of participants stay at home or with friends and relatives at little or no expense other than food which also may be provided by friends and relatives.

Lodging and added food expenditures together account for about half of the price of recreation, although this is highly variable among

Table 4-4. Average Expenditure Per Person Per Day on Recreation Trips of 100 Miles or More, United States

State	Lodging	Food	Transportation	Other	Total	Date of Data
Alabama	$ 4	$ 4	$ 3	$ 4	$15	1979
Alaska	7	5	71	9	93	1977
Arizona	7	10	9	6	32	1979
Arkansas	4	11	7	7	29	1977
California	6	14	26	8	54	1977
Colorado	7	12	14	9	41	1977
Connecticut	4	13	55	8	81	1977
Delaware	8	13	6	8	35	1977
District of Columbia	16	20	22	8	67	1977
Florida	9	11	5	10	34	1979
Georgia	6	13	23	8	51	1977
Hawaii	17	15	6	16	55	1977
Idaho	6	17	12	7	42	1977
Illinois	5	13	31	9	57	1977
Indiana	4	12	15	8	39	1977
Iowa	4	13	18	8	43	1977
Kansas	3	11	19	8	42	1977
Kentucky	5	13	22	8	49	1978
Louisiana	5	14	21	8	49	1977
Maine	11	13	8	7	39	1977
Maryland	6	15	22	8	50	1977
Massachusetts	11	14	31	8	64	1977
Michigan	7	11	15	8	42	1977
Minnesota	7	13	16	9	45	1977
Mississippi	4	12	11	7	34	1977
Missouri	2	3	6	2	14	1979
Montana	6	11	12	8	36	1977
Nebraska	4	4	4	2	14	1978
Nevada	12	17	18	7	54	1977
New Hampshire	16	12	8	8	44	1977
New Jersey	8	15	22	8	53	1977
New Mexico	5	15	13	8	41	1977
New York	10	18	30	8	66	1977
North Carolina	6	12	13	8	39	1977
North Dakota	3	12	17	7	38	1977
Ohio	3	14	26	8	51	1977
Oklahoma	3	12	12	8	35	1977
Oregon	3	14	17	8	42	1977
Pennsylvania	6	13	19	8	46	1977
Rhode Island	4	12	19	7	41	1977
South Carolina	6	5	2	4	17	1979
South Dakota	5	11	13	8	37	1977
Tennessee	6	13	12	8	39	1977
Texas	6	12	19	8	45	1977
Utah	3	4	4	4	14	1979
Vermont	8	16	3	8	35	1977
Virginia	2	4	2	1	10	1979
Washington	4	13	16	8	41	1977
West Virginia	7	12	10	8	37	1977
Wisconsin	7	13	10	9	39	1977
Wyoming	6	11	11	8	36	1977

Source: University of Colorado, Business Research Division.

Table 4-5. Distribution of Expenditures on Recreation Travel, United States

Category	Percent
Lodging	23%
Food and beverage	27
Recreation entrance fees	12
Transportation	9
Clothing and footwear	11
Jewelry and souvenirs	7
Drugs, cosmetics, and tobacco	7
Miscellaneous	4
Total	100

Source: Epperson.

individuals. Transportation costs and entrance fees together account for only about one-fifth of the price of recreation. Expenditures for a variety of consumable retail products and services constitute an important part of the price of recreation. In fact, these items together account for a larger share of the direct costs of recreation than do transportation costs and entrance fees.

Table 4-6 illustrates the range in prices of overnight lodging accommodations in selected recreation areas of the Rocky Mountains. Prices are shown per night for two persons occupying a double bed at five winter resorts and two summer resorts. Quality of service ranges from 2 to 5 stars based on the American Automobile Association rating system.

Seasonal Price Variation

Seasonal price variation is common in resort communities which supply recreation lodging services. As a general rule, whenever there is a large variation in seasonal demand for services, businesses will charge higher prices when demand is greatest. In effect, businesses surcharge customers during the peak season a premium price sufficient to cover fixed overhead costs and profits. They will continue to supply services during the rest of the year at a price sufficient to cover direct operating costs. If not, they will shut down during part of the year.

Individual consumers are willing to pay higher prices during peak seasons because their benefits are higher when conditions for outdoor recreation are most favorable. For most winter resorts, the high-price season is from December 15 to April 16, which coincides with favorable ski conditions. For example, the four star Lodge at Vail charged two persons $88 per night during the ski season, reducing this to $53 per night during the balance of 1980-81. For most summer resorts, the high-price season is from May 1 to September 15. For example, the five-star Broadmoor at Colorado Springs charged two persons $80-$110 per night during the summer and $60-$80 during the winter

Table 4-6. Seasonal Price Variation in Overnight Lodging at Selected Recreation Areas, Rocky Mountains, 1980-81

	for two persons	
Low accommodations	High season	Low season
Winter Resorts		
Aspen		
Boomerang Lodge***	$70- 74	$32- 36
Innsbruck Sports Motel***	54- 80	32- 42
Mountain Chalet-Snowmass****	60- 90	17- 26
Breckenridge-Dillon		
Holiday Inn****	50	30
Keystone Resort*****	80-100	44- 50
Ramada Silverthorne***	65	31- 45
Steamboat		
Best Western Ptarmigan Inn****	72	32
Nordic Lodge***	48- 52	28- 32
Thunderhead Inn***	78	38
Vail		
Christianian Motel***	45- 55	24- 30
Enzlan Lodge***	65	32
The Lodge at Vail****	88	53
Winter Park		
Beavers Village Ski Chalet & Guest Ranch***	98	71
Brookside Inn**	80	20
Summer Resorts		
Colorado Springs		
Embers Motel***	22	13
Best Western Palmer House***	30- 36	20- 26
The Broadmoor*****	80-110	60- 80
Estes Park		
Caribou Chalet***	28- 32	18- 22
Hobby Horse Motor Lodge****	30- 40	20- 30

Note: Number of stars refers to AAA rating system.
Source: Rocky Mountain Automobile Association.

of 1980-81. Low season prices often exclude some services such as a complimentary continental breakfast of beverage and roll.

Entrance Fees

In the past, entrance to most public parks and recreation facilities was free. For example, the National Park Service charged no entrance fees at nearly 300 national monuments and historic sites and only $1-$3 per vehicle or party at 49 national parks and recreation areas. The range in fees charged was based on the size of the park, as for example, $3 at Yosemite National Park and $1 at Appomattox.

It may be efficient to allow free admission to parks where fees generate less than $25,000 per year, as costs of collection are likely to exceed the revenue collected. Of the 49 national parks that charged an entrance fee, 22, or 45 percent that charged $1 per vehicle had fee receipts of less than $25,000 per year. Free admission to these parks would reduce revenues by $295,000, or only 3.6 percent of total entrance fee revenues of $8.2 million in 1976.

Most individuals have used recreation resources administered by the U.S. government without payment of entrance fees. The Forest Service, Bureau of Reclamation, Fish and Wildlife Service, and Army Corps of Engineers charge no entrance fees for admission to the national forests, wilderness areas, recreation areas, wildlife refuges, and reservoirs which these agencies administer. Fees of $2-$5 per night were charged per campsite with other charges for services such as boat-docking facilities.

While entrance to city parks has remained free, for the most part, the charge for use of recreation facilities such as swimming pools, zoos, tennis courts and golf courses within city parks has increased in recent years. Although such fees are generally small, $0.50-$2.50 per person, they may deter the participation of low-income people and the costs of collection represent a significant proportion of the revenue collected. Huszar and Seckler have reported on problems after an entrance fee was first charged at the California Academy of Sciences in Golden Gate State Park, San Francisco. The installation of a 50 cent entrance fee for adults and 25 cents for children over 12 raised net revenue of $0.3 million in 1971, the first year, and eliminated an operating deficit. However, the estimated loss in consumer surplus benefits of those who were not admitted because they were unwilling or unable to pay the fees was estimated as $0.4 million, or one-third more than the fee revenues generated. Thus, social welfare declined when a fee was charged for admission. They concluded that charging a fee for admission to museums is undesirable and not economically efficient, although it may be a better alternative than closing museums when general tax revenues and donations are insufficient to cover operation costs, in this case $1.7 million per year.

Nearly all state and local units of government have now initiated or increased entrance fees to recreational areas. Most states and counties charge entrance fees of $1-$2 per vehicle or party at public parks and reservoirs which they administer.

States own the wildlife in the United States and collect license fees for hunting and fishing, whether on public or private land. For example, in 1982 the state of Colorado charged residents $5 and nonresidents $20 for small game hunting compared to $7.50 and $25 for fishing, $13 and $90 for deer hunting, and $16 and $135 for elk hunting. Price discrimination between residents and nonresidents of states has been a controversial issue which remains unresolved. Munger reported that ranchers who control access roads to public land charged fees of $25 per hunter in northwest Colorado. Public access to private land for purposes of outdoor recreation is a problem which is partially resolved by the payment of entrance fees and state compensation for damages.

Table 4-7 shows the range in fees charged by over 8,000 private and public campgrounds. Over half of the campgrounds charged $5-$6 per campsite in 1979 compared with $2-$2.50 in 1968. Daily base rates for camping ranged from $3 or less to $9.50 per campsite in 1979. The Forest Service did not charge at campgrounds lacking drinking water, and camping fees were generally less at public than private campgrounds, which include more services in the base rate.

Some campgrounds include hookups for electricity, water, and sewer in their base rates while others charge extra for these services. Some have a base rate for two persons, with extra charges for each additional person, while others do not charge for extra persons. Some have a base rate for four persons or a family. Others charge per person in the party. Thus, the methods for calculating rates vary widely among campgrounds. Most include free use of some recreation facilities in the basic camping fee, for example, use of a recreation hall, outdoor pool or beach, and tennis, handball, or racquetball courts. Campgrounds charge extra for use of other recreation facilities and services such as boat rental, golf course, horseback riding, and river raft trip. Charges for these other recreation services are usually higher than fees for camping or entrance to public parks.

Table 4-8 illustrates the entrance fees charged for selected recreation services in the Rocky Mountains. Commercial charges for access to most of the activities shown ranged from $5-$20 per day or event in 1980. Charges to attend outdoor sports events are comparable to the

Table 4-7. Daily Fees Charged per Campsite at Public and Private Campgrounds, United States, 1979

Daily Fee per Campsite[a]	Number of Campgrounds	Percent
$3.00 or less	711	9%
$3.50	205	3
$4.00	740	9
$4.50	655	8
$5.00	1,787	22
$5.50	815	10
$6.00	1,526	19
$6.50	531	7
$7.00	573	7
$7.50	163	2
$8.00	178	2
$8.50	63	1
$9.00	54	1
$9.50	18	[b]
Total	8,019	100

[a]Average: $5.32.
[b]Less than 0.5%.
Source: Woodall Publishing Co.

Table 4-8. Entrance Fees for Selected Recreation Activities, Rocky Mountains, United States, 1980

Activity	Entrance Fee Dollars	Hours/Day	Dollars per Hour
Tennis	$ 0-16.00	2	$ 0-8.00
Golf	4.00-20.00	4	1.00-5.00
Downhill Skiing	11.00-16.00	5	2.20-3.20
Ice Skating	0- 3.00	2	0-1.50
Swimming	0- 3.25	2	0-1.63
River Raft Trips	27.00-47.00	8	3.38-5.88
Horseback Riding	16.00-24.00	4	4.00-6.00
Jeep Tours	12.00-21.75	4	3.00-5.44
Attend Professional Football	7.50-11.00	3	2.57-3.67
Attend College Football	10.00-15.00	3	3.33-5.00
Attend Hockey	6.00-12.00	3	2.00-4.00
Attend Opera	10.00-18.00	3	3.33-6.00
Attend Theatre	5.00-20.00	3	1.67-6.67
Attend Symphony	6.50-13.50	3	2.17-4.50

Source: University of Colorado, Business Research Division.

price of admission to opera, theatre, and symphony indoors. The range in admission fees reflects the difference between expensive country clubs and low priced municipal programs, the quality of services offered, the amenities included, and degree of price competition.

It is common for city park and recreation departments to offer tennis, golf, swimming, and ice skating at a nominal or low fee compared with commercial facilities offering these same opportunities in resort areas. It should be noted that many of the popular recreation activities are not shown in Table 4-8. These include, among others, picnicking, sightseeing, driving for pleasure, walking for pleasure, and playing outdoor sports, all of which are available without payment of an entrance fee.

Fees to play tennis at private courts exceed the charge per hour of most other recreation activities. The charge per day of skiing, golf, horseback riding, river raft trips, and jeep tours exceeds that for tennis. However, the consumer's conception of a day or event is typically 1-2 hours of tennis, 4 hours of golf, 4 hours of touring by jeep, 4 hours of horseback riding, 5 hours of skiing, and 8 hours of river rafting. Moreover, downhill skiers typically are actually skiing only one-third of the time; otherwise, they wait in lift lines, ride lifts, eat lunch, and spend time at the base facility. Thus, the charge per hour of actual skiing would exceed the fee for all other recreation activities.

Transportation Costs

Table 4-9 illustrates the trend in costs of operating large, medium and small automobiles in the United States. Average direct costs were estimated as 4.7 cents per mile in 1968 compared with 6.8 cents in

Table 4-9. Average Variable Costs per Mile to Operate an Automobile in the United States

Type of Automobile	Year	Variable Costs, Cents per Mile			
		Maintenance, accessories, repairs, tires	Gasoline and Oil (excluding taxes)	Taxes	Total
Standard					
	1976	4.2	3.3	0.9	8.4
	1979	5.5	5.5	1.6	12.6
	1981	6.0	7.3	1.5	14.8
Compact					
	1976	3.4	2.5	0.6	6.5
	1979	4.8	4.9	1.3	11.0
	1981	5.0	5.3	1.1	11.4
Subcompact					
	1976	3.1	1.8	0.5	5.4
	1979	4.1	4.1	1.1	9.3
	1981	4.8	4.5	1.0	10.3
Average					
	1968	2.2	1.8	0.7	4.7
	1976	3.6	2.5	0.7	6.8
	1979	4.8	4.8	1.3	10.9
	1981	5.3	5.7	1.2	12.2

Source: U.S. Dept. of Transportation.

1976, 10.9 cents in 1979, and 12.2 cents in 1981. Included are the variable costs of gasoline, oil, maintenance, repairs, tires, and taxes on these items. Not included are the fixed costs of auto ownership, such as depreciation, insurance, registration, etc., which were an additional 10.1 cents per mile in 1981. The estimates are based on studies conducted periodically by the U.S. Department of Transportation. To convert miles traveled to recreation travel costs, the federal guidelines recommend use of the most current study by the U.S. Department of Transportation. These costs may be adjusted for travel conditions. According to estimates by Haspel and Johnson, the variable cost of operating standard size cars on recreation trips in 1980 was 20 cents per mile.

The estimates in Table 4-9 are for the operation of typical suburban based vehicles in Baltimore, Maryland. Vehicles were 1981 models purchased at an average price of $7,323 to be driven an average of 10,000 miles per year for 12 years. Gasoline prices were $1.35 per gallon in 1981, consumed at a rate of 23 miles per gallon (range 17-28 MPG). A 30-cent increase in the price of gasoline to $1.65 per gallon would increase the average cost of operation by 1.36 cents per mile. The cost of oil change, lubrication, and repair would also rise proportionately.

Problems arise in application of average variable costs of suburban based auto travel in an Eastcentral U.S. State to recreation travel throughout the United States. Gasoline prices and repair costs vary among regions and are typically higher on the Interstate Highway System and in parks and resort areas.

In addition, the variable costs of operating passenger vans are omitted from the average variable costs recommended by the federal guidelines. Van costs are much higher than the costs of passenger cars. Average variable costs estimated by the U.S. Department of Transportation were 18.0 cents per mile in 1981, including gas and oil, 8.9 cents; maintenance, repairs and tires, 6.1 cents; and taxes, 1.9 cents. Gasoline consumption was at a rate of 14 miles per gallon and purchase price in 1981 was $12,877. These van costs are representative of a number of different types of recreation vehicles including: camper-pickups, recreation vehicles, and standard autos pulling a camper trailer. To include van costs in the average travel cost recommendations of the federal guidelines would increase the price estimate by 11 percent, from 12.2 to 13.7 cents in 1981 dollars.

Table 4-10 illustrates the roundtrip miles traveled to participate in recreation activities in Eastcentral United States. The average out of pocket cost of transportation can be estimated following the procedure

Table 4-10. Roundtrip Miles Traveled to Participate in Outdoor Recreation Activities, Maryland

Activity	Miles per Trip
Camping	239
Canoeing, Kayaking, River Running	85
Sailing	59
Waterskiing	93
Other Boating	93
Fishing	98
Nature Walks, Birdwatching, Photography	26
Outdoor Pool Swimming	22
Other Outdoor Swimming	218
Hiking or Backpacking	60
Other Walking for Pleasure	5
Jogging, Running	3
Bicycling	11
Horseback Riding	62
Driving Off-road Vehicles	61
Hunting	88
Picnicking	39
Golfing	48
Tennis Outdoors	9
Skiing, Downhill and Cross-country	156
Ice-skating, Lake or Pond	9
Sledding, Tobogganing	22
Playing Softball, Baseball	14
Skateboarding	9
Archery	24
Sightseeing	152
Driving for Pleasure	89
Attend Outdoor Sporting Events	28
Attend Outdoor Concerts, Plays	39

Source: Heritage, Conservation, and Recreation Service.

recommended by the federal guidelines. For example, the transportation costs of hunting average $5.87 per recreation day compared with fishing, $6.53; hiking and backpacking, $4.00; picnicking, $2.60; skiing, $10.40; and beach swimming, $14.59. These estimates assume single-purpose trips, three persons per vehicle, and direct transportation costs of 20 cents per mile. It should be noted the costs per mile tend to be higher on short trips in heavy stop-and-go traffic than longer trips on highways.

Table 4-11 illustrates the range in roundtrip miles traveled to participate in recreation in the United States. Nearly two-thirds of single-day trips are 50 miles or less, with transportation costs of less than $3.35 per recreation day. Twenty-two percent of single day trips are 51-100 miles, with average transportation costs of $5.00 per recreation day. Fifteen percent are over 100 miles with transportation costs of approximately $11.67 per recreation day. This shows that transportation costs increase and number of trips decrease with increasing number of roundtrip miles traveled to engage in recreation. This general attribute of recreation behavior is basic to the travel cost approach to demand for recreation.

Table 4-11. Distribution of Roundtrip Miles per Trip to Participate in Outdoor Recreation, United States

Distance	Vacation	Overnight	Day Outing
	----------- Percent -----------		
50 miles or less	2%	14%	63%
51-100 miles	3	21	22
101-250 miles	13	30	15[a]
251-500 miles	22	24	n.a.
501-1,000 miles	25	9	n.a.
Over 1,000 miles	35	2	n.a.
	----------- Miles -----------		
Average miles	1,285	253	62
Median miles	705	174	37

[a]Over 100 miles.
n.a. = not applicable.
Source: Bureau of Outdoor Recreation.

SUMMARY

Thus far, no standard proxy for the price of recreation has been developed that is suitable for all purposes of measurement. In this chapter we examined several measures that are used including: entrance fees, direct transportation costs, travel time costs, opportunity cost of recreation time, total direct costs, and fixed costs. The fact that out-of-pocket expenses are paid to many different businesses should not detract from the conclusion that together they constitute the necessary direct costs or price of recreation. Any individual time cost should be added to this monetary cost.

While each of these costs or a combination of them has provided a satisfactory measure of the price of recreation under particular conditions, we described several problems encountered in general application and demonstrated under what conditions each measure should be used. For example, entrance fees provide a satisfactory measure of the price of recreation where participation requires little or no travel or other out-of-pocket cost. Direct travel costs are a suitable measure of changes in price when there is information available on the number of visits from distance zones and total annual use of a recreation site. Travel time cost should be included in the price of recreation when there is dissatisfaction driving. Opportunity cost of recreation time on the site should be included in the price for those individual participants who would have worked or engaged in an alternative recreation activity. Total direct cost provides a suitable measure of the money price of recreation when other costs such as lodging, added food, and other services vary with distance traveled. Problems may arise when the direct cost or price perceived by individual consumers differs from the economic definition of price.

Next we distinguished between short-run and long-run prices of recreation. Short-run decisions to take an additional trip to a recreation site are affected by the direct out-of-pocket and time costs that change. Long-run decisions to purchase recreation equipment are based on fixed costs of depreciation, opportunity costs of the investment, and expected use levels over the life of the equipment.

We concluded the chapter with examples of price patterns. Recent regional and national surveys have established a number of distinguishing characteristics of recreation expenditures. Overnight lodging is the largest single expense for consumers who stay in commercial accommodations. Lodging and added food expenditures together account for about half of the price of recreation. Transportation and entrance fees are only about one-fifth. Expenditures for a variety of consumable retail products and services account for the balance of price.

Seasonal price variation is common in resort areas. As a general rule, whenever there is a large variation in seasonal demand for services, businesses will charge higher prices when demand is greatest. In effect, businesses surcharge customers during the peak season a premium price sufficient to cover fixed overhead costs and profits. They will continue to supply services during the rest of the year at a price sufficient to cover direct operating costs. If not, they will shut down during part of the year. Individual consumers are willing to pay higher prices during peak seasons because their benefits are higher when conditions are most favorable for the recreation activity.

The measures of the price of recreation introduced in this chapter are also used in empirical demand estimation. We shall refer to this material when demand studies are considered in Chapter 5.

READINGS

Arndt, Seifert. "The Time Price System: Its Application to the Measurement of Primary Outdoor Recreation Benefits." Ph.D. Dissertation, Michigan State University, East Lansing. 1971.

Brown, Gardner M., Jr. "Pricing Seasonal Recreation Services." *Western Economic Journal* 9(June 1971):218-25.

Brown, R. E., and William J. Hansen. "A Generalized Recreation Day Use Planning Model, Plan Formulation and Evaluation Studies-Recreation." Tech. Rep. No. 5. U.S. Army Corps of Engineers, Sacramento, Calif. 1974.

Brown, William G., Colin Sorhus, and Kenneth C. Gibbs. "Estimated Expenditure by Sport Anglers and Net Economic Values of Salmon and Steelhead for Specified Fisheries in the Pacific Northwest." Dept. of Economics, Oregon State University, Corvallis. 1980.

Bureau of Outdoor Recreation. "Federal Outdoor Recreation Expenditures Study." U.S. Dept. of the Interior, Washington, D.C. 1977.

Cesario, Frank J. "Value of Time in Recreation Benefit Studies." *Land Economics* 52(Febr. 1976):32-41.

Cicchetti, Charles J. "Some Economic Issues in Planning Urban Recreation Facilities." *Land Economics* 47(Febr. 1971):14-23.

Clawson, Marion, and Jack L. Knetsch. *Economics of Outdoor Recreation.* Johns Hopkins University Press, Baltimore, 1966.

Consumer Reports, *Buying Guide 1978.* Consumers Union of the United States, Inc., Mount Vernon, N.Y. 1977.

Daubert, John, and Robert A. Young. "Cost of Owning a Self-Contained Recreational Vehicle." Extension Service No. 9.127, Colorado State University, Fort Collins. 1976.

Epperson, Arlin. *Private and Commercial Recreation.* John Wiley, Inc., New York. 1977.

Garvey, Edward B. "Backpacking Gear: Shoes and Packs to Sleeping Bags." *Shopper's Guide,* Yearbook of Agriculture, U.S. Dept. of Agriculture, Washington, D.C. 1974.

Gibbs, Kenneth C. "The Economics of Water Oriented Recreation in Kissime River Basin." Technical Bulletin 769. Florida Agricultural Experiment Station, University of Florida, Gainesville. 1975.

Goeldner, Charles R., and Karen P. Duea. "Travel Trends in the United States and Canada." University of Colorado, Boulder. 1984.

Gordon, Douglas. "An Economic Analysis of Idaho Sport Fisheries." Idaho Cooperative Fishery Unit, Moscow. 1970.

Heritage Conservation and Recreation Service. "Third Nationwide Outdoor Recreation Plan." Four Volumes based on the 1977 National Recreation Survey. U.S. Dept. of the Interior, Gov. Print. Off., Washington, D.C. 1980.

Horvath, Joseph C. "Preliminary Executive Summary: Economic Survey of Wildlife Recreation, Southeastern States." Environmental Research Group, Georgia State University, Atlanta. 1973.

Huszar, Paul C., and David W. Seckler. "Effects of Pricing a 'Free' Good: A Study of Admission at the California Academy of Sciences." *Land Economics* 50(Nov. 1974):364-73.

Keith, John E., and J. P. Workman. "Opportunity Cost of Time in Demand Estimates for Nonmarket Resources." *Journal of Leisure Research* 7(No. 2, 1975):121-27.

LaPage, Wilbur. "The Role of Fees in Campers' Decisions." Research Paper NE-118, Northeast Experiment Station, U. S. Dept. of Agriculture, Washington, D.C. 1968.

Linder, Staffan B. *The Harried Leisure Class.* Columbia University Press, New York. 1970.

Manthy, Robert S., and Thomas L. Tucker. "Supply Costs for Public Forest Land Recreation." Research Report 158. Agricultural Experiment Station, Michigan State University, East Lansing. 1972.

McConnell, Kenneth E. "Problems in Estimating the Demand for Outdoor Recreation." *American Journal of Agricultural Economics* 57(May 1975):330-34.

McKean, John R., and Kenneth C. Nobe. "Sportsmen Expenditures for Hunting and Fishing in Colorado, 1981." Dept. of Economics, Colorado State University, Fort Collins. 1982.

Milam, R. L., and E. C. Pasour, Jr.. "Estimating the Demand for an On-Farm Recreational Service." *American Journal of Agricultural Economics* 52(Febr. 1970):127-31.

Morrison, Steven, and Clifford Winston. "An Econometric Analysis of the Demand for Intercity Passenger Transportation." Research in Transportation Economics: A Research Annual. Volume 2. JAI Press, Greenwich, Conn. 1985. 213-37.

Nobe, Kenneth C., and A. H. Gilbert. "A Survey of Sportsmen Expenditures for Hunting and Fishing in Colorado, 1968." Technical Publication No. 24, Division of Game, Fish and Parks, State of Colorado, Denver. 1970.

Noll, Roger G., ed. *Government and the Sports Business.* The Brookings Institution, Washington, D.C., 1974.

Norton, G. A. "Public Outdoor Recreation and Resource Allocation: A Welfare Approach." *Land Economics* 46(Nov. 1970):414-22.

Owen, John D. *The Price of Leisure.* Rotterdam University Press, Rotterdam. 1969.

Pearse, Peter H. "A New Approach to the Evaluation of Non-priced Recreational Resources." *Land Economics* 44(Febr. 1968):87-99.

Rocky Mountain Automobile Association. "Where to Vacation in Colorado." Rocky Mountain Motorists, Inc., Denver. 1980.

Ross, Lee Ann, Dwight M. Blood, and Kenneth C. Nobe. "A Survey of Sportsmen Expenditures for Hunting and Fishing in Colorado, 1973." National Resource Economics Report No. 20. Dept. of Economics, Colorado State University, Fort Collins. 1975.

Sanders, Larry D. "Economic Benefits of River Protection: A Study of Recreation Use and Preservation Values." Ph.D. Dissertation, Colorado State University, Fort Collins. 1985.

University of Colorado. "Travel Trends in the United States and Canada." Business Research Division in Cooperation with the Travel Research Association, Boulder. 1981.

U.S. Dept. of Agriculture. "National Outdoor Recreation Trends Symposium." Vols. 1 and 2. General Technical Report NE-57, Forest Service, Washington, D.C., 1980.

U.S. Dept. of Transportation. "Costs of Operating Automobiles and Vans." Federal Highway Administration. Office of Highway Planning, U.S. Gov. Print. Off., Washington, D.C. 1980 and 1982.

U.S. Dept. of Transportation. "Recreation Travel Impacts." Federal Highway Administration, Washington, D.C. 1977.

U.S. Travel Data Center. "The 1976 National Travel Expenditures Study, Summary Report." Washington, D.C. 1977.

Verhoven, Peter J., Jr. "An Evaluation of Policy-Related Research in the Field of Municipal Recreation and Parks." National Recreation and Parks Association, Washington, D.C., 1975.

Walsh, Richard G. "Effects of Improved Research Methods on the Value of Recreational Benefits." *Outdoor Recreation: Advances in Application of Economics.* Jay M. Hughes and R. Duane Lloyd, (eds.). General Technical Rpt. WO-2, Forest Service, U.S. Dept. of Agriculture, Washington, D.C., 1977.

Walsh, Richard G., Michael Retzloff, and Elliot Waples. "Economic Implications of Second Home Developments in Selected Areas of Colorado." *Man, Development, and Wildlands: A Complex Interaction.* Forest Service, U.S. Dept. of Agriculture, Washington, D.C. 1975. 98-107.

Ward, Frank A. "Specification Considerations for the Price Variable in Travel Cost Demand Models." *Land Economics* 60(Aug. 1984):301-305.

Wennegren, Boyd E. "Surrogate Pricing of Outdoor Recreation." *Land Economics* 43(Febr. 1967):112-16.

Wilman, Elizabeth A. "The Value of Time in Recreation Benefit Studies." *Journal of Environmental Economics and Management.* 7(Sept. 1980):272-86.

Winston, Clifford. "Conceptual Development in the Economics of Transportation: An Interpretive Survey." *Journal of Economic Literature* 23(Mar. 1985):57-94.

118

Chapter Five
Demand Curve

   This chapter distinguishes between total and marginal benefits; introduces the concept of diminishing marginal benefit; shows how individual demand curves are derived from the logic of consumer choice; and illustrates how to apply the information obtained from demand curves to recreation economic decisions.

   The primary purpose of recreation resource development and management is to provide the opportunity for consumers to benefit from recreation activities. Individual consumers tend to participate in recreation activities that provide them with the most benefits relative to direct costs or price. The federal guidelines recommend consumer surplus as an acceptable economic measure of the benefits of public recreation programs. Consumer surplus is defined as the area below a demand curve and above direct cost or price. Thus, recreation economists are frequently assigned the task of studying consumer demand for parks and other recreation areas.

   The focus of this chapter is on the relationship between a representative individual's willingness to pay for trips to a recreation site and the decision as to how many trips to take. We will see that the aggregate demand curve for a recreation site is the sum of the demand curves of individual consumers. Demand, of course, is also affected by other variables, such as consumer income, quality of the site, and prices of substitute sites. We will consider these influences in Chapter 6 on the demand function.

TOTAL AND MARGINAL BENEFITS

   We must first define what we mean by benefits and then consider how they are related to individual recreation economic decisions. Economists are concerned with two types of benefits — total and marginal. The total benefit to consumers of an activity, say, trips to a recreation area, is an economic measure of how much pleasure, usefulness, or utility consumers obtain from the experience. The trouble is that no one has yet invented a reliable sensory detector to tell us directly how much fun a recreation trip provides. Baumol and Blinder propose that to get around the problem, we can measure the total benefits to consumers by asking, "What is the largest sum of money you would be willing to pay rather than give up the experience?" Suppose, for example, an individual is considering the possibility of taking five trips to a recreation area this year. The individual is determined not to participate in the activity if it costs more than $200, but to participate if the trips cost $200 or less. Thus, the total benefits of five trips to the site are $200, the maximum amount that person is willing to pay for the experience.

Total benefit, as you can see, is an economic measure of the total satisfaction consumers derive from any purchase. The higher the total benefit obtained, the better off the individual. By definition, then, the best recreation economic decisions of consumers are those that make their benefits as large as possible. It is total benefit that really matters to the consumer. But to consider which decisions most effectively promote total benefit, we must consider the related concept of marginal benefit. This term refers to the additional benefit to individuals from consuming one more unit of any good or service. Table 5-1 helps clarify the distinction between marginal and total benefits and shows how the two are related. The first two columns show how much total benefit consumers derive from various numbers of trips per year, ranging from zero to seven. For example, a single trip is worth no more than $60, two trips are worth $110, and so on. The marginal benefit is the difference between any two successive total benefit figures. For example, if participants already have made three trips to a recreation site (worth $150), an additional trip would bring total benefits up to $180 for the year. The individual's marginal benefit is thus the difference between the two, or $30.

Table 5-1 illustrates a simple hypothesis about consumer behavior: the more trips to a recreation site a consumer has taken, other things being equal, the less marginal benefit an additional trip will bring. In general, this is a plausible proposition. Psychological studies, including photos of eye movements and measurement of electrical impulses in the brain, show that repetition of an event renders it less and less pleasurable. A sufficient number of repetitions can extinguish all reaction to it. This is the basis for the economic "law" of diminishing marginal utility, which means that additional units of a good or service yield successively smaller contributions to consumer well-being. As individual consumption increases, the marginal utility or benefits of each additional unit declines. The last column of Table 5-1 illustrates this concept.

If, for now, we hold constant variations in the quality of the site, sanitary conditions, insect populations, weather, crowding, and other conditions on individual trips, each successive trip adds less and less pleasure or satisfaction. Participants would be willing to pay the most for the first trip of the year when aesthetic satisfaction is at peak levels. The second trip provides substantial benefits but less than the first. With the third through the sixth trips, benefits diminish further;

Table 5-1. Total and Marginal Benefits of Recreation Trips by a Representative Individual

Number of Trips per Year	Total Benefits (Dollars)	Marginal Benefits (Dollars)
0	0	
1	$ 60	$ 60
2	110	50
3	150	40
4	180	30
5	200	20
6	210	10
7	210	0

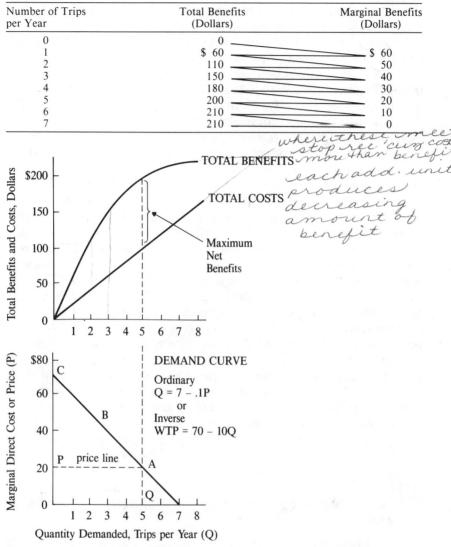

where these meet stop rec'cus costs more than benefits. each add. unit produces decreasing amount of benefit

Figure 5-1. Demand Curve for Recreation Trips by a Representative Individual

and, by the seventh trip, the experience provides no additional benefits. If an eighth visit is considered, marginal benefits would be negative, and the rational economic decision would be to choose an alternative recreation activity where benefits are positive.

The recreation economic rule is that consumers should participate more in any activity whose marginal benefits exceed its price or direct

121

costs, and avoid in any activity whose marginal benefits are less than its price. When possible, consumers should continue to participate until price and marginal benefits are equal, because this quantity will maximize the net benefits gained from the activity.

To see why this rule works, refer again to the table of marginal benefits for recreation trips (Table 5-1). Suppose that the price or direct cost of a trip is $20 per person, and our consumer considers taking only two trips. We see that this is not a wise decision, because the marginal benefits of a third trip ($40) are greater than its $20 price. If the consumer considers increasing the number of trips to three, the additional trip would cost $20 but yield $40 in marginal benefits; thus the additional trip would bring a clear net gain of the difference, or $20. Obviously, at a price of $20 per trip, the individual is better off with three trips than with two. Similarly, at this price, six trips is not the best recreation economic decision, because the $10 marginal benefit of the sixth trip is less than its $20 price. Our consumer would be better off with only five trips, since that would save $20 expense with only a $10 loss in benefits, a net gain of $10 from the decision to reduce trips from six to five. The recreation economic decision rule tells us that our consumer should take five trips per year, as more than five trips yields a marginal benefit that is less than price, and less than five trips leaves marginal benefit greater than price.

These concepts explain the behavior of most consumers of recreation goods and services. But there are exceptions. The more some people participate, the more they want. The trophy hunter who has a large and valuable collection of animal heads may be prepared to go to the ends of the earth for one more rare head. Similarly, the alcoholic in a resort bar cannot resist consuming another beer even though he has already consumed too many. However, economists generally consider such cases as exceptions. For most recreation activities, marginal benefits probably decline as consumption increases.

The marginal benefit information contained in Table 5-1 can also be summarized in what we call a demand curve, displayed in Figure 5-1. Each point in the graph corresponds to an entry in column three of the table.

DEMAND CURVE

A demand curve shows how the quantity demanded of some recreation activity during a specified period of time will change as the price of that activity changes, all other things held constant. Figure 5-1 depicts our representative individual's demand curve for trips to a recreation site. It is typical of graphs used in economics. The diagram shows the price or direct cost of recreation trips on the vertical (P) axis and the quantity of trips that the individual wants to take on the horizontal (Q) axis, starting from the origin point labeled zero. It shows the quantity of trips that will be demanded in a year at each possible price ranging from $10 to $70 per trip. The linear (straight line) form is used in order to make the illustration simple, but the same qualitative results would hold with nonlinear functions.

Economic diagrams are generally read as you would read latitudes and longitudes on a map. On the demand curve in Figure 5-1, the point marked A represents a hypothetical combination of price and quantity demanded by our individual consumer. Drawing a horizontal line leftward from that point to the vertical axis, we see that the average price of visiting a recreation site is $20 per trip. By dropping a line straight down to the horizontal axis, we find that five trips are wanted by our consumer at this price. The other points on the graph give similar information. For example, point B indicates that if the costs of visiting the site increase to $40 per trip, quantity demanded would be lower — it would fall to three trips per year. You can verify that this is, in fact, the case by drawing a horizontal line from point B to the vertical axis and by dropping a line straight down from point B to the horizontal axis. Going from point A to point B is defined as a movement along a demand curve.

Slope is one of the most important features of the diagrams used by economists, because the steeper the slope of a demand curve, the larger the price change required to bring about any given change in quantity demanded. The demand curve in Figure 5-1 clearly slopes downward as we follow it to the right. That is, as price falls more trips are demanded. In such instances we say that the curve has a negative slope, because one variable falls as the other one rises.

Learning how to calculate the slope of a demand curve will enable you to provide useful information for recreation economic decisions. The slope of a linear (straight line) demand curve is the same, no matter where on that line you choose to measure it. That is why you can pick any horizontal distance and corresponding vertical distance to measure slope. This is not true of lines that are curved, where the numerical value of the slope is different at every point. The slope of a curved line at a particular point is the slope of a straight line drawn tangent to the curve at that point.

The correct procedure for calculating the slope of a linear demand curve depends on whether the starting point intercepts the horizontal axis as in the case of ordinary demand curves, or the vertical axis as for inverse demand curves. Statistical demand curves for recreation have been estimated using both the travel cost and the contingent valuation methods. The travel cost method results in an ordinary demand curve in which the quantity demanded (Q) is dependent upon price (P). The contingent valuation approach typically provides an inverse demand curve in which willingness to pay (WTP) or price (P) is dependent upon the quantity demanded (Q). A detailed discussion of these methods is contained in Chapter 8. Application of either method results in identical demand curves; for example, our individual's demand curve for recreation trips illustrated in Figure 5-1. However, it is important to remember that the dependent variables, and therefore the intercepts, are reversed for the two approaches.

The equation for an ordinary demand curve is written

$$Q = a - bP \qquad \text{(5-1)}$$

where "Q" is the dependent variable number of trips, "P" is the independent variable price or direct cost, "a" is a constant representing the quantity demanded at zero price, and "b" is the rate of change in quantity with a one-unit change in price, which is the slope of the line.

Notice that the dependent variable, quantity demanded, is plotted on the horizontal axis of Figure 5-1 and the independent variable, price, is on the vertical axis. Mathematically, we would expect to see the reverse — the dependent variable on the vertical scale and the independent variable on the horizontal scale. However, the traditional practice in economics of plotting quantity on the horizontal axis and price on the vertical axis originated many years ago with the theory of competitive markets. In the case of competition, firms have no control over price but they can control output, and output of all producers determines market price. Hence, in the original model, price was the dependent variable and quantity (supplied, not demanded) was the independent variable. This is the reason price/quantity graphs appear as they do.

In the case of an inverse demand curve, price or marginal willingness to pay is the dependent variable. The equation is written

$$P = a - bQ \qquad \text{(5-2)}$$

where "Q" is the independent variable number of trips, "a" is a constant representing the price at which no quantity would be demanded, and "b" the rate of change in price with a one unit change in quantity, which is the slope of the line.

The slope of an ordinary demand curve is the ratio of the horizontal change to the corresponding vertical change as we move to the left along the line, or the ratio of the "run" over the "rise." Slope indicates how much the line rises as we move from right to left. Thus, in Figure 5-1, as we go from the horizontal intercept to zero, we go seven units to the left. But in that interval, the line rises from zero to a height of 70; that is, it rises 70 units. Consequently, the slope of this ordinary demand curve is $7/70 = -0.1$. Equation 5-1 for an ordinary demand curve becomes

$$Q = 7 - 0.1P \qquad \text{(5-3)}$$

This means that the individual demands seven trips when the price is zero and that the quantity demanded decreases by -0.1 trip with each one dollar increase in price.

The slope of an inverse demand curve is the familiar ratio of the vertical change to the corresponding horizontal change, or as is often said, the ratio of the "rise" over the "run". Slope indicates how much the line falls as we move from left to right. Thus, in Figure 5-1, as we go from the vertical intercept to zero the line falls 70 units. In that interval the line goes from zero to the horizontal intercept, seven units to the right. Consequently, the slope of this inverse demand curve is $70/7 = 10$. Equation 5-2 for an inverse demand curve becomes

$$P = 70 - 10Q \qquad\qquad (5\text{-}4)$$

This means that at a price of $70 the individual demands no trips, and that willingness to pay decreases by $10 with each additional trip per year.

The task remains to derive the site demand curve for a particular recreation area from individual demand curves. The procedure is straight forward if individual demand curves are additive as is the case when each individual pays no attention to other people's trip decisions when making his own. We simply add the individual demand curves horizontally. This means that the number of visits by the representative (average) individual user at any given price is multiplied by the total number of users of a particular site per year. This process is repeated for all alternative prices to obtain other points on the site demand curve.

Notice that information about price and quantity is all we can learn from the diagram. The demand curve will not tell us what kind of people visit the site or why. It tells us the price and quantity demanded at that price — no more, no less. A diagram abstracts from many details, some of which may be quite interesting, in order to focus on the two variables of primary interest — in this case, the price of wilderness trips and the number of trips demanded at each price. All of the diagrams used in this book share this basic feature. They cannot tell you the "whole story" any more than a map's latitude and longitude figures for a particular site can make you an authority on that site. Such information is useful to avoid getting lost when you are on unfamiliar ground.

COMPARING BENEFITS AND COSTS

One of the most important uses of demand curves is in the comparison of benefits and costs. Learning how to calculate benefit cost ratios will enable you to provide useful information for recreation economic decisions. A benefit cost ratio shows the dollar value of benefits for each one dollar of costs. Thus, at a benefit cost ratio of 1.0 the benefits are equal to costs, which represents the minimum justification for an expenditure. A benefit cost ratio of 2.0 indicates that two dollars worth of benefits are received for each one dollar of costs, and so forth. A prudent individual consumer or manager of recreation resources would choose those recreation activities and programs that yield the most benefits relative to costs and would continue to do so until benefits equal costs; that is, where the benefit cost ratio is 1.0. A benefit cost ratio of less than 1.0 indicates that benefits are less than costs and the proposed expenditure would reduce economic welfare.

In principle, benefit cost ratios for recreation activities of individual consumers have the same meaning as for public and private recreation programs. However, it is important to remember that the relevant definitions of benefits and costs differ. The benefit cost ratio for individual consumers is defined as the willingness to pay (total benefits) divided by the price or direct costs to consumers. For public recreation programs, the denominator in the benefit cost ratio is the sum of agency operating and opportunity costs and the numerator is the consumer surplus (net benefits) of individual users. The direct cost or price paid by consumers is subtracted from total benefit to obtain an estimate of the net benefit of the recreation opportunity provided by the agency.

It is also important to remember that the total benefit (willingness to pay) for a recreation activity is approximately equal to the area under the demand curve. If in Figure 5-1, five trips are taken to a recreation site with a direct cost or price of $20 per trip, total benefit would be measured as $200 or the area ●CA●. This includes the actual expenditure of $100 per year, area ●PA●, plus an approximation, PCA, of what consumers are willing to pay above price. This area PCA is referred to as consumer surplus, as it approximates net benefit to consumers, or the willingness of consumers to pay in excess of their actual payment. Economists define consumer surplus as the approximate area under the demand curve and above the price line. For the first trip, consumer surplus equals $40 or a willingness to pay of $60 less the price of $20. For the second trip, consumer surplus equals $30 or a willingness to pay of $50 less the price of $20. Applying the same procedure, the consumer surplus for the third trip is $20, for the fourth trip $10 and for the fifth trip zero. Summing $40, $30, $20, and $10 equals a total consumer surplus of $100 for the five trips per year. At this level of participation, the average consumer surplus per trip is $20 (= $100/5).

The benefit cost ratio of individual consumers is defined as willingness to pay (total benefits) divided by price or direct costs incurred by consumers. For example, the annual benefits of the recreation use of a site are maximized at five trips per year where the consumer benefit cost ratio equals 2.0 (= $200/ $100). The benefit cost ratio for the first trip is 3.0 (= $60/$20); the ratio continues to decline as additional trips are taken, until for the fifth trip the marginal benefit cost ratio falls to 1.0 (= $20/$20). A sixth trip would not be taken by a rational consumer because its marginal benefit cost ratio has declined to 0.5 (= $10/$20). Note that, although consumer benefit cost ratios depend on the level of consumer surplus, it does not enter the calculation directly.

The choice of an additional recreation trip is part of the process of choosing among the few alternative recreation activities available to an individual at any particular time. For example, the consumer's choice may be whether to attend an additional concert or to take an additional trip. Perhaps the individual has already been to two concerts this summer, so the estimate of benefits expected from the experience of a third concert may be somewhat less than the second which was less than the first. To maximize the total benefits of recreation, the consumer would choose whichever activity has the highest marginal benefit relative to price or direct cost at that particular point in time. In this way the consumer builds individual demand curves for each recreation activity day by day, incrementally. When possible, the individual should continue to participate in both activities until the benefit cost ratio of the last day of each equals 1.0.

The federal guidelines recommend consumer surplus as an acceptable economic measure of the benefits of recreation programs. For public recreation programs, the benefit cost ratio is defined as the consumer surplus (net benefits) of individual users divided by the sum of the agency's operating and opportunity costs. This means that if the average consumer surplus of recreation to our representative individual equals $20 per trip, the numerator in the benefit cost ratio is this amount times the total annual trips to the area by all recreation users. For 100,000 trips per year, benefits would be estimated as $2 million annually. If the opportunity costs of foregone development, the costs of environmental damages, and the agency's costs of managing the recreation site sum to $1.0 million annually, the benefit cost ratio to society would be 2.0 (= $2.0/$1.0 million).

For private recreation sites, the owner's benefit cost ratio would be defined as total revenue divided by the total costs incurred by the corporation. Note that the total and net benefits of consumers are not considered in benefit cost analysis by private companies. Their total costs include the opportunity costs of foregone development and the operating costs of the corporation. Private corporations may exclude external costs and benefits such as environmental effects shifted to other individuals, companies or agencies. For individual consumers, the price or direct cost of recreation also may exclude external costs such as environmental damages, opportunity cost of foregone development, and the agency's cost of managing recreation sites when user fees are lower than the sum of these costs.

CONSUMER SURPLUS ESTIMATES

Table 5-2 illustrates the average consumer surplus (net benefits) per recreation day for 23 recreation activities in the summer of 1982. The values should be considered approximations, as they are based on demand curves for the summer of 1972 and increased by the percent change in the consumer price index from 1972 to 1982. The dependent variable is the number of days per individual user during the summer season, and the price or direct cost variable is travel cost per day. Other direct costs such as entrance fees, lodging and related expenses are not included because answers to these questions are incomplete in the national household survey. As a result, the consumer surplus estimates from the recreation demand curves should be considered general indicators that may not be extremely precise.

The estimates range from an average of $6 to $22 per day and seem reasonable, for the most part. Consumer surplus varies depending upon whether participants are on vacation, a weekend trip, or a day outing. The net benefits of camping in wilderness areas exceed those of all other recreation activities except sailing, golfing, and attending outdoor sports events. Sailing on weekend trips provides the largest net benefits per day, followed by golfing while on vacations. Sightseeing by car on weekend trips is more beneficial than picnicking, as expected, since sightseeing is the single largest outdoor recreation activity in the United States and Europe.

Bicycling is more beneficial than riding motorcycles off the road, as expected, because the physical effort extended in bicycle riding is expected to provide more psychological stimulation, excitement, and benefits than motorcycle riding. Sailing is more beneficial than other water-based recreation activities, for the same reason, and is more beneficial on weekend trips than on day outings or vacations. Few persons would pull a sailboat on vacation because of reduced gas mileage and driving difficulty. Weekend sailing trips are more beneficial and provide the most frequent occasion for sailing. Water skiing on weekend trips and canoeing on day outings also have substantial benefits.

When the 23 recreation activities listed in Table 5-2 are classified according to the differences in psychological motivation of individual participants presented in Chapter 2, an interesting pattern begins to emerge. The consumer surplus from active outdoor recreation averages more than $14 per day compared to $12.75 for extractive, $12.50 for passive, $12 for appreciative, and $11.75 for socially interactive. These tentative estimates are consistent with recent psychological research findings that physically strenuous exercise heightens psychological stimulation, excitement, and benefits, whereas passive outdoor

Table 5-2. Approximations of Average Consumer Benefits per Recreation Day, United States, Summer 1982

Recreation Activity	Occasion	Recreation Days per Participant	Consumer Surplus per Day
Sightseeing by Car	Vacation	5.4	$11
	Weekend trip	3.9	13
	Day outing	3.5	n.a.
Picnicing	Vacation	4.7	11
	Weekend trip	4.6	9
	Day outing	4.1	n.a.
Camping in Developed Campgrounds	Vacation	8.0	14
	Weekend trip	6.5	15
	Day outing		n.a.
Camping in Remote Area, Wilderness	Vacation	5.3	17
	Weekend trip	7.2	13
	Day outing		n.a.
Walking for Pleasure	Vacation	6.4	10
	Weekend trip	4.4	12
	Day outing	7.7	11
Nature Walks	Vacation	7.5	10
	Weekend trip	4.7	13
	Day outing	4.3	n.a.
Bird Watching	Vacation	6.6	7
	Weekend trip	6.3	7
	Day outing	3.5	n.a.
Fishing	Vacation	4.6	10
	Weekend trip	5.1	9
	Day outing	6.8	n.a.
Water Skiing	Vacation	3.3	12
	Weekend trip	5.0	14
	Day outing	8.8	7
Canoeing	Vacation	5.2	8
	Weekend trip	2.6	12
	Day outing	2.5	14
Sailing	Vacation	5.0	9
	Weekend trip	3.4	22
	Day outing	10.1	6
Other (Power) Boating	Vacation	3.9	10
	Weekend trip	5.8	6
	Day outing	4.0	n.a.
Outdoor Pool Swimming	Vacation	5.2	10
	Weekend trip	5.3	10
	Day outing	8.7	n.a.
Natural Beach Swimming	Vacation	5.9	10
	Weekend trip	5.2	11
	Day outing	7.5	n.a.
Horseback Riding	Vacation	4.7	12
	Weekend trip	1.0	n.a.
	Day outing	7.2	n.a.
Bicycling	Vacation	5.6	10
	Weekend trip	3.2	9
	Day outing	15.3	n.a.
Riding Motorcycles Off the Road	Vacation	5.8	9
	Weekend trip	3.9	7
	Day outing	7.5	n.a.

Table 5-2. continued

Recreation Activity	Occasion	Recreation Days per Participant	Consumer Surplus per Day
Golf	Vacation	4.7	20
	Weekend trip	n.a.	n.a.
	Day outing	9.1	n.a.
Tennis	Vacation	3.9	12
	Weekend trip	3.3	n.a.
	Day outing	12.1	n.a.
Playing Other Outdoor	Vacation	6.2	11
Games or Sports	Weekend trip	4.8	11
	Day outing	9.0	n.a.
Going to Outdoor	Vacation	2.0	n.a.
Concerts, Plays	Weekend trip	2.1	14
	Day outing	2.5	n.a.
Going to Outdoor	Vacation	2.4	17
Sports Events	Weekend trip	3.0	7
	Day outing	5.6	15
Visiting Zoos, Fairs,	Vacation	2.6	13
Amusement Parks	Weekend trip	2.1	12
	Day outing	2.3	n.a.

n.a. = not available.
Source: Adapted from Adams, Lewis and Drake.

recreation requires relatively little physical effort and with less psychological stimulation, benefits are expected to be lower.

SUMMARY

In this chapter we distinguished between total and marginal benefits. Total benefit is the maximum amount of money consumers would be willing to pay rather than give up the recreation activity. It represents an economic measure of the total satisfaction of the experience. Marginal benefit is the change in total benefit resulting from a change in the number of trips. It is the willingness to pay for an additional trip. The concept of diminishing marginal benefit states that as consumers take more and more trips, other things being equal, the benefit of each additional trip will decrease. To make the most of it, consumers would continue to take additional trips until the benefit of the last trip equals the direct cost or price per trip.

Next we illustrated how individual demand curves are derived from this logic of consumer choice. A demand curve shows how the quantity demanded of some recreation activity during a specified period of time will change as the price of that activity changes, all other variables held constant. One of the most important features of demand curves is their slope. The steeper the slope, the larger the price change required to bring about any given change in quantity demanded. The correct procedure for calculating the slope of a linear demand curve depends on whether the starting point intercepts the horizontal axis as in the case of ordinary demand curves when quantity is the dependent variable, or the vertical axis as for inverse demand curves when price is the dependent variable. We showed that the aggregate demand curve for a recreation site is simply the horizontal summation of individual demand at the various prices.

Finally, we showed how to apply the information obtained from demand curves to recreation economic decisions. One of their most important uses is in the calculation of benefit cost ratios, which show the dollar value of benefits for each dollar of costs. The benefit cost ratio for individual consumers is defined as willingness to pay (total benefits) divided by price or direct costs to consumers. For public recreation and park programs, the denominator is the agency's operating and opportunity costs and the numerator is the consumer surplus (net benefits) of users. Consumer surplus is defined as the area below a demand curve and above the direct cost or price. It is recommended as an acceptable economic measure of the benefits of recreation and park programs.

The concepts of demand introduced in this chapter provide the basis for studies of the demand for recreation activities. We shall refer to this material in Chapter 6 when we look at empirical demand functions.

READINGS

Adams, Robert L., Robert C. Lewis, and Bruce H. Drake. "Outdoor Recreation in America: An Economic Analysis." Appendix A, Bureau of Outdoor Recreation, U.S. Department of the Interior, Washington, D.C. 1973.

Baumol, William J., and Alan S. Blinder. *Economics: Principles and Policy.* 2nd Edition. Harcourt Brace Jovanovich, New York. 1982.

Behr, Michael R., and Dennis L. Nelson. *Economics: A Personal Consumer Approach.* Reston Publishing Co., Reston, Va. 1975.

Cesario, Frank J. "Demand Curves for Public Facilities." *The Annals of Regional Science* 10(No. 1, 1976):1-13.

Clawson, Marion, and Jack L. Knetsch. *Economics of Outdoor Recreation.* Johns Hopkins University Press, Baltimore. 1966.

Davis, Robert K. "Research Accomplishments and Prospects in Wildlife Economics." *Transactions.* 49th North American Wildlife Conference. Wildlife Management Institute, Washington, D.C. 1984.

Gordon, Irene M., and Jack Knetsch. "Consumer's Surplus Measures and the Evaluation of Resources." *Land Economics* 55(Febr. 1979):1-10.

Loomis, John B., George L. Peterson, and Cindy F. Sorg. "A Field Guide to Wildlife Economic Analysis." *Transactions.* 49th North American Wildlife and Natural Resources Conference. Wildlife Management Institute, Washington, D.C. 1984. 315-24.

Marshall, Alfred. *Principles of Economics.* Macmillan Co., London. 1890.

Scitovsky, Tibor. *The Joyless Economy: An Inquiry into Human Satisfaction and Consumer Dissatisfaction.* Oxford University Press, London. 1976.

Wennegren, E. Boyd. "Valuing Non-Market Priced Recreation Resources." *Land Economics* 40(Aug. 1964):303-14.

Wennegren, E. Boyd, and Warren E. Johnston. "Economic Concepts Relevant to the Study of Outdoor Recreation." *Outdoor Recreation: Advances in Applications of Economics.* Jay M. Hughes and R. Duane Lloyd, (eds.). General Technical Report WO-2. Forest Service, U.S. Dept. of Agriculture. Washington, D.C. 1977. 3-10.

Chapter Six

Demand Function

> This chapter introduces the concept of a statistical demand function; shows how to derive a demand curve from a demand function; demonstrates how to estimate shifts in a demand curve with changes in each of the nonprice variables, and discusses a number of important statistical tests of the results.

Another important application of demand studies is to predict the effects of changes in circumstances. Because of these changes, demand curves often do not sit still; they shift around. If you look again at Figure 5-1, you can see clearly that any event that causes the demand curve to shift will also cause the consumer surplus estimate of benefits to change. Such events constitute the "other things" that we held constant in our definition of demand curves. We are now ready to consider how these nonprice forces affect demand.

Returning to our example of recreation trips, we might expect that in addition to price, demand will depend on such things as consumer income, quality of the resource, the price of trips to alternative areas, as well as other socioeconomnic variables. Should any of these circumstances change, the number of trips demanded will also change, even if their direct cost or price remains constant. Graphically, this means that the entire demand curve will shift.

Previously, we saw that a change in the direct cost or price of a recreation trip produced a "movement along" a fixed demand curve. By contrast, a change in any other variable that influences quantity demanded will produce a "shift" of the demand curve. If consumers want to buy more at any given price than they wanted previously, the demand curve shifts to the right (or outward). If they desire less at any given price, the demand curve shifts to the left (or inward).

In Chapter 5, we dealt with the relationship between two variables — price and quantity — as if the tradeoff could be decided separately from other determinants of demand. This is an over-simplification, for our choice of how many recreation trips to take depends on additional variables. The effect of direct cost or price is interdependent with other determinants of demand. When more than two variables are involved in the decision process, economists use multiple regression procedures to develop demand functions. Individual consumers rely upon a similar computation within the human brain, according to recent psychological studies reviewed by Scitovsky and Maslow. The quality of our judgment depends upon how accurate we are in estimating the simultaneous effects of each of our determinants of demand.

Learning how to calculate the effects of changes in the nonprice variables in the demand function will enable you to provide useful information for recreation economnic decisions. For example, it may be shown how much demand rises with increases in income, knowledge, or skill of the participant, direct cost or price of substitutes, quality of the recreation site, and population. At the same time, demand may fall with increases in travel time, age of participants, and family size. Some of these variables can be controlled by recreation resource managers — the location of recreation sites and the quality of services offered, for example — and it is important to know the effects of altering them if effective managerial decisions are to be made. The benefits of a change in the quality of a site can be estimated as the area between demand curves with and without the project.

Although other variables are outside the control of recreation managers, they can be influenced by effective promotional programs. For example, information can be directed to particular groups of consumers: the youth, generally, and young adults with small families. Training programs can be provided for those who lack the necessary skills to participate in particular recreation activities. In addition, estimates of the sensitivity of demand to long-run trends in consumer income, population, and family size can enhance a recreation manager's ability to predict future growth potential and to establish effective long-run programs. We will refer to the information in this chapter when we discuss projections of future demand in Chapter 11.

SHIFTS IN DEMAND AND CONTOUR MAPS

In Chapter 5, we presented a graphic illustration of a two-dimensional relationship between direct cost or price and the number of recreation trips demanded. Sometimes, when economnic problems involve more than two variables, a two-dimensional graphic illustration is not enough, which is unfortunate as paper is only two dimensional. When we study the decision-making process of consumers of recreation, for example, we may want to keep track simultaneously of three variables: how much income is received, how much direct cost or price is paid, and how much recreation is consumed. Baumol and Blinder suggest that we think of the shifts in demand resulting from the introduction of a third variable as analogous to the information presented on detailed maps of mountain areas in the United States.

The U.S. Geological Survey has developed a well-known device for collapsing three dimensions into two, namely a "contour map." Figure 6-1 is a contour map of Long's Peak, one of the highest mountains in

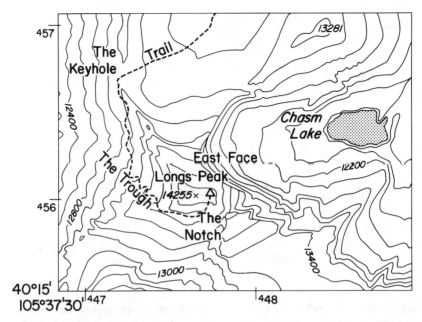

Figure 6-1. U.S. Geological Survey Map of Long's Peak in Rocky Mountain National Park, Colorado

the state of Colorado and a popular destination for hikers in Rocky Mountain National Park. On several of the irregularly shaped contour lines or "rings," we find a number indicating the height above sea level at that particular spot on the mountain. All points on any particular contour line represent geographic locations that are at the same height above sea level. Thus, unlike the more usual sort of map, which gives only latitudes and longitudes, this contour map exhibits three pieces of information about each point: latitude, longitude, and altitude.

Figure 6-2 looks more like the contour maps you will find in recreation economnics. It shows how some third variable, Y (think of it as consumer income, for example), affects the relationship between variable P (think of it as direct cost or price paid per trip) and variable Q (think of it as how much recreation is consumed). Just like the map of Long's Peak, any point on the diagram conveys three pieces of data. In this contour map, all points on a given contour line represent the different combinations of direct costs or price paid and recreation consumed by representative individuals receiving a given level of income. For example, all points on demand curve A with Y = \$25,000 represent the demand for trips at various levels of direct cost or price. Thus, five trips per year are demanded at a price of \$20, and four trips at a price of \$30, etc.

If incomes increase, consumers may decide that they can afford to buy more recreation and thus increase their number of trips even if

135

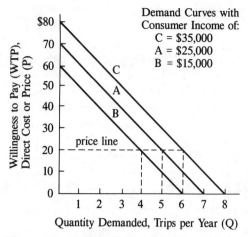

Figure 6-2. Income Shifts the Demand Curve for Recreation Trips by a Representative Individual

travel cost or price remains the same. That is, increases in income normally shift demand curves outward to the right, as depicted by demand curve C with Y = $35,000 per year. It is readily apparent that if direct cost or price remains unchanged at $20 per trip, and income increases to $35,000, demand would increase from five to six trips per year. Or, if the price increases from $20 to $30 per trip, individuals with higher incomes ($35,000) would demand more trips (five) than individuals with lower income ($25,000 income and four trips).

Everything works in reverse if consumer income falls. Figure 6-2 also depicts a leftward (inward) shift of the demand curve that results from a decline in consumer income. That is, decreases in income normally shift demand curves inward to the left, as depicted by demand curve B with Y = $15,000 per year. It is clear that if the direct cost or price remains unchanged at $20 per trip and income decreases to $15,000, demand would decrease from five to four trips per year. Or, if the price of recreation trips increased from $20 to $30 per trip, individuals with lower income ($15,000) would demand fewer trips (three) than individuals with higher income (four trips for $25,000 and five trips for $35,000). Economists define such effects as resulting from shifts in the demand curve.

While most of the information presented in this book will be based on the simpler two-variable diagrams, contour maps also find their applications in this chapter on the demand function.

STATISTICAL DEMAND FUNCTIONS

Demand functions for recreation sites can be estimated using the standard statistical procedures for multiple regression. This approach has been used because it fits an equation to a set of observed data providing statistical estimates of the effect of each variable, holding other variables in the demand function constant. There are limitations to the technique, but regressions frequently provides a reasonably good estimate of a demand function at a relatively small cost. The list of readings at the end of this chapter and Chapter 8 contain numerous examples of the application of regression analysis to estimate the demand functions for recreation sites.

Specify the Variables

The first step in regression analysis is to specify the variables that are expected to influence demand. In an ordinary demand function for a recreation site, the dependent variable to be explained is always the quantity demanded (Q), although it may be measured in different physical units: recreation trips, days, hours, and visitor days per person or per capita. The list of independent variables that influence demand always includes a proxy for direct cost or price (P) and generally includes such factors as consumer income (Y), travel distance or time (T), the price and availability of substitutes (S), other socioeconomnic variables such as age (G), quality or attractiveness of the site (A), population of the consuming group (K), individual taste or preference (D), expectations with respect to crowding or congestion (C), and other variables. If important determinants of demand are inadvertently omitted from the demand function, the equation will not predict demand accurately, as illustrated by Allen, Stevens and Barrett.

The individual demand function for a recreation site (x) is a statement of the relationship between the quantity demanded and all of these factors that affect this demand. Written in general form, the ordinary demand function may be expressed as:

$$Q_x = f(P_x, Y, T, S, G, A, K, D, C, \text{etc.}) \qquad (6\text{-}1)$$

The inverse demand function specifies willingness to pay (WTP) the direct cost or price of outdoor recreation as the dependent variable to be explained; and it includes the quantity demanded as one of the independent variables. Otherwise, the variables specified in the ordinary and inverse demand functions for a recreation site can remain approximately the same. Written in general form, the inverse demand function may be expressed as:

$$WTP_x = f(Q_x, Y, T, S, G, A, K, D, C, \text{etc.}) \qquad (6\text{-}2)$$

Collect the Data

The second step in regression analysis is to obtain information on the variables: measures of direct cost or price, travel distance or time, consumer income, and the like. The important determinants of demand must be measured correctly if the equation is to predict demand accurately, as discussed by McConnell with respect to the substitution variable. Obtaining accurate estimates of these variables is not always easy, especially if some key variables, such as consumer preferences and attitudes toward quality of the site (which are quite important in demand functions for many recreation sites) may have to be obtained by survey techniques as discussed in Chapters 7 and 8.

Structural Form

Once the variables have been chosen and the data gathered, the next step is to specify the form of the equation, or the manner in which the independent variables are assumed to interact to determine the level of demand. The generalized demand function expressed in Equation 6-1 is really just a listing of the variables that influence demand. For use in recreation economnic decisions, the demand function must be made explicit. That is, the nature of the relationship between the quantity demanded and each of the independent variables must be specified. To illustrate, let us assume that we are analyzing the demand for trips to a recreation area, and the demand function has been specified as a linear relationship:

$$Q = a + bP + cY + dT + eS + fG + gA + hK + iD + jC \qquad (6-3)$$

Linear demand functions, such as this, have great appeal in empirical work for two reasons. First, the regression coefficients (b through j), provide a direct measure of the marginal relationships in the demand function. That is, they indicate the change in quantity demanded caused by a one-unit change in each of the related variables. For example, if $b = -0.1$, demand will decline by 0.1 of a trip with each $1 increase in the direct cost or price per trip. Second, experience has shown that many demand relationships are in fact approximately linear over the range in which decisions are made. The demand curve derived from a demand function such as this, is a straight line as shown in Figure 6-2.

There are numerous other structural forms that can be used as the basis for regression analysis of demand for recreation. These include the nonlinear quadratic, semi- and double-logarithmic forms, all of which are consistent with the underlying theory of demand, in which the larger the price variable, the smaller the marginal effect of price on number of trips demanded. Figure 6-3 illustrates the most common

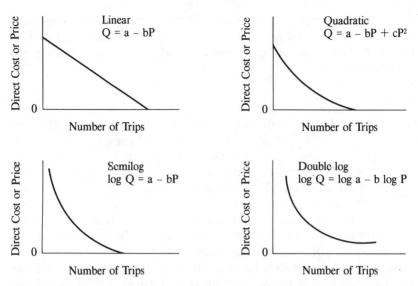

Figure 6-3. Functional Forms Used for Regression Analysis of Demand for Recreation

functional forms used in regressions of the demand for recreation.

The quadratic equation includes, in addition to the linear variables, squared terms for one or more of the independent variables:

$$Q = a + bP + bP^2 + cY + cY^2 \text{ etc.} \tag{6-4}$$

The quadratic form has been preferred for prediction because it provides the true arithmatic averages of the variables rather than the median values when using a semilog form. However, the quadratic curve may not reflect the true relationships among the variables in some cases.

The double-logarithmic equation takes the logarithmic form on both sides of the equation:

$$\log Q = \log a + b \log P + c \log Y \text{ etc.} \tag{6-5}$$

The double log form is most often used in regression analysis of the demand and supply of outdoor recreation (Kalter). Its unique advantage is the ease with which the regression coefficients can be compared. It is the only structural form in which the regression coefficients are the elasticities. In Chapter 9, elasticities are defined as the percent change in the dependent variable associated with a one percent change in each of the independent variables. Cheshire and Stabler suggest that the double log form is somewhat faulty because it fails to account for either the upper limit or lower limit of the demand curve, i.e., the double log demand curve approaches but does not touch either the price or quantity axis.

In specification of the semi-logarithmic form, either the dependent variable or one or more independent variables may be logged. In recreation demand studies, applications of the semilog form frequently convert number of trips per capita to a natural logarithm and leave all independent variables in their linear form. This semi-logarithmic equation is written:

$$\log Q = a + bP + cY \text{ etc.} \tag{6-6}$$

This has a unique advantage in estimating the average consumer surplus per trip; it is simply one divided by the regression coefficient for direct cost or price. Ziemer, Musser, and Hill compare the semilog form to the linear and quadratic, and conclude that the semilog is the preferred form for warmwater fishing demand in southeastern United States. They report household consumer surplus of $26 per trip or occasion for the semilog, compared to $29 for the linear and $20 for the quadratic. Cheshire and Stabler report, however, that the semilog form overpredicts visits to a recreation site in Great Britain at extreme distances (or prices) and underpredicts at middle distances. They suggest that a constant be added to the distance or price variable before the logarithmic transformation is performed. Smith and Kopp found that neither the semilog, linear, nor log-linear model provides a completely satisfactory representation of visits per capita to the Desolation Wilderness Area from 64 counties in California, Nevada, and Oregon. Hanemann discusses other forms that are available such as the 0-1 probit, logit, and Tobit models which are receiving more attention in recreation demand literature. They are used when the dependent variable is the probability of participating or paying. Smith and Munley compare the logit and probit models with the ordinary and generalized least squares methods of estimating the effect of the supply of recreation facilities on the proportion of the population who participate in beach swimming and fishing on vacation trips in the United States. They report no significant difference between these four methods in ability to identify key determinants of recreation behavior or to correctly predict actual behavior. They conclude that less attention should be given to the problems of the ordinary least squares approach and to apologies for failing to use a more sophisticated method. More attention, they suggest, should be given to the selection of realistic variables based on the underlying theory of consumer behavior.

The algebraic form of the demand function should always be chosen to reflect the true relationships among variables in the case being studied. That is, care should be taken to insure that the structural form chosen for an empirical demand function provides the best possible fit of the data. Scatter diagrams of the relationship between the dependent variable and each of the independent variables may suggest which form reflects the true relationships between them. In practice, several different forms may be tested, and the one that best fits the data should be selected as being most likely to reflect the true relationship.

Ordinary Least Squares Regression

Regression equations are typically fitted — that is, the coefficients a through j of Equation 6-3 are estimated — by the method of least squares. The method estimates the intercept and the slope of a line which minimizes the sum of the squares of the difference between each of the actual data points and the estimated line. The deviation of each data point from the fitted line, or error term, is squared because the deviations are both positive and negative. By squaring the deviations, we are summing a set of positive numbers. The line that minimizes this sum most accurately depicts the relationship between the dependent variable and each independent variable, holding constant the values of other independent variables in the demand function. The procedure is presented graphically in Figure 6-4. Here each point represents the direct cost or price and number of trips by an individual in our sample. It shows the vertical deviation of each data point from the fitted line.

A stepwise multiple regression is sometimes used to determine which independent variables included in a demand function are most highly correlated with the dependent variable, quantity or number of trips. Available computer programs select the independent variable that results in the greatest explanation of variation in the dependent variable. This process continues until all of the independent variables have been added to the regression in order of the amount of variation explained so long as they are significant at a predetermined level. Even if the regression coefficient for an important independent variation is not statistically significant, it may be included on the grounds that it is a better estimate than zero (which would be the value attributed to it if it were omitted from the equation).

When there is only one independent variable and one dependent variable, calculating the intercept and slope of a simple regression equation is not very difficult and is easily learned. However, it is sel-

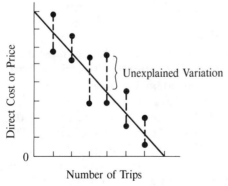

Figure 6-4. Vertical Deviation of Each Data Point from the Fitted Line

141

dom necessary to actually perform the calculations by hand because many calculators have routines to estimate simple regression equations and virtually all desk top computers can be loaded with regression programs. All you need to know is how to put the data into the calculator or computer. When many data points are involved, or when two or more independent variables are included in the demand function, then computers provide a much more practical means of implementing the least squares technique. Accordingly, we shall concentrate on setting up multiple regression problems for computer solution and interpreting the output, rather than dwelling on the mathematical process itself.

Regression Coefficients

Multiple regression techniques provide useful statistical estimates of demand functions for outdoor recreation. Learning how to interpret the many regression statistics which are typically provided by computer-based regressions can enable you to provide useful information for recreation economnic decisions. The important thing is how to interpret the values of the regression coefficients.

The most valuable information provided by statistical demand functions is the regression coefficient for each of the determinants of demand, b through j, in Equation 6-3. Each coefficient indicates the marginal relationship between the variable and the quantity demanded, holding constant the effects of all other variables included in the demand function. For example, assume that the computer printout of a statistical demand function for trips to a wilderness site provides us with the following information:

$$Q = 0.5 - 0.1P + 0.1Y - 0.4T + 0.054S - 0.088G$$
$$(-0.06) \quad (0.03) \quad (-0.16) \quad (0.04) \quad (-0.03)$$
$$+ 0.625A + 0.025K + 1.25D - 2.667C$$
$$(0.29) \quad (0.011) \quad (0.58) \quad (1.25) \tag{6-7}$$
$$N = 200 \quad R^2 = 0.82 \quad F = 126.4$$

Standard error of the estimate = 0.25

The values of the regression coefficients provide us with an estimate of the change in number of trips to the recreation site associated with a one-unit change in each of these independent variables, holding constant the effect of all other variables. For example, Equation 6-7 indicates that individual demand for trips to a recreation site falls by 0.1 of a trip with each $1 increase in average direct cost or price. The coefficient for income indicates that when we hold constant the effect of all other demand variables, a $1,000 increase in income will cause the quantity demanded to increase by 0.1 of a trip per year. Similarly, the regression coefficient for travel time indicates that demand will decrease by 0.4 of a trip with each 1-hour increase. The coefficient for the price of substitute sites shows that demand for trips to a recreation site increases by 0.054 of a trip with each $1 increase in the average direct cost or price of substitute sites. Similarly, demand decreases by 0.088 of a trip with a 1-year increase in age of participants. Demand increases by 0.625 of a trip with each 1-point (on a 5-point scale) increase in quality of the site. Demand increases by 0.025 of a trip with each 1,000 population increase. At 100 percent utilization of capacity of the recreation area, individual demand decreases by 2.667 trips per year.

The taste and preference variable is categorical (referred to as a dummy variable), meaning that 1 = active and 0 = passive. A regression coefficient of 1.250 indicates that individuals who prefer active outdoor recreation activities demand 1.25 more trips than those who prefer passive recreation activities. This illustrates the fact that multiple regression can be used to understand the effects of qualitative variables (that is, variables that do not have numerical values) as well as quantitative variables. The regression coefficient for taste and preference indicates that there are two regression lines, one for individuals with active preference and one for individuals with passive preference. These two regression lines have the same slope but different intercepts. It is assumed that the slope of the relationship between direct cost or price and number of trips is the same among individuals with active and passive preferences. This assumption may or may not be true. If a scatter diagram suggests this is not true, separate regression equations should be estimated for those with active and with passive preference. Or alternately, other techniques can be used such as the insertion of a categorical variable for slope or an interactive variable. To create a new interactive variable, multiply the categorical taste and preference variable by the direct cost or price variable. Then adding the regression coefficient for the interactive variable to the original coefficient for direct cost or price will show the effect of the preference for active outdoor recreation activities on the slope of the demand curve. Subtracting the coefficient for the interactive variable will show the effect of the preference for passive activities.

The constant or intercept term, a, from Equation 6-3 has a value of 0.5 in Equation 6-7. This can be interpreted as the expected number of trips demanded with zero values for all of the independent variables. This would represent the demand for trips to the site that is not explained by the independent variables included in the equation. Alternately, it may have no economnic meaning if the data points of observed values do not approach zero for each of the independent variables included. It is hazardous to generalize about the relationship beyond the range of observed values.

Tests of Regression Results

The coefficient of determination, identified by the symbol R^2, indicates that the regression explains 82 percent of the changes in the dependent variable. It is defined as the proportion (or percent) of the variation in the dependent variable that is explained by the full set of independent variables included in the equation. Accordingly, R^2 can have a value ranging from 0 indicating the equation explains none of the variation in the dependent variable, to 1.0, indicating that all of the variation has been explained by the independent variables. In demand functions for recreation, R^2 will seldom be equal to either 0 or 1.0. In empirical demand estimation, R^2 values of 0.50, indicating that 50 percent of the variation in demand is explained, are quite acceptable. For some zonal travel cost equations, R^2's as high as 0.90 are obtainable; for others, based on individual observations of consumer behavior, we must be satisfied with considerably less explanation of variation in demand. When the coefficient of determination is very low — say, in the range of 0.05 to 0.15 — it is an indication that the equation is inadequate for explaining the demand for recreation. The most general cause of this problem is the omission of some important variable or variables from the equation.

Two additional points should be made with respect to the coefficient of determination, R^2. First, most computer programs print out two coefficients of determination; one is adjusted for degrees of freedom (roughly the number of observations less one) and the other is not. The unadjusted R^2 is usually higher and the temptation should be avoided to rely on it rather than the adjusted R^2 which is the appropriate measure. Second, computer programs usually show the proportion of the variation in the dependent variable that is explained by each of the independent variables included in the equation, the sum of which equals the adjusted R^2. For example, direct cost or price may explain 20 percent of the variation, income 10 percent, etc. This valuable information is illustrated in Table 7-1 of the following chapter.

The numbers in parentheses below the regression coefficients in Equation 6-7 are the "standard errors of the coefficients" which provide a measure of the confidence we can place in the estimated regression coefficient for each independent variable. A frequent test is whether each regression coefficient is at least twice its standard error. This is equivalent, in most cases, to observing a "t-value" of approximately 2 for a regression coefficient, since the t-ratio is merely the regression coefficient divided by its standard error, adjusted for the degrees of freedom. If this is the case, we can reject at the 95 percent

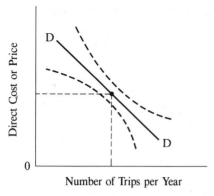

Figure 6-5. Use of the Standard Error of the Estimate to Define 95 Percent Confidence Intervals

significantly related to the dependent variable because zero is outside this range.

The "F-test" or "F-ratio" is used to estimate whether there is a significant relationship between the dependent variable and all the independent variables taken together. Tables are available in any statistical textbook, showing the values of F that are exceeded with certain probabilities, such as 0.05 and 0.01, for various degrees of freedom of the dependent and independent variables. The F-ratio of 126.4 indicates the overall equation is highly significant.

Another useful statistic printed out by the computer is the "standard error of the estimate," which tests the accuracy of the regression model as a whole. It is included as part of Equation 6-7. Assuming the errors are normally distributed about the regression equation, there is a 95 percent probability that future observations of the dependent variable will lie within the range of Q ± two standard errors of the estimate, or 0.5. There is a 99 percent chance that it will lie within Q ± three standard errors, or ± 0.75. It is clear, then, that greater predictive accuracy is associated with smaller standard errors of the estimate. This concept is illustrated in Figure 6-5. Here we see the least squares regression line, and the upper and lower 95 percent confidence limits. Ninety-five percent of all actual data observations will lie within two standard errors of the regression line. Thus, we are 95 percent confident that the actual number of trips will lie within the confidence interval.

APPLICATIONS: ESTIMATING DEMAND CURVES AND SHIFTS IN DEMAND

Table 6-1 shows how to estimate individual demand for trips to a recreation site using Equation 6-7. If we multiply each regression coef-

Table 6-1. Estimating Individual Demand for Trips to a Recreation Site Using a Demand Function

Independent Variables	Units	Estimated Mean Values of the Independent Variables (1)	Regression Coefficients for the Independent Variables (2)	(1 × 2) Estimated Total Demand, Trips per Year (3)
Direct Cost or Price (P)	Dollars per Trip	20.0	-0.100	-2.0
Consumer Income (Y)	Thousand Dollars	25.0	0.100	2.5
Travel Time (T)	Hours Round Trip	3.0	-0.400	-1.2
Price of Substitute Sites (S)	Dollars, Direct Cost/Trip	24.0	0.054	1.3
Age (G)	Years	25.0	-0.088	-2.2
Quality of the Site (A)	5-point Scale	4.0	0.625	2.5
County Population (K)	Thousand Persons	200.0	0.025	5.0
Taste or Preference (D)	1=Active 0=Passive	0.8	1.250	1.0
Daily Utilization/ Capacity Ratio (C)	1=Optimal	0.9	-2.667	-2.4
Constant (a)				0.5
Total Demand (Q)				5.0

ficient by the mean value of the variable and sum these products (plus the constant), we have the estimated individual demand for trips per year to the site. From Table 6-1 we see that the estimated individual demand for the site will be five trips per year, given the average values of the independent variables. It would be a relatively simple matter to aggregate individual demand to estimate the total demand for the site, multiplying five trips per individual user by the total number of users per year.

Deriving a Demand Curve from a Demand Function

A demand curve is defined as that part of the demand function showing the relation between the direct cost or price of a trip and number of trips demanded, holding constant the effects of all other independent variables. If we multiply each regression coefficient (except direct cost or price) by the mean value of the variable, sum these products, and add them to the value of the constant term, a, we have the number of trips intercept of the demand curve. To illustrate the process, consider the relationship depicted in Equation 6-7 and Table 6-1. Assuming that income, travel time, price of substitutes, etc., are all held constant at their average values, we can express the relationship between changes in direct cost or price and changes in number of trips demanded as:

$$Q = 0.1(P) + 0.1(25.0) - 0.4(3.0) + 0.054(24.0) - 0.088(25.0)$$
$$+ 0.625(4.0) + 0.025(200) + 1.25(0.8) - 2.667(0.9) + 0.5$$
$$= -0.1P + 2.5 - 1.2 + 1.3 - 2.2 + 2.5 + 5.0 + 1.0 - 2.4 + 0.5$$
$$= 7.0 - 0.1P \qquad (6\text{-}8)$$

This is presented graphically as demand curve A in Figure 6-2. The horizontal trips intercept is given by the demand equation which indicates that the representative individual demands seven trips when the direct cost or price is zero. The demand equation also indicates that the quantity demanded decreases by -0.1 of a trip with each $1 increase in price. Consequently, the vertical price intercept of this ordinary demand curve can be calculated as $7/0.1 = 70$. The graphic representation of this linear demand curve is obtained by drawing a straight line between the two intercept points, i.e., seven trips and $70.

As is typical of most demand curves, we see that a reduction in direct cost or price causes an increase in quantity demanded, and, conversely, an increase in price leads to a decrease in quantity demanded. For example, when the average price of visiting the recreation site is $20 per trip, we find that five trips per year are demanded by the representative consumer. If the average price of visiting the site increases to $40 per trip, demand would fall to three trips per year. This would be the effect on demand of doubling travel costs as a result of increased energy prices. Changes such as these are defined as movements along a demand curve.

Nonprice Variables Shift the Demand Curve

A change in demand — a shift from one demand curve to another — indicates a change in one or more of the other determinants of demand, the nonprice variables in the demand function. This means that at each price the number of trips demanded is either more or less than before, depending on whether the demand curve has shifted to the right or to the left. For example, consider again the effects of changes in consumer income presented in Figure 6-2. You will recall that demand curve A holds income at $25,000, which is the average value estimated for users of the recreation site. Individuals with $35,000 annual income, or $10,000 more than the average user, would demand one trip more, as shown by demand curve C. Those with $15,000 annual income would demand one less trip per year as shown by demand curve B. The result of income shifts in the demand curve is that, at a direct cost or price per trip of $20, those with $10,000 less income than the average demand four trips per year compared with six trips per year for those with $10,000 more income than the average. Alternately, if individual use of the recreation area is five trips per year, those with the lower income would be willing to pay $10 per trip compared with $30 per trip by those with the higher income.

The rule to calculate the shift in the demand curve caused by a change in any of the nonprice variables included in the demand function, is simply to multiply the regression coefficient for the nonprice variable by its change in value. For example, if average consumer income is assumed to change by $10,000 dollars per year and the regression coefficient for income is 0.1, then the income shift in demand is $10(0.1) = 1$ trip per year. This represents the effect of a change in income on demand for trips to the recreation site, holding constant the effect of all other variables included in the demand function. These so-called "partial" effects of each nonprice variable on demand can be estimated by applying the same rule.

UNDERSTANDING REGRESSION ANALYSIS

Mansfield, a noted authority on statistical applications in economics, cautions us to remember that regression analysis, like any tool, should not be applied blindly. It is important to check whether the assumptions underlying the approach are at least approximately correct, and to be aware of the problems that may arise in applications to recreation economic decisions. Although the assumptions underlying regression analysis are unlikely to be met completely, they are close enough in a sufficiently large number of cases that regression analysis is a powerful technique.

Potential Problems in Regression Analysis

There are a number of potential pitfalls that should be emphasized. First, it is by no means true that a high correlation between an independent and a dependent variable means that the former "causes" the other to vary. For example, if we regress travel cost on travel time to a recreation site, the correlation is bound to be high. But this does not mean that travel time causes travel cost to be as large or as small as it is. Two variables can be highly correlated without causation being implied. In this case, both travel cost and travel time are caused by a third variable, travel distance. Computer programs allow us to include dozens of independent variables with relative ease, which makes it extremely important that our reasons for including each of them be based on economic theory or on knowledge of the recreation economic behavior of consumers.

148

Second, even if an observed correlation is due to a causal relationship, the direction of causation may be the reverse of that implied by the regression. For example, suppose that we regress the profit of a recreation equipment manufacturer on its advertising expenditures. Profit is the dependent variable to be explained and advertising expenditure the independent variable. If the correlation between these two variables turns out to be high, does this imply that high advertising expenditures produce high profits? Obviously not. The line of causation could run the other way: High profits could enable management to spend more on advertising. Thus, in interpreting the results of regression studies, it is important to ask ourselves whether the line of causation assumed in the studies is correct.

Third, regressions are sometimes used to forecast values of the dependent variable lying beyond the range of sample data. For example, in Figure 6-2, a scatter diagram of observations of direct cost or price and trips may show that the data for the dependent variable, trips to a recreation site, range from 3 to 5. But the regression is used to forecast the dependent variable, number of trips per year, from 0 to 7 trips, both ends of which are outside this range. This procedure, known as "extrapolation," is dangerous because the available data provide no evidence that the true regression is linear beyond the range of the sample data. The true regression may be a curve rather than a straight line.

Fourth, you should be careful to avoid creating a spurious correlation by dividing or multiplying both the dependent variable and an independent variable by the same quantity. For example, we might want to determine whether a distance zone's trips to a particular recreation site is related to its trips to all recreation sites. To normalize for differences in population among distance zones, it may seem sensible to use trips per capita to a recreation site as one variable and trips per capita to all recreation sites as the other. This procedure may result in these ratios being highly correlated (because the denominator of the ratio is the same for both variables), even if there is little or no relationship between the number of trips to a particular recreation site and trips to all recreation sites.

Fifth, it is important to recognize that a regression is based on past data, and may not be a good predictor of future values due to changes in the relationships. For example, suppose that individual consumers experience considerable increases over time in the direct costs of outdoor recreation such as occurred during the 1970s. If so, the regression line relating direct costs or price to number of trips is likely to shift downward and to the left, and predictions based on historic data prior to the 1970s are likely to overestimate recreation trips. On the other hand, suppose that, while direct costs or price remain constant, the consumer experiences considerable productivity growth due to new technology (such as lighter weight tents, stoves, food, backpacks, sleeping bags, and clothing). If this happens, the regression line relating direct cost or price to number of trips is likely to shift upward and to the right. Predictions based on historic data are likely to underestimate future trips in a situation of this sort.

Assumptions of Regression Techniques

When we undertake a regression analysis of survey information, it is important to check whether the assumptions underlying the approach are at least approximately met. Essentially, this involves tests of misspecification of the model, heteroscedasticity, multicollinearity, and non-normal distribution of the sample values. Regression analysis makes the following assumptions.

First, the average value of the dependent variable, number of trips, is assumed to be a linear function of the independent variables. Or it can be transformed (using logs) to a linear function. This was discussed in the previous section.

Second, the distribution of sample observations around the predicted value of the dependent variable, number of trips, is the same for all values of an independent variable. This characteristic is called "homoscedasticity," and its violation, "heteroscedasticity," will be discussed below.

Third, the values of a variable are independent of one another and independent of the values of other variables. The individual values of a variable are generally independent of one another in the case of recreation trips by hundreds of individuals. However, the values of a single variable are not always independent of the values of other variables. Violation of this assumption is called "multicollinearity," discussed below.

Fourth, the values of the dependent variable, number of trips, are normally distributed (bell shaped) around their average values, although not all aspects of regression analysis require this assumption. It is worth noting that only the dependent variable, number of trips, is regarded as a random variable. The values of the independent variables are assumed to be fixed. For example, if regression analysis is used to estimate the number of trips when direct cost or price is $20, the true number of trips taken at this price can be predicted subject to confidence limits; but the direct cost or price ($20) is known precisely.

One important problem that can arise in multiple regression studies is "multicollinearity," which is defined as a situation in which two or more of the independent variables are very highly correlated. This violates the basic purpose of multiple regression to estimate the effect of one independent variable, holding the other independent variables constant. There is no way to tell how much effect each has separately when two independent variables move together in rigid, lockstep fashion. Their effects are hopelessly confounded. For example, researchers in outdoor recreation often encounter cases where the independent variables, travel cost and travel time, are so highly correlated that, although it is possible to estimate a regression coefficient for each variable, they cannot be estimated at all accurately.

To test whether multicollinearity is high, we can have the computer print out the simple correlations among pairs of independent variables and the multiple correlation coefficients of each of the independent variables on all of the others (Johnston). If some of these correlation coefficients are close to 1.0 (or -1.0), multi-collinearity is likely to be a problem. As a general rule, correlation coefficients of 0.8 (-0.8) or higher indicate the problem exists. Table 6-2 illustrates the computer printout of the simple correlation coefficients among pairs of independent variables. Note that several of the correlation coefficients exceed acceptable levels, indicating that corrective action should be taken.

In cases where multicollinearity exists, it is sometimes possible to alter the independent variables in such a way as to reduce the correlation between them to an acceptable level. For example, suppose that a researcher wants to estimate a regression equation where the number of trips per capita to a recreation site is the dependent variable, with travel cost and travel time as two of the independent variables. If travel cost is measured as round-trip miles times average travel costs of 20 cents per mile, and time cost is measured as round-trip miles divided by 45 miles per hour times $3 per hour (that is, without adjustment for individual variations), there may be a high correlation between the two independent variables. The values of both variables are extensions of distance traveled. But if travel cost per mile and time cost per hour are measured for each individual consumer, this correlation may be reduced considerably. Costs per mile vary among types of vehicle: standard, compact, and small cars, pickup truck, van, and mobile home. Time costs vary among individuals depending on the proportion of the trip that provides sightseeing benefits and the opportunity cost of work foregone, if any. There may be good reasons

Table 6-2. Computer Printout of Simple Correlation Coefficients Among Pairs of Independent Variables

Variables	Number of Trips	Direct Cost or Price	Income	Quality of Site	Substi- tution	Conges- tion
Direct Cost	-.2345					
Income	.2662	.2785				
Quality	.3913	.4548	.5839			
Substitution	.0811	.3062	.1122	.0589		
Congestion	-.1923	-.9218	.2863	.3436	.4658	
Preference	.2121	.8766	.2456	.3694	.6655	.9554

to measure transportation and travel time costs for individuals rather than to estimate them for large groups in distance zones. Another solution is to combine travel cost and time cost into a single price variable, since the disutility of overcoming distance is not travel cost alone but also the disutility of travel time involved in making the trip.

If multicollinearity cannot be avoided, there may be no alternative than to use only one of the variables in the regression analysis. Researchers in outdoor recreation often find that when income and education are both included as independent socio-economic variables in the multiple regression equation, they are highly inter-correlated. Education provides the skills that determine employment opportunities and income levels. Also, individuals born to higher income families can afford more education and often inherit wealth, which contributes to income levels.

In evaluating the results of a statistical demand function, it is useful to have the computer calculate the difference between each observation and what the model predicts this observation will be. These differences, often called "residuals," measure the extent to which the dependent variable cannot be explained by the independent variables included in the regression. A plot of the residuals can (1) test the assumption that the model is linear or some other functional form; (2) indicate whether the model excludes some important explanatory variables (specification error); and (3) detect the presence of departures from the assumptions underlying regression analysis. Heteroscedasticity may be present if the distribution of the sample observations around the predicted value of the dependent variable are not the same, regardless of the values of the independent variables. Plots similar to those in Figure 6-6 indicate these difficulties are present. confidence level the hypothesis that the independent variable is not

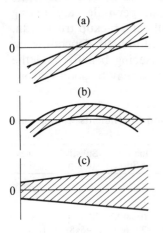

a. A positive or negative slope indicates the linear effect has not been properly accounted for, such as omission of a key variable.

b. A curved band indicates the need for a nonlinear term such as a quadratic or a logarithm.

c. A megaphone plot indicates the variance of the residuals is not constant. Corrective action is needed. Either use a weighted least squares regression technique or transform the dependent variable using a logarithm or a ratio.

Figure 6-6. Plots of Residuals

If you find evidence of heteroscedasticity, what can you do about it? One possible way to proceed is to perform a transformation of the data. In other words, rather than calculating the regression of trips on travel costs, you can calculate the regression of some function of the number of trips on travel cost. For example, Bowes and Loomis multiplied trips per capita by the square root of the population in each zone. They estimated the number of visits per capita as a function of travel costs from 28 distance zones to Westwater Canyon of the Colorado River on the Colorado-Utah border. They concluded that the demand for whitewater boating at this recreation site was linear, and the presence of heteroscedasticity was due to unequal population in distance zones, i.e., those with higher population had lower residuals.

Subsequently, Vaughan, Russell, and Hazilla re-evaluated the Westwater Canyon data and concluded that the appropriate functional form appeared more likely to be nonlinear, in which case heteroscedasticity essentially vanished. They also suggested an alternative approach to correcting for heteroscedasticity. The point is that if heteroscedasticity is detected, there are methods for handling the problem. However, you should first check for problems of variable omission and functional form of the model.

Similarly, if other complications exist, there are techniques for coping with these problems. This does not mean that the application of these techniques is cut-and-dried, or that it is possible to deal with any and all departures from the assumptions. But anyone who uses regression techniques should appreciate the importance of testing the assumptions on which these techniques are based, while realizing that when these tests indicate that the assumptions are violated, a variety of methods exist that are aimed at handling the problem. Descriptions of these methods can be found in more advanced books on statistical techniques.

SUMMARY

In this chapter we illustrated how to derive a demand curve from a demand function. A demand curve is defined as that part of the demand function showing the relation between the direct cost or price of a trip and the number of trips demanded, holding constant the effects of all nonprice variables in the function. If we multiply each regression coefficient (except direct cost or price) by the mean value of the variable, sum these products, and add them to the value of the constant term, we have obtained an estimate of the number of trips demanded when the direct cost or price is zero. The demand function also indicates the change in quantity demanded with a one-unit change in direct cost or price. Dividing the number of trips demanded when price is zero by the regression coefficient for direct cost or price provides an estimate of the price at which number of trips demanded is zero. The graphic representation of a linear demand curve is obtained by drawing a straight line between the two intercept points.

Statistical demand functions also provide estimates of the shifts in demand curves with changes in each of the nonprice determinants of demand, holding other things constant. Returning to our example of recreation trips, we might expect that in addition to the direct cost or price of trips, the number of trips demanded depends on such things as consumer income, quality of the resource, the price of trips to alternative areas, as well as socioeconomic variables. Should any of these circumstances change, the number of trips demanded will also change, even if the direct cost or price of trips remains constant. Graphically, this means that the entire demand curve will shift. The rule to calculate the shift in the demand curve caused by a change in any of the nonprice variables included in the demand function, is simply to multiply the regression coefficient for the nonprice variable by its change in value.

Demand functions for recreation sites can be estimated using standard statistical procedures for multiple regression. There are limitations to the technique, but regressions frequently provide a reasonably good estimate of a demand function at a relatively small cost. The necessary steps in regression analysis are to: choose the variables that are expected to influence demand; obtain information on the variables; and specify the form of the equation (linear or nonlinear). Multiple regression is a method of relating one variable (such as number of trips) to two or more other variables (such as direct cost or price, income, price of substitutes, quality of the site, etc.) which explain the number of trips. The least squares technique produces the smallest error between the actual values and those estimated by the regression. The computer printout provides regression coefficients for all of the independent variables. The dependent variable on the left hand side of the equation equals the sum of all of the explanatory independent variables on the right hand side, when the mean of each is multiplied by its regression coefficient.

We discussed several statistical tests of regression results provided by computer print outs. The coefficient of determination, R^2, is the best known indicator of success. It measures the percent of the change in the dependent variable that is explained by the full set of independent variables. The standard errors of the coefficients provide a measure of the confidence we can place in each independent variable. Each regression coefficient for the independent variables should be at least twice its standard error. This is equivalent, in most cases, to observing a t-value of approximately 2. The F-Test is used to estimate whether there is a significant relationship between the dependent variable and all of the independent variables taken together. Finally, the standard error of the estimate measures how close the fitted values are to the actual values.

Next, we discussed potential problems in regression analysis. High correlation between two variables may not mean causation if both are actually caused by a third variable. The direction of causation may be the reverse of that implied by the regression. Predictions beyond the range of sample data may not reflect the true relationship. A spurious correlation may occur when both the dependent variable and an independent variable are divided or multiplied by the same quantity. Regressions are based on past data, and may not be a good predictor of future values due to changes in the relationships.

We concluded the chapter with a discussion of the assumptions underlying regression analysis. When we carry out a regression of survey information, it is important to apply tests of mis-specification of the model, heteroscedasticity, multicollinearity, and non-normal distribution of sample values. The relationships are mis-specified if a linear form is used when the actual function is nonlinear. Heteroscedasticity is present when the distribution of sample observations around the predicted value of the dependent variable is not the same for all values of an independent variable. Multicollinearity occurs when two or more of the independent variables are very highly correlated with each other. If these and other complications exist, there are techniques for coping with them. Although the assumptions underlying regression analysis are unlikely to be met completely, they are close enough in a sufficiently large number of cases that regression analysis of demand functions is a powerful research technique.

READINGS

Allen, P. Geoffrey, Thomas H. Stevens, and Scott A. Barrett. "The Effects of Variable Omission in the Travel Cost Technique." *Land Economics* 57(May 1981):173-80.

Brown, William G., and Farid Nawas. "Impact of Aggregation on the Estimation of Outdoor Recreation Demand Functions." *American Journal of Agricultural Economics* 55(May 1973):246-49.

Burt, Oscar R., and Durwin Brewer. "Estimation of Net Social Benefits from Outdoor Recreation." *Econometrica* 39(Sept. 1971):813-27.

Cesario, Frank J., and Jack L. Knetsch. "A Recreation Site Demand and Benefit Estimation Model." *Regional Studies* 10(March 1976):97-104.

Cheshire, P. C., and M. J. Stabler. "Joint Consumption Benefits in Recreational Site Surplus: An Empirical Estimate." *Regional Studies* 10(No. 3, 1976):343-51.

Cicchetti, Charles J., Anthony C. Fisher, and V. Kerry Smith. "An Econometric Evaluation of a Generalized Consumer Surplus Measure: the Mineral King Controversy." *Econometrica* 44(No. 6, 1976):1259-76.

Gillespie, G. A., and Durwood Brewer. "Effects of Nonprice Variables Upon Participation in Water Oriented Outdoor Recreation." *American Journal of Agricultural Economics* 50(Febr. 1968):82-90.

Gum, Russell L., and William E. Martin. "Problems and Solution in Estimating Demand for and Value of Rural Outdoor Recreation." *American Journal of Agricultural Economics* 57(Nov. 1975):558-66.

Hanemann, W. Michael. "Discrete/Continuous Models of Consumer Demand." *Econometrica* 52(May 1984):541-61.

Hanemann, W. Michael. "Welfare Evaluations in Contingent Valuation Experiments with Discrete Responses." *American Journal of Agricultural Economics* 66(Aug. 1984):332-41.

Johnston, Jack. *Econometric Methods.* McGraw-Hill, New York. 1972.

Kalter, Robert J., and L. E. Gosse. "Recreation Demand Functions and the Identification Problem." *Journal of Leisure Research* 2(Winter 1970):43-53.

Mansfield, Edwin. *Statistics for Business and Economics.* W. W. Norton, New York. 1980.

McLagan, Donald L. "A Non-econometrician's Guide to Econometrics." *Business Economics* 8(May 1973):38-45.

Miller, Ronald J. "The Demand for Colorado Deer Hunting Experience." Ph.D. Dissertation, Colorado State University, Fort Collins. 1980.

Pappas, James L., and Eugene F. Brigham. *Fundamentals of Managerial Economics.* The Dryden Press, New York. 1981.

Smith, V. Kerry. "The Estimation and Use of Models of the Demand for Outdoor Recreation." *Assessing Demand for Outdoor Recreation.* National Academy of Science, Washington, D.C. 1975. 89-123.

Stynes, Daniel J., George L. Peterson, and Donald H. Rosenthal. "Log Transformation Bias in Estimating Travel Cost Models." *Land Economics* 62(Febr. 1986):94-103.

Vickerman, R. W. *The Economics of Leisure and Recreation.* MacMillan Press, London. 1975.

Walsh, Richard G., and Gordon J. Davitt. "A Demand Function for Length of Stay on Ski Trips to Aspen." *Journal of Travel Research* 22(Spring 1983):23-29.

Wetzstein, Michael E., and John G. McNeeley, Jr. "Specification Errors and Inference in Recreation Demand Models." *American Journal of Agricultural Economics* 62(Nov. 1980):798-800.

Ziemer, Rod F., Wesley N. Musser, and R. Carter Hill. "Recreation Demand Equations: Functional Form and Consumer Surplus." *American Journal of Agricultural Economics* 62(Febr. 1980):136-41.

Chapter Seven
Determinants of Demand

This chapter discusses the present state of knowledge about the determinants of demand: socioeconomic characteristics of users; attractiveness of recreation sites; availability of substitutes; travel time; congestion; and preferences. It also illustrates the effect of these nonprice variables in shifting the demand curve for recreation.

Increased attention has focused in recent years on improving our understanding of the determinants of demand for recreation. This is important because a change in any of the nonprice variables that influence quantity demanded will produce a shift of the demand curve. A positive relationship indicates that consumers want to buy more at any given price than they wanted previously and the demand curve shifts to the right (or outward). A negative relationship indicates that consumers desire less at any given price, and the demand curve shifts to the left (or inward). Learning how to accurately measure nonprice variables will enable you to provide useful information for recreation economic decisions.

Clawson and Knetsch presented the initial demand functions for recreation, using a single explanatory variable, the average direct cost of auto operation times distance, as a proxy for price. Information was not available on possible nonprice variables, and the use of travel cost as a single independent variable was sufficient to illustrate the method. By 1970, major advances had occurred with the introduction of several nonprice determinants, such as: (1) socioeconomic characteristics of the user population — notably, income, education, age, sex, and ethnicity; (2) attractiveness or quality of recreation sites; and (3) the availability of substitutes — alternative recreation opportunities in the market area. More recently, additional determinants of demand have been introduced, including: (4) travel time; (5) congestion or crowding at recreation sites; and (6) tastes and preferences. Also, notable improvements have occurred in measuring the nonprice variables included in recreation demand functions.

The people involved — both recreation managers and researchers — are interested in what can be learned from recent experience to help formulate realistic measures of the determinants of demand in the future. The purpose of this chapter is to describe the nature of several innovations in the "specification of variables" included in statistical demand functions, and to assess their effects on empirical estimates of demand for recreation. The important nonprice determinants of demand must be correctly measured and included in demand functions if they are to explain demand and estimate benefits accurately. Allan, Stevens, and Barrett have shown that differences in the variables included in demand functions are an important cause of divergent estimates of demand and benefits.

In a field of study where the general methodology is in a highly evolutionary state, a number of proposed innovations are embryonic and not so well developed or persuasive that there is general agreement on their application. Still others are so self-evident, reasonable, and realistic that they are immediately accepted.

SOCIOECONOMIC VARIABLES

Individuals vary in their response to recreation opportunities. In an attempt to account for these differences, demand functions usually have included one or more socioeconomic (demographic) measures as independent variables. Some examples are age, education, income, ethnicity, sex, vacation time, and size of city. Cesario and Knetsch used an index of a weighted combination of socioeconomic variables that may be useful in future efforts to account for individual differences in demand. It is not entirely clear what constitutes an appropriate index of the socioeconomic differences between individuals. Often, several variables are tried, and only those that are found to be significantly related to demand are retained in the demand function for a specific recreation site. While national household surveys of the entire population show that a number of socioeconomic variables affect demand for recreation, our surveys of participants at recreation sites do not always find a statistically significant relationship. For there is often insufficient variation in the characteristics of small samples of on-site users.

Table 7-1 suggests that several important socioeconomic variables are related to the demand for recreation. The table shows the results of a national survey of nearly 3,000 adults in the United States by the Heritage Conservation and Recreation Service in 1977. Individual participation in recreation was the dependent variable in a multiple correlation analysis that included 11 socioeconomic factors as independent variables. The correlation coefficients shown indicate the strength of the relationship between participation and each of the factors when all other determinants of participation included in the equation are held at their mean values.

Table 7-1. Socioeconomic Determinants of Adult Participation in Outdoor Recreation, United States

Socioeconomic Variables	Strength of the Relationship[a]	
	All Adults	Working Adults
Age	-.51***	-.43***
Education	.09***	.09***
Income	.08***	.06*
Race	.07*	.10**
Sex	.08***	.09***
Size of city	-.06***	-.07*
Type of dwelling	-.04	-.02
Hours worked	.02	.01
Vacation time	NC	.08***
Have yard	.07***	.06**
Have park nearby	.09***	.08***
Coefficient of determination, R^2	.63	.51
Sample size	2,970	1,709

[a]Significance: * = .05; ** = .01; *** = .001.
NC = Not calculated because vacation time data were not available for those not employed in a paid job.
Source: Heritage, Conservation, and Recreation Service.

Age

The most important socioeconomic variable appears to be age. It accounts for 51 percent of the variation in participation by all adults (over age 18) and 43 percent by working adults. The sign of the coefficient is negative indicating that the relationship is inverse; an increase in age results in a decrease in participation. Each of the other variables, such as education, income, race, sex, size of city, and vacation time, accounts for less than 10 percent of the variation in participation. The coefficients for each of the socioeconomic variables overstate somewhat the true correlation. Because they are unadjusted for degrees of freedom, their sum would exceed the coefficient of determination, R2, for the combined socioeconomic variables included in the multiple correlation. The 11 socioeconomic variables explain 63 percent of the variation in participation by all adults and 51 percent by working adults.

Age is negatively related to participation in most recreation activities. Table 7-2 shows that young people are more apt to participate in recreation activities than older people. In particular, more youth participate in physically strenuous activities, such as skiing, hiking, backpacking, horseback riding, sailing, waterskiing, driving off-road vehicles, playing tennis, and other outdoor games. Although these activities are clearly youth-oriented, participation in many others is only moderately related to age. Some recreation activities remain important in the lives of many people until late middle age, in particular: fishing, picnicking, sightseeing, driving for pleasure, nature walks,

Table 7-2. Effect of Age on Participation in Outdoor Recreation, United States

Activity	Age Group							Strength of Relationship[a]	
	12-17	18-24	25-34	35-44	45-54	55-64	65+	Simple Correlation	Multiple Correlation
Camping in Developed Area	40%	45%	38%	34%	23%	21	8%	-.23	-.26
Camping in Primitive Area	31	36	27	24	13	7	5	-.23	-.24
Canoeing, Kayaking, River Running	29	27	19	14	14	3	2	-.21	-.20
Sailing	19	17	13	8	8	4	2	-.17	-.10
Waterskiing	23	31	21	17	9	3		-.25	-.28
Fishing	72	60	57	56	52	46	30	-.20	-.20
Other Boating	48	39	41	37	31	19	17	-.19	-.16
Outdoor Pool Swimming and Sunbathing	90	82	78	73	51	41	19	-.48	-.39
Other Outdoor Swimming and Sunbathing	64	61	61	51	37	24	11	-.37	-.34
Nature Walks, Birdwatch, Photography	54	47	60	62	48	43	33	-.11	NC
Hiking or Backpacking	41	40	38	32	19	14	7	-.24	-.25
Other Walking or Jogging	87	79	78	62	57	53	53	-.27	-.22
Bicycling	89	67	59	46	32	16	10	-.49	-.39
Horseback Riding	30	23	20	15	9	2	1	-.26	-.21
Driving Off-road Vehicles	43	46	31	28	15	11	2	-.32	-.31
Hunting	24	25	18	27	17	15	8	-.11	-.10
Picnicking	77	74	84	81	75	64	47	-.21	-.18
Golf	21	18	17	15	14	14	8	-.05	-.02
Tennis Outdoors	65	53	43	34	18	7	2	-.43	-.36
Cross-country Skiing	5	4	3	3	1	1		-.09	NC
Downhill Skiing	13	14	8	7	4	1		-.19	-.17
Ice-skating Outdoors	33	22	22	18	10	4	1	-.25	-.18
Sledding	46	31	28	22	10	4	2	-.33	-.29
Snowmobiling	14	15	10	6	5	4	1	-.15	-.15
Playing Other Sports or Games	87	73	69	62	45	30	15	-.47	-.37
Sightseeing	61	63	70	73	64	59	44	-.10	-.07
Driving for Pleasure	52	83	80	79	64	66	51	-.13	-.18
Zoos, Aquariums, Carnivals, etc.	86	87	87	80	67	53	38	-.37	-.31
Attending Outdoor Sports Events	82	74	66	67	59	49	30	-.31	-.19
Attending Outdoor Concerts, Plays	57	62	45	36	31	21	18	-.28	NC

[a]All variables are significant at the .001 level.
NC = Value not calculated.
Source: Heritage, Conservation, and Recreation Service.

160

bird-watching, photography, visiting zoos and amusement parks, and attending outdoor sports events.

The cross-sectional data and simple correlation coefficients presented in Table 7-2 show the relationship between participation in recreation activities and age, where no other variables are held constant. This represents the total effect of individuals in a particular age group; it includes a number of related conditions, such as education, income, patterns of preference, and position in society. Earlier (in Chapter 6), we looked at the effect of age with all other socioeconomic variables held constant. The last column in Table 7-2 shows the strength of the relationship between age and participation when all other socioeconomic determinants of participating are held at their mean values.

Education

Education is positively related to participation in many recreation activities. Table 7-3 shows that more educated people generally participate in physically strenuous activities such as canoeing, sailing, swimming, hiking, backpacking, jogging, skiing, and playing golf and tennis. Although physically strenuous activities are clearly favored by those with higher education, participation in less active pursuits is only moderately related to education — for example, camping in developed areas, motor boating, driving for pleasure, and visiting zoos and amusement parks. In some cases, demand falls when education rises, all other things equal. As people gain knowledge of alternative recreation activities, they generally reduce participation in lesser preferred activities, notably: fishing, hunting, snowmobiling, and sledding.

Years of experience participating in a recreation activity or at a site can be used as a proxy for knowledge and skill. In a study of white water boating, Munley and Smith conclude that past experience tends to increase a participant's skill, which has been called "learning by doing." They reported a shift in the individual demand for recreation services as a result of the acquired skill. In other surveys, individual participants (skiers, for example) report their own ability according to categories such as beginner, intermediate, or advanced. McKean and Allen observe that subsidizing the learning of initial leisure skills may increase the economic welfare of society, for recreation education programs that enlarge society's stock of human capital may increase benefits from participation in preferred recreation activities.

Income

Normally, the more income consumers have to spend, the more they are willing and able to buy. For most recreation activities, this is

Table 7-3. Effect of Education on Participation in Outdoor Recreation, United States

Activity	Years of Education						Strength of Relationship[a]	
	8 and Below	9-11	12	13-15	16	17 and Over	Simple Correlation	Multiple Correlation
Camping in Developed Area	9%	23%	33%	37%	30%	33%	.08	.00
Camping in Primitive Area	5	14	22	27	22	25	.06	.02
Canoeing, Kayaking, River Running	3	7	15	20	21	22	.08	.09***
Sailing	2	3	8	15	24	24	.13	.13***
Waterskiing	2	6	16	23	19	21	.13	.02
Fishing	47	49	53	58	47	43	-.04	-.09***
Other Boating	15	24	32	43	40	40	.10	.01
Outdoor Pool Swimming and Sunbathing	25	43	63	74	74	77	.18	.09***
Other Outdoor Swimming and Sunbathing	16	31	45	58	55	57	.16	.10***
Nature Walks, Birdwatch, Photography	29	38	51	59	60	70	.16	.02
Hiking or Backpacking	8	14	27	36	36	45	.14	.15***
Other Walking or Jogging	48	61	65	75	76	77	.11	.12***
Bicycling	15	27	42	55	52	48	.06	.08**
Horseback Riding	4	8	14	18	15	19	.04	.03
Driving Off-road Vehicles	9	24	27	28	20	17	.02	-.06**
Hunting	22	15	20	20	13	11	-.06	-.14***
Picnicking	52	69	74	78	77	82	.14	.08***
Golf	3	8	14	23	25	28	.16	.08***
Tennis Outdoors	6	16	28	40	45	48	.16	.15***
Cross-country Skiing	(b)	2	2	3	3	8	.08	NC
Downhill Skiing	2	1	5	10	11	14	.09	.09***
Ice-skating Outdoors	3	7	16	18	17	18	.03	.05*
Sledding	7	6	21	22	19	19	-.01	-.01
Snowmobiling	3	6	9	9	6	5	.00	-.05*
Other Sports or Games	24	47	54	63	57	60	.08	.09****
Sightseeing	37	49	64	72	81	84	.22	.15***
Driving for Pleasure	46	69	76	77	75	76	.20	.04
Zoos, Carnivals, etc.	39	63	76	77	78	79	.15	.03
Attending Outdoor Sports Events	27	49	63	67	66	70	.13	.13***
Attending Outdoor Concerts, Plays	17	31	40	47	49	59	.15	NC

a* = .05; ** = .01; *** = .001; NC = value not calculated.
b Less than 0.5 percent.
Source: Heritage, Conservation, and Recreation Service.

162

true; but there appear to be exceptions. Table 7-4 shows that the correlation between income and participation is usually positive although not statistically significant in nearly two-thirds of the cases. The correlation is positive and statistically significant for sailing, motor boating, canoeing and white water boating, swimming in outdoor pools and beaches, sightseeing, playing tennis, bicycling, and attending outdoor sports events. The correlation also is positive but not statistically significant for walking, jogging, camping in developed areas, fishing, hunting, picnicking, downhill skiing, sledding, and waterskiing. Income is not related to participation in horseback riding, cross-country skiing, and snowmobiling.

An "inferior good" is defined as one whose demand falls when consumer income rises, all other things remaining equal. The reason is clear enough. As people become wealthier they generally reduce their purchases of inferior goods because a more desirable alternative is available. Examples include second-hand clothing, bus tickets, and retread auto tires. For most recreation activities, if incomes rise and prices do not change, there will be an increase in participation. But for a few inferior activities there will be a decrease. For example, the correlation between income and participation is negative and statistically significant for hiking and backpacking. It is also negative, although not statistically significant, for camping in primitive areas, driving off-road vehicles, and playing outdoor sports and games.

Other Socioeconomic Variables

Generally, whites are more likely to participate in recreation activities than blacks or other ethnic groups. Table 7-5 shows that more whites participate in canoeing, white water boating, camping, golfing, sledding, and ice skating. It appears that more whites participate in other activities also, although the strength of the relationship is not statistically significant. More nonwhites appear to participate in picnicking, playing outdoor sports and games, visiting zoos, carnivals, and amusement parks, driving for pleasure, and driving off-road vehicles, although the relationship is not statistically significant.

Table 7-6 shows that men are more likely than women to participate in most recreation activities. In particular, more men participate in consumptive activities — hunting and fishing — and in physically strenuous activities like hiking, backpacking, camping in primitive areas, outdoor sports and games, driving off-road vehicles, golfing, motor boating, and waterskiing. There is little or no significant difference between the sexes with respect to participation in beach swimming and sunbathing, snow sledding, attending outdoor sports events, horseback riding, and bicycling. Significantly more women than men

Table 7-4. Effect of Income on Participation in Outdoor Recreation, United States

Activity	Annual Household Income						Strength of Relationship[a]	
	Under $6,000	$6,001-$10,000	$10,001-$15,000	$15,001-$25,000	$25,001-$50,000	Over $50,000	Simple Correlation	Multiple Correlation
Camping in Developed Area	17%	30%	36%	36%	32%	31%	.11	.02
Camping in Primitive Area	12	25	21	25	19	26	.05	-.03
Canoeing, Kayaking, River Running	7	16	14	19	26	30	.12	.04*
Sailing	4	8	8	15	26	27	.19	.10***
Waterskiing	7	11	18	20	27	30	.17	.02
Fishing	40	55	61	58	52	49	.07	.02
Other Boating	18	30	35	42	46	51	.18	.09***
Outdoor Pool Swimming and Sunbathing	37	60	68	73	80	78	.29	.12***
Other Outdoor Swimming and Sunbathing	26	44	52	53	54	52	.19	.05**
Nature Walks, Birdwatch, Photography	39	50	50	57	55	51	.11	NC
Hiking or Backpacking	16	26	32	33	33	36	.12	-.04*
Other Walking or Jogging	59	68	70	70	76	70	.09	.01
Bicycling	27	43	52	55	53	58	.18	.05**
Horseback Riding	7	15	17	16	18	17	.08	.00
Driving Off-road Vehicles	16	28	29	28	26	25	.06	-.02
Hunting	14	19	20	22	18	23	.04	.03
Picnicking	55	74	79	80	74	67	.14	.02
Golf	6	11	13	22	34	26	.23	.18***
Tennis Outdoors	17	29	35	39	41	41	.19	.08***
Cross-country Skiing	1	2	3	2	4	6	.05	.00
Downhill Skiing	2	5	5	10	13	19	.13	.02
Ice-skating Outdoors	6	12	19	21	25	19	.17	.04*
Sledding	9	16	25	26	29	20	.16	.04
Snowmobiling	4	7	9	9	11	13	.08	.00
Other Sports or Games	36	57	62	62	58	61	.15	-.02
Sightseeing	42	59	66	74	73	81	.21	.15***
Driving for Pleasure	54	69	78	76	75	75	.15	.11***
Zoos, Carnivals, etc.	52	71	80	80	82	79	.21	.04
Attending Outdoor Sports Events	39	59	65	70	74	76	.21	.07***
Attending Outdoor Concerts, Plays	30	45	42	42	44	58	.08	NC

[a]* = .05; ** = .01; *** = .001; NC = value not calculated.
Source: Heritage, Conservation, and Recreation Service.

164

Table 7-5. Effect of Race on Participation in Outdoor Recreation, United States

	Ethnicity (Race)			Strength of Relationship[a]	
Activity	White	Black	Other	Simple Correlation	Multiple Correlation
Camping in Developed Area	33%	11%	29%	.13	.07*
Camping in Primitive Area	23	8	20	.10	.10**
Canoeing, Kayaking, River Running	17	11	8	.06	.11**
Sailing	12	8	8	.04	.02
Waterskiing	18	3	14	.12	.04
Fishing	54	48	53	.04	.01
Other Boating	36	18	30	.11	.04
Outdoor Pool Swimming and Sunbathing	65	44	65	.13	.03
Other Outdoor Swimming and Sunbathing	48	27	48	.13	.05
Nature Walks, Birdwatch, Photography	51	45	39	.05	NC
Hiking or Backpacking	30	16	27	.08	.05
Other Walking or Jogging	68	69	70	-.02	.01
Bicycling	46	51	56	-.06	.01
Horseback Riding	15	13	19	.01	.04
Driving Off-road Vehicles	26	25	27	.00	-.03
Hunting	20	8	18	.09	.04
Picnicking	73	71	78	.01	-.03
Golf	17	6	10	.10	.06*
Tennis Outdoors	33	31	36	.01	.04
Cross-country Skiing	3	2	4	.01	NC
Downhill Skiing	8	1	6	.08	.04
Ice-skating Outdoors	18	6	13	.09	.06*
Sledding	22	7	18	.11	.07*
Snowmobiling	9	3	3	.09	.05
Other Sports or Games	55	60	64	-.05	-.01
Sightseeing	55	43	62	.10	.00
Driving for Pleasure	70	64	66	.05	-.01
Zoos, Carnivals, etc.	73	70	84	-.02	-.03
Attending Outdoor Sports Events	61	60	72	-.02	.00
Attending Outdoor Concerts, Plays	40	49	55	-.09	NC

[a]* = .05; ** = .01; *** = .001; NC = value not calculated.
Source: Heritage, Conservation, and Recreation Service.

engage in the less strenuous activities of picnicking, walking or jogging, visiting zoos and amusement parks, and sightseeing.

Several other socioeconomic variables have been used in demand functions for recreation. Tables 7-7 through 7-11 illustrate the relationship between participation in 30 different recreation activities and number of vacation days per year, hours worked per week, occupation, region of the United States, and size of family. Annual vacation time appears to be positively related to participation in most activities except fishing, hunting, driving off-road vehicles, and sledding. Annual vacation is statistically significant for sightseeing, driving for pleasure, hiking, backpacking, camping in developed areas, motor boating,

Table 7-6. Effect of Sex on Participation in Outdoor Recreation, United States

| Activity | Sex | | Strength of Relationship[a] | |
	Male	Female	Simple Correlation	Multiple Correlation
Camping in Developed Area	35%	26%	.09	.05*
Camping in Primitive Area	29	18	.18	.11***
Canoeing, Kayaking, River Running	18	14	.07	.06**
Sailing	11	11	.00	.02
Waterskiing	20	12	.10	.08***
Fishing	65	43	.25	.18***
Other Boating	38	30	.10	.06**
Outdoor Pool Swimming and Sunbathing	62	64	-.02	.03
Other Outdoor Swimming and Sunbathing	48	44	.05	.00
Nature Walks, Birdwatch, Photography	47	53	-.05	NC
Hiking or Backpacking	34	23	.12	.07***
Other Walking or Jogging	65	71	-.06	-.05**
Bicycling	46	47	-.01	-.03
Horseback Riding	16	14	.04	.02
Driving Off-road Vehicles	31	21	.13	.06**
Hunting	33	7	.33	.26***
Picnicking	71	74	-.03	-.06***
Golf	22	11	.15	.15***
Tennis Outdoors	33	32	.00	.06**
Cross-country Skiing	3	2	.03	NC
Downhill Skiing	8	6	.04	.03
Ice-skating Outdoors	17	16	.03	.01
Sledding	21	20	.03	.00
Snowmobiling	10	7	.06	.02
Other Sports or Games	62	50	.13	.09***
Sightseeing	63	62	.02	-.03
Driving for Pleasure	69	70	-.01	-.05*
Zoos, Carnivals, etc.	73	72	.00	-.05*
Attending Outdoor Sports Events	67	56	.12	-.01
Attending Outdoor Concerts, Plays	42	40	.05	NC

[a]* = .05; ** = .01; *** = .001; NC = value not calculated.
Source: Heritage, Conservation, and Recreation Service.

and downhill skiing. The differences in participation rates among people working less than and more than a 40-hour week are generally mixed.

Participation by people engaged in different occupations is related to available leisure time, income, and age. Students (over 18 years of age) are more likely to participate in outdoor recreation activities than other adults. Retired persons are least likely to participate followed by those unemployed. Those with managerial and professional occupations are more likely to participate than farmers except for hunting. All occupations participate at about the same rate in: walking or jogging; picnicking; sightseeing; driving for pleasure; visiting zoos, car-

Table 7-7. Effect of Vacation Time on Participation in Outdoor Recreation, United States *no big difference*

Activity	Vacation Days per Year				Strength of Relationship[a]	
	0-6	7-14	15-31	32+	Simple Correlation	Multiple Correlation
Camping in Developed Area	32%	40%	40%	40%	.05	.06*
Camping in Primitive Area	24	31	29	30	.02	.05
Canoeing, Kayaking, River Running	14	17	17	22	.04	.02
Sailing	11	12	16	17	.08	.04
Waterskiing	19	27	21	23	.03	.04
Fishing	55	62	57	51	-.02	.02
Other Boating	32	43	44	42	.06	.06*
Outdoor Pool Swimming and Sunbathing	65	70	69	67	.03	.01
Other Outdoor Swimming and Sunbathing	NA	NA	NA	NA	.05	.04
Nature Walks, Birdwatch, Photography	NA	NA	NA	NA	NC	NC
Hiking or Backpacking	32	35	39	40	.06	.05*
Other Walking or Jogging	60	68	68	71	.05	.03
Bicycling	47	50	46	50	.04	.04
Horseback Riding	20	17	17	18	.00	.02
Driving Off-road Vehicles	29	36	26	26	-.02	.03
Hunting	25	26	28	23	-.03	.01
Picnicking	76	72	80	77	.05	.04
Golf	16	19	24	28	.09	.04
Tennis Outdoors	NA	NA	NA	NA	.02	-.01
Cross-country Skiing	NA	NA	NA	NA	NC	NC
Downhill Skiing	10	10	13	15	.08	.06*
Ice-skating Outdoors	16	15	21	16	.02	.01
Sledding	23	20	22	18	-.02	-.01
Snowmobiling	10	11	8	10	.01	.04
Other Sports or Games	58	62	59	50	.00	.01
Sightseeing	64	68	75	76	.13	.08**
Driving for Pleasure	72	50	73	75	.06	.07**
Zoos, Carnivals, etc.	74	79	77	88	.00	.00
Attending Outdoor Sports Events	NA	NA	NA	NA	.04	.02
Attending Outdoor Concerts, Plays	NA	NA	NA	NA	NC	NC

[a]* = .05; ** = .01; *** = .001; NA = data not available; NC = value not calculated.
Source: Heritage, Conservation, and Recreation Service.

nivals, and amusement parks; and attending outdoor concerts and plays. Participation by people living in different regions of the United States generally reflect differences in opportunities. Kalter reviewed a number of studies that show the relationship between population and participation in recreation tends to be one to one; that is, a one percent increase in population results in a one percent increase in participation, other things being equal. Single-person households generally are less likely to participate in recreation activities than are married

Table 7-8. Effect of Length of Workweek on Participation in Outdoor Recreation, United States

Activity	Hours per Week			Strength of Relationship[a]	
	Under 40	40	Over 40	Simple Correlation	Multiple Correlation
Camping in Developed Area	34%	41%	38%	.00	-.02
Camping in Primitive Area	22	25	33	.06	.04
Canoeing, Kayaking, River Running	17	16	21	.01	-.01
Sailing	14	13	16	.02	.00
Waterskiing	21	24	25	.00	-.02
Fishing	50	60	62	.06	.02
Other Boating	36	43	44	.05	.03
Outdoor Pool Swimming and Sunbathing	74	68	67	-.04	-.05*
Other Outdoor Swimming and Sunbathing	NA	NA	NA	-.08	-.05
Nature Walks, Birdwatch, Photography	NA	NA	NA	NC	NC
Hiking or Backpacking	35	35	39	.04	.03
Other Walking or Jogging	68	70	65	-.04	-.03
Bicycling	48	50	46	-.05	-.03
Horseback Riding	15	18	17	.04	.03
Driving Off-road Vehicles	28	30	31	.02	.02
Hunting	14	25	34	.14	.07**
Picnicking	76	80	78	.00	.01
Golf	19	22	24	.03	-.04
Tennis Outdoors	NA	NA	NA	.13	-.04
Cross-country Skiing	NA	NA	NA	NC	NC
Downhill Skiing	15	11	12	.00	.01
Ice-skating Outdoors	17	15	21	.05	.03
Sledding	21	19	23	.00	-.01
Snowmobiling	9	9	12	.05	.05*
Other Sports or Games	57	60	62	.04	.01
Sightseeing	73	71	71	.01	-.01
Driving for Pleasure	77	78	74	-.02	.00
Zoos, Carnivals, etc.	75	80	74	-.04	-.03
Attending Outdoor Sports Events	NA	NA	NA	.13	.05
Attending Outdoor Concerts, Plays	NA	NA	NA	NC	NC

[a]* = .05; ** = .01; NA = data not available; NC = value not calculated.
Source: Heritage, Conservation, and Recreation Service.

couples, particularly those with one to four children. Participation tends to decline for families with five or more children.

The relationships shown are suggestive of the strength and direction of the correlation of these variables with participation. Indeed, demand functions for recreation frequently have found that one or more of these variables are significant determinants of demand. However, the cross-sectional data and simple correlation coefficients do not hold the effects of other variables constant. Moreover, while the multiple correlation coefficients do hold the effects of other socioeconomic variables constant, the equation does not include the effects of other

Table 7-9. Effect of Occupational Status on Participation in Outdoor Recreation, United States

Activity	Profes-sional	Man-agers	Clerical & Sales	Craftsmen & Operatives	Service & Laborers	Farmers	Students	Retired	House-wives	Unem-ployed
Camping in Developed Area	39%	41%	33%	36%	38%	24%	41%	11%	26%	24%
Camping in Primitive Area	26	26	20	29	26	21	29	6	14	21
Canoeing, Kayaking, River Running	22	13	14	16	16	9	28	4	12	13
Sailing	19	14	14	8	6	(a)	20	3	7	13
Waterskiing	21	17	23	21	18	11	25	(a)	8	9
Fishing	51	64	47	68	56	54	67	37	46	52
Other Boating	40	46	39	39	31	8	43	18	27	27
Outdoor Pool Swimming and Sunbathing	78	69	76	60	60	29	90	23	59	53
Other Outdoor Swimming and Sunbathing	56	52	54	49	47	18	63	15	44	28
Nature Walks, Birdwatch, Photography	66	49	47	47	46	36	57	35	54	48
Hiking or Backpacking	43	32	28	30	29	20	42	10	20	23
Other Walking or Jogging	76	66	67	60	64	39	88	54	71	61
Bicycling	53	41	49	44	43	27	87	12	41	40
Horseback Riding	21	12	15	18	13	14	25	(a)	12	16
Driving Off-road Vehicles	27	26	25	38	31	24	40	4	18	24
Hunting	17	23	15	38	24	40	21	10	9	21
Picnicking	83	79	77	75	68	66	77	49	76	76
Golf	28	28	14	14	11	7	22	10	11	13
Tennis Outdoors	46	34	37	27	27	12	67	4	24	26
Cross-country Skiing	5	2	2	1	2	3	6	(a)	1	1
Downhill Skiing	12	7	9	7	7	1	15	(a)	3	1
Ice-skating Outdoors	19	15	19	16	14	9	32	2	14	10
Sledding	22	16	19	22	20	20	43	2	21	10
Snowmobiling	8	12	7	12	10	17	12	1	7	2
Other Sports or Games	63	56	55	59	65	49	88	19	48	42
Sightseeing	79	75	65	62	54	50	62	47	63	60
Driving for Pleasure	77	81	76	78	76	70	58	50	74	70
Zoos, Carnivals, etc.	83	73	77	80	76	56	85	42	71	68
Attending Outdoor Sports Events	73	72	69	70	61	47	82	34	48	46
Attending Outdoor Concerts, Plays	55	39	42	43	44	35	59	17	33	40

aLess than 0.5%.
Source: Heritage, Conservation, and Recreation Service.

Table 7-10. Effect of Region of Residence on Participation in Outdoor Recreation, United States

Activity	Standard Federal Region										Simple Correlation[a]
	Boston	New York	Phila-delphia	Atlanta	Chicago	Dallas	Kansas City	Denver	San Fran-cisco	Seattle	
Camping in Developed Area	25%	18%	24%	27%	33%	33%	36%	42%	38%	51%	.05
Camping in Primitive Area	20	13	15	19	22	21	22	34	28	41	.03
Canoeing, Kayaking, River Running	17	14	16	17	23	15	15	11	6	14	.03
Sailing	19	15	12	9	12	7	5	6	14	9	.03
Waterskiing	14	12	11	17	16	22	15	22	13	22	.03
Fishing	49	41	44	62	56	61	63	61	44	61	.06
Other Boating	36	35	31	34	37	33	30	36	27	40	.03
Outdoor Pool Swimming and Sunbathing	70	65	63	57	67	55	55	54	72	55	.03
Other Outdoor Swimming and Sunbathing	65	45	45	46	46	40	38	39	46	47	.02
Nature Walks, Birdwatch, Photography	57	51	52	43	59	44	43	48	47	52	.04
Hiking or Backpacking	34	26	26	23	30	22	25	39	35	40	.03
Other Walking or Jogging	71	70	67	68	70	64	59	66	73	68	.02
Bicycling	52	47	45	48	49	42	39	47	46	45	.02
Horseback Riding	14	14	14	13	15	17	13	18	16	18	.01
Driving Off-road Vehicles	23	19	25	25	27	28	28	32	31	31	.02
Hunting	15	9	21	23	20	27	22	25	11	26	.04
Picnicking	74	65	70	68	80	68	73	83	74	85	.04
Golf	19	11	13	12	23	10	19	15	18	18	.03
Tennis Outdoors	36	36	30	29	33	34	26	30	38	29	.02
Cross-country Skiing	8	4	1	1	4	1	1	7	2	4	.04
Downhill Skiing	15	10	6	5	10	2	2	14	7	14	.05
Ice-skating Outdoors	38	29	17	5	27	3	10	15	4	9	.09
Sledding	36	27	27	11	33	5	22	22	4	16	.08
Snowmobiling	15	12	8	1	15	1	7	16	2	7	.06
Other Sports or Games	59	51	56	59	62	48	54	55	50	54	.03
Sightseeing	69	62	65	58	62	56	64	68	67	69	.02
Driving for Pleasure	71	65	63	69	71	73	67	80	72	72	.02
Zoos, Carnivals, etc.	77	68	74	64	78	71	68	69	78	75	.02
Attending Outdoor Sports Events	66	55	61	62	63	63	63	63	58	56	.02
Attending Outdoor Concerts, Plays	55	45	35	38	43	39	40	41	43	26	.02

[a]Average correlation for Boston federal region vs. other nine regions; New York region vs. other nine regions; Seattle region vs. other nine regions; etc.

Source: Heritage, Conservation, and Recreation Service.

Table 7-11. Effect of Family Size on Participation in Outdoor Recreation, United States

Activity	Family Size, Persons				
	1	2	3-4	5-6	7 or More
Camping in Developed Area	21%	26%	34%	40%	24%
Camping in Primitive Area	15	16	25	26	18
Canoeing, Kayaking, River Running	7	12	19	21	21
Sailing	8	11	11	12	13
Waterskiing	10	12	19	18	16
Fishing	31	52	57	65	55
Other Boating	26	28	38	41	31
Outdoor Pool Swimming and Sunbathing	49	50	71	77	69
Other Outdoor Swimming and Sunbathing	36	36	52	54	47
Nature Walks, Birdwatch, Photography	47	44	53	57	53
Hiking or Backpacking	21	22	32	36	27
Other Walking or Jogging	63	61	71	76	82
Bicycling	25	33	55	63	75
Horseback Riding	8	11	18	20	16
Driving Off-road Vehicles	13	19	30	35	29
Hunting	6	17	22	27	13
Picnicking	58	69	77	82	77
Golf	9	18	16	18	16
Tennis Outdoors	22	22	39	43	45
Cross-country Skiing	3	2	2	3	5
Downhill Skiing	6	5	8	8	10
Ice-skating Outdoors	7	10	18	28	22
Sledding	6	11	26	35	34
Snowmobiling	4	6	9	12	10
Other Sports or Games	35	38	66	74	77
Sightseeing	56	60	67	62	63
Driving for Pleasure	59	72	73	66	59
Zoos, Carnivals, etc.	58	62	80	84	77
Attending Outdoor Sports Events	47	51	68	72	78
Attending Outdoor Concerts, Plays	36	33	45	46	50

Source: Heritage, Conservation, and Recreation Service.

important determinants of demand: direct cost or price, attractiveness or quality of the site, availability and price of substitutes, etc. Also, Knetsch observes that the variables explaining whether a person is a participant in outdoor recreation may differ from those determining the level of participation, i.e., number of recreation days or trips per year. Therefore, the tables in this section should be considered suggestive of the possible socioeconomic determinants of demand for recreation to include in an empirical demand function, which would provide an acceptable test of their effects and significance.

TRAVEL TIME

It can be reasonably argued that at least for some individuals, the value of travel time and on-site recreation time are important determinants of demand for recreation. The effect of both time variables is to shift the demand curve for a recreation site outward to the right and often to change its slope. Clawson and Knetsch observe that those who travel greater distances, and thereby incur higher direct costs or price, also have more travel time. If willingness to pay to avoid an hour of travel time is uniform per mile or increasing with miles traveled, those who travel greater distances also have proportionately higher travel time costs, and the demand curve will shift and become more negatively sloped. Figure 7-1 illustrates this effect. Note that the consumer surplus measure of benefits will change when time costs are included in the demand function. Whether consumer surplus increases will depend on the proportion of travel time devoted to sightseeing.

There is little or no reason to believe that the opportunity cost per hour of on-site recreation time of individuals will vary with distance traveled, i.e., the level of direct costs or price. However, those who incur larger direct costs or price per trip have an incentive to increase their length of stay at the recreation site, as shown by Jennings and Gibbs for trips to campgrounds in Florida. Thus, those who travel greater distances and thereby incur higher direct costs or price, would also have proportionately more opportunity cost of foregone income. When this is the case, the effect of including on-site recreation time in the demand function is to cause the demand curve to shift and to become more negatively sloped. Thus, the estimate of consumer surplus often will rise when on-site recreation time is included in the demand function. Exceptions would occur when all visitors are on single-day trips and when demand functions specify visitor days as the dependent variable, rather than trips.

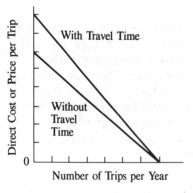

Figure 7-1. Effect of Travel Time Costs on Demand for a Recreation Site

Dwyer, Kelly, and Bowes observe that the travel time problem has been more easily recognized than solved. Thus far, there have been two main lines of approach. The first has been to include time as a separate independent variable in the regression equation in order to separate the effect of money and time costs on the number of trips to a recreation site. This approach has often been frustrated by high correlation between money and time costs of travel, precluding an accurate regression of the effect of each variable. Brown and Nawas overcame this problem by measuring travel cost and time cost for each individual consumer rather than estimating them on the basis of distance traveled and aggregating by zone.

The second approach has been to assume a monetary value of travel time and to add this to the direct money cost of auto travel to obtain a single combined price variable. An example is the Cesario and Knetsch study of trips to state parks in Pennsylvania. While the procedure appears to have provided acceptable results, an accurate estimate of the monetary value of travel time has yet to be established in empirical work. So far, the value of travel time has been assumed to be some fraction (25-50 percent) of individual wage rates, as recommended by the federal guidelines. Wilman suggests that a more accurate estimate of the value of travel time would be to ask individuals their willingness to pay to avoid it. Also, she recommends that on-site recreation time be valued in terms of opportunity cost in its best alternative use. For individuals whose work time is variable, the opportunity cost of on-site recreation time could be measured as income actually foregone while on site. In chapter four, we presented the empirical results of two tentative tests of the Wilman proposal, which resulted in much lower estimates of time costs than usually have been assumed in recreation demand functions in the past. It seems likely that the value per hour of travel time is a function of distance and other variables rather than a constant per mile traveled.

SUBSTITUTION

When substitute sites are available, it is likely that they will have a significant influence on demand for a particular recreation site. The effect of substitutes will depend on the extent to which the alternatives are perfect substitutes, the location of the user population relative to the recreation site and substitute sites. If individuals have a wider choice of substitutes, then the demand curve will have a flatter negative slope, as illustrated in Figure 7-2. On the other hand, if individuals have fewer substitutes, then the demand curve has a steeper negative slope. The reason is that the observed demand curve includes the effect of the availability of substitutes as well as the price of visiting the study site. When an effective measure of substitution is intro-

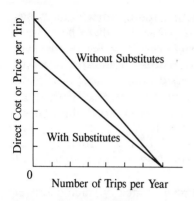

Figure 7-2. Effect of Substitute Sites on Demand for a Recreation Site

duced into the demand function as a separate independent variable, we can estimate its effect on the demand curve.

There are many recreation goods and services whose demand depends on the availability and prices of others. There are recreation goods and services that make one another less valuable. These are called substitutes. Ownership of an off-road vehicle, for example, may decrease the desire for a dirt bike. If there are reservoirs in the county where you live, you are less likely to go fishing at a site located in the next county. When the direct cost or price of a trip to a reservoir in the next county goes up, people demand fewer trips to the reservoir, and demand goes up for trips to reservoirs in the county where they live. When the price of downhill skiing at popular resorts goes up, people demand less downhill skiing; instead, they go cross-country skiing closer to home.

Certain recreation goods and services make one another more desirable. For example, restaurants and lodges increase the desirability of skiing at some resorts, and vice versa. The same is true of reservoirs and campgrounds. In some extreme cases, neither of the two has any use without the other — 4-wheel drive vehicles and mudtires, a pair of skis and ski boots, and so on. Such things, each of which makes the other more valuable, are called complements. The demand curves of complements are interrelated, meaning that a rise in the direct cost or price of skiing is likely to affect the quantity of restaurant meals and lodge rooms demanded. Why? When the direct costs or price of skiing at a site rises, less skiing will be demanded and therefore less overnight lodging and other services will be demanded at the ski site. A similar relationship holds for other complementary goods.

This result is really a matter of common sense. If the direct cost or price of anything goes up and there is a substitute available, some people will tend to switch to the substitute. On the other hand, if two goods or services are complements, a rise in the price of one will

Substitute - Price A↑ Demand B↑

174   *Complements   A↑   B↑*
A↓   B↓

discourage its own use and will also discourage use of the complementary item. Two recreation sites are called substitutes if an increase in the direct cost or price of trips to one increases the number of trips demanded to the other, all other things remaining constant. Two recreation sites are called complements if an increase in the direct cost or price of trips to one reduces the number of trips demanded to both sites. Kurtz and King show that some reservoirs in Arizona are substitutes and others are complements. One plausible explanation of a complementary relationship between reservoirs is the desire of individuals with motor boats to visit a variety of recreation sites each year. Caulkins, et al. suggest that the existence of two or more excellent bass fishing lakes may induce a fisherman to invest in more expensive equipment and fish more often, whereas the existence of only one such lake may not justify the investment.

The federal guidelines recommend that demand functions for recreation include a variable that takes into account the competition of other recreational opportunities within the area influenced by a recreation site. Early efforts by Cicchetti, Seneca, and Davidson characterized the recreation opportunities in counties of the United States in terms of water acreage, recreation land area, and miles to the nearest large body of water. Another early attempt to incorporate the substitution variable into a recreation demand function was a study of eight reservoirs in Texas by Grubb and Goodwin. The size of alternative reservoirs in surface acres of minimum pool was weighted by distance in miles to each reservoir within 100 miles of the center of counties where users live. In its simplest application, surface acres was divided by distance. To adjust for quality of substitute sites, fish catch has been divided by distance. The substitution variable was the sum of catch per mile for all sites exceeding the catch per mile of the study site. These are proxy measures of the capacity of the existing stock of recreation facilities in the market area centered at the respondent's home that are similar to those at the study site. They have been characterized by McConnell as rough measures which may not capture all of the substitution effects.

The substitution price variable has been measured as the distance from the home of each respondent to the nearest existing alternative facility offering recreation opportunities similar to those at the study site. Alternately, this variable has been measured from survey questions on the willingness to drive to the next most preferred recreation facility offering similar recreation opportunities if the study site became unavailable. In regional demand functions, the direct cost of trips to other sites in the region has been used as a proxy for the price of substitutes.

There is some dispute as to whether a quantity or a price measure is more appropriate. In theory, a distance or travel cost variable is most appropriate to estimate the substitution effects in an ordinary demand curve. However, the quantity of available substitutes may also influence actual user substitution. It seems likely that the supply of recreation resources and whether users consider them substitutes or complements may have an important influence on the demand for study sites. Work by social psychologists (Vaske, et al.), shows that researcher-defined substitutes are not statistically related to recreation user-defined substitutes. We conclude that more emphasis needs to be placed on consumer perceptions of suitable substitutes.

ATTRACTIVENESS OR QUALITY

The attractiveness of the site or the quality of the resource constitutes another important determinant of demand for recreation. In the past, a useful measure of attractiveness was simply size — for example, the surface area of a lake or park in acres (Brown and Hansen; Grubb and Goodwin). Experience has shown size to be an effective proxy for other variables that affect site attractiveness, such as: campsites, length of beach, acres of picnic area, miles of hiking trail, modern toilets and showers, visitor centers, boat launching ramps and rentals, and trailer sanitary stations. Knetsch concludes that size is a sufficiently good measure of attractiveness for purposes of estimating reasonably accurate demand functions in the case of Corps reservoirs where construction of recreation facilities tends to be related to size. However, it is too general a measure to effectively estimate the demand effects of specific site quality and design alternatives.

Recently, several measures of the quality of recreation resources have been included in demand functions in an effort to estimate their specific effects on demand and willingness to pay. Variables that have been tried include: air quality and visibility (Randall et al.; Schulze et al.), water quality (Bouwes and Schneider), water level (Daubert and Young), forest quality (Walsh and Olienyk), game and fish harvest (Stevens), weather conditions (McConnell), noise (McMillan, et al.), and congestion (discussed in the following section). Wherever possible, these quality variables have been measured in physical units — for example, cubic feet of instream flow, temperature, number of trees, number of persons, number and pounds of fish caught, etc. In other cases, quality has been estimated by experts, using a 10-point scale. Consumers may be asked to rate the quality of the physical characteristics of facilities and resources available at the recreation site or of color photos illustrating a range of quality. Cesario and Knetsch prepared an index of site quality that combined the subjective judgment of consumers and the physical characteristics of the site.

There are a large number of physical and biological characteristics of recreation sites that may influence recreation demand. Brown,

Haas, and Manfredo have studied consumer preferences for attributes of wilderness in the Rocky Mountains of the United States. They asked users of wilderness areas to rate each of the physical attributes shown in Table 7-12 on a Likert scale of satisfaction, from most strongly adds (1) to most strongly detracts (9). Attributes of the resource were grouped into eight categories. Attributes of the meadow, forest, water, and wildlife contributed most to satisfaction of using the recreation area. Nuisances and intrusions detracted from user satisfaction.

Interest in the study of the effects of site attractiveness has been stimulated by the development of a procedure to classify the supply of recreation land and related resources into six broad categories ranging from primitive to urban. The classification system, referred to as the recreation opportunity spectrum (ROS), has been adopted by the Forest Service, U.S. Department of Agriculture, and the Bureau of Land Management, U.S. Department of the Interior. Table 7-13 illustrates the essential elements of the system including: distance from a road, size in square miles, presence of buildings and other improvements, number of persons encountered, and visible management practices. These general indicators measure the naturalness of the setting in which recreation takes place. Essentially, larger and more remote sites, less developed, with lower density and less evidence of management are more likely to be classified toward the primitive end of the ROS scale. Thus, for those who desire a natural environment, hiking in a primitive roadless zone is expected to be more beneficial than hiking in a roaded or urban zone.

Studies of the demand for recreation sites should include the physical characteristics that are relevant. For downhill skiing, Morey observes that the physical characteristics most useful to individual skiers depend on ability (beginner, intermediate, or advanced), as they are not capable of skiing terrain that is more difficult than their ability allows. The appropriate measure of characteristics becomes the acres of terrain at the site suitable for the individual's skiing ability and the lift capacity (vertical transport feet) serving these ski runs. Other physical characteristics that affect demand for skiing include annual snowfall, snow quality, and weather conditions, such as sun, temperature, and, especially, wind.

In visiting a recreation site, a user acquires a bundle of physical services. Different recreation sites have different bundles of physical characteristics associated with them, and the user's demand and willingness to pay is a function of the physical services associated with the site. When there is a sufficient range of data on quality for different days at the same site or among a number of study sites, the effect of the quality variable on demand can be estimated statistically. The regression coefficient indicates the effect of one additional unit of quali-

Table 7-12. Consumer Ratings of the Quality of Resource Attributes at Indian Peaks Wilderness Area, Colorado

Resource Attribute	Value	Contribution to Satisfaction, Mean Score[a]
Meadow-Forest	Strongly Adds	1.8563
Alpine Meadows		1.8706
Aspen Groves		1.9301
Meadows Among the Forest		1.8951
Columbines		2.0421
Wildflowers in Bloom		1.5965
Diverse Scenery		1.8035
Water Related	Strongly Adds	2.1039
Mountain Springs		2.0351
Abundant Sources of Water		1.9509
A Variety of Different Sized Streams		2.3252
Waterfalls		1.6316
Lake Views		1.8702
Small Streams You Can Step Across		2.7359
Large Roaring Streams		2.1783
Wildlife	Moderately/	2.4844
Small Furbearers	Strongly Adds	2.4860
Grouse		2.7098
Squirrels		2.7028
Song Birds		2.2902
Ptarmigan		2.5614
Predatory Birds Such as Owls and Hawks		2.5000
Elk		2.3392
Mule Deer		2.5664
Big Horned Sheep		2.2035
Dense Vegetation	Moderately Adds	2.6203
Areas With Dense Vegetation		2.8421
Dense Stands of Pine		2.1614
Streams Lined With Brush		3.7958
Mature Virgin Forests		1.6818
Rugged Topography	Moderately Adds	2.6465
Steep Terrain		3.1579
Steep Terrain Areas		3.0211
Steep Gorges		2.6912
Boulder Fields		3.1404
Areas Above Timberline		2.2421
Glaciers		2.1263
Snowfields		2.4175
Rugged Terrain		2.3754
Rare or Unique Natural Features	Moderately Adds	2.8489
Wind Sculptured Rocks		2.5930
Fossil Outcrops		3.0455
Rock Towers		2.8386
A Variety of Rock Types and Minerals		2.5789
Unusually Shaped Rocks		2.7762
Caves		3.1408
Rock Outcroppings		2.7902
Rare Plants		2.8175
Indian Artifacts		3.0175
Hot Springs		2.8908

Table 7-12. continued

Resource Attribute	Value	Contribution to Satisfaction, Mean Score[a]
Fish Related	Moderately Adds	3.2033
Brown Trout		3.2702
Cutthroat Trout		3.3298
Brook Trout		3.0106
Rainbow Trout		3.1088
Slow Moving Streams With Deep Holes		2.9895
Naturally Reproducing Fish Populations		3.0386
Stocked Fish		3.6923
Nuisances	Neither Adds	5.3796
Insects That Bite	Nor Detracts	6.6912
Marshes		4.1084
Murky or Discolored Water		7.1895
Bears		4.0845
Streams With Many Fly Hatches		4.2289
Rainy Weather		5.9754
Intrusions	Slightly Detracts	5.8222
Evidence of Logging Activity		6.8182
Evidence of Mining Activity		6.1888
Reservoirs In The Backcountry		4.4596

[a]Nine-point scale, with 1 = most strongly adds and 9 = most strongly detracts.
Source: Brown, Haas, and Manfredo.

Table 7-13. Characteristics of Recreation Resources in a National Forest

Variable	Unit	Recreation Opportunity (ROS) Zones		
		Primitive	Semi-Primitive, Nonmotorized	Motorized
Buildings and Improvements	Number	None	Rare	Frequent
Distance from Roads	Miles	Over 3.0	0.5-3.0	Less than 0.5
Size of Sites	Acres	Over 5,000	2,500-5,000	Any size
Congestion on Trails	Parties Encountered/Day	Less than 6	6-15	Over 15
Persons at One Time, Maximum	Persons/Acre	0.025	0.083	0.083-7.6
Management Controls	Scale	Low	Moderate	High

Source: U.S. Forest Service.

ty on demand, all else held constant. Alternately, the value of an increment of quality can be estimated directly by asking users their willingness to pay or to participate with hypothetical changes in quality of the resource.

An example of the first approach is a study of water quality in southeastern Wisconsin. Bouwes and Schneider interviewed 195 households at eight lakes. Recreation user perception of water quality was included as an independent variable in an ordinary demand function, with trips as the dependent variable. Then the subjective estimates of water quality were related to technical measures from biological studies at the eight sites, in a two-step process. The authors estimated that household benefits from recreation use of Pine Lake would decline by $20 per year if water pollution increased from 3 to 10 points on a 23-point scale, with zero representing clean water.

Leuschner and Young applied the zonal travel cost approach to estimate the effect of southern pine beetle damage to ponderosa pine trees on demand for recreation use of 19 campgrounds located on the shore of two reservoirs in Texas. The demand function included pine tree density from aerial photos as one of the independent variables. The effect of the proportion of the recreation sites covered by pine crowns was isolated from other site characteristics such as the presence of hard wood trees, size of campground, facilities available, quality of access, and number of substitute sites available. They estimated the elasticity of demand with respect to pine trees as 0.64 to 0.68, nearly double the effect of number of pine trees at recreation sites in the northern Rocky Mountains. The variation in results may reflect differences in the value of shade from trees in the relatively cooler mountain states.

An example of a combination of both approaches is a study of air temperature at ocean beaches on the south shore of Rhode Island. McConnell interviewed 229 individuals at six ocean beaches. He found that a 1-degree increase in air temperature was associated with a 7.6 percent increase in the average individual's consumer surplus per day. Temperature is moderated by the ocean so that it may be significantly less than inland temperatures; for example, beach temperature may be 68 degrees and inland temperature 80 degrees. A 68-degree day would substantially reduce enjoyment of the beach and willingness to pay. Temperature is also a proxy for precipitation, as rainy days are also cool days. Including a precipitation variable in the inverse demand function added nothing to its explanatory power.

An example of the second approach is a study of forest quality at recreation sites in the Rocky Mountains. Walsh and Olienyk found that forest quality has a significant effect on demand for developed camping, semi-developed camping, backpacking, hiking, fishing, picnicking, driving off-road vehicles, and staying at resorts. Based on interviews with 435 users at six forest recreation sites, the relationship apparently is an inverted-U function. Annual recreation use increases at a decreasing rate from 9 days per year with no trees to nearly 19 days with 225 trees per acre. Beyond this level, participation decreases with additional trees.

CONGESTION

The level of congestion or crowding at a recreation site may have a significant effect on individual demand and willingness to pay. Congestion occurs when an individual user of a recreation area encounters increasing numbers of other users. Congestion enters the individual's demand function like any other nonprice variable. When congestion decreases the quality of the recreation experience, a downward shift in the demand curve results.

The effect of congestion on demand can be estimated either statistically or directly from consumer interviews. It can be estimated statistically when there is a sufficient range of data on number of users collected for different days at the same site or at a number of study sites, and observed congestion levels are what individuals anticipate when making their trip decisions. Then the regression coefficient for congestion indicates the effect of one additional user on demand, all else held constant. Alternately, the effect of incremental congestion can be estimated directly by asking users their willingness to pay or participate with hypothetical changes in congestion as for any quality variable.

Several alternative measures of congestion at recreation sites have been included in demand functions. Measures that have been tried include: (1) actual number of users per acre per day or at one time (McConnell); (2) number of encounters per day or per hour on the trail and in backcountry campsites (Cicchetti and Smith; Walsh and Gilliam); number of minutes of lift line wait (Walsh, Miller, and Gilliam); and (4) utilization of capacity, defined as a ratio of users per day to physical or economic capacity, as illustrated earlier in Chapter 6.

Users experience congestion in terms of number of individuals or groups encountered, other than members of their own party. Individuals seldom come into contact with all other users of the site. Thus, when number of encounters is the measure of congestion, it must be converted to the total number of users per day. Shechter and Lucas have simulated the relationship between encounters and number of users per day at the Desolation Wilderness in California. When the total number of users is known or can be estimated, it is substituted for the average number of encounters reported by a sample of users.

Table 7-14 illustrates the rate at which individual benefits diminish as the number of people encountered increases. When visitors are few, encountering other people provides a sense of safety, does not interfere appreciably with the quality of the experience, and benefits fall off slowly. Further increases in the number of people in a given space eventually result in crowding, a reduction in the quality of the experience, and benefits decrease more rapidly. This is true of most recreation activities for which data is available. With no encounters assigned

Table 7-14. Effect of Number of Other Parties Encountered per Activity Day on an Index of Individual Benefits from Wilderness Hiking, Camping, Fishing, and Boating, United States

Index of Benefits per Day of Recreation Activity	Number of Other Parties Encountered per Day[a]								
	0	5	10	15	20	25	30	35	40
Wilderness Areas									
Trails	1.0	.89	.79	.7	.6	0	0	0	0
Campgrounds	1.0	.81	.66	.53	0	0	0	0	0
River Fishing	1.0	.89	.79	.71	.55	.38	.33	.27	.12
Homestake Creek	1.0	.97	.95	.92	.88	.80	.70	.59	.32
Frying Pan River	1.0	.88	.78	.72	.60	.44	.38	.31	.12
Eagle River	1.0	.83	.68	.55	.27	0	0	0	0
River Kayaking	1.0	.95	.89	.83	.75	.66	.53	.31	.15
Crystal River	1.0	.91	.81	.69	.51	.35	.15	0	0
Roaring Fork River	1.0	.95	.88	.86	.84	.81	.77	.71	.64
Colorado at Glenwood	1.0	.98	.96	.93	.90	.84	.72	.36	0
River Rafting	1.0	.98	.65	.56	.33	.31	.25	.18	.16
Colorado at State Bridge	1.0	.95	.89	.81	.69	.60	.29	0	0
Roaring Fork River	1.0	.99	.98	.97	.94	.90	.87	.80	.72
Yampa River	1.0	.95	.80	.67	0	0	0	0	0
Colorado at Westwater	1.0	1.0	.13	0	0	0	0	0	0
Total, Western Rivers	1.0	.94	.74	.66	.49	.40	.33	.24	.15
Reservoir Fishing	1.0	.94	.88	.78	.55	.17	0	0	0
Small, 1-50 acres	1.0	.82	.61	.24	0	0	0	0	0
Medium, 51-150 acres	1.0	.93	.81	.65	.49	.22	0	0	0
Large, 151-400 acres	1.0	.97	.92	.85	.72	.51	.11	0	0
Reservoir Power Boating[b]	1.0	.96	.92	.88	.83	.77	.72	.66	.59

[a]A party was defined as one fisherman, one power boater, one kayaker, one hiker, one camper, and one raft containing an average of five persons.
[b]Large, over 400 acres.
Source: Wilderness data are from Fisher and Krutilla. Other data from studies by the author.

a value of 1.0, individual benefits of wilderness camping decline by half to 0.5 when 15 other persons are encountered. Encountering the same number of persons on a trail reduces benefits by about one-third to an index of 0.7. This illustrates the fact that wilderness campers tend to be more sensitive to congestion than hikers.

Perhaps it would be useful to consider a concrete example of a congestion survey. In a study of excess demand for the Indian Peaks wilderness area in the Rocky Mountains, we asked a representative sample of 126 hikers and backpackers to report the maximum amount of money they would be willing to pay rather than forego the experience. From this was subtracted direct costs or price to obtain consumer surplus. The number of persons (other than members of their own party) encountered in the wilderness area on the day of the interview was recorded as one of four observations. Willingness to pay also was reported when the number of persons encountered was zero, for an intermediate level, and for the maximum level of crowding that individuals would tolerate before discontinuing recreation use of the site. These four observations trace out the relationship between congestion and willingness to pay.

The demand function will yield a demand curve that holds congestion constant at the average observed level of use. This assumes that the observations represent the true average level of use for the sample period, which may not always be valid. Fortunately, whenever congestion enters as a variable in the demand function, it is possible to estimate a "family" of congestion-constant demand curves for the recreation site. For example, where there are different levels of congestion during weekdays and weekend peak days, a demand curve can be estimated for each subperiod or a combined site demand curve estimated for a weighted level of congestion for the entire season of use. On weekdays when total use is light, the reduction in congestion by itself has a positive effect on remaining individual user's demand which shifts outward to the right. However, the positive effect of low congestion would be overshadowed by other nonprice variables in the demand function, such as the opportunity cost of work foregone with weekday use, which causes the total site demand curve to shift inward to the left on weekdays.

Congestion may reduce the benefits received by individuals using the recreation area but it usually will not change the direct monetary costs or price to individual users. Each additional user considers his or her individual benefits of the experience, that is, net of the loss in benefits imposed by the presence of other users. But individuals ignore the fact that their presence increases congestion and reduces the benefits for other users, which creates a divergence between individual and social (or group) effects of congestion. As is generally true in cases of external effects, this will eventually result in overuse of the recreation site, reducing aggregate total satisfaction and benefits of the experience below efficient levels. Thus, the presence of congestion has implications for estimating the capacity of recreation areas.

As long as the gains from additional users exceed the losses due to congestion, aggregate total benefits increase. Beyond some point, the loss in benefits resulting from congestion exceed the gains experienced by additional users, and aggregate total benefits fall. Aggregate total benefits of a recreation area are maximized where the loss in benefits from incremental congestion equals the gain in benefits from incremental use. If there were no other effects of congestion, the recommended carrying capacity would be at this level. With the introduction of the costs of recreation use management and environmental degradation, the recommended carrying capacity would fall to a point where marginal benefits would equal marginal costs. See Figure 7-3.

The economic carrying capacity of recreation sites is the number of users where aggregate total benefits are maximized. This appears to be

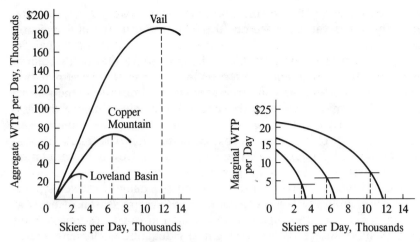

Figure 7-3. Effect of Number of Skiers per Day on Aggregate and Marginal
Willingness to Pay for Lift Tickets
Source: Walsh, Miller, and Gilliam.

consistent with the well known standard in forest management to seek
the greatest good for the largest number in the long-run. This general
goal was initially proposed by Gifford Pinchot, first chief of the U.S.
Forest Service. There are two points that should be made about its
implications for managers. Providing the greatest good for the largest
number of people does not mean serving the most people possible nor
providing the highest quality experience to individual users. Economic
studies of congestion show that serving the most people would eventually push benefits to zero. Providing the highest quality experience to
each individual would limit participation to fewer users than would
provide the greatest good for the largest number. The economic capacity of a recreation site represents a compromise solution in between
these two extreme objectives.

Congestion is an important consideration not only in estimating the
benefits of an existing recreation site and its carrying capacity, but
also in estimating the benefits of a new or expanded site. The regression coefficients for congestion at existing sites allow us to estimate
the external benefits of reducing congestion to optimal levels at these
sites as part of the benefits of the substitution of a new or expanded
site. Also, if congestion is taken into account when a demand function
derived from an existing site is applied to a new site, it is no longer
necessary to assume that congestion affects both sites in a similar
manner. If the level of congestion is expected to be different at the
new site, the demand curve would be shifted to reflect the change.
The amount of adjustment would be determined from the regression
coefficient for congestion such as presented in Chapter 6 (Table 6-1).
For example, if the rate of utilization of capacity of a new wilderness

area is expected to be 0.6 (60 per cent) rather than the 0.9 (90 percent) for the existing area, and the regression coefficient of -2.667 can be realistically applied to the new site, then expected individual demand would be increased by 0.8 of a day (= -0.3 × -2.667) to account for the increase associated with the reduced congestion. In some cases, the regression coefficient for congression at existing sites may be unique to those sites and, therefore, not useful in estimating demand for new sites (Smith).

The influence of congestion on demand and willingness to pay depends on the perception of individual users. Thus, recreation sites may be similar in physical characteristics and still have different congestion effects. For example, McConnell found substantially different congestion effects at each of six Rhode Island beaches. On average, an extra 100 people per acre reduced the average individual's consumer surplus per day by about 25 percent. However, he calculated the optimal number of users per acre (at maximum total benefits), based on the congestion effects, and found a wide range: from 59 people per acre for a beach near a wildlife sanctuary to a whopping 2,400 people per acre for a "singles" beach. The reason for this large divergence seems to be that the clientele of the two beaches differ greatly in their attitudes regarding the effect of crowding on their recreation benefits.

We can compare the economic capacity of several wilderness areas in the western states. The number of encounters, expressed as parties per day, which would maximize aggregate total benefits varies as follows:

Indian Peaks, Colorado	12-15
Other Colorado areas	6-8
Desolation, California	7-8
Spanish Peaks, Montana	4-7

These estimates suggest that if preferences for congestion avoidance were the same across wilderness areas in the west, the economic capacity of Indian Peaks would be nearly half the level estimated. Its higher capacity is associated with scarcity of wilderness recreation opportunities near large population centers where users have learned to accept higher levels of congestion.

It is interesting to compare the effect of congestion on demand and willingness to pay for lift tickets at a small and large ski area in the Rocky Mountains. On average, an additional 1-minute wait in a lift line decreases individual skier's demand by 0.25 of a day at the small ski area compared with 0.47 of a day at the large. An additional 1-minute wait in lift lines also decreases willingness to pay for lift tickets by 27 cents per day at the small ski area compared with 34 cents at the large (Figure 7-3). Also an extra skier per acre on the slopes decreases willingness to pay by 9 cents per day at the small ski area compared with 22 cents at the large. The reason for these differences seems to be that the clientele of the large ski area expect more services for the higher prices that they pay.

The results of these studies should be viewed as tentative and first approximations subject to further study. Much more research is needed before we will understand the relevant economic and noneconomic questions concerning congestion. We measured the effect of two important variables — lift line and slope congestion — on willingness to pay for lift tickets, and estimated the marginal costs of the ski areas from secondary data. As intensity of recreation resource use increases, congestion also occurs in the parking lot, lodge, restaurant, highway, and airport. Congestion research in the future should encompass all possible relevant variables and postpone the decision about which ones warrant consideration in the final analysis until knowledge of their relative significance has been developed. Also, there is a need to study the marginal costs of operating recreation sites and the external costs of environmental damages. The economic capacity of recreation sites is apt to prove much less than the available evidence suggests at the present time.

TASTES AND PREFERENCES

Tastes and preferences of individual consumers have been considered important nonprice variables in demand functions, at least since Marshall. Unfortunately, most empirical demand studies of recreation activities in the past have not included effective taste and preference variables. The omission is due to the lack of an accurate general measure, rather than any conscious decision by economists that the variable is unimportant as a determinant of demand. In the past, the federal guidelines have recommended that demand functions for recreation include the important socioeconomic characteristics of the user population as a proxy for taste and preference variables. While income, age, sex, etc., tend to be related to variations in tastes and preferences, they are indirect measures. The task remains to integrate direct measures into demand functions for recreation.

Tastes and preferences refer to the basic characteristics of individual personality. For example, some people like active or physically strenuous activities, such as hiking in a recreation area, while others prefer more passive or comfortable activities. Should many individuals suddenly decide that they like active recreation better, the demand curve for such recreation will shift to the right, as shown in Figure 6-2. The preference variable in Table 6-1 is categorical, meaning that 1 = active and 0 = passive. A regression coefficient of 1.25 indicates that individuals who prefer active recreation demand 1.25 trips more than those who prefer passive recreation.

Alternatively, should physical activity go out of style, the demand curve for such recreation would shift to the left, as in Figure 6-2. Again, these are quite general phenomena. If consumer preferences shift in favor of a particular activity, that activity's demand curve will shift outward to the right, as quantity demanded rises. Conversely, if consumer preferences go against a particular activity, that activity's demand curve will shift inward to the left, as quantity demanded falls.

Recently, a number of social scientists working in recreation, particularly Brown and Driver, have studied consumer preferences for recreation experiences. They found that patterns of individual preferences for recreation activities can be classified into the 19 categories illustrated in Table 7-15. They asked individuals participating in a wide variety of recreation activities to rate each of the preference variables on a Likert scale of satisfaction. The possible responses typically range from strongly adds to strongly detracts.

Table 7-15. Questions About Preference for Outdoor Recreation Experiences

1. Developing, applying, and testing skills and abilities for a better sense of self-worth and self-development.
2. Exercising to feel good physically.
3. Resting, both physically and mentally.
4. Associating with close friends and other users to develop new friendships.
5. Obtaining privacy, solitude, and tranquility in an outdoor setting.
6. Experiencing natural ecosystems in environments which are largely unmodified by human activity.
7. Gaining social recognition to enhance self-esteem.
8. Enhancing a feeling of family kinship or solidarity.
9. Teaching and leading others, especially to help direct the growth, learning, and development of one's children.
10. Reflecting on personal values and growing spiritually.
11. Feeling free, independent, and more in control than is possible in more structured home and work environments.
12. Enjoyment of scenic beauty.
13. Gaining a new mental perspective in a tranquil outdoor setting.
14. Self-testing and risk-taking for self-development and sense of accomplishment.
15. Applying and developing creative abilities.
16. Learning more about nature, especially natural processes, human dependence on them, and how to live in greater harmony with nature.
17. Gaining a greater appreciation of the nation's cultural heritage and resource endowment, which can contribute to development of more pride in that nation.
18. Exploring and being stimulated, to satisfy curiosity needs, and to meet the need for exploration.
19. Replenishing adaptive energies and abilities by temporarily escaping adverse social and physical conditions experienced in home, neighborhood, and work environments. These conditions include noise, too many things to do, demands of others, time pressures, crowdedness, insufficient green or open space, lack of privacy, pollution, unsafe environments, and demanding jobs.

Source: Driver and Rosenthal.

It is readily apparent that there are a large number of preference variables that can be significantly related to the recreation experience. Attempts have been made to combine these variables into meaningful groups reflecting types of individual personality, so-called O-types, such as passive, extractive, social, nature, etc. (Brown, Hautaluoma, and McPhail). Thus, far, grouped preference scores by personality types have provided encouraging results when included in demand functions for recreation. However, the complexity of the approach and the somewhat mixed results suggest that a simplifying modification must be developed before it will receive widespread adoption. Miller, Prato, and Young report that eight types of personalities explain 15 percent of the variation in willingness to pay for deer hunting. For example, values range from $29 per year for the group with minimum gratification to $108 for a group of gung-ho hunters who score highest on every attribute of the experience.

It may be possible to obtain direct estimates of willingness to pay for one or another of these psychological outcomes of the recreation experience. Recently, we asked a representative sample of 285 forest recreation users in the Rocky Mountains their willingness to drive additional miles to try a new recreation site. Table 7-14 describes this motivation as: "exploring and being stimulated, to satisfy curiosity needs, and to meet the need for exploration" (item 18), which is identical to Scitovsky's definition of novelty. We found that novelty shifted the demand curve outward and to the right for a substantial proportion of recreation users. Consumers reported that they were willing to drive about 30 percent more miles to try a new recreation site.

There may be other significant preference variables that are not included on this list and about which we know very little. For example, Leibenstein observed that a "bandwagon" effect — desire for social conformity — may make some recreation activities more desirable, and that a "snob" effect — desire for exclusivity — may favor other activities. This is an extension of the ideas of Thorstein Veblen in his earlier book, *The Theory of the Leisure Class.* Thus, if the bandwagon effect applies, the individual's demand curve will shift outward at all price levels as market demand in total increases. On the other hand, if the snob effect applies to an individual, his or her demand curve will shift back at all price levels as more and more consumers participate in the activity. As a recreation activity loses appeal with increased participation, some consumers will find the activity less desirable and take fewer trips than they would have if participation of others had been less. To estimate either the bandwagon or snob effect, a sample survey of consumers would be asked how much they would participate in a particular recreation activity when site or market demand is at various levels. Some consumers may exhibit bandwagon effects at the same time that others demonstrate snob effects.

Gibson was apparently the first economist to develop a general measure of the preference for the public good aspect of parks and recreation. She hypothesized that those who believe they do not have to use governmental services to derive benefits from them are more willing to pay taxes for the support of parks and recreational areas. She asked 182 registered voters in Santa Clara County, California, the five questions reproduced in Table 7-16. For example: "Some think that the only people who really benefit from state parks are people who use them. How much truth do you think there is to this way of thinking?" The possible responses were: (1) very little, (2) little, (3) some, (4) pretty much, and (5) a great deal. Responses to the five questions were combined, with scores summed into a single taste variable. The answers to questions 3 and 5 should be recoded, of course, to reflect the direction of strong preference consistent with questions 1, 2, and 4.

Then, two demand functions were estimated. In both, the dependent variable to be explained was willingness to pay taxes to support parks and recreational areas. One equation included price and income as independent variables, and the other, these two variables plus the preference variable. The results showed that the variable explained 15 percent of the variation in willingness to pay, with price and income effects held constant. On average, a 1-percent change in the preference variable resulted in a positive 0.32 percent change in willingness to pay taxes to support parks and recreational areas. We can conclude that general adoption of effective taste and preference measures would substantially increase our ability to explain willingness to pay for recreation.

Table 7-16. Questions About Preference for Public Goods

1. How much do you think state spending on education benefits those families without children in school?
2. Some people feel they benefit indirectly from a great many things state government does even though these programs don't help them directly very much. How much do you feel you benefit indirectly like this from things state government does?
3. Some think that the only people who really benefit from state parks are people who use them. How much truth do you think there is to this way of thinking?
4. How willing are you to pay taxes to support state programs which don't benefit you or your family but which do benefit other people in the state?
5. People sometimes say they only benefit from state government services when they use these services. How much truth do you think there is to the way these people feel?

Source: Gibson.

SUMMARY

This chapter addressed the problem of measuring the determinants of demand for recreation. We reviewed several approaches that have been used to measure the variables that shift demand for recreation. A demand curve shift — from one demand curve to another — indicates a change in one or more of the determinants of demand, the nonprice variables in the demand function. So that at each direct cost or price, the quantity demanded is either more or less than before, depending on whether the demand curve has shifted to the right or to the left. Information about the determinants of demand can help managers of private and public recreation resources make effective operating and planning decisions. What the recreation managers need to know is: how sensitive is demand to changes in the variables in the demand function?

It was shown that individuals vary in their response to recreation opportunities. In an attempt to account for these differences, demand functions have included socioeconomic or demographic measures, i.e., age, education, income, race, sex, vacation time, and size of city. Of these, the most important appears to be age. More youth participate in the physically strenuous activities while participation in other activities is only moderately related to age. Physically strenuous activities are also favored by people with higher education while participation in less active pursuits is only moderately related to education. In some cases, participation falls when education rises. Normally, the more income consumers have to spend, the more they are willing and able to buy. For most recreation activities, this is true; but there appear to be exceptions, and for some activities (so-called "inferior goods"), participation falls when income rises. Generally, whites are more likely to participate in recreation activities than blacks or other ethnic groups. However, more nonwhites appear to participate in some types of recreation. Men are more likely than women to participate in most recreation activities, particularly in consumptive and physical strenuous recreation activities. Significantly more women than men engage in the less strenuous recreation activities.

The value of travel time and on-site recreation time represent important determinants of demand for recreation sites, at least for some individuals. The effect of both of these time variables is to shift the demand curve for a recreation site and to change its slope. Those who travel greater distances, and thereby incur higher direct out-of-pocket costs, also have more travel time. If willingness to pay to avoid an hour of travel time is uniform or increasing with distance traveled, those who travel greater distances also have proportionately higher travel time costs. When this is the case, the demand curve will rotate and become more negatively sloped. Thus, the consumer surplus measure of benefits will change when time costs are included in the demand function.

When substitute sites are available, it is likely that they will have a significant influence on demand for a particular recreation site. The effect of substitutes will depend on the extent to which the alternatives are perfect substitutes, the location of the user population relative to the recreation site and substitute sites. If individuals have a wider choice of substitutes, then the demand curve will have a flatter negative slope. On the other hand, if individuals have fewer substitutes, then the demand curve has a steeper negative slope.

In visiting a recreation site, a user acquires a bundle of physical services which constitute the attractiveness of the site or quality of the resource. Each recreation site has a different bundle of physical characteristics, and user demand and willingness to pay is a function of them. When there is a sufficient range of data on quality variables for different days at the same site or among a number of study sites, the effect of the quality variable on demand can be estimated statistically. The regression coefficient indicates the effect of one additional unit of quality on demand, all else held constant. Alternatively, the value of an increment of quality can be estimated directly by asking users their willingness to pay or to participate with hypothetical changes in the quality of the resource.

It was shown that the level of crowding or congestion at a recreation site usually has a significant effect on individual demand and willingness to pay. Congestion occurs when an individual user encounters an increasing number of other users. The effect can be estimated statistically when there is a sufficient range of data for the number of users during different days at the same site or for a number of study sites, and observed congestion levels are what individuals anticipate when making their trip decisions. Alternatively, the effect of congestion can be estimated directly by asking users their willingness to pay or to participate with hypothetical changes in congestion as for any other quality variable.

The chapter concluded with a review of tastes and preferences for recreation. Most empirical demand studies of recreation in the past have not included an effective preference variable. The omission is due to the lack of an accurate general measure, rather than any conscious decision by economists that the variable is unimportant as a determinant of demand. In the past, the federal guidelines have recommended that demand functions for recreation include the important socioeconomic characteristics of the user population as a proxy for preference variables. While income, age, etc., tend to be related to variations in preferences, they are indirect measures. The task remains to integrate direct measures of preferences into demand functions for recreation.

The measures of the determinants of demand reviewed in this chapter were illustrated in an empirical demand function presented in Chapter 6. The reader may wish to look again at that demand function. Also, we shall refer to this material again when we look at elasticities of demand in Chapter 9.

READINGS

Bouwes, Nicolaas W., and Robert Schneider. "Procedures in Estimating Benefits of Water Quality Change." *American Journal of Agricultural Economics* 61(Aug. 1979): 535-39.

Brown, Perry J., and B. L. Driver. "A Social-Psychological Definition of Demand, With Implications for Recreation Resource Planning." *Assessing Demand for Outdoor Recreation.* National Academy of Sciences, Washington, D.C. 1975. 1-88.

Brown, Perry J., Glenn E. Haas, and Michael J. Manfredo. "Identifying Resource Attributes Providing Opportunities for Dispersed Recreation (Indian Peaks)." Department of Recreation Resources, Colorado State University, Fort Collins. 1977.

Brown, Perry J., Jacob E. Hautaluoma, and S. Morton McPhail. "Colorado Deer Hunting Experiences." *Transactions.* 42nd North American Wildlife and Natural Resources Conference. Wildlife Management Institute, Washington, D.C. 1977.

Brown, William G., and Farid Nawas. "Impact of Aggregation on the Estimation of Outdoor Recreation Demand Functions." *American Journal of Agricultural Economics* 55(May 1973):246-49.

Burt, Oscar R., and Durwin Brewer. "Estimation of Net Social Benefits from Outdoor Recreation." *Econometrica* 39(Sept. 1971):813-27.

Caulkins, Peter P., Richard C. Bishop, and Nicolaas Bouwes. "Omitted Cross-Price Variable Biases in the Linear Travel Cost Model: Correcting Common Misperceptions." *Land Economics* 61(May 1985):182-87.

Cesario, Frank J. "Congestion and Valuation of Recreation Benefits." *Land Economics* 56(Aug. 1980):329-38.

Cicchetti, Charles J. "Outdoor Recreation and Congestion in the United States." Population Resources and the Environment, by Ronald G. Ridker (ed.). Volume III, Research Reports, Commission on Population Growth and American Future. Washington, D.C. 1973.

Cicchetti, Charles J., Anthony C. Fisher, and V. Kerry Smith. "Economic Models and Planning Outdoor Recreation." *Operations Research* 21(No. 5, 1973):1104-13.

Cicchetti, Charles J., and V. Kerry Smith. *The Costs of Congestion: An Econometric Analysis of Wilderness Recreation.* Ballinger Publishing Co., Cambridge. 1976.

Clawson, Marion. "Methods of Measuring the Demand for and Value of Outdoor Recreation." Reprint No. 10, Resources for the Future, Washington, D.C. 1959.

Clawson, Marion, and Jack L. Knetsch. *Economics of Outdoor Recreation.* Johns Hopkins University Press, Baltimore, 1966.

Corey, D. C. "Equity-Efficiency Trade-Offs in Natural Resource Management: The Case of Congestion." *Journal of Environmental Systems* 9(No. 4, 1979-80):325-34.

Daubert, John T., and Robert A. Young. "Recreational Demands for Maintaining Instream Flows: A Contingent Valuation Approach." *American Journal of Agricultural Economics* 63(Nov. 1981):667-76.

Driver, B. L., and Perry J. Brown. "A Social-Psychological Definition of Recreation Demand, With Implications for Recreation Resource Planning." *Assessing Demand for Outdoor Recreation.* National Academy of Sciences, Washington, D.C. 1975. 1-88.

Driver, B. L., and D. H. Rosenthal. "Measuring and Improving Effectiveness of Public Outdoor Recreation Programs." George Washington University, Washington, D.C. 1982.

Fisher, Anthony C. "Economic Analysis and the Extinction of Species," in *Integration of Economy and Ecology: An Outlook, for the Eighties.* Ann-Mari Jansson (ed.). Asko Laboratory, University of Stockholm. 1984.

Fisher, Anthony C., and John V. Krutilla. "Determination of Optimal Capacity of Resource-Based Recreation Facilities." *Natural Resource Journal* 12(May 1972):417-44.

Gibson, Betty Blecha. "Estimating Demand Elasticities for Public Goods from Survey Data." *American Economic Review* 70(Dec. 1980):1,069-76.

Gillespie, G. A., and Durward Brewer. "Effects of Nonprice Variables Upon Participation in Water Oriented Outdoor Recreation." *American Journal of Agricultural Economics* 50(Feb. 1968):82-90.

Hanemann, W. Michael. "Entropy as a Measure of Concensus in the Evaluation of Recreation Site Quality." *Journal of Environmental Management* 18(Apr. 1984):241-51.

Hecock, Richard D. "Recreation Behavior Patterns as Related to Site Characteristics of Beaches." *Journal of Leisure Research* 2(No. 4, 1970):237-50.

Hendee, John C., and Robert W. Harris. "Foresters Perception of Wilderness Users Attitudes and Preferences." *Journal of Forestry* 68(No. 12, 1969):759-62.

Hendon, William S. *Evaluating Urban Parks and Recreation.* Praeger Publishers, New York. 1981.

Heritage Conservation and Recreation Service. "Third Nationwide Outdoor Recreation Plan." Four Volumes based on the 1977 National Recreation Survey. U.S. Dept. of the Interior, Gov. Print. Off., Washington, D.C. 1980.

Hotelling, Harold. "The Economics of Public Recreation." *The Prewitt Report.* Land and Recreation Planning Division, National Park Service, U.S. Dept. of the Interior, Washington, D.C. 1949.

King, David A. "Socioeconomic Variables Related to Campsite Use." *Forest Science* 14(No. 1, 1968):45-54.

Knetsch, Jack L. "Displaced Facilities and Benefit Calculations." *Land Economics* 53(Febr. 1977):123-29.

Kurtz, William B., and David A. King. "Evaluating Substitution Relationships Between Recreation Areas." *Tourism Marketing and Management Issues.* Donald E. Hawkins, Elwood L. Shafer, and James M. Rovelstad, (eds.). George Washington University, Washington, D.C. 1980. 391-403.

Leibenstein, Harvey. "Bandwagon, Snob and Veblen Effects in the Theory of Consumer Demand." *Quarterly Journal of Economics* 64(May 1950):183-207.

Leuschner, W. A., and R. L. Young. "Estimating the Southern Pine Beetle's Impact on Reservoir Campsites." *Forest Science* 24(Dec. 1978):527-43.

Loomis, John B., Cindy Sorg, and Dennis Donnelly. "Economic Losses to Recreational Fisheries Due to Small-head Hydro-power Development: A Case Study of the Henry's Fork in Idaho." *Journal of Environmental Management* 22(No. 1, 1986):85-94.

Lucas, Robert C. "Use Patterns and Visitor Characteristics, Attitudes, and Preferences in Nine Wilderness and Other Roadless Areas." Research Paper INT-253, Intermountain Forest and Range Experiment Station, Forest Service, U.S. Dept. of Agriculture, Ogden, Utah. 1980.

Marshall, Thomas L. "Trout Populations, Angler Harvest and Value of Stocked and Unstocked Fisheries of the Cache la Poudre River." Ph.D. Dissertation, Colorado State University, Fort Collins. 1973.

McConnell, Kenneth E. "Congestion and Willingness to Pay: A Study of Beach Use." *Land Economics* 53(May 1977):187-95.

McConnell, Kenneth E., and Ivar Strand. "Measuring the Cost of Time in Recreation Demand Analysis: An Application to Sport-fishing." *American Journal of Agricultural Economics* 63(Febr. 1981):153-56.

McConnell, Kenneth E., and John G. Sutinen. "A Conceptual Analysis of Congested Recreation Sites." Vol. 3, *Advances in Applied Micro-Economics.* V. Kerry Smith and A. D. Witte (eds.). JAI Press, Greenwich, Conn. 1984. 9-36.

McKean, John R., and Roy Allen. "A Note on the Demand for Skilled Leisure." *The American Economist* 20(Fall 1976):76-9.

McMillan, Melville L., Bradford G. Reid, and David W. Gillen. "An Extension of the Hedonic Approach for Estimating the Value of Quiet." *Land Economics* 56(Aug. 1980):315-28.

Michaelson, Edward L. "Economic Impact of Mountain Pine Beetle on Outdoor Recreation." *Southern Journal of Agricultural Economics* 7(Dec. 1975):42-50.

Miller, Ronald J., Anthony A. Prato, and Robert A. Young. "Congestion, Success and the Value of Colorado Deer Hunting Experience." *Transactions.* 42nd North American Wildlife and Natural Resources Conference. Wildlife Management Institute, Washington, D.C.

Morey, Edward R. "The Demand for Site-Specific Recreation Activities: A Characteristics Approach." *Journal of Environmental Economics and Management* 8(Dec. 1981):345-71.

Munley, Vincent G., and V. Kerry Smith. "Learning-by-Doing and Experience: The Case of White Water Recreation." *Land Economics* 52(Nov. 1976):545-53.

Pankey, V. S., and Warren E. Johnston. "Analysis of Recreation Use of Selected Reservoirs in California." in Plan Formulation and Evaluation Studies — Recreation. U.S. Army Corps of Engineers, Sacramento, Calif. 1969.

Ravenscraft, David J., and John F. Dwyer. "Estimating the Influence of Congestion on the Willingness of Users to Pay for Recreation Areas." Forestry Research Report No. 78-5. Agricultural Experiment Station, University of Illinois, Urbana. 1978.

Ravenscraft, David J., and John F. Dwyer. "Reflecting Site Attractiveness in Travel Cost Based Models for Recreation Benefit Estimation." Forest Research Report No. 78-6. Agricultural Experiment Station, University of Illinois, Urbana. 1978.

Smith, K., W. Desvousges, and M. McGivney. "The Opportunity Cost of Travel Time in Recreation Demand Models." *Land Economics* 59(1983):259-78.

Smith, V. Kerry, and John V. Krutilla. *Structure and Properties of a Wilderness Travel Simulator: An Application to the Spanish Peaks Area.* Johns Hopkins University Press, Baltimore. 1976.

Sutherland, Ronald J. "A Regional Approach to Estimating Recreation Benefits of Improved Water Quality." *Journal of Environmental Economics and Management* 9(Sept. 1982):229-47.

Sutherland, Ronald J. "The Sensitivity of Travel Cost Estimates of Recreation Demand to the Functional Form and Definition of Origin Zones." *Western Journal of Agricultural Economics* 7(1982):87-98.

Vaske, Jerry J., Maureen P. Donnelly, and Dan L. Tweed. "Recreationist-Defined Versus Researcher-Defined Similarity Judgments in Substitutability Research." *Journal of Leisure Research* 15(No. 3, 1983):251-62.

Vaux, Henry J., Philip D. Gardner, and Thomas J. Mills. "Methods for Assessing the Impact of Fire on Forest Recreation." Pacific Southwest Range and Forest Experiment Station, General Technical Report PSW-79, Forest Service, U.S. Dept. of Agriculture, Berkeley, Calif. 1984.

Veblen, Thorstein. *The Theory of the Leisure Class: An Economic Study of Institutions.* MacMillan Co., New York. 1899.

Vickerman, R. W. *The Economics of Leisure and Recreation.* MacMillan Press, London. 1975.

Walsh, Richard G., Robert Aukerman, and Robert Milton. "Measuring Benefits and Economic Value of Water In Recreation on High Country Reservoirs." Water Resources Research Institute, Colorado State University, Fort Collins. 1980.

Walsh, Richard G., Ray K. Ericson, Robert A. Young, and John R. McKean. "Recreation Benefits of Water Quality: Rocky Mountain National Park, South Platte River Basin, Colorado." Technical Report No. 12, Colorado Water Resources Research Institute, Fort Collins. 1978.

Walsh, Richard G., and Gordon J. Davitt. "A Demand Function for Length of Stay on Ski Trips to Aspen." *Journal of Travel Research* 22(Spring 1983):23-9.

Walsh, Richard G., and Lynde O. Gilliam. "Benefits of Wilderness Expansion with Excess Demand for Indian Peaks." *Western Journal of Agricultural Economics* 7(July 1982):1-12.

Walsh, Richard G., Ghebre Kelta, John P. Olienyk, and Eliot O. Waples. "Appraised Market Value of Trees on Residential Property with Mountain Pine Beetle and Spruce Budworm Damage in the Colorado Front Range." Report to the U.S. Forest Service by Colorado State University, Fort Collins. 1981.

Walsh, Richard G., Ghebre Keleta, John P. Olienyk, and Eliot O. Waples. "Dollars and Sense About Your Trees." Extension Circular, Colorado State Forest Service, Fort Collins, Colo. 1982.

Walsh, Richard G., Nicole P. Miller, and Lynde O. Gilliam. "Congestion and Willingness to Pay for Expansion of Skiing Capacity." *Land Economics* 59(May 1983):195-210.

Walsh, Richard G., and John P. Olienyk. "Recreation Demand Effects of Mountain Pine Beetle Damage to the Quality of Forest Recreation Resources in the Colorado Front Range." Report to the Forest Service by Department of Economics, Colorado State University, Fort Collins. 1981.

Walsh, Richard G., Olga Radulaski, and Li-Chin Lee. "Value of Hiking and Cross-Country Skiing in Roaded and Nonroaded Areas of a National Forest." Economic Value Analysis of Multiple-Use Forestry. Fred Kaiser, Dennis Schweitzer, and Perry Brown (eds.). International Union of Forestry Research Organizations. Department of Resource Recreation Management, Oregon State University, Corvallis. 1984. 1976-87.

Weithman, A. Stephen, and Mark A. Haas. "Socioeconomic Value of the Trout Fishery in Lake Taneycomo, Missouri." *Transactions of the America Fishery Society* 111(1982):223-30.

West, Patrick C. "A Status Group Dynamics Approach to Predicting Participation Rates in Regional Recreation Demand Studies." *Land Economics* 53(May 1977):196-211.

Wetzstein, Michael E., and John G. McNeeley, Jr. "Specification Errors and Inference in Recreation Demand Models." *American Journal of Agricultural Economics* 62(Nov. 1980):798-800.

White, Terrence H. "The Relative Importance of Education and Income as Predictors in Outdoor Recreation Participation." *Journal of Leisure Research* 7(No. 3, 1975):191-99.

Chapter Eight
Measures of Benefit

This chapter describes how to measure the benefits of recreation activities and resources; shows when each can be used; summarizes the results of recent studies; and discusses implications for recreation economic decisions.

Three methods have been recommended as providing acceptable economic measures of the benefits of recreation activities and resources. Federal guidelines establish uniform procedures for application of the contingent valuation, travel cost, and unit day value methods. The values developed by the three methods are considered to be equivalent to consumer surplus, defined as willingness to pay net of direct travel costs or price paid by individual users.

The *contingent valuation approach* relies on the stated intentions of a cross-section of the affected population to pay for recreation activities or resources contingent on hypothetical changes in their availability depicted in color photos or maps. The values reported represent the maximum willingness to pay rather than forego the recreation opportunity or resource.

The *travel cost approach* to the estimation of the value of recreation has traditionally been preferred by most economists, as it is based on observed market behavior of a cross-section of users in response to direct out-of-pocket and time cost of travel. The basic premise of the approach is that the number of trips to a recreation site will decrease with increases in distance traveled, other things remaining equal.

The *unit day value approach* relies on expert judgment to develop an approximation of the average willingness to pay for recreation activities. An estimate is selected from a range of values approved by the federal guidelines. Initially based on a survey of entrance fees at private recreation areas in 1962, the unit day values recommended by the guidelines have been adjusted for changes in the consumer price index since then.

Empirical research on the economic value of recreation has a relatively short history. Interest was stimulated by the authorization of Senate Document 97 in 1962, which established benefit cost methods to be used in planning water and related resource development by federal agencies. Supplement No. 1 to Senate Document 97 was signed by President Kennedy in 1964, authorizing use of the unit day value method. He also set up the Water Resources Council as an interagency committee to administer the guidelines. Subsequently, the Council revised the guidelines in 1973 under President Nixon to authorize use of the travel cost method. They were revised again in 1979, when use of the contingent valuation method was approved by President Carter. Authorization of the three methods were reaffirmed in a 1983 edition of the guidelines signed by President Reagan. It seems likely that future revisions in the guidelines will occur as improved methods are developed. The bipartisan political support for the guidelines in the past indicates their broad acceptability within and outside of government.

The purpose of this chapter is to describe these three approaches to empirical estimation of the value of recreation. While any one of them may provide a satisfactory measure of the value of a particular recreation site, a problem arises when the results of alternative approaches are compared. Thus far, no standard approach has been developed that is suitable for all purposes of measurement. Thus, it is important to understand when each measure should be used and how to adjust the results of each to compare it with the other measures. Accuracy of the alternative estimating procedures is a continuing problem, although considerable progress has been made in recent applications.

COMPARISON OF ALTERNATIVES

The first step is to decide when each measure should be used. This depends on the problem. There are three basic evaluation problems in recreation, namely, to estimate: (1) the benefits of recreation activities at existing sites of given quality; (2) the benefits of recreation activities with changes in the quantity and quality of the resource; and (3) the public benefits from preservation of resource quality. Table 8-1 summarizes the recommendations of the federal guidelines in 1983.

The travel cost method is the preferred approach for estimating the benefits from recreation activities at existing, new, and expanded sites. Also, it is often an acceptable approach for estimating the recreation benefits from changes in the quality of resources at recreation sites. However, it cannot be used to estimate the benefits to the general population, including users and nonusers, from the preservation of the quality of the resource.

The travel cost method has been successfully applied to intermediate areas located within 100-150 miles from the homes of most users, e.g., state parks and reservoirs. In 1983, the guidelines recommended that the method not be used to estimate the benefits of user-based or resource-based recreation sites. There usually is insufficient variation in travel distances to urban sites to allow statistical estimation of the relationship between distance (or price) and number of trips. Because

Table 8-1. Suitability of Alternative Methods of Measuring the Benefits of Recreation Activities and Resources

Valuation Problems	Contingent Valuation	Travel Cost	Unit Day
Benefits of recreation activities at site of given quality[a]			
User-Oriented Sites	yes	no	yes
Intermediate Sites	yes	yes	yes
Resource-Based Sites	yes	no	yes
Recreation benefits with changes in the quantity and quality of resources	yes	yes	yes
Public benefits from the preservation of resource quality			
Option Value	yes	no	no
Existence Value	yes	no	no

[a]Clawson and Knetsch classify the supply of outdoor recreation resources as: user oriented, intermediate, and resources based. User oriented sites include city and county parks, golf courses, tennis courts, swimming pools, zoos, playgrounds, and the like within 1 hour's travel from home. Intermediate sites include federal reservoirs and state parks which provide hiking, camping, fishing, boating, and hunting while on day outings and weekend trips within 2 hours' drive from home. Resource based sites include national forests, national parks, seashores, and major lakes which provide hiking and mountain climbing, fishing, and hunting while on vacation trips.
Source: U.S. Water Resources Council.

several resource-based recreation sites are usually visited on a single vacation trip, the distance-traveled proxy for price cannot be assigned to a single destination.

The limited applicability of the travel cost approach is a continuing problem in recreation economics. However, recent innovations in studies of resource-based national parks and user-based urban parks indicate that the travel cost method may soon be recommended in a revision of the guidelines as providing acceptable economic measures of the benefits of recreation activities and resources at these sites. Hendon, in a book entitled, *Evaluating Urban Parks and Recreation,* illustrated how the travel cost method could be applied to urban user-based recreation sites. The Corps of Engineers applied the travel cost method to a study of urban user-based sites near Sacramento, California.

Clawson and Knetsch illustrated how the travel cost method could be applied to resource-based sites. They assigned a decreasing proportion of the total distance traveled per trip to visit Yosemite National Park in California. More recently, Haspel and Johnson assigned an equal proportion of the total distance traveled on a single trip to each of several resource-based recreation destinations. They concluded that this procedure provides a reasonably accurate travel cost demand curve. Others have obtained satisfactory results by dividing the total distance traveled by the total number of recreation days per trip and allocating travel costs on the basis of the number of days at each site. In the past, attempts to allocate total travel costs among several resource-based recreation sites visited on a single trip have been somewhat arbitrary; however, they seem reasonably consistent with the behavior of consumers. In future travel cost studies, consumers could be asked to provide their perceived allocation of trip costs among alternative destinations.

The contingent valuation method is the preferred approach for estimating the effect of changes in the quality of resources at recreation sites. It is the only approach that can be used to estimate the value of environmental resources to the general population, including users and nonusers. It is also an acceptable approach for estimating the recreation demand for existing sites and the effects of changes in the availability of recreation opportunities, such as from the development of new and expanded recreation sites. The contingent valuation approach is gaining broad acceptance. It is generally recognized that the method requires careful wording of questions and well-defined hypothetical market situations with which respondents are familiar. Several procedures have been used, and none has emerged as superior in all cases. There is a need for further research to test the effectiveness of alternative willingness to pay questions.

The unit day value method is considered an acceptable approach for estimating the benefits from recreation activities at small sites. The guidelines recommend that its use be limited to general recreation activities at sites with fewer than 750,000 annual visits, where recreation specific costs do not exceed 25 percent of the expected total costs of multiple-purpose projects, and where annual costs to the agency for recreation management are less than $1 million (in 1982 dollars). The U.S. Forest Service has prepared unit day values for regions of the United States and the agency does not restrict their use to small projects. Expert evaluations of the effects of changes in quality of resources are not testable by accepted statistical methods, as are quality effects developed by the other two approaches. Also, in the past the unit day approach could not be used for estimating the public benefits from preservation of resource quality. However, as a number of contingent valuation studies are completed on the public benefits of various types of resource quality, unit day values may be developed in the future for option value and existence value to the general population, including users and nonusers.

Comparing the Results

The objective of each of the three approaches is to estimate consumer surplus of recreation activities. We have defined consumer surplus as the area below a demand curve above price, or the willingness to pay above actual payment. Thus, it is useful to estimate empirical demand curves for recreation sites. Statistical demand curves can be estimated, using both the travel cost and the contingent valuation

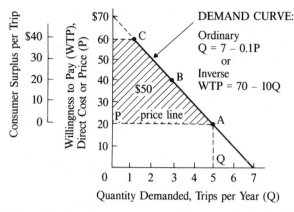

Figure 8-1. Consumer Surplus of Recreation Trips by a Representative Individual

methods. Application of either method can yield an identical demand curve — for example, our individual's demand curve for recreation trips illustrated in Figure 8-1. However, it is important to remember that the dependent variables, and therefore the intercepts, are reversed for the two approaches.

The individual travel cost method results in an ordinary demand curve in which the number of trips demanded (Q) is dependent upon price (P). Assume the equation for an ordinary demand curve is

$$Q = 7 - 0.1P$$

The equation indicates that if P = $60, individuals are willing to pay this amount for a single trip per year. By inserting other values for P, we can trace out the demand curve shown as Figure 8-1. It shows that the average individual will take five trips per year at a price of $20 per trip. Total consumer surplus of each individual is the sum of consumer surplus for all trips per year. For example, Table 8-2 indicates that our representative individual has consumer surplus for each of five trips of $40 + $30 + $20 + $10 + $0 = $100 total consumer surplus. This can also be found by integrating (estimating) the area of the right triangle under the demand curve and above the average direct cost or price shown in Figure 8-1. The area under a linear demand curve at any price is half of the base times the height. For example, from one to five trips per year, 2.5 × $40 = $100 total consumer surplus.

Contingent Valuation Method

The contingent valuation approach can provide an inverse demand curve either directly or indirectly, depending on how the valuation questions are worded. The federal guidelines recommend that questions be worded to obtain the added or marginal values directly. It is

Table 8-2. Total and Marginal Consumer Surplus of Recreation Trips by a Representative Individual

Number of Trips per Year	Total Willingness To Pay (Dollars)		Direct Cost Or Price (Dollars)		Total Consumer Surplus (Dollars)	Marginal Consumer Surplus (Dollars)
0	0		0		0	$ 0
1	$ 60	-	$ 20	=	$ 40	40
2	110	-	40	=	70	30
3	150	-	60	=	90	20
4	180	-	80	=	100	10
5	200	-	100	=	100	0

also an acceptable practice to derive marginal values indirectly from questions worded to obtain total consumer surplus per trip (on the average), or per year. Usually we ask individuals to report their added willingness to pay contingent on a one-unit increase in number of trips to a recreation site or in other variables. In this case, the responses provide a direct estimate of an inverse demand curve in which change in willingness to pay (WTP) is dependent on the change in number of trips (Q). The inverse demand equation for our representative individual's trips is

$$WTP = 70 - 10Q$$

The equation indicates that if $Q = 1$, individuals are willing to pay $60 for a single trip per year. By inserting other values for Q, we can trace out the demand curve shown as Figure 8-1. It shows that the average individual is willing to pay $20 for the fifth trip per year. Total consumer surplus of each individual is the sum of consumer surplus for all trips per year. For example, Table 8-2 indicates that our representative individual has consumer surplus for each of five trips of $40 + $30 + $20 + $10 + $0 = $100 total consumer surplus. This can be estimated by integrating the area of the right triangle under the demand curve and above the average direct cost or price shown in Figure 8-1. The area under a linear demand curve at any price is half of the base times the height. For example, from one to five trips per year, $2.5 \times \$40 = \$100$ total consumer surplus. As you can see, this estimate is identical to the one obtained by using the individual travel cost approach to derive an ordinary demand curve.

Recently, a number of contingent valuation studies have worded the question to obtain maximum willingness to pay per trip (on the average) for the current number of trips per year. In this case, the responses provide an indirect estimate of an inverse demand curve rather than a direct estimate. The responses represent the total willingness to pay per trip rather than the added or marginal willingness to pay for an additional trip. The equation for total willingness to pay per trip is

$$\frac{\text{Total WTP}}{\text{per trip}} = a - bQ$$

where "Q" is the independent variable number of trips, "a" is a constant representing the price at which no trips would be demanded, and "b" the rate of change in willingness to pay with a one unit change in quantity.

Total willingness to pay per year can be derived by multiplying both terms on the right side of the above equation by Q. Annual willingness to pay is

$$\frac{\text{Total WTP}}{\text{per year}} = aQ - bQ^2$$

Finally, the inverse demand curve representing the marginal willingness to pay for added trips can be derived from the total willingness to pay function. The resulting inverse demand equation for our representative individual's trips is

$$WTP = a - 2bQ$$

This can be interpreted in the same way as the inverse demand equation presented in the previous illustration. Assume the value of "a" = $70 and "b" = 5.0 The equation indicates that if Q = 1, individuals are willing to pay $60 for a single trip per year. By inserting other values for Q, we can trace out the demand curve shown as Figure 8-1. Total consumer surplus for each individual is the area of a right triangle under the demand curve and above the average direct cost or price. For example, from one to five trips per year, 2.5 × $40 = $100 total consumer surplus. As you can see, this estimate is identical to the one obtained when we used the question on added values that provided a direct estimate of the inverse demand curve.

The contingent valuation approach also can provide a direct measure of total consumer surplus — one you can calculate by hand. Suppose the question asked is the one proposed by Baumol and Blinder presented in Chapter 5. They suggest that we measure the total benefits of the experience by asking consumers: "What is the largest sum of money you would be willing to pay rather than give up the experience?" Suppose you sum the answers to this question by a random sample of recreation users at a site. You find the average individual is willing to pay a maximum of $200 for five trips per year, and that at this level of use, total direct costs are $100 annually. The consumer surplus of the average individual user of the site is simply the difference between total willingness to pay and total direct cost. Consumer surplus, as you can see, is $200 willingness to pay minus $100 direct cost which equals $100. Total consumer surplus from recreation use of the site is obtained by multiplying total consumer surplus of the average individual in your sample by the total number of users of the site.

Brookshire, Randall, and Stoll recommend direct questions on total consumer surplus to value increments in all of the services provided by natural resources. This is an extension of Bradford's concept of a total benefit function for public goods. The objective of the approach is to measure a total benefit (consumer surplus) function reflecting the representative individual's willingness to pay for increments in recreation activity or resource. An aggregate total benefit function is estimated by the vertical summation of individual values over the relevant population. Its slope represents the marginal rate of substitution between consumer surplus and increments in recreation activity or resource. Economists derive a compensated demand curve by taking the first derivative of total benefits with respect to trips.

Unit Day Value Estimates

To apply the unit day value approach, the expert's approximation of consumer surplus per recreation day is multiplied by the total number of recreation days per year at the study site. This so-called "rectangle" value has been criticized on the grounds that it may over- or understate the demand curve above price (Knetsch). It may be helpful to think of unit day values in the framework of individual demand for recreation. Unit day values are analogous to contingent values where the question is worded to obtain maximum willingness to pay per day (on the average) for the current number of days per year. Assume that unit day values represent total consumer surplus per day, with all else constant. To simplify the example, assume that we can estimate the average number of days per trip so that our unit day value equals $20 per trip for an individual who takes five trips per year to a recreation area. This may be interpreted as point B in Figure 8-1. With this information, it is a relatively simple task to estimate a demand curve for any recreation site from unit day values.

Total consumer surplus of the representative individual user is average consumer surplus of $20 per trip times five trips per year, which equals $100 per year. This is the total area under the demand curve and above the direct cost or price (which is unknown). You will recall the principle that the area of a right triangle is half the base times the height. Thus, to find the height, or price intercept, we divide the area, which is known to be $100, by half the base, which is known to be five trips. Thus, the height of the vertical intercept above the price line is calculated as $100/2.5, which equals $40 for the first trip. This is shown as point C in Figure 8-1. Drawing a line from the horizontal intercept of five trips to the vertical intercept for the first trip of $40 represents a linear demand curve for trips to the recreation area.

The slope of an ordinary demand curve derived from unit day value estimates can be calculated by simply dividing the change in quantity, five trips, by the change in price, $50 (the price at which no trips would be taken). Thus, the slope of the ordinary demand curve is -0.1, which means that a $1 change in price results in a decrease of 0.1 of a trip per year. Thus, the unit day value approach results in an ordinary demand curve in which the number of trips demanded (Q) is dependent upon price (P). The equation of an ordinary demand curve for our representative individual's trips becomes

$$Q = 5 - 0.1P$$

This is identical to the equation for the ordinary demand curve that we derived by the individual travel cost method, except that the horizontal axis now is located where the price line was formerly. This is of no importance in this case. What is important is the summation of consumer surplus below the demand curve and above the price, which remains the same in both cases. Similarly, when we know the total annual use of a recreation site, we can derive an aggregate demand curve for the recreation site from unit day values.

CONTINGENT VALUATION APPROACH

The direct interview (survey) approach can be used to provide acceptable measures of the economic value of recreation opportunities and resources. The federal guidelines authorized use of the contingent valuation method in 1979 and established procedures for its application to recreation problems. In this approach, a sample of the affected population is asked to report their maximum willingness to pay, contingent on hypothetical changes in recreation opportunities or resources. This is the basis for the term "contingent valuation."

Characteristics of the Approach

[Contingent valuation methods use simulated (hypothetical) markets to identify values similar to actual markets, if they existed.] The reliability of the estimates depends, in part, on the care with which the interviewer describes the nature of the hypothetical market; the change in the recreation activities or resources to be valued; the time period for which the valuation applies; the method of hypothetical payment; and the type of value question asked.

First, the institutional rules pertaining to the hypothetical market should be described in sufficient detail so that the respondent knows his or her rights and the rights of all others in the market. These rules should be realistic and credible; they should encourage market behavior with which consumers are familiar; and they should be viewed as just, fair, and ethically sound. Situations that threaten the respondents with a welfare shock that they may view as unfair should be avoided. For an example of a reasonably complete description of the hypothetical market, it may be stated that: "Designating wilderness for protection now would prevent economic development of these areas. Assume that the only way to protect the resource is for all of us is to pay into a special trust fund to be used exclusively for that purpose. Assume that if you do not pay, the resource will not be protected."

Second, the recreation activities or resources to be evaluated should be carefully described as to quantity, quality, time, and location. The description should be realistic and precise enough to give the respondent adequate information on which to base a valuation. To estimate the effect of possible changes in the availability of recreation opportunities and resources, the descriptions may be hypothetical in the sense that they may not precisely describe features of actual activities or resources. Still, they should be plausible, that is, within the realm of possibility. Also, the alternatives should be displayed in color photos, drawings, or maps. These should be selected with care to assure that the relevant attributes of the recreation activities or resources are clearly distinguishable while other possible variations (such as clouds) are held to a minimum.

For example, our study of the value of wilderness in the Rocky Mountains provided respondents with maps depicting four levels of wilderness designation. These included: the 1.2 million acres of wilderness at the time of the study in 1980; the 2.6 million acres proposed (and subsequently designated in 1981); double this amount or 5.0 million acres; and the 10.0 million acres of potential wilderness. These amounts were described as equivalent to about 2, 4, 8, and 15 percent of the surface land area of the state. Their general location and quality was familiar to most residents. Respondents were asked to assume that potential wilderness areas would be similar in quality to existing wilderness and would be designated for protection at the time of payment.

Third, respondents usually should be asked their willingness to pay for an increase (or increment) in a recreation opportunity or resource. It is the theoretically correct measure (Brookshire, Randall, and Stoll) and is preferred over asking respondents their willingness to pay to avoid a threatened decrease (or decrement) in a recreation opportunity or resource. It offers respondents the chance to value something they desire, and thus it is unlikely to provoke an offended reaction. On the other hand, asking respondents how much they would pay to avoid a change they do not want may seem unfair or morally offensive to some, and thus may result in unreliable values.

204

For example, a study of the annual value of two new parks found that the theoretically correct incremental value ($9) was less than half of the value reported ($24) when the question made no reference to existing parks. Majid, et al. interviewed a random sample of 140 households, divided into two groups of 70 households each, in Armidale, Australia (pop. 25,000). The problem was to estimate willingness to pay for recreation use and public preservation (option and existence) values for the addition of two parks to a nine-park system with 150,000 visitor days per year, mostly local day-users with moderate tourist use. No user fees were charged for recreation use of existing or new parks, and congestion was seldom a problem.

Fourth, contingent valuation studies generally obtain measures of individual or household willingness to pay annually or per year. Thus, respondents usually should be informed that what is being valued is the right to have or to use the recreation resource for one year. In some cases, however, it may be more realistic for respondents to value changes in the availability of recreation opportunities per day or per trip (when of uniform duration), given the continued availability of existing sites. Where willingness to pay per day or per trip is more appropriate, it can be used so long as information is available on the total number of recreation days or trips, to permit the calculation of annual values. Also, estimates of recreation use may be collected as part of a contingent valuation survey. To do so, the question should include how many trips were taken in the past 12 months, how many days were spent per trip to existing recreation sites similar to the proposed site, and how many household members participated in each trip. This question should be followed with one asking for the same use information if the proposed increment in recreation opportunity or resource were made available. The difference between number of trips with and without the proposed additional recreation opportunity or resource is the use attributed to it.

Fifth, a method of payment (called payment vehicle) should be selected that is most likely to provide correct evaluations by respondents. A number of alternative methods have been used in past studies. These include: payments into special trust funds, taxes (sales, property, or income), utility bills (water-sewer or electricity), entrance permits, hunting and fishing licenses, direct trip costs, general prices of goods and services purchased, and miles traveled. The federal guidelines suggest that several methods of payment should be tried in the pretest, including a neutral method, e.g., "The money collected will be placed in a trust fund and devoted entirely to providing the recreation opportunity or resource." Table 8-3 presents sample questions from a study of the willingness to pay for the protection of wilderness using the trust fund as method of payment.

Table 8-3. Contingent Valuation Questions About Willingness to Pay for the Preservation of Wilderness

Please keep in mind the next several questions are a hypothetical experiment intended to provide an economic measure of how strongly you value the protection of Wilderness Areas in Colorado.

A. Assume that the only way to protect Wilderness Areas is for all Colorado households to pay into a special fund to be used exclusively for that purpose. What is the maximum amount of money you would pay annually to protect Wilderness Areas? Answer all four parts.

    (1) Current Wilderness Areas (Map 1), 2% of Colorado, 1.2 million acres $_____

    (2) Proposed Wilderness Areas (Map 2), 4% of Colorado, 2.6 million acres $_____

    (3) Double the Proposed Wilderness Areas (Map 3), 8% of Colorado, 5 million acres $_____

    (4) All Potential Wilderness Areas (Map 4), 15% of Colorado, 10 million acres $_____

B. People value the protection of Wilderness Areas for several purposes. What proportion (percent of 100) of the highest dollar value you reported would you assign to each of the following purposes? Read the entire question first, then answer each of four parts; together, they should total 100 percent.

    (1) Payment to actually visit existing or potential Wilderness Areas each year. _____%

    (2) In addition to your recreation use value, how much of an "insurance premium" would you pay each year to guarantee your choice of recreation use in the future? _____%

    (3) Payment to preserve Wilderness Areas for reasons other than your own personal use:

        (a) The value to you from knowing there exists a natural habitat for plants, fish, wildlife, etc. _____%

        (b) The value to you from knowing that future generations will have Wilderness Areas. _____%

Source: Adapted from Walsh, Gillman, and Loomis.

The federal guidelines suggest that methods of payment such as taxes, utility bills, and hunting or fishing license fees usually should be avoided because they may result in an emotional reaction against the method of payment. Apparently, the subjective value of a dollar depends on what it is spent for. From the individual's perspective, a dollar spent on utility bills, entrance fees, or taxes may be valued differently than a dollar spent for direct trip costs or for the purchase of goods and services in general. Still, each method of payment may be used when it is the most realistic and provides reasonably correct evaluations by respondents in particular situations.

Davis, who originated the contingent valuation approach (then called "bidding game") more than two decades ago, initially used an entrance fee but abandoned it after a pretest showed that willingness to pay direct trip expenses proved more realistic and acceptable to households engaged in fishing, hunting, and camping in the Maine woods. Apparently, people would be unwilling to pay entrance permits equal to their consumer surplus. Concepts of "reasonable" and "proper" which may apply to entrance permits, taxes, and utility bills are diffused when applied to transportation, lodging, added food, and miscellaneous trip expenses. Direct trip costs also have been used successfully in studies of hiking, backpacking and other recreation activities. Table 8-4 presents sample questions from a study of the benefits of wilderness recreation, using direct trip costs as the method of payment.

Entrance permits have been used with apparent success to estimate changes in willingness to pay, even though they appear to be deficient in estimating total willingness to pay for the recreation experience. Examples include studies of the effect of instream flow of water (Daubert and Young), natural forest scenery (Thayer), congestion in downhill skiing (Walsh, Miller, and Gilliam), and propagation of such endangered wildlife species as grizzly bear and mountain sheep (Brookshire, Eubanks, and Randall).

The first study of the contingent value of environmental quality (Randall, Ives, and Eastman) found that households in New Mexico were willing to pay only about one-fourth as much for air quality (visibility) when the method of payment used was electric utility bills as compared to sales tax ($23 vs. $85 per year). A similar study also reported that households in Colorado (Greenley, Walsh, and Young) were willing to pay only about one-fourth as much for water quality when the method of payment used was a sewer water bill compared to a sales tax ($26 vs. $91 per year). Differences in the starting point in iterative estimating procedure used for both methods of payment accounted for less than one-third of the difference between the two.

Sixth, some respondents are likely to report that they are not willing to pay for a proposed change in recreation opportunity or resource. Thus, it is important to identify which of these represent true zero

Table 8-4. Contingent Valuation Questions About the Recreation Use of Wilderness

1.	Approximately how many trips did you take to visit wilderness areas during the past 12 months?
2.	On your last trip to a wilderness area, how many days were you away from home?
3.	How many days were you in a wilderness area?
4.	Please estimate what this trip cost in total, including transportation, food, accommodations, and miscellaneous expenses. $_____
5.	How many people in your party shared these costs?
6.	How much did you value this trip? Was it worth more than you actually spent?
7.	About how much was this trip worth? Assume that your trip became more expensive due perhaps to increased travel costs. What is the maximum you would have paid for this trip rather than do without? $_____

Source: Walsh, Gillman, and Loomis.

valuations and which, if any, represent a protest against the hypothetical market or method of payment. Questions should always be included in contingent valuation studies that ask, "Did you answer zero because (check one):

a. You do not receive any benefits from the recreation opportunity or resource and therefore see no reason to pay?
b. Your cost of living is already too high or you cannot afford it (i.e., income constraint)?
c. You believe the method of payment (tax, utility bill, etc.) is already too high?
d. You have a right to the recreation opportunity or resource, and it is unfair to expect you (as a utility customer, a fishing license holder, etc.) to pay for it."

Answers to (c) and (d) above should be recorded as protesting against the method of payment or hypothetical market and omitted from the calculation of average willingness to pay for the sample of respondents. The federal guidelines recommend that surveys with more than 15 percent protest response should not be used in decision-making because a high incidence of protest may indicate that other values are also distorted. Most contingent valuation studies have recorded protests that fall within this 15 percent limit.

Seventh, the question asked should be of a type that suggests the pragmatic "take it, or leave it" atmosphere of the marketplace. The wording, "Would you be willing to pay . . .?" should be avoided because some respondents may interpret it as an appeal for voluntary contributions, and the reported value would understate total willingness to pay. Respondents should be asked, "Would you pay a maximum of . . .?" with the clear understanding that, "if not, you would go without" the recreation activity or resource.

Finally, an iterative bidding technique is recommended by the guidelines to encourage respondents to report maximum values, representing the point of indifference between having the amount of money (income) stated vs. the recreation opportunity or resource. Following a description of the market and the recreation opportunity or resource to be valued, the respondent is asked to react to a series of dollar values posed by the interviewer. Respondents answer "yes" or "no" to whether they are willing to pay the stated amount of money to obtain the increment in recreation opportunity or resource. The interviewer increases or decreases the dollar value until the highest amount the respondent is willing to pay is identified.

The starting price (called "starting point") of the iterative process should be varied from one respondent to another on a random basis, to reduce the possibility that it may influence individual values. Early increases (or decreases) in the dollar value may be large (e.g., double the initial starting price) until the interviewer senses that the value is approaching the respondent's point of indifference; final changes in price should become smaller (e.g., $1 increments). This will avoid the possibility that respondents will get tired of answering "yes" or "no" to an excessive number of small price changes and end the process before their total willingness to pay is reached.

Iterative bidding questions are most effective in personal interviews, although they also have been used in mail surveys. In this case, respondents are asked to answer "yes" or "no" to a small number of increases in value and, finally, are asked an open-ended question: "Now, write down the maximum amount you would pay." At the present time, mail survey applications of iterative bidding questions have not been adequately tested and are not recommended. Noniterative questions are recommended for use in mail surveys.

Mail survey questions are usually noniterative. They may be either open-ended, asking respondents to write down the maximum amount they would pay, or to select their maximum willingness to pay from a list of alternative values shown. A list of average household expenditures for other goods and services may be provided to assist respondents in the process of assigning a dollar value to the particular recreation activity or resource being studied. Table 8-5 illustrates the use of a chart showing what a typical household spent in 1980 for various goods and services. Close-ended questions are increasingly used, asking respondents to answer "yes" or "no" to whether they would pay a single stated value. While close-ended questions do not provide a direct estimate of maximum willingness to pay, data on the proportion of the sample answering "yes" or "no" to each of a range of dollar values can be used to estimate a value function or demand function from which net benefits can be derived (Bishop and Heberlein).

In 1979 and 1983, the federal guidelines suggested that noniterative questions be used only for analysis of the value of small projects because noniterative questions may not be as reliable as iterative. More recently, studies have used iterative questions in personal interviews with half the sample and noniterative questions with the other half. The values obtained have been analyzed to determine if the two ap-

Table 8-5. Annual Expenditures for Goods and Services, and Taxes Paid for Public Programs by a Typical Household, United States, 1980

$25 Toothpaste	$450 Health (Public)
$75 Space Program	$500 Doctor, Dentist, Health Insurance
$100 Newspapers, Magazines	$750 Food Eaten Away From Home
$125 Pet Food	$1,100 Education
$250 Police and Fire	$2,000 National Defense
$300 Water Pollution Controls	$2,800 Transportation
$350 Highways	$3,500 Grocery Items
$400 Interest on Credit Purchases	$4,500 Housing

Source: Adapted from Mitchell and Carson; Randall, Hoehn, and Tolley.

proaches significantly influence the results. Several studies have shown that open-ended direct questions (noniterative) yield noticeably lower values, even though with small samples, they often are not statistically different at the .05 level of significance. While these tests are not conclusive, it appears that future studies using noniterative questions may provide somewhat lower more conservative estimates than the iterative approach.

Survey Design

The population to be sampled should be people in the market area who would be affected by the change in recreation opportunity or resource. If the market area is expected to exceed 120 miles, documentation of the reasons is required. Usually the basic sampling unit is the household, although individual participants, such as hunters and anglers, may be interviewed when appropriate. Samples of individuals or household groups may be drawn randomly from the population of on-site users, i.e., as they depart from a park or other recreation area, to avoid length of stay bias discussed by Lucas. Samples may be drawn from reliable lists of participants, such as hunting and fishing license holders, if available. Samples also may be drawn from the regional population of households, as listed in phone directories. Randomized cluster sampling is permissible to save travel time between interviews, provided that no cluster is larger than one-thirtieth of the sample size. Sample size should be no less than 200 households or individuals. The respondent selected to answer on behalf of the household should preferably be the head-of-household or spouse of the head. Another adult member of the household may be interviewed, provided he or she is sufficiently informed about household values.

Contingent valuation questionnaires must contain at least two sections, one for valuing the recreation opportunity or resource and the other for collecting appropriate demographic data on income, age, etc. Other useful data may be gathered, including recreation activities, attitudes, and preferences. The complete interview usually should not require more than 30 minutes in order to minimize inconvenience and fatigue of the respondent.

The questionnaire should be pretested, using a sample of at least 30 respondents, in order to permit appropriate statistical tests. The sample selected for pretest need not be drawn from the same population as the subsequent study. Sampling procedures for the pretest are not especially crucial, but an attempt should be made to obtain a cross section of users with respect to demographic characteristics. The purpose of the pretest is to check whether the questions are worded correctly. The number of nonresponses and protest zero responses should be tabulated; if they are equal to more than 15 percent of the sample, the questions should be redesigned and retested.

It is especially important that statistical tests be made of possible bias that may arise from the hypothetical information provided, the method of payment used, the starting points for the iterative process (Thayer), and over- or under-reporting of true values (called "strategic behavior"). When tests indicate the presence of any of these problems, the pretest questions should be redesigned and retested. Also, the final results of the sample survey should be tested later for the same types of bias, and any that remains should be reported along with the findings of the study. Users of contingent valuation techniques should appreciate the importance of testing for possible bias. The particular statistical tests are straightforward, and if bias is detected, there are methods for coping with the problem. Descriptions of some methods can be found in two reports (Schulze, d'Arge, and Brookshire; and Thayer) that review six contingent value studies and conclude that bias is not likely to be a major problem in carefully designed studies.

— The particular statistical tests for these possible biases (more properly, influences) include the following:

(1) Hypothetical: To test whether individuals respond as they would to an actual market situation, compare the results to other methods based on actual human behavior such as the travel cost or hedonic methods. Unfortunately, this test is limited to the use value of recreation activities and environmental resources. There are no behavior-based methods of estimating option, existence, or bequest values. In these applications, hypothetical bias is reduced if the contingent situation is realistic.

(2) Information: To show the effects of the type and amount of information available to individuals, provide each of three pretest subsamples with low, medium, and high levels of information, and then test for statistical difference in mean values. The influence of information can be minimized by ensuring that all respondents in the final survey have access to the same relevant information.

(3) Vehicle: To determine the effects of the payment vehicle, use three of the most likely payment vehicles with three pretest subsamples and then test for statistical difference in mean values. Also question pretest respondents about the acceptability of each. The influence of the payment vehicle is reduced if it seems appropriate to respondents.

(4) Starting point: The federal guidelines suggest that we vary the starting point randomly among respondents. Then starting point should be included as an independent variable in the statistical value function to adjust for any significant effect. The influence of starting point can be reduced by providing information on each respondent's actual payment for the environmental resource or recreation activity.

(5) Protest bidding: The federal guidelines suggest that we include a question asking respondents their reasons for answering zero to the value questions. Then, we should remove those who object to the hypothetical market or payment vehicle, not to exceed 15 percent of the sample. This was discussed previously.

(6) Strategic behavior: To obtain an indication of whether some respondents try to influence the outcome of the study, prepare a frequency distribution of dollar values, to test for the possibility of bimodal clustering of very high or very low values. Also, Randall suggests that we remove any very high outlying bids to obtain a solid core of estimates. Possible incentives for strategic behavior may be reduced in the case of university research for scientific rather than policy purposes.

(7) Incremental values: To test for the effect of the order in which several value questions are asked, start with the most important attributes of environmental resources or recreation activities for half of the sample and reverse the order for the other half. Then test for statistical differences in mean values. In addition, Randall suggests that we provide respondents the opportunity to go back and correct any prior values. Bohm considers the midpoint of the range in values reported to be the most acceptable. Of course, when the order in which environmental improvement programs will be implemented is known, then that would determine the proper order of the value questions, and no adjustment is needed.

(8) Interviewer: To test for possible influence of the interviewer on the values reported, identify them as categorical variables in the value function and test for possible statistical effect. The regression coefficient for each interviewer indicates the amount of adjustment in the values. Interviewer bias can be reduced by careful training and supervision or by using professional interviewers.

(9) Sampling and nonresponse: Several tests are recommended to determine the possible influence of the sampling procedure and the nonresponse of some individuals. They will be discussed below.

When a mail survey is used for a contingent valuation study, the guidelines developed by Dillman should be followed insofar as possible. Random sampling methods should be used, and at least two follow up mailings are necessary to reduce nonresponse. In addition, the federal guidelines recommend that after the second followup mailing, a random sample of 10 percent of the nonrespondents be contacted by phone. Responses to the telephone survey should be analyzed separately in order to test whether they are significantly different from the responses to the mail survey. An alternative test is possible in the case of state and national household surveys. Socioeconomic (demographic) information on the general population is available from the U.S. Census and can be compared to the socioeconomic characteris-

212

tics of responses to the mail survey. The regression coefficients for socioeconomic variables included in the value function can be used to adjust sample values to represent the intended population.

Dillman recommends four mailings rather than the three recommended by the federal guidelines. He has obtained response rates of 70-75 percent in statewide surveys by following the original mailing with a postcard reminder, a second letter and replacement questionnaire, and a final certified letter with replacement questionnaire. Many surveys omit the final certified mailing recommended by Dillman because of time and budget constraints. Moreover, a fourth certified mailing may irritate persons who prefer not to participate and consider repeated requests an intrusion on their privacy. Also, a study by Wellman et al. concludes that in mail surveys of recreation attitudes and behavior, repeated follow-ups are not justified, because differences between early and late responses are negligible. Thus, a response rate of 25-50 percent may represent the population as well as a response rate of 75-100 percent.

Dillman recommends that mail questionnaires be designed and pretested for clarity and ease of answering. They should be printed on good quality paper, photo-reproduced, visually uncluttered, and bound in booklet form. Letters should be typed individually and addressed to the individual by name. They should be individually signed by the project leader. In addition, the cover letter should be designed to motivate respondents by explaining the usefulness of the research and the importance of participation in the study. Interest may be stimulated by newspaper articles about the nature of the study. The reader is referred to the guidebook by Dillman for other helpful suggestions in designing mail surveys.

Telephone interviewing procedures also are described in the guidebook by Dillman. With improved telephone and computer equipment, the method is likely to become widely used for contingent valuation studies. A study of fish and wildlife values in Idaho successfully combined a mail survey with telephone interviews (Loomis et al.). A description of the legitimate scientific purpose of the study and the questions were mailed to a random sample of anglers and hunters. They were asked to identify where they fished and hunted on maps and to prepare additional information that would be collected by phone at a later date. The advantage of combining the two methods is that maps and other information can be supplied by mail. Then any problems can be clarified by telephone interviews. Answers can be typed directly into a console during the telephone interview. Also, the urgency of a phone call encourages more people to participate in the survey.

Accuracy of the Approach

Some economists share Freeman's reservations about the contingent valuation approach, primarily because of the potential for strategic behavior by respondents. If individuals believe that their answers might affect public decisions, they may respond in ways to maximize the likelihood of a preferred policy. Individuals may overstate true willingness to pay in order to gain a desired change or they may understate values in order to prevent a change they oppose. In addition, Samuelson has warned that ". . . it is in the selfish interest of each person to give false signals, to pretend to have less interest . . ." when they suspect that they may actually have to pay the amount they reveal as their willingness to pay. However, respondents usually are asked to reveal their willingness to pay in what is clearly a hypothetical situation. Respondents know that these studies are sponsored by universities for scientific purposes; thus they can infer that responses may have no direct effect on their payment obligation.

In addition, willingness to pay questions can specify that all households using a resource will pay, to reduce the "free rider" problem in which respondents may misrepresent values, expecting a third party to provide the service at no cost to themselves. Moreover, there is a relatively simple test of the possibility of biased responses. If respondents as groups bias their willingness to pay responses, a frequency distribution will show bimodal clustering of values at abnormally high and low levels. If this test does not indicate abnormal behavior, it suggests that there is little or no strategic bias of the results. Brookshire, Ives and Schulze applied a similar test and found no evidence of bias by recreation users of the Glen Canyon National Recreation Area. Rowe and Chestnut suggest, however, that without knowledge of the true underlying distribution of values, visual inspection for normal distribution does not constitute a completely satisfactory test of strategic behavior. Still, Schulze, d'Arge, and Brookshire reviewed six contingent valuation studies and tentatively concluded that "strategic bias in revealing consumer preferences is not likely to be a major problem."

It is notable that objections to the contingent valuation approach have been primarily theoretical, as empirical evidence of systematic bias is at best inconclusive. Davis, who pioneered the method in a study of the recreation benefits of the Maine woods, concluded that the reported values were not significantly different from those obtained by the market-related travel cost approach. More recently, other studies have shown similar results, for example, a study by Haspel and Johnson of recreation trips to Bryce Canyon National Park. Randall and associates developed refinements in the contingent valuation technique and present a persuasive case for its effectiveness in the valuation of environmental quality. They studied the benefits from improved air quality and other related visual amenities in the Four Corners area of New Mexico and the Glen Canyon National Recreation Area. They found no measurable strategic behavior by environmentalists compared to other respondents. Replication of the studies resulted in similar values. Replication in Canada of the Hammack and Brown study of waterfowl hunting in the western flyway of the United States also resulted in consistent values (Cocheba and Lanford). Bohm conducted a controlled experiment comparing five alternative measures of willingness to pay for a closed circuit public TV program, including actual payment in cash of the stated willingness to pay. He found no significant difference in values reported by five groups, each presented with an alternative willingness to pay question. Bohm concluded that the theoretical objections to the contingent valuation approach could be resolved by application of an interval method. Two questions would be asked with incentives to understate and overstate willingness to pay. The midpoint of the interval would represent the most acceptable value.

The federal guidelines recommend the willingness to pay measure of value over the alternative, willingness to sell or to accept compensation for reduced recreation opportunities and resources. The appropriate question depends on property rights and the resource decision to be made. Congress has determined that recreation areas are not for sale (although this may be changed in the future). Thus, the question of what level of compensation would be required to allow the user public to remain no worse off than before the sale of recreation areas is of only peripheral interest. A number of studies, including Bishop and Heberlein, have found that willingness to sell values including actual cash sales are considerably higher than willingness to pay, whether the latter is measured by the contingent valuation or the travel cost approach. This is the expected result, as willingness to pay would be constrained by limited household income and time budgets as well as other variables, as Gordon and Knetsch point out. More realistic estimates of values are expected under these constraints which are present when asking willingness to pay questions. The acceptance of compensation would increase the respondent's level of income and result in value estimates that are unrestrained by the utility of dollars normally earned as income.

Many of the initial questions about the validity of the contingent valuation approach are expected to be resolved with subsequent tests and improvements in research procedures. For example, Bishop and Heberlein challenged the approach when they tentatively concluded that the willingness to pay measure of the value of goose hunting permits underestimated by as much as 60 percent the acceptance of actual cash compensation to forego hunting. This would be a substantial underestimate, if true. The study along with others (notably Knetsch)

215

with similar findings stimulated a number of efforts to test these results. Especially interesting are two studies of deer hunting permits in the Sandhills of Wisconsin by the same authors (Heberlein and Bishop). In the first, they found significant differences between values involving actual cash payment and willingness to pay, similar to their earlier goose hunting permit study. However, in their second replication, more advanced research procedures resulted in no significant difference between values involving actual cash payment and willingness to pay. They concluded that the contingent valuation method may overestimate compensation demanded but provides relatively accurate measures of willingness to pay.

Other studies support these conclusions. Coursey, Hovis, and Schulze applied the Smith auction process to groups of students who reported the value of tasting sucrose oca-acetate, a bitter but harmless liquid. The Smith auction is a learning experience in which values are re-estimated a number of times. Individuals who may initially exaggerate their values, modify them incrementally, until a large majority (70 percent) reveal their true demand in laboratory settings. This means that the initial high estimates of willingness to accept compensation decline, and after several re-estimates are not significantly different from the initially lower willingness to pay.

In a related study, Brookshire and Coursey applied the Smith auction process in a study of the value of trees at a proposed neighborhood park serving a 1-square mile residential area of a western city with a population of about 100,000. They asked several groups of up to 9 residents their willingness to pay for additional trees and willingness to accept compensation for fewer trees. After individuals reported their initial values, they were told the average values of the group and their proportional share of total value. Final values were recorded when individuals agreed to average group values that were equal to or more than the cost of providing the trees. When agreement was reached, individuals received the public good and paid their share of its cost. Comparing the values after three interations of the Smith auction process, the authors concluded they could not reject the hypothesis that willingness to accept compensation for the loss of trees is a continuous function of the willingness to pay for more trees. This supports the continued use of willingness to pay questions in contingent valuation studies. Apparently, willingness to pay would not be significantly different from willingness to accept compensation in public good auctions.

The contingent valuation method has performed reasonably well when compared to the available empirical evidence from travel behavior, actual cash transactions, and controlled laboratory experiments. The question of accuracy is related to the nature of the problem of management to which the research is addressed. It seems unlikely that many decisions of wildlife managers will be changed significantly if the value of deer hunting is $30 or $40 per day. Methods are available to achieve levels of accuracy that are reasonable and consistent with levels obtained in other areas of economics and in other disciplines. Readers interested in a detailed discussion of the issue are referred to the book edited by Cummings, Brookshire, and Coursey. The authors caution us to remember that the contingent valuation method, like any other approach, cannot be applied blindly. It is important to check whether the assumptions underlying the approach are at least approximately correct, and to be aware of the problems that may arise in applications to recreation economic decisions. Although the assumptions underlying contingent valuation method are unlikely to be met completely, they are close enough in a sufficiently large number of cases that contingent valuation is a powerful technique.

TRAVEL COST APPROACH

The demand for recreation sites and resources is usually measured by the travel cost method. The procedure involves two steps: (1) estimating an individual or per capita demand curve; and (2) deriving the site or resource demand curve from it. The basic premise of the approach is that the number of trips to a recreation site will decrease as the direct out-of-pocket and time costs of travel increase, other things remaining equal. By calculating (integrating) the area for the demand curve, site or resource, the travel cost approach provides an indirect measure of consumer surplus benefits.

Individual and Per Capita Methods

The use of individual observations in the first step of the travel cost approach was illustrated in Chapters 5 and 6. The distinguishing feature of this approach is that the dependent variable in the demand function is the number of trips per year by individual users of a recreation site. This is an acceptable approach whenever most individuals take more than one trip per year and the objective is to estimate demand by the current population of participants. Individuals typically take several trips to recreation sites located within 100-150 miles from where they live. However, most individuals take a single trip per year on vacation to national parks or to hunt big game such as deer and elk. In these cases, the dependent variable does not exhibit sufficient variation to estimate a statistical demand function based on individual observations. When individuals take at most one trip per year, the dependent variable must be either the probability of participation or rate of participation per capita.

trip/Q neg. dist

The first stage of the travel cost method develops a statistical estimate of the relationship between distance or cost of travel and trips per individual or per 1,000 population in concentric zones or counties. Recreation use is usually defined as the number of trips to the recreation site in the past 12 months. The proxy for the independent variable, price, is usually the sum of direct out-of-pocket and time costs per trip. Travel costs per vehicle are divided by the number of persons per party. Other independent variables that should be included in the multiple regression are: socioeconomic characteristics, quality of the resource, congestion, and alternative recreation opportunities. These variables are the minimum necessary to estimate a correct individual or per capita demand curve.

In the second stage of the travel cost method, the statistical coefficients from the first stage are used to calculate each individual's or zonal population's demand for trips to the study site with increments in prices starting from the current price of each individual or zone and continuing until the estimated number of trips falls to zero. The observed number of trips by all individuals or from all distance zones represents the quantity demanded at current travel costs. Summed, this becomes one point on the demand curve for the site or resource, i.e., the number of trips with no price increase. The remainder of the demand curve for the site is estimated by calculating the number of trips by all individuals or zonal populations at each of several incremental prices. The area under the site demand curve plus any entrance fees measures the recreation use value attributed to the site or resource.

The per capita approach is more versatile than the individual approach. It can accommodate situations where participants take either one or several trips per year. In addition, the per capita approach introduces the effects of population, which is an important determinant of demand for recreation activities and resources. If some nonusers would become participants if prices fell, the quality of the resource improved, or for some other reason, then the use of data on the observed behavior of individuals to estimate demand provides only part of the necessary information. Only historical participants are counted, and those who have not participated historically have no opportunity to communicate their preferences. This means that the demand for the recreation use of a site is the product of two types of demand: (1) the number of trips per participant, and (2) the proportion of the population participating, or

$$\frac{\text{Quantity}}{\text{demanded}} = \frac{\text{Number of trips}}{\text{Number of participants}} \times \frac{\text{Number of participants}}{\text{Population}}$$

This states that demand for a site is a product of the number of trips per individual participant (discussed in Chapters 5, 6 and 7) times the

218

number of participants per capita. The zonal travel cost approach has a unique advantage in that it combines these two types of demand into a single concept. Note that the number of participants appears in both terms and thus cancels out. The single concept in the zonal travel cost method becomes trips per capita

$$\text{Quantity demanded} = \frac{\text{Number of trips}}{\text{Population}}$$

There are two basic types of per capita use or demand functions: the single-site and the multiple-site or regional. Both approaches develop statistical demand functions that relate trips per capita or per 1,000 population in origin zones to distance traveled, socioeconomic variables, characteristics of the site, congestion, and alternative recreation opportunities. The only difference between them is that the regional approach is based on data for all the similar recreation sites in the study area, rather than for a single site. The multiple-site method is preferred in the federal guidelines because it economizes on resources required for site-specific studies. The multiple-site methods also are more effective in measuring the effects of variation in resource quality and opportunities to substitute alternative sites (Sutherland). The federal government periodically publishes multiple-site studies for specific recreation activities and types of recreation resources in various regions of the United States. If regional studies are not available, per capita demand curves can be estimated readily from a site-specific study.

Illustration of the Zonal Method

The essentials of the zonal travel cost approach can be illustrated by using a simple hypothetical example involving recreation trips to a site from each of three zones of varying populations and distances from the site entrance.

Frequently the only information available is that provided by entrance station reports on the number of vehicles entering a park carrying license plates indicating the counties where visitors live. From the U.S. Census, we can identify the current population of each of these counties. Combining these two pieces of information provides our quantity variable, i.e., the number of visits or trips per capita or per 1,000 persons living in the counties of origin. The reason we divide number of visits from each zone by population is to obtain a visit rate that puts the number of visits from each zone on a comparable basis.

The federal guidelines recommend distance traveled as an acceptable proxy for the independent variable, direct cost or price per trip to the recreation site. This is particularly important because we can estimate the number of miles from the population center of each county

Table 8-6. Per Capita Demand for Visits to a Recreation Site

Origin Zone	Population	Distance, One-way Miles	Total Trips per Year	Trips per Capita
A	100,000	50	30,000	0.3
B	10,000	100	2,000	0.2
C	30,000	150	3,000	0.1
Total			35,000	

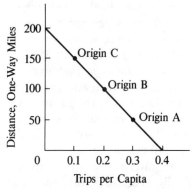

Figure 8-2. Trips per Capita from Distance Zones to a Recreation Site

to the recreation site from road maps which are readily available. Later, we will convert one-way distance traveled to round-trip miles, multiply this by travel and time cost per mile, and divide by the average number of persons per vehicle. For now, it is convenient to use one-way distance traveled.

Suppose that we know the number of trips per year taken by visitors to a recreation site from counties in three zones of origin with population centers located 50, 100, and 150 miles from the site entrance. Dividing the number of trips in each zone by its population tells us the visit rate, i.e., the number of trips per capita shown as the last column in Table 8-6. These visit rates for each zone are related to distance in Figure 8-2. The table shows a demand curve for trips per capita to the recreation site.

The next step is to calculate total use for increments in distance as illustrated in Table 8-7. The estimate of 35,000 trips from Table 8-6 represents the initial point of the demand curve for the recreation site or resource with zero increase in distance. To find sufficient points to determine the entire demand curve, it is necessary to make several increases in distance and measure the number of trips that would be demanded, given these changes. This is equivalent to moving the recreation site farther and farther away from the potential users, thus requiring them to pay more and more in travel costs. We have used increments of 50, 100, and 150 miles in Table 8-7 to keep the illustration

220

Table 8-7. Estimated Number of Trips with Increases in Distance from the Recreation Site

| Origin Zone | Estimated Number of Trips with Simulated Increases in Miles from the Site | | | |
	None (1)	50 Miles (2)	100 Miles (3)	150 Miles (4)
A	30,000	20,000	10,000	0
B	2,000	1,000	0	0
C	3,000	0	0	0
Total	35,000	21,000	10,000	0

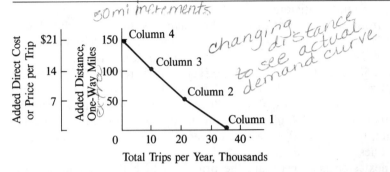

Figure 8-3. Aggregate Demand Curve for the Recreation Site or Resource

simple, although 10-mile increments are recommended by the Water Resources Council in actual applications of the method.

First, an added distance of 50 miles is assumed for each trip to the site from each zone of origin. The travel distance from the closest zone, A, was originally 50 miles, and an added 50 miles would make a total of 100 miles. The visit rate (trips per capita) from zone A, given this added 50 miles, can be read from Table 8-6, in this case 0.2 of a trip per capita, down from the original 0.3 of a trip per capita. Thus, 0.2 of a trip per capita times the 100,000 population of zone A equals 20,000 trips per year. Similarly, the visit rate from the next distance zone, B, would fall from the original 0.2 of a trip per capita to 0.1 of a trip per capita. Multiplying 0.1 of a trip per capita by the 10,000 population of zone B equals 1,000 trips per year. The trips per capita from the last distance zone, C, would fall from 0.1 of a trip per capita to zero as a result of the added 50 miles. The total number of trips that would be expected with an added distance of 50 miles would be 21,000, including 20,000 trips from zone A, 1,000 trips from zone B, and none from zone C. This represents a second point on the demand curve for the recreation site or resources.

Second, an added distance of 100 miles is assumed for each trip to the site from each zone of origin. The travel distance from the closest zone, A, was originally 50 miles, and an added 100 miles would make a total of 150 miles. The visit rate from zone, A, given this added 100 miles, can be read from Table 8-6, in this case 0.1 of a trip per capita,

221

down from the original 0.3 of a trip per capita. Thus, 0.1 of a trip per capita times the 100,000 population of zone A equals 10,000 trips per year. Similarly, the visit rates from zones B and C would fall to zero with an added distance of 100 miles because Table 8-6 implies that no trips are made by persons living 200 and 250 miles from the recreation site. Thus, the total number of trips that would be expected with an added distance of 100 miles would be 10,000, all from zone A. This represents a third point on the demand curve for the recreation site.

Third, an added distance of 150 miles is assumed for each trip to the site from each zone of origin. The travel distance from the closest zone, A, was originally 50 miles, and an added 150 miles would make a total of 200 miles. The travel distance from zones B and C would become 250 and 300 miles, respectively. As a result, the visit rate from all zones would fall to zero, because Table 8-6 implies that no trips are made by persons living 200 to 300 miles from the recreation site. This represents a fourth point on the demand curve for the recreation site, the added distance that drives the visit rate to zero from all origin zones.

The next step is to estimate the price at which the various quantities of use are demanded. The incremental increases in distance are simply converted to the costs that would be incurred by recreation users if they were required to travel the additional distances. The variable, or out-of-pocket travel costs are used as the proxy for money price, since these are the costs that users are most aware of when making decisions about whether to visit a particular recreation site. Such fixed costs as depreciation, insurance, and registration are not included, as these costs would generally not affect the recreation user's decision to travel additional miles to the recreation site. The federal guidelines recommend that the conversion of distance to money price should use the most current published results of studies conducted periodically by the U.S. Department of Transportation on the average cost of operating standard, compact, and subcompact automobiles. For example, average direct costs were reported as 12 cents per mile in 1981 (see Chapter 4).

Two adjustments must be made, however, before this travel cost can be used as the proxy for money price. The first adjustment is to account for round-trip miles. The distance measure used in Table 8-6 on per capita use was one-way miles, while recreation users must travel to and from the recreation site. So either the number of one-way miles must be doubled or the cost per mile doubled. A second adjustment is made to distribute the travel costs of a trip between the number of users traveling in each vehicle. This is done by taking the average number of recreation users per vehicle from entrance station reports or from a sample survey. Thus, the estimated money price for a simulated increase in distance of 50 miles in the above example would be equal to $4. This is derived as follows: 50 miles times 2 for round trip miles, times 12 cents per mile divided by 3 persons (average number of users per vehicle).

The final adjustment in travel cost recommended by the federal guidelines is to include the opportunity cost of time. Distances should be converted to dollar values, using both out-of-pocket and time costs per mile. For some individuals, the additional time required to travel the increased distance would seem to be a deterrent equal to or greater than the out-of-pocket money costs. But no generally accepted value of time has been established and empirically verified. A number of studies have used a method suggested in the guidelines. Travel time for adults is valued at 25 to 50 percent of average hourly income, and for children one-fourth of the adult value. For purposes of this illustration, assume that direct survey data show that individual time costs average $1.50 per hour for two adults and one child per vehicle. Thus, the individual time cost for a simulated increase in distance of 50 miles in the above example would equal $3. This is derived as follows: 50-miles times 2 for round trip miles, divided by 50 miles per hour, times $1.50 per hour.

Distances are converted to dollar values by summing out-of-pocket costs of $4 and time costs of $3 for 50-mile increments, equal to $7, illustrated in Figure 8-3. This allows us to make the final computation in the travel cost approach, which is to measure the area under the demand curve in Figure 8-3. This area is equal to the amount users would be willing to pay but do not have to pay for the opportunity to participate in recreation at the study site. The estimated benefits of the recreation site, represented by the area under this demand curve, are about $340,000 per year, equal to nearly $10 per individual recreation trip.

In this illustration, the visit rate from distance zones was considered to be a function of the distance-related travel costs and time. Actually, other variables would also influence trips per capita and would need to be considered in applications of the method. These include the determinants of demand discussed in Chapter 7.

Reliability of the Approach

The travel cost method has been thoroughly tested over more than 25 years and found to be a reasonably accurate way to estimate empirical demand functions and benefits of recreation. One of the important contributions of economists writing in professional journals is to challenge the theoretical basis and the reliability of all proposed innovations. The noted British philosopher of science, Karl Popper, has described this process of attempting to refute new ideas as the primary source of improvements and, therefore, of progress in science. The travel cost method has been evaluated in the professional economic journals and improved in a number of ways. The individual approach was added in the early 1970s (Brown and Nawas) and the individual per capita approach in the early 1980s (Brown et al); however, the zonal per capita approach continues to be very useful and remains essentially in the original form proposed by Clawson and Knetsch in the early 1960s.

In this section, we will consider several examples of ways that the travel cost method has been modified to improve the accuracy of results. Originally it was assumed that: (1) the characteristics of the population are the same from one distance zone to another; (2) groups of individual consumers would react similarly to increases in entrance fees as to increases in travel cost; (3) trips are of uniform duration and for the single purpose of visiting the recreation site; and (4) individuals travel the same speed regardless of road conditions, pay the same direct costs to operate private autos, and experience uniform opportunity costs of time.

These and related assumptions have been authorized by the federal guidelines. Where direct survey data are not available on individual variations, any one or all of the assumptions may be used to provide reasonably accurate demand and benefit estimates for specific types of recreation sites. However, the burden of proof is on researchers to document as best they can the extent of possible bias introduced by the assumptions made. Where effects on the reliability of the demand and benefit estimates are judged to be substantial, the research should adopt one or more of the following modifications in the travel cost method.

First, where direct survey data are not available, such as in the original travel cost studies, it is assumed that the characteristics of the population of consumers are essentially the same from one distance zone to another. This may include uniformity with respect to taste and preferences; income, and other socioeconomic variables; opportunities to substitute alternative recreation sites; travel time; and other characteristics of the population. The introduction and widespread availability of multiple regression computer packages make it relatively easy to modify this assumption. In most recent applications, standard statistical procedures are used to hold these variables constant in the demand function, and show the single effect of travel cost or price on quantity demanded. This means that the slope and location of the demand curve can be automatically corrected for variations in the characteristics of the population from one distance zone to another.

Second, even when direct survey data are available, the zonal per capita approach aggregates individual consumers into groups living in

224

origin zones. This means that each zone is associated with a single average travel cost or price, opportunity cost of time, income per household, age, etc. Individual variations are averaged out. The resulting zonal values for travel cost and time cost are more highly correlated with quantity demanded than are these values for individuals within zones. Thus, the zonal approach may appear to "explain" more of the variation in quantity demanded than the individual approach. This occurs because there is less variation to explain rather than because the approach is in any way superior in this respect.

When individual consumers are aggregated into groups living in origin zones, the socioeconomic variables usually have shown little or no significant relationship to quantity demanded. This results, in part, from the fact that aggregating zonal data tends to eliminate variability in the data, making it less likely that the variables will be revealed as having a statistically significant influence on demand. In general, tests of the influence of the socioeconomic characteristics of individual users, such as tastes and preferences, income, age, etc., will be more precise and significant in studies using individual observations than zonal averages. For example, Martin, Gum, and Smith used the individual travel cost approach to test the effect of 20 independent variables on demand for fishing, hunting, and other outdoor recreation in Arizona.

More recently, Brown et al. suggested a combination of the individual and per capita approaches in which each individual from an origin zone is allocated a proportion of the total population of the zone based on the number of individual users located in the zone. If there were ten users, zonal population would be divided by 10, and the number of trips by each user would be divided by one-tenth of total zonal population. This measure of individual trips per capita is treated as the dependent variable in a demand function that includes individual direct cost, time cost, and socioeconomic variables. This has the advantage of including population in the demand function and avoiding the use of zonal averages of independent variables.

Third, income has attracted the most attention of all the socioeconomic variables that have been considered for inclusion in demand functions. When income is included as an independent variable, the presumption is that it will result in parallel shifts in the demand curve, as is true of each of the nonprice variables included. If the income effect is positive, higher income groups are more willing and able to pay the direct cost or price for use of a recreation site; thus their demand curve shifts parallel to the right of the demand curve for lower income groups, resulting in greater consumer surplus for higher income groups. However, when there is unequal distribution of income among the participants in recreation at a study site, the slope of the demand curve also may depend on the level of income, as Seckler suggests.

A number of studies indicate that low income groups may have more elastic demand curves than higher income groups; thus their consumer surplus would be less than indicated by parallel shifts in demand curves. To test for this possibility, McConnell recommends that we separate the sample into income groups and estimate a demand function for each group. If the demand curves have significantly different slopes, the correct procedure to estimate total benefits of the site is to sum the consumer surplus under the demand curves of income groups. When sample size is insufficient to estimate separate demand curves for several income groups, interactive variables can be used. To create a new interactive variable, designate low income households equal to 1 and other income groups zero, and multiply by direct cost or price. Then adding the coefficient for the interactive variable to the original coefficient for direct cost or price will show the effect of low income on the slope of the demand curve.

Fourth, choosing the geographic boundary of the relevant market area for a recreation site can be an important problem in applying the zonal per capita travel cost approach. The boundary determines the price intercept of the per capita demand curve, defined as the point where the demand curve cuts the price axis. It represents the maximum direct cost or price anyone will pay for use of the recreation site and is based on the maximum distance people are willing to travel. The problem occurs when a few recreation users come a great distance and when nonlinear demand curves do not cut the vertical axis. Otherwise acceptable functional forms for the demand curve may imply unrealistic travel behavior and lead to infinite or gross overestimation of consumer surplus.

However, reasonable assumptions can be incorporated into the calculation of consumer surplus. For example, the Corps of Engineers uses distance zones that include approximately 95 percent of all visitors to the study site. Roughly 5 percent can live beyond the most distant zone, which represents the price intercept of the per capita demand curve. These users are excluded from the analysis, and their benefits are assumed equal to the average consumer surplus of those included. This is an acceptable procedure according to the federal guidelines. Other studies have limited the boundary of the relevant market so as to exclude out-of-state users who generally will have traveled farther than instate users. This practice has underestimated benefits of big game hunting, waterfowl hunting, cold water fishing, and boating. Further work on this problem may be expected to provide a more acceptable solution.

Fifth, the travel cost approach is designed to estimate demand for the recreation activities at a specific site. For a resource that provides a single recreation activity — for example, a campground — site demand is equivalent to demand for the recreation activity. However, most sites provide opportunities for more than a single recreation activity — for example, a reservoir may provide fishing, motor boating, waterskiing, sailing, swimming, camping, picnicking, and sightseeing. When information is desired on the demand for a specific recreation activity at a multipurpose site, studies have been limited to users who are primarily engaged in the activity of interest (i.e., more than 50 percent of on-site time). This approach may not be sufficiently precise when information is desired on demand by all users who engage in a single activity at the study site. The problem can be resolved by asking a sample of users to allocate total on-site time and travel cost among their various recreation activities at the study site. With this information, separate travel cost demand curves can be estimated for each recreation activity and summed to obtain demand for the site.

Sixth, the original travel cost studies stated that groups of individual consumers would react similarly to increases in entrance fees as to increases in travel cost. Therefore, an important problem concerns which travel costs should be included. Consumer surplus estimates are very sensitive to those direct out-of-pocket and time costs that vary with distance, for it has been demonstrated that increasing travel costs by any given proportion has the effect of increasing consumer surplus by the same proportion.

The federal guidelines suggest that uniform operating costs per mile for private autos be based on the latest U.S. Department of Transportation study. For some applications of the travel cost method this may be sufficient. The method derives its name from the basic proposition that distance traveled times the direct cost per mile to operate private autos is an effective proxy for the price of outdoor recreation. This is obviously true where the direct costs of auto operation represent most, if not all, of the necessary trip costs to such intermediate recreation resources as state parks and reservoirs located up to 150 miles from the residence of users. Even here, variation in types of vehicles and road conditions may affect costs per mile.

Additional costs of the trip should be included when they vary either among origin zones in relation to distance traveled or among individuals in relation to number of trips. Such costs will change the slope and the area under the demand curve above price. This may occur when some more distant or less frequent individual users are on overnight weekend trips, where payments for camping or resort lodging represent a substantial part of the necessary costs of the trip. In this case, lodging and related costs, such as added costs of restaurant meals, should be added to the direct cost of auto operation. An alternative procedure recommended by the federal guidelines is to separate the sample into day-users and overnight users and to estimate separate demand functions for each group.

It is not necessary to include an item of cost that does not vary either among origin zones in relation to distance traveled or among individuals in relation to number of trips; it will not change either the slope or the area under the demand curve. For example, if all users of a campground pay a daily fee of $10 for a campsite, the estimate of consumer surplus will not be affected, because both price and the demand curve shift upward by the same amount. Thus, the slope and the area under the demand curve above price remains the same. Where these costs are not known, reasonably accurate results often can be obtained by omitting them. It is often realistic to assume that individual users will react to these changes in direct costs in the same way that they react to changes in the direct costs of auto operation.

Finally, an extension of the travel cost method that has attracted particular attention is to include a variable allowing for time costs. Each additional mile traveled is assumed to increase both out-of-pocket costs and time cost. If time costs are omitted, the demand curve will be more elastic and consumer surplus will be lower. For example, Bishop and Heberlein report that the estimated consumer surplus of goose hunting at Horicon marsh in Wisconsin increased from $11 per trip with no time cost to $28 per trip with time valued at 25 percent, and to $45 per trip with time valued at 50 percent of median income, as suggested by the federal guidelines. However, a study of vacation travel by Morrison and Winston found that recreation travel time may be valued at closer to 6 percent of the wage rates, in which case consumer surplus would be about $15 per trip. Although this may be a low estimate for hunting trips, it compares more favorably with consumer surplus of $21 per trip estimated by the contingent valuation method (willingness to pay).

A pilot study suggests that future research on the demand for recreation travel time is likely to show that it is a function of distance rather than a constant for each mile traveled. The demand curve is expected to shift with changes in the quality of scenery along the route and other variables. Apparently, willingness to pay is often positive for short trips and when starting out on long trips. Sooner or later, willingness to pay reaches a breaking point and becomes negative. Willingness to pay becomes increasingly negative if distance traveled continues to increase.

These hypotheses are based on a pilot study of river-based recreation trips by 154 households in the Rocky Mountains of the United States (Sanders). Travel cost demand curves were estimated with and without the reported value of travel time. The results indicate that the demand curve for onsite recreation at study rivers shifts inward when the willingness to pay for travel time is included as an independent variable in the demand function. This results in an 18 percent loss of consumer surplus attributed to onsite recreation from $22 to $18 per day. However, the introduction of $8 in sightseeing benefits from river recreation trips shifts the total trip demand curve outward so that the combined benefit estimate increases to $26 per day.

Other modifications in the travel cost method have been suggested by a number of observers. For example, in 1983, the federal guidelines did not recommend the method for the study of single trips to more than one recreation site as is typical of vacation travel to national parks. However, Haspel and Johnson have demonstrated that a reasonable estimate of demand for a national recreation area can be obtained by dividing total direct trip costs by the number of recreation sites visited on the trip. Other adjustments also have been tried, and it seems likely that an acceptable procedure will be forthcoming. Another problem may arise from the assumption that trips are of uniform duration in terms of days at the study site. However, it seems that this variation among individual users could be determined by sample survey, and the number of days at the site could be included as an independent variable in individual demand functions. Finally, the distance zones may vary in size with typical applications using towns or cities for the zones close to the study site, counties for intermediate zones, and groups of counties for more distant zones. Sutherland has explored the effect of the choice of origin zones on the slope of the per capita demand curve. If the average distance to the population center of the most distant zone represents an extremely wide range of distance, the price intercept of the demand curve may be understated.

The federal guidelines do not preclude the use of new techniques as, for example, the hedonic method (Brookshire et al.; Bell) or a combination of the hedonic and travel cost methods. The hedonic travel cost method was developed by Brown and Mendelsohn, combining the hedonic procedures from the household production approach with the traditional travel cost method. The distinguishing characteristic of the approach is that travel cost is the dependent variable in the first step of a two-step process. The first step is to estimate the price individuals from each origin zone must pay to obtain each characteristic of the experience or recreation activity. A separate regression is run for each of 10 or more origin zones, in which the quantity of characteristics and recreation activities, are independent variables. The resulting regression coefficients for marginal prices of the characteristics and recreation activities along with the mean quantities are assigned to all individuals from each zone. When there is sufficient range in the prices and quantities of characteristics and activities between zones, it is possible in the second step to estimate a demand curve for each characteristic and activity for all individuals from the 10 or more zones. The hedonic travel cost approach has been used to estimate the effects of fish catch, congestion, scenic quality, and for the characteristics of hiking trails in Olympic National Park in Washington state. Although the hedonic approach has provided some very useful results

229

with respect to the quality of recreation sites, its application has been limited to situations where the most distant sites are also the highest quality with respect to the important characteristics. Otherwise, studies find an unacceptable large number of the regression coefficients for the marginal prices of characteristics have the wrong sign. Under certain circumstances (when users tend to be price takers in the market for outdoor recreation), the approach is indistinguishable from the travel cost approach according to McConnell.

UNIT DAY VALUES *subjective to expert opinion*

The unit day approach is the third method recommended by the federal guidelines as providing acceptable economic estimates of the value of recreation opportunities and resources. The approach may be used if application of the travel cost or contingent valuation methods would exceed budget constraints and if the recreation site studied is *other methods too expensive* *most IL sites* relatively small, with fewer than 750,000 recreation days per year. The method relies on expert judgment to develop an approximation of the average willingness to pay for recreation use. The values selected are considered to be equivalent to consumer surplus, i.e., net of travel cost or price.

The federal guidelines classify recreation into two categories: "general" and "specialized." General recreation includes the majority of activities requiring the development and maintenance of convenient access and developed facilities. Included are most picnicking, tent and trailer camping, warm water boating and fishing, swimming, and small-game hunting. Specialized recreation opportunities are more limited; intensity of use is low; and more skill, knowledge, and appreciation are required. Recreation use of wilderness areas is considered specialized, as are trout fishing, big-game hunting, upland bird and waterfowl hunting, pack trips, white water boating, canoeing, and specialized nature photography.

The guidelines recommended a range in value of $6.10 to $17.90 per day of specialized recreation, including wilderness use, in fiscal year 1982. General recreation values were much lower, $1.50 to $4.50 per day. Initially based on a survey of entrance fees at private recreation areas in 1962, unit day values have been adjusted for changes in the consumer price index to the present. For example, the recommended range of specialized recreation values was $2-$6 in 1962, $3-$9 in 1973, $4.29-$12.87 in 1979, and increased to $6.10-$17.90 in 1982. You can update these values to the present by adjusting for changes in the consumer price index.

Unit day values are adjusted to reflect quality considerations that prevail in various regions. For example, a reservoir that carries a heavy load of suspended silt or is used beyond capacity would be less

230

desirable, and therefore, of lower unit value than one with clear water and fewer users. The availability of alternative opportunities is also considered in assigning values. Higher values are assigned if the population served does not have similar recreation opportunities. On the other hand, if similar recreation opportunities are relatively abundant, lower unit values are assigned, even if a large number of people are expected to use a proposed site.

There are several problems with these guidelines for rating the quality of the recreation experience. The scale for the effect of crowding on the recreation experience should assign the highest value to the level of use which results in the maximum net benefit of users, rather assign the highest value to the least crowded as the federal guidelines recommend (Krutilla and Fisher). The scale for availability of substitutes assumes that alternative sites cannot be complements, however, they actually often are complements, particularly in resort areas such as Florida, Colorado, and Hawaii. The existence of two or more suitable recreation sites may induce a user to invest in more expensive equipment and participate more often, while the existence of only one such site may not justify the investment nor stimulate the increased use (Kurtz and King). The scale of the carrying capacity variable should assign the highest value to the level of facility development to maximize the net benefits of users, not necessarily the "ultimate facilities" which may have higher costs than the benefits they generate (Waring, et al.).

The guidelines recommend five criteria to rate at particular sites: (1) quality of the recreation experience as affected by congestion; (2) availability of substitute areas (in hours of travel); (3) carrying capacity as determined by level of facility development; (4) accessibility as affected by road and parking conditions; (5) environmental quality, including forests, air, water, pests, climate, adjacent areas, and aesthetics of the scenery. Individual sites are rated on a 100-point scale, in which recreation experience is assigned a weight of 30, availability of substitutes 18, carrying capacity 14, accessibility 18, and environmental quality 20 points. Table 8-8 is provided by the federal guidelines for converting the scaled values into unit day dollars representing estimated consumer surplus. For example, Table 8-9 shows that wilderness with a quality rating of 80 points out of a possible 100 would be assigned a value of $14 per user day, and one with a quality rating of 90 would have a value of $16 per user day. This compares to a value of $9 per user day for specialized recreation with a quality rating of 50.

These values recommended by the federal guidelines are comparable to the unit day values of the U.S. Forest Service. Table 8-10 shows that wilderness recreation, with standard service, was assigned a value of $12-$18 per recreation visitor day in 1985. This varied among re-

Table 8-8. Guidelines for Rating Quality of the Recreation Experience on a 100-Point Scale

Criteria	Quality of the Experience, 100-Point Scale				
Recreation Experience	Heavy use or frequent crowding or other interference with use	Moderate use, other users evident and likely to interfere with use	Moderate use, some evidence of other users and occasional interference with use due to crowding	Usually little evidence of other users, rarely if ever crowded	Very low evidence of other users, never crowded
Total Points: 30 Point Value:	0-4	5-10	11-16	17-23	24-30
Availability of Substitutes	Several within 1 hr. travel time; a few within 30 min. travel time	Several within 1 hr. travel time; none within 30 min. travel time	One or two within 1 hr. travel time; none within 45 min. travel time	None within 1 hr. travel time	None within 2 hr. travel time
Total Points: 18 Point Value:	0-3	4-6	7-10	11-14	15-18
Carrying Capacity	Minimum facility development for public health and safety	Basic facilities to conduct activity(ies)	Adequate facilities to conduct without deterioration of the resource or activity experience	Optimum facilities to conduct activity at site potential	Ultimate facilities to achieve intent of selected alternative
Total Points: 14 Point Value:	0-2	3-5	6-8	9-11	12-14
Accessibility	Limited access by any means to site or within site	Fair access, poor quality roads to site; limited access roads within site	Fair access, fair road to site; fair access, good roads within site	Good access, good roads to site; fair access, good roads within site	Good access, high standard road to site; good access within site
Total Points: 18 Point Value:	0-3	4-6	7-10	11-14	15-18
Environmental Quality	Low aesthetic factors[a] exist that significantly lower quality[b]	Average aesthetic quality; factors exist that lower quality to minor degree	Above average aesthetic quality; any limiting factors can be reasonably rectified	High aesthetic quality; no factors exist that lower quality	Outstanding aesthetic quality; no factors exist that lower quality
Total Points: 20 Point Value:	0-2	3-6	7-10	11-15	16-20

[a]Major aesthetic qualities to be considered include geology and topography, water, and vegetation.

[b]Factors to be considered in lowering quality include air and water pollution, pests, poor climate, and unsightly adjacent areas.

Source: U.S. Water Resources Council.

232

Table 8-9. Relation between Quality of the Experience and Unit Day Values

Recreation Activity	Quality of the Experience, 100-Point Scale										
	0	10	20	30	40	50	60	70	80	90	100
General Recreation	$ 1.50	$ 1.80	$ 2.00	$ 2.30	$ 2.80	$ 3.20	$ 3.50	$ 3.70	$ 4.00	$ 4.30	$ 4.50
General Fishing and Hunting	2.20	2.40	2.60	2.90	3.20	3.50	3.90	4.00	4.30	4.40	4.50
Specialized Recreation	6.10	6.50	7.00	7.50	8.00	9.00	10.00	12.00	14.00	16.00	17.90
Specialized Fishing and Hunting	10.50	10.80	11.00	11.30	11.60	12.70	13.80	14.70	15.80	16.90	17.90

Source: U.S. Water Resources Council.

gions, with the northwest, northeast, and Alaska assigned the higher values. Less than standard wilderness recreation was valued at $6-$10 per recreation visitor day or roughly one-half of standard service values. Standard service provided high quality recreation opportunities at sites with well maintained facilities for parking, drinking water, sanitation, health, safety, information, and environmental quality. Less than standard service was defined as the absence of one or more of these conditions. Unit day values for recreation activities with less than standard service were estimated as 53 percent of standard service values, based on a small sample (13) of recreation users who responded to the question: "What percent less do you feel your recreation experience will be at a below-standard service facility?" This preliminary estimate will be improved as additional studies are completed.

The Forest Service also estimated unit day values for general outdoor recreation activities in six recreation opportunity (ROS) zones. Table 8-11 shows that the highest values were assigned to recreation activities in the semi-primitive nonmotorized zone where the natural environment is mostly unmodified by development, with a minimum of controls and facilities, a low level of congestion, and located 1.5 miles or more from the nearest paved road. The next highest values were assigned to recreation activities in the semi-primitive motorized and urban zones. The lowest values were assigned to recreation activities in rural zone where the natural environment is substantially modified by development, activities are controlled, facilities provided for medium to high levels of congestion, and located within 1.5 miles of a paved road. These estimates were based on the values presented in Table 8-10 for forest recreation activities and information on the distribution of use within each of the 6 ROS zones. The values represent the weighted average value of all recreation activities occurring in each ROS zone, assuming that the value of a single activity does not vary among zones. These preliminary estimates will improve as information becomes available on the expected variation in benefits of

Table 8-10. Unit Day Values of ●utdoor Recreation Recommended by the U.S. Forest Service, United States, 1985

		Unit Day Value per Visitor Day (12 hours) in Forest Service Planning Regions								
Recreation Activity	Quality of Site[a]	Northern	Rocky Mountain	South Western	Inter Mountain	Pacific South West	Pacific North West	South Eastern	North Eastern	Alaska
Wilderness	Standard	$12	$12	$14	$12	$14	$18	$16	$18	$18
	Less than standard	6	6	7	6	7	10	8	10	10
Hiking	Standard	8	9	10	9	11	10	13	18	10
	Less than standard	4	5	5	5	6	7	7	10	5
Camping	Standard	5	6	9	5	8	6	10	11	5
	Less than standard	3	3	5	3	3	3	5	6	3
Picnicking	Standard	4	9	9	5	4	6	6	8	6
	Less than standard	2	5	5	3	3	3	4	4	3
Downhill Skiing	Standard	30	34	31	34	35	31	29	35	31
	Less than standard	16	18	16	18	19	16	15	19	16
Motorized Travel	Standard	7	8	7	6	8	8	7	9	8
	Less than standard	4	4	4	3	4	4	4	5	4
Motorized Boating	Standard	6	8	10	7	6	4	6	12	4
	Less than standard	3	4	5	4	3	2	3	6	2
Nonmotorized Boating	Standard	11	10	12	15	9	6	5	9	6
	Less than standard	6	5	6	8	5	3	5	5	6
Water Sports	Standard	6	8	9	8	9	8	9	11	8
	Less than standard	3	4	5	4	5	4	5	6	3
Wildlife & Fish	Standard	20	21	19	18	18	21	18	20	20
	Less than standard	13	14	13	12	12	14	12	13	13
Big Game Hunting		31	41	30	31	30	30	25	38	30
Wildlife Viewing		25	25	25	25	25	25	25	25	25
Anadromous Fishing		23	NA	NA	23	31	33	NA	38	33
Sport Fishing		11	11	13	11	12	15	13	13	11
●ther Game Use		21	19	18	19	18	19	18	21	19

[a]Standard service maintains high quality recreation opportunities. Less-than-standard service provides lower quality recreation opportunities.

234

Table 8-11. Unit Day Values of Outdoor Recreation in ROS Zones of the U.S. Forest Service, United States, 1985

Recreation Opportunity (ROS) Zone	Quality of Site[a]	Unit Day Value per Visitor Day (12 hours) in Forest Service Planning Regions[b]								
		Northern	Rocky Mountain	South Western	Inter Mountain	Pacific South West	Pacific North West	South Eastern	North Eastern	Alaska
Primitive	Standard	$ 9.50	$10.31	$11.25	$ 9.75	$11.75	$11.25	$10.94	$15.94	$11.19
	Less than standard	5.04	5.46	5.96	5.17	6.23	5.96	5.80	8.45	5.93
Semi-primitive, Nonmotorized	Standard	12.13	13.84	13.59	12.53	13.78	13.25	12.59	18.28	13.50
	Less than standard	6.43	7.34	7.20	6.64	7.30	7.02	6.67	9.69	7.16
Semi-primitive, Motorized	Standard	11.19	12.69	12.59	11.50	13.00	12.13	11.88	16.56	12.50
	Less than standard	5.93	6.73	6.67	6.10	6.89	6.43	6.30	8.78	6.63
Roaded, Natural	Standard	8.75	9.97	10.41	8.88	10.47	9.38	9.94	12.94	9.59
	Less than standard	4.64	3.72	5.52	4.71	5.55	4.97	5.27	6.86	5.08
Rural	Standard	7.75 (6.90)	9.19 (8.17)	10.25 (9.47)	8.13 (7.02)	9.75 (8.68)	8.47 (7.56)	9.75 (9.12)	12.19 (11.31)	8.44 (7.61)
	Less than standard	4.11 (3.65)	4.87 (4.33)	5.43 (5.02)	4.31 (3.72)	5.17 (4.60)	4.49 (4.00)	5.17 (4.84)	6.46 (5.99)	4.47 (4.04)
Urban	Standard	10.56 (6.61)	12.56 (7.92)	12.75 (9.24)	11.63 (6.60)	13.34 (8.48)	11.38 (7.27)	12.00 (9.17)	15.22 (11.17)	10.97 (7.22)
	Less than standard	5.60 (3.50)	6.66 (4.19)	6.76 (4.90)	6.16 (3.50)	7.08 (4.50)	6.03 (3.85)	6.36 (4.86)	8.07 (5.92)	5.81 (3.83)

[a]Standard service maintains high quality recreation opportunities. Less-than-standard service provides lower quality recreation opportunities.
[b]Values in parentheses are used in those areas without winter sports sites.

each recreation activity associated with the suitability of resources supplied in each R●S zone.

Forest Service unit day values are based on periodic reviews of recent studies using the travel cost and contingent valuation methods. These values are adjusted by the administration to reflect the concept of reasonable and proper levels for the purposes intended. For example, the 1985 resource planning values for recreation were based on a review of 60 studies adjusted to 1982 dollars (Sorg and Loomis). These empirical results were decreased by 37.5 percent to obtain the standard service values presented in Table 8-10. This adjustment was based on the national price elasticity of demand estimated as -.2 and information that the Forest Service provided 7.5 percent of the outdoor recreation consumed in the United States. Multiplying the price elasticity of demand by the 7.5 percent market share equals 37.5 percent decrease in price "to clear the market". Economists outside of the agency may not agree that this is a proper basis for valuing recreation programs. Nonetheless, it is noteworthy that most of the unit day values of the Forest Service are very similar to the unit day values recommended by the interagency federal guidelines. Thus, what may be questioned on economic grounds, may result in acceptable values for administrative purposes. Moreover, the 1985 unit day values represent a substantial improvement over the 1975 and 1980 resource planning values.

Reliance on unit day values can be expected to decrease as federal agencies gradually adopt such alternative methods as the travel cost and contingent valuation approaches. In recent years, these empirical methods have been encouraged through agency review procedures, demonstration projects, and educational workshops.

EMPIRICAL ESTIMATES ●F BENEFITS

The purpose of this section is to present the results of recent benefit studies and their implications for recreation economic decisions. Case studies of the consumer surplus of recreation activities at particular recreation sites are too numerous to review here. In the interest of brevity, Table 8-12 summarizes the results of a representative sample of more than 60 studies of various recreation activities. The values generally are within 50 percent of the average of $13 per recreation day, even though they are not adjusted for inflation or other variations, such as availability of substitutes, value of travel time, restriction of samples to instate residents, etc.

The federal guidelines recommend that wherever possible, we compare the values obtained from studies using each of the three methods: travel cost, contingent valuation, and unit day. Economists writing in the professional literature frequently have tested the reliability of

236

Table 8-12. Case Studies of the Consumer Surplus of Recreation Activities in States and Regions of the United States

Activity	Region or State	Research Method[a]	Consumer Surplus per Recreation Day	Source and Date of Study
Big Game Hunting	Arizona	TCM	$18-20	Martin, Gum, Smith (1970)
	Colorado	CVM	9	Miller (1974)
	Intermountain Region	CVM	12-23	Hansen (1975)
	Oregon	TCM	9	Brown (1968)
	Utah	TCM	14	Loomis (1979)
		TCM	9	Wennergren, Fullerton, Wrigley (1970)
Small Game Hunting	Arizona	TCM	14	Martin, Gum, Smith (1970)
	Intermountain Region	CVM	14	Hansen (1975)
Upland Gamebird Hunting	Intermountain Region	CVM	23	Hansen (1975)
Waterfowl Hunting	Arizona	TCM	6	Martin, Gum, Smith (1970)
	Intermountain Region	CVM	20	Hansen (1975)
	Wisconsin	CVM	21-63	Bishop, Heberlein (1978)
Fishing, Cold Water	Arizona	TCM	9	King, Walka (1980)
		TCM	10	Martin, Gum, Smith (1970)
	Colorado	CVM	11	Walsh, Aukerman, Milton (1978)
		CVM	11	Walsh, Ericson, Arosteguy, Hansen (1978)
		CVM	9	Walsh, Olienyk (1980)
	Idaho	TCM	18	Gordon (1968)
	Intermountain Region	CVM	10	Hansen (1975)
	Missouri	TCM	16	Weithman, Haas (1979)
	New York	TCM	9	Kalter, Gosse (1965)
Fishing, Warm Water	Arizona	TCM	12	Martin, Gum, Smith (1970)
	Florida	TCM	11	Gibbs (1970)
	Georgia	TCM	13	Ziemer, Musser, Hill (1971)
Fishing, Anadromous	Idaho	TCM	17	Gordon (1968)
	Oregon	TCM	22	Brown, et al. (1976)
		TCM	17	Brown, Sorhus, Gibbs (1977)
Fishing, Salt Water	Rhode Island	TCM	30-67	McConnell (1978)
Motorized Boating	New Mexico	TCM	11	Ward (1978)
	New York	TCM	15	Kalter, Gosse (1965)
Nonmotorized Boating	Arizona	TCM	24	Keith, et al. (1981)
	Colorado	CVM	11-13	Walsh, Ericson, et al. (1978)
	Idaho	TCM	10	Michaelson (1971)
	Utah	TCM	19	Bowes, Loomis (1978)
Water Sports	Arizona	TCM	14	Martin, Gum, Smith (1970)
	Florida	TCM	10	Gibbs (1970)
	New Mexico	TCM	11	Ward (1978)
	New York	TCM	9	Kalter, Gosse (1970)
	Texas	TCM	4	Grubb, Goodwin (1965)
Picnicking	Arizona	TCM	7	Martin, Gum, Smith (1970)
	California	TCM	3	Knetsch, Brown, Hansen (1969)
	Colorado	CVM	11	Walsh, Aukerman, Milton (1978)
		CVM	6	Walsh, Olienyk (1980)
	New Mexico	TCM	11	Ward (1978)
Camping	Arizona	TCM	14	Martin, Gum, Smith (1970)
	Colorado	CVM	11-14	Walsh, Aukerman, Milton (1978)
		CVM	6-8	Walsh, Olienyk (1980)
	Florida	TCM	11	Gibbs (1973)
	Idaho	TCM	9	Michaelson (1971)
	New Mexico	TCM	11	Ward (1978)
	New York	TCM	7	Kalter, Gosse (1970)
Wilderness	California	TCM	9	Smith, Kopp (1972)
	Colorado	CVM	10-18	Walsh, Gilliam (1979)
		TCM	14	Walsh, Gillman, Loomis (1980)
	Utah	TCM	12	Loomis (1978)
Hiking	Arizona	TCM	14	Martin, Gum, Smith (1970)
	Colorado	CVM	14	Walsh, Aukerman, Milton (1978)
		CVM	10	Walsh, Olienyk (1980)
	New Mexico	TCM	11	Ward (1978)
	New York	TCM	16	Kalter, Gosse (1970)
Motorized Travel (ORV)	Colorado	CVM	6	Walsh, Olienyk (1980)
Downhill Skiing	Colorado	CVM	24	Walsh (1980)

[a]TCM = travel cost method; CVM = contingent valuation method.
Source: Sorg and Loomis.

these approaches by comparing their results. Table 8-12 indicates that two-thirds used the travel cost method (TCM) and one-third the contingent valuation method (CVM), particularly the more recent studies. In order to compare these two approaches, it is necessary to adjust the values to a single base, January 1982, using the Gross National Product implicit price deflator. The average value becomes $22 per recreation day when adjusted for inflation to 1982. Studies using the travel cost method average nearly $24 per recreation day, approximately $5 more than the $19 per recreation day for studies using the contingent valuation approach. This relationship is consistent with the findings of case studies, showing that contingent valuation estimates are generally more conservative than travel cost estimates.

The values presented in Table 8-12 can be used to compare results of the travel cost and contingent valuation methods to unit day values. For example, the benefits of wilderness in Colorado have been estimated as $14 per recreation day, using a regional travel cost approach, and $10 to $18 per day on the basis of a contingent valuation study. If wilderness has a rating of 80 out of a possible 100 quality points, the unit day value recommended by the federal guidelines would be $14 per day. By comparison, the U.S. Forest Service recommends a unit day value of $12 for a 12-hour visitor day of wilderness recreation in the Rocky Mountain region. This comparison suggests that the unit day values of the Forest Service may under estimate recreation benefits somewhat. The implications for recreation economic decisions are readily apparent. When recreation activities are undervalued, insufficient public land will be allocated as wilderness.

In addition to the benefits of actual recreation use reported here, the general public may be willing to pay for the preservation of recreation resources. The environmental economics literature identifies several possibilities of willingness to pay for the preservation of natural resources in addition to consumer surplus from recreation use. Preservation values include option, existence, and bequest demands of the general public as discussed in chapter 3. You will recall that option value is defined as the willingness to pay to guarantee the opportunity for future access to resources of a given quality for recreation use. Existence value is the willingness to pay for the knowledge that a natural environment is protected even though no recreation use is contemplated. Bequest value is defined as the satisfaction derived from endowing future generations with a natural environment. These preservation values are nonmarket and public goods which means their consumption is nonexclusive. Additional beneficiaries can be added without diminishing the benefits of recreation users.

A number of studies suggest that these values may account for a substantial part of the benefits of recreation and environmental resources. In the interest of brevity, we will summarize the results of only a few.

Study	Resource	Annual Value
Randall, Ives, and Eastman	Air quality improvement in New Mexico	$23-85
Brookshire, Schulze, Thayer, and d'Arge	Air quality improvement in 4 cities	
	a. Poor to fair	$174
	b. Fair to good	$244
Mitchell and Carson	Water quality improvement in the U.S.	
	a. Boatable	$152
	b. Fishable	$194
	c. Swimmable	$225
Desvousges, Smith, and McGivney	Water quality improvement in Pennsylvania	
	a. Option	$10-38
	b. Existence	$42-66
Greenley, Walsh, and Young	Water quality improvement in Colorado	
	a. Option	$21
	b. Existence	$22-31
	c. Bequest	$16-31
Brookshire, Eubanks, and Randall	Wildlife protection in Wyoming	
	a. Bighorn sheep	$7
	b. Grizzly bear	$15-24
Stoll and Johnson	Whooping Crane, endangered species	
	a. Texas refuge visitors	$9-17
	b. Other households	$1-13
Boyle and Bishop	Wildlife protection in Wisconsin	
	a. Bald eagle	$13-44
	b. Striped shiner	$5-13
Walsh, Loomis, and Gillman	Wilderness protection in Colorado	
	a. Option	$9
	b. Existence	$11
	c. Bequest	$12
	d. Other states	$21

$32

239

Several of these studies include values for incremental improvement in the resource. This is illustrated for values of air and water quality in the United States. The four cities in the air quality study were Chicago, Denver, Albuquerque, and Los Angeles. The national water quality study was conducted by a private public opinion polling organization that routinely interviews random samples of U.S. households. On this basis, Mitchell and Carson estimated that the national benefits of water quality were larger than costs in past years, but that in the future, costs may exceed benefits. The results of some independent studies of similar resources are remarkably close; for example, the water quality studies of the Monongahela River in Pennsylvania and the South Platte River Basin in Colorado. The reliability of the studies of air quality in New Mexico and wilderness in Colorado have been tested by replication under similar conditions.

The values for bighorn sheep and grizzly bears are based on a survey of big game hunters in Wyoming. The lower figures represent existence values and the higher figures option price for hunting these species in 5-15 years. In the study of bald eagles and striped shiners (endangered species in Wisconsin), the range in values depends on whether respondents view bald eagles on recreation trips and whether they are active in environmental organizations. The range in values for water quality in Colorado depends on recreation use with lower values for nonusers. The whooping crane values include visitors to the Aransas Refuge in Texas and residents of Texas, Chicago, New York, Atlanta, and Los Angeles. The lower figures represent existence values and the higher figures option price for viewing whooping cranes. On this basis, Stoll and Johnson estimated the national benefits of protecting whooping cranes at $573 million per year. While these studies are encouraging, the reader should note that they are experimental and subject to verification by further research.

In the past, the benefit estimating procedures of state and federal agencies in the United States did not include preservation values. Their guidelines should be enlarged to include them. In the absence of information on preservation values to all of the people, insufficient public land will be protected as natural environment. The problem is especially acute in states where future development of subdivisions, roads, timber, mineral, energy, and water may irreversibly degrade environmental quality. Governments throughout the world face a similar problem of how much natural environment they can afford to protect as wildlife sanctuaries, national parks, and wilderness areas. This problem will be discussed in chapters 14 and 15.

There are two additional points that should be made about the limitations of the economic measures of the benefits of recreation activities and resources presented in this chapter. First, there may be psychological values associated with the preservation of recreation resources that exceed the economic measure of values reported here. The demand for recreation use of resources, and therefore our benefit estimates, is constrained by limited consumer income, availability of leisure time, and other variables. However, psychological values may not be constrained, i.e., demands for recreation use and preservation may be worth more than people are willing and able to pay.

Second, there may be long-run ecological values of preserving natural resources that are not included here. It is difficult for biologists to predict what these might be, let alone measure and incorporate them into a recreation economic value. For this reason, it seems that the benefits of recreation opportunities represent a conservative estimate of the total benefits to society from protecting recreation resources. The inability of economics to place a dollar value on unknown ecological values should be recognized in making decisions about recreation resource programs.

SUMMARY

In this chapter we distinguished between three approaches used to estimate the benefits of recreation activities and resources, as authorized by an interagency committee of the United States government. The federal guidelines provide uniform procedures for application of the contingent valuation, travel cost, and unit day value methods. The values developed by the three methods are considered equivalent to consumer surplus, net of direct travel costs or price paid by individual users.

The contingent valuation method uses simulated (hypothetical) markets to identify values similar to actual markets, if they existed. A sample of the affected population is asked to report their maximum willingness to pay, contingent on hypothetical changes in recreation opportunities or resources depicted in color photos or maps. The values reported represent the maximum willingness to pay rather than forego the recreation opportunity or resource.

The travel cost approach has been preferred by most economists, since it is based on observed market behavior of a cross-section of users in response to direct out-of-pocket and time cost of travel. The basic premise of the approach is that the number of trips to a recreation site will decrease with increases in distance traveled, other things remaining equal. The procedure involves two steps: (1) estimating an individual or per capita demand curve; and (2) deriving the site or resource demand curve from it. Calculating the area under the site demand curve provides an acceptable measure of consumer surplus benefits of recreation resource programs.

The unit day value method relies on expert judgment to develop an approximation of the average willingness to pay for recreation activities. An estimate is selected from a range of values approved by the federal guidelines. Initially based on a survey of entrance fees at private recreation areas in 1962, the unit day values recommended by the federal guidelines have been adjusted for changes in the consumer price index since then.

Next, we discussed when the alternative measures of economic benefits can be used and how to compare the results of each. Thus far, no standard approach to the estimation of the value of recreation has been developed that is suitable for all purposes of measurement. While any one of the three methods can provide a satisfactory measure of the value of a particular recreation site, a problem arises when the results of alternative approaches are compared. We discussed how to adjust the results of each to make them comparable to other measures. Accuracy of the alternative estimating procedures is a continuing problem although considerable progress has been made in recent applications.

We concluded the chapter with examples of the results of a large number of empirical studies of recreation benefits and discussed their implications for recreation economic decisions. Adjusted for inflation to 1982, average consumer surplus was estimated as $22 per recreation day. Studies using the travel cost method averaged nearly $24 per recreation day, compared to $19 for contingent valuation studies. This relationship is consistent with the findings of case studies showing that contingent value estimates are generally more conservative then those using the travel cost approach.

In addition to the benefits of actual recreation use, the general public may be willing to pay for the preservation of recreation resources. Preservation values include option, existence, and bequest demands of users and nonusers. It is proposed that the federal guidelines be enlarged to include these values.

READINGS

Andrews, Karen. "Recreation Benefits and Costs of the Proposed Deer Creek Reservoir." Wyoming Recreation Commission. Cheyenne, Wyoming. April 1984.

Baxter, Michael J. "Measuring the Benefits of Recreational Site Provision: A Review of Techniques Related to the Clawson Method." Sports Council for England and Wales, London. 1979.

Bell, Frederick W. "Recreational Benefits for the Atchafolaya River Basin." Report to U.S. Fish and Wildlife Service by the Dept. of Economics, Florida State University, Tallahassee. 1981.

Bentkover, Judith D., Vincent T. Covello, and Jeryl Mumpower. *Benefits Assessment: The State of the Art.* D. Reidel Publishing Co., Dordrecht, Holland. 1986.

Bergstrom, J. C., B. L. Dillman, and J. R. Stoll. "Public Environmental Amenity Benefits of Private Land: The Case of Prime Agricultural Land." *Southern Journal of Agricultural Economics* 17(July, 1985):139-49.

Bishop, Richard C. "Option Value: An Exposition and Extension." *Land Economics* 58(Feb. 1982):1-15.

Bishop, Richard C., and Thomas A. Heberlein. "Measuring Values of Extra-market Goods: Are Indirect Measures Biased?" *American Journal of Agricultural Economics* 61(Dec. 1979):926-30.

Bishop, Richard C., Thomas A. Heberlein, and Mary Jo Kealy. "Contingent Valuation of Environmental Assets: Comparisons with a Simulated Market." *Natural Resource Journal* 23(July 1983):619-33.
Bishop, Richard C., Thomas A. Heberlein, Michael P. Welsh, and Robert M. Baumgartner. "Does Contingent Valuation Work? Results of the Sandhill Experiment." Paper presented at the Annual Meeting of the American Agricultural Economic Association, Cornell, New York. 1984.
Bohm, Peter. "Estimating the Demand for Public Goods: An Experiment." *European Economic Review* 3(June 1972):111-30.
Bohm, Peter. "Estimating Willingness to Pay: Why and How?" *The Scandinavian Journal of Economics* 81(No. 1, 1979):142-53.
Bohm, Peter. "Revealing Demand for an Actual Public Good." *Journal of Public Economics* 24(July, 1984):135-51.
Bowes, Michael D., and John B. Loomis. "A Note on the Use of Travel Cost Models with Unequal Zonal Populations." *Land Economics* 56(Nov. 1980):465-70.
Boyle, Kevin J., and Richard C. Bishop. "Economic Benefits Associated with Boating and Canoeing on the Lower Wisconsin River." *Economic Issues,* No. 84. Dept. of Agricultural Economics, University of Wisconsin, Madison. 1984.
Boyle, Kevin J., and Richard C. Bishop. "The Value of Wildlife Resources: Conceptual and Empirical Issues." Workshop on Recreation Demand Modeling. Association of Environmental and Resource Economics, Boulder, Colo. 1985.
Boyle, Kevin J., Richard C. Bishop, and Michael P. Welsh. "Starting Point Bias in Contingent Valuation Bidding Games." *Land Economics* 61(May 1985):188-94.
Bradford, David F. "Benefit-Cost Analysis and Demand Curves for Public Goods." *Kyklos* 23(No. 4, 1970):775-91.
Brookshire, David S., and Don L. Coursey. "Measuring the Value of a Public Good: An Empirical Comparison of Elicitation Procedures." Paper presented at the Annual Meeting, American Economic Association, New York. 1985.
Brookshire, David S., and Thomas Crocker. "The Use of Survey Instruments in Determining the Economic Value of Environmental Goods: An Assessment." in Assessing Amenity Resource Values. Terry C. Daniel, Ervin H. Zube, and B. L. Driver, (eds.). RM-68. Rocky Mountain Forest and Range Experiment Station, Forest Service, U.S. Dept. of Agriculture, Fort Collins, Colo. 1979. 35-43.
Brookshire, David S., and Thomas D. Crocker. "The Advantages of Contingent Valuation Methods for Benefit-Cost Analysis." *Public Choice* 36(No. 2, 1981):235-52.
Brookshire, David S., Larry S. Eubanks, and Alan B. Randall. "Valuing Wildlife Resources: An Experiment." *Transactions.* 38th North American Wildlife and Natural Resources Conference. Wildlife Management Institute, Washington, D.C. 1978. 310-20.
Brookshire, David S., Larry S. Eubanks, and Alan B. Randall. "Estimating Option Prices and Existence Values for Wildlife Resources." *Land Economics* 59(Febr. 1983):1-15.
Brookshire, David S., Berry C. Ives, and William D. Schulze. "The Valuation of Aesthetic Preferences." *Journal of Environmental Economics and Management* 3(Fall, 1976): 325-46.
Brookshire, David S., Alan Randall, and John R. Stoll. "Valuing Increments and Decrements in Natural Resource Service Flows." *American Journal of Agricultural Economics* 62(Aug. 1980):478-88.
Brookshire, David S., Mark A. Thayer, William D. Schulze, and Ralph D. d'Arge. "Valuing Public Goods: A Comparison of Survey and Hedonic Approaches." *American Economic Review* 72(Mar. 1982):165-77.
Brown, Gardner M., and Henry O. Pollakowski. "Economic Valuation of Shoreline." *The Review of Economics and Statistics* 59(Aug. 1977):272-78.
Brown, Gardner M., and R. Mendelsohn. "Hedonic Travel Cost Method." *The Review of Economics and Statistics* 66(Aug. 1984):427-33.
Brown, William G., D. M. Larson, R. S. Johnston, and R. J. Wahle. "Improved Economic Evaluation of Commercially and Sport Caught Salmon and Steelhead of the Columbia River." Special Report 463. Oregon State University, Corvallis. 1976.
Brown, William G., Farid H. Nawas, and Joseph B. Stevens. "The Oregon Big Game Resource: An Economic Evaluation." Special Report No. 379, Agricultural Experiment Station, Oregon State University, Corvallis. 1973.
Brown, William G., A. K. Singh, and Emery N. Castle. "An Economic Evaluation of the Oregon Salmon and Steelhead Sport Fishery." Tech. Bull. No. 78, Agricultural Experiment Station, Oregon State University, Corvallis. 1964.
Brown, William G., A. K. Singh, and Jack A. Richards. "Influence of Improved Estimating Techniques on Predicted Net Economic Values for Salmon and Steelhead." Agricultural Experiment Station, Oregon State University, Corvallis. 1972.

Brown, William G., Colin Sorhus, Bih-lian Chou-Yang, and Jack A. Richards. "A Note of Caution on the Use of Individual Observations for Estimating Outdoor Recreational Demand Functions." *American Journal of Agricultural Economics* 65(Febr. 1983):154-57.

Calish, Steven, Roger D. Fight, and Dennis E. Teegarden. "How Do Nontimber Values Affect Douglas-Fir Rotations." *Journal of Forestry* 76(Apr. 1978):217-21.

Cesario, Frank J., and Jack L. Knetsch. "The Time Bias in Recreation Benefit Estimates." *Water Resources Research* 6(June 1970):700-4.

Charbonneau, J. John, and Michael J. Hay. "Determinants and Economic Values of Hunting and Fishing." *Transactions*. 43rd North American Wildlife and Natural Resources Conference. Wildlife Management Institute, Washington, D.C. 1978. 391-403.

Cocheba, Daniel J., and William A. Langford. "Wildlife Valuation: The Collective Good Aspect of Hunting." *Land Economics* 54(Nov. 1978):490-504.

Cocheba, Daniel J., and William A. Langford. "Direct Willingness to Pay Questions: An Analysis of Their Use for Quantitatively Value Wildlife." *Journal of Leisure Research* 13(No. 4, 1981):311-22.

Corps of Engineers. "Analysis of Supply and Demand of Urban Oriented Non-reservoir Recreation." Report 76-R2, Institute for Water Resources, U.S. Army Engineer District, Sacramento, Calif. 1976.

Coursey, Don L., J. J. Hovis, and William D. Schulze. "On the Supposed Disparity Between Willingness to Accept and Willingness to Pay Measures of Value." *The Quarterly Journal of Economics.* In press. 1986.

Cummings, Robert G., David S. Brookshire, and William B. Schulze. *Valuing Public Goods.* Rowan & Allenheld, Totowa, New Jersey. 1986.

Daubert, John T., and Robert A. Young. "Recreational Demands for Maintaining Instream Flows: A Contingent Valuation Approach." *American Journal of Agricultural Economics* 63(Nov., 1981):665-76.

Davis, Robert K. "Recreation Planning as an Economic Problem." *Natural Resources Journal* 3(Oct. 1963):239-49.

Desvousges, William H., V. Kerry Smith, and Matthew P. McGivney. "A Comparison of Alternative Approaches for Estimating Recreation and Related Benefits of Water Quality Improvement." Final Report to the Environmental Protection Agency by Research Triangle Institute, Research Triangle Park, N.C. 1983.

Dillman, Don A. *Mail and Telephone Surveys.* John Wiley and Sons, New York. 1978.

Donnelly, Dennis M., John B. Loomis, Cindy F. Sorg, and Louis J. Nelson. "Net Economic Value of Recreation Steelhead Fishing in Idaho." Resource Bulletin RM-9. Rocky Mountain Forest and Range Experiment Station, Forest Service, U.S. Dept. of Agriculture, Fort Collins, Colo. 1985.

Dwyer, John R., John R. Kelly, and Michael D. Bowes. "Improved Procedures for Valuation of the Contribution of Recreation to National Economic Development." Research Report No. 128, Water Resources Center, University of Illinois, Urbana. 1977.

Fischer, David W. "On the Problems of Measuring Environmental Benefits and Costs." *Social Science Information* 13(No. 2, 1974):95-105.

Freeman, A. Myrick III. *The Benefits of Environmental Improvement.* Johns Hopkins University Press, Baltimore. 1979.

Freeman, A. Myrick III. "Supply Uncertainty, Option Price, and Option Value." *Land Economics* 61(May 1985):176-81.

Garrett, J. R., O. J. Pon, and D. J. Arosteguy. "Economics of Big Game Resource Use in Nevada." Bulletin 25, Agricultural Experiment Station, University of Nevada, Reno. 1970.

Gibbs, Debby. "A Comparison of Travel Cost Models Which Estimate Recreation Demand for Water Resource Development: Summary Report." U.S. Bureau of Reclamation, Washington, D.C. 1983.

Gibbs, Kenneth C., Lewis Queirolo, and Craig Lumnicki. "The Valuation of Outdoor Recreation in a Multiple Use Forest." Research Bulletin 28. Oregon State University Forest Research Laboratory, Corvallis. 1979.

Greenley, Douglas A., Richard G. Walsh, and Robert A. Young. "Option Value: Empirical Evidence from a Case Study of Recreation and Water Quality." *Quarterly Journal of Economics* 96(Nov. 1981):657-72.

Greenley, Douglas A., Richard G. Walsh, and Robert A. Young. *Economic Benefits of Improved Water Quality: Public Perceptions of Option and Preservation Values.* Westview Press, Boulder, Colo. 1982.

Hammack, Judd M., and Gardner M. Brown. *Waterfowl and Wetlands, Toward Bioeconomic Analysis.* Johns Hopkins University Press, Baltimore. 1974.

Hansen, Chris. "A Report on the Value of Wildlife." Forest Service, U.S. Dept. of Agriculture, Washington, D.C. 1977.

244

Haspel, Abraham E., and F. Reed Johnson. "Multiple Destination Trip Bias in Recreation Benefit Estimation." *Land Economics* 58(Aug. 1982):364-72.

Hay, Michael J., and Kenneth E. McConnell. "An Analysis of Participation in Nonconsumptive Wildlife Recreation." *Land Economics* 55(Nov. 1979);460-71.

Heberlein, Thomas, and Richard Bishop. "Assessing the Validity of Contingent Valuation: Three Field Experiments." Paper presented at the International Conference, Man's Role in Changing the Global Environment. Milan, Italy. October, 1985.

Hendon, William S. *Evaluating Urban Parks and Recreation.* Praeger Publishers, New York. 1981.

Keith, John E., Phil Halverson, and Lon Furnworth. "Valuation of a Free Flowing River: The Salt River, Arizona." Report to the U.S. Army Corps of Engineers by Utah State University. 1982.

King, David A., and Ann W. Walka. "A Market Analysis of Trout Fishing on the Fort Apache Indian Reservation." Report to Forest Service, U.S. Dept. of Agriculture, by University of Arizona, Tucson. 1980.

Kneese, Allen V., and Stephen C. Smith (eds.). *Water Research.* Johns Hopkins University Press, Baltimore. 1966.

Kneese, Allen V. *Measuring the Benefits of Clean Air and Water.* Resources for the Future, Inc., Washington, D.C. 1984.

Knetsch, Jack L. "Outdoor Recreation Demands and Benefits." *Land Economics* 39(Nov. 1963):386-96.

Knetsch, Jack L. "Value Comparisons in Free-flowing Stream Development." *Natural Resources Journal* 11(Dec. 1971):624-35.

Knetsch, Jack L. *Outdoor Recreation and Water Resource Planning.* Water Resources Monograph No. 3. American Geophysical Union, Washington, D.C. 1974.

Knetsch, Jack L., R. E. Brown, and W. J. Hansen. "Estimating Expected Use and Value of Recreation Sites." In *Planning for Tourism Development Quantitative Approaches.* C. Gearing, W. Swart, and T. Var, (eds.). Praeger, New York. 1976.

Knetsch, Jack L., and Robert K. Davis. "Comparison of Methods of Recreation Valuation." *Water Research.* Allan V. Kneese and Stephen C. Smith (eds.). Johns Hopkins University Press, Baltimore. 1966.

Knetsch, Jack L., and J. A. Sinden. "Willingness to Pay and Compensation Demanded: Experimental Evidence of an Unexpected Disparity in Measures of Value." *Quarterly Journal of Economics* 99(Aug. 1984):507-21.

Livengood, Kerry. "Value of Big Game from Markets for Hunting Leases: The Hedonic Approach." *Land Economics* 59(1983):287-91.

Loomis, John B. "Use of Travel Cost Models for Evaluating Lottery Rationed Recreation: An Application to Big Game Hunting." *Journal of Leisure Research* 14(No. 2, 1982):117-24.

Loomis, John B. "Consistency of Methods for Valuing Outdoor Recreation." Ph.D. Dissertation, Department of Agricultural and Natural Resource Economics, Colorado State University, Fort Collins. 1983.

Loomis, John B., Dennis Donnelly, Cindy Sorg, and Lloyd Oldenburg. "Net Economic Value of Hunting Unique Species in Idaho: Bighorn Sheep, Mountain Goat, Moose and Antelope." Resource Bulletin, Rocky Mountain Forest and Range Experiment Station, U.S. Forest Service, Fort Collins, Colo. 1986.

Loomis, John B., Cindy F. Sorg, and Dennis M. Donnelly. "Evaluating Regional Demand Models for Estimating Recreation Use and Economic Benefits: A Case Study." *Water Resources Research* 22(No. 4, 1986):431-38.

Miller, Jon R., and Michael J. Hay. "Determinants of Hunter Participation: Duck Hunting in the Mississippi Flyway." *American Journal of Agricultural Economics* 63(Nov. 1981):677-84.

Lucas, Robert C. "Bias in Estimating Recreationists Length of Stay from Sample Interview." *Journal of Forestry* 61(1963):912-94.

Majid, I., J. A. Sinden, and Alan Randall. "Benefit Evaluation of Increments to Existing Systems of Public Facilities." *Land Economics* 59(Nov. 1983):377-92.

Martin, William E., Russell L. Gum, and Arthur H. Smith. "The Demand for and Value of Hunting, Fishing, and General Rural Outdoor Recreation in Arizona." Tech. Bull. 211. Ag. Exp. Sta., University of Arizona, Tucson. 1974.

McConnell, Kenneth E. "Values of Marine Recreational Fishing: Measurement and Impact of Measurement." *American Journal of Agricultural Economics* 61(Dec. 1979):921-25.

Mendelsohn, Robert, and Gardiner M. Brown. "Revealed Preference Approach to Valuing Outdoor Recreation." *Natural Resources Journal* 23(No. 3, 1983):607-18.

Mendelsohn, Robert, and Peter M. Roberts. "Estimating the Demand for Characteristics of Hiking Trails: An Application of the Hedonic Travel Cost Method." Paper presented at the American Economic Association Annual Meeting, New York. December, 1982.

245

Peterson, George L., B. C. Driver, and Robin Gregory (eds.). "Toward the Integration of Economics and Psychology in the Measurement of Non-Priced Values." Conference Proceedings, Rocky Mountain Forest and Range Experiment Station, Forest Service, U.S. Dept. of Agriculture, Fort Collins, Colo. 1986.

Popper, K. R. *The Logic of Scientific Discovery.* Translated 1959. Harper Torchbooks, New York. 1968.

Randall, Alan, John P. Hoehn, and George S. Tolley. "The Structure of Contingent Markets: Some Results of a Recent Experiment." Paper presented at the Annual Meeting of the American Economic Association, Washington, D.C. 1981.

Randall, Alan, Barry Ives, and Clyde Eastman. "Bidding Games for Valuation of Aesthestic Environmental Improvements." *Journal of Agricultural Economics* 61(Dec. 1979):921-25.

Randall, Alan, Glenn C. Bloomquist, John P. Hoehn, and John R. Stoll. "National Aggregate Benefits of Air and Water." Volumes I and II. Report to U.S. Environmental Protection Agency by the University of Kentucky, Lexington. 1985.

Rosenthal, Donald H., John B. Loomis, and George L. Peterson. "The Travel Cost Model: Concepts and Applications." Gen. Tech. Rpt. RM-109. Rocky Mountain Forest and Range Experiment Station, Forest Service, U.S. Department of Agriculture, Fort Collins, Colo. 1984.

Rowe, Robert D., and Lauraine G. Chestnut. "Valuing Environmental Commodities: Revisited." *Land Economics* 59(Nov. 1983):404-10.

Samples, Karl C. "A Note on the Existence of Starting Point Bias in Iterative Bidding Games." *Western Journal of Agricultural Economics* 10(July 1985):32-40.

Schulze, William D., Ralph D. d'Arge, and David S. Brookshire. "Valuing Environmental Commodities: Some Recent Experiments." *Land Economics* 57(May 1981):151-72.

Scott, Anthony. "The Valuation of Game Resources: Some Theoretical Aspects." *Canadian Fisheries Report* (No. 4, 1965):27-47.

Seckler, David W. "On the Uses and Abuses of Economic Science in Evaluating Public Outdoor Recreation." *Land Economics* 42(Nov. 1966):485-94.

Sellar, Christine, John R. Stoll, and Jean-Paul Chavas. "Validation of Empirical Measures of Welfare Change: A Comparison of Nonmarket Techniques." *Land Economics* 61(May 1985):156-75.

Shechter, M., and R. C. Lucas. *Simulation of Recreation Use for Park and Wilderness Management.* Johns Hopkins University Press, Baltimore. 1978.

Smith, Robert J., and N. J. Kavanaugh. "The Measurement of Benefits of Trout Fishing." *Journal of Leisure Research* 1(No. 4, 1969):316-32.

Smith, V. Kerry, and Raymond J. Kopp. "Spatial Limits of the Travel Cost Recreational Demand Model." *Land Economics* 56(Febr. 1980):64-72.

Sorg, Cindy F., and John B. Loomis. "Empirical Estimates of Amenity Forest Values: A Comparative Review." General Technical Report RM-107, Rocky Mountain Forest and Range Experiment Station, Forest Service, U.S. Dept. of Agriculture, Fort Collins, Colo. 1984.

Sorg, Cindy F., John B. Loomis, Dennis M. Donnelly, and George L. Peterson. "The Net Economic Value of Cold Water and Warm Water Fishing in Idaho." Rocky Mountain Forest and Range Experiment Station, Forest Service, U.S. Dept. of Agriculture, Fort Collins, Colo. 1985.

Sorg, Cindy F., and Louis J. Nelson. "Net Economic Value of Elk Hunting in Idaho." Resource Bulletin RM-12, Rocky Mountain Forest and Range Experiment Station, Fort Collins, Colo. 1986.

Stevens, Joe B. "Recreation Benefits from Water Pollution Control." *Water Resources Research* 2(2nd Qtr. 1966):167-81.

Stoll, John R., and L. A. Johnson. "Concepts of Value, Nonmarket Valuation and the Whooping Crane." *Transactions.* 49th North American Wildlife and Natural Resources Conference. Wildlife Management Institute, Washington, D.C. 1984. 382-92.

Sutherland, Ronald J. "A Regional Approach to Estimating Recreation Benefits of Improved Water Quality." *Journal of Environmental Economics and Management* 9(Sept. 1982):229-47.

Thayer, Mark A. "Contingent Valuation Techniques for Assessing Environmental Impacts: Further Evidence." *Journal of Environmental Economics and Management* 8(Mar. 1981):27-44.

Trice, Andrew II., and Samuel E. Wood. "Measurement of Recreation Benefits." *Land Economics* 34(Aug. 1958):195-207.

U.S. Water Resources Council. "Economic and Environmental Principles and Guidelines for Water and Related Land Resource Implementation Studies." U.S. Gov. Print. Off., Washington, D.C. 1983.

Vaughan, William J., and Clifford S. Russell. *Freshwater Recreation Fishing: The National Benefits of Water Pollution Control.* Resources for the Future, Washington, D.C. 1982.

Vaughan, William J., Clifford S. Russell, and Michael Hazilla. "A Note on the Use of Travel Cost Models With Unequal Zonal Populations: Comment." *Land Economics* 58(Aug. 1982):400-7.

Vickerman, R. W. *The Economics of Leisure and Recreation.* MacMillan Press, London. 1975.

Walsh, Richard G., and Lynde O. Gilliam. "Benefits of Wilderness Expansion with Excess Demand for Indian Peaks." *Western Journal of Agricultural Economics* 7(July 1982):1-12.

Walsh, Richard G., Richard A. Gillman, and John B. Loomis. *Wilderness Resource Economics: Recreation Use and Preservation Values.* American Wilderness Alliance, Denver. 1982.

Walsh, Richard G., Larry D. Sanders, and John B. Loomis. *Wild and Scenic River Economics: Recreation Use and Preservation Values.* American Wilderness Alliance, Denver. 1985.

Wellman, J. D., E. G. Hawk, J. W. Roggenbuck, and G. J. Buhyoff. "Mailed Questionnaire Surveys and the Reluctant Respondent: An Empirical Examination of Differences Between Early and Late Respondents." *Journal of Leisure Research* 12(No. 2, 1980):164-73.

Wennegren, E. Boyd, Herbert H. Fullerton, and James C. Wrigley. "Quality Values and Determinants for Deer Hunting." *Journal of Wildlife Management* 41(No. 3, 1977):400-7.

Chapter Nine
Elasticity of Demand

This chapter shows how to calculate the three most important elasticities of demand — price, income, and cross elasticity; summarizes the results of recent studies; and illustrates how elasticities can be applied to recreation economic decisions.

The concept is simple and straightforward. Elasticity of demand is defined as the percentage change in quantity consumed that is caused by a percentage change in a determinant of demand. Price elasticity of demand, for example, is a convenient way of comparing how price changes affect the quantity consumed. It is the ratio of two percentages — the change in quantity consumed that results from a change in the independent variable, price. When the percentage change in price results in a larger percentage change in quantity demanded, the demand is said to be elastic. Conversely, when the percentage change in price results in a smaller percentage change in quantity, demand is said to be inelastic.

Elasticity of demand has been widely used in recreation economic decisions because of its simplicity and convenience. When an elasticity is multiplied by an expected percentage change in a variable, it gives an estimate of the expected percentage change in demand. Thus, it is clear that estimates of elasticities of demand can play an important role in understanding the consequences of socioeconomic trends and management alternatives. Economists are asked by recreation agencies to help draw up long-term investment plans based on the projected future demand for recreation. The National Park Service and the U.S. Forest Service call on economists to review their systems for leasing recreation resource development rights to private firms. Whether, and to what extent, entrance fees will help ease the deficits of city and state parks are questions that cannot be answered correctly without a knowledge of the price elasticity of demand. When managers of private or public recreation resources want to estimate demand for specific recreation activities and sites, they need to know the elasticities of demand with respect to price, income, substitution, and other variables. Many resort operators need to know the cross elasticities of demand for their goods and services with petroleum products in order to estimate the effect of changes in travel costs. Reliable measurement of demand elasticities would be valuable in a wide variety of applications involving recreation decisions. The value of this information to decision makers is the ultimate proof of the usefulness of recreation economic research.

Fortunately, a great deal of information is available on elasticities of demand. Many of the statistical problems associated with the measurement of demand for recreation were solved early in the 1960s. Since that time, large quantities of data on demand elasticities have been accumulated. In this chapter, we will look at some of the estimates that have been made over the last couple of decades. Even where information is not already available, it is often possible to obtain it without great cost or difficulty. The appropriate methods have been carefully worked out to calculate elasticities of demand.

If you have access to the computer printout of a demand function for a recreation site, elasticities of demand are usually shown for each independent variable, at the point where the quantity demanded and each independent variable are at their mean values. In this case, no additional computation is necessary when expected changes in the independent variables are small. However, you are more likely to have access to a published work showing the demand function for the study site or a similar site. In this case, you probably will need to compute elasticities from the information that is available.

The first thing to do is check the functional form of the demand function, whether it is linear, quadratic, semilog, or double-log. When the functional form is double-log no additional computation is necessary, because the regression coefficients are also the elasticities. However, the other three functional forms are more commonly used in studies of demand for recreation. The following section illustrates how to compute elasticities when the demand function is linear. Then, a simple geometric method is presented for estimating elasticities when the demand function is nonlinear as in the quadratic and semilog forms.

PRICE ELASTICITY OF DEMAND

Price elasticity of demand is a measure of the responsiveness of quantity demanded to changes in the direct cost or price of trips to a recreation site, holding constant the values of all other variables. Price elasticity of demand is defined as the percentage change in quantity demanded resulting from a 1 percent change in price. For example, suppose that a 1 percent increase in the direct cost or price of recreation trips results in a 0.4 percent decrease in number of trips. Then the price elasticity of demand for wilderness trips is -0.4.

Note that the price elasticity of demand will always be negative, since price and quantity change in opposite directions. However, you will notice that when economists discuss elasticities, they ignore the

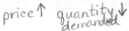
price ↑ quantity demanded ↓

minus sign. Thus, economists say an elasticity of -1.0 is greater than an elasticity of -0.5, and an elasticity of -2.0 is greater than an elasticity of -1.0.

Calculating the Price Elasticity of Demand

The price elasticity of demand for recreation is a very important concept and one that economists often use, so it is worthwhile to spend some time learning how it is computed. There are many acceptable procedures, and choice among them will depend on the information available to you. First, suppose that you have access to a linear demand function for a recreation site as presented in Table 9-1. In this case, you can estimate the price elasticity of demand for any point on the demand curve using the following formula:

$$\text{Price elasticity} = \frac{\text{change in quantity demanded}}{\text{change in price}} \times \frac{\text{original price}}{\text{original quantity demanded}}$$

Table 9-1. Estimating Elasticity of Demand for Trips to a Recreation Site Using Regression Coefficients from a Demand Function

Independent Variables	Units	Estimated Mean Values of the Variables (1)	Regression Coefficients for the slope Independent Variables (2)	Elasticities Of Demand (3) $\frac{(1)}{Q}$
Direct Cost or Price	Dollars/ Trip	20.0	-0.100	-0.4
Consumer Income	Thousand Dollars	25.0 × 5	0.100 =	0.5
Travel Time	Hours Round Trip	3.0	-0.400	-0.24
Price of Substitute Sites	Dollars Direct Cost/Trip	24.0	0.054	0.26
Age	Years	25.0	-0.088	-0.44
Quality of the Site	5-point Scale	4.0	0.625	0.5
County Population	Thousand Persons	200.0 5 ×	0.025 =	1.0 sensitize to demand
Taste or Preference	1=Active 0=Passive	0.8	1.250	0.2
Daily Utilization/ Capacity Ratio	1=Optimal	0.9	-2.667	-0.48
Constant			0.5	
Total Demand		5.0		

The first expression in this formula, change in quantity demanded divided by change in price, is equivalent to the regression coefficient for price. Thus, the formula can be rewritten as:

$$\text{Price elasticity} = \frac{\text{regression coefficient for price}}{} \times \frac{\text{original price}}{\text{original quantity demanded}}$$

The regression coefficient for direct cost or price per trip is shown in Table 9-1 as -0.1 for recreation trips. The average direct cost or price is shown as $20 per trip; at this price, the representative individual user takes 5 trips per year. If we insert these values in the formula:

$$\text{Price elasticity} = -0.1 \times \frac{\$20}{5} = -0.4$$

Thus, dividing the original price, $20, by the original quantity demanded, 5 trips, equals 4, and multiplying this by the regression coefficient, -0.1, equals -0.4 price elasticity of demand. This means that a 1 percent increase in price from the original level results in a 0.4 percent decrease in quantity demanded, or conversely for a price decrease. Now you are familiar with the preferred procedure when statistical demand functions are available; however, this may not always be the case.

For many recreation areas in the United States, managers do not have access to the necessary data to calculate price elasticity for a single point on the demand curve for their site. Often only two data points on the demand curve are available. Fortunately, you can estimate an "arc" or average elasticity of demand between these two points. Arc elasticities provide a useful approximation of the responsiveness of demand to price changes, providing all other variables that influence demand remain unchanged.

Suppose that you notice that the direct cost or price of trips to a recreation site increases by 50 percent and at the same time the number of visits falls by 20 percent. Assuming other variables are unchanged, what is the price elasticity of demand? You can use the following formula to obtain a reasonable approximation:

$$\text{Price elasticity} = \frac{\text{percentage change in quantity demanded}}{} \div \frac{\text{percentage change in price}}{}$$

Thus, the percentage change in demand, -0.2, divided by the percentage change in price, 0.5, equals -0.4 price elasticity of demand.

Suppose that all you have is a table showing various points on a demand curve for a recreation site. For example, Table 9-2 shows the number of visits to a recreation site demanded at various levels of direct cost or price. Given these data, how do you go about computing the price elasticity of demand? Because the price elasticity of any site generally varies from point to point on a linear demand curve, you must first determine at what point on the demand curve you want to measure the price elasticity of demand.

Table 9-2. Effect of Direct Cost or Price on the Number of Visits to a Wilderness Recreation Site

Number of Visits per Year	Direct Cost or Price per Visit (dollars)
0	$70
100,000	60
200,000	50
300,000	40
400,000	30
500,000	20
600,000	10
700,000	0

Let us assume that you want to estimate the price elasticity of demand for this site when the direct cost or price is between $20 and $30 per visit. To do this, you can use the following formula:

$$\text{Price elasticity} = \frac{\text{change in quantity demanded}}{\text{original quantity demanded}} \div \frac{\text{change in price}}{\text{original price}}$$

Table 9-2 shows that the quantity demanded equals 500 thousand visits when the price is $20 per visit, and that it equals 400 thousand visits when the price is $30. But should we use $20 and 500 thousand visits as the original price and quantity? Or should we use $30 and 400 thousand visit as the original price and quantity? If we choose the former, we have:

$$\text{Price elasticity} = \frac{400 - 500}{500} \div \frac{30 - 20}{20} = -0.4$$

The price elasticity of demand is estimated to be -0.4. But we could just as well have used $30 and 400 thousand visits as the original price and quantity. If this had been our choice, the answer would be:

$$\text{Price elasticity} = \frac{500 - 400}{400} \div \frac{20 - 30}{30} = -0.76$$

which is somewhat different from the answer we got in the previous paragraph.

To get around this difficulty, the generally accepted procedure is to use the average values of price and quantity as the original price and quantity. In other words, we use as an estimate of the price elasticity of demand:

$$\text{Price elasticity} = \frac{\text{change in quantity demanded}}{\text{sum of quantities}/2} \div \frac{\text{change in price}}{\text{sum of prices}/2}$$

This is the so-called average arc elasticity of demand. In the specific case we are considering, the average arc elasticity is:

$$\text{Price elasticity} = \frac{400 - 500}{\dfrac{400 + 500}{2}} \div \frac{30 - 20}{\dfrac{30 + 20}{2}} = -0.56$$

The answer to our problem is -0.56. Needless to say, it is hard to estimate price elasticities with pinpoint accuracy. Fortunately, pinpoint accuracy is seldom necessary. In this case, knowledge that the answer probably lies between -0.4 and -0.76 and is closest to -0.56 is useful for many practical purposes.

Arc elasticity between two different points on a demand curve represents an approximation. The farther apart the points between which arc elasticity is calculated, the greater the discrepancy between the two estimates of elasticity, and the less reliable either will be. Arc elasticity can be reasonably accurate when: (1) it is computed between points on the demand curve that are close together, or (2) when the points are by necessity far apart, the formula is modified to provide an average arc elasticity. The concept of point elasticity is more precise than that of arc elasticity. As the two points between which arc elasticity is measured are moved closer and closer together, they merge into a single point. Point elasticity is simply arc elasticity when the distance between the two points approaches zero. Proper use of point elasticity is limited to cases of very small changes in price and other variables. Arc elasticity is a better approach for measuring the average elasticity over an extended range of the demand curve.

If you have access to a graph showing an empirical demand curve for recreation, a simple geometric method can be used to estimate elasticity at any point along the curve. If the demand curve, D, is a straight line (linear), shown as Panel 1 in Figure 9-1, simply drop a perpendicular line from the intersection of price on the demand curve to the horizontal axis. Label the intersection with the quantity axis point B. The rule is that elasticity of demand at price, P, equals BD/OB or 2/5 = -0.4.

The geometric technique for measuring point elasticity of demand can be applied to demand curves derived from empirical studies using the nonlinear quadratic and semilog functional forms. Suppose elastic-

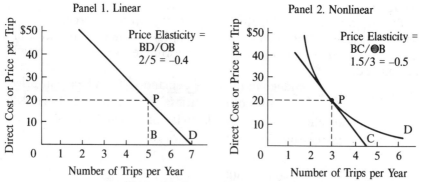

Figure 9-1. Price Elasticity of a Point on Linear and Nonlinear Demand Curves

ity is to be measured at point P on the demand curve shown as Panel 2 in Figure 9-1. First, draw a tangent to the demand curve at point P and extend it so that it cuts the quantity axis at point C. The important principle is that at point P the demand curve and the tangent line coincide and have the same slopes; therefore, their elasticities must be the same at that point. Then the measurement of elasticity can proceed as for linear demand curves. Drop a perpendicular from P to the horizontal axis. Label the intersection with the quantity axis point B. Elasticity of demand at point P is equal to BC/●B or 1.5/3 = -0.5.

To obtain a more precise estimate of the elasticity of demand at any point on a nonlinear demand curve derived from a semilog function, you should use a more advanced text for the algebraic derivation. For a nonlinear demand curves derived from a quadratic function, the equation may be written:

$$\text{Elasticity of demand} = \frac{b + 2cP(P)}{Q}$$

where b is the regression coefficient for the linear expression of price, c is the regression coefficient for the squared expression of price, and Q is the mean of quantity demanded, as shown for a quadratic equation in Chapter 6.

In the discussion of how to calculate price elasticity of demand for a point on the demand curve, we assumed that a regression coefficient for price was available from an ordinary demand curve, where quantity demanded is a function of price and other independent variables. How do we estimate the price elasticity of demand if all we have access to is an inverse demand curve where willingness to pay or price is a function of quantity demanded and other variables? In this case, the price elasticity of demand can be estimated for any point on a linear demand curve using the following formula:

$$\text{Price elasticity} = \frac{1}{\text{regression coefficient for quantity}} \times \frac{\text{original price}}{\text{original quantity demanded}}$$

The first expression in this formula, one divided by the regression coefficient for quantity in an inverse demand curve, is equivalent to the regression coefficient for price in an ordinary demand curve. That this is so can be easily demonstrated. In Chapter 5, the regression coefficient for quantity demanded in an inverse demand curve is shown as -10 trips per year to a recreation area. The representative individual user takes 5 trips per year and, for the fifth trip, is willing to pay a price of $20. If we insert these values in the formula:

$$\text{Price elasticity} = \frac{1}{-10} \times \frac{\$20}{5} = -0.4$$

Thus, dividing 1 by the regression coefficient for quantity demanded,

-10, equals -.1, and dividing the original price, $20, by the original quantity demanded, 5 trips, equals 4. Multiplying -0.1 by 4 equals -0.4 price elasticity of demand. This is identical to the price elasticity of demand estimate from the ordinary demand curve.

Elastic and Inelastic Demand

In applying price elasticity of demand, economists use three terms — price elastic, price inelastic, and unitary elasticity. The demand for a recreation site is "price elastic" if it is greater than 1. The demand is "price inelastic" if it is less than 1. And the demand is of "unitary elasticity" if it equals 1. Figure 9-2 illustrates these three concepts with each line passing through the same mean value of price and quantity.

There are two problems with this diagram. First, it does not indicate any units of measurement along either axis. This may be deceptive, because it could be that the units selected would be such that a demand curve appearing inelastic is actually elastic, and vice versa. For example, the line in Figure 9-2 drawn to illustrate an elastic demand curve looks elastic because it seems to show that the percentage change in the quantity demanded is proportionately greater than the percentage change in price. But suppose the units were actually those shown as Panel 1 in Figure 9-3 for an individual demand curve for trips to a local city park. Now we can see that at a direct cost or price of $2 per trip, the quantity demanded is 10 trips per year, and at a price of $1 it is 15 trips. In other words, a 50 percent decrease in price has been accompanied by the same percentage increase in the quantity demanded. That is unitary elasticity of demand, not an elastic demand. Furthermore, if you sketch in with pencil the result of dropping the price from $1 to 50 cents, you will see that a further

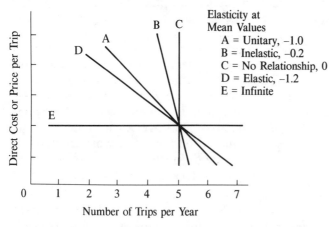

Figure 9-2. Price Elasticities of Demand

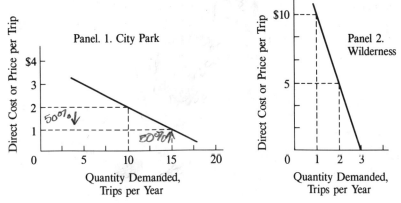

Figure 9-3. Effect of Price on the Number of Trips per Year to a City Park and a Wilderness Area

drop in price of 50 percent will bring an increase in the quantity demand from 15 trips to something less than 18 trips, or approximately 20 percent. The latter is a smaller percentage increase and therefore reveals an inelastic demand (0.2/-0.5 = -0.4).

Hence, before deciding whether or not a demand curve is elastic, you have to be careful to consult the actual prices and quantities that the graph shows. Here is another example (Panel 2, Figure 9-3). The demand curve looks inelastic; but when we read the actual changes in prices and quantities, we find that a 50 percent decrease in price, from $10 to $5, is accompanied by a 100 percent increase in the quantity demanded, from 1 trip to 2. Actually the graph shows a condition of highly elastic demand for individual trips to a wilderness area in a National Forest for which there are a large number of substitutes nearby. The units of measurement on the axes make the line appear steeper (have less elasticity).

Another problem in using elasticities is that they generally vary from point to point along the demand curve. Therefore, you must first determine at what point you want to measure the price elasticity of demand. For example, the price elasticity of demand for recreation trips may be higher when a trip costs $40 than when it costs $10. Note on Figure 9-4 that if a price of $50 falls to $40 — a drop of 20 percent — quantity demanded increases from 2 to 3 trips, or 50 percent. That's certainly an elastic demand, 50/20 = -2.5. But, if the price falls from $20 to $10 — a drop of 50 percent — the quantity demanded increases only from 5 trips to 6, or a rise of 20 percent. That's an inelastic demand, 20/50 = -0.4. In other words, the relation between proportional changes in price and corresponding proportional changes in quantity varies according to where you are on the demand curve. At the top of any straight line demand curve, demand is always more elastic than at the bottom.

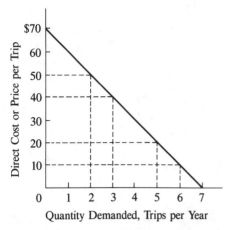

Figure 9-4. Demand Curve for Recreation Trips by Individual Users

Determinants of the Price Elasticity of Demand

Many studies have been made of the price elasticity of demand for particular recreation goods and services. Table 9-3, 9-4, and 9-5 present the results of some of them. Note the substantial differences among them. For example, the estimated price elasticity of demand for 23 outdoor recreation activities in the United States generally appears to be quite inelastic, ranging from -0.12 to -0.32. By comparison, Table 9-4 shows that the estimated price elasticity of demand for outdoor recreation activities in seven planning regions of Arizona tends to be less inelastic, ranging from -0.25 to -0.65 for the most part. Table 9-5 shows that the estimated price elasticity of demand for many recreation goods and services is even less inelastic, in the range of -0.4 to -1.0, or elastic — for example, pleasure boats, -1.3; airline travel, -2.4; radio and TV sets, -1.2; and automobiles, -1.2 to -2.1.

The purpose of this section is to explore the reasons why the price elasticity of demand is low for one product and high for another. Price elasticity of demand for recreation is generally low when it is considered a necessity, when substitutes are not available to satisfy the perceived need, when the proportion of income spent on it is low, or when it is purchased frequently. Economic studies have identified other determinants of the price elasticity of demand for particular products, including number of uses and quality of the product. The more specialized the use and the higher the quality of the experience, the lower the price elasticity of demand.

A relatively constant quantity of such necessities as access to recreation resources that provide opportunities for physical exercise and viewing nature will be purchased almost irrespective of price, at least within the price ranges customarily encountered. For these experi-

Table 9-3. Estimated Elasticity of Demand for Selected Outdoor Recreation Activities, United States

Recreation Activity	Occasion	Average Number of Days per Participant	Price Elasticity of Demand[a]
Sightseeing	Vacation	5.42	-0.21
	Weekend trip	3.89	-0.17
	Day outing	3.51	
Picnicking	Vacation	4.67	-0.21
	Weekend trip	4.55	-0.26
	Day outing	4.05	
Camping in Developed Campgrounds	Vacation	7.99	-0.16
	Weekend trip	6.52	-0.15
Camping in Remote Areas, Wilderness	Vacation	5.26	-0.14
	Weekend trip	7.19	-0.18
Walking for Pleasure	Vacation	6.35	-0.22
	Weekend trip	4.43	-0.19
	Day outing	7.73	-0.20
Nature Walks	Vacation	7.48	-0.22
	Weekend trip	4.73	-0.18
	Day outing	4.27	-0.07
Bird Watching	Vacation	6.55	-0.32
	Weekend trip	6.30	-0.32
	Day outing	3.52	
Fishing	Vacation	4.63	-0.24
	Weekend trip	5.06	-0.27
	Day outing	6.79	
Water-skiing	Vacation	3.34	-0.20
	Weekend trip	5.02	-0.17
	Day outing	8.75	-0.32
Canoeing	Vacation	5.17	-0.29
	Weekend trip	2.58	-0.19
	Day outing	2.54	-0.16
Sailing	Vacation	4.96	-0.25
	Weekend trip	3.44	-0.11
	Day outing	10.07	-0.40
Other Boating	Vacation	3.87	-0.23
	Weekend trip	5.76	-0.18
	Day outing	3.95	
Outdoor Pool Swimming	Vacation	5.16	-0.23
	Weekend trip	5.33	-0.23
	Day outing	8.72	
Natural Beach Swimming	Vacation	5.87	-0.24
	Weekend trip	5.21	-0.20
	Day outing	7.52	
Horseback Riding	Vacation	4.69	-0.20
	Weekend trip	1.02	
	Day outing	7.18	
Bicycling	Vacation	5.55	-0.23
	Weekend trip	3.22	-0.25
	Day outing	15.26	
Riding Motorcycles Off the Road	Vacation	5.83	-0.27
	Weekend trip	3.90	-0.35
	Day outing	7.48	
Golf	Vacation	4.72	-0.12
	Weekend trip	9.05	
Tennis	Vacation	3.88	-0.20
	Weekend trip	3.35	
	Day outing	12.08	
Playing Other Outdoor Games or Sports	Vacation	6.15	-0.21
	Weekend trip	4.76	-0.22
	Day outing	9.01	
Going to Outdoor Concerts, Plays	Vacation	1.96	-0.17
	Weekend trip	2.07	
	Day outing	2.47	
Going to Outdoor Sports Events	Vacation	2.37	-0.14
	Weekend trip	2.99	-0.33
	Day outing	5.61	-0.16
Visiting Zoos, Fairs, Amusement Parks	Vacation	2.59	-0.19
	Weekend trip	2.12	-0.20
	Day outing	2.29	-0.06

[a]From double log functions with days during the summer season as the dependent variable and travel cost as the price variable.
Source: Adams, Lewis, and Drake.

Table 9-4. Estimated Price Elasticities of Demand for Recreation Activities in Arizona[a]

Arizona Regions	Hunting			Fishing		General Rural Outdoor Recreation
	Deer	Other Big Game	Small Game	Cold Water	Warm Water	
Northeast	-0.43	-0.33	-1.06	-0.40	-0.48	-0.12
Northcentral	-0.30	-0.39	-0.52	-0.38	-0.65	-0.15
Northwest	-0.44	—	-0.74	-0.41	-0.31	-0.35
Southwest	-0.21	—	-0.68	—	-0.33	-0.56
Central	-0.87	-0.23	-0.54	-0.74	-0.44	-0.30
Southcentral	-0.27	-0.40	-0.36	-0.59	-0.83	-0.14
Southeast	-0.27	-0.62	-0.52	-0.97	-0.85	-0.36

[a]Elasticities are computed at the mean variable cost per household trip and mean number of household trips taken in 1970.
Source: Gum and Martin.

Table 9-5. Estimated Price Elasticities of Demand for Selected Recreation Products and Services, United States

Product or Service	Price Elasticity
Automobiles	-1.2 to -2.1
Gasoline	-0.2 to -0.6
Tires	-0.6
Public transportation	-0.4
Airline travel	-2.4
Electricity	-1.3
Shoes	-0.4
All clothing	-0.6
Pleasure boats	-1.3
Radio and TV sets	-1.2
Furniture	-1.2
Newspapers	-0.1
All food	-0.4
Beer	-0.9 to 1.1
Cigarettes	-0.5
Golfing, club members	-0.7
Camping, Rocky Mountains	-0.4
Skiing, Aspen	-0.7

ences, there are no close substitutes. Other recreation activities — attending outdoor sports events, for example — while desirable, face considerably more competition, and the demand for them will be much more dependent on price.

Similarly, the demand for high-priced goods and services which account for a large portion of purchasers' incomes will be relatively sensitive to price. The price elasticity of demand for boats, automobiles, and air travel is higher than that for matches to light a campfire. The demand for less expensive products will not be so sensitive to prices. The small percentage of income spent on these goods and services means that it simply will not be worthwhile to waste time and energy worrying about their prices.

How, then, can we explain the relatively low price elasticity of demand for most recreation activities? First, most are unique, having few close substitutes, thus their demand is likely to be inelastic, i.e., price elasticity is likely to be low. If the direct cost or price of a recreation activity increases, few of its participants will turn to the close substitutes that are available. If its price decreases, few participants in substitute activities will switch to this recreation activity.

Second, the price elasticity of demand for a recreation activity is not the same as the elasticity of demand for the opportunities provided by a single recreation site. Since each recreation industry includes a large number of sites where the activity can take place, the price elasticity of demand for each site providing the opportunity will usually be less inelastic than for the activity in the national market. This is because most recreation sites have some close substitutes in the regional market. Trout fishing at Rocky Mountain sites, for example, has been estimated to have a price elasticity of -0.4. In contrast, all fishing tends to be even less price elastic, -0.2.

Price elasticity of demand is related to the quality of the resource. Table 9-4 shows that price elasticities for deer hunting in Arizona are low in all regions except the rather poor hunting Central region surrounding Phoenix, the population center of the state. Similarly, elasticities for cold-water fishing are lowest in the northern regions, which include the high mountain areas of the state with superior resources.

It is often asserted that the price elasticity of demand for recreation activities also depends on the importance of the recreation expenditure in consumer budgets. The demand for recreation activities like nature walks on a day outing may be quite inelastic. Typical consumers spend a very small portion of their income for recreation activities on day outings near home, and the quantity they demand may not be influenced much by changes in price within a reasonable range. The price elasticity of demand for recreation activities is often less elastic for day outings than for weekend or vacation trips in the United States. For example, the price elasticity of demand for nature walks was estimated as -0.07 for day outings, compared with -0.18 while on weekend trips and -0.22 on vacation trips. This relationship may result in the fact that the direct cost or price of nature walks on day outings is usually lower than for nature walks on weekend or vacation trips and, thus, are less important in the consumer's budget.

Although a tendency of this sort is often hypothesized, there is no guarantee that it always exists. It is also true that price elasticity of demand is related to the frequency of purchase and availability of substitutes. The availability of small blocks of leisure time during a typical workweek results in more frequent nature walks on day outings and the necessity to minimize driving time results in fewer substitutes available near where people live. However, if the opportunity to walk in one park is exactly like that provided by other suitable open space in the neighborhood, and if the park establishes an entrance fee (that raises the price above the price of substitute sites), the park's use will be reduced.

Price Elasticity and Total Expenditure

Many important decisions depend on the price elasticity of demand for recreation. One reason why this is so is that the price elasticity of demand determines whether a given change in price will increase or decrease the amount of money spent on a recreation activity — often a matter of basic importance to consumers and managers of private and public recreation resources. In this section, we show how the price elasticity of demand determines the effect of a price change on total expenditures for a recreation activity.

First, consider a recreation activity where demand is price elastic. In this case, if the price is reduced, the total amount spent on the activity will increase. To see why, suppose that the price elasticity of demand for outdoor jazz concerts at a site near where you live is -2.0 and that the price of concerts is reduced by 1 percent. Because the price elasticity of demand is -2.0, the 1 percent reduction in price results in a 2 percent increase in attendance at jazz concerts. Because the total amount spent on concerts equals the quantity demanded times the price, the 1 percent reduction in price will be more than offset by the 2 percent increase in quantity demanded. The result of the price cut will be an increase in the total amount spent.

On the other hand, if the price of a recreation activity is increased, the total amount spent on the activity will fall. For example, if the price of outdoor jazz concerts is raised by 1 percent, this will reduce the quantity demanded by 2 percent. The 2 percent reduction in the quantity demanded will more than offset the 1 percent increase in price, the result being a decrease in total expenditures.

Next, consider a recreation activity where demand is price inelastic. In this case, if the price is reduced, the total amount spent on the activity will decrease. To see why, suppose that the price elasticity of demand for recreation activity is -0.5 and the direct cost or price of trips is reduced by 1 percent. Because the price elasticity of demand is -0.5, the 1 percent price reduction results in a 0.5 percent increase in the number of trips demanded. Since the total amount spent on trips equals the quantity demanded times the price, the 0.5 percent increase in the quantity demanded will be more than offset by the 1 percent reduction in price. The result of the price cut will be a decrease in the total amount spent.

On the other hand, if the price of a recreation activity is increased, the total amount spent on the activity will increase. For example, if the direct cost or price of recreation trips is raised by 1 percent, this will reduce the number of trips demanded by 0.5 percent. The 1 percent price increase will more than offset the 0.5 percent reduction in quantity demanded, the result being an increase in the total amount spent.

Finally, consider a recreation activity where demand is of unitary elasticity. In this case, a price increase or decrease results in no difference in the total amount spent on the activity. Why? Because a price decrease (increase) of a certain percentage always results in a quantity increase (decrease) of the same percentage, so that the product of the price times quantity is unaffected.

Why Elasticities Are Useful

It may initially appear based on the discussion in Chapters 5, 6, and 7, that the regression coefficients for the independent variables included in a demand function are sufficient measures of the responsiveness of the quantity demanded to changes in the determinants of demand. For example, the regression coefficient for direct cost or price of -0.1 when multiplied by a $10 increase in the price of recreation trips tells us that individual demand will decrease by 1 trip per year. The regression coefficient for price represents the slope of the demand curve for recreation trips, i.e., the change in quantity demanded resulting from each $1 change in price.

Suppose we redraw the demand curve, measuring price in cents rather than dollars. The slope of the demand curve is now -0.001, or 100 times less than before. A shift from dollars to cents in measuring price causes a drastic decrease in the downward slope of the demand curve, even though there has been no real change in the demand curve itself. Suppose we redraw the demand curve, again measuring price in dollars and quantity demanded in hours (with 10 hours per trip). The slope of the same demand curve now becomes -1.0, or 10 times greater than initially. Slope of the demand curve is a very unreliable indicator of how responsive quantity demanded is to changes in price. Similarly, comparisons of the absolute changes in other determinants of demand can be ambiguous, as they depend on the units in which the independent variables and quantity demanded are measured.

There is an additional disadvantage to the use of regression coefficients as a measure of how responsive quantity demanded is to changes in the value of the independent variables such as price. Suppose we want to compare the demand curve for a city park with the demand curve for a national park. We want to know which recreation activity is more responsive to a change in direct cost or price. Comparative slopes of the two demand curves tell us nothing in this respect. A $1 increase in the price of recreation at the city park may decrease the quantity demanded by 100 thousand visits per year. A $1 increase in the price of visits to a national park may decrease the quantity demanded by 5 thousand visits per year. But this does not mean that the demand for the city park is more responsive to price changes than is the demand for the national park. $1 change in the price of visits to a city park is a tremendous change. A $1 change in the price of trips to a national park is of little consequence.

To overcome these problems, the noted British economist, Alfred Marshall, defined the concept of elasticity as the percentage change in quantity demanded divided by the percentage change in a determinant of demand. Dividing a percentage by a percentage results in a measure of responsiveness that is independent of the units of measurement. Thus, the percentage increase in the price of recreation trips is the same, regard less of whether price is measured in dollars or cents. And the percentage reduction in the quantity demanded is the same, regardless of whether it is measured in trips, days, or hours. Thus, elasticities provide useful measures of the responsiveness to price and nonprice variables included in a demand function for a recreation site, as well as facilitating comparisons between recreation sites and activities.

Estimating Regression Coefficients from Elasticities

When information is available on the price elasticity of demand for similar recreation resources, it is possible to estimate the slope of a demand curve for a particular recreation site. Regression coefficients can be derived from the elasticities for each of the independent variables in a linear demand function using the following formula:

$$\text{Regression coefficient for price} = \text{price elasticity of demand} \times \frac{\text{quantity demanded}}{\text{price}}$$

Note how this formula relates to the one used to estimate the price elasticity of demand from a regression coefficient. First, the position of these two values changes from one side to the other side of the equation. Then, quantity demanded is divided by price; formerly, price was divided by quantity demanded.

Suppose that you have access to the elasticities presented in Table 9-1. In this case, the price elasticity of demand is -0.4 for recreation trips. The average direct cost is shown as $10 per trip and, at this price, the representative individual user takes 5 trips per year. If we insert these values in the formula:

$$\text{Regression coefficient for price} = -0.4 \times \frac{5}{\$20} = -0.1$$

Thus, dividing the quantity demanded of 5 trips, by the average price,

264

of $20 per trip, equals 0.25, and multiplying this by the price elasticity of demand, -0.4, equals the -0.1 regression coefficient for price. This is identical to the value shown in Table 9-1 as the regression coefficient for price of recreation trips by individual users.

The necessary information (in addition to elasticities) is often readily available or can be estimated. Quantity demanded can be represented as the current number of visits to the recreation site and price, as the average direct costs per visit. The latter can be approximated from information on average distance traveled and direct costs per mile, discussed in Chapter 4. If the only available information on quantity demanded is the current number of visitors per year, say, 100 thousand, the regression coefficient for price or slope of a site demand curve can be estimated by inserting this value in the formula:

$$\text{Regression coefficient for price} = -0.4 \times \frac{100{,}000}{\$20} = -2{,}000$$

This means that each $1 increase in price causes demand for the recreation site to fall by 2,000 visits per year. This is approximately the same as the demand of 20,000 individual users taking an average of 5 trips per year (Table 9-1). That this is the case can be seen by multiplying the regression coefficient for price in the individual demand function by the number of individual users taking an average of 5 trips. Thus, $-0.1 \times 20{,}000 = -2{,}000$, which is the regression coefficient for price and the slope of the demand curve for the recreation site.

The regression coefficients for all of the independent variable in demand functions can be estimated in the same way from their elasticities.

INCOME ELASTICITY OF DEMAND

So far this chapter has dealt almost exclusively with the price elasticity of demand. But price is not, of course, the only variable that influences the demand for recreation. Another important variable is the level of money income among consumers in the market. The income elasticity of demand is a measure of the sensitivity of quantity demanded to the money income of consumers. Income elasticity of demand is defined as the percentage change in the quantity demanded resulting from a 1 percent change in consumer income, holding constant the effect of all other variables that influence demand.

The income elasticity of demand for recreation is a basic concept used by economists. Fortunately, it is calculated in the same way as price elasticity. First, suppose that you have access to a statistical demand function for a recreation site as presented in Table 9-1. In this case, the income elasticity of demand can be estimated using the following formula:

$$\text{Income elasticity} = \frac{\text{regression coef-}}{\text{ficient for income}} \times \frac{\text{original income}}{\text{original quantity demanded}}$$

The regression coefficient for income (in thousands) is shown in Table 9-1 as 0.1 for trips to a recreation site. The average household income is shown as $25 thousand and, at this income level, the representative individual user takes 5 trips per year. If we insert these values in the formula:

$$\text{Income elasticity} = 0.1 \times \frac{\$25}{5} = 0.5$$

Thus, dividing household income, $25 thousand, by the original quantity demanded, 5 trips, equals 5, and multiplying this by the regression coefficient for household income, 0.1, equals 0.5 income elasticity of demand. This means that a 1 percent increase in household income from the average level results in a 0.5 percent increase in quantity demanded, or conversely for a decrease in income.

This is the recommended procedure when statistical demand functions are available; however, sometimes you may have only two data points on an income consumption curve for a recreation site from which you can estimate an arc or average income elasticity of demand between the two points. Suppose you notice that household income increases by an average of 20 percent at the same time that the number of visits to the study site increases by an average of 10 percent. Assuming that all other variables are unchanged, you can use the following formula to obtain a reasonable approximation:

$$\text{Income elasticity} = \frac{\text{percentage change}}{\text{in quantity demanded}} \div \frac{\text{percentage change}}{\text{in income}}$$

Thus, the percentage change in demand for the study site, 0.1, divided by the percentage change in household income, 0.2, equals 0.5 income elasticity of demand.

When information is available on the original and ending incomes and quantities, the generally accepted procedure is to use the average income and quantity demanded. In other words, we use as an estimate of the income elasticity of demand:

$$\text{Income elasticity} = \frac{\dfrac{\text{change in quantity demanded}}{\text{sum of original and ending quantities/2}}}{\dfrac{\text{change in income}}{\text{sum of original and ending income/2}}}$$

This provides a measure of the average responsiveness of demand to the change in income.

For most recreation goods and services, increases in income lead to increases in demand and income elasticity will be positive. These are called "normal goods." Those few for which consumption decreases in response to a rise in income have negative income elasticities and are called "inferior goods." The income elasticity of normal goods is considered low (inelastic) when it is between zero and one, or high (elastic) when it is greater than one. Elasticity is defined as unitary when a 1 percent increase in income leads to a 1 percent increase in the quantity demanded. These and related concepts are illustrated in Figure 9-5.

It should not be surprising that different recreation goods and services have different income elasticities (as the studies summarized in Table 9-6 show). Those that consumers regard as necessities tend to have lower income elasticities than do luxuries. The reason is that as incomes rise it becomes possible for households to devote a smaller proportion of their income to meeting basic needs and a larger proportion to buying things they have always wanted but could not afford. Indeed, one way to define luxuries and necessities is to say that luxuries have high income elasticities of demand and necessities, low.

Examples of recreational luxuries include African safaris, yachting, foreign travel, mobile home camping, owning condominiums at ski areas and ocean beaches, and possibly vacation trips to national parks in the western states. Examples of recreation necessities include pic-

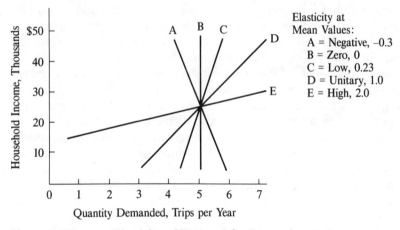

Figure 9-5. Income Elasticity of Demand for Recreation

Table 9-6. Estimated Income Elasticities of Demand for Selected Recreation Goods and Services, United States

Goods and Services	Income Elasticity	Goods and Services	Income Elasticity
Swimming Trips	0.31	Restaurant Meals	1.48
Boating Trips	0.34	Liquor	1.0
Camping Trips	0.42	Wine	1.4
Fishing Trips	0.47	Automobiles	3.0
Skiing	0.5	Gasoline	1.1
Recreation Expenditures	1.4	Housing	0.6
Theatre, Live	1.98	Cigarettes	0.8
All Food	0.2	Consumer Durables	1.8

nicking and playing outdoor games and sports, and possibly swimming. Many other recreation goods and services are not very responsive to income changes, rather they are purchased in fairly constant amounts regardless of changes in income. If the income elasticity of demand for a recreation site is close to zero, we would not expect recreation use to increase very much on account of increases in income.

Table 9-6 suggests that the income elasticity of demand for food in restaurants (1.48) exceeds that for food served at home (all food is 0.2). Semiprocessed food purchased in retail grocery stores is combined with household labor in its preparation for eating in the home primarily for nourishment and palatability. Food eaten away from home on recreation trips provides nourishment, palatability, and entertainment. The entertainment value of food eaten away from home probably has a higher income elasticity of demand.

The reaction of demand to changes in income is extremely important. In most Western economies, growth in productivity has caused the level of income to double every 20 to 30 years over a sustained period of at least a century. This rise in income is shared to some extent by most households, regardless of initial income level. As they find their incomes increasing, they demand more recreation goods and services. But the demand for some commodities, such as food and basic clothing, will not increase very much as incomes rise, while the demand for other goods and services increase rapidly.

As household incomes rise, causing demand for a particular recreation activity to increase rapidly, demand for the recreation equipment necessary to participate increases even more rapidly. Demand for services necessary to participate is also rising rapidly. However, once the growth in demand for the activity levels off (matures), the demand for recreation equipment falls sharply, while the demand for services may level off or continue to grow at a more moderate level. Thus, the uneven impact of increased income on the demand for different recreation goods and services has important effects on different groups in the economy.

The income elasticity of expenditures on recreation is expected to be different at widely different income levels. Thompson and Tinsley estimate that the income elasticity of expenditures on recreation in North Carolina averages an elastic 1.4. However, for low income households, recreation demand is inelastic, 0.8. It is an elastic 1.3 for households with middle income and 2.0 for upper middle income, then levels off at 1.4 for upper income. Consider how a family's recreation demand may change as its income level rises. When incomes are very low, households may participate in games and sports, picnicking, swimming, and warm-water fishing. At higher levels of income, they may participate in the relatively inexpensive forms of recreation, such as tent camping and sightseeing along with their participation in picnicking, swimming, games, and sports. At yet higher levels of income, they are likely to participate in more expensive recreation activities requiring the purchase of special equipment such as snow skiing and backpacking. In this sequence, the income elasticity of low cost recreation activities may be high at low levels of income, but decrease as income rises and more costly recreation activities replace the less costly ones. Different recreation activities will show different patterns (as illustrated in Chapter 7, Table 7-4). Ice-skating and sledding are likely to exhibit low income elasticities, while downhill and cross-country skiing prove to be income-elastic over a wide range of income. Figure 9-6 shows one particular pattern of income elasticity varying with income.

Many studies have been made of the income elasticity of demand for particular recreation activities and sites. Generally, they have found that the effect of income on demand for recreation activities is inelastic, less than 1. Studies of demand for some particular recreation sites show that income elasticity is zero with no measurable effect on site demand.

Table 9-6 illustrates the findings of empirical studies. Consider the following results obtained by Kalter and Gosse. Based on a national Census survey, the income elasticity of demand in the United States is estimated as 0.31 for swimming, 0.34 for boating, 0.42 for camping, and 0.47 for fishing trips on weekends. These estimates seem reasonable. We would expect the income elasticity of demand to be lower for swimming than for other water-based recreation activities that may require substantial investments in recreation equipment.

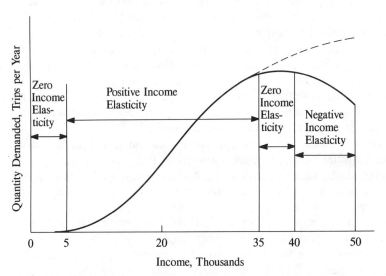

Figure 9-6. Effect of Income Levels on Income Elasticity of Demand for a Recreation Activity

How can the income elasticity of expenditure for recreation be elastic, 1.4, and the income elasticity of demand be an inelastic 0.3 to 0.5 for important recreation activities? The reasons are straightforward. First, as incomes rise, households participate in additional recreation activities while the number of days per year in any one activity remains about the same for most activities. Second, with higher income, they tend to spend more money per day on overnight recreation trips and on recreation equipment. These relationships are shown in Chapter 2, Tables 2-1 and 2-2.

For most recreation activities, the income elasticity of demand is positive, indicating that as the economy expands and national income increases, demand for recreation will also increase. However, the actual size of the elasticity coefficient is also important. Suppose, for example, that the income elasticity of demand for a particular recreation site is 0.4. This means that a 1 percent increase in income will cause demand for this site to increase by only 4/10 of 1 percent. The recreation resource would not be maintaining it's relative importance in the economy. Another recreation site might have an income elasticity of 1.5. For this product, demand will increase 1.5 times as fast as income. We see, then, that if the income elasticity is less than 1.0 for a particular recreation resource, the operator will not share proportionately in increases in national income. On the other hand, if income elasticity is greater than 1.0, the operator will gain more than a proportionate share of increases in income.

These relationships have important policy implications for both private and public managers. Recreation resources whose demand functions have high income elasticities will have good growth opportunities in an expanding economy. Recreation resources with low income elasticities, on the other hand, are not so sensitive to the level of economic activity. This may be desirable in that such an economic activity is, to a large extent, recession proof. But, since private managers cannot expect to share fully in a growth economy, society may be forced to rely on government agencies to provide such recreation resources. Private managers may seek entry into other industries that provide better long-run growth opportunities.

The income elasticity of demand for recreation has figured significantly in national policy. Congress and most presidents of the United States have stated that improving the nation's supply of recreation resources is one of our primary national goals. If income elasticity of demand for recreation were high (something in excess of 1.0), an improvement in the supply of recreation resources would be a natural by-product of a prosperous economy from World War II to the present. However, the fact is that the income elasticity of demand for particular recreation activities and resources is low, which means that a relatively small percentage of additional income is spent on it. As a result, the supply of recreation resources will not improve much even if the economy is booming and incomes are increasing. In this case, direct governmental actions such as public recreation programs, subsidies to the private sector of the recreation industry, and the like are necessary to bring the stock of recreation resources up to the desired level. Income elasticity of demand for recreation provides an important input in debates on national recreation policy, and these debates have stimulated research to measure income elasticities. Many other considerations enter the debate, of course, and they will be introduced in subsequent parts of this book.

CROSS ELASTICITY OF DEMAND

Besides the direct cost or price of recreation and the level of consumer income — the factors discussed in previous sections of this chapter — the demand for recreation also depends on the price of other goods and services. Suppose the direct cost or price of camping is held constant. The amount of camping demanded will be influenced by the price of commercial accommodations such as motels and lodges in the region of the campground. Cross elasticity of demand is used to measure the sensitivity of the former's demand to changes in the latter's price. Cross elasticity is defined as the percent change in the quantity demanded of one good or service resulting from a 1 percent change in the price of another good or service.

The cross elasticity of demand for recreation is a very important concept and one that economists often use, so it is worthwhile to spend some time considering how it is computed. Fortunately, it is calculated in the same manner as price elasticity, previously described. The distinguishing characteristic of cross elasticity is that the direct cost or price of trips to the second site is substituted for price of trips to the study site.

First, suppose that you have access to a statistical demand function for a recreation site as presented in Table 9-1. In this case, the cross elasticity of demand for recreation can be estimated using the following formula:

$$\text{Cross elasticity} = \frac{\substack{\text{regression coefficient} \\ \text{for substitutes}} \times \text{original price of substitutes}}{\text{original quantity demanded at this site}}$$

The regression coefficient for cross elasticity is shown in Table 9-1 as 0.054 for trips to a recreation site. The average direct cost or price of substitute sites is shown as $24 per trip and, at this price, the representative individual user takes 5 trips per year to this site. If we insert these values in the formula:

$$\text{Cross elasticity} = 0.054 \times \frac{\$24}{5} = 0.26$$

Thus, dividing the original price of substitute sites ($24) by the original quantity demanded for this site (5 trips) equals 4.8, and multiplying this by the regression coefficient for substitution (0.054) equals 0.26 cross elasticity of demand. This means that a 1 percent increase in the price of substitutes from the original level results in a 0.26 percent increase in quantity demanded at the site, or conversely for a price decrease.

This is the recommended procedure when statistical demand functions are available, however, sometimes you may have only two data points on a recreation site's substitution function from which you can estimate an arc or average cross elasticity of demand between the two points. Suppose you notice that the direct cost or price of trips to substitutes increases by 20 percent at the same time the number of visits to the study site increases by 5.2 percent. Assuming that all other variables are unchanged, you can use the following formula to obtain a reasonable approximation:

$$\text{Cross elasticity} = \frac{\text{percentage change}}{\text{in quantity demanded}} \div \frac{\text{percentage change in}}{\text{price of substitutes}}$$

Thus, the percentage change in demand for the study site, 0.052, divided by the percentage change in the price of substitutes, 0.20, equals 0.26 cross elasticity of demand.

When information is available on the original and ending prices of trips to the second site and the number of trips to the study site, the generally accepted procedure is to use the average price of substitutes and quantity demanded. In other words, we use as an estimate of the cross elasticity of demand:

$$\text{Cross elasticity} = \frac{\dfrac{\text{change in quantity demand}}{\text{sum of original and ending quantities/2}}}{\dfrac{\text{change in price of substitutes}}{\text{sum of original and ending price of substitutes/2}}}$$

This provides a measure of the average responsiveness of demand at the study site to the change in price of substitutes.

Pairs of goods and services are classified as substitutes or complements, depending on the sign of the cross elasticity of demand. If the cross elasticity of demand is positive, two goods or services are substitutes because a decrease in the price of motels, for example, will result in a decrease in the demand for camping — many campers may really prefer the more comfortable motel accommodations. Panel 1 of Figure 9-7 illustrates the effect on demand for camping of the construction of low cost motels in a resort area. If the price of commercial accommodations is decreased from $40 to $20 per night, the demand for camping declines from 6 to 2 nights. Motel and campground operators are

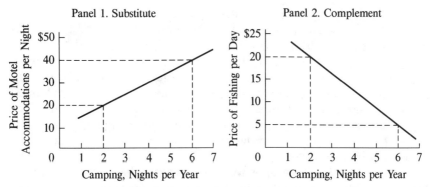

Figure 9-7. Hypothetical Cross Elasticity of Demand for Camping with Changes in the Price of a Substitute and a Complement

competitors in resort areas; when the price of motels goes down, campground use declines.

On the other hand, if the cross elasticity of demand is negative, two goods or services are complements. For example, camping and fishing may be complements because an increase in the price of fishing licenses will decrease the demand for fishing. This, in turn, decreases the demand for camping because recreation resources that provide camping and fishing opportunities tend to be used together. Panel 2 of Figure 9-7 illustrates the effect on demand for camping of an increase in the direct cost or price of fishing at the same site. If the direct costs of fishing are increased from $5 to $20 per day, the demand for camping will decline from 6 to 2 nights.

When cross elasticity of demand is zero, or nearly zero, we can conclude that the goods or services are unrelated and in separate and distinct markets. We would know this because variations in the price of one good or service would have no effect on demand for the second.

When products are always used together — as for skis, ski boots, and ski poles — the demand for each item is referred to as being in "joint demand" with the other products. A price increase of a joint product such as skis typically leads to a reduction in demand for the complete package of skis, boots, and poles. Joint products represent the extreme case of complements.

Many studies have been made of the cross elasticity of demand for various pairs of goods or services. After all, it frequently is very important to know how a change in the price of one good or service will affect the demand for another. For example, what would be the effect of a 1 percent increase in the direct cost or price of boating on one reservoir on the demand for boating on another reservoir located in the same region? According to a study by Kurtz and King of motor boating on large reservoirs in Arizona, the cross elasticity of demand between pairs of reservoirs is sometimes positive and sometimes negative, depending on the characteristics of the reservoirs and the preferences of recreation users.

Table 9-7 illustrates the relationships that may occur. The negative sign for the relationship between Bartlett and Canyon reservoirs indicates that a 1 percent increase in the price of trips to one of these reservoirs reduces the number of trips demanded for recreation use of the other reservoir by -2.9 to -4.4 percent. This complementary relationship indicates that users desire a variety of motor boating opportunities at both reservoirs.

On the other hand, the positive signs suggest that a substitute relationship exists between Apache and Canyon reservoirs. A 1 percent increase in the price of trips to one of these reservoirs increases the number of trips demanded for recreation use of the other reservoir by 1.87 to 2.6 percent. For substitutes, recreation opportunities provided by the respective reservoirs are perceived by consumers to be reasonably comparable (the same), so that they will tend to use the least cost resource.

The relationship between the Saguaro and Carl Pleasant reservoirs illustrates a case where one is a substitute and one a complement of the other. A 1 percent increase in the price of trips to the Carl Pleasant reservoir increases the number of trips demanded for recreation use of the Saguaro reservoir by 1.5 percent. On the other hand, a 1 percent increase in the price of trips to the Saguaro reservoir reduces the number of trips demanded for recreation use of the Carl Pleasant reservoir by 3.4 percent. This relationship indicates that recreation users of both reservoirs consider the recreation opportunities provided by the Saguaro reservoir (for water skiing and cruising) more desirable than the Carl Pleasant reservoir (for fishing). Both reservoirs are located 35 miles from Phoenix, Arizona.

Table 9-7. Estimated Cross Elasticity of Demand for Motor Boating on Selected Reservoirs in Arizona

Pairs of Reservoirs	Cross Elasticity of Demand[a]	Relationship
Canyon to Barlett	-4.40	Complement
Barlett to Canyon	-2.98	Complement
Canyon to Apache	1.87	Substitute
Apache to Canyon	2.60	Substitute
Saguaro to Carl Pleasant	3.44	Substitute
Carl Pleasant to Saguaro	-1.54	Complement

[a]Cross elasticity of demand is defined as the percentage change in the number of trips demanded to the first reservoir listed, resulting from a 1 percent change in the direct cost or price of trips to the second reservoir listed.
Source: Kurtz and King.

LONG-RUN ELASTICITY OF DEMAND

Time may have an important effect on elasticity of demand for rec-reation. One of the general characteristics of consumer demand is the lack of an instantaneous response. Individuals often react slowly to changes in price and other conditions. To illustrate this delayed (or lagged) effect, consider the demand for recreation travel. Suppose the direct cost or price of a trip increased by 10 percent relative to the price of other goods and services, primarily owing to the increased price of gasoline. What effect will this have on demand for recreation travel? In the very short-run, the effect will be slight. Tourists may be more careful to avoid unneeded side trips, but total demand for recreation travel, which is highly dependent on the established patterns of recreation behavior and recreation equipment owned, will probably not be greatly affected. Prices will go up and demand will not fall very much. In other words, the short-run demand for recreation travel is relatively inelastic.

Over the long-run, however, the increase in direct costs of travel has more substantial effects. Consumers will reduce their purchases of travel trailers and other recreation equipment, and those products that are purchased will be more energy efficient. When their present auto is replaced, it may well be by a more economical model. Similarly, the travel industry itself will tend to switch to other energy sources, will employ less energy-intensive methods, or will relocate in areas where energy requirements are less.

Consumer adjustments to changes in the price and nonprice determinants of demand for recreation often takes time to accomplish. We have all seen instances in which individuals seem to respond to price increases by apparently not reducing consumption very much, if at all. Obviously, tastes and preferences differ substantially among consumers, causing the rational response of some to be a very slight adjustment in number of trips demanded. Also, they must first be assured that the price increase is real and not simply nominal (consistent with the general inflation rate).

Every empirical demand curve in recreation pertains to a certain time interval such as the summer season or, at most, a calendar year. In general, demand is likely to be more sensitive to price over a long period of time than a short one. Thus, the ultimate effect of a price increase on demand may be substantial, but it will take a number of years before the full impact is felt. The phenomenon of long-run elasticity exceeding short-run elasticity is typical for most determinants of demand.

Table 9-8 illustrates the expected sensitivity of the long-run quantity demanded to a change in direct cost or price in year 1. The hypothesis is that while empirical studies show the price elasticity of demand for

Table 9-8. Cumulative Price Elasticity of Demand for Outdoor Recreation in the Long Run

Year	Cumulative Price Elasticities of Demand in the Long Run[a]	Percentage of Total Long Run Demand Effect
First	-0.20	15.7
Second	-0.45	19.3
Third	-0.69	19.3
Fourth	-0.90	16.4
Fifth	-1.06	12.9
Sixth	-1.17	8.6
Seventh	-1.24	5.0
Eighth	-1.27	2.9
Ninth	-1.27	0
Total	-1.27	100.0

[a]First year demand elasticity is for outdoor recreation; years 2-9 have the same relationship to year 1 as for other products.
Source: Adapted from Waugh.

recreation to be inelastic (less than -1.0) in the short-run, it is expected to be elastic (greater than -1.0) in the long-run. This is based on empirical studies by the distinguished statistician, Waugh, who demonstrated the phenomenon for a large number of products in the United States. On this basis, a 10 percent increase in the price of recreation travel would result in a 2 percent decrease in demand in the first year when price is very inelastic, -0.2. Thus, the immediate effect on recreation travel would be insignificant. But if the direct cost or price of recreation travel is raised 10 percent and held at the higher level for a decade, price elasticity of demand for recreation travel would likely increase from -0.2 in the first year, to approximately -0.45 in the second year, -0.69 in the third year, and so on, until the ninth year when it reached a level of about -1.27. Thus, the long-run price elasticity of demand for recreation travel is expected to be elastic. On this basis, a 10 percent increase in price would have a significant 12.7 percent effect on the demand for recreation travel and the total revenue of the travel industry might decrease in the long-run.

Table 9-8 also shows the proportion of the long-run elasticity of demand over the nine years that is expected to occur each year. Price elasticity of demand increases to a peak in the second and third years, then declines at a decreasing rate from the fourth to eighth years. This long-run effect is similar to an ordinary "decay curve" in physics. It seems to fit observed consumer behavior in recreation. Consumers gradually shift to substitutes if a price increase is continuous over the long-run, all else equal.

The National Park Service applied this concept in a study of the visual effect of power plants and air pollution on recreation demand for the Indiana Dunes National Lakeshore located on Lake Michigan near the industrial city of Gary, Indiana. Coal-fired power plants are located on two sides of the recreation area. The agency study relied on work by Brookshire, Ives, and Schulze that estimated the visual effect of power plants and air pollution on willingness to pay for the recreation use of Lake Powell and Glen Canyon National Recreation Area in southern Utah. A random sample of 104 households reported they were willing to pay an average of $2.77 per day in admission fees to avoid seeing the Navajo power plant south of Lake Powell and associated air pollution (in 1973 dollars). Updated, the visual effect at Indian Dunes was estimated as 15.3 percent (= $3.82/$25) of the direct cost or price of $25 per household visit (1977 dollars).

The price elasticity of demand for lakeshore swimming has been estimated to range from -0.19 to -0.24 and average -0.22 (Adams, Lewis, and Drake). Thus, if the visual effect of the power plants continued for a decade, recreation visits to the lakeshore would be expected to decrease by 3.4 percent (= 15.3 × 0.22 in the first year), by 7.5 percent in the second year, and so on, until it reached a level about 21.4 percent (15.3 × 1.4) below what it was originally. This is calculated from the accumulated long-run elasticities of demand over the 9 years shown in column 1 of Table 9-8. Thus, the long-run visual effect of the power plants is expected to substantially reduce recreation demand for the Indiana Dunes National Lakeshore, assuming other factors such as population do not change.

These estimates should be treated as first approximations, to be verified by future studies of the long-run demand for specific recreation activities and resources. Little or no research has been undertaken thus far because of two problems. First, time-series demand studies used to estimate the effect of time often confound the long-run price effects with other residual effects. Second, cross-sectional demand studies have been unable to include the effect of time because respondents cannot remember the relevant information for past years.

When time-series data are used in demand analysis, the year can be entered as a separate independent variable to account for long-term trends in demand, such as might result from changing consumer preferences and other conditions (residuals not included as separate variables). The effect of time can also be estimated for specific conditions by the use of lagged variables such as the previous year's direct costs to explain this year's demand.

Cross-sectional data from a sample of individual consumers in a single year are usually used in recreation demand analysis, and it is even more difficult to include an effective measure of time. Respondents have difficulty recalling the direct costs of recreation trips during the past 12 months and would be unable to accurately report direct costs for the past 5 to 10 years. To overcome this problem in future studies of the effect of time, it may be possible to develop a panel of respondents who would report their direct costs and trips each month for 5 to 10 years, similar to the pioneering study by LaPage and Ragain of demand for camping in the northeastern region of the United States. Their work suggests that long-run demand is more sensitive to changes in direct costs than data on the trends in aggregate demand for camping would suggest.

PRICE ELASTICITY FOR DERIVED DEMAND PRODUCTS

The demand functions for some goods and services contain as one of the independent variables the quantity demanded of another product. This relationship indicates that the quantity of the good or service purchased is derived from the demand for the final product, so we use the term "derived demand". The demand for air transportation is an example. The quantity of air transportation to major resort areas is not a direct demand but rather is derived from the demand for recreation. Similarly, the quantity of mortgage credit demanded for the purchase of second homes and condominiums at resort areas is not determined autonomously or directly; rather it is derived from the more fundamental demand to stay in seasonal recreation housing. The consumer demand for recreation equipment such as skis, boots, poles, and special clothing is derived from the final demand for skiing. The final demand for recreation determines, in large part, the demand for the goods and services used as inputs in the production process. None of these goods and services is demanded because of its direct value to consumers but rather because of the role it plays in the production of recreation activity.

Although the demand for recreation activities may or may not be derived (Driver and Brown discuss demand derived from basic psychological motivations) the demand for all producer goods is derived. Producer goods are defined as those products used in the manufacture of goods and services for final consumption. Consumer demand for goods and services determines, in large part, the demand for the capital equipment, materials, labor, and energy used in producing them. For example, the demands for steel, aluminum, and plastics are all derived demands, as are the demands for machine tools and labor. None of these producers' goods is demanded because of its direct value to consumers but rather because of its input into the production of consumer goods and services.

Since the demand for producers' goods is related to consumer demand for the final products they are used to make, an examination of the final product's demand is an important part of the study of demand for intermediate or producers' goods. This relationship is not always a direct one-to-one basis. For example, the demand for intermediate goods is typically less price elastic than is the demand for the resulting final product. This is because the intermediate good represents only one input in the production process. Unless its cost represents a major part of the total cost of the final product, any given percentage price change for intermediate goods will result in a smaller percentage change in the cost (and price) of the final product.

McCallum and Adams point out that the price elasticity of demand for skiing may appear to be misleadingly low if measured simply in terms of ski lift ticket prices, since skiers could be more sensitive to changes in total direct costs. A skier pays for a ski lift ticket but also has to pay for travel, added food, overnight accommodations, equipment rental, and the like. Since the price of the ski lift ticket is often only a relatively small part of the total direct cost of skiing, the skier may not be particularly sensitive to the cost of the ticket.

This relationship can be illustrated by looking at the demand for lift tickets used in the production of downhill skiing in the United States. Assume the total direct cost to consumers of vacation ski trips to major winter resorts is $160 per day, and $20 of this is the cost of lift tickets. Assume the price of lift tickets is doubled (a 100 percent increase) so that it now requires $40 of this input for each recreation day of skiing produced. In this situation, the total direct cost of the final product — and presumably its price — will increase by only 12.5 percent (= $20/$160). If the price elasticity of demand for an additional day of downhill skiing is -0.7 (as reported by Walsh and Davitt), this 12.5 percent increase in price would result in an 8.75 percent reduction in final demand. Assuming that the purchase of a daily lift ticket or its multi-day equivalent is necessary to ski, the 100 percent increase in the price of lift tickets would result in only an 8.75 percent reduction in its demand. That implies a price elasticity of little more than -0.08 percent (= -8.75/100). In other words, a 1 percent increase in the price of lift tickets would cause vacation skier's demand for them to decline by only eight-hundredths of 1 percent. The vacation skier's demand for lift tickets is extremely price inelastic even though the demand for the final product is much less so. See Table 9-9.

Contrast the price elasticity of derived demand for lift tickets by day users who live in the region of the ski resort. In this case, assume

Table 9-9. Derived Price Elasticity of Demand for Ski Lift Tickets

Direct and Derived Demand	Price Elasticity of Demand
Downhill skiing	-0.7
Ski lift tickets	
Day use	-0.35
Weekend use	-0.22
Vacation trips	-0.087

Source: Calculated from Walsh and Davitt.

the total direct cost to consumers of 1-day ski trips to winter resorts is $40 per day, and $20 of this is the cost of lift tickets. If the price of lift tickets is doubled (a 100 percent increase), it now requires $40 of this input plus $20 direct cost of travel for each recreation day of skiing produced. This means that the total direct cost of the final product will increase by 50 percent (= $20/$40). If the price elasticity of demand for 1-day ski trips is also -0.7, this 50 percent increase in price would result in a 35 percent reduction in final demand. Assuming that the purchase of a daily lift ticket is necessary to ski, the 100 percent increase in the price of lift tickets would result in a 35 percent reduction in its demand. That implies a price elasticity of -0.35 percent (= -35/100). In other words, a 1 percent increase in the price of lift tickets would cause day user demand for them to decline by thirty-five hundredths of 1 percent. The day user demand for lift tickets is not as extremely price inelastic as that for vacation skiers. This is because its cost represents a major part of the total direct cost of the final product, one day of skiing. The total direct cost of the final product, skiing, is one-fourth as much for day users as for vacation skiers; thus the price of lift tickets accounts for four times more of the total direct cost or price of the final product, and the derived price elasticity of demand for lift tickets is four times greater.

OTHER ELASTICITIES OF DEMAND

The concept of elasticity is a useful way to measure the effect of a change in any of the independent variables on the dependent variable in a demand function. The dependent variable in an ordinary demand function is the quantity demanded or number of trips, so it is possible to calculate the demand elasticity of any variable in the function.

We have emphasized the three most common demand elasticities — price, income, and cross elasticity — but other demand elasticities are also important to recreation economic decisions. For example, Table 9-1 illustrates the elasticities of demand for the age of participants, quality of the site, population, taste and preference, and congestion or crowding. The elasticity for any determinant of demand is defined as the percentage change in quantity demanded resulting from a 1 percent change in the variable, holding constant the effect of all other variables that influence demand.

Other elasticities of demand for recreation are important, so it is worthwhile to spend some time considering how they are computed. Fortunately, they are calculated in the same way as price elasticity, previously described. First, suppose that you have access to a statistical demand function for a recreation site as presented in Table 9-1. In this case, the age elasticity of demand for a recreation site can be estimated using the following formula:

$$\text{Age elasticity} = \frac{\text{regression coef-}}{\text{ficient for age}} \times \frac{\text{original age}}{\text{original quantity demanded}}$$

The regression coefficient for age is shown in Table 9-1 as -0.088 for trips to the site. The average age is shown as 25 years, and at this age level, the representative individual user takes 5 trips per year. If we insert these values in the formula:

$$\text{Age elasticity} = -0.088 \times \frac{25}{5} = -0.44$$

Thus, dividing average age (25 years) by the original quantity demanded (5 trips) equals 5, and multiplying this by the regression coefficient for age (-0.088) equals -0.44 age elasticity of demand. This means that a 1 percent increase in the age of participants from the average level results in a 0.44 percent decrease in quantity demanded, or conversely for a decrease in age.

This is the recommended procedure when statistical demand functions are available. However, sometimes you may have only two data points on a function relating quantity consumed to another variable from which you can estimate an arc or average elasticity of demand between the two points. Suppose you notice that the average age of participants decreases by 5 percent at the same time the number of visits to the study site increases by an average of 2.2 percent. Assuming that all other variables are unchanged, you can use the following formula to obtain a reasonable approximation:

$$\text{Age elasticity} = \frac{\text{percentage change}}{\text{in quantity demanded}} \div \frac{\text{percent change}}{\text{in age}}$$

Thus, the percentage change in demand for the study site, 2.2, divided by the percentage change in age, -5.0, equals -0.44 age elasticity of demand.

When information is available on the original and ending ages and quantities, the generally accepted procedure is to use average age and quantity demanded. In other words, we use the following formula to estimate the age elasticity of demand:

$$\frac{\dfrac{\text{change in quantity demanded}}{\text{sum of original and ending quantities/2}}}{\dfrac{\text{change in age}}{\text{sum of original and ending ages/2}}}$$

This provides a measure of the average responsiveness of demand to the change in age.

Many studies have been made of other elasticities of demand for recreation. Table 9-10 summarizes the results of a U.S. Census survey of several thousand participants in hiking, camping, boating, fishing, and swimming in the United States. Note the substantial differences among elasticities of demand with respect to age, education, and sex. For example, age elasticity of demand is inelastic and positive for hik-

Table 9-10. Other Elasticities of Demand for Outdoor Recreation

Independent Variable	Activity	Elasticity of Demand
Population	Outdoor Recreation	1.0
Age	Hiking, Vacation	0.98
	Camping, Trip	0.37
	Boating, Trip	-0.37
	Fishing, Overall	-0.41
	Swimming, Trip	0.89
Education	Hiking, Overall	0.33
	Camping, Vacation	0.39
	Boating, Overall	0.51
	Fishing, Vacation	0.58
	Swimming, Overall	0.44
Sex, Male	Hiking, Vacation	-0.14
	Camping, Trip	0.19
	Boating, Trip	0.32
	Fishing, Overall	0.10
	Swimming, Overall	-0.07

Source: Kalter and Gosse.

ing, camping, and swimming. However, it is negative for fishing and boating. Education is inelastic and positive for all of these recreation activities, especially fishing and boating. Elasticity of demand with respect to sex (male) is inelastic and positive for camping, fishing, and boating, while it is negative for swimming and hiking.

Bouwes and Schneider used the individual travel cost approach to estimate the shift in demand for water-based recreation with pollution from a storm sewer at Pike Lake in southeastern Wisconsin. It is one of many small lakes in the state less than one square mile in size that are suitable for day use, with boat launching facilities and swimming beaches with lifeguards. On-site interviews with a sample of 195 households visiting eight lakes, including Pike Lake, provided the basic data for the study. The elasticity of demand with respect to water quality was estimated as 0.31 which means that a 1 per cent change in lake water quality results in a 0.31 percent change in the number of trips demanded to Pike Lake.

A number of studies have been made of the elasticity of demand with respect to quality of recreation resources. For example, consider three studies that estimated the effect of forest quality on demand for recreation in the United States. Walsh and Olienyk interviewed a sample of 500 households at forest recreation sites on the Front Range of the Rocky Mountains. The sample was stratified to include developed camping, semideveloped camping, backpacking, hiking, fishing, picnicking, driving off-road vehicles, staying at resorts, and living in mountain homes. The study estimated the demand effect of the number of live ponderosa pine trees 6 inches dbh (diameter breast high) or more per acre surviving mountain pine beetle infestation. Results of the analysis show that the travel cost and contingent value methods provide comparable estimates of the effect of number of trees on recreation demand for Front Range forests. The elasticity of demand with respect to trees was estimated as 0.34 by the travel cost method and 0.28 by the contingent valuation approach.

A second study, by Leuschner and Young, applied the zonal travel cost method to estimate the elasticity of demand with respect to pine tree cover as 0.64 to 0.68 at campgrounds located at reservoirs in Texas, nearly double the elasticity in Colorado. The variation in results may reflect differences in the value of shade from trees in the relatively hot southern state compared to the cooler mountain region. In a third study, Michaelson applied the individual travel cost approach in a study of the demand effect of mountain pine beetle damage to ponderosa pine at campgrounds in Idaho forests. The average elasticity of demand with respect to trees on forest campgrounds was estimated as 0.27, which is comparable to the effect of number of trees at recreation sites in Colorado. The elasticity of demand with respect to trees also varies among recreation activities and over the range of the functions.

Information on elasticities of demand can help a ski resort make effective operating and planning decisions. For decision-making purposes, what the ski resort needs to know is: How sensitive is demand to changes in the independent variables in the demand function? A sample of 837 skiers were interviewed in Aspen, Colorado, on vacation trips averaging 8 days with expenditures of $96 per day, in 1978 dollars (Walsh and Davitt). Elasticities of demand for an additional day of skiing are estimated as: -0.73 with respect to price, 0.53 income, 0.37 skiing ability, 1.50 distance traveled, 0.11 state population, 0.18 preference for Aspen relative to substitute ski areas, -0.11 party size, and -0.34 package plan.

Some of these variables can be controlled by the ski resort — the range in prices and quality of services offered, for example — and it is important to know the effects of altering them if effective price and service decisions are to be made. Knowledge of the effect of the price of services on demand is essential in establishing a suitable range of food, lodging, and skiing services at alternative prices. Knowledge of the effects of existing package plans on demand for length of stay is important in appraising the desirability of new, more flexible package plans.

Although other variables are outside the control of the ski resort, they can be influenced by effective promotional programs. For example, advertising can be directed to particular groups of skiers: smaller parties, with advanced skiing ability, higher income, living in more populous states, located farther from Aspen. In addition, estimates of the sensitivity of demand to long-run trends in population, family size, and income can enhance a ski resort's ability to predict future growth potential and to establish effective long-run programs.

SUMMARY

The noted British economist, Alfred Marshall, defined the concept of elasticity as a measure of the responsiveness of demand to changes in the price and nonprice variables included in a demand function. The concept is a particularly useful one to recreation economic decisions. It facilitates comparison among recreation resources and activities independent of the units of measurement. In this chapter we distinguished between the three most important elasticities of demand — price, income, and cross elasticity.

Price elasticity measures the sensitivity of demand to changes in price; it is defined as the percentage change in quantity demanded resulting from a 1 percent change in its own price. Demand for most recreation activities is price inelastic, meaning that a 1 percent change in direct cost or price results in less than a 1 percent change in quantity demanded. This means that substitutes are usually not available to satisfy the perceived need, the proportion of income spent on it is low, and it is purchased frequently. We showed why the price elasticity of demand is likely to vary from one point to another on the curve. Thus, elasticity may be computed either for a single point or as an average arc elasticity between two points on the curve.

Income elasticity measures the sensitivity of demand to changes in total income; it is defined as the percentage change in quantity demanded resulting from a 1 percent change in money income. Income elasticity for recreation expenditures as a whole is positive and high, meaning that a 1 percent change in income results in more than a 1 percent change in recreation expenditures. However, income elasticity of demand for most recreation activities is positive but low, meaning that a 1 percent change in income results in less than a 1 percent change in quantity demanded. In fact, income elasticity is often zero, meaning that a change in income does not affect the quantity demanded by users. Income elasticity has important policy implications. Since some recreation industries cannot expect to share fully in a growth economy, society often must rely on government to provide recreation resources.

Cross elasticity measures the sensitivity of demand to changes in the price of a second product; it is defined as the percentage change in quantity demanded resulting from a 1 percent change in the price of any other product. If the cross elasticity of demand is positive, the two products are substitutes; if it is negative, they are complements. If cross elasticity is zero, the demands for the two products are independent of one another, i.e., they are in separate markets.

Next, we discussed the impact of time on elasticity of demand. While the short-run demand for recreation is relatively inelastic, over the long run, demand becomes more elastic. The frictions in the economy typically cause short-run response to a price change to be smaller than over the long-run when the full influence of a change in price has run its course. Thus, the ultimate effect of a price increase on demand may be substantial, but it will take a number of years before the full impact is felt.

Another important aspect of elasticities is the concept of derived demand, which refers to the fact that the demand for one product may be derived from a more fundamental demand for another. Recreation goods and services are not demanded because of their direct value to consumers but rather because of the role they play in the production of recreation activities by consuming households. It was shown that the demand for these intermediate goods and services is typically less price elastic than is the demand for the resulting final product, unless its cost represents a major part of total direct cost or price.

We concluded the chapter with examples of other kinds of elasticities of demand for recreation. Other elasticities of demand measure the sensitivity of the amount demanded to changes in each of the other determinants of demand; it is defined as the percentage change in quantity demanded resulting from a 1 percent change in the value of each variable. Other kinds of elasticities that have been used in recreation economic decision-making include: age, education, sex, family size, skill or ability, quality of the resource, population, congestion, and preferences. Some of these variables can be influenced by recreation managers through special service and promotion programs in the short run. Knowledge of the sensitivity of demand to these variables is important in planning long-run programs.

READINGS

Adams, Robert L., Robert C. Lewis, and Bruce H. Drake. "Outdoor Recreation in America: An Economic Analysis." Appendix A. Bureau of Outdoor Recreation, U.S. Department of the Interior, Washington, D.C. 1973.

Bouwes, Nicolaas W., and Robert Schneider. "Procedures in Estimating Benefits of Water Quality Change." *American Journal of Agricultural Economics* 61(Aug. 1979): 535-39.

Gum, Russell L., and William E. Martin. "Problems and Solutions in Estimating Demand for and Value of Rural Outdoor Recreation." *American Journal of Agricultural Economics* 57(Nov. 1975):558-66.

Kalter, Robert J., and Lois E. Gosse. "Outdoor Recreation in New York State: Projections of Demand, Economic Value, and Pricing Effects for the Period 1970-1985." Special Series Number 5. Cornell University, Ithaca, N.Y. 1969.

Kurtz, William B. "The Demand for Motorboat Use of Large Reservoirs in Arizona." Ph.D. Dissertation, University of Arizona, Tucson. 1972.

Kurtz, William B., and David A. King. "Evaluating Substitution Relationships Between Recreation Areas." *Tourism Marketing and Management Issues.* Donald E. Hawkins, Elwood L. Shafer, and James M. Rovelstad, (eds.). George Washington University, Washington, D.C. 1980. 391-403.

LaPage, Wilbur F., and Dale P. Ragain. "Family Camping Trends — An Eight-Year Panel Study." *Journal of Leisure Research* 6(Spring, 1974):101-12.

Leuschner, W. A., and R. L. Young. "Estimating the Southern Pine Beetle's Impact on Reservoir Campsites." *Forest Science* 24(Dec. 1978):527-43.

National Park Service. "Analysis of Kaiparowits Power Plant Impacts on National Recreation Resources." U.S. Department of the Interior, Washington, D.C. Mar. 1976.

National Park Service. "Special Study of Indiana Dunes National Lakeshore." Report to the Congress of the United States, Department of the Interior, Washington, D.C. June, 1977.

Thompson, C. Stassen, and A. W. Tinsley. "Income Expenditure Elasticities for Recreation: Their Estimation and Relation to Demand for Recreation." *Journal of Leisure Research* 10(4, 1978):265-70.

Walsh, Richard G., and Gordon J. Davitt. "A Demand Function for Length of Stay on Ski Trips to Aspen." *Journal of Travel Research* 22(Spring 1983):23-9.

Waugh, Frederick V. "Demand and Price Analysis." Technical Bulletin No. 1316, Economic and Statistical Analysis Division, U.S. Department of Agriculture, Washington, D.C. Nov. 1964.

Chapter Ten

Risk, Uncertainty, and Information

This chapter reviews existing knowledge about the extent of risk and uncertainty in recreation; shows how to calculate expected value and apply it to decision making by consumers and managers; illustrates how decision makers search for information to reduce risk to acceptable levels; and discusses the problem of waiting time or queueing for recreation services.

In previous chapters it was implicitly assumed that individuals make recreation economic decisions in an environment characterized as risk free. That is, we assumed that when individuals decide to take a recreation trip they know what they are getting, what it will cost, and how much benefit it will yield. Substantial insight into decision-making procedures was gained by treating the problem as though individuals and managers had reasonably complete information concerning the outcomes of possible alternative decisions. Recreation economic decisions are somewhat more complex under conditions of risk and uncertainty.

In this chapter, we will see how recreation economic decisions are based on the expected value of alternatives. Expected value depends on conditions of risk and uncertainty and is adjusted for the decision maker's attitude toward risk. The riskiness of a decision depends, in part, on the information available to the decision maker. We will see how individuals search for information to reduce price uncertainty in the purchase of recreation goods and services. Finally, we consider the problem of how much information service to provide at a recreation site.

PERCEPTIONS OF RISK

Existing knowledge about the extent of risk and uncertainty in recreation suggests that it is pervasive. Vacation travel, for example, is riskier than the purchase of many other goods and services. It takes considerable discretionary dollars and time. The recreation experience cannot be examined before purchase as would be true for most other goods and services. Travelers tend to visit new destinations and try new things in the search for variety in recreation. Recreation economic decisions are less effective under conditions of risk and uncertainty. This often results in reduced benefits.

We know more about the physical risks of recreation than other types. A national survey of 750 participants in selected recreation activities found that 80 percent suffered frequent physical accidents and illnesses during recreation trips. The sample was limited to individuals who participated in at least two of the following recreation activities for 3 weeks or more per year — hunting, hiking, angling, backpacking, canoeing, mountain climbing, biking, and skiing.

Table 10-1 shows the proportion of the sample reporting that they were affected by 16 physical hazards. The probability of insect bites each year was 95 percent among those surveyed, followed by sunburn and the effects of drinking unpurified water, each with a probability of 77 percent. Blisters, stings, deep cuts, traumatic experiences, skin rash, sprained ankles, embedded fishhooks, and burns were reported by 32 to 70 percent of the sample. Getting lost, suffering broken bones, food poisoning, and sunstroke were reported by 8 to 16 percent. Only 5 percent reported that they had ever suffered from snakebite. The probability of death from snakebite is 8 percent for timber rattlesnakes, and 15 percent for large diamondbacks. Almost 75 percent of respondents reported that they take a first aid kit with them on recreation trips, but the average kit lacks many essential first-aid supplies. Outdoor recreation participants in the South were least likely to take along a first-aid kit, yet they suffer the most accidents and illnesses of the four geographic regions of the United States.

Economics is primarily concerned with the risk and uncertainty of future benefits and costs. We have seen that benefits represent the willingness to pay for satisfactions of the recreation experience. The economic meaning of the term "satisfaction" includes all of the physical, psychological, social, leisure, and technological aspects of recreation. Consider a study that related individual perceptions of economic or financial risk to the other measures. Cheron and Ritchie studied seven types of risk perceived by participants in 20 recreation activities in Alberta, Canada, in 1980. The results are summarized in Table

Table 10-1. Percent of Participants in Selected Outdoor Recreation Activities Affected by 16 Physical Hazards, United States

Physical Hazards	Percent of Users Affected[a]	Physical Hazards	Percent of Users Affected[a]
Insect Bites	95	Sprained Ankle	34
Sunburn	77	Embedded Fishhook	43
Drink Unpurified Water	77	Burns	32
Blisters	70	Got Lost	16
Wasp Stings	70	Broken Bones	14
Deep Cut	52	Food Poisoning	10
Traumatic Experience[b]	52	Sunstroke	8
Poison Ivy Rash	45	Snakebite	5

[a]The 95 percent confidence limit is ± 4 percent.
[b]Near-drowning, falls, encounters with bears and snakes, and bad storms.
Source: Desner, Morris, and Tortorello Research, Inc.

10-2. Because the authors interviewed a nonrandom sample of 68 college graduates, the findings of the study cannot be generalized to a broader population. Nonetheless, they are indicative of the varying levels of risk likely to be associated with different recreation activities. Individual risk was measured on a 9-point scale with 1 = lowest and 9 = highest.

The seven types of risk considered were: (1) financial, the possibility that the activity will not provide value for the money spent; (2) time, the possibility that the activity will take too much time or will waste time; (3) satisfaction, the possibility that the activity will not provide personal satisfaction or self-actualization; (4) functional, the possibility of problems with mechanical equipment or the organization while performing the activity; (5) physical, the possibility of physical danger, injury, i.e., detrimental to health; (6) psychological, the possibility that the activity will not be consistent with the individual's self-image, life style, or personality; and (7) social, the possibility that participation will adversely affect others' opinions of the individual. An overall risk, the possibility that when all types of risk are considered, participation will result in disappointment, was also considered.

Snowmobiling was clearly viewed as the recreation activity having the highest overall risk (6.1) and cross-country skiing was viewed as

Table 10-2. Importance of Seven Types of Perceived Risk Associated With 20 Leisure Activities, Alberta, Canada

Leisure Activity	Types of Perceived Risk[a]							
	Finan-cial	Func-tional	Phys-ical	Psycho-logical	Social	Satis-faction	Time	Overall Risk
Snowmobiling	7.1	7.2	6.7	6.6	4.6	6.7	5.2	6.1
Shopping	6.3	3.2	2.2	5.8	3.2	5.7	5.8	5.0
Bowling	5.3	3.1	2.0	5.9	3.8	6.0	4.6	4.9
Golfing	5.2	3.3	2.2	4.8	3.5	4.8	5.2	4.4
Playing Cards	4.3	2.3	1.7	4.9	3.4	5.0	4.3	4.4
Alpine Skiing	4.9	5.0	6.3	3.9	2.8	3.4	3.8	4.3
Making Handicrafts	4.7	4.0	1.7	4.7	3.0	4.4	4.8	3.9
Gardening	3.3	3.0	1.5	3.8	2.7	3.5	4.0	3.9
TV Viewing	4.3	2.4	2.3	3.8	2.7	4.6	4.8	3.8
Doing Odd Jobs	3.3	4.0	2.9	3.4	2.7	3.2	4.0	3.6
Swimming (Pool)	3.5	3.0	2.9	3.4	2.4	3.4	3.1	3.6
Swimming (Lake)	3.4	3.3	4.0	3.5	2.6	3.7	3.0	3.6
Skating	3.8	2.8	3.1	3.3	2.4	3.1	2.8	3.4
Attending Movies	4.2	2.5	1.7	2.8	2.1	2.9	2.7	3.3
Visiting Friends	2.9	2.9	1.9	2.5	2.4	2.6	3.1	3.3
Playing Tennis	3.2	3.0	2.7	3.0	2.2	2.8	2.7	3.1
Walking	2.6	2.3	1.9	1.9	2.8	2.7	2.9	2.9
Reading	2.5	1.7	1.3	2.3	2.1	2.3	2.7	2.6
Bicycling	2.5	2.8	3.1	2.5	2.0	2.6	2.3	2.5
Cross Country Skiing	2.2	2.6	2.9	2.1	2.0	2.1	2.8	2.4

[a]Based on a 9-point scale; 1 = lowest, 9 = highest.
Source: Cheron and Ritchie.

the lowest (2.4). The level of risk perceived by individuals participating in any single activity was generally uniform across all types of risk. Snowmobiling, for example, was rated as the most risky for six of the seven types, and cross-country skiing was considered among the lowest risk activities across all seven types. There were a number of variations for specific activities. For example, downhill or alpine skiing was considered the second most risky activity with respect to the possibility of physical injury, yet it was rated medium to low for other types of risk. You can compare your own perception of the risk while participating in these and other recreation activities shown in the table to the average rating of respondents to the Canadian study.

Results of this study suggest that an economic measure of risk can provide an effective proxy for the psychological and social perceptions of risk by individuals participating in recreation activities. The authors tested the correlation between overall risk and each of the seven types perceived by participants in the 20 recreation activities. They found that financial risk — the possibility that the activity will not provide value for the money spent — was highly correlated (.94) with overall risk, as were personal satisfaction (.94), psychological self-image (.96), social opinion (.95), and use of time (.85). Such high correlation between two or more variables suggests that they are measuring the same thing, and it is acceptable practice to adopt a single proxy, such as the expected economic value measure introduced in this chapter.

SOME IMPORTANT CONCEPTS

All recreation economic decisions are made in the present based on expectations about the future. The actual experience will seldom turn out exactly as expected when a decision is made. Since none of us knows for certain what the future holds, we are all forced to guess what the most likely outcome of any of our decisions will be. Though we would be unlikely to think of a decision in these terms, what we in fact do when we guess is to assign a statistical probability to the likelihood that future events will occur, based on our knowledge and experience of the situation. You may prefer to talk about "degrees of belief" instead of probabilities. That's fine, so long as it is understood that we operate with degrees of belief in exactly the same way as we operate with probabilities; the two terms are working synonyms. To say that you believe an event has a high or low probability is simply to make a statement that forecasts the future. Probability may range between 0 and 1. Zero means that you estimate that there is no chance of the event happening, and 1 means you are sure it will happen.

Probability is defined as the chances, odds, or frequency that an event will occur. For example, an individual consumer may read the weather forecast in a local paper and conclude that the odds are 3 in 10 we will get rain during a softball game and 7 in 10 we will not. If all possible relevant outcomes are considered, and if the probability is assigned to each possible outcome, then this is defined as a probability distribution. For our softball example, we could set up the following probability distribution:

Outcome		Probability of Occurrence		
Rain	3 in 10	—	0.3	—	30%
No rain	7 in 10	=	0.7	=	70%
Total	10 in 10	=	1.0	=	100%

The possible outcomes are listed in column 1, and the probability of each, expressed as chances, decimals, and percentages are given in column 2. Notice that the probabilities sum to 10, 1.0, or 100 percent, as they must if the probability distribution is complete. A probability estimate of .3 means that you think the chances are 3 in 10 (odds of 3 to 7) that the event will happen. A probability estimate of .3 indicates that you think there is twice as great a chance of the event happening than if you had estimated a probability of .15.

Certainty is defined as knowing the outcome of a decision in advance. For many simple recreation economic decisions, the outcomes are known with certainty. In these cases, the expected value is equal to the actual consumer surplus realized when the event occurs. For example, you may observe as you walk out the door with a picnic lunch under your arm that there is not a cloud in the sky. You may conclude that there is virtually a 100 percent chance that sunny skies will prevail while you are picnicking at a city park during the next 2 hours. The probability of a single "state of nature" is equal to 1.0. Thus, the expected value of picnicking is equal to the full value of the experience under sunny skies. If the consumer surplus of picnicking at city park is $15 with sunny skies, then its expected value is $15 × 1 = $15. In some cases, such as this, the amount of risk is so small that it can be ignored. You are sure that the event will happen as expected. However, in reality the vast majority of consumer and managerial decisions are made under conditions of risk or uncertainty where benefits and costs cannot be predicted exactly. Consumers and managers must select a course of action from the alternatives available with less than full knowledge about the events affecting the outcome.

Uncertainty is defined as a situation in which two or more possible outcomes may result from a decision, but the precise nature of these outcomes is not known, or the probability of each occurring cannot be assigned objectively. That is, not all of the possible outcomes can be accurately foreseen; and their probabilities cannot be based on previous empirical data. Instead, the decision maker must use intuition, judgment, experience, and whatever other information is available to assign probabilities to the outcomes considered possible in such a situation.

Most individual consumers and managers of private and public recreation resources operate in a continuing state of uncertainty. With uncertainty, consumers and managers have no information concerning the probabilities of possible outcomes of alternative decisions. The expected value of a recreation activity with a number of uncertain outcomes is simply the consumer surplus that the individual will realize, on average, if the decision is repeated many times. Suppose, for example, that we have no information at all about the probability that it will rain or not during a softball game. In this case, we must proceed on a subjective basis, and the most simple method of assigning probabilities when there is no information is to assume "equi-probability of the unknown." That is, since we are uncertain about the relative likelihood that it will rain or not, we assign each equal probabilities of occurring. We assume that there is a 50 percent chance that it will rain and a 50 percent chance that it will not. If there are two or more possible outcomes (n), the probability of each outcome under the equi-probability method is $1/n$. Thus, with two possible outcomes, the probability of each is $1/2 = .5$; with three possible outcomes, the probability of each is $1/3 = .33$; with four possible outcomes, the probability of each is $1/4 = .25$; etc.

Risk is defined as a situation in which two or more possible outcomes may result from a decision and the probability of each occurring is known to the decision maker. The actual outcome of a particular decision is not known in advance, of course. But given a sufficiently large number of decisions, the proportion of each possible outcome is known. This objective knowledge is based either on mathematical and physical principles or on past experience under similar circumstances. Thus, the major distinction between risk and uncertainty is that probability has an objective basis in the case of risk, rather than a subjective basis in the case of uncertainty.

For example, the National Weather Service keeps extensive data on previous wind patterns, temperatures, cloud formations, and rainfall. Meteorologic data show the relative incidence of various outcomes in past situations. On finding that a particular weather pattern is similar in all major respects to those of the data base, the service is able to assign a probability to the chances of a particular event (state of nature) occurring in the near future. On this basis, the probability of snow, rain, wind, and flood is forecast daily by the service. Similarly, the probabilities of personal injury and death are prepared by insurance companies as actuarial tables. Risk of personal injury to downhill skiers has been calculated for ski areas by the U.S. Forest Service. State wildlife management agencies have developed a historic data base on hunting and fishing success in each region of their states. If hunting and fishing conditions are similar to those of the data base, recreation decision makers can assign a probability to the chance of bagging an animal or catching a fish in the near future.

Any decision is only as good as the information on which it is based, in particular, the accuracy of the probability of the event occurring. There is no logical difference between the probabilities that an insurance company estimates on the basis of the frequency of past death rates or weather service estimates on the basis of past weather patterns, and the individual angler's seat-of-the-pants estimate of whether the fish will be biting. No frequency data can speak for itself in a perfectly objective manner. Many judgments go into compiling every frequency series, in deciding which series to use for an estimate, and in choosing which part of the data to use. For example, should anglers use only their recorded catch from last year, which will be too few observations to give as much data as they would like, or should they also use catch records from years further back, when conditions were different? They can ask friends and acquaintances and rely on the judgment of the most experienced among them. But in the end, their own subjective estimate of the likely variability in the expected outcome of the decision is all that they have upon which to base a recreation economic decision. Tourists may purchase a 5-day fishing license only to find that the fish are not biting during August when they are on vacation at a resort area. Similarly, the weather forecast may be for scattered showers, but the microclimate where they choose to fish may have heavy rain all afternoon. Tens of thousands of deer and elk hunters have an unsuccessful hunt each year because of unforeseen circumstances.

DECISION MAKING PROCESS

We can now outline the major steps involved in decision making under conditions of risk and uncertainty. The decision maker should develop an understanding of the (1) alternatives, (2) outcomes, (3) economic benefits, (4) probabilities, (5) expected values, and (6) adjustments for the decision maker's attitude toward risk. First, because all decisions involve a choice among alternatives, we must have at least two possible alternatives or projects between which to choose. If there is only one possible course of action available, then obviously no decision is necessary. Second, for each alternative recreation activity or program, we have a number of possible outcomes that may occur depending on the "state of nature," or other conditions encountered. Only one of these outcomes will occur, although we do not know which one. Third, we have estimates of the economic benefits associated with each possible outcome for each alternative recreation activi-

ty or program. Fourth, we have estimates of the likelihood or probability of each particular outcome occurring. Fifth, we calculate the expected value of consumer surplus at the time the decision is made,
which equals the weighted average value of possible outcomes for each
alternative considered. Finally, we adjust the expected value for the
decision maker's attitude toward risk, whether he or she tends to be
neutral, cautious, or a gambler.

We can illustrate the approach by applying it to a simple recreation
economic problem in which a consumer must decide whether to take
a trip or to devote the equivalent leisure time to some other unspeci-
fied alternative activity. The treatment of two or more alternative activities will be considered in subsequent cases considered in this
chapter. This initial problem is purposely limited in order to emphasize the other important steps in decision making under conditions
of risk and uncertainty.

Brookshire and Crocker present an example of the effects of visibility (as measured by the distance that users can see in and around a national park) on demand for recreation use. A coal-fired power plant
nearby either operates effective air quality control devices or shuts
them down for maintenance periodically during the recreation season
of park use. As a result, visibility in and around the park will be clear
(c) or murky (m) during an individual recreation trip. The direct costs
of trips to the park are not affected by the availability of atmospheric
visibility in the park. However, the ability to observe distant mountains from the site enhances individual satisfaction and benefits from
recreation use. Economists depict such effects as shifts in the demand
curve for trips to the park. If the relationship between a nonprice variable, such as visibility, and demand is not familiar to you, review the
first section of Chapter 6 on shifts in the demand curve.

Figure 10-1 reproduces our representative individual's demand
curve (D) for trips to a recreation site from Chapters 5 and 6. With
seasonal average conditions as to visibility, users would demand five
trips per year at a price of $20 per trip. Net benefits to consumers
would equal the area below the demand curve above price. The total
consumer surplus for one to five trips would be $100 which, divided
by five trips, yields average consumer surplus of $20 per trip with
average visibility. With clear visibility, consumers would be willing to
take more trips for the same travel costs or price. That is, magnificent
vistas normally shift the demand curve outward to the right as depicted by demand curve Dc with clear skies. Demand would increase
from five to seven trips per year and total consumer surplus for one to
seven trips per year becomes $210 which, divided by seven trips,
yields an average consumer surplus of $30 per trip with clear skies.
However, when skies are murky with low visibility, the demand curve
(Dm) for trips shifts inward to the left. At the same direct costs or

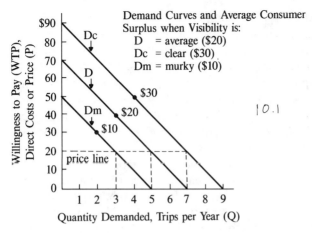

Figure 10-1. Visibility Shifts the Demand Curve for Trips to a Park by a Representative Individual User

price of trips, demand would decrease from five to three trips per year. Total consumer surplus for one to three trips becomes $30 which, divided by three trips, yields an average consumer surplus of $10 per trip with murky sky.

Recreation economic decisions under conditions of risk and uncertainty are based on the "expected value of consumer surplus," E(CS), which is defined as the average benefits that individuals will end up with who take repeated trips to a recreation site. To estimate this weighted average expected value, economists multiply the consumer surplus for each possible outcome by its probability of occurrence and then add these products. For example, if individuals contemplating trips do not have access to information about visibility at the park, they may be assumed to have a fair chance with a 50-50 probability of obtaining clear vistas valued at $30 or murky visibility valued at $10. The calculation of expected value becomes

$$\$30 \times 0.5 = \$15$$
$$\$10 \times 0.5 = \$\ 5$$
$$E(CS)\quad\ = \$20$$

For uncertain park users, the recreation economic decision would be to take 5 trips per year with an expected value of $20 per trip. This is the average consumer surplus of individual users who take repeated trips if half are clear and half are murky.

Now assume that park managers initiate a program to supply prospective park users with visibility forecasts. Individuals considering trips on the July 4th weekend are provided with the information that there is a 75 percent chance of clear visibility and a 25 percent chance of murky skies. The calculation of expected value becomes

$30 \times 0.75 = \$22.50$
$10 \times 0.25 = \$\ 2.50$
E(CS) $\quad = \$25.00$

The improvement in knowledge converted the decision from one of uncertainty to one of risk. Now the recreation economic decision by informed park users would be to take six trips per year with an expected value of $25 per trip. This is the average consumer surplus of individual users who take repeated trips if 75 percent of the trips are under clear skies and 25 percent, murky.

The probabilities of the outcomes have been changed by recreation resource managers so that there is a greater chance of clear vistas, increasing from 0.5 to 0.75. The recreation benefits of the park are increased as a result of the improved information. Now individuals choose to visit on days when the probability of clear vistas is high. Since many trips are taken to the recreation site, individual users will end up big winners. In fact, users may be willing to pay considerably more for the opportunities to realize improved visibility. The benefits of the visibility forecasting program are equal to the increase in the expected value of recreation use, $5 (= $25 - $20) per trip, and the increase in individual demand for use of the park, from five to six trips per year, or by 20 percent. Users might even be willing to pay as much as $50 per year for the site improvement (= $25 + [$5 × 5]). This $50 is a measure of the improvement in the welfare of recreation users by introduction of the improved resource management program, assuming they have a neutral attitude toward risk.

The final step involved in decision making under conditions of risk and uncertainty is to adjust the expected value to users for their attitude toward risk — whether risk neutral, risk averse, or risk seeking. This is based on Bernoulli's insight that individuals are usually risk averse; thus high-risk recreation activities and programs have an expected value that is less than for individuals who have a neutral attitude toward risk. Individuals who are neutral toward risk, value a dollar gained equal to a dollar lost (as assumed in the visibility example above). Individuals who tend to be risk averse value a dollar gained less than a dollar lost, and those who are risk seeking value a dollar gained more than a dollar lost.

Figure 10-2 illustrates the three possible attitudes toward risk. The expected value of each outcome is shown on the horizontal axis and the "adjusted" expected value of each outcome (for individual attitudes toward risk), on the vertical axis. Note that the relationship is linear for risk-neutral individuals represented by a straight line drawn at a 45° angle from the origin at zero. The relationship is nonlinear for risk-averse and risk-seeking individuals, represented by a curve drawn convex from the origin for risk aversion and by a curve drawn concave from the origin for risk seeking. The illustration assumes equal,

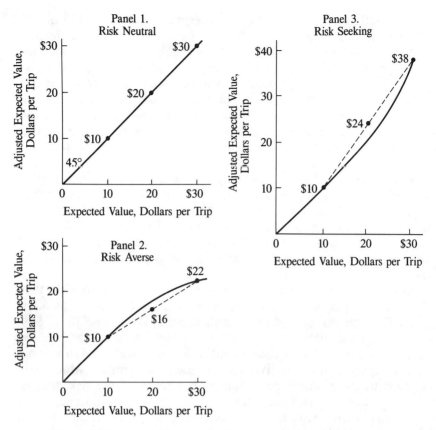

Figure 10-2. Adjusting the Expected Value of Consumer Surplus for Individual Attitudes Toward Risk

50-50, probabilities of each of two possible outcomes (states of nature) for trips to a park, continuing the previous example.

Suppose that we ask recreation users how much they would be prepared to pay to take recreation trips offering a 50-50 chance of realizing outcomes with benefits of either $10 or $30 per day. If they are neutral in their attitudes toward risk, they might reply that they would be prepared to pay $20 per day, because the $20 is a "bird in the hand," which they are prepared to give up in the hope of gaining the "two in the bush" on average. Then we can say that they regard $20 as being equivalent to a 50-50 chance of realizing outputs with benefits of either $30 or $10. It is possible to offer individuals a number of 50-50 chances, such as the previous one, in order to construct the functions shown in Figure 10-2. The neutral attitude toward risk is depicted in panel 1.

If recreation users are risk-seekers, who in fact gain a positive consumer surplus from taking a chance on visibility, then they might regard a 50-50 chance of gaining outcomes with benefits of $30 or $10 as being the equivalent to, say, $24 with certainty. The $4 difference between the $20 expected value of risk-neutral individuals and the $24 willingness to pay of risk-seeking individuals represents a risk premium that gamblers would be willing to pay for the chance to outwit nature by arriving at the park when skies are clear. This is shown as the panel 3 of Figure 10-2. Similarly, risk-seeking anglers on trips to high mountain rivers and lakes in the park may value a dollar of consumer surplus gained from catching one large fish more highly than a dollar of consumer surplus lost by not catching fish of any size. This attitude toward risk was clearly the central plot in Hemingway's last novel, *The Old Man and the Sea,* in which the many dreary days the old man and the boy fished without success were more than offset by the satisfaction of a final solitary catch of a very large fish even though when lashed to the side of the small boat, its bones were all that survived repeated shark attacks on the trip home in the Caribbean Sea.

Conversely, if individuals are to some extent averse to risk, then they might be prepared to pay only $16 to take recreation trips offering a 50-50 chance of outcomes with benefits of either $30 or $10. This is shown as panel 2 of Figure 10-2. The $4 difference between the $20 expected value of risk-neutral individuals and the $16 willingness to pay by cautious individuals represents a premium which risk-averse individuals would be willing to pay to avoid the risk, that is, the 50-50 chance of realizing clear or murky skies on wilderness trips to the park. Economists refer to this $4 risk premium as the "option value" of air quality to risk-averse users of the park. Option value is defined as a kind of insurance premium in addition to the $16 expected value of recreation use of the park. The purchase of options is a common practice in real estate and securities markets. The same kind of individual motivations exist for environmental and recreational resources even though markets are absent. Randall concludes that it makes sense to quantify these values and to include them in public benefit cost analysis. Managers of private downhill ski areas recognize the option value motivation of risk-averse individuals when they lower the price of lift tickets to encourage skiers to participate early and late during the ski season when snow conditions are most risky.

CASE STUDIES OF RISKY DECISIONS

Next, we will see how consumers and managers can apply the expected value approach to recreation economic decisions and, in particular, how risk-averse attitudes affect the choice of alternatives that maximize adjusted expected values. We will begin with a simple illustration of the effect of risky weather conditions on consumer decisions. It involves choosing between two alternative winter recreation activities, downhill skiing and cross-country skiing. This is followed by a more complex decision by the superintendent of a national park who considers alternative ways to expand visitor services in the face of variability in general economic conditions (business cycles). Finally, managers of a private ski resort review alternative programs to increase sales and profits which may result in various possible reactions by its competitors. You will see that we apply the expected value approach to all of these recreation economic decisions in the same way.

Consumer Recreation Decision

A skier is making plans for a weekend trip. The problem is to decide between downhill and cross-country skiing under risky weather conditions. Recreation benefits of downhill skiing are $20 with sun and a negative $10 in a blizzard. Benefits of cross-country skiing are $12 with sun and $5 in a blizzard. The morning weather forecast is an 80 percent chance of sun and a 20 percent chance of a blizzard. The problem is to estimate the expected value of each alternative with (1) certainty of good weather, (2) uncertainty, (3) risk as defined by the National Weather Service, and (4) adjusting expected value for an averse attitude toward risk.

(1) Certainty of good weather:
Choose the highest net benefits of $20 for downhill skiing.

(2) Uncertainty, with a .5 chance of either state of nature occurring:
Downhill skiing
$20(.5) - $10(.5) = $10 - $5 = $5
Cross-country skiing
$12(.5) + $5(.5) = $6 + $2.50 = $8.50
Cross-country skiing has the higher expected value.

(3) Risk with a .8 probability of good weather and a .2 probability of a blizzard:
Downhill skiing
$20(.8) - $10(.2) = $16 - $2 = $14
Cross-country skiing
$12(.8) + $5(.2) = $9.60 + $1 = $10.60
Downhill skiing has the higher expected value.

(4) Adjusting expected value for an averse attitude toward risk: (from Figure 10-2; for example, $16 becomes $10)
Downhill skiing
$16 = $10   -$2 = -$2 $10 - $2 = $8

Cross-country skiing
$9.60 = \$8$ $\$1 = \$1$ $\$8 + \$1 = \$9$

Cross-country skiing has the highest expected value adjusted for risk aversion.

Studies show that downhill skiing is the more favored winter recreation activity if the weather is good. With uncertainty as to weather conditions, cross-country skiing would be the favored activity because snow conditions are usually better on trails in dense forests. With known risk, downhill skiing again becomes the more favored activity since the chance of good weather is high (.8). For risk-averse individuals, however, cross-country skiing remains the more favored activity because they tend to be pessimistic about the effects of good weather (the sun may turn the snow to slush) and as a result they heavily discount the higher benefits of downhill skiing under good weather conditions.

Public Recreation Agency Decision

Suppose that the superintendent of Yosemite National Park in California is considering alternative programs to increase public recreation use and benefits. The agency has limited resources and is preparing a risk analysis of its management plan. Suppose park managers are considering three alternative programs which would result in more recreation opportunities — (1) expand the size of the park by the acquisition of land; (2) rehabilitate facilities to provide more intensive park use for existing recreation activities; or (3) construct new facilities to provide a greater variety of recreation activities.

The park managers would like to know: What the public use and benefits will be from each alternative? How will these effects change with variability in economic conditions of (1) normal economy; (2) boom economy; or (3) recession? What is the probability that each of these conditions will occur in the future 10 years? With this information, they could adjust the expected recreation benefits from each management program for risk. Knowing something about the economic health of the U.S. economy may lead to different recreation economic decisions by the agency.

Begin the analysis by estimating the public use and benefits of each alternative program under different economic conditions as shown below. Set up the problem with the alternatives you want to consider displayed on the left margin, and the possible economic conditions horizontally along the top. The recommended structure of the decision follows:

Alternative Management Programs	Conditions in U.S. Economy		
	Normal	Boom	Recession
	(Public Benefits in million dollars)		
Land acquisition, park expansion	$60	$125	-$10
Rehabilitation of existing facilities	$10	$200	-$ 5
Construction of new facilities	$50	$140	$10

Suppose that a recent empirical study of the demand for recreation use of the park provides forecasts of net benefits (total benefits minus total costs) in millions of dollars. The park will receive more use and public benefits will be higher when the national economy is booming, and less when the national economy is in a recession. If future prosperity of the economy is a certainty, the alternative that would maximize benefits of $200 million is to rehabilitate existing facilities. Rehabilitation and expansion of facilities for existing uses, such as sightseeing by car or bus, staying at a resort lodge, pool swimming, and playing golf, would meet the needs for developed recreation by a growing population in the California market area served. The recreation economic decision is to rehabilitate existing facilities under risk-free conditions of prosperity in the economy. Public benefits exceed that of either alternative. Of course, the risk-free decision would change if it were certain the economy would be either normal or in a recession.

What would be the decision if park managers are uncertain about future conditions in the economy? Perhaps the future of the economy depends on forces outside the United States such as the OPEC (Organization of Petroleum Exporting Countries) oil cartel. With an inability to predict what the Arab leaders will do in the future, park managers may decide that they are uncertain about the variability in the economic health of the U.S. economy. Whether the economy is normal, booms, or enters a recession may be equally probable. When each possibility has an equal chance of occurring, multiply each benefit estimate by .33, or equal probability. When the resulting values for each alternative park program are summed, the total represents the weighted average of the outcomes under uncertainty. This weighted average is defined as the expected value of benefits flowing from each alternative park program adjusted for uncertainty:

Land acquisition, park expansion:
$60(.33) + $125(.33) - $10(.33) = $20 + $41.3 - $3.3 = $58

Rehabilitation of existing facilities:
$10(.33) + $200(.33) - $5(.33) = $3.3 + $66 - $1.7 = $67.6

Construction of new facilities:
$$\$50(.33) + \$140(.33) + \$10(.33) = \$16.5 + \$46.2 + \$3.3 = \$66$$

With uncertainty, rehabilitation of existing park facilities has the highest expected value of $67.6 million compared with $66 million for new facilities construction and $58 million for land acquisition to expand the park. The recreation economic decision under uncertainty would be to choose to rehabilitate existing park facilities.

What would be the decision by park managers if they could convert uncertainty to risk? It is possible to convert uncertainty to a risk whose probability can be calculated from variability in the past. Suppose an economic forecast by the U.S. Department of Commerce shows that, given current trends in economic indicators, the odds are only 1 in 10 that a recession will occur, 6 in 10 that the economy will be normal, and 3 in 10 that there will be a boom. Redefining these odds as probabilities, we estimate that the probability of a recession is 0.1 or 10 percent. The probability of normal times is 0.6 or 60 percent, and the probability of a boom is 0.3 or 30 percent. Note that the probabilities add up to 1.0 or 100 percent.

Next, calculate the expected value of benefits from each alternative by multiplying each benefit by its probability of occurrence. When the values for each alternative are summed, the result represents a weighted average of the outcomes under variable conditions in the U.S. economy. This weighted average is defined as the expected value of benefits from each alternative park program adjusted for risk:

Land acquisition, park expansion:
$$\$60(.6) + \$125(.3) - \$10(.1) = \$36 + \$37.5 - \$1 = \$72.5$$

Rehabilitation of existing facilities:
$$\$10(.6) + \$200(.3) - \$5(.1) = \$6 + \$60 - \$.5 = \$65.5$$

Construction of new facilities:
$$\$50(.6) + \$140(.3) + \$10(.1) = \$30 + \$42 + \$1 = \$73$$

Converting uncertainty about economic conditions to risk changes the outcome of the analysis. When adjusted for risk, the construction of new facilities has the highest expected value of $73 million compared with $72.5 million for land acquisition and $65.5 million for rehabilitation of existing facilities. The recreation economic decision adjusted for the risk of variability in the economy would be to construct new facilities.

What if the managers of Yosemite National Park are risk averse? This means that they would receive diminishing marginal benefits from additional use of the park. Managers will suffer more loss of benefits from a decision that leads to an outcome in which public use and benefits turn out to be lower than expected, than they will derive gain in benefits from an outcome in which public use and benefits turn out to be higher than expected. Thus, they will be opposed to risk and will require high public use and benefits from any alternative program that is subject to much risk.

Suppose that the composite benefit function for managers of Yosemite National Park looks like that in Figure 10-3 for a risk-averse individual. Recalculate the above payoff matrix for risk into expected benefits adjusted for risk aversion, as follows.

Land acquisition, park expansion:
$36 = $31; $37.5 = $32; -$1 = -$1; $31 + $32 - $1 = $62

Rehabilitation of existing facilities:
$6 − $6; $60 − $37; -$0.5 = -$0.5; $6 | $37 - $.5 = $42.5

Construction of new facilities:
$30 = $25; $42 = $35; $1 = $1; $25 + $35 + $1 = $61

Now, select the alternative that maximizes the expected benefits adjusted for risk-averse managers. The recreation economic decision would be to choose park expansion through acquisition of additional land. It has the highest expected benefits of $62 million per year. Introducing the managers' averse attitude toward risk into the problem has changed the recreation economic decision. The construction of new facilities would be the recreation economic choice only when managers have a neutral attitude toward risk. Acquisition of additional park land, particularly private inholdings, appeals to risk-averse managers because park users and citizens generally favor the policy as it reduces incompatible land uses within the park boundary. Moreover, expansion of the park land is visible and has an immediate payoff for politicians who face reelection every few years. Rehabilitation of existing facilities is less visible to citizens generally, and the construction of new facilities is often controversial, particularly when it conflicts with the park's objective of environmental protection. Park managers have been dismissed or transferred when they have advocated controversial projects to construct new facilities, a possibility which is particularly unappealing to risk-averse individuals.

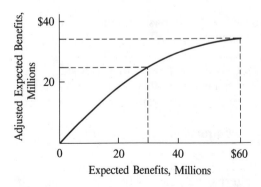

Figure 10-3. Adjusting Expected Benefits for Managers' Averse Attitudes Toward Risk, Yosemite National Park

Private Resort Decision

Assume that the management of Aspen Ski Corp., a division of Twentieth Century Fox, wants to increase its sales and profits. In 1976, Aspen Ski Corp. was the largest and most profitable company in the ski industry with sales of $15.5 million and profits (after corporate income taxes) of $2.87 million, or an 18.5 percent return on sales. Profits were equal to about 18.5 percent of net investment, which was approximately twice the rate of interest on risk-free investments in U.S. industry. The Aspen Ski Corp. is not risk free, as it experienced a loss of $1.4 million in 1977, resulting from reduced sales ($7.1 million) with poor snow conditions. Sales rebounded in 1978, and profits exceeded 15 percent on sales and stockholders equity, prompting an executive in Twentieth Century Fox to state that any business that returns over 15 percent on sales is a good investment. Its profits from the movie Star Wars were used, in part, to acquire the Aspen Ski Corp. in 1978. Management is seeking to increase the division's sales and profits.

Suppose Aspen Ski Corp. is considering three alternative projects: (1) expand existing facilities by developing new ski slopes at Aspen; (2) enter a new territory with a new ski resort; or (3) design a new ski pricing system which would charge skiers per lift trip rather than per day or half-day as has been the general practice in the industry. Charging all skiers the same price per day discriminates against beginning and intermediate skiers relative to advanced skiers because direct costs tend to be proportional to lift operation. Typically, a beginning skier takes 6 rides per day, an intermediate skier 12, and an advanced skier 24. At an average price of $1 per ride, a beginning skier would pay $6 per day, an intermediate skier $12, and an advanced skier $24, which would be more proportional than a flat rate to cost of service. Moreover, studies show that more people would begin skiing and fewer drop out at middle age if they were able to pay lower prices for shorter ski days.

All of the managers agree, based on their past experience in the ski industry, that competitors of Aspen Ski Corp. may retaliate against whatever strategy the resort pursues to increase its sales and profits. The managers are confident that rival ski areas will either cut prices or increase promotion and advertising. They also recognize, however, that competitors may do nothing at all in retaliation. Uncertainty about the reaction of competitors results in variability of expected profits from the alternative market strategies, a condition which is defined as risk.

The corporate managers would like to know the following: What will be the profits from each alternative? How will profits change if competitive reactions vary, i.e., cut price, advertise, or do nothing? What is the probability each of these reactions will occur? With this information, the managers could adjust the expected profits from each alternative for risk. Knowing something about risk of competitive reactions may lead to different recreation economic decisions.

Begin the analysis by setting up the problem. The alternatives are displayed on the left margin and the possible competitor reactions horizontally along the top. The recommended structure of the decision follows:

| | Possible Competitor Reactions | | |
Alternative Projects	Cut Price	Advertise	Do Nothing
	(Profits, Thousand Dollars)		
Expand existing facilities	$100	$500	$1,400
New ski area	-$50	$100	$2,000
New pricing strategy	-$100	$600	$1,250

Analysts in the accounting department of Aspen Ski Corp. provide estimates of normal annual profits of each alternative project or program if competitors do nothing. Under risk-free conditions in which managers are certain competitors will do nothing in reaction to the corporation's entering a new territory with a new ski resort, profits would increase by $2 million annually. This alternative would be the risk-free recreation economic decision because profitability exceeds either of the other alternatives. The marketing department provides estimates of normal annual profit expected from each of the alternative programs if competitors react by increasing their advertising and promotion, which lures potential Aspen skiers to other ski areas such as Vail and Beaver Creek. If the managers are certain that competitors will react by advertising, the recreation economic decision would be to charge skiers for each lift ride rather than per day. This would increase profits by $600,000 per year, which exceeds the profitability of either of the other alternatives. In addition, the marketing department provides an estimate of normal annual profit expected from each of the alternative programs if competitors react by cutting prices for lift tickets, which would reduce total sales and profits. If they are certain that competitors will react by cutting prices, the recreation economic decision would be to expand existing ski slopes at Aspen to raise the quality of service (less congestion). This alternative would show profits of $100,000 because of its efficiency in spreading existing overhead costs with the expanded operations in Aspen. Each of the other alternatives would result in negative profit or loss if competitors cut prices.

What would be the decision if managers are uncertain about competitive conditions? Perhaps the corporate headquarters of Twentieth Century Fox has few executives who are experienced in the ski industry. They may be uncertain about the variability in competitive conditions in the industry. With limited knowledge, they may decide that each possible competitive reaction has an equal chance of occurring and multiply the profits of each possible outcome by .33. The sum of the resulting values for each possible outcome represents the weighted average of the outcomes under uncertainty. This weighted average is defined as the expected value of profits from each alternative project adjusted for uncertainty:

Expand existing facilities:
$100(.33) + $500(.33) + $1,400(.33) =
$33 + $65 + $462 = $660

New ski area:
-$50(.33) + $100(.33) + $2,000(.33) =
-$16.5 + $33 + $660 = $676.5

New pricing strategy:
-$100(.33) + $600(.33) + $1,250(.33) =
-$33 + $200 + $413 = $580

With uncertainty, building a new ski area in a new territory has the highest expected profit of $676,500 compared with $660,000 for expansion of existing facilities at Aspen and $580,000 for the new pricing system. The recreation economic decision under uncertainty would be to build a new ski area.

What would be the decision if managers could convert uncertainty to risk? It is possible to convert uncertainty to a risk whose probability can be calculated from the variability in the outcome of past occurrences. Suppose that a study of competitive behavior in the ski industry shows that given current trends toward economic concentration of conglomerate firms, the odds are only 1 in 10 that competitors will cut price. The odds are 6 in 10 that they will increase advertising and 3 in 10 that they will do nothing. Redefining these odds as probabilities, we say that the probability of a cut in price is 0.1 or 10 percent. The probability of advertising and promotion is 0.6 or 60 percent, and the probability that competitors will do nothing is 0.3 or 30 percent. Notice that the probabilities add up to 1.0, or 100 percent.

Calculate the expected profits from each alternative by multiplying the profits of each outcome by its probability of occurrence. The sum of the values for each alternative represents the weighted average of the outcomes under variable competitive conditions. This weighted average is defined as the expected value of profits from each alternative project adjusted for risk.

Expand existing facilities:
$100(.1) + $500(.6) + $1,400(.3) = $10 + $300 + $420 = $730

New ski area:
-$50(.1) + $100(.6) + $2,000(.3) = -$5 + $60 + $600 = $655

New pricing strategy:
-$100(.1) + $600(.6) + $1,250(.3) = -$10 + $360 + $375 = $725

Converting uncertainty about competitive conditions to risk changes the outcome of the analysis. When adjusting for risk, the plan to expand existing facilities at Aspen has the highest expected value of $730,000 compared with $725,000 for the new pricing system and $655,000 for building a new ski area in a new territory. The recreation economic decision adjusted for risk would be to expand existing facilities at Aspen.

What if the managers of Aspen Ski Corp. are risk averse? This means that they will receive diminishing marginal benefits from additional profits. They will suffer more loss of benefits from a decision that leads to profits that turn out to be lower than they will gain in benefits from profits that turn out to be higher than expected. Thus, they will be opposed to risk and will require high profits from any alternative that is subject to much risk.

Suppose that the composite benefit function for the managers of Aspen Ski Corp. looks like that in Figure 10-4 for a risk averse individual. Recalculate the above payoff matrix for risk into expected profits adjusted for risk aversion, as follows:

Expand existing facilities:
$10 = $10; $300 = $250; $420 = $350; $10 + $250 + $350 = $610

New ski area:
-$5 = -$5; $60 = $60; $600 = $370; -$5 + $60 + $370 = $425

New pricing strategy:
-$10 = -$10; $360 = $310; $375 = $320; -$10 + $310 + $320 = $620

Now, select the alternative that maximizes the expected profits adjusted for risk-averse private resort managers. The recreation economic decision would be to choose a new pricing program that would charge skiers for each lift trip rather than per day, a more equitable pricing practice. It has the highest expected profit of $620,000 per year. Introducing the managers' averse attitude toward risk into the problem has

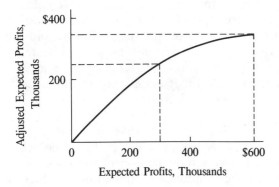

Figure 10-4. Adjusting Expected Benefits for Managers' Averse Attitude Toward Risk, Aspen Ski Corp.

changed the recreation economic decision. The project to expand existing facilities at Aspen would be the recreation economic choice only when managers have a neutral attitude toward risk. The unit pricing policy appeals to risk-averse managers because it can be easily changed at little or no cost to the corporation if it fails. However, the other two alternatives would require a substantial long-run commitment of capital investment funds, which could be lost if the projects fail.

OTHER APPROACHES TO THE PROBLEM

In this chapter, we have illustrated the basic principles and how to apply them without presenting the details of all possible approaches to the problem. The reader is referred to any managerial economics book for a discussion of the several approaches that have been used to estimate the effect of risk and uncertainty on decision making by consumers and managers. Among these are degree or risk, decision tree, maximin and minimax strategies, risk premium, and simulation.

The degree of risk is indicated by the spread or variation in the probability distribution of the possible outcomes for each alternative (see Chapter 6). A useful statistical measure of the degree of risk for each alternative activity or project is to calculate the coefficient of variation, which is the ratio of the standard deviation to the mean, expressed as a percent. Activities that have a wide spread or variation in distribution of possible outcomes may be rejected in favor of those with a narrower range.

When a sequence or series of decisions is to be made, a decision tree enables the decision maker to visualize the ultimate outcome of all possible alternative activities or projects. It shows the sequence over time of the possible choices open to consumers or managers of private and public recreation resources.

The maximin strategy is to choose the activity or project that yields the best of the worst possible outcome. It is designed to avoid a possible catastrophic outcome that might endanger the survival of the individual, corporation, or government agency. The minimax regret strategy is to choose that activity or project whose expected value is least different from the highest possible benefit. It is designed to minimize the regret or opportunity cost of incorrect decisions.

Managers of private recreation resources will make risky decisions only if there is a commensurate risk premium. Investors adjust interest rates to reflect perceived risk. A risk premium is the difference between the expected profit on a risky activity or project and profit on one that is risk-free. Finally, another approach is simulation in which a computer is used to generate random distributions of costs and benefits for each alternative activity or project and to estimate the probability distribution of possible outcomes. Full-scale application may involve hundreds of computer runs and is not feasible except on large projects or programs.

It is rarely possible to avoid risk and uncertainty in recreation. Weather conditions and the biological nature of the production process cannot be controlled, particularly in the case of fishing and hunting. There are, however, a number of approaches that consumers and managers commonly use to reduce risk and uncertainty. Among these are acquiring additional information, referring to authority for guidance, attempting to control the environment, modifying goals, introducing flexibility into plans, diversifying interests, and purchasing insurance. Recreation equipment can be insured to recover property damages from fire, wind, hail, avalanche, flood, and theft. Individuals and corporations can purchase liability, personal injury, and medical insurance.

In the next section of this chapter, we will emphasize the importance of information. The more information gathered about the future, the less uncertain it will be. However, this is only true up to a point, after which the law of diminishing returns takes over. The collection of information is costly, and the benefits to be derived from additional information must be weighed against the additional cost of obtaining it. Hasty decisions made before sufficient information is gathered can be very costly. On the other hand, a recreation economic decision delayed too long in the pursuit of information may put the consumer or manager in the position of "too little, too late."

SHOPPING OR SEARCH

Individual consumers may be careful shoppers during most of the year, but when on holiday, many tend to expect the time not only be leisurely, but also carefree. Some hardly bother to look out for their own interests by shopping for the best quality or the lowest price and seldom bother to complain. Served a poorly prepared dish at a restaurant, too many would rather swallow their anger or disappointment, along with the bad food, in silence (Scitovsky). Effective consumption of recreation goods and services involves physical effort, time, and especially care. Care consists of the mental effort of planning, remembering, judging, deciding, and taking responsibility. It also involves nervous energy spent in bargaining arguing, comparing — in short, seeking the best buy at the lowest price. It contributes to keeping producers on their toes, merchants honest, and the market competitive.

The prices of recreation goods and services change with varying frequency in all markets, and few consumers know all the prices which various sellers quote at any given time. Consumers who desire information on the most favorable price must search alternative sellers, an activity known as shopping (Stigler). The alternative is for consumers to pay the price asked by the first seller they happen to contact. If the range of price quotations by sellers in the market is at all large relative to the cost of shopping, it would pay the consumer to comparison shop several sellers. Recreation goods and services typically have a price range of 20 to 40 percent. Inexperienced buyers such as tourists pay higher prices in a market than do experienced buyers. Tourists have no accumulated knowledge of asking prices. When buyers enter a wholly new market, they estimate the amount of price dispersion based on their experience in other markets.

The expected benefits from shopping will be approximately the quantity purchased times the expected reduction in price as a result of the search. There will be, in addition, the savings on the additional purchases resulting from the lower price. Most neglect this quantity, which will generally be small. The savings from shopping will be greater the larger the expenditure on the product or service. Saving will also be greater the larger the dispersion of prices. The frequency distribution of asking prices is probably skewed, because some sellers will have a minimum but no maximum limit on the price they will accept. Whatever the precise distribution of prices, increased shopping by consumers of recreation goods and services will yield substantial benefits as measured by the expected reduction in the prices paid.

The costs of search seem to be approximately proportional to the number of sellers approached, for the main cost is time. Cost would not be equal for all consumers because time will be more valuable to a person with a larger income. Consumers often pool their knowledge and thus reduce the effective cost of search; however, because two buyers who compare prices will likely live in the same area and have similar preferences, duplication will often occur. The costs of search will be larger, as the geographical size of the market increases, because travel cost and time will increase. The more repetitive the purchase, the lower the price of search per unit purchased.

Shopping For the Lowest Price Gasoline

Consider tourists on trips to a recreation area. As a party of tourists traveling in a private automobile approaches a village not far from their destination, they notice that the gas gauge shows less than one-fourth full. Prudence suggests that they fill the tank before entering the park. As tourists, they have no idea of the prices of gasoline in the recreation area. However, they know that gasoline prices in the United States generally cluster around two levels, with major brand stations often 20 cents per gallon higher in price than self-service and other cut-rate stations. The problem is to decide whether or not it is worth their time to look for several gasoline stations in search of the most favorable price, an activity known as shopping. The alternative is to pay the price asked by the first station they happen to see. They would like to know the range (dispersion) of prices charged by sellers in the market, because if it is at all large relative to the cost of shopping, it would pay them to comparison shop several sellers. They would also like to know their chances of paying the most favorable price if they shop at one, two, three, or more dealers. With this information, they could estimate their benefits from additional shopping and compare that to their expected costs of search.

They begin by estimating the range of price quotations of sellers in the market. Based on general knowledge, they expect that sellers are about equally divided between two price levels. They may figure that the prices of major brand stations will be around $1.50 per gallon of lead-free gasoline, while the prices of self-service and other cut-rate stations will be about $1.30 per gallon. Thus, the range of price quotations in the market is expected to be 20 cents per gallon.

How much gasoline do they expect to buy? This is an important question because, for any consumer, the expected saving from additional shopping will be approximately the quantity to be purchased times the expected reduction in price as a result of the search. With less than one-quarter tank left, it is likely that they will need to purchase at least 10 gallons.

What are their potential benefits from gaining reasonably complete knowledge of the location of stations with the most favorable prices? Multiplying the range in gasoline prices of 20 cents per gallon by the 10 gallons to be purchased equals $2. Their potential benefit from shopping on a single occasion is $2 per fill-up.

What are their chances on the average of paying the most favorable price? When sellers are equally divided between two asking price levels, the probability they will pay the most favorable price at the first station they see is 50-50, on the average. Table 10-3 shows the probability they will pay the most favorable price as the number of stations searched is increased from one to two, three, and four. With each increase in the number of stations canvassed, the probability of paying the most favorable price is calculated as one-half the difference between the previous probability and 1. To find the expected minimum price per gallon, multiply the probability of paying the maximum price by the price dispersion, 20 cents in this case, plus the minimum price, which in this case is $1.30.

What are their expected benefits from shopping? Table 10-3 shows that if they follow the practice of buying from the first dealer they see, their average price of gasoline will be $1.40 per gallon, or $14.00 for a 10-gallon fill-up. If they search two stations, their average price will fall to $1.35 per gallon, or $13.50 for 10 gallons. Subtracting $13.50

Table 10-3. Effect of Shopping on the Probability of Paying the Most Favorable Price for Gasoline at a Recreation Area When Sellers are Equally Divided Between Two Price Levels

Number of Stations	Probability Paying Prices of		Expected Minimum Price		Marginal Benefits From Shopping
	$1.30/ gallon	$1.50/ gallon	Per gallon	10 gallons	
First Station	.50	.50	$1.40	$14.00	
Second Station	.75	.25	1.35	13.50	$0.50
Third Station	.875	.125	1.325	13.25	0.25
Fourth Station	.9375	.0625	1.3125	13.125	0.125
All Other Stations	1.0	0.0	1.30	13.00	

from $14.00 equals 50 cents. Their expected benefits from shopping additional stations would yield diminishing benefits. Added benefits from shopping at a third station average 25 cents and from shopping at a fourth station, 12.5 cents.

What are their costs of shopping? For consumers, the main cost is the time it takes, which will be proportional to the number of sellers approached. Of course, time costs would not be equal for all consumers because incomes and personalities vary. Also, the time and travel costs of shopping will rise with increases in the geographical size of the market. An approximation of tourists' time costs in this case is based on the federal guidelines that recommend 50 percent of the wage rate. Studies have shown that the time costs of commuter driving range between 25 and 50 percent of the driver's average wage rate. Multiplying tourists' average hourly income of $10 by 50 percent equals shopping costs of $5 per hour. Dividing $5 per hour by 60 minutes equals 8.3 cents per minute. Tourists' shopping costs are thus estimated as 8.3 cents per minute.

What is their recreation economic decision? Should tourists decide to shop for gasoline at two or more stations? To recommend a decision, review the findings of the analysis. When sellers are equally divided between $1.50 and $1.30 per gallon, with a range of price quotations in the market of 20 cents, and they purchase 10 gallons, their potential benefits are $2. Their chances of paying the most favorable price are 50 percent if they buy from the first station they see, 75 percent if they shop at two stations, and 87.5 percent if they shop at three stations. Increasing search yields diminishing benefits. The benefits from shopping at two stations is estimated as 50 cents. This compares to costs (or disbenefits) of 8.3 cents per minute of shopping. Dividing benefits of 50 cents by cost per minute of 8.3 cents equals about 6 minutes. Thus, applying the rule that benefits should be equal to or exceed costs, indicates that they should decide to spend only about 6 minutes shopping for a second station. Six minutes is not enough time to drive more than 2 miles off the interstate highway and return. Thus, chances are that the costs of shopping would exceed its benefits. Their recreation economic decision would be to pay the price asked by the first gasoline station they happen to see at an interstate highway interchange and not to shop for a second or third station. Similar consumer decisions explain why higher priced major brand gasoline stations have prospered, particularly along the interstate highway system.

How does the gasoline shopping decision of tourists differ from that of residents of the recreation area? Assume that the tourists stop to visit a friend who lives in a village near the park. They ask where he or she buys gasoline and the reply is at a minimum price station near home. Local residents such as their friend have accumulated knowledge of the location of minimum price stations and realize benefits of $2 on each 10-gallon purchase. If their friend is a typical driver, he or she has annual auto mileage of 10,000 miles at about 20 miles per gallon and purchases 500 gallons per year. With average savings of 20 cents per gallon, minimum price purchasing results in benefits of $100 per year to residents of the recreation area.

How sensitive are the results to changes in the variables? If the range of prices doubles from 20 to 40 cents per gallon, benefits of shopping at two stations would double from 50 cents to $1 per 10 gallons purchased, and maximum time shopping would increase from 6 to 12 minutes, which probably would not modify tourists' buying behavior. If tourists drive large cars, a fill-up of gasoline may average 15 gallons rather than 10 gallons for small cars. Benefits of shopping at two stations would increase from 50 cents to 75 cents and maximum shopping time, from 6 to 9 minutes. If tourists are retired or less than 30 years of age and have lower income, the time cost of shopping may be reduced by approximately one-half from $5 to $2.50 per hour, with the result that maximum shopping time would increase from 6 to 12 minutes. If these three changes in the variables are fortuitously combined, maximum search time would increase from 6 to 33 minutes. These and related changes in the variables explain the fact that some tourists shop for the most favorable price of gasoline. For them, the benefits of shopping exceed its costs.

Searching for a Place to Stay Overnight

Consider tourists on trips to a recreation area. As the party of tourists traveling in a private auto approach their destination at the end of a day's traveling on the interstate highway system, they need to find a place to stay overnight. As tourists, they have no idea of prices of lodging in this recreation area. However, they know from previous experience that costs of a place to stay overnight vary greatly. Also, road traffic has been relatively heavy and experience has shown that if they

313

delay the decision until late in the evening, their choice will be limited to either unacceptably high-priced or low quality facilities. The problem is to decide whether or not it is worth their time to look for alternative places to stay overnight in search of the most favorable price, an activity known as shopping. They would like to know the range of price quotations by sellers in the market, because if it is at all large relative to the cost of shopping, it would pay them to comparison shop several lodging establishments. They would also like to know their chances of paying the most favorable price, if they shop at one, two, three, or more places. With this information, they could estimate their benefits from additional shopping and compare their benefits to their expected costs of search.

Begin the analysis by estimating the dispersion of price quotations among sellers in the market. Based on their general knowledge of other recreation areas, they may expect that prices of places to stay overnight in this market will range from zero to $100 per day, as startling as that may seem. A recent study of tourists showed that approximately 20 percent stayed with friends and relatives, for the most part at no cost to themselves. Many public campgrounds are free, as are unimproved campsites on backcountry trails and roads. Improved campgrounds of the National Park Service, Forest Service, State Park and Recreation Departments, and other governmental and private operators have daily fees of $5 to $10 per campsite. Motel and lodge rates typically range from $20 per night at an economy motel to approximately $70 per night at deluxe motels and lodges. Rental rates for condominiums at ski resorts range from $30 to $100 per night, as do rooms and suites in deluxe lodges and hotels. Thus, the market dispersion or range of prices for places to stay overnight is expected to be $100 per day.

How many nights of lodging do they intend to buy? This is an important question because, for any consumer, the expected savings from additional shopping will be approximately the number of nights lodging purchased times the expected reduction in price as a result of the search. Assume in this case that only one night of lodging is being purchased in this market, after which the party may drive 350 miles to another recreation area.

What are tourists' chances on the average of paying a favorable price for a place to stay overnight? When alternatives are uniformly distributed between zero and $100 per night, the chances that they will pay the most favorable price at the first lodging establishment they see are 50-50, on the average. Table 10-4 shows the probability they will pay the most favorable price as the number of lodging alternatives searched is increased from one to two, three, four, and so forth. With each increase in the number of alternatives canvassed, the probability of paying the highest price is calculated as follows: divide

Table 10-4. Effect of Shopping on the Probability of Paying the Most Favorable Price to Stay Overnight in a Recreation Area When Sellers are Uniformly Distributed Between the Lowest and Highest Price Levels

Number of Establishments	Probability of Paying Prices of		Expected Minimum Price per Night	Marginal Benefits From Shopping
	Zero	$100		
First	.50	.50	$50.00	
Second	.67	.33	33.00	$17.00
Third	.75	.25	25.00	8.00
Fourth	.80	.20	20.00	5.00
Fifth	.8333	.1667	16.67	3.33
Sixth	.857	.1429	14.29	2.38

1 by the result of the number of searches plus 1. The probability of paying the most favorable price is calculated by subtracting the result of this calculation from 1. For example, the probability of paying the highest price at the second seller they see is $1/(2 + 1) = .333$. Subtracting .333 from 1.0 equals .667, which is the probability of paying the lowest price at the second seller they see. To find the expected minimum price per night, multiply the probability of paying the maximum price by the price dispersion, $100 in this case, plus the minimum price, which in this case is zero.

What are their expected benefits from search? Table 10-4 shows that if they follow the practice of staying at the first lodging establishment they see, their average price of overnight lodging will be $50 per night. If they search two alternatives, their average price will fall to $33 per night. Subtracting $33 from $50 equals $17. Thus, their expected benefits from shopping at two lodging establishments averages $17 per night. Increasing the search to three or four alternatives would yield diminishing benefits. Added benefits from shopping at a third alternative averages $8 per night and from shopping at a fourth alternative, $5.

What are their costs of searching alternative places to stay overnight? For any consumer, the main cost of searching is time, which will be proportional to the number of alternative sellers approached. Of course, time costs would not be equal for all consumers because income and personalities vary. Also, the time and travel costs of shopping will rise with increases in the geographical size of the market. Again, using the federal guidelines rule-of-thumb, we apply a time cost of 8.3 cents per minute.

What is their recreation economic decision? Should tourists decide to search for a place to stay overnight at two or more alternatives? To recommend a decision, review the findings of the analysis. When sellers are uniformly distributed between zero and $100, the range of price quotation in the market is $100, and their potential benefits are

$100 per night. Their chances of paying the most favorable price are 50 percent if they buy from the first lodging establishment they see, 67 percent if they shop at two places, 75 percent if they shop at three, and so forth. Increasing the search yields diminishing benefits. Benefits from shopping at two alternatives is estimated as $17 per night, a third as $8, and a fourth as $5. This compares to costs of 8.3 cents per minute or $5 per hour of search.

Assume that each alternative searched has time costs (or equivalent costs for long-distance telephone calls) of 15 minutes equal to $1.25. Dividing benefit by cost results in a benefit cost ratio of 13.6 (= $17/1.25) for a second search. Even the fifth alternative searched has a marginal benefit cost ratio of about 2.7 (= $3.33/1.25). Chances are that these benefit cost (B/C) ratios for searching alternative places to stay overnight exceed the B/C ratios of using the 15 minutes required for each of five or six searches in any practical alternative recreation activity in the park. Their recreation economic decision would be to search at least six alternative places to stay overnight.

Similar consumer decisions explain why public libraries contain a guide to hotels and motels, which contains prices and other information; the American Automobile Association provides similar information for specific trip itineraries; and travel agencies provide package travel plans with favorable lodging rates. Recreation lodging reservations are often made a month or more in advance, and prepayment is common. Long-distance telephone calls have become a better buy and increasingly substitute for search time.

How sensitive are the results to changes in the variables? If their decision is limited to staying in a motel, lodge, condominium, or hotel with a range of prices from $20 to $70 per night, the benefits of shopping at two alternatives would decline by one-half, from $17 to $8.50 per night, which would have a B/C ratio of 6.8 (= $8.50/1.25). Even the fifth search would have a favorable B/C ratio of 1.3 (= $1.66/1.25). A sixth search would have an unfavorable B/C ratio.

If their decision is to camp out with a range of prices from zero to $10 per night, benefits of shopping two alternative campgrounds would decline to one-tenth, from $17 to $1.70 per night, which would have a B/C ratio of about 1.4 (= $1.70/1.25). Applying the rule that benefits should be equal to or exceed costs, they would not rationally decide to spend $1.25 of time cost or equivalent searching for a third campground, as the marginal B/C ratio of 0.64 (= $0.80/1.25) is unfavorable. However, if their trip plans are to stay in the campground for two nights, it would pay to search for a third campground, as benefits slightly exceed cost with a B/C ratio of 1.3 (= 2 × $0.80 = 1.60/1.25). If their income is higher than $10 per hour, they would be less likely to search for a place to stay. At an income of $20 per hour the cost of a 15-minute search doubles to $2.50. At an income of $40 per hour, the cost of a 15-minute search doubles again to $5. Increasing cost of search with income explains, in part, why higher priced lodging establishments have prospered in recreation areas. The best economic decision of higher income consumers is to pay the price asked by the first or second commercial lodging establishment they happen to see and avoid their high cost of search.

WAITING TIME OR QUEUEING

Many problems of consumers and recreation resource managers involve waiting time or queueing. The two terms may be used interchangeably. Europeans prefer the word "queueing," while in the United States, we use the phrase, "waiting time." It is defined as time beginning when you enter a waiting line and ending when services begin. Waiting time or queueing problems occur whenever there is: (1) variation in the number of people arriving for service; (2) variation in the time required to provide the service; or, (3) an arrival rate that exceeds the capacity of the resource, so that a bottleneck is created. These conditions are characteristic of many recreation activities. People often wait for service at a park entrance, museum, visitor center, restaurant, grocery store, hotel, motel, airline, gas station, repair shop, stop sign, tunnel, train station, bus depot, bus stop, subway stop, golf course, tennis court, boat ramp, swimming pool, beach, campground, ski lift, sporting event, concert, and theater. For example, people wait in line at restaurants during meal time on peak demand days, and they experience delays in receiving their food order from the kitchen. Similarly, people wait to tee off at a golf course and wait for the foursome ahead to clear the green before chipping on.

Becker has suggested that a reservation or appointment system is a type of queue, in which the waiting is done at home rather than in line. Examples include making advance reservations at campgrounds, theaters, and airlines. People reserve tennis courts to minimize the time waiting their turn to play. Limits on playing time are often set to allow more people to use the facilities and to minimize the wait. Advance purchase of hunting licenses is a form of reservation, and limitations on the number of licenses sold are designed to provide sustained yield management of the herd. The state of California and several other states use a campsite reservation system. The National Park Service experimented with a national reservation system for campsites; however, discontinued the program because of the inconvenience resulting from an overloaded telephone reservation service. Hotels, motels, and lodges routinely accept advance reservations. Airlines encourage advance reservations, but 30-minute check-in lines are still common during the peak holiday season. Planes themselves often wait in a holding pattern for their turn to land at the largest airports.

How many rangers should be employed by managers to obtain the best economic balance between the cost of idle employee and/or facility time, and delay in serving visitors who line up and wait for service? How long should consumers wait in line for a recreation service? The answer depends on the balance between the costs of waiting time and the benefits of the recreation service. An entrance station to a park can become a bottleneck, even though sufficient capacity for additional visitors is available inside the park. In this case, additional booths and standby employees may be provided to handle peak demand at additional cost to the park but with considerable benefit to park visitors. Time costs are especially burdensome to society because they are a "dead weight" loss. Time is a cost to people who wait in line, but it is not a revenue to the suppliers of the service.

There are several alternative solutions to queueing problems, including changes in the:

(1) number of service employees;
(2) number of service stations or counters;
(3) queue discipline such as first-class and second class-airline ticket counters; and
(4) self-service to reduce employee time per customer.

Waiting Time at a Park Information Center

Consider individuals on recreation trips to Yellowstone National Park. Suppose that as they approach the entrance, they consider the possibility of stopping at the headquarters building where there is an information booth which provides, free of charge, a brochure containing a map of the park and advice about where to go and what to see. Increased knowledge of geysers, flora, fauna, trails, and other features of the park would enhance their enjoyment. However, road traffic has been relatively heavy, and it is expected that there will be many other visitors present. The problem is to decide whether or not to visit the information center. They would like to know: What are the chances they will have to wait in line? How many people will be in line? What is the average waiting time? With this information, they could estimate their own waiting time cost and compare that to their expected benefits from the added information about the park.

Begin the analysis by estimating the number of visitors to the information booth and its capacity per day. Any convenient unit of time could be used, but park visitor centers are known to be staffed from 8 A.M. to 5 P.M. for a 9-hour day. A recent study of the operation of the information booth shows that visitors arrive at an average rate of 60 per day and that service time per visitor averages 5.4 minutes. To calculate capacity of the information booth, divide total time available in a day by the service time per visitor. Multiplying 9 hours by 60 minutes per hour equals 540 minutes of total time per day. Dividing the 540 minutes of total time available by 5.4 minutes per visitor served equals 100. Thus, capacity of the information booth is 100 visitors per day.

What are the chances that visitors have to wait in line? Obviously, they will have to wait if they arrive when the information center is occupied serving other visitors. To calculate the proportion of time the information booth is occupied, simply divide the number of visitors in a day by capacity. Dividing 60 visitors by capacity of 100 equals 0.6. Thus, the information booth will be occupied serving visitors 60 percent of the time. The chance they will have to wait in line are 60 out of 100.

How long will visitors have to wait in line? To calculate the average waiting time, first divide the number of visits per day by the result of daily capacity times idle capacity.

$$\frac{60}{100(100 - 60)} = 0.015 \text{ day}$$

Then, convert the 0.015 proportion of a day to minutes of waiting time. Multiplying the 540 minutes in a 9-hour day by 0.015 of a day equals 8.1 minutes. Visitors can expect to wait an average of 8.1 minutes to be served by the information center.

How many people will be waiting in line? To calculate the average number of persons waiting in line, multiply the visitor arrival rate by the average waiting time per visitor. Multiplying the arrival rate of 60 persons per day by the average waiting time of 0.015 day equals 0.9 person. Thus, the average number of people waiting in line is slightly less than one.

What are visitors' waiting time costs? A useful approximation is their opportunity costs. This means their waiting time costs are equal to the loss in benefits from recreation opportunities given up to wait in line. Assume they are typical users with benefits equal to approximately $20 per day in the park. Dividing $20 by 540 minutes in a 9-hour day equals benefits valued at 3.7 cents per minute. Thus, their opportunity costs of waiting time are found by multiplying 8.1 minutes by 3.7 cents per minute, which equals 30 cents. Their opportunity costs of 13.5 minutes at the visitor center (including waiting time of 8.1 minutes and service time of 5.4 minutes) are found by multiplying 13.5 minutes by 3.7 cents per minute, which equals 50 cents. Their waiting time costs are 30 cents and their total waiting time and service time costs are 50 cents.

What are the visitors' expected benefits from the added information? With such a small proportion of their available recreation time at stake (13.5 minutes out of 540 minutes, or 2.5 percent), it may be sufficient to ask whether benefits are expected to exceed waiting and service time costs of 50 cents. A missed turn on a trail or road could easily waste 10 to 15 minutes of time or 50 cents of gas, and a good map and information about road and trail conditions could prevent this. Some consumers would estimate the expected dollar value of the benefits from the additional information. They may estimate that with the additional information, the total benefits of the visit to the park would amount to $22 per day compared with $20 without the added information. Thus, benefits increase by $2 per day with additional information.

What is the recreation economic decision? Should visitors decide to wait at the information booth? To make a decision, review the findings of the above analysis. Although the chances are 6 out of 10 that visitors will have to wait in line, the average length of the waiting time is only one person. They can expect to wait an average of 8.1 minutes, which is probably within their range of tolerance, even when we add 5.4 minutes for receiving the information, or a total time at the visitor center of 13.5 minutes. This is a small proportion (2.5 percent) of their total available time in the park. Benefits were estimated at $2 compared with costs (or disbenefits) of 50 cents. Dividing benefits by costs ($2/$0.50) results in a benefit cost ratio of 4.0. Chances are that this B/C ratio for stopping at the visitor center would exceed the B/C ratio of using the 13.5 minutes in any practical alternative recreation activity in the park. Their recreation economic decision would be to stop at the visitor center for the additional information.

How sensitive are the results to changes in the variables? For example, what if visitors underestimated the number of other people who want to visit the information center? What if the number of people arriving at the information center increases from 60 to 80, to 90, or even 95 on a holiday weekend with peak demand? If capacity of the information center remains unchanged at 100 visitors per day, utilization of capacity would increase from 60 percent to 80 percent, 90 percent, and 95 percent. It is a simple task to calculate the effect of these changes in this key variable on the chances that visitors have to wait in line, number of people in line, and waiting time. Table 10-5 was prepared using these procedures.

Note that the probability that visitors will have to wait in line increases from 60 in 100 to 80 in 100, etc., and is identical to the rate of capacity utilization of the information center. At 90 percent utilization, the average number of people in line is 8 and the average waiting time becomes 48.6 minutes. It seems that most people would not wait when waiting time ranges from 20 to 50 minutes, or between 80 and 90 percent utilization of capacity. Multiplying average waiting time plus service time of 5.4 minutes by time costs of 3.7 cents per minute equals $1 at 80 percent utilization, and rises to $2 at 90 percent utilization. The point at which benefits of $2 equals costs (or disbenefits)

Table 10-5. Effect of Capacity Utilization on Average Waiting Time Cost to Visitors at an Information Center, Yellowstone National Park

Rate of Capacity Utilization	Probability Visitors Will Have To Wait in Line	Average Number of Visitors Waiting in Line	Average Waiting Time Per Visitor		Average Waiting Time plus Service Time Costs
			Fraction of a Visitor Day	Minutes	
60 percent	.60	1	0.015	8.1	$0.50
80 percent	.80	3	0.04	21.6	1.00
90 percent	.90	8	0.09	48.6	2.00
95 percent	.95	18	0.19	102.6	4.00

of $2 occurs at 90 percent utilization, where the average wait equals 48.6 minutes plus service time of 5.4 minutes. However, many people would leave the line before this point is reached, simply because their benefit cost ratio from using the time in any practical alternative recreation activity in the park would exceed unity or 1.0 (= $2/$2). It seems unreasonable to expect that 95 percent utilization of capacity could occur, because it would result in an average of 18 visitors waiting in line at an information center for 1 hour and 42 minutes plus a service time of 5.4 minutes. Waiting time costs of $4 result in an unacceptable benefit cost ratio of only 0.5 (= $2/$4).

Changes in other variables may alter the results of the analysis. If this is their first trip to the park, the information provided may be more critical to their beneficial use of its facilities than if they have accumulated some knowledge from previous visits. Thus, their benefit from waiting in line may exceed $2 on their first visit. Moreover, they may realize that knowledge gained now has a holdover effect and will contribute to benefits from future park visits. But knowledge gained does not last forever; thus benefits to future visits will decay more or less rapidly as they lose maps, conditions change, and they forget what they once could easily recall. Perhaps their benefits from information now would be $3 on this visit, totaling $8 for five visits over the following year. In this case, their recreation economic decision would be to wait in line longer than the average visitor who has been to the park many times before.

Thus far, this analysis has considered a situation in which there is only one person per car. What if there are other persons in the party? If the others are typical tourists, the costs and benefits shown above may not change. The reason is that they also serve who wait in the car rather than in line. Moreover, the value of the information provided those waiting in the car may be approximately equal. Also, they could stand in line and question the interpretive expert at the information booth. However, persons in the party could do other things while one member stands in line, in which case their waiting costs may be lower.

They could take the occasion to use other facilities at the visitor center — for example, have a beverage on the garden deck, watch the nature movie, or use the public toilet.

What if members of some parties are of varying sex, age, and income? Persons who are retired, under 30 years of age, women, and children may have lower time costs of waiting. Studies of people waiting in line have shown that these groups are more likely to wait longer. This reflects a lower opportunity cost of time. The economic decision would be to wait in line longer than other park visitors.

What if some visitors are unlucky (walk under a dark cloud as did the little man in Al Capp's Li'l Abner comic strip), and invariably arrive everywhere when the service counter is occupied and a waiting line exists? In the initial problem, they had lots of company, as 60 percent of the users arrived when the visitor center was occupied serving other visitors. It is important to note here that the average waiting time of 8.1 minutes included the zero waiting time of the lucky ones (the 40 percent of the visitors who did not wait at all). What you have intuitively sensed is confirmed. Their waiting time will be substantially longer than the average. This can be shown by dividing the average waiting time of all visitors by the proportion of visitors who have to wait. This shows that their average wait increases from the user average of 8.1 minutes to 13.5 minutes ($= 8.1/0.60$), or two-thirds, because they arrive when the service counter is serving other visitors. Their waiting time costs increase from 30 cents to 50 cents, or by 20 cents. The unlucky ones walk the face of the earth burdened with two-thirds more waiting time costs, thus lower benefits relative to costs of everything that they do. They indeed stand and wait under a black cloud of perpetual gloom!

What if visitors have an opportunity to drive by the information center more than once during their visit to the park? As they approach the parking lot of the information center, they can observe parked cars indicating people presumably waiting in line. The initial problem dealt with the usual situation for park visitors, in which each visitor passes by the visitor center only once during the day. However, if they stay at a campground nearby or sightseeing by car takes them by the visitor center a second time, what are the chances they will have to wait in line? The 40 percent probability of finding the visitor center unoccupied on the first visit increases on the second visit to 64 percent ($= 60 \times 40 = 24 + 40$), on the third visit to 78.4 percent ($= 36 \times 40 = 14.4 + 64$), on the fourth visit to 87 percent ($= 21.6 \times 40 = 8.6 + 78.4$), and on the fifth visit to 92 percent ($= 13 \times 40 = 5.2 + 87$).

These calculations are based on the rule that the probability of an event occurring with repeated callbacks is the constant 40 percent of the time the information center is unused, multiplied by the remaining difference between the probability of the previous event occurring and 100, added to the probability of the previous event. It is evident that the chances of avoiding waiting in line increase rapidly with repeated visits. Visitor benefits from repeated visits until the information center is unoccupied are the average waiting time saved of 13.5 minutes (= 8.1/0.60) multiplied by their opportunity cost of waiting time of 3.7 cents per minute, which equals benefits of 50 cents. The recreation economic decision would be to limit the time and travel costs of repeated visits to less than or equal to the 50 cents in benefits.

Waiting Time Costs and Alternative Levels of Park Information Service

Assume that the superintendent of Yellowstone National Park is concerned about waiting time at the visitor information center in the park headquarters building. Park managers wish to investigate the severity of the problem and to consider alternative levels of information service to provide an efficient level of public recreation use and benefit. The agency is considering three alternative staffing levels to increase the output of information services: (1) continue the current program with increased utilization of idle time of the single employee assigned to the information desk from 8 A.M. to 5 P.M. daily; (2) double the capacity by increasing the number of employees assigned to the information desk from one to two; and (3) triple the capacity by increasing the number of employees assigned to the information desk from one to three. Under all three alternatives, the information center would continue to have one line for all customers, perhaps marked out with metal posts on stands and nylon rope. Visitors would be serviced by the first available employee in the order of first come, first served.

The problem, in brief, is to decide how to expand visitor information services to provide an efficient level of public use and benefits. When the waiting is done by the agency's employees, the cost is more easily calculated than when the waiting is done by visitors. In the latter case, the cost of waiting time and of the visitor information and visitor goodwill of those who refuse to wait is harder to estimate. We need to know the effects of the number of visitors and the number of service employees on the waiting time costs of visitors. A useful approach is to hold one of these variables constant and to calculate the effect of changes in the other on waiting time costs. First, holding number of employees constant, what is the effect of changes in the number of visitors on waiting time costs? Second, holding number of visitors, constant, what is the effect of changes in the number of service employees? With this information, we could estimate the total or social cost of waiting time and compare that to the benefits from the information provided by the park program. Waiting in line does not usually change the direct cost or price of a recreation activity, but it has the same effect on the number of visitors, because it increases the indirect time costs until demand for the resource or program is curtailed to the limited supply.

Utilization of Existing Capacity

Begin the analysis by holding the number of employees constant and estimating the effect of changes in the number of visitors on waiting time costs. This will show the effects of the first alternative of continuing the current program with increased utilization of idle time of the single employee assigned to the information center. From the previous section, we know that capacity with a single employee is 100 visitors per day, which provides an average service time of 5.4 minutes per visitor. Also we know the effect of changes in the number of visitors, from 60 per day to threshold levels of 80, 90, and 95, on the average waiting times costs per visitor.

What is the effect of changes in the number of visitors on total waiting time cost? It is a simple task to calculate total waiting time costs once average waiting time costs are known. For example, multiplying average waiting time per visitor of 8.1 minutes by the number of visitors per day, say 60, equals 486 minutes of total waiting time. Likewise, multiplying average waiting time costs per visitor of 30 cents by 60 visitors per day equals about $18 of total waiting time costs of all visitors. This is shown in Table 10-6 along with identical calculations for increases in the number of people arriving at the information center from 50 to 60, 70, 80, 90, and 95 as might occur on a holiday weekend with peak demand. For example, with 80 visitors per day, total waiting time rises to 1,728 minutes at a total cost of about $64 per day. And with 90 visitors per day, total waiting time climbs to 4,374 minutes at a total cost of about $162 per day.

What is the incremental or marginal effect of changes in the number of visitors on changes in total waiting time costs? It is a simple task to calculate incremental or marginal waiting time costs once total waiting time costs are known. For example, dividing the change in number of visitors as utilization increases from 50 to 60 (60 - 50 = 10) by change in total waiting time costs of $8 (= $18 - $10) equals 80 cents (= $8/10) per additional visitor. Thus, the incremental or marginal waiting time costs of one additional visitor in the range of 50 to 60 visitors averages 80 cents. This is shown in Table 10-6, along with identical calculations for the incremental or marginal waiting time costs in the range of 60 to 70, 70 to 80, 80 to 90, and 90 to 95 visitors. For example, in the range of 60 to 70 visitors, incremental or marginal waiting time costs increase to $1.41 per additional visitor. In the range of 70 to 80

Table 10-6. Effect of Capacity Utilization on Average, Total and Marginal Waiting Time Cost of Visitors to an Information Center, Yellowstone National Park

Rate of Capacity Utilization	Average Time Per Visitor		Total Waiting Time Costs		Marginal Waiting Time Costs[d]
	Minutes per day	Dollars per day [a]	Minutes per day[b]	Dollars per day[c]	
50 percent	5.4	$0.20	270	$ 10.00	—
60 percent	8.1	0.30	486	17.98	$ 0.80
70 percent	12.4	0.46	868	32.12	1.41
80 percent	21.6	0.80	1,728	63.94	3.18
90 percent	48.6	1.80	4,374	161.84	9.79
95 percent	102.6	3.80	9,747	360.64	39.76

[a]Average waiting time multiplied by opportunity cost of waiting time of 3.7 cents per minute (= $20/540 minutes).
[b]Average waiting time per visitor multiplied by number of visitors per day.
[c]Total waiting time multiplied by opportunity cost of waiting time of 3.7 cents per minute.
[d]Change in total waiting time costs per day divided by change in number of visitors per day.

Table 10-7. Effect of Capacity Utilization on Idle Time Cost of a Single Employee at an Information Center, Yellowstone National Park

Rate of Capacity Utilization	Average Idle Time		Average Idle Time Cost	
	Proportion of Day	Minutes per Day	Per Day[a]	Per Visitor[b]
50 percent	.50	270	$45.00	$0.90
60 percent	.40	216	36.00	.60
70 percent	.30	162	27.00	.39
80 percent	.20	108	18.00	.23
90 percent	.10	54	9.00	.10
95 percent	.05	27	4.50	.05

[a]Total idle time of single employee multiplied by wage rate of $10 per hour, equivalent to 16.666 cents per minute.
[b]Total idle time cost of single employee divided by number of visitors serviced per day.

visitors, incremental or marginal waiting time costs increase to $3.18 per additional visitor. As the number of visitors rises, incremental or marginal waiting time costs rise at an increasing rate. Incremental costs increase to $9.79 per additional visitor in the range of 80 to 90 visitors per day. Incremental costs increase to $39.76 per additional visitor in the range of 90 to 95 visitors per day.

What are the benefits to the agency from reduced idle time as the rate of capacity utilization is increased? Table 10-7 shows the effect of number of visitors served on idle time costs of a single employee at the information center. Increasing the number served increases the efficiency of the agency. For example, the average costs of idle time decline from 90 cents per visitor to 60 cents as utilization of capacity is increased from 50 to 60 percent. Idle time costs continue to decline to zero at 100 percent utilization of capacity of the single employee. Service time costs remain constant at 90 cents per visitor. Adding the two costs, service time and idle time, indicates that total agency costs of providing information service declines as utilization of capacity is increased up to physical capacity.

Begin the analysis by calculating the amount of idle time. It is the inverse of the proportion of time the information center is occupied serving visitors. For example, subtracting the 0.6 utilization of capacity from 1.0 equals 0.4. Thus, idle time at 60 percent utilization of capacity is 40 percent. Multiplying 40 percent by the total 540 minutes in a 9-hour day equals idle time of 216 minutes per day.

The next step is to find out what it costs the agency to operate the information center. Suppose we find that labor and related costs amount to $90 for a 9-hour day or $10 per hour, including primarily salary and labor overhead, such as social security contribution, training, vacation, sick leave, and other fringe benefits. Assume that other costs that are relatively fixed, such as administration, building maintenance and repairs, and utilities (which would be relatively minor in this case), are included as part of the $90-per-day labor costs. Ignored here are the costs of printing maps and brochures that are given out free, which would remain constant per visitor. Also some brochures, booklets, and topographical maps are sold at prices that cover costs of printing and acquisition. Sales may contribute some revenue toward operation of the information center. These costs and revenues could be included at the end of the analysis.

The final task is to calculate the costs of service time and idle time at the information center. Dividing costs of $10 per hour by 60 minutes equals costs of 16.67 cents per minute. With average service time of 5.4 minutes per visitor, agency labor costs equal 90 cents (= 16.67 cents × 5.4 minutes) per visitor served at the information center. Average service time and service time cost are unaffected by the number of visitors served, and they are constant per visitor.

It was previously determined that when service time equals 60 percent of capacity, idle time equals 40 percent, or 216 minutes in a 9-hour day. Multiplying idle time of 216 minutes by 16.67 cents per minute equals $36 idle time costs per day. Dividing this idle time cost of $36 by 60 visitors per day equals 60 cents idle time costs per visitor. This is shown in Table 10-7 along with identical calculations for decreases in idle time from 50 to 40, 30, 20, 10, and 5 percent of capacity of a 9-hour work day. For example, with 80 visitors per day, idle time falls to 108 minutes at a cost of $18. With 90 visitors per day, idle time falls to 54 minutes at a cost of about $9. Thus, idle time and its costs fall as number of visitors increase up to capacity of the information center.

What would be the recreation economic decision? Should the managers of Yellowstone National Park choose the alternative that increases utilization of the obvious idle time of the single employee at the information desk? To make a recommendation, review the findings of the analysis. Table 10-8 summarizes the results thus far. It shows the effect of capacity utilization on combined visitor waiting and agency idle time costs. The social or total costs of visiting an information center would increase substantially, for it is the sum of the private consumer's costs of waiting in line and the direct costs to the government of providing the service. As utilization of capacity increases from 50 to 70 percent, waiting time costs of visitors and idle time costs to the agency combined decline from $1.10 to $0.85 per visitor. Seventy percent utilization is the least-cost level, with 60 percent utilization only slightly higher. Up to 70 percent utilization, savings to the agency from reduced idle time offset increased costs to visitors from added waiting time. At higher rates of utilization, combined waiting and idle time costs increase rapidly. For example, at 80 percent utilization, combined waiting and idle time costs rise to $1.03 per visitor. At 95 percent utilization, they amount to $3.85 per visitor.

Indications are that a park program to freeze the number of information service employees, and to increase utilization of the idle time of existing employees at information desks, could not possibly succeed. The reason is that the visitors would refuse to bear the time cost burden of waiting in line more than an average of about 10 to 15 minutes at 65 to 75 percent utilization of capacity. They have the option of visiting the park without the advantage of the special information provided at information centers. Thus, under this alternative, the size of the waiting line outside the information center would grow until the expected time costs of standing in line discouraged the excess demand. In queueing language, the time costs of waiting in line are a discouragement that stabilizes the length of the queue. As shown in Table 10-8, incremental or marginal waiting time costs per additional

Table 10-8. Effect of Capacity Utilization on Combined Visitor and Agency Waiting and Service Time Costs, Compared to Benefits of an Information Center, Yellowstone National Park

Rate of Capacity Utilization	Average Waiting Time Cost per Customer			Average Waiting & Service Time Cost per Customer[b]			Benefit/ Cost Ratio[c]
	Visitor	Agency[a]	Total	Visitor	Agency	Total	
50 percent	$0.20	$0.90	$1.10	$ .40	$1.80	$2.20	.89
60 percent	.30	.60	.90	.50	1.50	2.00	1.0
70 percent	.46	.39	.85	.66	1.29	1.95	1.04
80 percent	.80	.23	1.03	1.00	1.13	2.13	.88
90 percent	1.80	.10	1.90	2.00	1.00	3.00	—
95 percent	3.80	.05	3.85	4.00	.95	4.95	—

[a]Total idle time per day multiplied by $10 per hour, and divided by number of visitors serviced per day.
[b]Average service time of 5.4 minutes per visitor valued at 3.7 and agency service employee wage rate of $10 per hour, equivalent to 16.666 cents per minute, plus waiting time.
[c]Benefits to visitors from added information estimated at $2 per day minus average visitor waiting and service time cost divided by agency waiting and service time costs per customer.

visitor equal benefits in the range of 65 to 75 percent capacity utilization. At higher levels, incremental or marginal waiting time costs per additional visitor exceed benefits. People leave the line before utilization reaches 80 percent. Most customers arriving during a period of high congestion are lost. The agency should be particularly concerned about the characteristics and number of lost customers. Influential, higher income visitors are more likely to leave the park if delayed longer than some critical time and also more likely to complain to their congressional representatives.

The last column in Table 10-8 shows the combined agency and visitor benefit cost ratios. B/C ratios were calculated for alternative rates of capacity utilization from 50 to 95 percent. For example, at 70 percent utilization, dividing visitor benefits previously estimated at $2 (minus visitor waiting and service time costs of $0.66) by the costs to the agency of $1.29 per visitor served results in a benefit cost ratio of 1.04. This is only slightly more than the benefit cost ratio at 60 percent utilization calculated as 1.0. All other utilization levels have benefit cost ratios of less than 1.0 and are not considered cost-effective. Thus, the agency's recreation economic decision would be to limit utilization of visitor information service to around 60 to 70 percent of capacity.

Changes in Size of Staff

Begin the analysis by holding the rate of utilization constant and estimating the effect of changes in the number of employees. This will show the effects of the second and third alternatives — change service capacity by increasing the number of employees assigned to the information desk from one to two or three persons. From the previous section, we know that 60 to 70 percent utilization of capacity provides a cost-effective level of public recreation use and benefit. To be on the safe side, utilization of capacity is held constant at 60 percent.

Table 10-9 shows that capacity of the information center increases by 100 visitors with each additional service employee. With one service employee, capacity is 100 visitors per day; with two employees, to 200 visitors per day; and with three employees, capacity increases to 300 visitors per day. Holding utilization of capacity constant at 60 percent means that when one service employee is present at the information center the average number of visitors is 60 per day; with two service employees, the number of visitors doubles to 120; and with three service employees, triples to 180.

The reason this assumption is necessary should be clarified. The purpose of Table 10-9 is to show the effect of number of service employees at the information booth on the waiting time costs of visitors. To do so requires that the effect of the rate of capacity utilization be

Table 10-9. Effect of Increases in the Size of Staff on Waiting Time Costs of Visitors to an Information Center, Yellowstone National Park

Waiting Time Variables	Number of Employees Present at One Time		
	One	Two	Three
Capacity, visitors per day	100	200	300
Average number of visitors per day	60	120	180
Rate of capacity utilization[a]	.6	.6	.6
Proportion of visitors who wait	0.60	0.45	0.35
Proportion of time facility is completely idle	0.40	0.25	0.15
Average waiting time per visitor			
Proportion of day	0.015	0.006	0.003
Number of minutes	8.1	3.24	1.62
Average waiting time costs per visitor			
Waiting time costs	$0.30	$0.12	$0.06
Service time costs[b]	0.20	0.20	0.20
Total	0.50	0.32	0.26
Total visitor waiting time, minutes	486	389	292
Total visitor waiting time cost	$17.98	$14.39	$10.80
Benefits per day			
Visitor waiting time, minutes	—	583	1,116
Visitor waiting time costs[c]	—	$21.57	$43.14
Benefits per year			
Visitor waiting time, hours	—	3,547	7,093
Visitor waiting time costs	—	$7,873	$15,746

[a]Rate of capacity utilization equals 60 percent for all three alternatives.
[b]This is 5.4 minutes multiplied by 3.7 cents per minute.
[c]Benefit calculation: With two employees: $2 \times \$17.98 = \$35.96 - \$14.39 = \$21.57$. With three employees: $3 \times \$17.98 = \$53.94 - \$10.80 = \$43.14$.

held constant. Some may object that this assumption violates conditions in the real world. Not necessarily, as it would be the natural result of the increased attractiveness of shorter waiting time. With the number of visits to Yellowstone National Park estimated at 3 million per year or about 8,200 per day, it is not unreasonable to expect that an average of 180 visitors per day would stop at this particular information center, although it is only one of several in the park. Moreover, a special promotion program at the entrance gate could emphasize the increased service at the information center, so that more visitors are made aware of its existence. Finally, the experience of most recreation resource management agencies has been that whatever service is provided tends to be used by park visitors; i.e., to a considerable extent, supply creates its own demand under these circumstances.

What is the effect of number of service employees at the information center on the proportion of visitors who will have to wait in line? When visitors arrive, they will receive immediate service if one of the employees present is not occupied serving other visitors. They will have to wait if all employees present are occupied serving other visitors. Table 10-9 shows that the probability that visitors will have to wait in line is .6 when a single service employee is at the information center. With two service employees, the probability of waiting falls to .45, and with three employees, to .35. Thus, the chances of a waiting line forming at the information center are nearly one-half as great with three employees as with a single employee.

What is the effect of number of service employees at the information center on visitor waiting time? Table 10-9 shows that the average waiting time per visitor is 8.1 minutes when a single service employee is at the information center. With two employees, average waiting time declines to 3.24 minutes, and with three employees, to 1.62 minutes. Thus, average waiting by visitors to an information center with a single service employee is five times the average waiting time with three service employees and 2.5 times the waiting time with two service employees. A procedure for calculating the effects of number of employees on waiting time is illustrated in Barish.

Multiplying average waiting time per visitor by number of visitors equals total waiting time. With a single service employee, the total waiting time of 60 visitors is 486 minutes per day. When the number of service employees is increased to two, the total waiting time of 120 visitors is 389 minutes per day. Increasing the number of service employees to three reduces the total waiting time of 180 visitors to 292 minutes per day.

What is the effect of the number of service employees at the information center on waiting time costs? Table 10-9 shows that the average waiting time cost per visitor decline at the same dramatic rate as waiting time. Waiting time costs are 30 cents per visitor with a single service employee at the information center; however, this falls to 12 cents with two service employees and to 6 cents with three service employees.

Multiplying average waiting time costs per visitor by number of visitors equals total waiting time costs. With a single service employee, the total waiting time cost incurred by 60 visitors is about $18 per day. When the number of service employees is increased to two, total waiting time costs incurred by 120 visitors is $14.39 per day. Increasing the number of service employees to three reduces total waiting time costs borne by 180 visitors to $10.80 per day.

What are the expected benefits from increasing the number of service employees at the information center? Table 10-9 shows benefits to visitors as the difference in waiting time with and without the added service employees. From Table 10-6 you know that waiting time costs to 60 visitors served by a single employee are $17.98 per day. In order to hold constant the number of visitors served, it is necessary to consider the practical alternatives of adding service employees at two or three additional information centers each with a single employee.

Thus, multiplying the waiting time costs of $17.98 per day by 2 so that waiting costs are equivalent to two separate information centers, each with a single employee, serving a total of 120 visitors, equals $35.95 per day. Subtracting from $35.96 the $14.39 total waiting time costs with two employees serving 120 visitors at a single information center equals $21.57 per day savings in visitor waiting time costs. This represents the estimated daily benefits of adding a second service employee and is equivalent to $7,873 benefits per year.

The benefits from adding a third service employee to the visitor information center are similarly calculated. Multiplying the waiting time costs of $17.98 per day by 3 so that waiting costs are equivalent to three separate information centers each with a single employee serving a total of 180 visitors, equals $53.94 per day. Subtracting from $53.94 the $10.80 total waiting time costs with three employees serving 180 visitors at a single information center equals $43.14 per day savings in visitor waiting time costs. This represents the estimated daily benefits of three service employees rather than one and is equivalent to $15,746 benefits per year.

The incremental benefits of a third service employee are the difference in benefits with two employees compared with three employees. Subtracting $21.57 benefits with two employees from $43.14 benefits with three employees equals benefits of $21.57 per day from adding a third service employee. This is equivalent to $7,873 benefits per year.

What are the expected costs of increasing the number of service employees at the information center? Agency costs per visitor would not vary with two or three service employees because utilization of capacity would remain identical. From the previous section, we know that agency costs at 60 percent utilization of capacity average $1.50 per visitor, including $0.90 service time of 5.4 minutes per visitor plus 40 percent idle time cost of $0.60 per visitor. Average agency costs per day are $90 with a single employee, $180 with two employees, and $270 with three. These are 9-hour days at $10 per hour. However, the managers of the park should put these total costs in perspective by noting that if visitor benefits from the added information average $2 per day, the increased use of the center increases total visitor benefits per day from $120 with one service employee to $240 per day with two employees, and to $360 with three. Moreover, visitor waiting time costs are reduced, which increases visitor benefits.

What would be the recreation economic decision? Should the managers of Yellowstone National Park favor either of the alternatives of increasing the number of service employees to two or three? To recommend a decision, review the findings of the analysis. Increasing the number of service employees from one to two or three would increase public use and benefits. The number of visitors provided with information would increase from 60 per day with one service employee to 120 per day with two employees, and to 180 with three. The proportion of visitors who must wait in line is reduced from 60 percent with a single service employee to 45 percent with two employees and to 35 percent with three employees. In addition, average waiting time per visitor is reduced from 8.1 minutes with a single service employee to 3.2 minutes with two employees and to 1.6 minutes with three employees. Together, these results of increased number of service employees would lead to enhanced customer goodwill, as more visitors are served and fewer elect to leave the shorter waiting line.

Increasing the number of service employees from one to two or three would lead to a more favorable benefit cost ratio. In the previous section, we found that the benefit cost ratio was unity or 1.0 with 60 percent utilization of capacity of a single service employee at the information center. This was based on average visitor benefits of $2 less average visitor waiting and service time costs of $0.50 divided by average agency costs of $1.50 per visitor. On an average daily basis, this is equivalent to total benefits of $120 less average visitor waiting and service time costs of $30 divided by daily agency costs of $90. Adding a second employee increases net benefits from zero to $7,873 annually and the average daily benefit cost ratio from 1.0 to 1.12 (= [$240 - $38.43]/$180). Adding a third employee increases net benefits to $15,746 annually and the average daily benefit cost ratio to 1.16 (= [$360 - $46.86]/$270). The recreation economic decision by managers of the park would be to employ three rangers at the visitor information center.

How sensitive are the results to changes in the variables? For example, what if we overestimate agency costs? Nearly all of the visitor waiting time at the information center occurs during the peak summer weekend and holidays. Labor costs could be reduced in two possible ways. First, perhaps (as is customary) temporary summer employees could be hired at approximately one-half the cost, or $5 per hour for total labor and related visitor service costs compared with $10 per hour assumed in this case. This would have the effect of reducing agency costs by one-half; however, the relationships throughout the problem would not change sufficiently to change the recreation economic decision, which would remain the same. Wherever benefits are compared to agency and visitor costs, the ratio would increase, when agency costs are reduced by one-half. For example, the benefit cost ratio with a single employee becomes 2.0 (= [$120 - $30]/$45). With two employees, the B/C ratio becomes 2.24 (= [$240 - $38.43]/$90). With three employees, the B/C ratio becomes 2.32 (= [$360 - $46.86]/$135).

A second possible change on the cost side would be to reorganize the information center so that employees may perform other productive activities when they are idle. Like a receptionist at the entrance to an office, employees of the information center may work at a typewriter when no visitors are waiting for information services. Thus, information center employees may be assigned multiple functions rather than the single function of providing visitor information. The other functions could be such that they do not take employees away from the information desk, so they can easily shift from performing the alternative work to serving visitors the moment they arrive. This could have the effect of eliminating idle time costs of agency employees at the information center.

For example, elimination of the 40 percent idle time of one service employee reduces agency costs from $90 per day to approximately $54, or by $36 per day. This is somewhat overestimated because approximately 10 minutes per hour are necessary for coffee break and lunch break. However, for purposes of this problem, it is assumed that other employees in the park headquarters fill in during breaktime so that the information center is staffed on a continuous basis from 8 A.M. to 5 P.M. daily. The effect of reduced idle time could be easily calculated for two- and three-employee information centers. The result would be a more favorable benefit cost ratio; however, the relationship would not change sufficiently to change the recreation economic decision, which would remain the same.

SUMMARY

In this chapter, we addressed the problem of risk and uncertainty and learned how to apply the concept of expected value to decision making by consumers and managers. Expected value of recreation use, E(CS), was defined as the average consumer surplus that an individual will end up with who takes repeated trips to a recreation site. The consumer surplus from each possible outcome is multiplied by its probability of occurrence and these products are summed to obtain a weighted average expected value. The problem of risk and uncertainty is important for two reasons. First, all decisions by consumers and managers of private and public recreation resources are made in the present, based on expectations about the future. Second, the actual experience will seldom turn out exactly as expected when a decision is made.

For many simple recreation economic decisions, of course, the outcomes are known with certainty. In these cases, the expected value is equal to the actual consumer surplus realized when the event occurs. However, the vast majority of consumer and managerial decisions are made under conditions of risk or uncertainty in which benefits and costs cannot be predicted exactly. The major distinction between risk and uncertainty is that probability has an objective basis in the case of risk, rather than a subjective basis in the case of uncertainty. Uncertainty was defined as a situation in which two or more possible outcomes may result from a decision, but the precise nature of these outcomes is not known or the probability of each occurring cannot be assigned objectively. Risk was defined as a situation in which the probability of each possible outcome is known to the decision maker. Objective knowledge is either based on mathematical and physical principles or on past experience under similar circumstances.

We outlined the major steps involved in decision making under conditions of risk and uncertainty. First, because all decisions involve a choice among alternatives, identify the two or more possible alternatives or projects between which to choose. Second, for each alternative recreation activity or program, define the possible outcomes that may occur, depending on the state of nature or other conditions encountered. Third, estimate the economic benefits associated with each possible outcome for each alternative. Fourth, estimate the probability of each particular outcome occurring. Fifth, calculate the expected value of consumer surplus at the time the decision is made, which equals the weighted average value of possible outcomes for each alternative considered. Finally, adjust the expected value for the decision maker's attitude toward risk, whether he or she tends to be neutral, cautious, or a gambler.

What decision makers actually decide depends largely upon their attitude toward risk. Individuals who are neutral toward risk value a dollar gained equal to a dollar lost. Those who tend to be risk averse value a dollar gained less than a dollar lost, and those who are risk seeking value a dollar gained more than a dollar lost. This is an important distinction because consumers and managers of private and public recreation resources are usually risk averse. This means that high risk recreation activities and programs have an expected value that is less than those with low risk. Economists define "option value" as a kind of insurance premium that risk-averse individuals would be willing to pay to avoid risky conditions. Randall has concluded that it makes as much sense to measure option value and include it in public benefit cost analysis as in private decision making.

Individual consumers may be careful shoppers during most of the year, but when on holiday, want their time to be not only leisurely, but carefree. Inexperienced buyers, such as tourists, pay higher prices in a market than do experienced buyers because they have no accumulated knowledge of asking prices by alternative sellers. The problem is to decide whether or not it is worth their time to search for the most favorable price among alternative places to buy recreation goods and services, an activity known as shopping. The economic benefits of improved information are equal to the added expected value of recreation use plus the added use demanded with the added information. We learned that most tourists do not shop for gasoline; but they will shop for a place to stay overnight because the savings from shopping are greater for larger expenditures and for larger price ranges among sellers.

Finally, we looked at the problem of waiting time or queueing for service at a park information center. It is characteristic of many such problems of congestion on recreation trips. Time costs are especially burdensome to society because they are a dead weight loss. This means that time is a cost to people who wait in line, but it is not offset by benefit to the suppliers of the service. How long should consumers wait in line for a recreation service? The answer depends on the costs of waiting time and the benefits of the recreation service. Waiting in line does not usually change the direct cost or price of a recreation activity, but it has the same effect on demand because it increases time costs until demand for the resource or program is curtailed to the limited supply. How many rangers should be employed by park managers depends on a comparison of user benefits to agency costs plus time costs of users who wait in line for the recreation service. The conclusion was that efficiency in the utilization of park service employees occurs between 60 and 70 percent of capacity. Beyond this rate, the social costs of information services increase substantially. Social costs were defined as the sum of the private consumer's costs of waiting in line and the direct costs to the government of providing the service.

READINGS

Barish, Norman K. *Economic Analysis for Engineering and Managerial Decision-Making.* McGraw-Hill, New York. 1962.

Becker, Gary S. "A Theory of the Allocation of Time." *The Economic Journal* 75(Sept. 1965):493-517.

Bernoulli, Danial. "Exposition of a New Theory on the Measurement of Risk." *Econometrica* 22(Jan. 1954):25-36.

Brookshire, David S., and Thomas D. Crocker. "The Advantages of Contingent Valuation Methods for Benefit-Cost Analysis." *Public Choice* 36(No. 2, 1981):235-52.

Buse, Reuben C., and Nava Enosh. "Youth Experience: Effect on Participation in Recreation Activities." *Land Economics* 53(Nov. 1977):468-82.

Cheron, Emmanuel J., and J. R. Brent Ritchie. "Leisure Activities and Perceived Risk." *Journal of Leisure Research* 14(No. 2, 1982):139-54.

Cox, D. R., and W. L. Smith. *Queues.* John Wiley and Sons, New York. 1961.

Desner, Morris, and Tortorello Research, Inc. "Outdoorsmen Surveyed: Frequency of Mishaps Shows First Aid Items to Stock." *Campground Management* (Apr. 1983):18-19.

Gitelson, Richard J., and John L. Crompton. "The Planning Horizons and Sources of Information Used by Pleasure Vacationers." *Journal of Travel Research* 11(No. 3, 1983):2-7.

Lindsay, Cotton M., and Bernard Feigenbaum. "Rationing by Waiting Lists." *American Economic Review* 74(June 1984):404-17.

Mann, Leon. "Queue Culture: The Waiting Line as a Social System." *American Journal of Sociology* 75(Nov. 1969):340-54.

Mann, Leon, and K. R. Taylor. "Queue Counting: The Effects of Motives Upon Estimates of Numbers in Waiting Lines." *Journal of Personality and Social Psychology* 12(June 1969):95-103.

Nichols, D., E. Smolensky, and T. N. Tideman. "Discrimination by Waiting Time in Merit Goods." *American Economic Review* 61(June 1971):312-23.

Porter, R. D. "On the Optimal Size of Underpriced Facilities." *American Economic Review* 67(Sept. 1977):753-60.

Rothschild, Michael. "Searching for the Lowest Price When the Distribution of Price is Unknown." *Quarterly Journal of Economics* 89(Aug. 1974):689-12.

Schwartz, Barry. *Queuing and Waiting.* University of Chicago Press, Chicago. 1975.

Scitovsky, Tibor. *The Joyless Economy: An Inquiry into Human Satisfaction and Consumer Dissatisfaction.* Oxford University Press, London. 1976.

Smith, V. Kerry, and Vincent G. Munley. "Learning-by-Doing and Experience: The Case of Whitewater Recreation." *Land Economics* 52(Nov. 1976):545-53.

Stigler, George J. "The Economics of Information." *Journal of Political Economy* 69(June 1961):213-15.

Chapter Eleven

Forecasting Future Consumption

This chapter introduces the concept of time; describes several important methods of forecasting "with" and "without" effects, including extrapolation or trend projection, and forecasting demand from multiple regression coefficients and elasticities of demand; summarizes recent trends and forecasts of the future consumption of recreation; and discusses implications for improving the application of forecasting techniques to recreation economic decisions.

Up to now we have assumed that the consequences of most recreation economic decisions occur in the short-run rather than long-run, a simplification that was useful for purposes of understanding decisions with immediate effects. At this point we modify this assumption in order to consider important long-run recreation economic problems. Decisions made now by managers of private and public recreation resources will have consequences next year and in the years that follow. Some will have effects that are felt for decades or even centuries. Once the decision was made by the State of California and the U.S. government to protect Yosemite as the first National Park, for example, the government was committed to pay not only the initial acquisition and development costs but all future development, operation, and maintenance costs. That decision more than a century ago (1872) committed public funds to be used for recreation purposes for decades yet to come. It is useful, then, to consider the problem of forecasting the future effects of current recreation economic decisions.

In this chapter, we will consider historic trends in the consumption of recreation and the prospects for future growth. Thus far, no standard method of forecasting future participation has been developed that is suitable for all purposes. We will examine a variety of methods that are used, including time-series, simple regression, multiple regression, resource capacity, expert judgment, and market survey. Although each of these approaches has provided satisfactory estimates of the amount of recreation that will be consumed in future years under particular conditions, each also has its drawbacks. We will discuss the problems of each approach and demonstrate under what conditions it should be used. Accuracy of the alternative forecasting methods is a continuing problem, although considerable progress has been made in recent years.

The purpose of forecasting is to estimate what future benefits and costs would be with a proposed project compared to what they would be without it. The difference is the increment in net benefits of the proposal. Thus, we forecast consumption both with and without a project. Such estimates are useful to anyone planning future development of recreation resources. The availability of private financing depends on reliable forecasts of future revenues and costs of proposed projects in order to determine if they will be financially feasible. The availability of public financing also depends on reliable forecasts of future benefits and costs of proposed public projects in order to determine if they will be socially beneficial. With the renewed emphasis on accountability in government, there is a special concern about the expected benefits of expenditures on recreation programs.

HISTORIC TRENDS AND FUTURE PROSPECTS

Trends in the consumption of recreation have changed decisively since World War II. Table 11-1 illustrates the declining annual growth in the use of public parks and recreation areas from the 1940s to the 1980s. Growth rates exceeding 10 percent per year were typical of the early postwar period to the mid-1960s. We were all growth-oriented then. The chief governmental concern was to meet the need for development of access roads and facilities at new recreation sites. Clawson and Knetsch were correct in characterizing the United States as a "more so" society and economy. In their book *Economics of Outdoor Recreation,* published in 1966, they forecast more people, more leisure, more income, more travel, more opportunity for individual choice and growth, and more varied activities generally. At that time, it was safe to predict rapid increases in recreation, as consumers ex-

Table 11-1. Compound Annual Growth Rates of Public Recreation Consumption in the United States

Government Agency	Compound Annual Growth, Percent			
	1945-67	1967-75	1975-80	1980-83
National Park Service	9.0	7.0	3.0	3.4
U.S. Forest Service	12.0	3.7	2.3	0.6
Reservoirs, Corps of Engineers	23.0	7.9	4.0	1.7
Reservoirs, Bureau of Reclamation		3.9	3.9	3.3
National Wildlife Refuges	12.0	6.9		
Reservoirs, Tennessee Valley Authority	12.0	1.2		
Bureau of Land Management		6.4		
State Parks	8.0		3.4	
City and County Parks	5.0			

Source: Years 1945-67, Clawson and Knetsch, p. 122; 1967-75, U.S. Department of Transportation; 1975-80 and 1980-83 from agency reports.

perienced newfound affluence, leisure time, and increased environmental awareness. Rapid growth also resulted from expanded opportunities provided by government development and subsidization of participation in recreation. Development of new technology and commercial production was also important, particularly for skiing, snowmobiling, white-water boating, camping, and backpacking.

Long-run forecasts based on the data base provided by the era of rapid growth were overly-optimistic for the 1970s and 1980s. Table 11-1 shows that annual growth rates declined from more than 10 percent during the early postwar period to about 5 percent in the 1970s, then tumbled to approximately 2 percent in the early 1980s. For example, annual growth in the recreation use of the national forests declined from an average of 12 percent per year in the early postwar years to 3.7 percent in the period 1967-75; 2.3 percent, 1975-80; and 0.6 percent, 1980-83. The decline in annual growth was even more dramatic for water-based recreation at reservoirs constructed by the Corps of Engineers. The growth rate declined from an average of 23 percent per year in the early postwar years to 7.9 percent in the period, 1967-75; 4.0 percent, 1975-80; and 1.7 percent, 1980-83. As a result, forecasts made in the late 1970s and early 1980s were much more conservative than previously.

Recreation consumers and managers became less optimistic in their expectations about the future. The publication in 1972 of Meadows, et al., *The Limits to Growth,* had a sobering effect on expectations in the United States and throughout the Western world. The conclusion was that we would run out of essential mineral and energy resources in the foreseeable future if exponential growth rates in consumption continued at the high levels of the early postwar years. Their predictions were controversial and disputed by other forecasters. However, since that time has come an awareness of the complexity of demand and limits to growth in the recreation industry. With the renewed emphasis on efficiency in government, managers are more concerned about forecasts of the benefits of expenditures on recreation programs. Recreation planners and managers are faced with the problem of allocating increasingly scarce resources among competing uses. The people involved have become more interested in the application of economics to improve the decision making process.

Conditions have changed decisively; the United States of the 1970s and 1980s could not be characterized as a "more so" society. For example, the rate of population growth declined by nearly half, from 1.8 percent per year in the early postwar baby boom years to a rate of less than 1.0 percent. The rate of increase in real household income (adjusted to remove inflation) fell precipitously from an average increase of about 3 percent per year in the early postwar years to near zero. The average number of hours in the workweek tended to stabilize at about 40 hours, and unemployment levels reached postwar highs. With record high interest rates, the purchase of most types of recreation equipment declined sharply. Travel, which had been increasing rapidly, actually declined as a result of the energy crisis and increased price of gasoline. With reduced travel, recreation was often limited to activities that could be pursued close to home.

In 1986, a decrease in interest rates and energy prices stimulated the sale of recreation equipment and recreation travel in the United States. Future growth in the recreation industry will be affected by changes in these and related variables that affect consumption.

Historic Trends in Sports

Let's look at trends in the number of persons participating in several important recreation activities and sports during the 1970s and early 1980s. Table 11-2 shows estimates by A. C. Nielsen Company (worldwide market research) based on telephone interviews with the heads of 3,000 households who reported the participation of 9,000 persons living in these homes. Using the nationwide survey for 1973 as the base year, the 3-year intervals between each subsequent survey provide a trend in participation to 1982.

Swimming is the number one sport, although the number of persons participating shows a moderate decline. Bicycling maintained the number two position. This activity grew rapidly from 1973 to 1976 as a result of the energy crisis. Subsequently, participation in bicycling declined from 1976 to 1979, but experienced renewed popularity in 1982, with another sharp rise in energy prices. Fishing was ranked third in 1973, 1976, and 1982. This activity has been holding steady in terms of number of participants with moderate fluctuations from year to year. Camping was the fourth most popular activity in 1973, 1976, and 1982. This activity has been growing steadily in the number of participants during the 1970s and early 1980s. Camping grew rapidly from 1973 to 1976 as a result of the energy crisis and associated price rise, with subsequent declining rates of growth to 1982. Others in the top-ten ranking of popularity are boating, jogging, roller skating, softball, tennis, and basketball.

Overall, nine of the top 10 sports have shown increases in the number of participants from 1973 to 1982. Boating, in particular, has shown steady growth. Boating, other than sailing, increased at a compound annual rate of 2.9 percent and sailing, 4.7 percent. The growth in popularity of tennis during the 1970s appears to have peaked, with a significant decline in the number of participants in the early 1980s. The same trend is evident to a lesser degree for jogging, softball, and basketball. Roller skating shows a rapid growth in the number of participants into the early 1980s.

340

Table 11-2. Trends in the Number of Persons Participating in Outdoor Recreation Activities and Sports, United States

Activity	Number of Persons Participating, Millions				Percent Change 1973-82	Compound Annual Percent Change 1973-82
	1973	1976	1979	1982		
Swimming	107.2	103.5	105.4	102.3	-4.6	-0.5
Bicycling	65.6	75.0	69.8	72.2	10.1	1.1
Fishing	61.3	63.9	59.3	63.7	3.9	0.4
Camping	54.4	58.1	60.3	61.6	13.2	1.4
Boating (Other than Sailing)	32.6	35.2	37.9	42.0	28.8	2.9
Jogging and Running	—	—	35.7	34.3	—	—
Roller Skating	—	—	25.4	30.2	—	—
Softball	26.4	27.3	28.4	28.0	6.1	0.7
Tennis	20.2	29.2	32.3	25.5	26.4	2.6
Basketball	22.1	25.8	24.0	25.3	14.5	1.5
Snow Skiing (Downhill and Cross-country)	7.7	11.0	15.4	19.5	153.2	10.9
Hunting	20.0	20.5	19.7	18.7	-6.5	-0.7
Ice Skating	24.9	25.8	18.9	18.0	-17.7	-1.8
Water Skiing	14.0	14.7	16.9	18.0	28.5	2.5
Golf	17.0	16.6	15.9	17.4	2.4	0.3
Baseball	15.2	15.7	15.0	13.6	-10.6	-1.1
Football	14.2	14.9	14.3	14.0	-1.4	-0.2
Raquetball	—	2.8	10.7	12.1	—	—
Motorbiking and Motorcycling	11.3	9.7	10.5	12.1	7.1	0.8
Sailing	7.0	7.3	8.7	10.6	51.4	4.7
Snowmobiling	7.8	9.2	8.6	8.6	10.3	1.1
Soccer	—	—	6.5	8.0	—	—
Hardball	—	5.5	5.6	2.6	—	—
Archery	5.8	5.5	5.5	—	—	—
Ice Hockey	3.3	2.7	1.7	1.4	-54.5	-5.0
Total U.S. Population	206.0	210.0	215.0	225.6	9.5	1.0

Source: A. C. Nielsen Co.

The fastest growing recreation activity in the 1970s and early 1980s was snow skiing, both downhill and cross-country. From a relatively small base of 7.7 million skiers in 1973, participation increased at a compound annual rate of 10.9 percent to 1982 when nearly 20 million persons participated in downhill and/or cross-country skiing. Skiing was the 11th most popular activity in the early 1980s and showed no indication that the increase in participation was slackening. Apparently, participants have substituted downhill and cross-country skiing for other winter sports activities. Snowmobiling participation increased from 1973 to 1976, declined to 1979, and held steady the 1982. Other winter sports, such as ice skating and ice hockey, were on a downward slide in terms of number of participants in the 1970s and early 1980s.

Among the team sports included in the Nielsen surveys, softball was the most popular, with a total of about 28 million players in 1982. This estimate was up about 6 percent from the 26.4 million participants in 1973. Basketball participation (including both indoor and outdoor play) was at a level of 25.3 million in 1982, which was about 14.5 percent higher than the 22.1 million figure reported in the 1973 base-year study. The trends in baseball and football are down — in particular, baseball. This is believed to be a result of the decline in number of teenagers that took place in the late 1970s. Softball, on the other hand, continued to be played by both males and females beyond the high school and teenage years. Soccer, measured for the first time in 1979, appears to be coming on strong in the United States; the estimate of participation in 1982 was about 8 million.

Future Prospects

Long-run forecasts of the growth in recreation consumption average about 2 percent and range from 1 to 3 percent per year. This is shown in Table 11-3, which illustrates the results of a 1980 forecast by Hof and Kaiser prepared for use in long-run planning by the U.S. Forest Service. The authors forecast the number of participants in 19 outdoor recreation activities for 10-year intervals to the year 2030. Their results are presented as an index (or percent), with 1977 equal to 100. For example, an index of 159 for hiking in the year 2030 means that participation in the activity is forecast to increase to 159 percent of its level in 1977, or a total increase of 59 percent in 53 years.

To enable us to compare Hof and Kaiser's forecasts with historic growth rates, Table 11-3 contains a conversion of their estimates of total growth to compound annual growth rates (in percent) using the compound growth tables in Gittinger. The average annual growth rates are shown as the right hand column of Table 11-3. There are two points that should be made about this comparison. First, even very low growth rates would result in substantial increases in participation over the 50-year planning period to the year 2030. A compound annual growth rate of 2 percent doubles every 35 years, and 3 percent, every 24 years. Second, if there is a difference between the historic trend and forecast of recreation consumption, this does not necessarily mean that the forecast is wrong, because of the growth cycle in recreation activities. The hypothesis is that some recreation activities go through a life cycle of growth, maturity, and decay. Camping at developed sites is forecast to grow by 1.9 percent per year and camping at undeveloped sites by 1.5 percent. This seems consistent with the 1.4 percent annual growth in number of persons camping during the 1970s and early 1980s (Table 11-2). On the other hand, downhill skiing is forecast to grow by 2.4 percent per year and cross-country

Table 11-3. Forecasts of the Number of Persons Participating in ◉utdoor Recreation in the United States, 1977 to 2030

Recreation Activity	Projection Level	Projections by Year, Percent						Compound Annual Growth Rate, Percent
		1977	1990	2000	2010	2020	2030	
Population Index	Medium	100	112	120	127	134	139	0.7
Land Based Total	High	100	122	144	175	208	245	1.9
	Medium	100	111	121	135	149	161	1.0
	Low	100	105	109	113	118	120	0.4
Camping (Developed)	High	100	130	180	236	297	369	2.6
	Medium	100	118	150	181	214	245	1.9
	Low	100	116	133	149	167	181	1.3
Camping	High	100	130	161	207	254	311	2.3
(Undeveloped)	Medium	100	116	133	157	182	205	1.5
	Low	100	111	121	132	145	155	0.9
Driving Off-road	High	100	118	134	154	177	201	1.4
Vehicle	Medium	100	108	118	128	139	147	0.8
	Low	100	108	115	120	125	126	0.5
Hiking	High	100	124	149	187	225	270	2.1
	Medium	100	109	117	132	146	159	0.9
	Low	100	101	102	103	107	109	0.3
Horseback Riding	High	100	125	151	194	233	284	2.1
	Medium	100	109	118	137	155	173	1.2
	Low	100	102	102	105	113	119	0.4
Nature Study	High	100	123	146	176	210	247	1.9
	Medium	100	110	110	133	145	155	0.9
	Low	100	106	111	117	125	131	0.6
Picnicking	High	100	119	140	166	196	230	1.7
	Medium	100	112	124	137	150	162	1.0
	Low	100	107	114	119	125	127	0.5
Pleasure Driving	High	100	118	136	159	186	215	1.6
	Medium	100	110	120	130	141	149	0.8
	Low	100	105	111	114	117	118	0.4
Sightseeing	High	100	121	143	171	202	237	1.7
	Medium	100	112	123	136	148	159	0.9
	Low	100	105	111	115	118	120	0.4
Water Based Total	High	100	131	164	218	261	322	2.4
	Medium	100	118	134	158	181	206	1.5
	Low	100	108	115	124	134	144	0.8
Canoeing	High	100	140	182	243	305	384	2.8
	Medium	100	121	140	170	200	233	1.8
	Low	100	109	117	128	141	155	0.9
Sailing	High	100	159	221	305	396	511	3.4
	Medium	100	144	182	231	281	337	2.5
	Low	100	130	155	183	212	242	1.9
Other Boating	High	100	132	164	209	257	315	2.3
	Medium	100	119	136	159	182	207	1.5
	Low	100	110	110	127	137	147	0.8
Swimming Outdoors	High	100	123	150	189	229	278	2.1
	Medium	100	114	127	146	164	183	1.3
	Low	100	106	111	117	125	131	0.6
Water Skiing	High	100	127	156	204	249	308	2.3
	Medium	100	109	117	137	155	175	1.2
	Low	100	98	96	96	101	105	0.3
Snow and Ice	High	100	139	179	239	300	377	2.7
Based Total	Medium	100	123	143	175	207	240	1.8
	Low	100	113	124	137	155	170	1.1
Cross-Country Skiing	High	100	154	211	290	376	479	3.0
	Medium	100	133	161	200	241	280	2.1
	Low	100	118	134	151	172	190	1.3
Downhill Skiing	High	100	162	227	318	416	538	3.4
	Medium	100	142	178	228	279	334	2.4
	Low	100	125	146	171	199	226	1.6
Ice Skating	High	100	137	176	234	293	367	2.6
	Medium	100	123	143	174	205	237	1.8
	Low	100	113	124	138	155	170	1.1
Sledding	High	100	131	165	218	268	334	2.5
	Medium	100	117	132	160	187	215	1.6
	Low	100	109	116	126	140	154	0.9
Snowmobiling	High	100	126	151	191	229	277	2.1
	Medium	100	109	120	141	161	181	1.2
	Low	100	107	114	122	133	141	0.8

Source: U.S. Forest Service.

343

skiing by 2.1 percent. This is substantially less than the annual growth of 15.1 percent for downhill and cross-country skiing during the 1970s and early 1980s. This suggests that growth in skiing will slow down as the industry matures.

It is clear from the results presented in Table 11-3 that substantial increases in participation are expected in all of the recreation activities studied. There are noticeable differences in the size of projected increases for land-based, water-based, and snow- and ice-based activities. Winter sports activities are expected to have the largest increases in participation, 1.8 percent per year, especially downhill skiing, with 2.4 percent growth per year. Participation in water-based activities is expected to increase at 1.5 percent per year, a somewhat lower rate than for winter sports. However, larger increases are forecast for participation in white water boating such as canoeing, rafting, kayaking, and for sailing. Other water-based activities show moderate increases. Participation in land-based activities is expected to increase at a rate of 1.0 percent per year, a somewhat slower rate than the other activities. Those with the smallest increase in participation are driving off-road vehicles, picnicking, and sightseeing. Even here, it is expected that participation will double by the year 2030, based on the "high" projection. Also, considering only percentage increases can be somewhat misleading. Land-based activities include larger numbers of participants. Thus, the smaller percentage growth will mean much larger growth in numbers of participants in land-based activities than for either winter sports or water-based activities.

Figures 11-1 and 11-2 illustrate the projections of participation in the activities of picnicking and downhill skiing. Cordell and Hendee prepared these comparisons of information on participation from several sources. They show the index of actual participation in 1965 and 1977 (= 100) drawn from the national participation surveys for those years. Note that in the case of picnicking, actual growth in participation during this period of time was much less than that forecast by the Bureau of Outdoor Recreation (BOR), U.S. Department of the Interior, to the year 2000 based on the 1965 National Participation Survey. Also, note that for skiing, actual growth in participation from 1965 to 1977 period of time was much more than the forecast by the Bureau of Outdoor Recreation. Cordell and Hendee show the high, medium, and low projections for the year 2030 based on the analysis of the 1977 National Participation Survey by Hof and Kaiser. Actual growth in number of participants from 1965 to 1977 seems consistent with the medium projection of picnicking and the high projection for skiing. Finally, they show the U.S. Census mid-level population projection to provide perspective.

The forecasts by Hof and Kaiser are based on multiple regressions using data from personal interviews with a random sample of 4,029

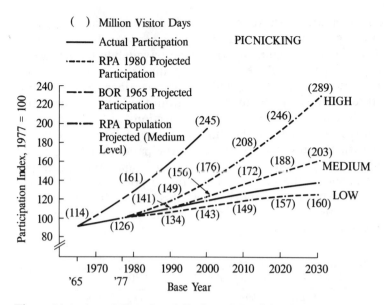

Figure 11-1. Actual Trend and Projected Participation in Picnicking to 2030, United States

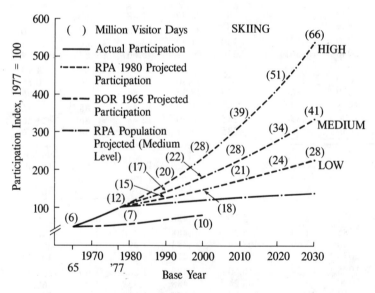

Figure 11-2. Actual Trend and Projected Participation in Skiing to 2030, United States

households participating in the 1977 National Outdoor Recreation Survey conducted by the U.S. Department of the Interior. The dependent variable is the probability that the average citizen will participate in an activity. The explanatory variables include type of residence (urban, rural, or suburban), age, years of education, race, length of workweek, number of vacation days per year, family income, sex, number of close proximity parks, supply availability, and participation price. In the second step, these explanatory variables are projected based on high, medium, and low expectations. For example, there are three different population series from the U.S. Census. Table 11-4 shows the high, medium, and low projections of the explanatory variables to the year 2030. In the third step, the projections of the independent variables are used to forecast participation. Each regression coefficient is multiplied by its expected future value and the results summed to arrive at the percent of the future population that is expected to participate in an activity. Then, this percent is multiplied by the projected future population to obtain the estimated number of participants in any future year.

Table 11-4. Projections of Explanatory Variables in the Consumption of Outdoor Recreation, United States, 1977 to 2030

Scenario	Year	Percent Urban Residence	Percent Rural Residence	Age, Years	Education, Years	Race, Percent, White	Work Hours/ week
Initial Condition	1977	.334	.285	38.49	12.487	.896	21.565
High	1985	.314	.325	39.65	12.97	.887	20.70
	2000	.301	.350	41.57	13.87	.860	19.09
	2030	.301	.350	40.41	15.66	.833	19.09
Medium	1985	.354	.245	40.80	12.64	.887	21.13
	2000	.366	.220	45.80	12.94	.860	20.86
	2030	.366	.220	48.88	13.54	.833	20.86
Low	1985	.334	.285	41.57	12.48	.887	21.56
	2000	.334	.285	48.50	12.48	.869	21.56
	2030	.334	.285	55.81	12.48	.842	21.56

Scenario	Year	Vacation, Days/ Year	Income, $100's	Sex, Percent Male	Parks, Number "close"	Participation Price Index	National Population, Millions
Initial Condition	1977	9.955	173.279	.488	1.219	1.0	216.8
High	1985	14.73	218.33	.488	1.316	1.60	240.4
	2000	23.69	308.44	.483	1.499	1.97	282.8
	2030	41.61	571.82	.478	1.865	1.97	392.8
Medium	1985	12.34	216.60	.488	1.268	1.60	233.3
	2000	16.82	303.24	.488	1.359	1.97	260.4
	2030	25.78	585.68	.483	1.359	1.97	300.3
Low	1985	9.95	211.40	.488	1.219	1.60	228.2
	2000	9.95	284.18	.488	1.219	1.97	245.9
	2030	9.95	537.16	.488	1.219	1.97	249.8

Source: Hof and Kaiser.

Explanatory Variables

Multiple regression forecasting depends on the accuracy of projections of the explanatory variables. Table 11-4 shows the high, medium, and low projections of the explanatory variables used by Hof and Kaiser. The income per capita projections are based on the gross national product forecasts by the Bureau of Economic Analysis of the U.S. Department of Commerce. For example, the medium projection represents a 2.2 percent compound annual increase to the year 2030. Although admittedly optimistic, it was adopted in order to be consistent with projections for other uses of the national forests. The population projections are probably the most accurate, as they are based on three different population series from the U.S. Census. For example, the medium population projection represents a compound annual increases of nearly 1.0 percent to the year 2030. At a minimum, a 1 percent increase in population will result in a proportionate 1 percent increase in participation in recreation. Thus, population is one of the more important variables increasing demand. Projections of other explanatory variables are admittedly judgmental. For example, the authors assume that the supply of facilities will increase at a linear rate of 8 percent per year.

Anticipated increases in population and income are expected to increase participation in all recreation activities studied. The same is true to a lesser extent for increases in education and for increases in leisure time. In the 1960s and 1970s, the workweek changed very little if at all, and it is expected that it will remain relatively stable in future years. However, vacation time has increased substantially, and the assumption is that this trend will continue in the future. A potential negative influence on participation is the expected future increase in travel costs with energy price rises. Another potential negative influence on participation is the expected increase in the average age of the population.

Average age in the medium projection is expected to increase from 38.5 years in the base year (1977) to 45.8 years in 2000, and to 48.9 years in 2030. In the short run, the distribution of the population among age categories may be more important than the average age. The biggest upward shifts in population from 1970 to 1980 took place among those persons in the age categories of 18 to 24 years (up 26.4 percent) and 25 to 34 years (up 42.7 percent). Because these age classifications also account for a high proportion of participants, we can conclude that age shifts had a significant impact on the growth of recreation during the decade. One of the most dramatic age changes of the 1980s is the decline in persons between the ages of 14 and 24. The bulge in the 1970s population for the age categories of 18 to 24 years and 25 to 34 years during the 1970s moves up primarily to the age category of 35 to 44 years (up 50.1 percent) during the 1980s. Of course, the 25 to 34 year old group is still expected to increase in numbers by 21 percent during the 1980s. So, when relating the age shifts for the 1980s to the age profiles of recreation participants as we know them to have been in 1980, it appears that age changes may continue to have a favorable impact on growth during the early 1980s, but this trend may begin to have a slowing influence by 1990.

Of course, at the same time, marketing of recreation during the 1980s may also change the trends in participant age profiles. If the participant profile change happens to be similar in nature to the age shifts that are expected to be upward, the net result would continue to have a favorable implication on the future of recreation. The aging American population may actually stimulate some areas of recreation participation as a result of better health care, concern for fitness, and greater lifelong commitments to recreation activity.

The availability of recreation facilities appears to be an important determinant of participation in general; it is especially important to those activities that require specialized facilities. Table 11-5 illustrates the effect of the supply of recreation resources and facilities on forecasts of participation in recreation activities in 1990 and the year 2030. Activities requiring specialized facilities, such as downhill skiing and developed camping, are highly sensitive to the availability of facilities. For example, participation in developed camping is expected to increase to 279 percent (1977 = 100 percent) by the year 2030 if the supply of campsites increases by 10 percent per year. However, if supply is fixed at 1977 levels, participation in camping will increase only to 109 percent, resulting in virtually no change during this period of time (53 years). The 170 percent difference between participation with and without the increase in camping facilities represents the effect of increased supply on willingness to participate in the recreation activity, assuming no other explanatory variables change. Of course, activities that do not require specialized recreation facilities, such as sightseeing and driving off-road vehicles, are not constrained by the available supply.

Let's look at the supply trends in a water-based recreation agency. Supply of recreation facilities and resources provided by the Corps of Engineers has been reflected in recreation use trends. Development of new recreation areas at Corps reservoirs increased during the early postwar years to a peak during the mid-1960s and then declined to virtually no development in the years 1979-82.

Years	Acres	Years	Acres
1955-58	183	1971-74	303
1959-62	511	1975-78	191
1963-66	1,454	1979-82	34
1967-70	723		

Table 11-5. Medium Forecast of Participation in Outdoor Recreation With and Without a 10 Percent Annual Increase in the Supply of Recreation Resources, United States, 1990 and 2030

Recreation Activity	Supply Assumption, Increase per Year	Index of Participation 1977=100, Medium Forecast	
		1990	2030
Camping (Developed)	Fixed	99	109
	10%	133	279
Camping (Primitive)	Fixed	94	92
	10%	122	233
Hiking or Backpacking	Fixed	98	106
	10%	111	172
Horseback Riding	Fixed	97	121
	10%	112	196
Driving Off-road Vehicles	Fixed	104	128
	10%	109	152
Picnicking	Fixed	105	127
	10%	114	171
Sightseeing	Fixed	110	154
	10%	112	166
Canoeing, Kayaking	Fixed	106	172
	10%	125	264
Sailing	Fixed	120	245
	10%	151	398
Other Boating	Fixed	110	175
	10%	121	231
Swimming (Outdoors)	Fixed	104	140
	10%	117	203
Downhill Skiing	Fixed	108	179
	10%	151	395
Snowmobiling	Fixed	88	75
	10%	114	207

Source: Hof and Kaiser.

Meanwhile, annual growth in recreation use of Corps reservoirs declined from an average of 23 percent per year in the early postwar years to 7.9 percent in 1967-75; 4.0 percent, 1975-80; and 1.7 percent, 1980-83. You can clearly see that the development of new recreation facilities was closely associated with recreation use trends since the 1960s.

WITH AND WITHOUT COMPARISON

The basic purpose of forecasting is to identify what the future benefits and costs would be "with" a proposed project compared to what they would be "without" it. The difference is the increment in net benefits of the proposed project. For example, if we forecast consumption both with and without a project, the difference represents the effects of the proposal. Note that these with-and-without comparisons are not the same as comparing the situation "before" and "after" the project. The before-and-after comparison does not account for changes in future recreation demand that would occur without the project and thus may lead to an over- or understatement of the benefits attributable to it. This point has been developed by the federal guidelines and by Gittinger.

Figure 11-3 illustrates the five situations likely to be encountered in forecasting the consequences of alternative recreation programs: (1) consumption is growing without the project which will provide additional growth; (2) consumption is declining without the project which will restore consumption to its former level; (3) consumption is declining without the project which will avoid the loss and increase recreation use; (4) consumption is stable without the project which will increase recreation use; and (5) there is little or no consumption without the project which will initiate growing recreation use.

The most common (see panel 1) is when recreation demand in the area is already growing, if only slowly, and would probably continue to grow during the life of the proposed project. The objective is to increase benefits by providing additional opportunities to participate in recreation activities. For example, in a mountain region, participation in recreation in primitive roadless areas was forecast to grow at about 2 percent a year without designation of the areas as wilderness. It was proposed to designate and manage these areas as wilderness to protect

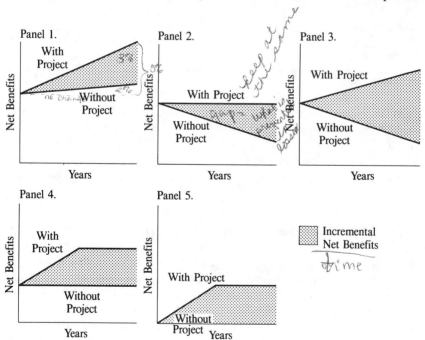

Figure 11-3. Variations in Net Benefits With and Without Proposed Projects
Source: Gittinger.

the natural environment and to increase recreation benefits. If with designation, recreation use is forecast to grow at a rate of 5 percent a year and the project analysts simply compare the recreation use before and after the project, they would erroneously attribute the total increase to wilderness designation. Actually, what can be attributed to the proposal is only the 3 percent increase in recreation use in excess of the 2 percent that would have occurred anyway. Net recreation benefits are the gains minus the losses.

The federal guidelines caution that many proposed projects involve both recreation gains and recreation losses. Consider the following examples of existing site use displaced or destroyed by new project facilities. River use, such as for sightseeing, hiking, camping, fishing, boating, and swimming , may be lost because of a proposed reservoir that would flood many miles of river. Or the development of a large ski resort may result in the loss of the habitat of an elk herd with the subsequent loss of elk hunting opportunities over the life of the ski area. In the case of wilderness expansion, the prohibition of motorized use would result in the loss of opportunity for off-road vehicle use in the designated area.

A second situation (see panel 2) occurs when recreation use would actually fall in the absence of the proposed project. Near Chicago, on the south shore of Lake Michigan, the Indiana Dunes National Lakeshore is located on a 20-mile strip of sand edging the lake. The shoreline has been subject to erosion from wave action. Under a federal project, the government has built seawalls to prevent the erosion. The benefits from this project, then, are not from increased recreation use but from avoiding the loss in recreation opportunity resulting from erosion of the swimming beach and scenic highway. A similar situation may characterize state wildlife management programs, where recreation opportunities would actually fall without the regulation of annual harvest and other management programs. A simple before-and-after comparison would fail to identify these benefits.

A third situation (see panel 3) occurs when a proposal to increase recreation use also avoids a loss. In this case, benefits would include both the increased use and the loss avoided. In many areas, river fishing and boating opportunities are diminished during the late summer months. This is in part attributable to the natural reduction in flow such as occurs with the end of the snow melt and runoff. In addition, water increasingly is diverted from rivers for irrigation, domestic, and industrial uses. If nothing is done to halt the process, recreation use will decline. Consider a proposal to build a high mountain storage reservoir to capture excess runoff during the spring snow melt and to utilize a recreation river as a natural canal to provide irrigation water on the plains below during the late summer months. This would provide sufficient instream flow for fishing and boating in the river to ex-

351

tend through the late summer months of peak tourist demand. The proposed project is expected to provide additional opportunities for fishing and boating on the high mountain reservoir, constructed in an otherwise little-used canyon located off the main stem of the river, and, in addition, to arrest the decline in river flow. The proposal would not only increase recreation opportunity but also avoid a loss. A simple before-and-after comparison of the reservoir site would fail to identify the benefits realized by avoiding the loss from reduced in-stream flow.

There is a more general situation in which projects that increase recreation use may also avoid a loss. Demand often exceeds supply of existing sites in regions where new or expanded capacity is proposed. Availability of the new or expanded recreation site would encourage some participants to substitute the new site for the old. This would reduce congestion at existing sites with excess demand. Reduced congestion would increase willingness to pay by those who continue to use the existing sites. Since reducing the use of existing sites toward benefit-maximizing levels would be a consequence of the new or expanded site, the increased willingness to pay would be counted as an external benefit and added to the benefits from recreation use of the proposed project.

A fourth situation (see panel 4) occurs when no change in recreation use is expected in the project area without the project. In this case, the distinction between the before-and-after comparison and the with-and-without comparison is less important. In some recreation areas, the prospects for increasing recreation use without new investments are minimal. At a major ski resort, a symphony orchestra permitted the resort to increase recreation use during the summer months. It was impractical to extend the concert series to other seasons of the year because the concerts were performed outdoors in an open tent and the artists were contracted to metropolitan orchestras during the rest of the year. Winter use of the ski resort was not likely to increase because of the limited amount of suitable mountain terrain for downhill skiing. With the summer music project in operation, more of the resort's facilities were used year round and costs per recreation day fell, increasing both consumer and producer surplus. Of course, the value of the summer recreation use could not be taken as the total benefit from the music project. From this value must be deducted the value of such summer recreation activities as fishing, rafting, hiking, sightseeing, and camping nearby.

A fifth situation (see panel 5) is another instance where there may be no change in output without the project. In the Alaska Lands Bill, national parks were established in many areas where there had been virtually no prior development for recreational use. Nor was there likely to be significant recreation use, at least for many years, in the absence of the national parks. With the National Park designation, the government will develop access and visitor facilities to provide opportunities for sightseeing, fishing, hiking, camping, and related uses. In this case, recreation use without the project would be virtually the same as the output before the project.

METHODS OF FORECASTING

Several methods have been used to forecast future consumption of recreation. These include (1) time-series or extension of past trends in use; (2) simple regression of past trends in use on one important determinant of demand; (3) multiple regression of consumption by a cross-section of households related to several important determinants of demand; (4) resource capacity which provides an upper limit on recreation consumption; (5) informed judgment of those directly involved in management; and (6) market surveys of user intentions and preferences. Although each of these approaches has provided satisfactory estimates of the amount of recreation which may be consumed in future years under particular circumstances, each also has its drawbacks. In this section, we will discuss these problems and demonstrate under what conditions each approach can be used. Later in this chapter, we will look at the two principal methods of forecasting and show how to apply them without presenting the details of all possible approaches to the problem. Any marketing research book will provide a discussion of the several approaches that have been used to estimate future consumption of goods and services.

Extension of Past Trends

Extension of past recreation use trends has been widely adopted as a method of forecasting future use of local, regional, and national recreation resources. The method assumes that whatever has caused recreation consumption in the past will continue to operate in the same way in the future. A time-series is a set of observations of a variable, such as the number of recreation visitor days at a campground, over a number of years. If a time-series shows regularity, we may expect that it would continue in the same manner next year and the years that follow. Using the trend in past visitor rates, we can extrapolate the series into the future. Computer programs are available that fit a curve to time-series data fed into the computer, and then produce extrapolations for future years.

Successful forecasting requires that there be enough information within the time-series to explain its behavior. Many methods of time-series analysis are extremely sophisticated, but they only use information within the series itself. Looking for regular patterns in recreation behavior is, of course, quite sensible. It is the way in which we discover the "laws of motion" in economic events, which is the study of business cycles. The studies of patterns in human behavior have something to commend them. They are successful in some cases. However, they do not appear to deal very well with changes in the pattern. In the case of camping, for example, a time-series would not be able to predict the effect of sudden increases in oil prices. The reason is that time-series say how things have changed rather than why.

The method assumes that past growth trends will continue without change in the future. Clawson and Knetsch conclude that where past growth has been relatively stable, the method has often been both useful and reliable. Whatever variables are operating to produce a regular trend, the assumption is that they will continue to be effective in the future. However, the method should not be relied upon for long-run projections. Estimates based on a constant growth rate tend to become unrealistic in the long run, due to changes in the determinants of demand. For short-run forecasts, up to perhaps 5 years, it may yield more accurate estimates than any other method, and its simplicity has much to commend it. Later in this chapter, we will see how to apply the time-series method.

Simple Regression Method

one-to-one relation
time not involved
height-weight   corn yield - rainfall

Another way of forecasting is to look for a variable that acts as a barometer for the variable we are interested in such as consumption of recreation. A barometer measures the changes in atmospheric pressure which take place before the weather changes. Similarly, some economic variables are considered "leading indicators" which change direction before consumption of recreation. For example, changes in income, leisure time, and travel have been used to forecast upswings or downswings in recreation demand. To apply this method, information on the level of consumption for a series of past years is plotted against one important determinant of demand, such as income. Then, through the application of a statistical technique known as least squares regression, we obtain a line that "best fits" the relationship between consumption and income.

A number of studies have used this simple regression method. McIntosh and Goeldner illustrate the technique in their book on Tourism. One interesting example of the method was contained in the Outdoor Recreation Resources Review Commission (ORRRC) Report No. 26. This report presented a simple correlation between per-capita income and the number of visits per-capita to national parks from 1929 to 1960. Ninety-five percent of the variation in consumption was explained by income, which represents a very high correlation.

Separate regressions were also run correlating the number of national park visits to per-capita leisure time and to per-capita mobility, measured as miles of inter-city auto travel. The percentage of the variation in per-capita visits explained by each of these variables taken singly was also 95 percent. Whenever each of several variables are so highly correlated with recreation use, we can conclude that they are measuring the same thing, and the practical procedure is to use a single explanatory variable for prediction purposes, such as per-capita income.

Thus, if per-capita income is forecast to increase by $10,000 in the next 5 years, we can estimate with a high degree of statistical confidence that per-capita visits to national parks will increase to a level equal to $10,000 times the coefficient for income. For example, if the regression coefficient for income is 5.0 and the constant 75,000, the predicted number of visits to the recreation site 5 years hence is 125,000 $(= 75,000 + (10,000 \times 5.0)$. This means that the number of visits increases by 5 with each $1 increase in per-capita income from a base of 75,000 visits explained by other variables.

Since income is known to be one of the major determinants of demand, simple regression explains demand to some extent. It is superior to trend analysis for this reason. The method is relatively easy to apply with the available software for desktop computers, and data are readily available. The major drawback of simple regression is that only one explanatory variable can be considered at a time. In reality, demand is affected by many variables, not just one. To put this in concrete terms, if income increased 3 percent last year and demand for recreation remained the same, this does not mean that income elasticity of demand is zero. What this probably means is that the income increase was matched by a price rise in an inflationary economy, which had a dampening effect on demand for recreation. Thus, we need to make our forecasting model a little more complex.

Multiple Regression Method *multiple variables*

The federal guidelines recommend that forecasts of recreation consumption be based on multiple regressions, which provide coefficients indicating how much each of the explanatory variables causes demand to vary. Multiplying the projected values of the explanatory variables by their coefficients and summing the results provides the best available forecasts of future demand. The approach provides decision makers with reasonably accurate predictions of the amount and type of recreation use that an area is likely to receive at a particular level of facility development and price. Changes in socioeconomic characteristics of the population, user preferences, management policy, recreation supply, price, and other variables can be incorporated into the model to determine their potential effects on consumption. In short, the approach shows the reasons why future demand will change. This means that if one or more of the determinants of demand is expected to change in future years, its effect on consumption can be easily estimated. This is why the federal guidelines recommend the method over the time-series method or extension of past trends in use. They cannot predict the effect of changes in several determinants of demand.

Forecasting the future recreation use of a new park or other recreation site relies on a demand function for the region or for a similar site. This is known in the profession as forecasting from an econometric model, participation function, or use-estimating model. Potential use of a new site is the expected quantity demanded at prevailing prices unconstrained by supply. Forecasts of the total recreation use should be made for each activity currently provided at other sites in the region that will be provided at the new site. The recreation use of the proposed site will depend not only on the quality of its resources and its proximity to population centers, but also on its location in relation to other sites providing similar types of recreation within the region. Some participation functions have had to omit direct cost or price from the equation because the survey variable was not available in the data source. In the past, surveys of participation in recreation often were not designed to provide all of the necessary information for demand analysis. Thus, some participation functions represent "consumption functions" rather than demand functions, which require that direct cost or price be included.

The technique in all of its forms basically assumes that the relationship between demand and its determinants, as shown by their regression coefficients, will remain sufficiently stable so that inserted changes in their values will accurately predict the future. These models implicitly assume that the variables determining recreation behavior in the future will be the same as those at the time of the study. Most models also implicitly assume a constant relationship between demand and recreation facility supply over time. Thus, the method cannot foresee the effect of large changes in preferences and technology.

Clawson and Knetsch observe that the method did not forecast the boom in boating and camping following World War II. It probably will not forecast the current increase in recreation activities related to physical fitness, such as skiing, hiking, jogging, and some outdoor sports. Technological advance will continue to influence recreation consumption. Major breakthroughs are expected in lightweight clothing, backpacking equipment, hang gliders, white-water craft, hot-air balloons, recreation-equipped vans, more economical four-wheel-drive vehicles, and mass transit. For this reason, the authors recommend that national participation surveys should be undertaken at least every

5 years to provide the data base necessary to update multiple regression forecasts.

The technique relies upon projections of the determinants of demand, such as population, income, age, price of substitutes, tastes and preferences, and other traditional demand shifters. The Bureau of the Census, U.S. Department of Commerce, routinely prepares long-run forecasts for some of these values. An advantage of the uniform application of recognized and acceptable sources is that any two studies can be compared. However, other values are less readily available and must be estimated by the individuals conducting the studies, as did Hof and Kaiser. Faulty projections of explanatory variables may introduce some error in the forecasts of recreation consumption.

It is important to remember that forecasts based on national participation in recreation activities cannot be used to estimate the recreation use of particular recreation sites. It would not be correct to assume that all recreation areas providing facilities for a particular activity will receive an identical proportion of use. There are several reasons why facilities do not receive similar use intensity. The amount of recreation consumed differs between areas depending on characteristics of the population served, climatic variation, and transportation available. Different recreation areas vary in quality which affects their attractiveness. Finally, the supply of substitute recreation facilities within a particular region will influence the use of a particular recreation site.

Reasonably accurate forecasts of future consumption can probably be obtained from a single multiple regression. However, Cicchetti correctly observes that the decision making process of consumers involves two steps: (1) whether to participate in a particular recreation activity; and (2) how much to participate per year. Cicchetti suggests that we adopt a two-step approach to forecasting recreation consumption. The first equation would predict the probability of an individual's choosing to participate in a particular recreation activity. The second would predict the number of trips per year by the average individual participant. This two-step approach may improve future applications of the multiple regression approach to forecasting consumption of recreation. The reason is that different variables are likely to influence one decision more than the other. For example, age and income influence the decision whether to participate at all. But price, leisure time, and the availability of substitutes may be more important in determining the number of trips to a recreation site. In the application of this approach, the forecast would represent the sum of the two multiple regressions.

Resource Capacity Approach

The use of this approach is authorized by the federal guidelines when it can be demonstrated that sufficient excess demand exists in the market area of a recreation site to fully utilize the additional capacity supplied by a proposed project. This means that the forecast of future consumption is assumed to be equal to the maximum practical capacity of recreation sites. As unique recreation resources become increasingly scarce, the resource capacity approach will become more and more applicable. Already, there are many national parks in which recreation use exceeds carrying capacity (for example, Yosemite), and it is well known to decision makers that expanded supply would increase use to capacity of the new resource.

Application of the resource capacity approach usually begins with the preparation of an inventory of the resource to determine its physical development potential. This establishes an upper limit on the amount of recreation use that a site can sustain based on the amount of physical resource that can be developed for recreational purposes. Once carrying capacity is established and resources are developed to that level, recreation use is kept within resource capability limits. This means that user controls are initiated to maintain the quality of the resource. Thus, in this approach, forecasts of recreation consumption in the usual sense are simply not needed.

Problems arise when the resource capacity approach is applied to situations where it is inappropriate. It is important to remember that the approach applies only when known excess demand is greater than the capacity of proposed projects, as for example, when current turnaways exceed the proposed additional capacity. This was generally true for the early post World War II years, and it was hardly necessary to forecast demand. Whatever was built was used. In more recent years, this has not been the case. Poorly located, inappropriate, and excess capacity facilities have received very low levels of use. Thus, accurate forecasts of recreation demand are needed for the majority of recreation development decisions for the future.

A related concept, described by Clawson and Knetsch, is the satiation principle. This means that at some point, individuals will have their fill of a recreation activity, no matter how much income or leisure they have. This puts an upper limit on forecasts of growth in future consumption.

Informed Judgment Approach (Delphi method)

The judgment approach to forecasting uses all of the data and analysis available, but the final estimates also are based on subjective appraisal of variables that are not measured. The resulting forecasts

358

depend on the personality and experience of the individuals involved. At its best, the approach brings to bear the accumulated knowledge of managers and administrators. The approach was developed because, quantitative methods often cannot directly incorporate the special insights and the informed judgments of those involved with management of recreation sites. No statistical method can forecast the influence of variables explicitly excluded from the analysis. Managers can contribute a great deal to forecasting of the use of a recreation site or planning unit. They often know the history of the particular recreation site and region, have observed changing recreation use patterns, understand resource capabilities, and can subjectively evaluate regional political and economic conditions that are likely to prevail at some future time.

The essential advantage of the approach is that forecasts of recreation use derived from quantitative methods can be tempered by informed judgments and special individual insights. For example, informed judgment can be used to incorporate into national forecasts those regional changes that are likely to occur and to identify realistic limits such as the practical carrying capacity of resources. Moeller and Echelberger reviewed past applications of forecasting methods and concluded that the quantitative methods should take advantage of informed judgment whenever possible. For example, Hof and Kaiser relied on informed judgment in estimating some of the high, medium, and low projections of explanatory variables. All empirical approaches require informed judgment at numerous points — for example, which data to use, what model is appropriate, how to interpret statistical results, and the like.

The Delphi method is one form of the judgment approach. It consists of a systematic survey of a group of experts asked about the determinants of future demand. The results of the first round are reported to each member of the group, and values are re-estimated in subsequent rounds. A final consensus is reached, based on the most persuasive reasoning within the group. Unpredictable variables, such as the fuel situation, changes in preferences, amounts of leisure, and the effectiveness of promotion programs, obviously have an impact on future demand. Also, Moeller and Shafer describe use of the Delphi method to forecast technological change. Campground design standards are based on forecasts of the type of camping vehicles most likely to be used in the year 2000. In the Delphi method, the combined effects of all such variables can be carefully considered from the viewpoint of the experts.

Informed judgment, by itself, is not a reliable approach to forecasting recreation consumption. It can create special problems if relied upon too much. Individual biases can easily enter into the process, and past short-term use trends can be misinterpreted as long-run trend. Evidence suggests that resource managers are not always able to accurately perceive consumer preferences and behavior (Hendee and Harris). Moreover, rapid turnover in management personnel means that reliable informed judgment is not always available.

Market Survey Approach

One of the obvious methods of short-run forecasting is to ask people what they are going to do. For example, commercial market survey organizations ask households what trips they intend to take and recreation equipment they intend to purchase over the next 6 months or 1 year. These surveys are often reasonably accurate, but their use by equipment manufacturers and resort areas can be disappointing. The intentions of recreation consumers seldom require much advance planning and are easily postponed. Moreover, while consumers are often accurate about their intentions to purchase equipment and to take recreation trips, they are much less sure about specific destinations or the brands of equipment they will buy. Asking questions about specific brand names and trip destinations often produces reticence and uncertain response. Thus, consumer intention surveys are more useful for market forecasts than for specific recreation sites and products.

Social psychologists and sociologists are concerned with human motivation and have produced a number of studies of recreation consumers. These behavioral sciences pioneered the use of questionnaires to gather data on the variables that appear to affect human behavior. They can identify the kind of consumers who will use a particular recreation site or engage in one activity rather than another. They can also identify the characteristics of recreation sites that appear to affect the behavior of users. Such studies can be used in planning facilities and marketing programs. Although they are difficult to incorporate into long-run forecasting techniques, considerable progress has been made, and eventually they will become a routine part of multiple regression forecasts.

Test marketing is another way to forecast the demand for recreation. In this approach, new recreation facilities and opportunities are introduced at a typical site, and the results analyzed to see if they are likely to be acceptable nationally. Similarly, we could test the reaction of consumers to changes in entrance fees, and thus obtain direct estimates of the price elasticity of demand. The problem is that most users of a recreation site will have chosen it without prior knowledge of the change in facilities, services, or entrance fees. Rather than change destinations, they will tend to accept the experimental conditions in the short-run. We cannot be sure that the long run will show the same pattern as our 2- or 3-month experiments. Test marketing experiments in recreation often must be continued over 2 or 3 years to allow sufficient time for consumers to change their decisions about subsequent trips to the site with experimental conditions.

A related problem with test marketing is the "Hawthorn effect," first discovered in a series of studies of working conditions. It was found that the people being experimented on came to enjoy the experience and eventually reacted favorably to almost any stimulus they were offered. Thus, continued and prolonged use of a particular group of people for test-marketing may produce a good reaction to almost any new service, facility, or program. Fortunately, there is sufficient turnover in visitors to most recreation sites that the same people are seldom interviewed twice in the same study.

PROJECTING LINEAR AND NONLINEAR TRENDS

Probably the most frequently used method of forecasting is to project linear and nonlinear trends. This is known in the profession as the time-series, extrapolation, trend projection, curve fitting, or, affectionately, the lost-horse method. The technique basically assumes that future events will follow along a path established in the past. This is realistic when past patterns of consumption are sufficiently stable that changes in the historic consumption rate accurately predict the future. The technique acquired the "lost-horse" label because it is analogous to the way dude ranch operators would search for a lost horse. They would proceed to the spot where the horse was last seen and then search in the direction it was heading. Economic forecasters using this technique look at the historical pattern of consumption and then forecast that it will continue moving along the path described by its past movement.

There are many variations in the method, including: (1) long-run trends, the secular increase or decrease in consumption over many years; (2) cyclical fluctuations, the rhythmic variations in consumption from year to year; (3) seasonal variations, the patterns caused by changes in the weather and by consumer habits or preferences; (4) irregular or random influences, the unpredictable changes in consumption caused by wars, strikes, natural catastrophies, and the like. We will consider the case of projecting long-run trends in visits to a park and see how these results can be adjusted to account for seasonal variations in park use.

Forecasting by extension of past trends assumes the historic relationship between consumption and the passage of time will continue in the future. Applying either graphic paper methods (by eye fitting) or regression techniques based on time-series data, we use historical observations to determine the average increase or decrease in consumption each year and then project this annual rate of change into the future. Since extrapolation techniques assume that consumption will follow its established path, the problem is to determine accurately the appropriate trend curve. We typically find linear and exponential growth curves used for economic forecasting by trend projection.

A "linear" trend line means that the variable increases by a constant amount each year. For example, assume that visits to a city's parks 20 years ago were 500,000 and have increased to 1,000,000 today. Growth in number of visits from year -20 to the present would be 25,000 per year (= 500,000/20). With growth calculated as an annual increase by a constant absolute amount of 25,000, projected growth to 10 years in the future would be a straight line drawn from 1,000,000 in the present to 1,250,000 (= [25,000 × 10 years] + 1,000,000). See Figure 11-4.

An alternative approach is to calculate the "proportional" rate of change or annual percent change. The change over time in visits to parks often is proportional rather than constant in absolute amount. Application of this approach involves determining the average historical rate of change in the number of visits as a percent and projecting that percentage rate into the future. This is identical to the compounding of value. For example, if a city's park department is projecting visitation for 10 years into the future and if it has determined that visits are increasing at an average annual rate of 3.6 percent (equal to compound growth in the past 20 years), the projection would involve multiplying the 3.6 percent interest factor for 10 years times the current annual visits. Assuming current visits are 1,000,000, the forecast of visits 10 years hence would be:

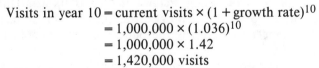

$$\text{Visits in year } 10 = \text{current visits} \times (1 + \text{growth rate})^{10}$$
$$= 1,000,000 \times (1.036)^{10}$$
$$= 1,000,000 \times 1.42$$
$$= 1,420,000 \text{ visits}$$

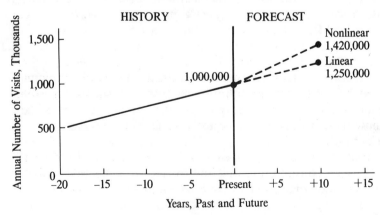

Figure 11-4. Forecasting the Number of Visits to a Park with Linear and Nonlinear Growth Projections

362

This would be an exponential growth curve on graph paper. Figure 11-4 shows that forecasts based on a linear trend may become less and less accurate the further into the future we project. The difference in the near-term forecasts is quite small relative to the difference in the 10-year projections, which equals 170,000 visits.

Visits to most parks are seasonal, and often it is useful to convert annual demand projections to a monthly or daily basis. There are several techniques for estimating seasonal variations in demand. For example, if monthly-visit data for a particular park indicate that, on the average, July visits are 20 percent above the trend line, a seasonal adjustment factor of 1.20 can be applied to the trend projection to forecast visits in that month. Likewise, if it is found that February visits are, on average, 20 percent below the trend, an adjustment factor of 0.80 would be applied in projecting February visits. For example, assume annual visits are forecast as 1.2 million in a given year, or 100,000 a month. When the seasonal factor is introduced, however, July visits will be projected at 120,000 (= 100,000 × 1.20) and February visits at 80,000 (= 100,000 × 0.8).

Peak day use of most parks occurs on the July 4th weekend, and we may want to convert annual and monthly visit or projections to a daily basis. For example, if daily-visit data for a particular park indicate that, on the average, daily visits on the July 4th weekend are 40 percent above the trend line, a daily peak adjustment factor of 1.40 can be applied to the trend projection. Likewise, if it is found that visits during the week, say Tuesdays, are, on average, 40 percent below the trend, an adjustment factor of 0.60 would be applied to project those days when park visits would be least. To illustrate, monthly visits in July might be forecast at 120,000, or 3,871 per day. When the peak day factor is introduced, however, July 4th weekend visits would be projected at 5,419 (= 3,871 × 1.40), and July Tuesday visits at 2,323 (= 3,871 × 0.60). Information on the seasonal variation in demand is useful in setting employee work schedules to service peak day use and to avoid bottlenecks and slack time.

The exponential (or compound) growth in consumption of recreation is very important in determining the scope of recreation programs. The higher the growth rate, the greater the effect of compounding on forecasts of future consumption. Figure 11-5 shows, for example, a park with 1 million visits currently and annual growth of 1 to 10 percent during its 25-year expected life. Consumption 25 years in the future is forecast at about 2.7 million with a growth rate of 4 percent and 10.8 million at 10 percent. Thus, the recreation use of a park forecast 25 years in the future can be changed by more than a factor of 4.0 when the compound rate of growth changes by a factor of only 2.5 (= 10/4).

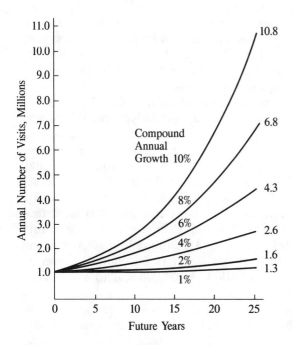

Figure 11-5. Effect of Compound Growth of 4-10 Percent on Annual Visits to a Park
Source: Table 15-2.

FORECASTING FROM A DEMAND FUNCTION

In multiple regression forecasting, we are simply predicting shifts in the demand curve for a recreation site or activity. If incomes increase, for example, consumers may decide that they can afford to engage in more recreation and thus increase the number of recreation trips, even if travel cost and other determinants of demand remain the same. Increases in income normally shift demand curves outward to the right. Figure 11-6 shows two demand curves for the recreation use of a recreation area: (1) demand in the current year (from Chapter 6); and (2) demand forecast 25 years in the future. A shift from one demand curve to another indicates a change in one or more of the nonprice variables in the demand function. The forecasted shift in the demand curve would be caused by the expected changes in all of the independent variables.

You will recall from the discussion in Chapter 6 that demand functions for recreation sites are estimated using standard statistical procedures for multiple regression. This approach is used because it fits an equation to a set of observed data providing statistical estimates of the effect of each variable, holding other variables in the demand function constant. The most valuable information provided by statisti-

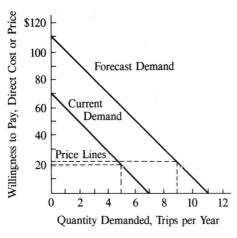

Figure 11-6. Forecasting Shifts in the Demand for Trips to a Recreation Area by a Representative Individual User

cal demand functions is the regression coefficient for each of the determinants of demand. The regression coefficients provide us with an estimate of the change in number of trips to the recreation site associated with a one-unit change in each of these independent variables. For example, column 3 of Table 11-6 indicates that individual demand for trips to a recreation site falls by 0.2 of a trip with each $1 increase in average direct cost or price. The coefficient for income indicates that when we hold constant the effect of all other variables, a $1,000 increase in income will cause the quantity demanded to increase by 0.1 of a trip per year.

The first step in forecasting future consumption from a demand function is to estimate the expected changes in the average values of each of the determinants of demand. Assume that careful long-run forecasts of these values are available from the Census Bureau and other agencies. On this basis, the direct cost or price is expected to increase from $20 to $24 per trip in constant dollars. Consumer income is expected to increase from $25,000 to $30,000 in constant dollars. Travel time is expected to fall from 3 to 2 hours with improved roads, autos, and increased speed limits. The price of substitutes is expected to increase from $24 to $30 per trip in constant dollars. The average age of users is expected to increase from 25 to 30 years, with the gradual aging of the population. Quality of the site is expected to deteriorate somewhat with the number of users exceeding the biological carrying capacity of the natural environment. Daily utilization of capacity is expected to exceed the economic optimum by 20 percent. The population of counties where users reside is expected to double in the next 25 years. Individual preferences for active recreation are ex-

Table 11-6. Forecasting Individual Demand for Trips to a Recreation Area Using a Demand Function

Independent Variables	Units	Estimated Mean Values of the Independent Variables		Regression Coefficients for the Independent Variables	Estimated Total Demand, Trips per Year	
		Current (1)	Forecast (2)	(3)	Current (4)	Forecast (5)
Direct Cost or Price	Dollars per Trip	20.0	24.0	-0.100	-2.0	-2.4
Consumer Income	Thousand Dollars	25.0	30.0	0.100	2.5	3.0
Travel Time	Hours Round Trip	3.0	2.0	-0.400	-1.2	-0.8
Price of Substitute Sites	Dollars per Trip	24.0	30.0	0.054	1.3	1.6
Age	Years	25.0	30.0	-0.088	-2.2	-2.6
Quality of Site	5-point Scale	4.0	3.0	0.625	2.5	1.9
County Population	Thousand Persons	200.0	400.0	0.025	5.0	10.0
Taste or Preference	1=Active 0=Passive	0.8	0.9	1.250	1.0	1.1
Daily Utilization Capacity Ratio	1=Optimal	0.9	1.2	-2.667	-2.4	-3.2
Constant					0.5	0.5
Total Demand					5.0	9.0

Source: Chapter 6.

pected to increase with the rising concern for physical fitness and personal health. These values are shown in column 2 of Table 11-6.

The second step in forecasting future consumption from a demand function is to multiply the average values for each of the determinants of demand by their regression coefficients and sum them all (including the value of the constant term in the demand function, which does not change). The result of this procedure is shown as column 5 in Table 11-6. The bottom line (sum) shows that demand for trips to the site is forecast to increase from five trips per year currently to nine trips per year 25 years in the future.

The final step in forecasting future consumption from a demand function is to convert this estimate for the representative individual user to total annual use by multiplying it by the total number of users. For example, if it is known that 100,000 individuals currently use the site, total demand is estimated as 500,000 recreation days per year. Assume that a separate study has estimated that 200,000 individuals will use the site in 25 years; then the combined demand forecast is 1.8 million recreation days (= 9 × 200,000). This is equivalent to a compound annual growth rate of 5.3 percent.

Earlier in this chapter, we illustrated a U.S. Forest Service forecast of the number of individuals who are expected to participate in recreation activities. Similar studies have estimated the number of individuals who are expected to visit a particular recreation site. These studies are known in the profession as consumption functions, which predict the proportion of the population who will participate. The demand for a recreation site is the sum of two demand functions, predicting how many individuals will participate in recreation at the site and how many trips per year the average individual will make to the site.

Table 11-7 illustrates an alternative procedure to the one just described. Identical results can be obtained by forecasting individual demand for trips to a recreation area using elasticities of demand. Instead of using the average values and regression coefficients, the average values are converted to percentage changes and the regression coefficients are converted to elasticities. You will recall from the discussion in Chapter 9 that elasticity of demand is defined as the percentage change in quantity consumed (number of trips) that is caused by a percentage change in each of the determinants of demand. It is a

Table 11-7. Forecasting Individual Demand for Trips to a Recreation Area Using Elasticities of Demand

Independent Variables	Units	Forecast Percent Change in Mean Values of the Variables (1)	Elasti- cities of Demand (2)	Estimated Percent Change in Total Demand, Trips per Year (3)	Estimated Total Demand, Trips per Year (4)
Direct Cost or Price	Dollars per Trip	0.20	-0.4	-0.480	-2.4
Consumer Income	Thousand Dollars	0.20	0.5	0.600	3.0
Travel Time	Hours, Round Trip	-0.33	-0.24	-0.160	-0.8
Price of Substitute Sites	Dollars per Trip	0.25	0.26	0.325	1.6
Age	Years	0.20	-0.44	-0.528	-2.6
Quality of Site	5-point Scale	-0.25	0.5	0.375	1.9
County Population	Thousand Persons	1.00	1.0	2.000	10.0
Taste or Preference	1=Active 0=Passive	0.125	0.2	0.225	1.1
Daily Utilization/ Capacity Ratio	1=Optimal	0.33	-0.48	-0.638	-3.2
Constant					0.5
Total Demand					9.0

Source: Table 9-1 and Table 11-1.

367

ratio of two percentages — the change in demand that results from a change in an independent variable.

Elasticities for each of the variables in the demand function for trips to an area are shown in column 2 of Table 11-7. The percentage change in the average value of each of the variables in the next 25 years is shown in column 1 of the table. The procedure is simply to multiply the percentage change (plus 1) by the elasticity to obtain the percentage change in demand caused by each variable. This is shown in column 3. The next step is to multiply the percentage change in demand attributed to each variable by the current five trips per year and sum them all, as shown in column 4. The bottom line of this column is nine trips per year for the representative individual. This result is identical to the previous procedure presented in Table 11-6.

Much information is available on elasticities of demand. Many of the statistical problems associated with the measurement of demand for recreation were solved early in the 1960s. Since that time, large quantities of data on demand elasticities have been accumulated. Even where information is not already available, it is often possible to obtain it without great cost or difficulty. The appropriate methods for calculating elasticities of demand have been carefully worked out and were presented in Chapter 9. If you have access to the computer print-out of a demand function for a recreation site, elasticities of demand are usually shown for each independent variable, at the point where the quantity demanded and each independent variable are at their mean values. No additional computation is necessary when expected changes in the independent variables are small. However, you are more likely to have access to a published work showing the demand function for the study site or a similar site. In this case, you probably will need to compute elasticities from the information that is available.

SUMMARY

In this chapter, we addressed the problem of time and described methods of forecasting the long-run effects of recreation economic decisions. The purpose of forecasting is to estimate what future benefits and costs would be with a proposed project compared to what they would be without it. The difference represents the effect of the proposal. Such estimates are useful to anyone planning future development of recreation resources. The availability of private financing will depend on reliable forecasts of future revenues and costs of proposed projects in order to determine if the proposals will be financially feasible. The availability of public financing also depends on reliable forecasts of future benefits and costs of proposed projects in order to determine if they are socially beneficial. With the renewed emphasis on accountability in government, there is a special concern about the expected benefits of expenditures on recreation programs.

We described the historic trends in consumption of recreation and the prospects for future growth. Trends have changed decisively since World War II. Growth rates exceeding 10 percent per year were typical of the early postwar period to the mid-1960s. We were all growth-oriented then, in a "more so" society and economy. Growth rates declined to about 5 percent in the 1970s, and then tumbled to approximately 2 percent in the early 1980s. Long-run forecasts of the growth in recreation consumption average about 2 percent, ranging from nearly 1 percent to slightly more than 3 percent. Clearly, recreation consumers and managers have become less optimistic in their expectations about the future. Since the 1960s, we have become aware of the complexity of demand and the limits to growth in the recreation industry. With the renewed emphasis of accountability in government, managers are increasingly concerned about forecasts of the benefits of expenditures on recreation programs. Recreation planners and managers are faced with the problem of allocating increasingly scarce resources among competing uses. The people involved have become more interested in improving the application of economic methods to assist in the decision making process.

Thus far, no standard method of forecasting recreation consumption has been developed that is suitable for all purposes. In this chapter we examined a variety of methods that are used. These include time-series or extension of past trends in use; simple regression of past trends in use on one important determinant of demand; multiple regression of consumption by a cross section of households related to several important determinants of demand; resource capacity which provides an upper limit on recreation consumption; informed judgment of those directly involved in management; and market surveys of user intentions and preferences. Although each of these approaches has provided satisfactory estimates of the amount of recreation that may be consumed in future years under particular circumstances, each also has its drawbacks. In this chapter, we discussed the problems of each approach and demonstrated under what conditions each can be used.

The extension of past recreation use trends has been widely adopted as a method of forecasting future use of local, regional, and national recreation resources. The method assumes that whatever has caused recreation consumption in the past will continue to operate in the same way in the future. In the simple regression method, information on the level of consumption for a series of past years is plotted against one important determinant of demand, such as income. Then, through the application of a statistical technique known as least squares regression, we obtain a line that "best fits" the relationship between consumption and income. The federal guidelines recommend that forecasts of recreation consumption be based on multiple regressions which provide coefficients indicating how much each of the explanatory variables causes demand to vary. Multiplying the projected values of the explanatory variables by their coefficients and summing the results provides the best available forecast of future demand. The approach shows the reasons why future demand will change. This means that if one or more of the determinants of demand is expected to change in future years, its effect on consumption can be easily estimated.

The resource capacity approach is authorized by the federal guidelines when it can be demonstrated that sufficient excess demand exists in the market area of a recreation site to fully utilize additional capacity supplied by a proposed project. This means that the forecast of future consumption is assumed to be equal to the maximum practical capacity of recreation sites. The informed judgment approach to forecasting uses all of the data and analysis available, but the final estimates also are based on subjective appraisal of variables that are not measured. The resulting forecasts utilize the accumulated knowledge of managers and administrators. The market survey approach to forecasting is to ask people what they intend to do. Commercial market survey organizations routinely ask households what trips they intend to take and what recreation equipment they intend to purchase over the next six months or a year.

All forecasts need periodic checking and refinement, as consumer preferences will change and new substitute activities and sites will enter the market. As a recreation site is developed and put into operation, more information will become available about recreation use, and as the site goes through its life-cycle, different management policies may become appropriate. A change in political leadership may change the availability of tax revenues and user fees for operation and maintenance. Thus, the forecasts need periodic review to keep their predictions on target.

In the following chapter, we will see that future recreation expenditures can be forecast using a regional input-output model. The implications of future growth on costs will be considered in Chapter 13. Finally, Chapter 15 will illustrate the important role of forecasts in comparing the benefits and costs of new projects and programs.

READINGS

Arosteguy, D. J. "Socio-Economic Based Projections of Wildlife Recreation in Colorado to 1985." Ph.D. Dissertation, Colorado State University, Fort Collins. 1974.

Archer, Brian H. *Demand Forecasting in Tourism.* University of Wales Press, Cardiff, England. 1976.

Boyet, Wayne E., and George S. Tolley. "Recreation Projection Based on Demand Analysis." *Journal of Farm Economics* 48(Nov. 1966):984-1001.

Brown, Tommy L., and Bruce T. Wilkins. "Methods of Improving Recreation Projections." *Journal of Leisure Research* 7(No. 3, 1975):225-34.

Cicchetti, Charles J. *Forecasting Recreation in the United States.* D.C. Heath and Co., Lexington, Mass. 1973.

Cicchetti, Charles J., J. J. Seneca, and P. Davidson. "The Demand and Supply of Outdoor Recreation." Bureau of Economic Research, Rutgers University, New Brunswick, N.J. 1969.

Clawson, Marion, and Jack L. Knetsch. *Economics of Outdoor Recreation.* Johns Hopkins University Press, Baltimore. 1966.

Cooper, R. B., A. Somerson, N. Enosh, and S. McKinney. "Upper Great Lakes Regional Recreation Planning Study, Part 2, Recreation Demand Survey and Forecasts." Recreation Resources Center, University of Wisconsin Extension, Madison. 1974.

Cordell, H. Ken, and John C. Hendee. "Renewable Resources, Recreation in the United States: Supply, Demand, and Critical Policy Issues." American Forestry Association, Washington, D.C. 1982.

Davidson, Paul, F. G. Adams, and Joseph Seneca. "The Social Value of Water Recreational Facilities Resulting from an Improvement in Water Quality: The Delaware Estuary." in *Water Research.* Kneese, A. V., and S. C. Smith (eds.), The Johns Hopkins University Press, Baltimore. 1966. 175-211.

Drake, Ronald, L. T. Wallace, Oliver R. Stanton, and Harry S. Hinkley. "Selected Economic Consequences of Recreation Development: Tuolumne County, Case Study." Information Series in Agricultural Economics No. 68-4, Agricultural Extension Service, University of California, Davis. 1968.

Hof, John G., and H. Fred Kaiser. "Long-term Outdoor Recreation Participation Projections for Public Land Management Agencies." *Journal of Leisure Research* 15(No. 1, 1983):1-14.

Johnston, Warren E. "Predicting Future Outdoor Recreation Demands and Uses." Outdoor Recreation and the Public Interest. Proceedings of the 1979 Meeting of W-133, Russell L. Gum and Louise M. Arthur (eds.). Special Report No. 610, Oregon State University, Corvallis. 1981.

Kalter, Robert J., and Lois E. Gosse. "Outdoor Recreation in New York State: Projections of Demand, Economic Value, and Pricing Effects for the Period 1970-1985." Special Cornell Series No. 5. College of Agriculture, Cornell University, Ithaca, N.Y. 1969.

LaPage, Wilbur F. (ed.). "Proceedings, National Outdoor Recreation Trends Symposium." Vol. 1 and 2. General Technical Report NE-57, Northeastern Forest Experiment Station, Forest Service, Upper Darby, Pa. 1980.

LaPage, Wilbur F., and Dale P. Ragain. "Trends in Camping Participation." Research Paper NE-183, Northeastern Forest Experiment Station, Forest Service, U.S. Dept. of Agr., Upper Darby, Pa. 1971.

Manning, R. "Resource Use When Demand is Interdependent Over Time." *The Economic Record* 54(Apr. 1978):72-77.

McIntosh, Robert W., and Charles R. Goeldner. *Tourism Principles, Practices, and Philosophies.* 4th Edition. Grid Publishing Co., Columbus, Ohio. 1984.

Meadows, Dennis L., Donnella H. Meadows, Jorgen Randers, and William W. Behrens III. *The Limits of Growth.* A Report for the Club of Rome, Universe Books, New York. 1972.

Michigan Survey Research Center. "Prospective Demand for Outdoor Recreation." Study Report No. 26. Outdoor Recreation Resources Review Commission. Washington, D.C. 1962.

Moeller, George H., and Herbert E. Echelberger. "Approaches to Forecasting Recreation Consumption." Outdoor Recreation Research: Applying the Results. Technical Report NC-9, North Central Forest Experiment Station, Forest Service, U.S. Dept. of Agriculture, St. Paul, Minn. 1974. 43-55.

Moeller, George H., and Elwood L. Shafer. "The Use and Misuse of Delphi Forecasting." *Recreation Planning and Management.* Stanley R. Lieber and Daniel R. Fesenmaier, (eds.). Venture Publishing Inc., State College, Pa. 1983. 96-104.

Outdoor Recreation Resources Review Commission. "Prospective Demand for Outdoor Recreation." Report No. 26. U.S. Gov. Print. Off., Washington, D.C. 1962.

Owen, Elizabeth. "The Growth of Selected Leisure Industries." Office of Consumer Goods and Services Industries, U.S. Dept. of Commerce, Washington, D.C. 1979.

Steinnes, D. N., and R. L. Raab. "A Time Series Approach to Forecasting Angling Activity at a Recreational Site Based on Past Successes." *Canadian Journal of Fisheries and Aquatic Sciences* 40(No. 12, 1983):2189-93.

Stynes, Daniel J. "An Introduction to Recreation Forecasting." *Recreation Planning and Management.* Stanley R. Lieber and Daniel J. Fesenmaier, (eds.). Venture Publishing Inc., State College, Pa. 1983. 87-95.

371

Tadros, M. E., and Robert J. Kalter. "A Spatial Allocation Model for Projected Outdoor Recreation Demand." *Search,* Cornell University, Ithaca, New York. January 1971.

U.S. Dept. of Agriculture. "An Assessment of the Forest and Range Land Situation in the United States." Forest Service, U.S. Dept. of Agriculture, Washington, D.C. 1980.

Chapter Twelve
Regional Economic Impact

This chapter introduces the concept of regional economic impact of recreation economic decisions on the growth in business output or sales, jobs, net income, tax revenues, and government spending; summarizes the results of empirical studies of the regional economic impact of recreation; and discusses policy implications for recreation economic decisions.

Economists distinguish between the primary benefits and secondary impacts of recreation economic decisions. In previous chapters, we considered the primary benefits to individual users of recreation programs. Substantial insight into decision making was gained by treating the problem as though there were no other effects. Understanding recreation economic decisions of individual consumers provides the foundation for comparing benefits and costs. The net benefits of individual consumers represent the social benefits of public recreation programs. The consumer surplus of individual users may not be spent in the region of the recreation site or spent at all, but this does not make it any less real to individual consumers. It is a measure of the economic value that people place on recreation activities and resources.

In this chapter, we introduce another closely related concept, regional economic impact. It is defined as the economic activity generated by the recreation use of resources. It is a measure of the secondary effects of the actual expenditures by individual consumers and managers of private and public recreation resources. These are the regional economic impacts on business output or sales, employment, net income, tax revenues, and government spending. The essential idea is that the primary costs to individual consumers and managers become secondary gains, in part, to the regional economy supplying recreation goods and services. Studies of regional economic impact do not measure the value to the primary users of a recreation site but rather the value to those who are involved in supplying the primary users with goods and services.

Every local community is concerned about regional economic development to create job opportunities, raise incomes, and contribute to the community's social viability and general economic prosperity. The hundreds of local economic development organizations in each state are testimony to the importance communities place on regional economic impacts. These organizations cooperate with the state and federal government in programs aimed at attracting new employers and retaining current ones. Examples of economic development activities in resort areas include acquiring parks and other recreation areas, open space, upgrading sewer-water systems, roads, labor training, small business assistance, theme zoning, and store front renovation. It is not surprising that nearly all communities welcome additional job opportunities. Community members worry that young people finishing school and other unemployed residents will be forced to commute elsewhere or move away to find work. This concern is not only for the individuals unable to find work locally, but also regards a broader issue — a significant loss of residents would threaten the community's social and economic viability. The ghost towns from an earlier era are stark reminders that not all local economies survive.

In this chapter, we will examine the methods used in conducting empirical studies of the regional economic impact of recreation. We will also look at the results of these studies, in particular, the policy implications for recreation economic decisions.

SOME IMPORTANT CONCEPTS

The federal guidelines recommend that regional economic impacts should be treated as income transfers in a separate account to distinguish them from benefits that contribute to general welfare or national economic development. Conceptually, employment anywhere in the nation of otherwise unemployed or underemployed resources represents a valid benefit. However, they are not counted as such because of problems of identification and measurement and because unemployment is regarded as temporary. The guidelines allow one major exception to the rule. If the regional economy of a proposed project has substantial and persistent unemployment of labor, then the benefits of the project may include the income (salaries and wages) of otherwise unemployed labor working onsite in the construction of a project or a nonstructural improvement.

These benefits will be determined at the time a project is submitted for authorization and for appropriation of funds to begin construction. Substantial and persistent unemployment exists in an area when unemployment in the previous year was 6 percent or more; and was at least 50 percent above the national average for 3 of the previous four years, or 75 percent above the national average for 2 of the previous 3 years, or 100 percent above the national average for 1 of the previous 2 years. The guidelines provide that the percentage of project construction labor estimated to come from the local unemployed labor pool will be 30-43 percent for skilled labor, 47-58 percent for unskilled; and 35 percent for other labor, depending upon whether there is a local hire rule.

In the 1960s and 1970s the regions of the United States in which these conditions prevailed were the Appalachian Mountains, the Northern Lake states, and the Four Corners area of the Southwest. In these cases, secondary economic benefits measured by direct and indirect gains in net income from the construction of park facilities would be counted as benefits representing real economic gains to the national economy. But these cases are infrequently encountered in recreation economic decisions. This is not to downplay the economic importance of regional economic impacts to the economic and political considerations in the region of a park or other recreation area. Much of the political motivation for the development of public and private recreation resources represents an attempt to capture regional gains, which in many cases are reflected in large increases in property values.

Most secondary gains to a particular region will be offset by actual or potential losses elsewhere. This means that recreation programs redistribute income from other regions and the nation to the regional economy of parks and other recreation sites. Whether such redistribution is desirable is a political decision beyond the scope of economics. The essential point is that these changes in the distribution of income represent transfers of income and not social benefits, i.e., not real welfare gains to the nation. Beardsley, for example, illustrates the problem as follows. Recreation spending in Colorado by Nebraska tourists may result in a net economic loss to the plains region of Nebraska and to other areas where the money would have been spent had Nebraskans not taken a Colorado vacation. He suggests caution when interpreting the regional economic gains from a new park or other recreation development. What is a gain to the local region may be a loss to another region, and the national economic welfare may not change. Economists refer to such transfers of income as pecuniary impacts to distinguish them from technological impacts which result in real national secondary benefits in regions with long-run unemployment, immobility of resources, and economies of large scale.

Regional economic impact studies provide the states with useful information about the social and economic effects of proposed new projects and programs. In the 1970s and 1980s, many such studies were undertaken to comply with the National Environmental Policy Act (NEPA). The law requires that all major projects, defined as those having a significant effect on environmental quality, include information on social and economic effects. As a result, environmental impact studies have included a study of the regional economic impact in the immediate vicinity of the project or park. These studies show the effect of the construction and operation of the proposed project and of the change in tourist consumption. Included are the estimated changes in direct and indirect output or sales of each industry and trade in the region. Income and employment effects are either estimated directly or as a proportion of the added output or sales. Population effects are estimated on the basis of the number of new jobs created. The effects on tax revenues and expenditures for social services are estimated from changes in population or in output. Effects on environmental quality, such as air and water pollution, can be estimated from technical studies of the effect of changes in population and output on aspects of environmental quality.

The distinguishing characteristic of a regional economic impact study is that it answers questions about the distribution of economic gains and losses. What industry receives the gains and what industry loses, and how much? How is the income of various economic groups affected by alternative park development proposals? Thus, a regional economic impact study asks a different question than does a benefit cost study, which deals with the question of the efficiency of a proposed project, i.e., do total benefits exceed costs to society? The distribution of economic benefits and costs is not usually asked in benefit cost studies. Studies of income distribution ask which industry gains and which industry loses and by how much. It is important to recognize the limitation of the answer to that question by a regional economic impact study. For example, an impact study can show how much a change in skier demand in a county contributes to the output of lodging and other industries. However, an impact study does not show such important information about income distribution as (1) the effect of a change in demand on the output of particular individuals or corporations which provide lodging services; (2) whether lodging prices, profits, and wage rates are competitive; (3) whether lodging operations are efficient in size, utilization of the capacity of facilities, or the level of services by lodging operators; and (4) the distribution of income between small business and large corporate operations. These questions will be addressed in Chapters 13 and 14.

Studies of regional economic impacts have often emphasized the gains and failed to count the secondary losses or costs. We should remember that local economic impact involves not only pluses (gains) but also minuses (losses), which should be subtracted from the gains to find the net regional impact. Millard and Fischer review several categories of local secondary costs. First, development of a recreation site usually means that the natural resources cannot be used for other purposes, such as agriculture and forestry. These lost opportunities lead to foregone local income and employment. Second, increases in local tax rates may be necessary to provide medical, fire protection, and police services to the additional tourists entering the area. The seasonal nature of tourist demand for these public services may lead to underutilization by regional residents during the balance of the year. Third, the markets for private recreation land, housing, repair and maintenance, food, clothing, and general merchandise may be bid up by tourists who are willing to pay higher prices than local residents are accustomed to paying. Fourth, increased congestion on the roads and in local businesses may result in inconvenience and discomfort to local residents and adversely alter local lifestyles. Finally, many individuals affected by higher rents, congestion, and poorer public services may not gain from the additional employment opportunities, increased business sales, larger profits, and rising property values.

Obviously the relevant region of economic impact extends beyond the boundary of the park or recreation site. The geographic area depends on the type of park decision, its magnitude, and the size of the relevant regional economy associated with a particular site. Most of the data to be used in assessing regional impacts must be assembled from sources outside the park. The concept of a functional economic area (Fox and Kumar) appears to offer the most useful definition of a geographic region for recreation impact studies. The ideal region is people- and job-oriented, recognizing that essential services and regional employment opportunities are offered in a central city, with a perimeter based on the maximum time a resident will spend commuting to work, estimated to be about 60 minutes. The central city usually must have at least 10,000 inhabitants in order to be viable, because there are scale economies and minimum thresholds in the production of certain goods and services such as medical services. The surrounding low density rural area includes agriculture and the smaller towns that serve as bedroom communities and limited service centers. Some low population counties which lack commuting linkages to a central city would be included in an adjacent functional economic area. In practical applications, it has been shown that little is lost by defining functional economic areas to include combinations of two to six entire counties, thus making standard Census data sources useful to the analysis. The functional economic area for Yosemite National Park, for example, includes the five counties immediately adjacent to and surrounding its perimeter.

REGIONAL ECONOMIC MULTIPLIERS

The most important concept with respect to regional economic impact, and the most elusive, is the multiplier. It is defined simply as the total effects (direct plus indirect) divided by the direct effects:

$$\text{Multiplier} = \frac{\text{Direct} + \text{Indirect effects}}{\text{Direct effects}}$$

It is not difficult to comprehend the "direct effect" on the sales of businesses from which park visitors and the park agency purchase goods and services. However, the concept of "indirect effects" may be more elusive. It is simply the effect on the sales of these and other businesses in the region, as a portion of the recreation dollars are

377

spent and respent, leading to a multiple increase in the sales of all businesses in the region.

As a general rule, the multiplier for business output or sales is equal to 1 divided by the inverse of value added expressed as a percent of direct sales:

$$\text{Multiplier} = \frac{1}{1 - \text{value added in percent}}$$

where "value added" is defined as the proportion of total direct sales that remain in the region as wages, salaries, interest, profits, rents, and local taxes. The difference between total sales and value added is defined as "leakage," which is the payment for wholesale and retail products and services brought in from outside the region, plus the interest, profits, rents, and taxes paid outside the region. Furthermore, only part of the income earned by residents of the region is respent locally. Some is saved, taxed away, or spent outside the region. Thus, we could also say that the multiplier is equal to 1 divided by the percent of regional sales that are leaked outside the region, i.e., lost to businesses in the region.

The more value added by businesses in the region, the higher the multiplier. If, for every dollar spent on recreation goods and services, value added is equal to 40 percent, the regional output multiplier is 1.67:

$$1.67 = \frac{1}{1 - 0.4}$$

If value added increases to 50 percent of expenditures for recreation goods and services, the regional output multiplier becomes 2.0:

$$2.0 = \frac{1}{1 - 0.5}$$

If value added rises to 60 percent of each dollar spent for recreation goods and services, the regional output multiplier rises to 2.5:

$$2.5 = \frac{1}{1 - 0.6}$$

Table 12-1 illustrates the multiplier process. It shows the direct and indirect impact on regional output of an increase of $100 in direct demand for recreation goods and services when value added is 40, 50, and 60 percent. The important thing to note is that the value added portion of recreation dollars is spent and respent through 12 rounds, at which time their effect approaches zero. Most of the indirect effect of tourist spending occurs during the first calendar year in about five or six rounds. The first-round direct impact on the regional economy is an increase of $100 in demand for recreation goods and services. Consider the case in which 50 percent is value added by the region and 50 percent is payment for products and services brought in from outside the region. In the second round, the $50 of value added is

378

Table 12-1. Direct and Indirect Impact on Regional Output or Sales From an Increase of $100 in Demand for Recreation Goods and Services

Number of Times Part of the $100 is Re-spent in the Region	Total Direct and Indirect Impact on Output or Sales When Local Income or Value Added in the Region Equals		
	40 Percent	50 Percent	60 Percent
Tourist Expenditure	$100.00	$100.00	$100.00
Second	40.00	50.00	60.00
Third	16.00	25.00	36.00
Fourth	6.40	12.50	21.60
Fifth	2.56	6.25	12.96
Sixth	1.024	3.125	7.776
Seventh	0.4096	1.5625	4.6656
Eighth	0.1638	0.7812	2.7994
Ninth	0.0655	0.3906	1.6796
Tenth	0.0262	0.1953	1.0078
Eleventh	0.0104	0.0977	0.6047
Twelfth	0.0042	0.0488	0.3628
Total Direct and Indirect	$166.67	$199.58	$249.45

respent for goods and services in the region. In the third round, $25 of value added is respent in the region, in the fourth round, $12.50, and so on until the effect on regional output becomes negligible.

When the value added by businesses in the region averages 50 percent of expenditures for recreation goods and services in the region, the indirect spending in the region by another $99.58 is rounded to $100. Dividing the sum of total direct and indirect spending, $200, by the $100 of direct spending yields a multiplier of 2.0. Similarly, when value added is 40 percent, direct spending of $100 results in indirect spending of $66.67, rounded to $67. Dividing the sum of direct and indirect spending of $167 by the $100 of direct spending yields a multiplier of 1.67. In the same way, when value added is 60 percent, direct spending of $100 results in indirect spending of $149.45, rounded to $150. Dividing the sum of direct and indirect spending of $250 by the $100 of direct spending yields a multiplier of 2.5.

It is important to note that these results are approximately the same as those obtained from applying the general rule above. Actual studies of the regional economic impact of recreation development rely on input-output analysis to obtain a more precise estimate of the multiplier effect. Input-output procedures will be illustrated in a later section of this chapter. It is sufficient here to understand the concept and how it operates.

Some Recreation Multipliers

Regional output or sales multipliers for expenditures on recreation goods and services average about 2.0 and range from 1.5 to 2.6 in the

United States. Table 12-2 shows the results of several regional economic impact studies during the 1960s, 1970s, and early 1980s. Several of the studies summarized in Table 12-2 also estimate regional multipliers for local income or value added and regional employment. Although these multipliers vary somewhat from regional output or sales multipliers, they are generally similar. This means that income and employment multipliers for expenditures on recreation goods and services also range from about 1.5 to 2.6 and average 2.0.

Since regional multipliers are expressed as a ratio, changes in the general price level do not appreciably affect their application to current regional economic development problems. Thus, we would not expect a regional output multiplier from an input-output study in 1970 to be significantly different from a study in 1980 or 1990 for the same recreation activity and region. Regional output multipliers for expenditures on recreation goods and services have averaged about 2.0 for two decades, and there is little or no reason to expect this to vary in the near future. This will remain the case if regional employment patterns, relative prices for goods and services, and economies of scale do not change appreciably. Most recreation areas have a rela-

Table 12-2. Regional Output or Sales Multipliers for Expenditures on Recreation Goods and Services, United States

Regions	Sources	Types of Recreation Development	Output or Sales Multipliers
Teton County, Wyoming	Rajender, et al.	Tourism	1.46
Southwest Counties, Wyoming	Kite and Schultz	Fishing, Flaming Gorge Reservoir	2.07
Sullivan County, Pennsylvania	Gamble	Summer homes	1.60
Itasca County, Minnesota	Hughes	Summer resorts	2.23
Ely County, Minnesota	Lichty and Steinnes	Boundary Waters Canoe Area, Tourism	2.23
Wadsworth County, Wisconsin	Kalter and Lord	Tourism	1.87
Baldwin County, Alabama	Main	Tourism	2.58
Montana	Haroldson	Winter resorts	2.40
Grand County, Colorado	Rhody and Lovegrove	Hunting and Fishing	2.00
Colorado Counties	McKean and Nobe	Hunting and Fishing Resident Nonresident	1.75 2.60
Yaquina Bay, Oregon	Stoevener, et al.	Fishing	2.06
United States	National Marine Fisheries Services	Saltwater Fishing	1.90

tively stable economy with modest growth rates. However, some resort areas have experienced substantial growth causing the relationships between industries and multipliers to change. In prosperous areas where value added is rising, tourist multipliers will also rise, as illustrated in Table 12-1. The reverse would be expected for declining areas.

The empirical results of past studies provide several clues to the reasons multipliers vary in amount. Size of the region has an important effect; for example, a typical county may have a recreation multiplier of 1.6 compared to a five-county region with 1.9; the entire state, 2.2; and the United States, 2.5. This reflects the fact that the value added within a region rises as its geographic area is increased and a smaller proportion of the expenditures on recreation goods and services are purchased outside of the region. Wholesalers are more likely to be located within a region as its size increases. The manufacture and processing of recreation goods and services also are more likely to be included in the region, as are the individual owners of business outlets, corporate headquarters, etc.

Table 12-3 illustrates another important reason why regional multipliers vary. They represent a weighted average of the multipliers for each type of business from which tourists purchase goods and services. Over half of the direct spending by recreation visitors is typically for retail, wholesale, and automotive products. Businesses selling these products to recreation visitors purchase more of their inputs outside of the county than do some other businesses. Consequently, their business output or sales multipliers (1.80 and 1.76) are less. If a larger proportion of expenditures by recreation visitors is for services, lodging, food, and beverages, with much higher output or sales multipliers (2.41, 2.19, and 2.18), then the regional multiplier will be higher because it represents a weighted average for all recreation expenditures.

Thus, regional multipliers vary among types of recreation activities. Day users of a park who bring a picnic lunch from home have very

Table 12-3. Distribution of Direct Expenditures for Hunting and Fishing Among Industries with Multipliers for Output and Employment

Industries	Percent of Direct Expenditures	Output or Sales Multiplier	Employment Multiplier (Jobs per $1 Million)
Retail and Wholesale Trade	27.8	1.80	59
Services	15.1	2.41	44
Lodging	8.5	2.19	97
Eating and Drinking	20.3	2.18	97
Automotive	27.8	1.76	63
Communication and Transportation	0.5	2.05	31
Total	100.0	2.00	69

Source: Rhody and Lovegrove.

low impact on regional output or sales multipliers. Recreation visitors who stay overnight in campgrounds typically spend little or no money for services, lodging, or restaurant meals, and as a result have low regional multipliers. Tourists who stay overnight in resort lodges, eat in restaurants, and purchase local services have much higher regional multiplier effects. Owners of seasonal homes have higher multipliers because they purchase repairs from the local construction industry and they pay local property taxes. Ski resorts have higher regional multipliers than wilderness areas. However, the presence of wilderness areas near ski resorts stimulates summer visits and expenditures for lodging, restaurant meals, and services at ski resorts.

The recreation industry tends to have somewhat lower regional multipliers than agriculture, forestry, or light manufacturing industry. For example, logging multipliers range from 2.2 to 3.0 and average about 2.5, while sawmill multipliers range from 2.5 to 3.1. However, in many rural counties with substantial recreation industries, the somewhat lower regional multiplier effect of tourist spending is more than offset by the large absolute level of tourist expenditures. For example, in Teton County, Wyoming, tourist spending to visit Jackson Hole Ski Area and Teton National Park accounts for nearly two-thirds of the regional economy. Ranching and forestry are relatively minor, despite their more favorable regional multipliers. However, this is not typical of most of the rural counties in the United States where recreation expenditures are relatively small and the industry complements basic farming, ranching, and timber industries. For example, Polzin and Schweitzer conclude that most counties in Montana could not generate sufficient growth in tourism to counter-balance even moderate declines in the timber industry.

INPUT OUTPUT METHOD

The purpose of this section is to describe briefly the input-output method of estimating the multiplier. The distinguishing characteristic of the method is that it provides information on the direct and indirect impact of tourist spending on the output or sales of each industry in the local economy. This provides a more precise calculation of the regional tourist multiplier as a weighted average of the multipliers for each local industry where tourists purchase goods and services. A regional economy consists of a number of businesses, which are classified into industries according to type of output or sales. These industries or trades buy from and sell to each other and to industries in other regions. They also sell goods and services for household consumption. Input-output analysis involves the development of an inter-industry table showing the distribution of all purchases and sales. An input-output table is a set of double-entry accounts for the regional economy. It maps the interconnections among various lines of businesses. The essential idea is that part of the output of one business becomes input to another.

Table 12-4 illustrates the first step in applying the method, to collect the basic information used in the analysis. This includes the transactions identified as (1) intermediate sales between industries A, B, and C in the region, (2) payments for capital, labor, and other inputs, and (3) sales to final buyers, such as tourists, etc. It identifies each industry's annual dollar value of sales to other industries, and each industry's purchases of inputs from the other industries. Thus, the table represents double-entry accounting in which every sale constitutes a purchase, and the total output or sales of each industry equals the total inputs purchased.

Reading across a row in Table 12-4 shows the total dollar value of output or sales by each industry, including the intermediate sales to other industries and to final buyers. For example, if industry B represents the food and lodging industry, the table shows total annual sales of $25 million, including sales to industry A, $2 million; industry B, $6 million; industry C, $0.2 million; and to consumers, $16 million. Reading down the column shows the total dollar value of inputs each industry buys from other industries and payments for capital, labor, and other inputs. For example, the table shows that industry B, the food and lodging industry, purchases total annual inputs of $25 million. This includes purchases from industry A, $2.25 million; industry B, $6 million; industry C, $3 million; and payments for capital, labor, and other inputs, $13.75 million.

Table 12-5 illustrates the second and simplest step in input-output analysis. This is to estimate the direct inputs required per dollar of output or sales by each industry. These coefficients are calculated from the information contained in Table 12-4. The procedure is straightforward in that each entry in a column for a single industry is divided by its column total. The resulting coefficients show the direct purchases necessary from each supplier (at the left of the table) in order for the industry (at the head of the column) to produce one dollar's worth of output or sales. For example, if industry B represents the food and lodging industry, the table shows for each dollar of output or sales, the industry must buy inputs from industry A valued at 9 cents; industry B, 24 cents; industry C, 12 cents; plus capital, labor, and other inputs, 55 cents. Thus, Table 12-5 converts the dollar information in Table 12-4 to the equivalent percentages.

Table 12-6 illustrates the third step in applying the input-output method. This is to calculate the multipliers for each industry in the region. The sum of each column shows the direct plus indirect impacts of $1 of output or sales by each industry. They are based on high-speed computer iterations of successive rounds of transactions in the region. For example, from Table 12-5, we see that if industry B in-

Table 12-4. Inter-industry Transactions in a Regional Economy

Output or Sales by Industry	Purchases by Industry to (Million Dollars)			Final Demand	Total Output or Sales
	A	B	C		
A	$1.00	$ 2.25	$ 0.20	$ 1.55	$ 5.00
B	2.00	6.00	1.00	16.00	25.00
C	.20	3.00	1.80	15.00	20.00
Payments	1.80	13.75	17.00	3.00	35.55
Total Input	5.00	25.00	20.00	35.55	85.55

Table 12-5. Coefficients of Direct Inputs Required per Dollar of Output or Sales in a Regional Economy

Output or Sales by Industry	Direct Purchases by Industry (Cents per Dollar Sales)		
	A	B	C
A	$0.20	$0.09	$0.01
B	.40	.24	.05
C	.04	.12	.09
Payments	.36	.55	.85
Total Input	1.00	1.00	1.00

Table 12-6. Output or Sales Multipliers, Total Direct and Indirect Impact per Dollar of Final Demand in a Regional Economy

Output or Sales by Industry	Direct and Indirect Purchases (Cents per Dollar Final Demand)		
	A	B	C
A	$1.33	$0.16	$0.02
B	.71	1.41	.09
C	.15	.19	1.11
Output or Sales Multipliers	2.19	1.76	1.22

Source: McKean.

creases output by $1, it must buy 9 cents of input from industry A. In turn, industry A must buy inputs from other industries, and so on. As a result, industry A eventually will supply 16 cents of direct and indirect inputs. This figure is noticeably larger than the 9 cents of direct inputs because industries depend on each other. The table shows that the total business or sales multiplier for industry B is 1.76, which indicates that, as tourist spending for food and lodging increases by $1, total sales of $1.76 are generated in the regional economy. The recreation multiplier would be the weighted average of multipliers for each industry from which tourists purchase goods and services.

In this example, we see a highly aggregated version of a transaction table for a regional economy. Headings for three industries, plus aggregate payments and aggregate final demand, are sufficient to illustrate the input-output method. In empirical studies of regional economies, the extent of disaggregation will depend on the purpose of the study, the availability of data, and the time and resources budgeted for the study. It is common practice to have 20 or more industries and 5 to 10 payment and final demand categories.

The payments row in Table 12-4 represents the value added by the regional economy. These are the payments to the factors of production that contribute to the output of goods and services. Labor is paid wages and salaries; capital is depreciated and receives interest; land is paid rent; and enterpreneurs (or owners) are paid dividends based on profitability. Also included are payments of taxes to governments in and outside the region and payments for goods and services imported from outside the region. The latter represents leakage from the regional economy.

Regional economic development is based on changes in final demand such as tourist spending. An increase in final demand stimulates the economy and leads to increased output or sales, income, and employment. Final demand includes sales for end use. Included are tourist spending in the region, nonlocal government expenditures for construction and operation of parks in the region; new private investments, and other sales of products and services outside the region. Final demand also consists of sales to regional households for consumption, sales to regional governments, sales of goods and services outside the region (exports), inventory changes, and investments.

Other effects can be estimated from the inter-industry transactions table. For example, there are two types of income multipliers. Type I is the ratio of the direct plus indirect income to the direct income paid to households in the region, primarily in the form of wages and salaries. Type II multipliers show not only the direct plus indirect changes in income but also the induced increases in income generated by additional consumer spending. They show the chain reaction beginning with increased demands, increased output, increased income, increased household purchases induced by increased household income, increased output, and so on. The Type II multiplier is obtained by including households as an "industry" in the input-output table. Note that the income multipliers are sometimes reported as per dollar change in direct income paid to households, and sometimes as per dollar change in direct business output or sales.

Employment multipliers are closely related to business output or sales multipliers. If the direct labor inputs required per dollar of sales are measured for each industry, it is simply a matter of multiplication to find the employment effects of a change in output or sales for each industry. Suppose that the direct labor inputs per $1,000 of sales for industry A are .06 of a workyear, compared with .02 for industry B and .01 for industry C. For example, assume a $100,000 increase in sales to tourists (final demand) by industry B, food and lodging. Table 12-5 shows that output or sales by industry A rise by $16,000 (= $100,000 × .16), output or sales by industry B rises by $141,000 (=$100,000 × 1.41), and industry C sells an added $19,000 (= $100,000 × .19). In this case, where sales to tourists increase by $100,000 per year, employment will rise by 4 workers (= [.06 × $16] + [.02 × $141] + [.01 × $19]).

The input-output method is an expensive and time-consuming process. In order to develop a transactions table showing the sales and purchases of each local industry, data are obtained from businesses, governments, and consumers. This task involves many hours of research, including the use of mail questionnaires, personal interviews, and published reports. Once the data is collected, it must be cross-checked and verified to assure reliable results. For example, one test of consistency is the requirement that industry sales equal purchases. The alternative to collecting detailed regional data is to use national data and assume that the average relationships between industries will be approximately the same in each county or regional economy. National data provides the basis for the U.S. Forest Service IMPLAN, a 466 industry input-output model. It is used to produce detailed estimates of the direct, indirect, and induced economic impacts on regional economies that result from alternative resource management plans.

The input-output method has a long history. An early input-output table was developed by the French economist Quesnay in 1758. His *Tableau Economique* (economic table) attempted to diagram the flow of money and goods in a nation. Also a physician, Quesnay was inspired by Harvey's discovery in 1616 of the human circulatory system. The first empirical input-output study in the United States was published by Leontief in 1936. A Harvard economist, Leontief won the Nobel Prize in economics for his pioneering effort, which described the structure of the U.S. economy for 1919. It has been followed by other studies for the years 1947, 1958, 1968, 1972, and subsequent years. Since then, the method has been used to describe the economies of most nations and of smaller regional economies within their borders. The method has become an important tool for studying such economic problems as energy development, water use, and recreation demand in the United States, Europe, and other countries.

In the following section we will apply the time-tested approach to a hypothetical problem.

A REGIONAL IMPACT PROBLEM

Suppose the governor of a tourist state has asked its Division of Recreation and Parks to estimate the regional economic impact of alternative recreation use of a roadless area proposed by the U.S. Forest Service for designation as a wilderness area. The governor is interested in the economic development of the state. Three alternative management plans have been proposed:

(1) Minimum development with wilderness designation;
(2) Intermediate development; and
(3) Maximum development.

The governor has requested a regional economic impact study of the alternative levels of recreation development on (1) direct and indirect output or sales, income, and jobs, (2) water quality, (3) tax revenues and government spending, and (4) whether government revenues exceed the costs of government services.

The first step is to designate the region influenced by the recreation development. Assume that the geographic area of the region includes the three counties in the immediate vicinity of the recreation site.

The next step is to estimate the effect of each alternative on direct output or sales within the region. Assume that with wilderness designation, consumption is forecast at 100,000 visitor days per year and average expenditures, at $15 per visitor day. Intermediate development would provide access roads and public campgrounds with an estimated 250,000 visitor days per year and average expenditures of $20 per visitor day. The full development alternative would provide concessioner-operated campgrounds, lodges, restaurants, and curio shops, attracting 500,000 visitor days per year with average expenditures of $30 per visitor day. Assume that expenditures by recreation users represent the total direct output or sales resulting from each alternative development. This means that the costs of construction and operation of facilities are included in the recreation use fees paid by recreation users. This simplifies the problem but does not change its essential nature. However, note that it is often desirable to make a separate regional impact estimate for the construction cost phase of recreation development (Frick and Coddington).

The third step is to select an existing input-output study similar to the economy of the region of the recreation site. Rhody and Lovegrove studied the direct and indirect impact of fishing and hunting in a county similar to those in the region of the proposal. They allocated recreation expenditures into six standard categories: retail and wholesale trade, services, lodging, eating and drinking places, automotive, and communication and transportation. An input-output analysis provided the multipliers for the output or sales and for employment in each of these types of business. Table 12-3 shows that over half of the direct spending by recreation visitors was for retail, wholesale, and automotive products. Businesses selling these products to recreation visitors purchased more of their inputs outside of the county than did some of the other businesses. Consequently, their business output or sales multipliers (1.80 and 1.76) were less, as were their employment multipliers (59 and 63 jobs) per million dollars of direct additional spending by recreation visitors. The average multipliers for total business output or sales (2.0) and for employment (69 jobs) were higher because they represent a weighted average including recreation expenditures on services, lodging, food, and beverage with much higher output and employment multipliers.

The next step is to calculate the total direct and indirect output for each alternative level of development for the study site. Column 1 of Table 12-7 shows that total direct expenditures are $1.5 million with minimum development and wilderness designation, $5 million with intermediate development, and $15 million with maximum development. These values are equal to average expenditures per day in the region, multiplied by the average number of visitor days per year forecast for each alternative. Then, these total expenditures are allocated into the six categories according to the percentage distribution shown

Table 12-7. Regional Economic Impact of Recreation Development on Industry Output or Sales

Industries	Direct Dollar Expenditures	Output or Sales Multiplier	Total Direct and Indirect Output or Sales
Minimum Development			
Retail and Wholesale	$ 417,000	1.80	$ 750,600
Services	226,500	2.41	545,865
Lodging	127,500	2.19	279,225
Eating and Drinking	304,500	2.18	663,810
Automotive	417,000	1.76	733,920
Communication and Transport	7,500	2.05	15,375
Total	$1,500,000		$2,988,795
Intermediate Development			
Retail and Wholesale	$ 1,390,000	1.80	$ 2,502,000
Services	755,000	2.41	1,819,550
Lodging	425,000	2.19	930,750
Eating and Drinking	1,015,000	2.18	2,212,700
Automotive	1,390,000	1.76	2,446,400
Communication and Transport	25,000	2.05	51,250
Total	$5,000,000		$9,962,650
Maximum Development			
Retail and Wholesale	$ 4,170,000	1.80	$ 7,506,000
Services	2,265,000	2.41	5,458,650
Lodging	1,275,000	2.19	2,792,250
Eating and Drinking	3,045,000	2.18	6,638,100
Automotive	4,170,000	1.76	7,339,200
Communication and Transport	75,000	2.05	153,750
Total	$15,000,000		$29,887,950

in Table 12-3. The output or sales multipliers for each of the six categories are then multiplied by the direct dollar expenditures in each category and summed for each alternative level of development. The total direct and indirect output is $3 million with minimum development and wilderness designation, $10 million with intermediate development, and $30 million with maximum development, rounded from column 3 of Table 12-7.

The next task is to calculate the impact of each alternative recreation development on employment. The employment multipliers for each of the six categories are the number of jobs per million dollars of direct output or sales. This times the multiplier are summed for each alternative level of development. On this basis, the total direct and indirect employment is 103 jobs with minimum development and wilderness designation, 343 jobs with intermediate development, and 1,030 jobs with maximum development (column 3 of Table 12-8).

The next task is to calculate the effect of each alternative level of development on water pollution. Assume that studies by the Environmental Protection Agency show the pounds of waterborne pollution per $1 million of direct and indirect output for each alternative as follows

Table 12-8. Regional Economic Impact of Recreation Development on Employment

Name of Industry	Direct Dollar Expenditures (Millions)	Employment Multiplier (Jobs per million)	Total Employment (Number of Jobs)
Minimum Development			
Retail and Wholesale	$ 0.417	59	25
Services	0.236	44	10
Lodging	0.127	97	12
Eating and Drinking	0.304	97	30
Automotive	0.417	63	26
Communication and Transport	0.008	31	0
Total	1.500		103
Intermediate Development			
Retail and Wholesale	$ 1.390	59	82
Services	0.755	44	33
Lodging	0.425	97	41
Eating and Drinking	1.015	97	98
Automotive	1.390	63	88
Communication and Transport	0.025	31	1
Total	5.000		343
Maximum Development			
Retail and Wholesale	$ 4.170	59	246
Services	2.265	44	100
Lodging	1.275	97	124
Eating and Drinking	3.045	97	295
Automotive	4.170	63	263
Communication and Transport	0.075	31	2
Total	15.000		1,030

Minimum development, 50 pounds × 3.0 = 150 pounds
Intermediate development, 500 pounds × 10.0 = 5,000 pounds
Maximum development, 2,000 pounds × 30.0 = 60,000 pounds

These wastes pour untreated into the major rivers of the region from faulty septic tank operations in thin mountain soils and from soil erosion caused by the construction of roads and trails. A careful modeling of the watershed in the region shows the contribution of these wastes to water quality (in parts per million)

Minimum development,
  1 ppm/pound × 150 pounds = 150 ppm
Intermediate development,
  3 ppm/pound × 5,000 pounds = 15,000 ppm
Maximum development,
  7 ppm/pound × 60,000 pounds = 420,000 ppm

This is the effect of each alternative level of development on river water quality.

The next step is to estimate the effect of each alternative level of development on income, tax revenues, and government spending in the region. An input-output analysis of a similar regional economy shows that value added or local income represents 50 percent of direct output or sales and has a multiplier of 2.0. Tax revenues are expected to be approximately 10 percent of regional income, according to budget analysts in the governor's office. They also estimate the government spending necessary to provide the social capital (public expenditures for roads, schools, police and fire protection, etc.) per $1 million of direct and indirect output as follows:

Minimum development, $20,000 × 3.0 = $60,000
Intermediate development, $50,000 × 10.0 = $500,000
Maximum development, $100,000 × 30.0 = $3,000,000

On this basis, the following estimates of economic impact have been prepared for each alternative:

Minimum development
  Regional income, .50 × 2.0 × $1,500,000 = $1,500,000
  Tax revenue, $1,500,000 × .10 = $150,000
  Government gain-loss ratio, $150,000/$60,000 = 2.5

Intermediate development
  Regional income, .50 × 2.0 × $5,000,000 = $5,000,000
  Tax revenue, $5,000,000 × .10 = $500,000
  Government gain-loss ratio, $500,000/$500,000 = 1.0

Maximum development
  Regional income, .50 × 2.0 × $15,000,000 = $15,000,000
  Tax revenue, $15,000,000 × .10 = $1,500,000
  Government gain-loss ratio, $1,500,000/3,000,000 = 0.5

We could conclude, from the point of view of financial efficiency in government, that the alternative designating the study site as wilderness with minimum development should be recommended over the other alternatives. Wilderness has a favorable gain-loss ratio of 2.5, compared with intermediate development, 1.0. This indicates that tax revenues would just equal government spending on the intermediate alternative. Maximum development would be rejected on the basis of financial efficiency in government as its gain-loss ratio is only 0.5. This indicates that the tax revenue recovered would be only half of the necessary government spending for maximum development.

From the viewpoint of regional economic development, we could conclude that the alternative that would provide maximum recreation development should be recommended over the other alternatives. Maximum development results in far more regional output, income, and employment. It would generate total direct and indirect output of $30 million per year, income of $15 million, and employment of 1,030 persons. This is 10 times the wilderness alternative, which would generate total direct and indirect output of $3 million per year, income of $1.5 million, and employment of 103 persons. Maximum development would be three times greater than intermediate development in these categories of regional economic impact. However, there are substantial social costs to provide the 1,030 jobs measured by the deficit spending, meaning the amount by which the loss (government expenditures) exceeds the gain (tax revenue). This subsidy amounts to nearly $1,500 per year for each job provided by maximum development (= $1,500,000/1030). The governor may have less costly alternative methods to stimulate employment in the regional economy.

From the viewpoint of environmental quality, we could conclude that the alternative providing maximum recreation development should be rejected because it is expected to result in water pollution levels that violate public health standards. Intermediate development would generate pollution levels unsafe for human contact but satisfactory for fish life. Minimum development would not appreciably affect water quality in the region. On this basis, the alternative that would designate the study site as wilderness with minimum development should be recommended over the other alternatives. In addition to a favorable environmental impact, it represents a reversible decision. If the demand for commercial recreation development increases or the technology and costs of pollution control improve in future years, the site can be restudied for possible development. However, if either the intermediate or maximum recreation development alternative is selected at the present time, it would be very expensive, if not impossible, to reverse the decision at some future time, if demand for wilderness recreation with minimum development may increase.

You should remember that this is a hypothetical example of a region with these unique circumstances. It seems likely that the maximum development alternative generally would have the most favorable regional economic impact by these measures.

SUMMARY

In this chapter, we distinguished between the primary benefits and secondary impacts of recreation economic decisions. Secondary effects include the regional economic impacts on business output or sales, employment, net income, tax revenues, and government spending. The essential idea is that the primary costs to individual consumers and managers become secondary gains to the regional economy supplying recreation goods and services. Every local community is concerned about regional economic development — to create job opportunities, raise incomes, and contribute to the community's general economic prosperity.

The federal guidelines recommend that regional economic impacts be treated as income transfers in a separate account to distinguish them from benefits. The single exception is when the regional economy of a proposed project has substantial and persistent unemployment of labor. Then the benefits of the project may include the income (salaries and wages) of otherwise unemployed labor working on-site in the construction of a project or a nonstructural improvement.

The most important concept with respect to regional economic impact is the multiplier. It is defined as the total effects (direct plus indirect) divided by the direct effects. The multiplier includes: (1) the direct effect on the sales of businesses from which park visitors and the park agency purchase goods and services; and (2) the indirect effects on the sales of these and other businesses in the region, as a portion of the recreation dollars are spent and respent, leading to a multiple increase in sales. We saw that the value added portion of recreation dollars is spent and respent through approximately 12 rounds, at which time the effect approaches zero. Value added is defined as the proportion of total direct sales that remain in the region as wages, salaries, interest, profits, rents, and local taxes. The difference between total sales and value added is defined as leakage, meaning the payments for wholesale and retail products and services brought in from outside the region, plus the interest, profits, rents, and taxes paid outside the region. The more value added by businesses in the region, the higher the multiplier.

Next, we illustrated the steps involved in the input-output method of estimating the multiplier. A regional economy consists of a number of businesses which are classified into industries according to type of output or sales. These industries or trades buy from and sell to each

392

other and to industries in other regions. They also make payments for capital, labor, and other inputs, and they sell to final buyers such as tourists, etc. An input-output table is a set of double-entry accounts for the regional economy. It maps the interconnections among various lines of business. The advantage of the method is that it provides information on the indirect and induced impact of tourist spending on the output or sales of each industry in the local economy. This provides a more precise calculation of the regional tourist multiplier as a weighted average of the multipliers for each local industry from which tourists purchase goods and services.

Regional output or sales multipliers for expenditures on recreation goods and services have averaged approximately 2.0 and ranged from 1.5 to 2.6 in the United States. Past studies provide several clues as to the reasons regional multipliers vary in amount. Size of the region has an important effect; the value added within the region rises as its geographic area is increased and a smaller proportion of the expenditures on recreation goods and services are purchased outside of the region. Also, regional multipliers represent a weighted average of the multipliers for each type of business from which tourists purchase goods and services. If a large proportion of expenditures by recreation visitors are for services, lodging, food, and beverages, with much higher output or sales multipliers, then the regional multiplier will be higher because it represents a weighted average for all recreation expenditures. Day users of a park who bring a picnic lunch from home have very low regional output or sales multipliers. Recreation visitors who stay overnight in campgrounds typically spend little or no money for services, lodging, or restaurant meals, and as a result have low regional multipliers. The recreation industry tends to have somewhat lower regional multipliers than agriculture, forestry, or light manufacturing industry. However, in many rural counties with resorts, the somewhat lower regional multiplier effect of tourist spending is more than offset by the large absolute level of tourist expenditures.

Finally, we learned how to apply regional economic impact methods to the problem of alternative recreation development, from the point of view of maximizing the economic development of the state.

READINGS

Beardsley, Wendell G. "Comments on 'Travel and the National Parks: An Economic Study.'" *Journal of Leisure Research* 2(No. 1, 1970): 78-81.

Beardsley, Wendell G. "The Economic Impact of Recreation Development: A Synopsis." Recreation Symposium Proceedings. Northeastern Forest Experiment Station, Forest Service, U.S. Dept. of Agriculture, Upper Darby, Pa. 1971. 28-32.

Bell, Clive, Peter Hazell, and Robert Slade. *Project Evaluation in Regional Perspective.* Johns Hopkins University Press, Baltimore. 1982.

Booz, Allen, and Hamilton, Inc. "A Procedures Manual for Assessing the Socioeconomic Impact of the Construction and Operation of Coal Utilization Facilities in the Old West Region." Report to the Old West Regional Commission. Washington, D.C. 1974.

Brown, Nicholas, and James A. MacMillan. "Recreation Program Development Impacts: A Dynamic Regional Analysis." *American Journal of Agricultural Economics* 59(Nov. 1977):750-54.

Davulis, J. P., C. T. K. Ching, G. E. Frick, and R. L. Christensen. "Economic Effects of Pawtuckaway State Park." Research Report No. 34, New Hampshire Agricultural Experiment Station, University of New Hampshire, Durham. 1974.

Dean, Gillian, Malcolm Getz, Larry Nelson, and John Siegfried. "The Local Economic Impact of State Parks." *Journal of Leisure Research* 10(No. 2, 1978):98-112.

Epp, Donald J. "The Economic Impact of Recreational Water Reservoir Development on Land Use, Business Enterprises, and Land Values." Agricultural Experiment Station Bulletin 764. Pennsylvania State University, University Park. 1970.

Fox, Karl A., and T. Krishna Kumar. "The Functional Economic Area: Delineation and Implications for Economic Analysis and Policy." in *Research and Education for Regional and Area Development.* Iowa State University Press, Ames. 1966.

Frick, F. C., and D. C. Coddington. "The Contribution of Skiing to the Colorado Economy." Colorado Ski Country USA, Denver. 1982.

Frick, G. E., and C. T. K. Ching. "Generation of Local Income from Users of a Rural Public Park." *Journal of Leisure Research* 2(No. 4, 1970):260-63.

Fullerton, Herbert H., W. Cris Lewis, and B. Delworth Gardner. "Socio-Economic Data and Methods in Environmental Analysis of National Park Service Actions." Report to the National Park Service, by Utah State University, Logan. 1975.

Gamble, Hays B. "Community Income from Outdoor Recreation." A paper presented at the Maryland Governor's Recreation Conference, Ocean City, Md. 1965.

Garrison, C. B. "A Case Study of the Local Economic Impact of Reservoir Recreation." *Journal of Leisure Research* 6(No. 1, 1974):7-19.

Gittinger, J. Price. *Economic Analysis of Agricultural Projects.* Second Edition. Johns Hopkins University Press, Baltimore. 1982.

Gramann, James H. "An Ex Post Facto Analysis of the Regional Economic Impact of Expenditures for Reservoir Recreation." *Journal of Environmental Management* 16(No. 2, 1983):357-67.

Gray, James R., and Garrey E. Carruthers. "Economic Impact of Recreational Developments in the Reserve Ranger District." Agricultural Experiment Station Bulletin No. 515. New Mexico State University, Las Cruces. 1966.

Haroldson, Ancel D. "Economic Impact of Recreation Development at Big Sky, Montana." Research Report No. 75, Agricultural Experiment Station, Montana State University, Bozeman. 1975.

Herr, Philip B., and Associates. "Cape Cod National Seashore Economic Impact Study." Report to the National Park Service, U.S. Dept. of the Interior. Washington, D.C. 1969.

Hughes, Jay M. "Forestry in Itasca County's Economy: An Input-Output Analysis." Agricultural Experiment Station Miscellaneous Report No. 95, Forestry Series No. 4. University of Minnesota, St. Paul. 1970.

Jewett, Frank I. "The Impact of a National Park Upon a County's Economy." *Annals of Regional Science* 2(Dec. 1968):274-87.

Johnson, Maxine C. "The Tourist Industry: Some Second Thoughts." *Montana Business Quarterly* 12(No. 2, 1968):3-6.

Kalter, Robert J., and William B. Lord. "Measurement of the Impact of Recreation Investments on a Local Economy." *American Journal of Agricultural Economics* 50(May 1968):243-55.

Kite, Rodney C., and William D. Schultz. "Economic Impact on Southwestern Wyoming of Recreationists Visiting Flaming Gorge Reservoir." Research Report No. 11, Agricultural Experiment Station, University of Wyoming, Laramie. 1967.

Lichty, Richard W., and Donald N. Steinnes. "Ely, Minnesota: Measuring the Impact of Tourism on a Small Community." *Growth and Change* 13(No. 2, 1982):36-9.

Main, Alden. "Impact of Forestry and Forest-related Industries on a Local Economy, Baldwin County, Alabama." Ph.D. Dissertation, Auburn University, Auburn. 1971.

McIntosh, Robert W., and Charles R. Goeldner. *Tourism: Principles, Practices, and Philosophies.* 4th Edition. Grid Publishing Co., Columbus, Ohio. 1984.

McKean, John R., and Kenneth C. Nobe. "Direct and Indirect Economic Effects of Hunting and Fishing in Colorado, 1981." Technical Report No. 44, Colorado Water Resources Research Institute. Colorado State University, Fort Collins. 1984.

McKean, John R. "Impact of Mountain Pine Beetle and Spruce Budworm on the Economies in the Front Range Foothills of Colorado." Report to the Rocky Mountain Forest and Range Experiment Station, Forest Service, U.S. Dept. of Agriculture, Fort Collins, Colo. 1981.

McKean, John R. "An Input-Output Analysis of Sportsman Expenditures in Colorado." Colorado Water Resources Research Institute Technical Report No. 26. Colorado State University, Fort Collins. 1981.

Millard, Frank W., and David W. Fischer. "The Local Economic Impact of Outdoor Recreation Facilities." *Land and Leisure: Concepts and Methods in Outdoor Recreation.* Carlton S. Van Doren, George B. Priddle, and John E. Lewis (eds.). 2nd edition. Maaroufa Press, Chicago. 1979. 244-58.

Milliken, J. Gordon, and H. E. Mew, Jr. "Recreation Impact of Reclamation Reservoirs." Bureau of Reclamation, U.S. Dept. of the Interior, Washington, D.C. 1969.

Nathan Association. "Recreation as an Industry in Appalachia." A Report Prepared for the Appalachian Regional Commission, Washington, D.C. 1966.

Polzin, Paul E., and Dennis L. Schweitzer. "Economic Importance of Tourism in Montana." Research Paper, INT-171, Intermountain Forest and Range Experiment Station, Forest Service, U.S. Department of Agriculture, Ogden, Utah. 1975.

Rajender, G. R., Floyd K. Harston, and Dwight M. Blood. "A Study of the Resources, People, and Economy of Teton County, Wyoming." Division of Business and Economic Research, University of Wyoming, Laramie. 1967.

Rhody, Donald D., and Robert F. Lovegrove. "Economic Impact of Hunting and Fishing Expenditures in Grand County, Colorado, 1968." GS916, Colorado State University, Fort Collins. 1970.

Rockland, David B. "The Economic Benefits of a Fishery Resource: A Practical Guide." Sport Fishing Institute, Washington, D.C. 1985.

Stoevener, H. H., R. B. Retting, and S. D. Reiling. "Economic Impact of Outdoor Recreation: What Have We Learned?" *Water and Community Development: Social and Economic Perspectives.* Donald R. Field, J. C. Barron, and B. F. Long (eds.). Ann Arbor Science Publishers, Ann Arbor, Mich. 1974. 235-55.

Swanson, Ernest W. "Travel and the National Parks." National Park Service, U.S. Dept. of the Interior, Washington, D.C. 1969.

U.S. Dept. of Agriculture. "Secondary Impacts of Public Investment in Natural Resources." Proceedings of a Symposium. Economic Research Service, U.S. Dept. of Agriculture, Washington, D.C. 1968.

U.S. Dept. of Transportation. "Recreation Travel Impacts." Federal Highway Administration, Washington, D.C. 1977.

Chapter Thirteen

Resource Supply and Costs

> This chapter introduces the concept of recreation resource supply and the various types of fixed and variable costs including capital construction, land, operation, maintenance, external costs, and associated costs; describes the three sources of cost information: engineering economic, cross-sectional, and time-series methods; distinguishes between financial costs and economic cost; summarizes the results of several empirical studies of costs; and discusses the effects of costs on recreation economic decisions.

Resource supply and costs are important in recreation economics, because decisions by private and public managers require a comparison between the costs of alternative courses of action and their benefits. For example, the expected benefits of programs to upgrade services provided at a campground are compared with the costs of the programs. Likewise, a decision to expand a boat marina or campground involves a comparison of the benefits expected from the capital improvement with its costs. Even a decision about whether to improve park employees' living quarters requires a comparison between the cost of the project and the subjectively estimated benefits expected to result from improved employee morale. In each case, the benefits resulting from the decision are compared with its costs.

In this chapter, we introduce the concept of economic costs. We show that the distinction between financial costs and economic or social costs is based on the idea of opportunity costs. You will see what economists mean by short-run, long-run, fixed, variable, and marginal costs. The latter is the supply curve for recreation. We review in some detail the types of costs including capital investment, land, operation and maintenance, external costs, and associated costs. This is followed by a review of three methods that have been used to measure recreation costs. Using the results of recent empirical studies, we draw several important implications for improving the study of costs in future recreation economic decisions. In the past, most studies provided summaries of the average costs of providing opportunities for recreation. More recently, considerable progress has been made both in recreation agency cost accounting and in the development of incremental cost functions. The widespread availability of computer software enables us to show how costs change with improvements in design, size, utilization of capacity, and level of service provided. Such studies are particularly useful in recreation economic decisions because they show how future costs are expected to change with alternative policies.

SHORT-RUN AND LONG-RUN COSTS

The supply of parks and other recreation resources is determined by the cost of production. Supply is also affected by other variables, of course, such as availability of public funds, quality of potential sites, the price of inputs such as labor, energy, and other factors of production. But for now, we will consider cost and quantity supplied. The purpose of this section is to introduce the concepts of short-run and long-run production costs. In the short-run, costs of production vary with changes in the rate of utilization of capacity of facilities, such as the proportion of existing campsites rented. In the long-run, costs of production vary with changes in the size of facilities, such as the number of campsites in a campground, which defines maximum capacity. In addition, long-run costs of production vary with changes in the level of technology or development. For example, there are three basic levels of technology in campgrounds: fully developed with utility hookups, primitive with pit toilets, and undeveloped backcountry sites where everything is carried in and out by the user. If the relationship of short-run to long-run costs is not familiar to you, review the microeconomic theory section of any economic textbook.

Total cost (TC) means the total cost of producing any given level of output. Total cost is divided into two parts, total fixed costs (TFC) and total variable costs (TVC). Fixed costs are those that do not vary with changes in the recreation use of a site in the short run. They will be the same if output is 100 visits or 10,000. Managers often refer to fixed costs as overhead costs or unavoidable costs. Fixed costs include capital investment, general administration, and external costs. Variable costs are those that vary directly with changes in the recreation use of a site, rising with more visits and falling with less. Managers often refer to variable costs as direct costs or avoidable costs. Variable costs cover operation and maintenance (O&M) including direct labor, expendable supplies, and utilities. Panel 1 of Figure 13-1 illustrates these concepts. Note that total fixed cost does not vary with output, while total variable cost and total costs $(TC = TFC + TVC)$ rise with more visits, first at a decreasing rate, and then at an increasing rate.

Average total cost (ATC), also called average cost (AC), is the cost per visit. The total cost of producing any given level of use is divided by the number of visits produced. Average total cost may be separated into average fixed costs (AFC) and average variable costs (AVC) in the same way that total costs were divided. Thus, the total cost curves in panel 1 of Figure 13-1 provide the basis for the average cost curves shown in panel 2. AFC declines continuously as output increases. A doubling of output always leads to a halving of fixed costs per unit of output. This is the process popularly known as spreading the overhead. ATC curves are usually U-shaped; they fall and then rise as output increases. This reflects the fact that productivity is increasing

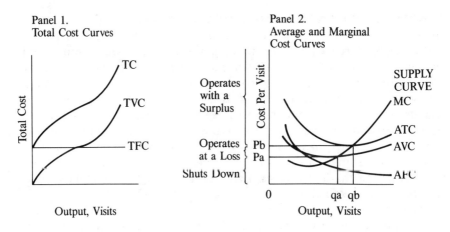

Figure 13-1. Total, Average, and Marginal Cost Curves for Park and Recreation Programs in the Short Run

Source: Walsh, Keleta, Waples, and Olienyk.

when output is low but at some level of output, productivity begins to fall enough to cause AVC to increase faster than AFC falls. When this happens, ATC increases.

Marginal cost (MC), sometimes called incremental cost, is the increase in total cost resulting from increasing production by 1 visit. Because fixed costs do not vary with output, marginal fixed costs are always zero. Therefore, marginal costs are necessarily marginal variable costs, and changes in fixed costs will not affect marginal costs. For example, the marginal cost of producing a few more skier days by utilizing a given ski site more intensively is the same, whatever the rent paid for the fixed amount of land in ski slope. Panel 2 of Figure 13-1 shows that MC falls and then rises as output increases and intersects the ATC and AVC at their minimum points. The intersection of the MC and AVC curves defines the shut down point, below which there is no incentive to continue operation of the site. Note that above this point, the MC curve represents the supply curve for the site.

Economic capacity of a park or other outdoor recreation site is defined as the level of output at the minimum ATC. This is not an upper limit on what can be produced. Instead, it is the largest output that can be produced without encountering rising average total costs per visit. In Figure 13-1, economic capacity output is qb visits, but output could be higher, provided the manager is willing to accept the higher costs per visit that accompany output above economic capacity. For outputs less than the point of minimum average total cost, the site is said to have extra or excess capacity. This definition of capacity may differ from that in everyday speech, but it is widely used in economic and financial discussions.

Short-run cost curves show how costs vary with the number of visits to a park or other recreation site of a given size. There is always some limiting factor of production that is fixed such as acres of land or size of facilities. In any regional market for outdoor recreation, there is a different short-run cost curve for each park or other recreation site of a given size. A small city park will have its own short-run cost curve. A medium-sized state park and a very large national park will each have its own short-run cost curve. If a park or recreation program expands and replaces a small site with a medium-sized one, it will move from one short-run cost curve to another. The change from one size to another is a long-run change. How short-run cost curves for sites of different sizes are related to each other is shown in Figure 13-2. Economists define the long run as a situation in which all factors of production can be varied, i.e., all costs become variable costs.

The long-run planning decisions are important because once a new recreation site is acquired and new facilities constructed, it becomes fixed for a long time. Managers must anticipate what methods of production will be efficient not only today but in the years ahead, when costs of labor and other direct expenses may have changed. The decisions are also difficult because managers must estimate how many visitors will use the facilities. The long-run average cost curve shown in Figure 13-2 falls at first and then rises. This curve is often described as saucer shaped. Over the range of output from zero to q, the industry has falling long-run average costs. An expansion in size of facilities results in a reduction of costs per visit. Over the range of size greater than q, the industry encounters rising costs. An expansion in size of facilities will be accompanied by a rise in average cost per visit. Such an industry is said to suffer long-run increasing costs or diseconomy of scale (or size). At output q in Figure 13-2, the industry has reached its lowest possible long-run costs per visit. In a competitive industry, each supplier would produce at the minimum point on its LRAC curve. See Chapter 14 for a full discussion of this proposition.

The discussion so far shows how cost varies with changes in output and size, assuming constant prices of the factors of production and

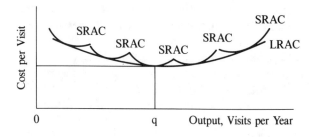

Figure 13-2. Relationship Between the Long-Run Average Cost Curve and Short-Run Average Cost Curves for Park and Recreation Programs

fixed technology. Changes in either technological knowledge or factor prices will cause the short-run and long-run cost curves to shift. Technological change normally works in only one direction, to shift cost curves downward. Improved ways of providing existing recreation opportunities will mean that lower cost methods of production become available. Changes in the price of the factors of production can exert an influence in either direction. If an agency has to pay more for any input, the cost of producing each level of output will rise; if the agency has to pay less, costs will fall.

Lipsey and Steiner reviewed three major changes that have affected production costs in the long run. All are related to technology, broadly defined. The first is the change in the techniques available for producing existing recreation opportunities, products, and services. Over an average person's lifetime, these changes often can be dramatic. Seventy years ago, recreation roads and trails were built by gangs of workers using buckets, spades, and draft horses; today bulldozers, steam shovels, giant trucks, and other specialized equipment have completely banished the workhorse from construction sites and to a great extent have displaced the workers with their shovels.

Second is the change in new products and services that become available. Electronic equipment, nylon clothing, fiberglass boats, freeze dried food, lightweight running shoes, and many other consumer products of today did not exist two generations ago. Other products are so changed that they are hardly the same product as in the past. A new front-wheel drive auto is very different from the early autos. Modern jet planes are revolutionary compared with the planes of World War II.

Third, improvements in nutrition, health care, and education increase the quality of labor services. Today's managers and workers are in better health, are better clothed, and better housed than their counterparts in your grandparents' generation. On the average, they are better educated. Even unskilled workers today tend to be literate and competent in arithmetic, and their managers are trained in modern methods of recreation economic decision making. These kinds of technological changes have been vital features of the so-called developed or industrialized countries throughout the world.

TYPES OF FIXED AND VARIABLE COSTS

To economists, the total cost of a park or recreation program includes: the cost of program planning or design; the cost of land and related natural resources; the cost of capital construction or installation; operation and maintenance costs; external costs to other agencies and individuals; and the associated cost to users. The purpose of this section is to review these types of fixed and variable cost and to distinguish social costs from the financial costs of private and public agencies.

The economic evaluation of public recreation projects differs from financial analysis in that social costs rather than accounting costs are used. The social cost of producing recreation is what must be given up by society as a whole to make that production possible. To economists, the concept of social cost always means opportunity cost. The opportunity cost of using a resource is the value of the resource in its next best alternative use. When measuring the opportunity cost of recreation, all consequences of its production must be identified and incorporated into the measurement. We estimate the opportunity costs for all inputs, whether they are correctly or incorrectly priced by markets or not priced at all.

There are a number of reasons why financial cost differs from economic cost. The standard accounting practice in both private and public agencies is to record only the costs of those inputs purchased from others. This can lead to a substantial divergence between accounting measures of financial cost and social cost. In neither case do accounts measure the implicit costs of factors of production owned by the firm or public. Certain planning and overhead costs may be paid by other agencies that do not require reimbursement by the agency operating the park or recreation program. For example, federal agencies may participate in capital installation cost but not in annual costs of operation. Nor do accountants include external costs defined as those opportunity costs of production that fall on others and for which the firm or agency bears no responsibility. The recreation agency may not be legally required to reimburse those individuals and agencies that bear the external costs or may be legally unable to collect external benefits. Financial cost may benefit others, for example, when a low quality road to the site is replaced with a high quality access road. Recreation agencies are not financially responsible to pay the associated costs of recreation users, but should include them in site location decisions.

Although economists and accountants define costs differently, both definitions are correct since they are used for different purposes. In describing or predicting the actual behavior of managers, economists should use the accounting information that managers actually use. But in helping managers make the best decisions they can in pursuing their goals and evaluating how well they use scarce resources, economists should substitute social cost rather than financial or accounting costs. Fortunately, the evaluation of most public recreation projects can proceed on the assumption that the relevant markets reasonably accurately measure the true social costs of goods and services employed by public agencies. In smoothly functioning markets, wage rates and the prices of material and equipment are a close approximation of the opportunity cost of resources. Some possible exceptions are noted below.

402

Capital Construction Costs

Parks and other recreation programs usually require the construction of facilities such as buildings, roads, campgrounds, and trails. Preconstruction costs include design, contract preparation, environmental assessment, site survey, feasibility analysis, vegetative treatment, and other functions. Construction costs include clearing and grading, roads, spurs, and barriers; water development and distribution; wastewater disposal, signs and bulletin boards; visitor information facilities, electrical connections, fee collection facilities, campsite facilities, trails, contract administration and inspection; and other construction costs.

Estimating the social costs of capital construction is relatively more straightforward than valuation of social benefits, and often is little different from comparable estimation of costs in private financial decisions. Well established markets usually exist for construction material, equipment, and services. Thus, information on market prices is generally available or can be obtained through estimating procedures based on past construction costs in the region of the site. The National Park Service publishes "Construction Cost" guidelines for long-run planning. Included are the costs of roads, trails, landscaping, sitework, buildings, structures, campgrounds, fences, incinerators, concrete items, electrical, gas, water, sewage, miscellaneous items, planning, and administration. These national estimates are adjusted for remoteness of the site, elevation, difficulty of terrain, season, material suppliers, labor availability, and wage rates. For example, the productivity of construction workers at 11,000 feet elevation is about half that at sea level.

The federal guidelines for evaluating the costs of capital construction include planning costs since they are incurred only once in the lifetime of the park or other recreation site. Planning and design costs include preparing specifications and construction drawings, field surveys, and special investigations as part of the planning and design of facilities. Planning and design costs are based on the actual current costs incurred by the public agency or private contractor for similar projects. They may be estimated as a percentage of construction costs based on the ratio for similar projects (30 percent) and adjusted to reflect special circumstances of the proposed project.

Administration costs associated with construction include review of the engineering plans and inspection during construction to ensure that facilities are installed in accordance with the plans and specifications. Also included are the administrative services to secure the necessary permits for construction, representation at public hearings, and testimony in court when legal disputes arise. Administrative costs associated with construction should be based on the actual current costs of the public agency or private contractor to carry out these activities for similar projects. They may be estimated as a percentage of construction costs based on the ratio for similar projects (15 percent) and adjusted to reflect special circumstances of the proposed project.

The costs of actual construction include site preparation; purchased materials delivered to the site; equipment rental or purchase; construction wages or salaries including social security and fringe benefits; and contractor management, supervision, overhead, and profit. The costs of construction are usually based on current contract bids in the region of the proposed project or on the current market value of purchased materials and services, etc., to install the facilities. Contingency costs are normally added to allow for unforeseen construction problems. They may be estimated as a percentage of construction costs, depending on the variability of site conditions and the type of project proposed. Some specified amount (often, 10 percent) is added to the initial cost estimates. These funds are set aside to allow for the uncertainty of project cost estimates. They help insure that funds will be adequate to complete the project. They are not an allowance for inflation or for the omission of the costs of facilities that are known to be required.

Construction costs also should include the interest on the construction loan of private contractors and an equivalent amount of opportunity cost for public projects. Compound interest is calculated at the applicable agency interest rate from the date the costs are incurred to the end of the construction or installation period. Finally, construction costs may be adjusted to allow for the expected salvage value of facilities at the end of the life of the recreation project. For example, the access road to a campground may be valuable for other uses at the end of 20 years.

Problems may arise when monopolistic conditions prevail in the local market, so that the prices for construction materials do not accurately measure their opportunity cost. In this case, an appropriate downward adjustment of construction costs would be required to accurately reflect true social costs. In other cases, a project might increase the demand for local construction materials sufficiently to affect their prices in local competitive markets. Where the project purchases a sufficiently large proportion of the available supply of the necessary factors of production to influence the price at which the total can be marketed, the increase in price calls for special treatment in estimating the cost of project construction (Krutilla and Eckstein).

The opportunity cost of the total input required to construct the project would be less than the amount estimated by costing all units of input at the level needed to attract the final unit required. The aggregate value of the construction materials is represented by the amount which could be paid if each unit of the block of input demanded could be purchased separately at the price it would command. Successive units of input purchased during the specified construction period would be available at prices above the level of preceding units in the sequence. Accordingly, neither the price which would prevail in the absence of the project, nor the price which would be necessary to bring forth the last unit from the market, would accurately indicate the value of each unit of input. The social cost of the total increase in input required could be approximated by using an average price midway between that prevailing with the project demand and without it. This would be an acceptable procedure when the supply function for the construction materials is linear.

Economists distinguish between explicit and implicit costs. Explicit costs are the costs of inputs purchased from others such as direct labor, expendable supplies, rent and general administration. Implicit costs are capital or labor services purchased during an earlier accounting period. Capital investment foregoes interest and loses value, i.e., depreciates. This distinction has important implications because public agencies own land, buildings, and equipment that they use in production of recreation opportunities. The conventional practice is that if they were purchased in the past, there is no payment during this year to show up on the accounting records. This means that there is no explicit cost associated with the use of existing land and capital improvements by public agencies. Also, if some of these assets are purchased during the current accounting period (1 year), the expenditure to acquire them is not a valid explicit cost of this period's production of recreation opportunities, because the assets will still be able to contribute to the production of recreation opportunities in future periods. Until government recognizes the implicit cost of its capital investment, private recreation site operators will be under more pressure than public agencies to increase the number of users (Clawson and Knetsch). The reason is that a small change in the number of users of private facilities has a substantial effect on implicit costs per user. The implicit cost of the land, buildings, and equipment of public recreation agencies is its opportunity cost, i.e., what has been foregone by society in order to use the assets for this purpose.

Problems may arise when converting the initial capital investment costs to annual fixed costs over the life of the facility. Depreciation and interest on capital investment are generally overlooked by public agencies. Managers of private recreation sites realize that depreciation, which means setting aside enough money to replace facilities when they wear out, is a cost which must be recovered if they are to continue to operate. Depreciation includes both the loss in value due to physical wear and that due to obsolescence. Accountants use several conventional methods of depreciation based on the price originally paid for the asset. One of the most common is straight-line depreciation, in which the same amount of historical cost is deducted in every year of useful life of the asset. While historical costs are often useful approximations, they may differ from depreciation required by the opportunity cost principle. The economic cost of using an asset for a year is the loss in value of the asset during the year. Economists consider interest on the value of assets as the opportunity cost of capital necessary to keep the assets employed.

There are several additional points that should be made with respect to depreciation and interest on capital investment. They should be counted as an economic cost when: (1) they are part of a proposed new facility and have not yet been expended; (2) when their value is reduced by continuing to use them; and (3) there is a question whether users are being charged enough to repay total costs to perpetuate the program indefinitely. This is the situation for most recreation programs. On the other hand, depreciation and interest on capital investment should not be counted as an economic cost when: (1) facilities have already been installed and they will have the same value whether or not they continue to be used; (2) there is a question whether to continue to incur a program's direct costs of operation; and (3) the program is not a perpetual one.

Managers should not overlook the fact that when parks and other recreation facilities are built, there is a loss of property tax base to the community. For example, a city operating its own golf course foregoes the tax revenue it could have earned if the golf course were supplied by private operators who pay property taxes. Since a public recreation facility consumes municipal services in much the same way as a private one, the costs of services provided results in a higher tax load on the rest of the community. Economists consider the foregone tax as an economic cost of the capital investment by the public recreation agency. As a result, a number of states and federal agencies make annual payment to local units of government in lieu of taxes.

Finally, managers who have been growth oriented in the past should consider the social benefits of zero or low growth in the future. Growth affects the rate of utilization of recreation facilities and their costs (Walsh, Soper, and Prato). The reason is that recreation facilities have a long life. They are designed to have sufficient excess capacity in the early years to serve users 20 years in the future. The more use is expected to grow, the more excess capacity is necessary in the early years of operation with resulting higher costs. With zero growth, utilization of capacity of facilities such as a wastewater treatment system can be nearly 100 percent over 20 years with no increase in costs. With 3 percent annual growth in use, costs 10 years hence, midyear in the planning period, are increased by 35 percent. With 10 percent growth, midyear costs increase by 160 percent. A 15 percent annual growth increases midyear costs to a level 305 percent higher than with zero growth.

Not all costs increase with growth. For example, most variable costs of wastewater treatment vary directly with the volume of wastewater processed and thus per capita costs remain virtually unaffected by underutilization of the wastewater system. It is the capital costs that are affected by underutilization of capacity. These include investment in the treatment plant, land, collection lines and transmission lines. The challenge to managers is to phase investment in capital improvements consistent with growth. For example, construction of campgrounds could be phased with the first loop build in year 1, the second loop in year 5, the third and final loop in year 10. Managers could install the first loop of a second campground in year 15, and continuing so long as growth in demand is present (Lime).

Opportunity Cost of Land

Parks and other recreation programs usually require a substantial amount of land and related natural resources such as forests, rivers, and lakes. Estimating the social costs of these natural resources is one of the most difficult problems in recreation economics. Land set aside for public recreation use has an opportunity cost. Often it could be devoted to other productive uses if it were not set aside. The value of the land in the best alternative use represents the economic cost of land for recreation use. Hof, et al., discuss the problem of allocating joint costs under conditions of multiple use such as for recreation, fish, wildlife, timber, forage, water, and minerals. Here we limit the discussion to a single use which is typical of most park land in the United States and around the world. Reiling and Anderson provide a useful discussion of the problem of valuing recreation land in the state of Maine.

Land used for publicly provided recreation may be acquired in several ways. It may be purchased from private landowners at market prices or through the process of eminent domain, through which government condemns the land of an unwilling seller and the courts decide its fair market value. The concept of opportunity cost is relevant in determining fair market value since its purchase price should reflect the rate of return the land would earn in its highest and best use. If the land or the right to use it, is to be purchased, the value placed on the land by government real estate appraisors may understate the real opportunity costs. The assessed value of the site may be different from the value assigned by existing owners who may have an aversion to risk, a higher interest rate, and differing price expectations (Herfindahl and Kneese).

Some land used for recreation sites has been donated to government for the expressed purpose of recreation. But it may not in fact be free if it could have been put to other productive uses such as timber production, mining, or urban development. Reiling and Anderson suggest that in the case of donation, its opportunity cost is not clear. In principle, it has an opportunity cost; however, the donor has sacrificed the potential return from alternative use in exchange for the satisfaction of knowing the land will be preserved for the recreation enjoyment of future generations. They argue that alternative uses of the land have been rejected by the donor, and the agency cannot consider alternative uses under terms of the bequest. So its opportunity cost may be zero. Land may or may not have an opportunity cost, depending on whether it would have been used for other productive uses or would have been an unemployed resource if the agency had not accepted the gift.

If, as is usually the case, the recreation site is already publicly owned, no capital outlay is required, but valuable alternative uses may be foregone. If alternative uses of the land are sacrificed for recreation uses, estimates of the value of the land in previously allowable uses should approximate its opportunity cost. For example, the opportunity cost of land set aside as part of the National Wilderness Preservation System should be based on the alternative uses that were previously allowed under the multiple-use concept of management, but are disallowed with wilderness designation. For example, the social opportunity cost of land removed from timber harvesting for wilderness use may range from zero for lands that are at the margin for timber harvesting, to an upper limit represented by the annualized stumpage value of timber net of access road construction costs. Reiling and Anderson suggest that the correct measure of the social opportunity cost of wilderness is equal to this economic rent or net benefit associated with the removal of land from timber harvesting plus the loss of consumer surplus from motorized recreation which is no longer allowed.

Land that is already part of the public domain may have very little opportunity cost when used for recreation purposes other than wilderness. If recreation facilities are constructed on land managed under the multiple-use concept, opportunity cost may be negligible because few, if any, alternatives may be sacrificed. For example, timber can mature and be harvested after the useful life has ended for recreation facilities such as campgrounds. Hiking trails are an example of recreation improvements with essentially a zero opportunity cost of land. Timber management practices may be enhanced by the improved access provided by the recreation trails. Recreation access roads can be used jointly for timber removal and other management purposes. Some consumer surplus from hunting may be lost when hikers push some species out of otherwise productive habitat. Hiking and other recreation use may result in some deterioration in water quality and reduce the quality of fishing.

Some park and recreation agencies of city, county, and state government may be allowed to sell surplus recreation land on the open market. In that case, the opportunity cost of its continued park and recreation use is the competitive market value for alternative use by private buyers. However, for most levels of government, in particular state and federal, regulations prevent the sale of land on the open market. This means that its market value is not an appropriate basis for estimating opportunity cost. Legislators are aware of the option, existence, and bequest value of public natural resources to the voters within their jurisdictions. As a result, most public lands were not for sale in the past, a policy which is likely to be continued in the future.

Opportunity costs are based on what would — not what should — be done with the resource in its next best alternative use. For example, suppose an energy development is proposed for an existing state owned natural roadless area. The development plan calls for a coal fired power plant and surface strip mine to use half of the land in the natural area. A government land appraisor estimates that the surface rights to the land could be sold for $250,000 to private purchasers. The present value of net benefits for future recreation use of the site with all its land are $1 million and with only half its land are $600,000. What value should be placed on half of the land required for the energy development?

To answer this question, we must first know what the alternative use of the land would be if not used for the energy development. Given the potential sales price of $250,000, we know the land is worth a minimum of $250,000. However, if the land would be maintained as a natural area, the half of the area in question would have present value of net benefits of $400,000 (= $1,000,000 minus $600,000). The land is thus worth $400,000 if maintained as a natural area. Since this is more than the $250,000 that would be received if the land were sold, the land — if not used for energy development — should be kept as a natural area. The net benefits foregone by taking the land from recreation use is the opportunity cost of the land, $400,000, not the potential sales price of $250,000. The opportunity cost of the land would be $250,000 only if the public agency would sell the land rather than keep it as a natural area if the energy development does not occur.

Previous studies have estimated the opportunity cost of land in a number of ways. Guldin used total acquisition costs, including purchase price and closing costs, to estimate the opportunity cost of land purchased in Eastern states for inclusion in the wilderness system. For existing public lands that were designated as wilderness, he based the land value on current stumpage value of timber production, net of road construction costs. Gibbs and Reed, Gibbs and van Hees, and Tyre also used timber production on U.S. Forest Service land as a basis for estimating the opportunity cost of recreation use. On the other hand, Reiling et al., Downing, and Manthy and Tucker did not include the opportunity cost of land in their studies of recreation use of U.S. Forest Service land. This was based on the proposition that recreation use generally does not exclude other uses under the multiple-use concept of forest land management. Hence, they concluded that the opportunity cost of the land may be very low, in most cases. Finally, the studies were designed, for the most part, to measure the financial costs of the agency rather than social costs.

More recently, a number of studies have estimated the value of natural resources such as forest quality. Trees are one of the most important determinants of land values in mountain subdivisions in the Rocky Mountains. According to a sample of real estate appraisers, they are about as important as nearness to water and quality of the view. Figure 13-3 shows that in general, the optimum number of trees is between 120 and 140 per acre for both a healthy forest and the maximum economic value of private property. If density is more than 140 trees per acre, land value decreases in proportion to the additional trees. Value continues to decline as density increases. Studies of the value of trees at campgrounds and other recreation sites indicate a similar relationship between trees and willingness to pay for the recreation experience.

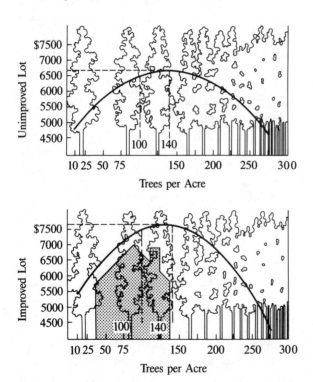

Figure 13-3. Effect of Number of Trees 6 Inches dbh or More on the Appraised Market Value of Land in the Rocky Mountains, United States

Source: Walsh, Keleta, Waples, and Olienyk.

Operation and Maintenance Costs

Parks and other recreation programs usually require expenditures for the operation and maintenance of facilities. They include both variable and fixed costs. Variable costs are for cleaning, contacts with visitors, collection of fees, law enforcement, vandalism, utilities, and maintenance that is dependent on the amount of use of the facilities. Fixed costs are for annual opening and closing of facilities, scheduled maintenance not dependent on the amount of use, and administration. These costs include the current value of materials and services needed to operate the facility and to make repairs necessary to maintain it in good condition during its useful life. Included are the salaries and fringe benefits of operating personnel, custodial services, repairs, replacements, inspection, engineering, supervision, and administrative overhead. Also included are the costs of vehicles, vehicle accidents, per diem, travel time, training, vacation, housing, and other incidental costs. If road maintenance or fire patrols in the vicinity of the site will be increased because of visitor use, then these increased costs should be included in the costs of operation and maintenance. When any of these tasks are contracted outside of the agency, the costs should include an allowance for contingencies.

In most cases, accurate estimates of operation and maintenance costs for a recreation site can be obtained from historical records and the knowledge of agency employees. Labor costs may be obtained for a facility from employee logs of their time, and the actual use of supplies, materials, and equipment. However, these costs are often difficult to estimate for a specific facility such as a campground or trail located in a larger management unit, such as a ranger district in a national forest. Costs to be included are those that are incurred only if the park or other recreation site is opened for visitor use. Costs that would be incurred whether or not the site is open should not be included. Costs of general administration would be increased by opening the site to visitors and therefore should be included.

Generally, administrative overhead costs do not vary with the level of output and are considered fixed costs. Administrative overhead includes an allocated portion of the agency supervisory, personnel services, legal services, computer services, accounting and budget services, purchasing division, motor pool, and other general expenses. Problems may arise in estimating the costs of administrative overhead for a recreation site. How far up the administrative structure of the agency should we go? For example, should a fraction of the cost associated with recreation planning by the National Park Service staff in Washington, D.C., be allocated to a specific camping facility in a national park? Reiling et al. suggest that managers are in the best position to resolve this problem. Some administrative services are always shared with other recreation sites. They have the same directors, auditors, training programs, computer services, and the like.

Some of these common or joint costs could be allocated on the basis of time studies, in which employees would keep an hourly time diary during several typical weeks of the year. Other common costs could be allocated on the basis of the agency budget for direct operation and maintenance costs. If the O&M costs of a recreation site accounted for 10 percent of total O&M costs of the agency, 10 percent of the administrative overhead costs would be allocated to the site. Shabman and Kalter applied this procedure to allocate the general administrative costs of recreation programs in New York state. The federal guidelines recommend the separable costs remaining benefits method. In this case, the direct O&M costs of each recreation site would be subtracted from the benefits of each site. Then the administrative overhead of the agency would be allocated to each site on the basis of its remaining benefits as a proportion of the total remaining benefits of all sites operated by the agency. Allocating costs on this basis appeals to many observers because of the inherent fairness of each site's users paying in proportion to benefits.

The contribution of the different types of fixed and variable cost to total cost varies for specific park and recreation programs, but labor cost comprises the largest share. Labor cost typically accounts for over 80 percent of operation and maintenance cost and over 50 percent of total cost. Market wage rates generally provide an acceptable measure of the opportunity cost of labor. The reason is that in competitive markets, workers tend to be paid the value they produce (the marginal revenue product). Both public and private employers have to pay the going market wage rates to hire workers. Of course, minimum wage laws, union bargaining, or exploitation by employers may cause the earnings of some workers to differ from their true social contribution. Moreover, unpaid family workers and volunteers may have a social opportunity cost if they forego other jobs or devote less time to other enterprises. Nonetheless, the operational rule is: in the absence of clear-cut market imperfections, actual wage rates may be assumed to be the true social costs of labor.

For most project evaluation in the United States, it is sufficient to assume that the pursuit of an effective economic stabilization policy, consistent with the intent of the Full Employment Act of 1946, will result in relatively full employment throughout the economy. It is true, however, that the business cycle results in periodic pockets of unemployment in some local areas and regions. Examples in the past, include the Appalachian region of the Northeast, the upper Great Lakes region of the Midwest, and the Four Corners region of the Southwest. Regions of high unemployment often have natural resources which are suitable for recreation development. In this case, the market wage may not accurately reflect the opportunity cost of labor in the region of a proposed project, and an appropriate downward adjustment in the wage rate would be required to accurately estimate opportunity cost. The opportunity cost of underutilized human resources would be less than the market wage rate when little or no production would be foregone if they were employed in the recreation project.

For most recreation projects, we need not be concerned with this problem. However, it may be important for large projects. Haveman and Krutilla estimated that the true social costs of multipurpose water development projects have been from 5 to 30 percent less than their monetary costs, based on the probability of projects drawing from the pool of unemployed. But economists have been skeptical of attempts to forecast regional unemployment between the time of project planning and construction or the longer period of time over the project's lifetime. They note that measurement of with or without conditions are particularly difficult, given the prospect of labor migration from other regions. As a result, the federal guidelines limit adjustments in the value of underutilized resources to the construction period of project life. The market wage would be multiplied by one minus the probability (P) of drawing workers from the unemployment pool (1 - P). See Chapter 12 for additional information on this adjustment.

Manpower programs such as CETA and the Job Corps have contributed labor services to the operation of public recreation facilities. When human resources devoted to a recreation program would otherwise be unemployed, their opportunity cost may be zero or some amount between zero and the market wage rate. Thompson suggests that in this case, the effective cost to the government is the difference between any unemployment payments and the wage rates in the recreation program. The job training program in the United States was designed to prepare up to a million unemployed people annually for permanent work. Participants were economically disadvantaged adults and youths, including those on welfare and workers displaced by automation and technological change. When a forest recreation manpower training program upgrades work skills of labor that would be otherwise unemployed, their on-the-job production of recreation services should be valued at zero added cost to the government.

A study of labor costs at forest recreation sites in Oregon and Washington (Gibbs and Reed) concluded that work time valued on the basis of the compensation received by individuals participating in manpower training programs was nearly one-fourth of the total costs of labor at developed recreation sites. This may somewhat overstate the true social costs. Since labor was in short supply, the social value of the work time of individuals taking part in manpower training programs should have been the difference between the compensation they received for participating in the training program and the income they would have received if they would have worked instead of participating.

Thompson suggests that an added wrinkle is introduced if workers have a preference for one type of work over another — independent of monetary considerations. Opportunity costs depend not just on where the resource is coming from but also where it might go. Opportunity costs would be lower if workers moved to more desirable work than if the same workers moved to less desirable work. For example, workers might prefer being outdoors in forest recreation work rather than in a resort lodge, and thus be indifferent to working at a public campground for $11,500 per year or at a private resort for $12,000 per year. In this case, it would appear to make sense to subtract $500 from the opportunity cost of public campground workers. If, on the other hand, they preferred the inside lodge work to the outside campground work by the same amount, it would seem sensible to add $500 to the opportunity cost of public campground employees. Opportunity cost methods have traditionally neglected the preferences of workers and thus have often overlooked a possibly important welfare effect.

Problems may arise in the long run, if the productivity of labor in recreation does not increase or lags behind productivity in other industries. Productivity is defined as the amount of input required for a given amount of output, and is measured as output per man-hour. Baumol observed that productivity is rising in agriculture, manufacturing, and most other industries. This enables wages in these industries to rise at about the same rate as productivity without increasing prices of the output. However, productivity gains are lower in recreation where personal services and natural environments are necessary inputs. Yet wages in recreation employment rise at about the same rate as in other industries. As a result, labor costs per unit of output will rise in recreation, while they remain constant in other industries. User fees or subsidies will have to increase to pay the higher wage costs in recreation. This is known as "Baumol's Disease." The public will pay higher and higher prices for recreation in the long run unless managers can improve productivity. This is a considerable challenge to the recreation industry and to the leisure arts in general.

Not all variable costs are directly proportional to changes in the number of visits. As buildings and equipment age, maintenance and repair costs rise. This is particularly important in the case of recreation facilities where the preservation of historic buildings can override efficiency goals. Historic buildings may be maintained well beyond a point in time when it would be more economic to replace them. It is not unusual to have higher maintenance and operating costs for equipment and buildings as they get older. Taking a simple arithmetic average of these costs may sometimes overstate the value. This is especially true when there is a sharply increasing pattern in later years. For example, assume that the anticipated maintenance costs of a proposed visitor center are as follows:

Year	Anticipate Maintenance	Year	Anticipate Maintenance
1	0	7	2,000
2	0	8	2,000
3	0	9	3,000
4	0	10	3,000
5	$1,000	Total	$12,000
6	1,000		

Total anticipated maintenance over the 10-year period is $12,000, or an arithmetic average of $1,200 per year. The equivalent annual cost, taking time into account, would be considerably less than the simple arithmetic average because it discounts future payments, giving them less value than the current one. In this case, the present value of the total maintenance cost over the 10-year period would be only $5,574 with a 10 percent discount rate, and the equivalent annual cost becomes $907 per year. Discounting and present value concepts are discussed in Chapter 15.

Operation and maintenance costs cannot be classified as permanently fixed or variable. Any cost can be altered by a decisive manager, or become fixed as the result of failure to act. For example, the park supervisory work force is usually not reduced or increased with fluctuations in the number of visits. However, given a large enough or long enough decrease in number of visits, the supervisory work force may be intentionally reduced. Similarly, the costs of heat and light can be reduced by closing sections of park facilities, such as some toilets or part of the visitor center building. Direct labor is considered a variable cost, however, it becomes temporarily fixed in a situation where a cutback in number of visits owing to adverse weather conditions, cannot be accompanied by a reduction in the direct labor force. When sunny weather returns, a full complement of direct labor will be needed. Also, some costs are partly fixed and partly variable. For example, part of the maintenance costs of a trail may be proportional to its use, whereas certain routine inspection and maintenance costs may continue so long as it is open regardless of the level of use.

The definition of fixed and variable costs depends entirely on the planning horizon, i.e., the time period over which managers make decisions. In the short-run, for example, during a skiing season, some costs are usually fixed while others are variable. In the long-run, all costs are variable since individuals could simply liquidate the resources they use for the recreation enterprise and invest them in some entirely different enterprise. Randall discussed costs in the short-run and long-run. Whether an item of cost is fixed or variable is all a matter of time. If ski resorts have already prepared for opening day by cleaning and repairing equipment and other facilities, the costs of performing those tasks are no longer relevant to any decisions during the operating season. For the rest of the year, the costs of initial cleaning and repairing equipment must be considered fixed. As the season progresses, managers will make many more decisions, one by one. They will decide how much to spend on artificial snow-making, at what time and manner to groom the slopes, and how much to invest in marketing strategies that may increase the total revenue they receive. After each of these various tasks is completed, the expenditures for them must be considered fixed for that operating season. Decisions of managers will be based only on the costs that face them in the future, that is, those costs that are still variable in that operating season.

If they encounter adverse climatic conditions or a sharp fall in the demand for their services, it may become apparent to them that the total revenue they can expect during the entire season will be less than the total costs, fixed plus variable, of operations. However, they will continue to operate as long as the total revenue from current operations seems likely to exceed the current direct costs. At any point in the ski season, they will base operating decisions on total revenue and variable costs. Only if their expected total revenue is so low that they cannot recover daily direct costs will they simply abandon the campaign and close down.

But what about next year's ski season? Before they begin to prepare the ski facility for opening day, they will make their best estimate of the total revenue from the season. They will perform the first task of the new ski season if, and only if, the expected total revenue exceeds its total direct costs. At the very start of the skiing season, all the direct costs of the season are variable. However, they still have some fixed costs; for example, the costs of owning the land, facilities, and equipment. Those costs are fixed, until such time as they seriously consider whether to sell out. If they take a very long view of their decision problem, even the costs of owning the land, facilities, and equipment are variable.

External Costs

The social costs of recreation programs often include external costs, defined as those costs of production that fall on others and for which the agency bears no financial responsibility. These are the uncompensated adverse effects. A recreation program may cause a decrease in the output or additional costs to continue production of livestock grazing or timber production. Also included are increases in the cost of local governmental services directly resulting from the recreation program, and adverse effects on the local economy such as increased transportation costs resulting from road congestion. The recreational agency is not legally required to reimburse those individuals and agencies that bear these external costs. External costs are outside of the financial accounting and decision making framework of the agency whose actions cause them. As a result, the recorded accounting costs of recreation agencies underestimate social costs. The social cost of producing recreation should include all of the consequences of its production. Thus, all external costs should be identified and incorporated into the measurement of total social costs.

Fishing and hunting opportunities are produced by both internal costs of the wildlife agency in each of the states and external costs to individual landowners and other government agencies. The supply cost of big game hunting in a western state, for example, was estimated to include the following internal and external costs per hunter day in 1982:

Internal Cost, State Wildlife Agency	$ 8
External Cost, Federal Feed and Habitat	6
External Cost, Private Feed and Habitat	6
Total Internal and External Costs	$20

Although the responsibility for wildlife management lies with the state, few of the costs of land, food, and habitat are paid by the state. The majority of habitat both in terms of acreage and animal unit months of food consumed is provided by private and federal land. Of the 66 million acres of land in the state, 63 million acres are used by wildlife for feed and habitat. About 60 percent is privately owned compared to about 4 percent owned by the state. Some 36 percent is in federal ownership, nearly all of which is used by big game. More than 80 percent of the food supply for deer and elk is provided by federal land compared to about 20 percent for waterfowl and upland game birds.

In some cases, the development of park and other recreation sites may damage fish and wildlife habitat. For example, a ski resort or reservoir may result in the permanent loss of 200 elk and other wildlife. Also, during construction of facilities, water pollution may damage the fishery. If the developer of the recreation site is a federal agency, mitigation measures must be included in project plans. The Fish and Wildlife Coordination Act (P.L. 85-625) requires the recreation agency to coordinate with the Federal and State Fish and Wildlife agencies in developing programs to reduce external costs. Costs of mitigation measures include: planning and design, construction, construction contingency, administration, relocation, land, water, and mineral rights, operation, maintenance, and replacement. These costs should be based on actual current costs incurred for carrying out these activities for similar projects. For example, a ski resort or reservoir development might include the cost of purchasing a nearby ranch with sufficient habitat to support an additional 200 elk and other wildlife equal to the loss. Providing public access for hunting and fishing could fully compensate for the loss resulting from the ski resort or reservoir development.

In other cases, the development of park and other recreation sites may damage historical and archaeological resources. Access roads, trails, buildings, campsites, and other recreation facilities may be located on sites that have values defined in the Preservation of Historic and Archaeological Data Act (P.L. 93-291). The developer of the recreation site is required to undertake salvage operations to reduce the external costs of damage to these types of resources. These costs should be based on current market prices of salvage operations carried out just prior to or during construction of the recreation facilities.

Another important external cost is congestion. It occurs when individual users of a recreation site encounter increasing numbers of other users. When visitors are few, encountering other people provides a sense of safety, does not interfere appreciably with the quality of the experience, and benefits fall off slowly. Further increases in the number of people in a given space eventually results in crowding, a reduction in the quality of the experience, and benefits decrease more rapidly. This is true of most recreation activities for which data is available (see Chapter 7).

The level of congestion enters individual demand functions like any other nonprice variable decreasing the quality of the recreation experience, and net benefits fall. Individuals tend to ignore the fact that their presence increases congestion and reduces the benefits of other users. This creates a divergence between individual and social costs. As is generally true in cases of external costs, this will eventually result in overuse of the recreation site, reducing aggregate total satisfaction and benefits of the experience below optimum levels.

The development of parks and other recreation sites always affects the level of congestion or crowding of visitors at the sites. A number of studies have shown that size of a park, lake, or other recreation facility is an important determinant of demand. Thus, to a considerable extent, managers and planners determine the number of recreation users on peak days when they decide what size of recreation facilities to develop. When evaluating alternative size of parks and other recreation sites, the costs of congestion are equal to the loss in recreation user benefits with additional use.

As long as the gains from additional users exceed the losses due to congestion, aggregate total benefits increase. Beyond some point, the loss in benefits resulting from congestion exceed the gains experienced by additional users, and aggregate total benefits fall. Aggregate total benefits of a recreation site are maximized where the loss in benefits from incremental congestion equals the gain in benefits from incremental use. If there were no other effects of congestion, the recommended carrying capacity of facilities would be at this level. With the introduction of the costs of recreation use management and environmental degradation, the recommended carrying capacity would fall to a point where marginal benefits would equal marginal costs.

Congestion at an existing recreation site is an important consideration when estimating the external benefits of new or expanded sites.
Introducing new capacity may reduce the use of existing sites nearby.
If these other sites are heavily used and congestion is reduced by the
opening of the new site, the increase in willingness of users of those
sites to pay resulting from the reduction in congestion to optimum
levels should be considered a benefit of the new or expanded site.
However, sometimes a new or expanded site may increase congestion
of facilities such as roads, restaurants, shops, and motels. This increase in congestion of neighboring facilities may be a cost or a benefit.

Associated Costs

The social cost of parks and other recreation programs also includes
the associated cost of users. Associated costs are defined as the costs
of goods and services, in addition to agency project costs, needed to
make the recreation activity available. These are the costs which must
be incurred before consumer benefits can be realized from the project.
The associated costs of using recreation sites include the added costs
of food, transportation, and lodging at or near the recreation site that
would not otherwise have been incurred. In addition, uses of recreation sites may incur time costs of traveling to and from the sites and
while engaged in on-site recreation activities. Some users would be
willing to pay to avoid the travel time and some would forego opportunities to earn income if they were not occupied in recreation pursuits. Both may be considered associated costs. Also, to become recreation participants, consumers must obtain the minimum amount of
equipment necessary, either through rental or purchase. When the
agency or a concessioner supplies recreation equipment, the consumer
has the option of rental which would be an associated cost.

There are two approaches to the treatment of associated costs. Some
observers have noted that the associated cost of recreation users already have been subtracted from total benefit to obtain an estimate of
net benefit for purposes of benefit cost studies of the recreation programs of public agencies (as illustrated in Chapter 5 and 15). Thus,
they argue that associated costs have been accounted for in the benefit
estimate and need not be reintroduced in the estimation of cost. This
would be an acceptable procedure when savings in associated user
costs of visiting a new recreation site are considered benefits of the
project. For example, if one proposed site is located nearer its user
clientele than an alternative site, decreased travel costs will accrue as
benefits of the nearer site. When users save travel time, the value of
time saved is another measure of benefits. If travel time of a successful fishing trip formerly taking 12 hours can be compressed into 10
hours without loss of fishing success, then savings in income foregone

are additional benefits. As a result, the net benefits of recreation sites located closer to where users live should have higher net benefits, all else equal, than sites located more distant (Mishan).

Others have noted that the associated costs of recreation users are often ignored in benefit estimation. This would occur whenever estimates of net benefits per recreation visitor day do not take into account effects of the location of recreation sites. In this event, it would be appropriate to estimate the associated cost of users and include it in total social costs of sites. This would be especially important when decisions are being made about the location of sites. The reason is that the minimum cost facility based solely on agency costs will not be the same location and size as the minimum cost facility based on total social cost, including the associated cost of users.

Figure 13-4 illustrates two average and marginal cost curves for a recreation site, one with associated costs and one without. Note that the usual cost curves for recreation sites are lower and to the right of cost curves which include associated costs. It is generally true that when only the internal production costs of recreation agencies are included, minimum costs will be lower at larger outputs. As a result, it appears efficient for recreation sites to be of larger size and, for any given density of population, located further away from where users live. The appearance is deceiving. The transportation economic literature has shown that the minimum cost location and size of recreation sites is really a function of optimizing the sum of agency costs and associated user costs. This means that the correct social cost curves for recreation sites are higher and to the left of where they are usually drawn. As a result, it is more efficient for recreation sites to be small and, for any given density of population, located closer to where users live. Schumacher popularized this solution in his book, *Small Is Beautiful.*

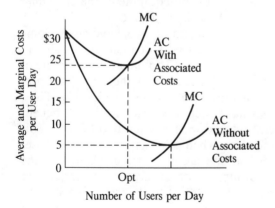

Figure 13-4. Average and Marginal Cost Curves for a Recreation Site With and Without Associated User Costs
Source: Adapted from Fischer.

420

Figure 13-5 illustrates the advantage of locating recreation sites closer to users. Consider a public recreation beach on a lake or ocean where bathers are uniformly distributed along the shore. Hotelling suggested that two private ice cream vendors on the beach would locate their stands back to back in the center of the beach. This way the two vendors could share the market equally without colluding. The two vendors supply identical quality and variety of flavors. So bathers view the situation as equivalent to being served by a single vendor. The horizontal axis of the left panel illustrates the location of vendors A and B in the center and the distance from each to the outer limits of the beach or the maximum distance walked to purchase an ice cream cone. The vertical axis represents the associated cost of increasing time and effort walking to a vendor's stand plus the price of the cone.

Now assume that some beach users approach the manager of the public beach, and suggest that the ice cream vendors be asked to relocate at the quartiles in order to minimize the distance walked to purchase a cone. The lower panel on the right of Figure 13-5 illustrates the proposed relocation. If all beach users purchase the same number of cones, the shaded area represents the benefits from reduced walking time of most bathers and the dotted area is the increase in distance walked by some bathers in the center of the beach. The efficient recreation economic decision is clear. The reduced costs of locating suppliers of recreation goods and services convenient to most users exceed the added costs by four times. This problem is simplified to illustrate the principle involved. In reality, of course, bathers close to the vendors would be expected to buy a greater quantity than those further away due to differences in the walking distance. Also, the density of the population of beach users would not be uniform, as larger families with children may tend to locate nearer to the vendors for convenience of access to its goodies. This would reduce the advantage of relocating vendors closer to users somewhat.

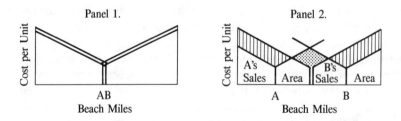

Figure 13-5. Associated User Costs and Location of Ice Cream Vendors on a Beach
Source: Reekie and Crook, adapted from Hotelling.

SOURCES OF COST INFORMATION

Several methods have been used to measure the costs of developing and operating parks and other recreation sites. These include the following: (1) engineering economic estimates of the optimum combination of inputs to produce a range of output levels; (2) cross-sectional comparison of the costs of several existing facilities with varying output levels at one point in time; and (3) time-series observations of costs for varying output levels of a single recreation site over a period of time. While each of these methods has provided satisfactory estimates of costs under particular circumstances, each also has its drawbacks. In this section, we will discuss the problems of each approach and demonstrate under what conditions they can be used successfully. Later in this chapter, we will illustrate the two principle methods of cost analysis and show how to apply them to recreation economic decisions. Accuracy of the alternative methods is a continuing problem, although considerable progress is evident in recent years.

Engineering Economic Method

The engineering economic approach probably comes closest to the least-cost combination of inputs expressed in economic cost functions. Conditions that affect costs, such as the quality of management and age of facilities, can be held constant to show the separable effects of size or capacity, rate of capacity utilization, changes in technology, and the quality of services provided. Variations in accounting procedures and the price of inputs can distort the results of cross-sectional and time-series studies. Both methods rely on current or historic accounting records of costs. These need adjusting to be relevant to recreation economic decisions about future operations. The engineering economic approach avoids these drawbacks and can be used to make reasonably accurate estimates of future costs. Also, its results can be compared to information on the costs of actual park operations to reveal the efficiency gap between what is and what could be.

The engineering economic method is based on the physical relationships expressed in the production function. Costs represent engineering estimates of the optimum combination of inputs to produce a range of output levels, with each input multiplied by its cost or price per unit and the results summed for each output level. The technique is discussed in the federal guidelines as cost estimating from engineering economic, synthetic, or budgeted data. The method is particularly useful for estimating costs for new parks or recreation facilities where the historical data necessary for statistical cost analysis are unavailable. The technique, in all of its forms, assumes that the relationship between the inputs and outputs will remain sufficiently stable so that inserting expected changes in their values into the cost function will accurately predict future costs.

Anyone can apply the engineering economic method with little or no training in economics and statistics. The first step is to interview three to nine engineers with construction companies and equipment suppliers who have been involved in planning recreation facilities near the study area. Engineering estimates of facility construction costs may be available to recreation managers from recent contract construction bids or from the record of construction costs for similar facilities. Interviewing three to nine engineers with experience in the planning and construction of recreation facilities in the study area helps avoid the possible bias or adverse experience of a single engineering company.

Each engineer should be asked to estimate the costs of equipment and construction for a range of small, medium, and large facilities of uniform design and specification. The design can be based on the latest available technology for recreation facility construction and operation. Physical conditions, such as location, elevation, topography, and soil type, should be specified. The expected rate of capacity utilization should be determined in order to estimate the labor required for operation and maintenance. Costs of labor and material costs are usually available for local markets. Alternatively, the cost of labor and materials for operation and maintenance can be estimated from a cross-sectional study of several existing recreation facilities or from the operation of a similar recreation facility over a period of time.

This approach is not without problems. Economists and statisticians have raised a number of questions about applications of the method. First, the small size of the sample and its lack of randomness, which are characteristic of the approach, prevent application of the usual statistical tests of the reliability of the estimates. As a result, some observers recommend use of the cross-sectional or time-series method with a random sample of 30 or more observations, which facilitates statistical tests of reliability. However, reliability can be tested by replication (repeating the study under similar conditions and comparing the results). Second, inaccurate cost estimates may result in extending the engineering cost functions beyond the range in size of existing facilities, or in going from small experimental to full-scale operations.

These problems are not common to recreation applications. Proposed projects and programs are usually within the range of size and type of existing facilities elsewhere in the United States. The engineering economic method can provide a useful alternative to statistical cost estimation. The technique comes the closest of any of the estimation procedures to reflecting the theoretical cost function. It abstracts from all of the complications of existing operations in favor of engineering estimates of the required quantities of various inputs and current price quotations from suppliers.

Cross-Sectional Method

The cross-sectional approach is used by public agencies to compare the operating costs of existing parks and other recreation areas. It is also used by trade associations of private recreation companies. For example, the national ski area operators association compares the average costs of small-, medium-, and large-size ski sites each year. With available computer software, it is possible to develop statistical functions showing the relationship between costs and a set of independent variables determining costs. A multiple regression can show the effect of recreation output, input prices, facility capacity, level of service, quality of natural resources, weather conditions, and the like. Multiple regression can account for the effect on costs of factors other than level of output.

This method is based on the accounting records of public agencies and private companies. The method relies on costs that have actually occurred in the past. Usually a sample of 30 or more similar recreation sites are selected to represent small-, medium-, and large-size operations. Cost-accounting data is classified into categories of fixed, variable, and semivariable costs. From this basic data, statistical cost functions are estimated usually with little attention to variation in the price of inputs or other conditions that may affect costs. Because the empirical cost curve is an average of past relationships, it is not an exact replica of the theoretical cost curves discussed in economics.

Problems arise when input prices vary in different recreation areas and regions of the nation. Labor and fuel costs, for example, should be adjusted using the U.S. Department of Commerce index of input prices and wage rates in the various states. A second problem can be traced to variations in accounting procedures. This is less likely to be a problem in comparing sites managed by a single recreation agency, such as the U.S. Forest Service, with uniform accounting practices. However, differing depreciation schedules among private ski site operators and varying techniques for amortizing major expenses, such as development costs, can substantially distort the true cost-output relationship. A similar distortion can arise if the recreation sites that are compared use different means of paying for land, labor, or capital.

Finally, a basic assumption of the cross-sectional method is that all recreation sites are operating at points along the long-run cost curve at which costs are minimized. That is, the cross-sectional technique assumes that all recreation areas are operating in an efficient manner and are using the latest technology available, whatever their output. If this assumption is violated, the regression line will lie above the true long-run average cost curve, and recreation costs will be overstated. Moreover, it is possible that the true curvature in the long-run cost curve may be accentuated and thereby overstate any economies or diseconomies of scale available to recreation areas. For example, if more of the smaller recreation areas are operating well below their optimum output, the estimated long-run average cost curve will have a downward slope much steeper than the true long-run average cost curve, and this will lead to an overestimation of economies of scale in recreation facilities and parks. It is possible to overcome this problem by including both capacity and output as independent variables in the cost function. Then the long-run average cost curve can be estimated for the optimum output of each site.

Time-Series Method

The time-series method is based on observations of the costs of a single park or other recreation site for a relatively short period of time. Although the best length of time will vary from situation to situation, 1 month is the period most frequently used. In other words, the various costs incurred during each month are collected and related to the number of visits during the month. A total period of perhaps 30 months can provide enough observations for statistical analysis, yet still be short enough that the recreation activities provided have remained relatively unchanged.

This approach is the most popular method used to estimate the short-run cost functions for private recreation companies. Variable costs are regressed on output, in a cost function that typically includes a number of other variables affecting cost, such as wage rates, material prices, weather, fuel costs, input quality, and so on. Including these variables in the model allows us to isolate their effects and obtain a better estimate of the relationship between variable costs and output. The time-series method uses recorded historical data, and during most of the period for which data is available, the costs of labor, raw materials, and other items may have been rising. To remove this bias, historic data is deflated for price level changes. Time-series are usually applied to variable costs rather than fixed costs. This has the advantage of avoiding the difficult problem of allocating fixed costs to a particular recreation activity. Moreover, it is a relatively simple matter to add alternative estimates of fixed costs to the basic variable cost function.

Problems may arise when an increase in the number of visits during one time period causes additional maintenance expenses not in that period but, rather, in subsequent periods. During a period of high production, actual maintenance expenditures will be unusually low because the recreation facilities are being used at full capacity, so that maintenance must be postponed when possible. Repairs that are made will usually be temporary in nature, aimed at getting the facilities back into operation rapidly until a period when some slack exists in the number of visits. Without careful adjustment, this problem can cause errors in statistically estimated cost functions from time-series data.

Another problem is that accounting data usually fail to record opportunity costs, which are frequently the largest and the most important costs in short-run decisions. Because managerial decisions pertain to future operations, the relevant costs are future costs as opposed to current or historical costs found in accounting records. Accounting costs usually should be modified to reflect likely changes before they are used for making important decisions about future operations.

The three approaches discussed in this section should not be regarded as mutually exclusive or even competitive in all cases, but rather as generally complementary to one another. As always, the emphasis placed on any one method depends on the purpose of the study, that is, determining what management really needs and wants, as well as the time and expense involved, considering the availability of data.

SOME COST STUDIES

In the past, most cost studies by state and federal agencies were cross-sectional. Their objective was to provide summaries of the average costs of recreation programs of an agency for one point in time. During the 1970s, considerable progress was made in improving the traditional public cost-accounting procedures so that they would show the operating costs associated with each major type of recreation activity. Historical line item accounting practices show types of expenses, such as total agency or park labor, materials, maintenance and repair, and contract services. Functional accounting practices are an improvement over line item accounting, in that they show expenses by type of program. Typically, these include total agency or park fire control, safety, conservation, visitor interpretation, recreation services, and the like. Unfortunately, neither line item nor functional accounting reveals the costs allocated to each recreation activity, nor how costs vary with changes in design, size, utilization of capacity, or level of services provided. More recently, several cost studies have attempted to remedy these deficiencies in the available cost information.

This section presents examples of the many average cost studies by state and federal agencies during the 1970s. Also, we will examine the few studies that have developed cost functions or supply curves. These studies are particularly useful in recreation economic decision making, for they show how future costs are expected to change with alternative levels of program or budget.

Average Costs per User Day

An interesting example of the cross-sectional method is a study of the average costs of recreation activities at state parks in Pennsylvania by Strauss. Table 13-1 shows the average costs statewide for 17 recrea-

Table 13-1. Average Annual Operating and Maintenance Costs per Recreation Activity Day, Pennsylvania State Parks

Recreation Activity	Percent of Annual Operations and Maintenance Costs	Percent of Annual Activity Days	Costs per Activity Day
Tent and Trailer Camping	21.8	6.7	$1.30
Group Tent Camping	2.4	0.3	2.71
Group Camping	2.4	0.5	1.87
Primitive Cabin	3.6	0.5	2.77
Swimming, Beach	13.2	16.7	0.32
Swimming, Pool	4.7	3.4	0.56
Picnicking	22.2	38.3	0.23
Boating	7.8	6.7	0.47
Fishing	7.4	11.8	0.25
Environmental Education	4.6	4.9	0.38
Hiking	3.6	8.6	0.17
Hunting	1.7	1.0	0.66
Pleasure Driving			0.07
Ice Sports	0.9	0.2	
Snowmobiling	0.7	0.1	2.16
Sledding	0.2	1.1	
Skiing	2.7	1.1	

Source: Strauss.

tion activities. Included are the costs in 110 parks for direct and indirect labor, allocated on a time basis, and contract services for operation, maintenance, and minor development. These costs represent the essential variable costs of park operations. Strauss purposely omitted fixed costs in the belief that they might be used as a convenient catchall for many park expenditures, resulting in an inaccurate allocation of total costs. Note that output is measured in activity days of service, which represent use by one person for any portion of a given day.

The preliminary results of the study show that average variable costs range from 7 cents per activity day of pleasure driving to $2.77 for lodging in primitive cabins. Picnicking was the most popular activity in the state parks with average costs of 23 cents per day, followed by beach swimming, 32 cents; fishing, 25 cents; hiking, 17 cents; and tent and trailer camping, $1.30. The average costs for all recreation use of the state parks were not reported but appear to have been less than 50 cents per day at the time of the study, 1974. These costs have increased substantially to the present time; however, the relationships would probably remain much the same. You can estimate how much these costs have increased by referring to a later section of this Chapter for changes in the general price level.

A number of studies have attempted to calculate the average fixed costs as well as the variable costs of recreation activities. Table 13-2 shows average fixed and variable costs for several recreation activities in two regions of the U.S. Forest Service. Variable costs include operation and maintenance, similar to the Pennsylvania state parks

Table 13-2. Average Annual Fixed and Variable Costs of Recreation Activities on the National Forests

| | Costs per Recreation Visitor Day | | |
Region and Activity	Variable Costs	Fixed Costs	Total Costs
Northern Rocky Mountain Region			
Camping, Total	$0.66	$1.08	$1.74
Wilderness	0.14	0.14	0.28
Semiprimitive Motorized	0.79	0.86	1.65
Roaded Natural	0.68	1.05	1.73
Semiurban	0.59	1.27	1.86
Picnicking	1.11	1.80	2.91
Boating	0.76	2.29	3.05
Swimming	0.73	1.57	2.30
Interpretation, Minor	0.15	1.31	1.46
Observation	0.48	0.82	1.30
Southern Region			
Camping	0.74	0.54	1.28
Picnicking	1.31	0.83	2.14
Boating	2.11	1.26	3.37
Swimming	2.50	1.76	4.26
Observation	1.04	0.58	1.62

Source: Tyre; Gibbs and Reed; Gibbs and van Hees.

study. Because output is measured in 12-hour recreation visitor days (RVDs), the variable cost results are not directly comparable to the state data. For example, it would take nearly two RVDs to equal one activity day of camping. This means that the variable costs of camping in the northern Rocky Mountains reported as 66 cents per RVD should be doubled to $1.32 per activity day. This compares favorably with the state data for camping of $1.30 per activity day. In the case of picnicking, nearly four activity days are required to equal one 12-hour RVD. This means that variable costs of picnicking in the northern Rocky Mountains reported as $1.11 per RVD should be divided by four to equal about 28 cents per activity day. This compares favorably with the state data for picnicking of 23 cents per activity day.

Fixed costs include the opportunity cost of timber, overhead, and the amortized construction costs of facilities at replacement cost. As you can see by reading down the fixed cost column of Table 13-2, if we have to replace all of our capital investment in outdoor recreation facilities on federal land, costs would increase by a substantial amount. For example, in the case of camping in the northern Rocky Moutains, fixed costs would be $1.08 per RVD and would account for nearly two-thirds of total camping costs of $1.74 per RVD with all new facilities. Including fixed costs does illustrate the magnitude of the long-run costs when new facilities are added as demand increases in future years.

Incremental Cost Functions

The best example of an application of the engineering economic method is a study of pleasure boat marinas on the Chesapeake Bay, Maryland, by Lyon, et al. It shows costs for marinas with capacities of 50, 100, 150, 200, and 300 boats, and costs for rates of utilization from 50 to 100 percent of capacity. The marinas are standardized in all respects except size. Each provides the same services — dock rental, fuel, showers, rest rooms, and hookups for electricity and drinking water. The study excludes the maintenance and repair of boats, dry storage, hauling and launching services, restaurant operations, and boat sales.

Information on necessary investment costs was obtained from marina engineering and construction firms based on uniform specifications of materials used in the construction of piers, docks, electrical systems, water systems, and buildings for the office, equipment, showers, and rest rooms. Commercial companies serving marinas provided information on the prices of necessary marina equipment, materials, and insurance. Public utilities in the area provided information on electricity, natural gas, water, and sewage rate schedules and use by marinas. A survey of the operating costs of 17 marinas provided information on average wages and miscellaneous expenses. See the footnotes to Table 13-3 for additional information.

The first marina in Maryland was developed in 1696. From this early beginning, marinas increased to 25 in 1920 and 78 in 1940. Most of the 308 marinas in Maryland at the time of the study (1965) were small, with an average capacity of 64 boats. Pleasure boating on the Chesapeake Bay occurred during a 6-month period between May 1 and November 1. Most boats were stored at marinas during winter months, so marina utilization was year round. Annual marina charges averaged $167 per boat. Marinas were operating at nearly 90 percent of capacity and, with rapid increases in the demand for marina services, operators reported they would need 30 percent more capacity in the next 5 years. Thus, the problem was to estimate the effect on costs of changes in the utilization and size of marinas.

Table 13-3 shows the effect of size on average annual fixed and variable costs per boat. Note that the data are for 100 percent capacity operation. Fixed costs fall continuously from $126 for marinas with 50-boat capacity to $85 for 200 boats. Variable costs fall from $86 for marinas with 50-boat capacity to $53 for 150 boats and then rise to $62 for 200 boats. Total costs, which are the sum of fixed and variable costs, fall from $212 for marinas with 50-boat capacity to $142 for 150 boats and then rise to $147 for 200 boats. The authors also included costs for a 300-boat marina, which are omitted here to simplify the example without changing the results.

Table 13-4 shows the effect on costs of rate of capacity utilization. Average total costs increase sharply as utilization of capacity falls

Table 13-3. Effect of Size on Average Annual Fixed and Variable Costs per Boat for Recreation Marinas, Chesapeake Bay, Maryland

Costs per Boat	Marina Size, Number of Boats at Capacity			
	50	100	150	200
Fixed Costs				
Buildings[a]	$ 5.37	$ 3.07	$ 2.34	$ 1.98
Piers[a]	26.22	19.85	19.78	19.75
Bulkheading[a]	12.31	7.47	6.29	5.11
Equipment[a]	12.17	6.26	4.67	4.97
Water System[a]	1.46	1.36	1.35	1.32
Electrical System[a]	3.15	2.87	2.90	2.75
Taxes[b]	9.58	8.09	7.91	7.85
Insurance	8.31	5.99	5.52	5.13
Maintenance[c]	2.91	2.16	2.04	2.03
Interest[d]	43.97	36.38	35.20	34.40
Subtotal	126	94	88	85
Variable Costs				
Labor[e]	61.75	42.30	31.84	41.37
Electricity[f]	14.40	12.64	11.54	10.75
Water-Sewer[f]	1.04	0.59	0.58	0.53
Telephone[g]	4.50	4.50	4.50	4.50
Fuel for Heat[h]	2.43	1.33	0.98	0.80
Miscellaneous[i]	3.03	3.27	4.22	3.83
Subtotal	86	64	53	62
Total Costs	$212	$158	$142	$147

[a]Depreciation was calculated by the straight line method, assuming a 20-year life for buildings, piers, and bulkhead, 10 years for the water and electrical systems, and 5 years for equipment.
[b]Average tax of $9.58 per $1,000 of investment for the 50-slip marina, declining $0.0073 per slip for the larger size marinas.
[c]Maintenance at 5 percent of investment.
[d]Interest at 5 percent of one-half of facilities investment and all of land investment.
[e]Labor based on survey of 17 marinas at $1.62 per hour. Manager salary was omitted as a cost because managers are assumed to receive a share of profits.
[f]Public utility services for electricity, fresh water, and sewage were available to marinas.
[g]Based on average telephone costs of 17 marinas adjusted for marina size.
[h]Based on average heat costs of 17 marinas adjusted for building volume.
[i]Includes office supplies, toilet supplies, laundry, rags, legal fees, and other minor supplies.
Source: Lyon, et al.

Table 13-4. Effect of the Rate of Capacity Utilization on Average Total Costs for Recreation Boating Marinas, Chesapeake Bay, Maryland

Marina Size	Percent of Capacity Utilization					
	50	60	70	80	90	100
50 Boats						
Number of Slips Rented	25	30	35	40	45	50
Average Cost	$338	$296	$266	$244	$227	$212
100 Boats						
Number of Slips Rented	50	60	70	80	90	100
Average Cost	$252	$220	$198	$182	$169	$158
150 Boats						
Number of Slips Rented	75	90	105	120	135	150
Average Cost	$230	$200	$179	$164	$151	$142
200 Boats						
Number of Slips Rented	100	120	140	160	180	200
Average Cost	$232	$204	$184	$168	$157	$147

430

from 100 percent to 50 percent. For example, costs of the 150-boat marina rise from $142 at 100 percent capacity utilization to $230 at 50 percent, or by 62 percent. You can verify this result by multiplying average fixed costs of $88 by 150 boats (= $13,200), dividing by 75 boats (= $176), and adding variable costs of $53 which vary directly with output and do not change (= $230, rounded). Similar procedures were used to estimate the effect on costs of rate of capacity utilization for each marina.

Figure 13-6 illustrates the relationship between marina size and rate of capacity utilization. The short-run average cost curves are formed by varying the utilization of marinas from 50 to 100 percent of capacity. Costs decline sharply over this range. The long-run average cost function represents the effect of varying the size of marinas from 50 to 200 boats. Drawing a line through the minimum cost points of the short-run average cost curves for each marina provides a close approximation of the long-run average cost curve for the marina industry.

The long-run average cost curve is characterized by three distinct phases — decreasing, constant, and increasing costs. The initial phase of the curve shows decreasing costs resulting from more efficient use of capital equipment as size of the enterprise increases. Also, expansion allows more labor specialization, which increases labor efficiency and reduces average costs. Constant costs along the horizontal segment of the curve indicate that costs cannot be decreased through improved management organization or techniques of operation to reduce material inputs. The final phase of the curve shows increasing costs, which result from decreases in labor efficiency as employees are required to walk greater distances to perform their work in large marinas. Marinas extend their operations either along the waterfront or perpendicular to the waterfront. In either case, expansion adds to the distance that personnel cover when going back and forth between their

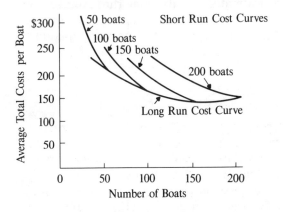

Figure 13-6. Short Run and Long Run Average Cost Curves for Recreation Boat Marinas, Chesapeake Bay, Maryland

central station and the boat docks, resulting in additional labor costs per boat.

Engineering economic cost information can help managers make several important recreation economic decisions. For example, what dock rental fee would be required to cover the total costs of a small 50-boat marina? Table 13-3 shows that a fee of $212 per boat would cover total costs, which is considerably more than the average fee of $167 at the time of the study. What is the minimum fee required to cover the total costs of a large 200-boat marina? With 200 boats, a fee of $147 would cover total costs, which is $20 below the average fee at the time of the study. If rate of capacity utilization fell to 80 percent, what is the minimum fee necessary to cover the total costs of the large marina? According to Table 13-4, $168 would be required. If utilization of capacity of the large marina fell to 50 percent, a fee of $232 would be required to cover total costs, which exceeds the fee required to cover the total costs of the small marina operated at 100 percent of capacity. At what price would small and large marinas shut down? Small marinas would shut down at a price of $85 per boat and large marinas at a price of $61 when they could no longer recover average variable costs.

What is the optimum or most efficient number of boat docks (usually termed "slips" in marina terminology) per marina in the long run? Optimum size occurs at the minimum of the long-run average total cost curve. A 150-boat marina has average total costs of $142, the lowest of the four marinas shown. However, Figure 13-6 suggests that the lowest cost marina may be somewhat larger, as the following discussion demonstrates.

Many managers of private and public recreation resources are developing computerized management information systems. To illustrate the possible use of engineering economic data in statistical cost analysis, seven points were estimated on the long-run average cost function shown in Table 13-3 and Figure 13-6. Ordinary least-squares regression procedures were used to estimate the following quadratic average cost curve

$$AC = a - bQ + cQ^2$$

$$AC = 290.25 - 1.85Q + 0.0057Q^2 \qquad F = 235.5 \quad R^2 = .98$$
$$(7.46) \quad (0.13) \quad (0.0005) \qquad \text{Cases} = 7$$

where AC refers to average costs per boat; Q is the size of marinas or the quantity of boats at capacity; and a, b, and c are the regression coefficients determined by the statistical analysis. Standard errors are shown in parenthesis and indicate that all coefficients are highly significant. A comparison of the actual and statistical (in parentheses) estimates of average costs for 50 boats were $212 ($212); for 100 boats, $158 ($162); for 150 boats, $142 ($141); and 200 boats, $147 ($148). This represents a close relationship. Note that the quadratic form includes both a linear and a squared term for the size of marina. Figure 13-7 depicts the average, total, and marginal costs per boat for recreation marinas in the long run. The curves were all plotted from the regression results for average costs.

The quadratic form is widely used in empirical cost studies, because it is a relatively simple matter to derive the cubic total cost function once a quadratic average cost function is known. The cubic total cost (TC) function becomes

$$TC = aQ - bQ^2 + cQ^3$$
$$TC = 290.25Q - 1.85Q^2 + 0.0057Q^3$$

The total cost curve shows that the first dollars spent on providing boat marina services produce a large output of boating opportunities. However, as more and more dollars are spent, less additional output is produced by each additional dollar, i.e., increasing marginal costs. The marginal cost function can be easily derived from a quadratic average cost function. The marginal cost (MC) function becomes

$$MC = a - 2bQ + 3cQ^2$$

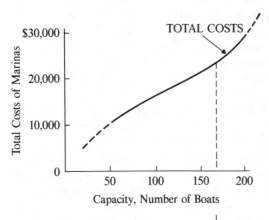

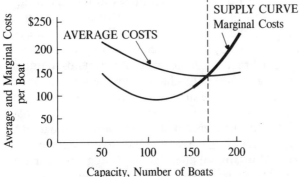

Figure 13-7. Total, Average, and Marginal Costs per Boat at Recreation Marinas, Chesapeake Bay, Maryland

433

$$MC = 290.25 - 3.7Q + 0.0171Q^2$$

The marginal cost curve represents the long-run supply curve for boat marinas, as indicated by the darkened portion of the curve. Finally, the optimum size of marinas can be precisely estimated as the least-cost point on the average cost curve. Optimum size (OPT) becomes

OPT = b/2c

OPT = 1.85/0.0114

OPT = 162.3

The optimum size marina is estimated at about 162 boats, which is a more precise estimate than the 150 boats based on engineering economic budgets for the four marinas. Optimum size occurs at the lowest point on the long-run average total cost curve where marginal cost is equal to average cost.

Cross-Sectional Cost Functions

Managers also can use cross-sectional data in statistical cost analysis. The necessary information is readily available to anyone who is interested. Often, all that is required is information from a sample of sites operated by public agencies in the state where you live. Recall from the discussion in an earlier section of this chapter that the approach is based on accounting records for a cross section of sites operating in a representative year. All that is required is a sample of 30 or more similar recreation sites. With available computer software, it is possible to develop statistical functions showing the relationship between costs and the independent variables determining costs. A multiple regression can show the effects on costs of level of technology or development, size or capacity, rate of utilization of capacity, and other variables. The regression coefficient for each independent variable indicates the marginal relationship between that variable and cost, holding constant the effect of all other variables in the function.

The purpose of this section is to show the effect of a reduction in campground services. This is the typical case when budgets for operation and maintenance are sharply reduced. Figure 13-8 shows empirical-based shifts in average variable cost (AVC) and marginal cost (MC) curves for campgrounds with changes in the level of management service. This illustrates a possible application of the computerized information system of the U.S. Forest Service. The cross-sectional data are from the Recreation Information Management (RIM) system for campgrounds in the Arapaho and Roosevelt National Forests in the Rocky Mountains of the U.S. By using data for one region from a single agency, it is possible to avoid several potential problems of cross-sectional analysis.

First, the variable costs reported in RIM appear to be reasonably complete. In this study, AVC includes unadjusted RIM data for opera-

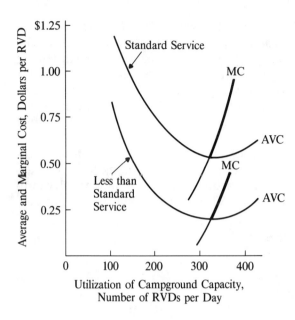

Figure 13-8. Shifts in the Short Run Costs of Campgrounds in the Arapahoe and Roosevelt National Forests, Colorado, 1980

tion, maintenance, roads, trails, and administration of the campgrounds. The agency's accounts include the cost of cleaning, contact with visitors, collection of fees, law enforcement, vandalism, utilities, and materials to operate the campgrounds and to make repairs necessary to maintain standard service. Not included in the agency's accounts are the external costs of unpaid labor such as volunteers, fire control, and other offsite costs. Omitting them here does not preclude meaningful analysis as will be demonstrated below.

Second, the variable costs reported in RIM appear to be uniform. The prices of inputs such as labor, fuel, and repairs are generally the same across the sample of campgrounds. We can test for the possibility that campgrounds located at a greater distance from the headquarters of the forests and at higher elevations may have higher prices of inputs than those more favorably located. We simply include them as independent variables in the cost function. In this case, variables measuring location or distance, elevation above sea level, and quality of the access road are not statistically significant. Therefore, they are omitted from the final cost function. The reason is a lack of sufficient variation among the study sites. We conclude that the prices of inputs are generally uniform.

Third, several important problems of cross-sectional analysis can be avoided in selecting the sample. The possible effect of environmental quality, in particular, the location of campgrounds along the shore of a river or lake, is controlled by excluding the few sites otherwise located. Also, the sample is limited to the agency's Roaded Natural (class 3) campgrounds. This means that capital improvements at all of the sites are rustic, being constructed of native materials. Facilities are designed to protect environmental quality and to provide comfort for users. Visitor information services are informal. Access is by gravel or hard surface roads. As a result of these two adjustments, the sample is limited to 47 of the 58 campgrounds located in the two national forests.

Fourth, there is sufficient variation in output that the effects of capacity and its utilization can be estimated by including them as independent variables in the cost function. Output of individual campgrounds varies from a low of 5 RVDs to nearly 900 RVDs per day. The size distribution is:

Number of Campsites	Number of Campgrounds
Less than 10	15
10-19	17
20-29	5
30-39	4
40 and Over	6

The average campground is small with 22.8 campsites and capacity of 228 RVDs at one time (i.e., 10 RVDs per campsite). Overall, 14.4 campsites are occupied per day which represents 63.2 percent utilization of capacity during the 142-day summer season. This is reasonably efficient, given the peak use on weekends, holidays, and during the months of July and August.

Fifth, there is sufficient variation in the quality of service so that its effects can be estimated by including it as an independent variable in the cost function. The sample includes 21 campgrounds with standard service and 26 without. The categorical variable is set equal to 1 if standard services are provided and equal to 0 if less than standard services are provided. The campground service variable is specified as the attractiveness of a recreation site in terms of management service level including capital improvements. Standard service is defined to include the availability of drinking water, toilets, tables, fireplaces, trash removal, tent pads, parking spaces, and access roads to develop campgrounds where fees are charged. Less than standard service omits drinking water, with other services at minimal levels. No camping fees are charged at less than standard service campgrounds.

Finally, one problem that could not be avoided is the possibility that some or all of the sites are not operating efficiently. For example, they may be using more than the optimum combination of resources. If this is the case, the regression line for existing campgrounds will lie above the potential efficient cost curve. Recreation costs will be overstated. This is an inherent limitation of the cross-sectional approach.

436

However, violation of the assumption of optimum combination of resources does not preclude meaningful analysis. When the purpose of the study is to describe or predict the actual behavior of managers, we should use the accounting information that managers actually use.

Once the information is prepared and put into the computer, software packages are available to automatically perform the analysis. Following the usual procedure in recreation cost analysis, we use the ordinary least squares statistical method to estimate the relationship of costs to output and other important variables including size and services provided. The average cost function is:

$$AVC = a - bQ + cQ^2 + dS - eS^2 + fM$$

$$AVC = 0.6666 - 0.0843Q + 0.00013Q^2 + 0.0322S$$
$$\qquad (0.1419) \quad (0.0226) \quad\;\; (0.00002) \quad\;\;\; (0.0126)$$
$$\quad - 0.000015S^2 + 0.3471M$$
$$\qquad (0.000007) \quad\;\; (0.2135) \qquad\qquad R^2 = 0.60 \quad F = 14.98$$

where AVC refer to average variable costs per RVD; Q is utilization of capacity in RVDs per day; S is size or capacity in RVDs per day; M is a categorical variable for standard service of management; and a, b, c, e, and f are the regression coefficients determined by the statistical analysis. Note that the quadratic form of the equation includes both a linear and a squared term for the rate of utilization and capacity of the campgrounds. It provided the best fit of the actual data points.

The coefficient of determination, R^2, adjusted for degrees of freedom, indicates that 60 percent of the total variation in costs is explained by the variables included in the function, which is considered a satisfactory level of explanation for cross-sectional data from operating sites. The number of observations, 47, is sufficient for statistically significant analysis. The overall equation is significant at the 0.01 level, as indicated by an F value of 14.98. Furthermore, the regression coefficients for each independent variable are highly significant. The numbers in parentheses below each regression coefficient represent standard errors of the coefficients. The regression coefficients included in the equation are significantly different from zero at the 0.01 level except for capacity squared at the 0.06 level and standard service at the 0.11 level. That is, we can reject at the 99 percent confidence level the hypothesis that the independent variables are unrelated to cost, except capacity squared at the 94 percent confidence level and standard service at the 88 percent confidence level. This is an acceptable level of significance.

The cost curves shown in Figure 13-8 can be easily derived from the statistical cost function. The short-run AVC curve is that part of the AVC function that expresses the relation between cost and rate of utilization of capacity, holding constant the effects of all other independent variables. For example, we hold constant size or capacity (32.3

437

campsites) and standard service (1), then examine the relationship between changes in campground utilization (Q) and changes in average variable cost (AVC). This procedure results in the following condensed equations:

$$AVC = a - bQ + cQ^2$$

With standard service:

$$AVC = 1.89 - 0.0843Q + 0.00013Q^2$$

Without standard service:

$$AVC = 1.54 - 0.0843Q + 0.00013Q^2$$

Figure 13-8 depicts how short-run AVC varies with the number of visits to a campground of a given size. Note that the curves are U-shaped; they fall at first and then rise as output increases.

The marginal cost equation can be easily derived from the quadratic AVC equations. The marginal cost (MC) equations become:

$$MC = a - 2bQ + 3cQ^2$$

With standard service:

$$MC = 1.89 - 0.168Q + 0.00039Q^2$$

Without standard service:

$$MC = 1.54 - 0.1686Q + 0.00039Q^2$$

The marginal cost curves represent the short-run supply curves indicated by the heavy portion of the curves above the point of intersection with the average variable cost curves. As is typical for the supply curve for most goods and services, we see that an increase in supply is associated with an increase in marginal cost. Changes such as this represent movements along the supply curves.

Figure 13-8 also shows the shift from one supply curve to another for campgrounds with and without standard service. The regression coefficient indicates that AVC and MC increase by $0.3471 per RVD with standard service. Thus, the constant or "a" terms in the condensed AVC and MC equations are increased by $0.35 from 1.54 to 1.89 as shown above. This means that the level of service results in parallel shifts in the AVC and MC curves. We can test for the possibility that the effect of service may vary with level of output by including interactive variables in the cost function. In this case, the interactive variables are not statistically significant and therefore are omitted from the final function. We conclude that the shift is parallel in the vicinity of mean values, which is the important area of decision making.

Figure 13-8 shows that at its lowest point the AVC of standard service campgrounds is $0.54 per RVD compared with $0.19 per RVD for campgrounds without standard service, or $0.35 per RVD lower. This provides managers with a more accurate estimate of the cost of standard service than could be obtained by alternative procedures. For example, taking the difference between the simple average costs of campgrounds grouped by level of service, we would have concluded that standard service costs about $0.43 rather than $0.35 per RVD. This would overstate the cost of providing standard service by about 23 percent because the difference in AVC also is caused by differences in size or capacity and utilization of campground capacity. The average campground with standard service contains 36 campsites compared with only with 12 campsites in campgrounds without standard service. Standard service campgrounds utilize 70 percent of capacity compared with 45 percent for campgrounds without standard service. The chief advantage of using a statistical cost function is that it can show the cost of standard service with these other determinants of costs held constant.

For other applications of cross-sectional data to statistical cost analysis, see (1) the pioneering study by Gibbs and van Hees of 47 campgrounds in roaded natural forests of Oregon and Washington; and (2) the study by Gibbs and Reed of 94 roaded natural campgrounds in Northern Idaho, Montana, and North and South Dakota. The authors adjusted labor costs to account for the contribution of CETA trainees, volunteers, and shared workers. In their northern Rocky Mountain study, for example, the opportunity costs of this unbudgeted labor was estimated as $0.11 compared to budgeted labor costs of $0.30 per RVD. Total variable costs were $0.68, including contract services, $0.11; vehicles, $0.09; and materials, $0.05 per RVD.

BREAKEVEN CHARTS

Empirical cost functions are used in a variety of ways in making recreation economic decisions. One important practical application by managers of private companies and government agencies is to prepare linear breakeven charts. They are a simplification of the nonlinear total cost and total revenue functions shown previously. The charts are used to estimate the number of customers necessary to break even. They simply show that if recreation sites are going to break even or make a profit, total revenue must rise fast enough to get above total cost before running out of customers. This is an important consideration for recreation sites. By the time most sites are set up to open for visitors, they have already incurred substantial fixed cost. So the sites must serve a lot of customers to break even. But beyond the breakeven point, additional customers add to profits. There is nothing new or novel about this basic idea; the first such chart was developed in the early 1900s at Columbia University in New York City.

A breakeven chart is a graphic representation of the relationship between total cost and total revenue for all levels of output or sales.

As shown in Figure 13-9, output is measured on the horizontal axis, with total revenue and total cost shown on the vertical axis. Since fixed costs are constant regardless of output, they are indicated by a horizontal line. Variable costs at each level of output are measured by the distance between the total cost and the constant fixed costs.

The total cost function is simply a straight line drawn from fixed cost at zero output through total cost at current output. Since total revenue is proportional to output, it is usually shown as a 45° straight line from zero to current output. The breakeven point is depicted as the level of output and sales where total revenue equals total cost.

Linear analysis is appropriate for many uses. To assume a linear total revenue function means that all units of output can be sold at the same price. A constant price per unit of output would be true of companies in a competitive industry, and for many other companies in situations where the product can be sold without a break in price over a wide range of output. To assume a linear total cost function means that additional units of each input can be purchased at the same price and the production function also is linear. These assumptions may be reasonable for a wide range of output for most recreation goods and services, as shown by a number of empirical studies of costs. Finally, it should be noted that even though the charts are drawn from zero output to current output, managers who use them would not ordinarily consider the high and the low extremes. Linear functions are probably reasonably accurate within the relevant range near current output.

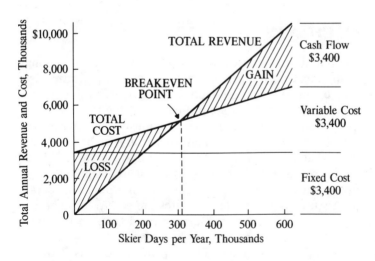

Figure 13-9. Breakeven Chart for Large Ski Areas in North America

440

A Breakeven Chart for Skiing

The ski industry provides a good example of the effective use of breakeven analysis. Figure 13-9 shows a typical linear breakeven chart for large ski areas in North America based on the data contained in Table 15-5. Fixed costs of $3.4 million are represented by a horizontal line. Variable costs are estimated to be $5.50 per skier day, so total costs rise by $5.50 for each additional skier day of output. At the time of the study, average revenue was reported to be $16.50 per skier day, so total revenue is a 45° straight line through the origin. The slope of the total revenue line is steeper than of the total cost line. This follows from the fact that large ski areas receive $16.50 in revenue for every $5.50 spent on labor, materials, and other variable costs.

The breakeven point is found at the intersection of the total revenue line and the total cost line. Figure 13-8 indicates a breakeven point at a sales and cost level of slightly over $5.0 million which occurs at an output level of roughly 300,000 skiers per year. Up to this point, the ski area suffers losses. Beyond this point, it begins to make a profit or cash flow. Both gains and losses are shown as the shaded areas in Figure 13-9. For example, if large ski areas had only 200,000 skier days of output in a year of very poor snow, they would have lost an average of one-half million dollars. On the other hand, if fair snow conditions increased demand to 400,000 skier days, they would have made a profit of one-half million dollars. In 1983, with fair to good snow conditions, demand increased to more than 600,000 skier days, and large ski areas made a profit (or cash flow) of $3.4 million. In this way, the breakeven chart shows approximately how much profit or loss will result from each output level.

An algebraic technique for solving breakeven problems can be illustrated using the cost and revenue shown in Figure 13-9. The breakeven output, defined as that quantity at which total revenue is exactly equal to total cost, is found as follows:

$$Q = \frac{TFC}{P - AVC}$$

Where P = price per unit of output; Q = quantity of output; TFC = total fixed cost; and AVC = average variable cost per unit of output. In the example illustrated in Figure 13-9, $P = \$16.50$, $AVC = \$5.50$, and $TFC = \$3.4$ million. So the breakeven quantity is found as follows:

$$Q = \frac{\$3,400,000}{\$16.50 - \$5.50}$$

$$= 310,000 \text{ skier days (rounded)}$$

This is identical to the breakeven output shown geometrically in Figure 13-9.

Breakeven charts are used by private companies and other groups to estimate the effect of output on revenues, costs, and profits. A manager may use a breakeven chart to estimate the effect on profits of a projected increase in output or how much output must be produced to break even. For instance, managers of ski areas may want to find the effect on breakeven and price if they install new equipment (such as triple or quad chair lifts) that would increase their fixed costs to $4.0 million per year and reduce their average variable cost to $5 per skier day. The new breakeven quantity is found as follows:

$$Q = \frac{\$4,000,000}{\$16.50 - \$5.00}$$

$$= 350,000 \text{ (rounded)}$$

Under these circumstances, the breakeven point would be nearly 350,000 skiers rather than 310,000, a growth of more than 10 percent. Without an increase in the number of skiers, lift ticket prices would have to be increased from $16.50 to $17.90 per skier to equal costs after installation of the new equipment. The new breakeven price is found as follows:

$$\$4,000,000/310,000 = \$12.90$$

$$\$17.90 = \$12.90 + \$5.00$$

This information is of considerable value to managers of ski companies. It means that, if they install the new equipment, they must sell at least 40,000 more ski tickets or increase the price of each ticket by $1.40 to stay in the black.

Operating leverage is a useful concept which refers to the profit contribution of increased output and sales. The degree of operating leverage is defined as the percentage change in profit resulting from a percentage change in number of skiers. Algebraically, this may be expressed as:

$$\text{Operating Leverage} = \frac{\text{Percentage Change in Profit}}{\text{Percentage Change in Output}}$$

For large ski areas in Figure 13-9, the degree of operating leverage at 620,000 skiers is calculated as follows:

$$= \frac{\$68,000/\$3,400,000}{6,200/620,000}$$

$$= \frac{0.2}{0.1}$$

$$= 2.0$$

This means that a 1 percent increase in output would result in a 2.0 percent increase in cash flow. This elasticity represents a substantial incentive for growth. Note that to calculate percentage change in profit, the profit contribution of an additional 6,200 skiers is divided by cash flow with 620,000 skiers. Profit contribution is defined as the difference between total revenue and variable cost; it is therefore equal to the price of a lift ticket minus average variable cost per skier.

The most difficult problem in drawing an accurate breakeven chart is estimating which costs are fixed and which are variable with changes in output. Fixed cost will not be affected by short-run changes in the number of skiers within the relevant range of operation. Table 13-5 shows that fixed cost in the ski industry includes the usual elements — general administrative, marketing, rent, and property taxes. Variable cost includes ski lift direct expenses such as wages, payroll taxes, and property operation (materials, electricity, fuel, etc.).

The accuracy of the allocation of costs into fixed and variable categories varies from industry to industry. In the ski industry, some types of costs are neither fully fixed nor fully variable. Take, for ex-

Table 13-5. Total Revenue and Cost of North American Ski Areas, 1983

Revenue and Cost, Thousand Dollars	Size, Vertical Transport Feet (1,000 VTF/hour)				
	Under 2,500	2,500- 3,999	4,000- 5,499	5,500 9,999	10,000 and over
Sample Size	31	25	19	22	21
Revenue					
Ski Lift Gross-Winter	$376	$ 910	$1,296	$3,047	$ 8,057
Ski Lift Gross-Summer	1	4	45	20	58
Supporting Margin-Winter	179	245	368	471	1,172
Supporting Margin-Summer	61	40	50	21	30
Year Round Margin	18	22	29	282	949
Total Revenue	$635	$1,221	$1,788	$3,841	$10,266
Variable Cost					
Ski Lift Direct Expense	$101	$ 289	$ 387	$ 887	$ 2,206
Payroll Taxes	35	63	77	178	242
Property Operation	84	123	196	228	542
Total Variable Cost	$220	$ 475	$ 660	$1,293	$ 2,990
Semi-Variable Cost					
Insurance (property, liability)	$ 36	$ 64	$ 80	$ 127	$ 301
Land Use Fees (public)	12	21	26	67	220
Snowmaking	58	88	103	101	252
Snow Removal	4	3	5	21	34
Miscellaneous	2	16	15	18	100
Total Semi-Variable Cost	$112	$ 192	$ 229	$ 334	$ 907
Fixed Cost					
General & Administrative	$120	$ 205	$ 335	$ 712	$ 1,870
Marketing (advertising, public relations, promotion, etc.)	47	71	121	261	601
Land Rent (private)	15	4	23	14	49
Property Taxes	15	15	28	68	214
Other Taxes (except income)	7	19	12	36	233
Total Fixed Cost	$204	$ 314	$ 519	$1,091	$ 2,967
Cash Flow					
Interest	$102	$ 93	$ 198	$ 297	$ 931
Depreciation & Amortization	104	171	258	613	1,638
Profit (Loss) Before Tax	(107)	(24)	(76)	213	833
Total Cash Flow	$ 99	$ 240	$ 380	$1,123	$ 3,402
Profitability					
Cash Flow on Sales	15.59%	19.66%	21.25%	29.24%	33.14%
Profit (BT) on Equity	Loss	Loss	Loss	3.74%	8.33%

Source: Goeldner, Buchman, and Duea.

ample, insurance costs. Normal accounting practice would probably lump property and liability insurance together as a fixed expense. Actually, however, property insurance is a fixed cost and liability insurance tends to be a variable cost since rates vary with the level of liability which is a function of output, i.e., number of skiers. Constructing an accurate breakeven chart, then, is largely dependent upon proper cost allocation. As a first approximation, we estimate that semi-variable cost includes insurance, land use fees, snowmaking, snow removal, and miscellaneous expenses. We assume for illustrative purposes that semi-variable costs are allocated one-half to fixed costs and one-half to variable costs. This means that fixed cost includes one-half of semi-variable costs or $450,000. Variable cost includes one-half of semi-variable cost or $0.72 per skier day (= $450,000/623,000).

Managers usually think of profit as cash flow rather than as simply total revenues less total costs. For short-run decisions where a portion of the company's capital is already a sunk investment and hence immobile, the appropriate profit concept is known as contribution margin or cash flow. This is defined in various ways for different purposes. One useful approach is to define cash flow as the cost of capital including profit, interest, and depreciation. This means that it is equal to total revenue less total cash outlay for fixed, semi-variable, and variable costs. In other words, cash flow is the cash available to owners as profit on their investment, depreciation on fixed assets, and interest to debt holders. Thus, unprofitable ski areas in Table 13-5 may continue to operate because their cash flow equals 15-20 percent of total revenue. This contribution to the cost of capital may be considered superior to shutting down which would provide no contribution.

Profitability of all ski areas is an increasing function of size. The larger the ski area, the larger the profit and cash flow. This conclusion is based on financial data presented in Table 13-5 for a sample of 118 North American ski areas grouped into five size classes ranging from about 1,500 to 10,000 skiers on peak days of operation. An interesting exercise would be to draw new breakeven charts for small and medium size ski areas. The charts would show that the increase in cash flow with size is related to price and revenue rather than cost or efficiency. Apparently large ski areas have been able to command a premium price by differentiating their product.

The effect of size is also shown in Table 13-6 where the total revenue and cost information from Table 13-5 is converted to the equivalent average values per skier. On this basis, the cash flow of large ski areas averaged about $5.50, considerably more than small ski areas. The profit of large ski areas averaged $1.33 while small ski areas experienced a loss. The depreciation of large ski areas averaged $2.63 which was more than small and medium-size areas. Total fixed costs of large ski areas averaged about $5 per skier which was more than small ski areas owing to higher general and administrative expenses.

Table 13-6. Economic Characteristics of North American Ski Areas, 1983

Revenue and Cost/Skier	Size, Vertical Transport Feet (1,000 VTF/hour)				
	Under 2,500	2,500- 3,999	4,000- 5,499	5,500 9,999	10,000 and over
Sample Size	31	25	19	22	21
Size					
VTF/Hour, Thousands	1,579	3,282	4,534	7,400	16,785
Skiable Acres	67	295	514	930	1,239
Gross Fixed Assets, Thousands	$1,878	$3,591	$3,786	$9,532	$22,840
Net Worth, Thousands	$ 132	$ 899	$1,203	$5,691	$ 9,999
Business Characteristics					
Operating With USFS Permit	19%	44%	74%	68%	62%
Engaged in Land Development	20%	16%	39%	46%	52%
Operational Characteristics					
Average Days of Operation/Year	83	110	128	141	138
Average Peak Day Use/Day	1,446	2,870	3,314	4,893	9,701
Average Skier Visits/Year[a]	52,000	99,000	141,000	262,000	623,000
Economic Characteristics					
Average Revenue/Skier Visit	$ 12.32	$ 12.38	$ 12.69	$ 14.68	$ 16.49
Average Lift Ticket Revenue/Skier Visit	$ 8.83	$ 9.76	$ 10.13	$ 12.83	$ 14.56
Average Adult Lift Ticket Price					
Weekend	$ 14.36	$ 14.87	$ 16.63	$ 17.73	$ 19.77
Weekday	$ 12.02	$ 12.86	$ 14.50	$ 17.14	$ 19.12
Average Adult Season Ticket Price	$217	$264	$335	$381	$499
Revenue/Skier					
Ski Lift Gross	$ 8.83	$ 9.76	$10.13	$12.83	$14.56
Ski School Margin	0.43	0.44	0.53	0.36	0.51
Food Service Margin	0.66	0.53	0.61	0.52	0.61
Bar Margin	0.31	0.29	0.34	0.21	0.20
Ski Shop Margin	0.35	0.22	0.22	0.26	0.28
Ski Rental Margin	1.44	0.81	0.60	0.51	0.25
Other Margin	0.30	0.33	0.26	(.01)	0.08
Total Revenue/Skier	$12.32	$12.38	$12.69	$14.68	$16.49
Ski Lift Department					
Direct Labor/Skier					
Ski Lift	$ 0.59	$ 0.85	$ 0.75	$ 0.85	$ 0.88
Ski Patrol	0.12	0.40	0.23	0.50	0.46
Slope Maintenance	0.13	0.29	0.30	0.40	0.32
Maintenance & Repair	0.38	0.56	0.49	0.51	0.54
Ticket Sales	0.14	0.19	0.16	0.21	0.20
Other Payroll	0.13	0.13	0.12	0.05	0.22
Total Direct Labor/Skier	$ 1.48	$ 2.42	$ 2.04	$ 2.52	$ 2.62
Other Direct Cost/Skier	0.96	0.76	0.88	1.26	1.19
Total Direct Cost/Skier	2.44	3.18	2.92	3.78	3.81
Gross Margin/Skier	6.39	6.58	7.20	9.05	10.75
Variable Cost/Skier					
Ski Lift Direct Expense	$ 1.96	$ 2.93	$ 1.60	$ 3.39	$ 3.54
Payroll Taxes	0.68	0.64	0.55	0.68	0.39
Property Operation	1.63	1.25	1.39	0.87	0.87
Total Variable Cost	$ 4.27	$ 4.82	$ 3.54	$ 4.94	$ 4.80
Gross Margin/Skier	8.05	7.56	8.01	9.74	11.69
Semi-Variable Cost/Skier					
Insurance (property, liability)	$ 0.70	$ 0.65	$ 0.57	$ 0.49	$ 0.48
Land Use Fees (public)	0.23	0.21	0.18	0.26	0.35
Snowmaking	1.13	0.89	0.73	0.39	0.40
Snow Removal	0.08	0.03	0.04	0.08	0.05
Miscellaneous	0.04	0.16	0.11	0.07	0.16
Total Semi-Variable Cost	$ 2.18	$ 1.94	$ 1.63	$ 1.29	$ 1.44
Fixed Cost/Skier					
General & Administrative	$ 2.33	$ 2.08	$ 2.38	$ 2.72	$ 3.01
Marketing (advertising, public relations, promotion, etc.)	0.91	0.72	0.86	1.00	0.97
Land Rent (private)	0.29	0.04	0.16	0.05	0.08
Property Taxes	0.29	0.15	0.20	0.26	0.34
Other Taxes (except income)	0.14	0.19	0.08	0.14	0.37
Total Fixed Cost	$ 3.96	$ 3.18	$ 3.68	$ 4.17	$ 4.76
Cash Flow/Skier					
Interest	$ 1.98	$ 0.94	$ 1.40	$ 1.13	$ 1.49
Depreciation & Amortization	2.02	1.73	1.83	2.34	2.63
Profit (Loss) Before Tax	(2.08)	(0.24)	(0.54)	0.81	1.33
Total Cash Flow	$ 1.92	$ 2.43	$ 2.69	$ 4.28	$ 5.45

[a]Adjusted.
Source: Goeldner, Buchanan, and Duea.

445

Large ski areas operated more days per year, were more likely to operate on Forest Service land, and engage in land development at the base of the ski areas.

Prices of lift tickets were an increasing function of size. The larger the ski area, the higher the price. Lift ticket prices of large ski areas averaged nearly $20 in 1983, which was one-third more than small areas. After discounts, average lift ticket revenue for all ski areas was about $5 per skier less than list price. But ski areas received an additional margin of $2-3 per skier for other services such as food and beverage, ski school, ski rental, and ski shop.

Medium-size ski areas, with average peak day output of 3,300 skiers, had the lowest variable costs of $3.50. Variable costs of small and large ski areas did not appear to be systematically related to size. When one-half of semi-variable costs were added to variable costs, medium-size ski areas had variable costs of approximately $4.35 per skier which was substantially lower than for large and small areas. Usually, low variable costs are achieved by substituting capital investment for direct operating labor and other expenses. However, medium-size ski areas also had the lowest investment, as measured by gross fixed assets (at purchase price) per skier. Medium-size ski areas were not the most profitable, however, because competition and lack of product differentiation forced average lift ticket revenue down to a level considerably below large areas.

COST EFFECTIVENESS

Cost effectiveness is a way to make recreation economic decisions when costs can be measured but benefits cannot be measured in dollar values. It is usually presented as a ratio in which the nonmonetary measure of effectiveness is divided by the costs. Measures of costs are the same as for benefit cost studies, although measures of benefits may be in physical units or effectiveness scores. In the past, benefit cost studies defined some benefits from nonmarket output, such as historic and environmental preservation, as intangible and not quantifiable in dollar terms; and thus they were omitted from the benefit cost ratio. Cost effectiveness is a way to study the most efficient way to achieve such objectives.

The National Park Service authorized use of the cost-effectiveness method in 1976. Since then, it has been applied to the evaluation of alternative park management plans under the able leadership of George Nez. Its acceptance by park managers should not be surprising. Our ability to measure the benefit of recreation programs varies and is possible to different degrees for different programs. There are three types of programs or services. The output of Type I programs has a market value, or if nonmarket, dollar values can be calculated. Either the service is sold, as overnight camping in the parks, or the service increases the value of other outputs, as a visitor interpretation program or backcountry camper registration, which increases the willingness to pay of park users. Also, the service may reduce the costs associated with other activities, as development of park programs near population centers saves visitors' travel time and costs. The output of Type II programs can be measured in physical terms but no market or nonmarket valuation procedure has been developed. Examples include site beautification through regrassing, road maintenance, law enforcement, and so forth. Type III programs are those for which no useful estimate can be made of either the level of output or its value. Program objectives can be defined and the level of activity of such programs can be measured only in terms of costs or workhours. Examples include some of the programs undertaken to protect a natural environment or historic site. The general public benefits from Type III programs, although there is no market in which demands of the general public can be expressed. Nonetheless, the general public would be willing to pay, for example, to preserve the option to visit national parks in the future, for the knowledge that national parks exist, and to bequest national parks to future generations.

The distinguishing characteristic of the cost-effectiveness approach to decision making is that measures of benefits may be in units other than dollar values, such as physical units of output or a scale of effectiveness prepared by informed managers. For example, given the choice between cross-country skiing and snowmobile winter use of a backcountry road system in a national park or forest, a manager may decide among alternative uses by determining how many cross-country ski visits and how many snowmobile visits can be provided for the same amount of money. Usually, the choice is between more complex outputs than visitor days, so the analyst may have trouble discovering what the different outputs are and then communicating this information to the decision maker. The only physical measure of the output of historic site preservation devised so far is the square footage of buildings preserved and the number of acres of battleground protected. These measures do not differentiate between the value of preserving relatively minor sites compared to those of national historic significance such as Plymouth Rock or the Gettysburg battleground. In this case, Nez has devised an elaborate system in which park managers estimate effectiveness scores for alternative programs.

Least-Cost and Constant-Cost Methods

Cost effectiveness is a way to compare alternative recreation projects and programs by (1) minimizing dollar cost subject to some required output level that is not measurable in dollar terms, or (2) maximizing some output level of a recreation program subject to a fixed budget constraint, such as appropriation levels. These are the least-cost and constant-cost methods of cost-effectiveness analysis.

A typical least-cost effectiveness study begins with a statement of an objective, such as the protection of a viable herd of mountain sheep, then estimates the costs of achieving this objective under different management systems. Some of the alternatives that might be examined in this case would include zoning of habitat area to prevent the intrusion of people, hunting restrictions, disease control, and restocking from domesticated herds produced under controlled conditions. The problem is to determine the effectiveness of each alternative and then to calculate the cost of the program needed to reach the objective.

For example, let's simplify the problem of preserving bighorn sheep. Assume there are two alternative projects with the following costs and effectiveness scores.

	Effectiveness, Number of Sheep Protected	Costs, Thousand Dollars	Cost Effectiveness
Project A	100	$100	1.0
Project B	100	50	2.0

We see that project B has a cost-effectiveness ratio of 2.0 compared with 1.0 for project A. Project B is the preferred alternative with the highest cost-effectiveness score.

The constant-cost effectiveness study tells decision makers what they can buy for their money. The objective is to determine the maximum level of output that can be produced with different systems, all of which require the same commitment of resources. This shows the consequences of alternative policies with a fixed budget appropriations. For example, continuing the example of the problem of preserving a herd of bighorn sheep, the cost-effectiveness scores are —

	Effectiveness, Number of Sheep Protected	Costs, Thousand Dollars	Cost Effectiveness
Project A	100	$100	1.0
Project B	200	100	2.0

We see that project B again has the highest cost-effectiveness score — 2.0 compared with 1.0 for project A. Thus, project B would be the preferred alternative.

Many government agencies find themselves asked to provide more recreation services without proportionate increases in budget and under conditions of inflating costs. Thus they have no alternative but to seek ways to improve efficiency, that is, to reduce the costs of providing existing services as well as new ones. Constant-cost effectiveness is a technique to evaluate alternative systems or to determine whether a new design can provide the same benefits as other alternatives and at reduced costs.

A third type of cost-effectiveness analysis is to estimate the costs of achieving several alternative levels of effectiveness for a single objective. This may be illustrated with the case of preserving a herd of bighorn sheep. Assume that the budget for project A, disease control, can be varied as follows.

Effectiveness, Number of Sheep Protected	Costs, Thousand Dollars	Cost Effectiveness
50	$ 75	0.67
100	100	1.0
150	200	0.75
200	400	0.5

Protecting a herd of 100 sheep is the most cost-effective level of operation for the disease control program. A herd of 50 sheep is less cost effective than 100 sheep. As the size of the herd is increased above 100 sheep, the costs of disease control increase at a much more rapid rate than does the level of effectiveness.

This illustrates an important economic fact of life for many programs. The added costs of protecting the last 50 sheep is as great as the cost of protecting the first 150. This may give the decision maker the information needed to make expenditure decisions. For example, it may be clear that the $100,000 expenditure needed to protect the first 100 sheep is reasonable. It may be far less clear that protecting an additional 100 sheep is worth the required incremental expenditure of $300,000. Thus, we can see that cost-effectiveness studies provide decision makers with studies of program costs in relation to measurable but unvalued estimates of program outputs. This modest accomplishment may be of substantial aid in the decision-making process.

A Case Study of Cost Effectiveness

Let's consider a case study drawn from the real world in which cost effectiveness played a decisive role in the final outcome of an important decision about the use of natural resources. The problem is whether to route a section of the Interstate highway system through an environmentally sensitive area. Figure 13-10 shows two alternative routes for Interstate 70 just west of the Continental Divide in the Rocky Mountains about 75 miles west of Denver. The Vail Pass route would, for the most part, follow the existing U.S. Highway 6 right-of-way. The Red Buffalo route, farther north, would cut through what is now the Eagles Nest Wilderness Area. It would take about 7,000 acres for actual construction, and it would destroy the wilderness quality of nearly 25,000 acres.

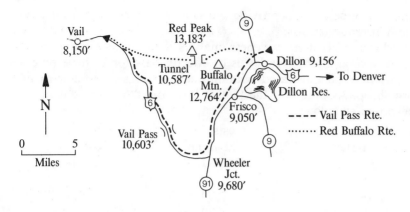

Figure 13-10. Map of Alternative Routes for Interstate 70 via Vail Pass or
Red Buffalo Gap
Source: Neuzil.

Table 13-7 summarizes the design characteristics and costs of the
two alternatives presented by Neuzil. The Red Buffalo route is nearly
11 miles shorter than the Vail Pass route but has steeper grades. Both
routes were designed for speeds of 50-60 miles per hour. The net effect is that auto driving costs would be about $1.14 per trip less for
the Red Buffalo route. The Red Buffalo route would cost $40 million
more, nearly three times as costly to construct as the Vail Pass route.
The difference is attributed to the need to construct a twin-bore tunnel. Construction costs were converted to annual equivalent costs using a discount rate of 3.5 percent and useful lives of 20 years for the
pavement, 40 years for the roadway, and 60 years for the tunnel and
right-of-way. Road user costs were based on 20-year projections of
10.8 to 12.4 thousand vehicles per day and standard auto costs per
mile.

Note that a unique contribution of this cost study is that the state
highway department included external costs as well as costs internal to

Table 13-7. Design Characteristics and Costs of Alternative Routes for Interstate 70 via Vail Pass or Red Buffalo Gap

Variable	Vail Pass	Red Buffalo
Length, Miles	27.3	16.5
Average Grade, Percent	3.1	5.1
Average Daily Traffic, Thousand Vehicles	12.4	10.8
Auto Driving Costs, Dollars per Trip	2.90	1.76
Construction Costs, Millions of Dollars	22.8	63.1
Annual Costs, Millions of Dollars		
Construction Costs	1.1	2.7
Maintenance Costs	0.1	0.2
Total	1.2	2.9
Road Users Costs	11.8	8.5
Total, Highway Department and User	13.0	11.4

the agency, that is, road user costs as well as agency costs of construction and maintenance. Recreation agencies, such as the National Park Service and U.S. Forest Service, could learn an important lesson from highway engineers. The travel costs of recreation users should be included as an external cost in planning the location of parks and other recreation sites.

Normally, the route with the lowest highway cost is assumed to be the most economically desirable unless it can be shown that a more expensive alternative would produce offsetting savings in the form of lower user costs. The state highway department prepared a benefit cost ratio for the Red Buffalo route in which social benefits were the lower annual road user costs and social costs were the higher annualized costs of construction and maintenance, as compared to the Vail Pass route. The benefit cost ratio of the Red Buffalo alternative was calculated to be

$$\frac{\$3.3 \text{ million}}{\$1.7 \text{ million}} = 1.94$$

This means that for each additional dollar of annual highway costs, over and above the annual highway costs of the Vail Pass alternative, the Red Buffalo route is expected to save motorists $1.94 in user costs. On this basis, the state highway department recommended construction of the Red Buffalo route.

The Red Buffalo route was opposed by many citizens of the state. As a result, the U.S. Forest Service decided to study the cost effectiveness of the two routes. Each was evaluated by a study team on the basis of environmental impacts, recreation, regional economic impact, and highway efficiency. The interdisciplinary study team included experts in engineering, economics, fish and wildlife biology, recreation resource management, and community impacts. They prepared a report which rated the effect of alternative routes on a scale from plus-seven to minus-seven. The most important point to remember about estimating an effectiveness score is that the panel of experts representing each of the major effects of the project reaches a group consensus as to the effectiveness score for each variable (through discussion and old-fashioned horse trading). A simple average of the values assigned by each individual independently should be avoided, because the extreme values will cancel each other around the mean score. Table 13-8 summarizes the effectiveness ratings and weights assigned by the study team to 11 variables. The effectiveness ratings are multiplied by the weights to obtain the effectiveness scores. The total effectiveness score for each alternative is the sum of the 11 variables considered. The bottom line in Table 13-8 shows an effectiveness rating for the Vail Pass route of 53 compared with 15 for Red Buffalo.

The cost-effectiveness ratios for the alternative routes are

Vail Pass $\qquad 4.1 = \dfrac{53}{13.0}$

Table 13-8. Effectiveness Ratings for Alternative Routes of Interstate 70 via Vail Pass or Red Buffalo Gap

| Variable | Rating of Alternatives | | Weight Factor | Weighted Effectiveness Rating | |
	Vail Pass	Red Buffalo		Vail Pass	Red Buffalo
Environmental and Recreational					
Wilderness Loss	-1	-3	5	-5	-15
Driving for Pleasure	+7	+6	1	+7	+6
Physical Environment Damage	-1	-3	5	-5	-15
Fish and Wildlife Damage	-1	-4	2	-2	-8
Other Recreational Effects	+2	+1	2	+4	+2
Impacts on Economy					
Local	+3	+2	3	+9	+6
State	+3	+3	4	+12	+12
National	+2	+1	5	+10	+5
Roadway Efficiency					
Annual Direct Cost	+1	+1	5	+5	+5
Traffic-Carrying Ability	+2	+1	1	+2	+1
Safety	+4	+4	4	+16	+16
Total, Effectiveness Rating				+53	+15

Source: Libeau.

$$\text{Red Buffalo} \quad 1.3 = \frac{15}{11.4}$$

This means that for each $1 million of annual cost for highway construction, maintenance, and road user costs, Vail Pass has an effectiveness score of 4.1 compared with 1.3 for Red Buffalo. The cost effectiveness of Vail Pass is three times that of Red Buffalo.

As a result of this cost-effectiveness study and other evidence prepared by citizens opposed to the Red Buffalo route, the Vail Pass route was chosen by the governor of the state. The Red Buffalo route is now part of the Eagles Nest Wilderness Area. This result should not be surprising. The Vail Pass route results in a small loss of natural resources compared to Red Buffalo. It is more open, with better visibility, and offers greater variety to sightseers. It results in less damage to streams and lakes and less scarring of the landscape. Fewer big-game animals are lost. It encourages the development of skiing and camping areas, principally south, down the Blue River Valley. It is safer and more dependable, particularly in the winter.

By the time the Vail Pass route was completed in 1980, construction costs had escalated from $22.8 to $68.5 million. However, it is likely that the costs of Red Buffalo would have increased even more because of the unforeseen costs of tunnel construction. Revised estimates of highway use doubled for 1990 and nearly tripled for the year 2000. Highway planners did not foresee the rapid increase in recreation traffic, particularly skiers.

TREATMENT OF INFLATION

In the 1970s and early 1980s, inflation became a fact of life in most nations. Very likely, inflationary pressure will return and we should learn how to measure its effects. Table 13-9 shows two measures of the annual rate of inflation in the general price level in the United States. The consumer price index increased at a compound annual rate of 7.0 percent per year between 1970 and 1980, somewhat more than the gross national product implicit price deflator, which increased at a compound annual rate of 6.3 percent during the same time period. Since recreation benefits and costs are for productive investments, the U.S. Forest Service considers the gross national product implicit price deflator more appropriate than the consumer price index for converting recreation values to constant dollars.

Table 13-10 shows that construction costs, measured by the U.S. Department of Commerce index, increased 8.9 percent per year between 1970 and 1980, compared with the Engineering News Record index, which increased at an average rate of 8.0 percent. Unfortunately, these are based on prices in 20 cities and may not fully reflect price level changes in remote rural areas where recreation facilities are often located. The U.S. Bureau of Public Roads highway construction cost index increase averaged 9.7 percent during the same time period. The public transportation (air, bus, train, and ship) cost index of the Department of Commerce increased by an average 6.2 percent, compared to private vehicle costs, which increased by 7.6 percent per year, somewhat more than the rate of inflation in the general price

Table 13-9. Annual Rate of Inflation in the General Price Level, United States, 1970-85

Year	Gross National Product Implicit Price Deflator 1972=100.0	Inflation Rate, Annual Percent Change	Consumer Price Index 1967=100.0	Inflation Rate, Annual Percent Change
1970	92.4		116.3	
1971	96.9	.049	121.3	.043
1972	100.0	.032	125.3	.033
1973	105.7	.057	133.1	.062
1974	116.1	.098	147.7	.109
1975	127.2	.096	161.2	.091
1976	132.5	.042	170.5	.058
1977	140.7	.062	181.5	.064
1978	150.4	.069	195.4	.076
1979	163.4	.086	217.4	.113
1980	178.6	.093	246.8	.135
1981	195.5	.095	272.4	.104
1982	206.9	.058	289.1	.061
1983	215.3	.041	298.4	.032
1984	223.4	.038	311.1	.043
1985	230.8	.033	322.2	.039

Source: U.S. Department of Commerce.

Table 13-10. Annual Rate of Inflation in Transportation and Construction Price Levels, United States, 1970-85

Year	Transportation				Construction					
	Public Index 1967=100	Inflation Rate	Private Index 1967=100	Inflation Rate	Department of Commerce 1977=100	Inflation Rate	Engineering News Record 1967=100	Inflation Rate	Bureau of Public Roads 1977=100	Inflation Rate
1970	128.5		111.1		56.9		128.9		59.6	
1971	137.7	.072	116.6	.049	60.6	.065	146.7	.138	62.5	.049
1972	143.4	.041	117.5	.008	64.8	.069	163.0	.111	65.6	.049
1973	144.8	.010	121.5	.034	70.9	.094	176.5	.077	72.3	.102
1974	148.0	.022	136.6	.124	80.6	.137	188.0	.082	95.5	.321
1975	158.6	.071	149.8	.097	88.3	.096	205.7	.094	96.5	.010
1976	174.2	.098	164.6	.099	91.9	.040	223.4	.086	92.1	-.046
1977	182.4	.047	176.6	.073	100.0	.088	240.0	.074	100.0	.086
1978	187.8	.030	185.0	.047	113.3	.133	258.4	.077	122.6	.226
1979	200.3	.067	212.3	.149	128.7	.136	279.5	.082	142.6	.163
1980	251.6	.256	249.2	.174	143.2	.113	301.4	.078	163.0	.143
1981	312.0	.240	277.5	.114	151.9	.061	328.9	.091	156.7	-.039
1982	346.0	.109	287.5	.036	154.1	.014	356.1	.083	146.8	-.063
1983	362.6	.048	293.9	.022	157.1	.019	378.6	.063	146.5	-.002
1984	385.2	.062	306.6	.043	163.7	.042	386.2	.020	155.0	.058
1985	402.8	.046	314.2	.025	168.8	.031	389.0	.007	172.1	.110

Source: U.S. Department of Commerce.

454

level. Note that public transportation costs increased very rapidly during the early 1980s relative to the general price level, which had a dampening effect on long distance recreation travel.

Inflation creates an illusion of high interest rates. For example, from 1960 to 1980, market interest rates on private recreation investments doubled, increasing from less than 8 percent to 15 percent and more. Yet in real terms, the 1980 interest rate of 15 percent was much lower than the 1960 interest rate of 8 percent. The reason is that in 1960, there was virtually no inflation, with prices typically rising at less than 2 percent a year; however, in 1980 inflation was rampant, with consumer prices rising over 13 percent in a single year.

Consider a loan of $100 for 1 year at a rate of 8 percent interest a year when prices are rising only 2 percent a year. The lender gets back the original $100 plus $8 in interest, and loses only $2 in purchasing power, for a net gain of $6, or a 6 percent interest on the loan. Now consider a loan of $100 at 15 percent interest when the inflation rate is 13 percent. At the end of the year the lender gets back $100 plus $15 interest. But with inflation, the $100 has lost $13 in purchasing power. Thus, the lender is left only $2 richer in terms of what the $100 can buy now. In terms of purchasing power, the lender gains only 2 percent interest on the loan. While the nominal dollar value of the $100 investment grows at 15 percent, inflation is eating up the investment at an annual rate of 13 percent, leading to a real interest rate of only 2 percent. Thus, any decisions based on a direct comparison of the two interest rates, without adjusting for inflation are illusory.

Note that the precise economic adjustment for inflation is arithmetically straightforward. The real interest rate is simply the market rate of interest divided by the rate of inflation (adding 1 to each variable). For example, the precise calculation of the real interest rates for 1960 would be

$$1.0588 = \frac{1.08}{1.02} \text{ or 5.88 percent, rather than 6.0 percent.}$$

In 1980, it would be

$$1.0177 = \frac{1.15}{1.13} \text{ or 1.77 percent, rather than 2.0 percent.}$$

Economists distinguish between market (inflating) dollar values and real or constant values. In benefit cost studies, we assume a stable price level for the life of the project. Usually all estimates of the costs and benefits for each year of the planning period of a proposed project are in constant (current or present) dollars, i.e., the purchasing power of the dollar at the time of the decision. So long as future benefits and costs of public projects are valued at constant prices, the social discount rate should be the real rate of interest, before inflation, not the monetary (nominal or market) rate. The President's Office of Management and Budget has established this policy for treatment of inflation in benefit cost studies.

Use of constant or current dollars in benefit cost studies provides satisfactory results when the value of benefits and costs changes at approximately the same rate over the life of the project. The relative values of inputs and outputs do not change with a uniform rise in the price level. Using current prices is equivalent to deflating all prices to the present. Howe demonstrated that in the case of general inflation, it makes no difference whether we use: (1) benefits and costs in constant (current) dollars and a discount without inflation, or (2) benefits and costs in inflating dollars of the year in which they are incurred and a discount rate that fully compensates for the expected rate of inflation. Assuming a rate of general inflation of 5 percent, then the value of benefits and costs each year of the expected life of the project would be multiplied by $(1 + 0.05)$. The value of benefits and costs will increase over time by the rate of general inflation. Also, the discount rate will be multiplied by $(1 + 0.05)$ to incorporate an inflationary premium because interest rates will increase to protect lenders from a loss of purchasing power on the funds they lend. Because the inflationary adjustment is introduced into both the numerator and denominator, they cancel out, and we are left with the same present value calculation as without inflation.

On the other hand, if the relative prices of some inputs or outputs are expected to change, with some prices expected to rise more than others, their prices may be inflated over the life of the project. This practice is authorized by the Office of Management and Budget when there is a reasonable basis for estimating such changes. For example, early in the 1980s camping fees increased more than the general price level. From 1979 to 1982, the average fee at over 7,500 private campgrounds in the United States increased from $5.39 to $7.28 per campsite, or 35 percent. During the same period of time, the gross national product price deflator increased 26.8 percent. Thus the real rate of increase in fees for camping averaged nearly 2.7 percent per year. If this relative price increase continues for a 5-10-year period and is expected to continue during the 20-year life of a proposed campground project, it could be included in the calculation of benefits. However, it is unlikely that this is a long-run trend, rather it probably represents a lagged adjustment to the business cycle. Over time, campground fees rise and fall relative to the general price level.

Recent experience suggests that even long-run changes in the relative prices of inputs and outputs may prove of limited reliability in forecasting future price trends. In 1970, Krutilla and others testified before the Federal Power Commission on the relative value of benefits and costs of a proposed hydroelectric dam at Hells Canyon on the Snake River in Idaho. It is the deepest canyon in the United States and represents one of the last great rivers unchanged by man. For several decades before 1970, technological advances in the production of electricity resulted in falling relative prices. As a result, economists predicted that the benefit of the hydroelectric development would tend to decrease over time with continued advances in the technology of producing alternative sources of energy. The construction application was denied. However, the relative prices of energy actually increased sharply from 1970 to 1980, and prospects were for continued increases in the long run. This raised a question as to the continuing validity of the earlier analysis.

The economists also predicted increases in the value of recreation use of the Hells Canyon if it were protected in its natural condition (Krutilla and Fisher). Since the services of the natural environment are gifts of nature, not produced by humans, we cannot expect gains in productive efficiency to augment the present supply of such resources as the Hells Canyon. Thus, the increasing scarcity of unique environmental resources is expected to increase their relative value in the future. There is a need to develop an empirical basis for the expected increase in the relative value of benefits from recreation use and preservation demands by the general population, including users and nonusers. When a reasonable basis for estimating such changes becomes available, we may find that their relative values increase over the planning period of proposed projects.

SUMMARY

In this chapter, we presented the results of recent empirical studies of costs, and discussed several implications for improving future recreation economic decisions. In the past, most studies provided the average costs of recreation programs of an agency. More recently, considerable progress has been made both in recreation agency cost accounting and in the development of incremental cost functions. The widespread availability of computer software enable us to show how costs change with improvements in design, size, utilization of capacity, and level of service provided. Such studies are particularly useful in recreation economic decisions because they show how future costs are expected to change with alternative policies.

We saw the distinction between the concepts of short-run and long-run production costs. In the short-run, costs of production vary with changes in the rate of utilization of capacity of facilities, such as the proportion of existing campsites rented. In the long-run, costs of production vary with changes in the size of facilities, such as the number of campsites in a campground, which defines maximum capacity. In addition, long-run costs of production vary with changes in the level of technology or development. Improved ways of providing recreation opportunities will result in lower cost methods of production.

We reviewed the concepts of fixed and variable cost and distinguished social costs from the financial costs of private and public

457

agencies. The total cost of a park or recreation program includes: the cost of program planning or design; the cost of land and related natural resources; the cost of capital construction or installation; operation and maintenance costs; external costs to other agencies and individuals; and the associated cost to users.

The economic evaluation of public recreation projects differs from financial analysis in that social costs rather than accounting costs are used. The social cost of producing recreation is what must be given up by society as a whole to make that production possible. To economists, the concept of social cost always means opportunity cost. The opportunity cost of using a resource is the value of the resource in its next best alternative use. When measuring the opportunity cost of recreation, all consequences of its production must be identified and incorporated into the measurement. We attempt to estimate the opportunity costs for all inputs, whether they are correctly or incorrectly priced by markets or not priced at all. Although economists and accountants define costs differently, both definitions are correct since they are used for different purposes. In describing or predicting the actual behavior of managers, economists should use the accounting information that managers actually use. But in helping managers make the best decisions they can in pursuing their goals and evaluating how well they use scarce resources, economists should substitute social cost rather than financial or accounting costs.

Next, we described the sources of information on costs of developing and operating recreation sites: (1) engineering economic estimates of the optimum combination of inputs to produce a range of output levels; (2) cross-sectional comparison of the costs of several existing facilities with varying output levels at one point in time; and (3) time-series observations of costs for varying output levels of a single recreation site over a period of time. Although each of these methods can provide satisfactory estimates of costs under particular circumstances, each also has its drawbacks. We discussed the problems of each approach and demonstrate under what conditions each can be used successfully. Accuracy of the alternative methods is a continuing problem, although considerable progress has been made in recent years.

We illustrated the principles of empirical cost analysis for boat marinas. The total cost curve showed that the first dollars spent providing marina services produced a large output of boating opportunities. However, as more and more dollars were spent, less additional output was produced by each additional dollar, i.e., increasing marginal costs. Optimum size occurred at the lowest point on the long-run average total cost curve where marginal cost were equal to average cost. The marginal cost curve represented the long-run supply curve for boat marinas.

Managers have simplified empirical cost studies in a number of ways. We demonstrated how they prepare breakeven charts, which are simple linear representations of the relationship between total cost and total revenue for all levels of output or sales. Managers who use them would not ordinarily consider the high and the low extremes. Linear functions are probably reasonably accurate within the relevant range near current output. The charts are used to estimate the number of customers necessary to break even. The breakeven point is described as the level of output and sales where total revenue equals total cost. The accuracy of a breakeven chart is largely dependent upon proper cost allocation. The allocation of costs into fixed and variable categories varies from industry to industry. In the ski industry, we saw that some types of costs are neither fully fixed nor fully variable.

Cost effectiveness is a way to make recreation economic decisions when costs can be measured but benefits cannot be measured in dollar values. It is usually presented as a ratio in which the nonmonetary measure of effectiveness is divided by the costs. Measures of costs are the same as for benefit cost studies, while measures of benefits may be in physical units or effectiveness scores. Cost effectiveness is a way to compare alternative recreation projects and programs by (1) minimizing dollar cost subject to some required output level that is not measurable in dollar terms, or (2) maximizing some output level of a recreation program subject to a fixed budget constraint such as appropriation levels. In the past, benefit cost studies defined some benefits from nonmarket output, such as historic and environmental preservation, as intangible and not quantifiable in dollar terms; thus, they were omitted from the benefit cost ratio. Cost effectiveness is a way to study the most efficient way to achieve such objectives.

Economists distinguish between market (inflating) dollar values and real or constant values. In benefit cost studies, we assume a stable price level for the life of the project. Usually all estimates of the costs and benefits for each year of the planning period of a proposed project are in constant (current or present) dollars, i.e., the purchasing power of the dollar at the time of the decision. Use of constant or current dollars in benefit cost studies provides satisfactory results when the value of benefits and costs change at approximately the same rate over the life of the project.

The concepts introduced in this chapter are used in Chapter 14 where we show that supply curves influence recreation economic decisions with respect to user fee policy. We shall refer to the concepts again in the discussion of benefit cost studies in Chapter 15.

READINGS

Angus, James, Cornelius Corssmit, and John H. Foster. "Criteria for Public Supply of Outdoor Recreation Facilities." Research Bulletin 592, Massachusetts Agricultural Experiment Station, Amherst. 1971.

Baumol, William J. "Macroeconomics of Unbalanced Growth: The Anatomy of Urban Crisis." *American Economic Review* 57(June 1967):415-26.

Clawson, Marion, and Jack L. Knetsch. *Economics of Outdoor Recreation.* Johns Hopkins University Press, Baltimore. 1966.

Cornell, George W. "Conducting a Feasibility Study for a Proposed Outdoor Recreation Enterprise." Circular 1011, Cooperative Extension Service, Virginia Polytechnic Institute, Blacksburg. 1966.

Downing, Kent. "Costs of Providing Dispersed Recreation Along Forest Roads: A Pilot Study." Report to U.S. Forest Service. Logan, Utah: Utah State University. 1979.

Fight, R. D. "Planners Guide for Estimating Cost per User-day of Proposed Recreational Facilities." General Technical Report PNW-110. Pacific Northwest Forest and Range Experiment Station, USDA Forest Service, Portland, Ore. 1980.

Fischer, David W. "Planning for Recreation Investments." Ph.D. Dissertation, Colorado State University, Fort Collins. 1968.

Gibbs, K. C. "Public Campgrounds: Are They Profitable?" *Journal of Forestry* 78(Aug. 1980):466-68.

Gibbs, K. C., and W. W. S. van Hees. "Cost of Operating Public Campgrounds." *Journal of Leisure Research* 3(No. 3, 1981):243-53.

Gibbs, K. C., and F. L. Reed. "Estimation and Analysis of Costs for Developed Recreation Sites in U.S. Forest Service Region One." Forest Research Lab. Research Bulletin 42, Oregon State University, Corvallis. 1983.

Goeldner, Charles R., T. A. Buchman, and K. P. Duea. "Economic Analysis of North American Ski Areas." Business Research Division, University of Colorado, Boulder. 1984.

Gray, James R., and Larry D. Bedford. "Economic Analysis of Commercial Ranch Recreation Enterprises." Station Bulletin 559, New Mexico Agricultural Experiment Station, University of New Mexico, Las Cruces. 1970.

Guldin, Richard W. "Wilderness Costs in New England." *Journal of Forestry* 9(Sept. 1980):548-52.

Harrison, A. Price. "The Ski Resort and Its Feasibility." *Journal of Travel Research* 4(No. 1, 1972):1-4.

Haveman, Robert H., and John V. Krutilla. *Unemployment, Idle Capacity and the Evaluation of Public Expenditures.* Johns Hopkins University Press, Baltimore. 1968.

Hof, John G., Robert D. Lee, A. Allen Dyer, and Brian M. Kent. "An Analysis of Joint Costs in a Managed Forest Ecosystem." *Journal of Environmental Economics and Management* 12(No. 2, 1985):338-52.

Jones, J. Greg, Wendell G. Beardsley, David W. Countryman, and Dennis L. Schweitzer. "Estimating Economic Costs of Allocating Land to Wilderness." *Forest Science* 24(No. 3, 1978):410-22.

Kaiser, H. Fred. "Interindustry Model of the U.S. Forest Product Economy." *Forest Product Journal* 18(Nov. 1968):15-18.

Libeau, Clayton. "Cost-Effectiveness Analysis." Forest Service, U.S. Dept. of Agriculture, Washington, D.C. 1969.

Lime, David W. "Locating and Designing Campgrounds to Provide a Full Range of Camping Opportunities." in Outdoor Recreation Research: Applying the Results. General Technical Report NC-9, North Central Forest Experiment Station, St. Paul, Minn. 1974. 56-66.

Lipsey, Richard G., and Peter O. Steiner. *Economics.* 6th Edition. Harper and Row, Publishers, New York. 1981.

Lyon, Gale H., Dean F. Tuthill, and William B. Matthews, Jr. "Economic Analysis of Marinas in Maryland." MP 673, Agricultural Experiment Station, University of Maryland, College Park. 1969.

Manthy, Robert S., and Thomas L. Tucker. "Supply Costs for Public Forest Land Recreation." Research Report 158, Agricultural Experiment Station, Michigan State University, East Lansing. 1972.

Mishan, E. J. *Cost-Benefit Analysis.* 3rd Edition. George Allen and Unwin, London. 1982.

Neuzil, Dennis R. "Uses and Abuses of Highway Benefit-Cost Analysis." *Sierra Club Bulletin* 53(Jan. 1968):16-21.

Nez, George. "A Method of Cost-Effectiveness Analysis for Joint Consideration of Quantities and Qualities in Parks and Conservation Areas." National Park Service, U.S. Dept. of the Interior, Washington, D.C. 1983.

460

Nienaber, Jeanne, and Aaron Wildavsky. *The Budgeting and Evaluation of Federal Recreation Programs.* Basic Books, Inc., New York. 1973.

Peterson, Rodney D. "The Anatomy of Cost-Effectiveness Analysis." *Evaluation Review* 1(Febr. 1986):29-44.

Randall, Alan. *Resource Economics: An Economic Approach to Natural Resource and Environmental Policy.* Grid Publishers, Inc., Columbus, Ohio. 1981.

Reekie, W. Duncan, and Jonathan N. Crook. *Managerial Economics.* 2nd Edition. Philip Allan Publishers, Ltd., Oxford, England. 1982.

Reiling, Stephen D., Mark W. Anderson, and Kenneth C. Gibbs. "Measuring the Costs of Publicly Supplied Outdoor Recreation Facilities: A Methodological Note." *Journal of Leisure Research* 15(No. 3, 1983):203-18.

Reiling, Stephen D., and Mark W. Anderson. "Estimation of the Cost of Providing Publicly-Supported Outdoor Recreation Facilities in Maine." Bulletin 793, Maine Agricultural Experiment Station, University of Maine, Orono. 1983.

Schumacher, E. F. *Small is Beautiful: Economics as if People Mattered.* Harper and Row, Publishers, Inc., New York. 1973.

Shabman, L. A., and Robert J. Kalter. "The Effects of New York State Administered Outdoor Recreation Expenditures on the Distribution of Personal Income." Agricultural Economic Research Report No. 298, Cornell University, Ithaca, N.Y. 1969.

Singer, Neil M. *Public Microeconomics: An Introduction to Government Finance.* 2nd Edition. Little, Brown and Co., Boston, Mass. 1976.

Strauss, Charles H. "Management Study for Pennsylvania Parks." *Guidelines* (July-Sept., 1975):44-48.

Thompson, Mark S. *Benefit Cost Analysis for Program Evaluation.* Sage Publications, Beverly Hills, Calif. 1980.

Tyre, Gary L. "Average Costs of Recreation on National Forests in the South." *Journal of Leisure Research* 7(No. 2, 1975):114-20.

U.S. Dept. of Commerce. *Survey of Current Business.* Washington, D.C. Various years.

Walsh, Richard G. "Efficiency of Resorts in National Forests." Report to the Forest Service, U.S. Dept. of Agriculture, Washington, D.C. 1972.

Walsh, Richard G. "Relationship Between Price and Costs of Ski Area Operation." Outdoor Recreation and Ski Permits on National Forest Lands. Hearings, U.S. Senate, Washington, D.C. 1976. 224-38.

Walsh, Richard G., Ghebre Keleta, John P. Olienyk, and Eliot O. Waples. "Appraised Market Value of Trees on Residential Property with Mountain Pine Beetle and Spruce Budworm Damage in the Colorado Front Range." Report to the U.S. Forest Service by Colorado State University, Fort Collins. 1981.

Walsh, Richard G., Li-Chin Lee, Olga Radulaski, and Gary H. Elsner. "Value of Standard Service Campgrounds in a National Forest." *Economic Value Analysis of Multiple-Use Forestry.* Fred Kaiser, Dennis Schweitzer, and Perry Brown, (eds.). International Union of Forestry Research Organizations. Department of Resource Recreation Management, Oregon State University, Corvallis. 1984. 163-75.

Walsh, Richard G., and John P. Olienyk. "Recreation Demand Effects of Mountain Pine Beetle Damage to the Quality of Forest Recreation Resources in the Colorado Front Range." Report to the Forest Service by Department of Economics, Colorado State University, Fort Collins. 1981.

Walsh, Richard G., Jared P. Soper, and Anthony A. Prato. "Efficiency of Wastewater Disposal in Mountain Areas." Environmental Resources Center Technical Report No. 10, Colorado State University, Fort Collins. 1978.

Waring, Michael R., Ronald W. Hodgson, Thomas M. Walski, and Anita K. Lindsey. "Computing Cost-Effectiveness of Alternative Sanitary Facilities." Institution Report R-83-1, Recreation Research Program, Environmental Laboratory, U.S. Army Engineer Waterways Experiment Station, Vicksburg, Miss. 1983.

461

Chapter Fourteen
Pricing Practices and Market Structure

This chapter introduces the problem of charging users for part of the cost of park and recreation programs and the protection of natural, historic, and cultural resources; evaluates pricing patterns in terms of agency policy, costs, benefits, comparable prices, and feasibility of collection; illustrates the effect of alternative levels of demand on the three basic pricing problems, namely, when marginal costs are less than, equal to, or exceed average costs; distinguishes between several types of price discrimination and related practices such as peak load pricing; summarizes the results of recent studies of user fee policies in public agencies; and discusses the implications for improving future fee practices.

If the issues of scarcity and choice are the basic problems of economics, demand and supply functions are the basic empirical tools. This book described demand and supply in steps. We began with demand, then added supply, and finally we will put the two sides together in this chapter. Demand and supply curves — simply graphs that relate price to quantity demanded and supplied — are explained and used to show how prices and quantities are determined. This depends on a great many other variables, of course. But, for now, let us concentrate on the relationship between the price of a recreation activity and the quantity of it that consumers demand and agencies supply. This chapter reviews the pricing practices of public agencies and private companies from the perspective of economic decision making.

MULTIPURPOSE USER FEES

Economists generally recommend that user fees be set where the added costs of producing recreation opportunities equal the added benefits. This means that prices equal the point of intersection of the demand and supply curve. In other words, the efficient pricing solution for a government agency would be to attempt to provide the competitive industry result. In this way, public recreation opportunities would be supplied at efficient minimum-cost levels, that is, at the lowest point on the average total cost curve. Resources would be efficiently used, consumers would get the largest possible total supply, benefits would be as large as possible, and operating deficits or surpluses would not occur.

In a broad social context, there are other goals that we expect to be served by pricing policy. In addition to economic efficiency, pricing policies can be designed to contribute to: equity in the distribution of income and opportunity; fairness in apportioning joint fixed costs among users; community stability through subsidy of the tourist industry; conservation of natural resources; protection of environmental quality; and other external effects. A number of studies, notably the work of Clawson and Knetsch, reviewed these and related arguments that have been put forward with respect to pricing policy.

First, user fees contribute to economic efficiency because those who choose to participate have higher benefits than those who do not, believing the experience is not worth the cost of the service. However, the cost of collecting user fees is often more than the value of the fees collected, and fee revenues often are not a significant amount relative to the cost of service.

Second, user fees contribute to equity because those who participate pay and nonusers avoid payment. However, public recreation resources belong to all of the people and each individual is entitled to a fair share without penalty. User fees exclude some people who are entitled to use recreation resources. Moreover, free admission is often a more gracious treatment of users as guests of the government.

Third, user fees contribute to fairness because fees are charged for other resource uses such as livestock grazing, timber harvesting, and mining. However, these other resource users often do not pay the market clearing price and are subsidized by the general treasury. Under these conditions, charging higher recreation fees would discriminate against recreation users.

Fourth, user fees contribute to regional economic development because they encourage private companies to compete with government in providing facilities such as campgrounds when prices are not artificially low. However, if user fees are increased when the local tourist industry provides ancillary services such as lodging and food to users of public recreation sites, consumers would have less left over to purchase the goods and services provided by private companies.

Finally, when the external benefits of publicly provided recreation resources are low, costs should be recovered by user fees rather than by taxing the general public. However, user fees should be low when external benefits are high. External benefits of park and recreation programs include environmental protection, reduced crime, increased work productivity, etc. If recreation is a merit good, then children, the aged, the disabled, and the poor should pay reduced or no fees. The defenders of pricing argue that these groups can be helped without lowering user charges for everyone else.

The pricing decision of most park and recreation agencies is no longer, "Should we put a price on outdoor recreation?" Rather it is,

464

"How much should we charge?" Managers are required to justify their pricing decisions by demonstrating that they are neither arbitrary nor inequitable. For example, the Land and Water Conservation Fund Act (1965) authorized user fees at federal recreation sites provided that they are consistent with:

(1) the public policy or interest served by the agency;
(2) the direct and indirect costs to the government and the general public;
(3) the benefits to users and the general public;
(4) comparable prices charged by private, other federal, and non federal public agencies;
(5) the economic and administrative feasibility of fee collection; and
(6) other pertinent matters such as effects on public health, safety, and welfare.

Properly interpreted, this enabling legislation provides the necessary criteria to evaluate the pricing practices of recreation and park agencies at the state and local levels of government as well as federal agencies. The purpose of this chapter is to illustrate how to apply these pricing criteria. We will draw on several studies of user fee policies in public agencies and discuss implications for improving fee practices in the future.

In this chapter, we will adopt the term "user fee" to refer to all types of charges paid by users of parks and other recreation sites. These include direct user charges such as entrance fees, admission fees, rental fees, licenses and permits, and payment for special services. Also included are the revenues from the sale of retail products, although this is not strictly a user fee, and indirect user charges such as rental income from concessioners selling to users.

The National Recreation and Parks Association has adopted the following classification of charges: (1) entrance fees to enter a park, botanical, or zoological garden, historical area or other developed recreation area; (2) admission fees to enter a building or structure offering an exhibit, show, or demonstration including grandstand, museum, zoo, monument, historic building, etc.; (3) rental fees for use of equipment such as boats, golf clubs, lawn chairs and meeting rooms; user fees for use of a facility such as golf course, campsite, swimming pool, boat launching ramp, trapshooting range, etc.; (4) sales revenues from the operation of retail stores and rental income from concessioners selling food, beverage, souvenirs, fireplace wood, educational materials, sports equipment, photo supplies, etc.; (5) licenses and permits for fishing, hunting, cutting firewood, exhibiting, flying light aircraft, etc.; (6) special service fees for instruction and materials, making reservations, equipment storage, night lighting, pay telephone booths, etc. As you can see, our concept of user fees is a broad one. We intend it to include all of the types of fees collected by park and recreation agencies. This is necessary in order to apply Census data.

PRICE PRACTICES AND COSTS

The pricing guidelines recommend that recreation agencies compare user charges to direct and indirect costs. While cost recovery from recreation user fees is not the only basis for pricing decisions by public agencies, it is obviously the most important. Manager of city, county, and state park and recreation programs rank costs of operation and maintenance as the most important consideration in making decisions about user charges. Capital investment costs rank fifth behind user benefits, comparable public fees, and collection costs. The five most important variables are the following:

	City	County	State
Costs of Operation	1	1	1
User Benefits	2	2	5
Comparable Public Charges	4	3	2
Fee Collection Costs	3	4	6
Capital Investment Costs	5	5	7

This is based on a survey of 36 California recreation agencies by Economic Research Associates in 1978.

The purpose of this section is to discuss the results of several studies of user charges and costs of local, state, and federal government. Total government expenditures on park and recreation programs amounted to $8.9 billion in 1982, according to the U.S. Census. This was equal to about 0.72 percent of the total spending by all levels of government in the United States in 1982. Recreation spending was 4.5 percent for cities; compared with all local government, 2.0 percent; state government, 0.6 percent; and federal government, 0.02 percent. Table 14-1 shows that total government spending on park and recreation programs was equivalent to a cost per-capita of slightly more than $38. For the average family of 2.7 persons, this was equal to about $104 per year. Data on the trend in per-capita expenditures indicate that government programs grew rapidly during the 1960s. Growth slowed in the 1970s, followed by no growth in the early 1980s. After removing the effects of inflation, annual growth in spending per capita was:

1967-1972	7.2%
1972-1977	3.7
1977-1982	0

The slow down was of major concern to recreation consumers and managers. In a period of inflating costs and growing scarcity of tax

Table 14-1. Park and Recreation Expenditures by Federal, State, and Local Government, United States, 1967, 1972, 1977, and 1982

Level of Government	Government Expenditures				Percent Change in Per Capita Expenditures[a]		
	1967	1972	1977	1982	1967-1972	1972-1977	1977-1982
All Government, Total							
Million Dollars	$2,110	$3,540	$5,698	$8,876			
Dollars per Capita	$10.69	$16.92	$25.93	$38.29	67.8	60.1	47.7
Federal							
Million Dollars	434[b]	608[b]	782	1,375			
Dollars per Capita	2.20	2.91	3.56	5.93	40.8	28.6	66.6
State							
Million Dollars	385	614	1,025	1,362			
Dollars per Capita	1.95	2.93	4.66	5.98	50.8	59.0	28.3
Local, Total							
Million Dollars	1,291	2,318	3,891	6,140			
Dollars per Capita	6.54	11.08	17.71	26.49	69.4	59.8	49.6
City							
Million Dollars	905	1,561	2,504	4,009			
Dollars per Capita	4.58	7.46	11.39	17.30	62.9	52.7	51.9
County							
Million Dollars	200	430	822	1,224			
Dollars per Capita	1.01	2.05	3.74	5.28	103.0	82.4	41.2
Township							
Million Dollars	61	114	199	282			
Dollars per Capita	0.30	0.54	0.91	1.22	80.0	68.5	34.1
Special District							
Million Dollars	125	213	366	625			
Dollars per Capita	.063	1.02	1.67	2.70	61.9	63.7	61.7

[a]Inflation measured by the gross national product implicit price deflator increased 26.5 percent from 1967 to 1972, 40.1 percent from 1972 to 1977, and 47.7 percent from 1977 to 1982.
[b]Estimate based on growth in total federal expenditures from 1965 to 1975 of 80 percent.
Source: U.S. Census.

revenues to support park and recreation programs, there was increased interest in user charges.

In the past, most observers of public pricing practices in the United States and elsewhere throughout the world concluded that user charges were "excessively low or zero" (Vickerman) with virtually all of the costs of public recreation programs paid by general tax revenues rather than user fees. There were many cases where this was true in the past and continue to the present time. However, since their beginning, park and recreation programs have paid a part of their costs from entrance fees, licenses, permits, and other kinds of charges, particularly for special services such as camping. In the 1970s and 1980s, public agencies began to rely on recreation use fees to cover a larger proportion of their costs.

States recovered more of the costs of park and recreation programs from users than did either local or federal government. In the early 1980s, user charges paid 37 percent of state operating costs; compared with local government, 18 percent; U.S. Forest Service, 24 percent; Corps of Engineers, 10 percent; and National Park Service, less than 5 percent. This may be related to the suitability of user fee collection at intermediate type recreation facilities of the states compared with user-oriented facilities of local government, and with resource-based facilities of the federal government. For a description of the relevant characteristics of these three types of recreation supply, see Table 8-1.

Local Government Park and Recreation Programs

Local governments have had park and recreation programs since the earliest organization of city states. In ancient Greece, public gardens and forests were provided on temple grounds. One of the earliest recorded private endowments of a public park was Julius Caesar's bequest of his private gardens to the people of Rome. During the Middle Ages, there was little or no concern about public parks.

The modern parks movement began with the industrial revolution in the growing urban centers of Europe during the late 18th and early 19th centuries. The word "parc" originally meant enclosure of animals for hunting by the nobility. Most of them were converted to parks for the people. Investigations by the British Parliament emphasized the benefits of parks to industrial workers. The history of parks was described by Knudson, noted authority on outdoor recreation management at Purdue University.

In North America, public squares were set aside in the earliest settlements. The Boston Commons, established in 1634, is one of the oldest parks in the United States. Central Park was established in New York City in 1858. Local parks were developed in most cities during the latter half of the 19th Century. Many public works programs benefited city parks during the economic depression of the 1930s. After World War II, the sustained period of economic prosperity led to renewed interest in the balanced growth of urban and suburban parks. With the migration of many middle- and upper-income people to the suburbs, more recreation programs in the large cities served low-income people who could least afford to pay user fees.

Local government park and recreation sites vary in size, design, facilities, and programs. They are planned to meet the needs of the people of a neighborhood or section of town rather than the state or nation. They include vest pocket parks on 30-foot lots between two large buildings with playground equipment, concrete surfaces, and a minimum of landscaping. They also include large parks (3,000 to 14,000 acres) with a natural environment except for access roads, trails, picnic sites, etc. Despite the unique nature of each park, some recreation facilities are common to most park systems. Verhoven and Lancaster surveyed 1,123 cities in the mid-1970s with parks having the following facilities: tennis courts, 76.0 percent; baseball and softball diamonds, 72.8 percent; basketball courts, 71.3 percent; recreation centers, 59.8 percent; athletic fields, 54.9 percent; outdoor swimming pools, 53.6 percent; outdoor ice skating rinks, 27.2 percent; boat-launching facilities, 25.3 percent; day camps, 26.2 percent; bathing beaches, 19.1 percent; 18-hole golf courses, 18.3 percent; outdoor theaters, 14.4 percent; nature centers, 12.6 percent; indoor pools, 10.8 percent; outdoor recreation centers, 9.9 percent; museums, 9.5 percent; zoos, 8.9 percent; marinas, 8.4 percent; resident camps, 6.5 percent; artificial ice-skating rinks, 6.4 percent; outdoor ice skating rinks, 5.7 percent; portable pools, 4.5 percent; combined indoor-outdoor pools, 2.3 percent; and indoor tennis courts, 2.8 percent.

The park and recreation programs of local government represent the most important public supply of recreation opportunities in the United States. Table 14-1 shows that the total expenditures of local government was $6.1 billion in 1982. Cities were the most important, accounting for about 65 percent of this amount; compared with counties, 20 percent; special recreation districts, 10 percent; and townships, 5 percent. This was equivalent to a per-capita cost of $26.50 for all park and recreation programs of local government including cities, $17.30; counties, $5.28; special districts, $2.70; and townships, $1.22. This compares to a per-capita cost of nearly $6.00 for state programs and an identical amount, $6.00, for federal programs. Local government spending is higher because three-fourths of all participation in recreation occurs close to where people live. Nearly one-fourth occurs during the few available hours of a day within 1-5 miles from the residence of participants, and an additional one-half on single-day outings within 50 miles of home, as shown in Chapter 3.

Table 14-1 also shows the trend in per-capita expenditures by local government, which has been of major concern to recreation managers

469

and consumers. The Census data show that local recreation expenditures grew rapidly during the 1960s. Growth slowed in the 1970s and there was little or no growth in the early 1980s. After removing the effects of inflation, annual growth in spending per capita was:

1967-1972	7.4%
1972-1977	3.7
1977-1982	0.4

These growth rates were calculated from the information presented. From 1967 to 1972, local government spending increased 69.4 percent, or 42.9 percent more than inflation of 26.5 percent. From 1972 to 1977, local government spending increased 59.8 percent, or 19.7 percent more than inflation of 40.1 percent. From 1977 to 1982, local government spending increased 49.6 percent, or only 1.9 percent more than inflation of 47.7 percent.

Table 14-2 shows that expenditures for park and recreation programs accounted for about 2.0 percent of total spending by local government in 1982. Local park and recreation spending ranged from

Table 14-2. Park and Recreation Expenditures and User Charges by Local Government, United States, 1967, 1972, and 1977

Level of Government	Park and Recreation Expenditures			Park and Recreation User Charges		
	1967	1972	1977	1967	1972	1977
Local Government, Total						
Million Dollars	$1,290.8	$2,318.1	$3,890.8	$194.6	$356.6	$633.3
Percent	2.2%[a]	2.2%	2.3%	15.1%[b]	15.4%	16.3%
Within Metro Areas						
Million Dollars	1,132.5	2,090.9	3,421.6	174.8	324.6	579.0
Percent	2.6	2.5	2.6	15.4	15.5	16.9
Cities						
Million Dollars	787.0	1,402.5	2,200.1	123.8	216.8	373.9
Percent	4.8	4.5	4.5	15.7	15.5	17.0
Counties						
Million Dollars	179.1	388.5	706.7	26.2	57.2	97.0
Percent	2.4	2.4	2.5	14.6	14.7	13.7
Townships						
Million Dollars	50.3	98.3	173.8	6.3	12.9	23.2
Percent	3.5	3.6	3.8	12.5	13.1	13.3
Special Districts						
Million Dollars	116.2	201.6	341.0	18.5	37.7	84.9
Percent	5.4	4.5	5.0	15.9	18.7	24.9
Outside Metro Areas						
Million Dollars	158.3	227.2	469.1	19.8	32.0	54.4
Percent	1.0	1.0	1.2	12.5	14.1	11.6
Per Capita						
Local Government, Total	$6.59	$11.41	$18.26	$0.99	$1.75	$2.97
Within Metro Areas	8.70	14.59	22.07	1.34	2.27	3.73
Outside Metro Areas	2.41	3.79	8.08	0.34	0.53	.094

[a]Park and recreation expenditures as a percentage of total local government expenditures for all services.
[b]User charges as a percentage of park and recreation expenditures.
Source: U.S. Census.

1.8 to 2.6 percent of total spending during the 60-year period from 1922 to 1982 with no apparent trend up or down. There was considerable variation, however, among levels of local government. Spending for recreation and parks programs ranged from 1.2 percent of total expenditures by local governments outside metropolitan areas to 2.6 percent within. For large metropolitan areas, park and recreation spending rose to 3.0 percent, compared to 2.5 percent for medium sized, and 2.0 percent for small. Cities within metropolitan areas spent 4.5 percent of their total budgets for park and recreation programs; special recreation districts, 5.0 percent; townships, 3.8 percent; and counties, 2.5 percent.

Table 14-3 illustrates the trend in user charges for the park and recreation programs of city governments in each of the states from 1967 to 1982. User fees were 15.3 percent in 1967 and virtually an identical proportion, 15.2 percent, in 1972. This means that during the 5-year period, user charges increased at about the same rate as expenditures on park and recreation programs. Then began a slowly rising trend during the next 10 years. User fees increased to 16.2 percent in 1977 and to 17.8 percent in 1982. This means that user fees as a proportion of expenditures increased 7 percent from 1972 to 1977 and by 10 percent from 1977 to 1982. The trend was for the user fees of cities to increase in more and more states. From 1972 to 1977, user fees rose in 19 of the 50 states while from 1977 to 1982, they increased in 35 states.

The increase in user charges by the cities was less than expected during a period of inflating costs and growing scarcity of tax revenues to support park and recreation programs (Crompton). In California cities, for example, where Proposition 13 sharply curtailed property tax revenues for local government programs, user fees increased less than for those in the rest of the nation. User charges by California cities increased from 19.2 percent in 1977 to 20.6 percent in 1982, or by 7 percent compared with a 10 percent increase for the nation. In California, city government spending for park and recreation programs was $790.1 million in 1972, more than double that for cities in any other state. From 1977 to 1982, city government spending on park and recreation programs in the state increased by 80 percent, or 32 percent more than inflation of 47.7 percent. Apparently, city governments were able to obtain most of this increase in funding from sources other than property taxes or user fees. This is discussed in a later section.

There was considerable variation among the states in the revenue from user fees as a proportion of expenditures for city park and recreation programs. In 1982, the states where user fees of cities were the highest included North Dakota, 43.0 percent; and West Virginia, 42.2 percent. The states where user fees of cities were the lowest included

Table 14-3. User Charges as a Percent of Total Park and Recreation Expenditures by City Government, United States, 1967 to 1982

City Governments in the State of	Total Expenditures, Million Dollars				Percent User Charges			
	1967	1972	1977	1982	1967	1972	1977	1982
United States	$913.8	$1,572.6	$2,515.4	$4,041.9	15.3	15.2	16.2	17.8
Alabama	9.1	18.1	37.3	60.9	21.1	13.3	12.2	15.3
Alaska	0.8	3.1	10.7	33.8	4.0	6.7	4.1	2.9
Arizona	11.3	35.0	46.1	83.0	12.6	8.7	13.5	16.5
Arkansas	2.9	3.9	11.1	13.3	16.0	19.6	11.7	18.2
California	171.8	266.6	438.5	790.3	17.5	19.3	19.2	20.6
Colorado	14.4	21.3	69.4	96.0	15.9	25.6	17.4	22.7
Connecticut	12.1	20.2	20.8	33.5	12.5	12.1	29.7	36.4
Delaware	1.1	2.6	3.7	4.1	13.6	—	1.3	3.7
District of Columbia	15.9	16.3	23.1	26.3	7.3	9.1	10.1	10.9
Florida	43.9	64.7	136.2	288.0	21.2	22.3	21.4	19.6
Georgia	14.1	33.4	38.6	62.8	15.4	11.7	18.3	19.9
Hawaii	9.0	14.8	29.6	33.5	13.9	14.4	11.7	11.2
Idaho	1.8	3.3	8.7	10.2	19.1	17.9	11.6	19.4
Illinois	16.3	26.2	49.9	78.9	10.3	13.9	13.3	19.4
Indiana	20.5	34.8	47.5	58.4	16.0	16.1	17.6	26.0
Iowa	12.3	16.2	35.7	54.7	20.1	26.9	19.4	22.4
Kansas	8.9	10.1	18.7	38.4	13.5	18.0	19.0	17.7
Kentucky	4.9	11.8	19.9	27.5	13.7	14.3	12.0	17.2
Louisiana	11.1	22.3	47.7	71.2	17.5	16.7	12.6	17.5
Maine	1.3	2.7	6.0	5.9	16.8	9.0	10.7	14.1
Maryland	13.2	24.3	39.3	52.1	16.8	14.9	9.8	12.4
Massachusetts	20.1	48.4	50.9	59.6	5.6	3.3	3.3	6.6
Michigan	48.0	71.4	125.5	164.2	18.4	18.6	19.5	15.4
Minnesota	23.2	42.2	79.7	139.5	19.6	20.2	22.3	20.3
Mississippi	3.7	4.4	12.7	17.1	6.6	13.4	10.8	9.2
Missouri	23.4	35.0	72.3	65.5	18.0	19.5	13.4	26.3
Montana	2.6	2.4	5.6	7.3	4.2	14.2	5.9	14.9
Nebraska	6.2	10.8	21.8	31.0	19.4	22.0	18.3	20.1
Nevada	3.0	5.5	9.7	19.4	11.8	12.0	17.2	14.7
New Hampshire	1.3	2.7	3.8	5.7	13.4	12.2	11.4	19.9
New Jersey	25.8	35.2	52.1	53.2	12.5	13.2	10.1	15.3
New Mexico	3.8	12.7	15.8	30.4	16.7	9.5	13.4	12.2
New York	115.7	175.4	190.6	294.2	10.0	9.3	9.9	8.1
North Carolina	12.3	24.1	46.6	80.7	16.7	16.9	14.2	19.9
North Dakota	0.6	3.0	1.3	2.2	27.8	29.3	18.5	43.0
Ohio	43.1	68.4	111.0	162.8	18.1	19.3	18.6	18.6
Oklahoma	8.1	19.5	40.2	54.6	26.9	18.6	14.7	19.9
Oregon	16.0	16.1	28.5	58.2	14.0	22.0	22.4	20.4
Pennsylvania	38.5	66.4	86.7	110.7	6.6	8.2	10.9	11.1
Rhode Island	2.4	9.0	7.2	8.4	4.4	1.0	6.7	7.3
South Carolina	4.0	5.3	13.6	20.1	8.4	9.8	8.0	13.6
South Dakota	2.4	4.3	8.8	13.9	12.8	19.9	15.4	20.4
Tennessee	16.2	33.7	52.1	96.7	24.8	18.3	24.4	17.8
Texas	40.5	109.5	147.9	312.8	16.4	10.9	19.2	19.2
Utah	3.4	6.1	12.4	22.8	26.2	25.3	21.6	23.4
Vermont	0.5	0.9	1.6	2.0	20.8	9.7	20.1	25.0
Virginia	12.6	32.4	45.5	68.4	6.2	15.2	18.2	14.4
Washington	15.0	39.9	67.1	107.7	22.4	14.4	13.5	17.0
West Virginia	2.8	4.2	7.9	11.8	71.8	68.2	19.1	42.2
Wisconsin	20.8	31.0	53.8	77.1	10.7	13.1	11.6	17.5
Wyoming	1.0	1.2	4.1	21.1	12.5	17.5	9.7	8.1

Source: U.S. Census.

472

Alaska, 2.9 percent; and Delaware, 3.7 percent. It was reported that the park and recreation department of the industrial city of Wheeling, West Virginia, was 98 percent self sufficient. Some nonfee programs were subsidized by user fees from other programs. On the other hand, municipal governments in Alaska apparently considered it an essential public service to subsidize recreation programs to avoid "cabin fever" during the long winter months.

User fees for city park and recreation programs were higher within metropolitan areas than outside. User fees were nearly 17 percent of per capita park and recreation expenditures within metropolitan areas compared with about 12 percent in rural areas of the country (Table 14-2). Within large metropolitan areas, smaller suburban cities and counties recovered more of costs from user fees than did the large central city, according to a national urban recreation study. The city of Denver, for example, recovered only about 4 percent of the cost of city park and recreation programs in 1985, compared with an average of 40 percent in smaller cities within the metropolitan area and 100 percent in a suburban recreation district. In Denver, it cost $6 to rent a softball field for a 2-hour game compared with $50 in two smaller cities within the metropolitan area. Table 14-2 shows that special recreation districts in suburban areas of metropolitan regions recovered 25 percent of cost from user fees, which was more than any other type of local government. Suburbs with more medium- to high-income residents were more able to pay for recreation services. Older neighborhoods in the central cities have had immigration of poorer people and loss of medium- and high-income residents. From an income distribution viewpoint, it may be desirable that large cities continue to recover less of cost from user fees than do suburban areas.

In the past, the primary reason that user fees did not equal the cost of local government programs was that most managers believed they should not do so. This was the finding of an Economic Research Associates survey of a sample of managers about agency user fee policies and practices in 1975. They reported that the pricing structure preferred by a majority of local government agencies was to offer resource-based activities free and to charge user fees for selected recreation activities requiring developed facilities. Fifty-five percent of the managers believed that users should pay only for special facilities such as golf courses, campgrounds, boat-launching ramps, etc. About 20 percent reported users should not pay any of the costs. As a result, entrance fees were charged at only 16 percent of the large multiple-use parks operated by cities and 14 percent of the counties. In 36 percent of the cities and 53 percent of the counties, user fees were charged for some recreation activities at developed sites.

In Oakland, California, for example, Odell reported that historically, the city subsidized children' recreation activities from general tax revenues on the principle that recreation activities are wholesome and build character. Also, several of the programs for senior citizens were fully supported through general tax revenues. Overall, the recreation and parks department recovered one-third of total expenditures. The balance was subsidized from general tax revenue and grants from federal and state government. There was considerable variation among recreation activities in the proportion of costs recovered by user fees. Golf courses were operated on a self-supporting basis which means that golfers of working age subsidized persons under 18 and over 65 who paid reduced green fees. The city recovered 70 percent of the operation cost of facilities at a camp for day and overnight use. The costs of the children's day camp were extensively subsidized; fees recovered only part of the costs of serving noon luncheons. The fees for family campers recovered all costs other than capital investment in land and facilities. Excluding capital costs, charges for sailing and boating recovered 30 percent of operating costs of the programs. There were no charges for tennis facilities which were mostly used by high school students, or for lawn bowling facilities for senior citizens. The city subsidized special recreation classes by providing facilities, maintenance, publicity, and various other overhead costs. The instructors received the registration fees to provide them an incentive to excel as their income would be closely related to instructional quality.

Several points should be made about the quality of information presented here from the Census of Government. While the data from census reports are generally considered the most reliable available, they do not provide a competely satisfactory measure of either outdoor recreation and parks expenditures or user fees. As a result, outdoor recreation spending by local government is overestimated somewhat. The estimates presented here are sufficient, nonetheless, to indicate overall trends.

First, some unknown portion of the park and recreation expenditures by local government is for indoor recreation and omits related forestry and natural resource programs, as noted in Chapter 2. Since the 1960s, nearly all cities have combined park and recreation departments. This means that a portion of the budget has been spent for indoor recreation at schools, community centers, museums, art galleries, auditoriums, and other convention and exhibit centers, as well as parks. The natural resource programs of local government are in a category separate from the park and recreation programs. Natural resource programs include soil, water, forests, minerals, irrigation drainage, flood control, forestry and forest fire protection, soil reclamation, soil and water conservation, fish and wildlife management programs, and agricultural fairs. Many of these programs also contribute to the enjoyment of outdoor recreation activities. Most notable are local government expenditures for fish and wildlife programs, forestry and forest fire protection, water resource development, and protection of water quality.

Second, the Census category, "current charges," includes rental revenues from concessioners, gross retail sales, and the sale of surplus equipment, etc., as well as user fees. While the rents from concessioners providing goods and services to recreation users may be considered an indirect user charge, there is some question about classifying gross retail sales to consumers as user fees, and the sale of surplus property obviously has no relation to user charges. Fortunately, concession revenues and retail sales usually make up a small portion of this category. However, some local governments operate retail stores, restaurants, and overnight accommodations, the gross revenue from which cannot be considered equivalent to user fees for access to park and recreation facilities. Crompton illustrated the problem in the case of the city of Miami which presumably included such items as retail sales and rents from concessioners at the Orange Bowl as current charges. This helps explain why Miami reported user charges were 55.1 percent of expenditures compared with only 21.4 percent for all municipal governments in the state of Florida.

Finally, for neighborhood parks, which are used mostly by local residents, general tax revenue from local sources may be viewed as an indirect form of user fee because participation in the service hinges on local residence for the most part. A substantial portion of the costs of park operation and maintenance are paid from the general funds of local government, which are financed by property and sales taxes paid by local residents. Often, the capital costs of new neighborhood parks can be paid by the developer of new residential units based on the value of each residence. But many cities also provide park and recreation services to persons who reside and pay taxes in the suburbs. User fees can recoup some of the costs of serving suburban users and tourists by charging higher rates for nonresidents and during the peak tourist season. Thus, some observers believe that from a practical viewpoint, most of the costs of local park and recreation facilities can be recovered by a combination of local tax assessments and user fees. Unlike most state and federal recreation programs, local park and recreation programs can be financed largely by either direct or indirect user charges.

Intergovernment transfers or grants from state and federal government also have helped local government finance park and recreation programs. Their purpose has been to cover the capital costs of construction and rehabilitation of neighborhood park and recreation facilities, and to pay some of the costs of serving nonresidential users and tourists. The Census data show the trend in sources of revenue for all local government operations. Unfortunately, the data do not show the amount of each type of revenue allocated to the park and recreation program. Still the overall finances of local government indicate the trend in funds available for specific programs. The percentage of total revenue from selected sources is the following:

	1972	1977	1982
Intergovernmental Transfers	34.6%	39.1%	37.0%
Local Government Sources	65.4	60.3	63.0
Property Taxes	36.3	30.7	25.0
Sales Taxes	3.7	4.2	4.7
User Charges	13.8	13.9	19.2

During the 10 years from 1972 to 1982, the relative importance of local property taxes declined sharply while local sales taxes increased somewhat, as did revenues from user charges. Intergovernmental transfers, mostly federal grants to local government or to the states for transfer to local governments, increased somewhat from 1972 to 1982, although they were higher in 1977 than 1982. We know from a 1975 study of recreation expenditures by federal, state, and local government discussed in Chapter 2 that intergovernmental transfers or grants accounted for about one-third of total expenditures by state and local government agencies for park and recreation programs. The trend in total intergovernment transfers suggests that federal and state grants to local government continued to be a substantial source of revenue for park and recreation programs in 1982 as well as in more recent years.

State Park and Recreation Programs

The first state recreation areas were set aside by the Massachusetts Bay Colony in 1641. Public rights were established for access to 2,000 lakes with 90,000 surface acres for recreation use by the people. The California state parks system may be the earliest in the nation. Yosemite was granted to the state in 1864 for preservation and public recreation use. State protection was less than desired, however. In 1890, John Muir and other concerned citizens persuaded Congress to establish a national park which included the state lands. In 1905, the state returned Yosemite Valley and Mariposa Grave to the federal government as part of Yosemite National Park.

Until the 1930s, state park and recreation programs were relatively minor compared with the historic role of state programs in health, education, transportation, and police protection. Few state parks or recreation areas were purchased from private owners using state tax revenues. Some recreation sites were located on land originally held by the colonies and not turned over to the federal government, federal school land turned over to the states, tax-delinquent private land, and land received as gifts. For example, Pennsylvania obtained nearly 3 million acres of tax-delinquent forest and wildlife lands. Illinois obtained lands at low prices that were neither productive for agriculture nor useful for residential and commercial development. Maine, Florida, Mississippi, Louisiana, and other states leased private timber lands for public recreation use.

After World War II, state park and recreation programs expanded rapidly. During the 30 years from 1950 to 1980, state recreation land more than doubled from about 4 million acres to over 9 million acres. States acquired the additional recreation land primarily with special bond issues and special taxes which provided matching funds for federal grants. During the same time period, recreation use increased from 114 million to 618 million visits. With an average of 5 hours per visit, this was equivalent to 257 million 12-hour recreation visitor days in 1980. This enables us to gain some perspective as to the role of states by comparing them to national park and forest recreation programs, as follows:

	Surface Acres, Million	Recreation Visitor Days, Million	RVDs per Acre
State Park and Recreation Areas	9	257	28.6
National Park Service	57	106	1.9
U.S. Forest Service	185	230	1.2

This shows that with considerably less land area, the states provided more recreation use than either of the federal agencies. Apparently, the state acreage was much more effectively used, with 28.6 recreation visitor days per acre compared to only 1.9 for the National Park Service and 1.2 for the U.S. Forest Service. But contrary to popular belief, state lands do not provide more total recreation than the federal lands.

State parks differ from national parks in the appeal and significance of their features. Usually a state park must have either scenic or historic value to residents of the state. Local attractions that have state significance are recommended for state acquisition and management. As is true for all functions of state government, the management of park and recreation programs differs among the states. Most state parks are managed solely for the dual purpose of recreation use and preservation of the resource, similar to the national parks. Others are managed for multiple use including recreation, timber, range, and wildlife, similar to the national forests. Others are highly developed resort communities with lodges, golf courses, and marinas, such as in Kentucky.

All 50 states have some state parks. They range from small highway rest stops of a few acres to huge natural areas, such as in Alaska. State parks are especially important in the eastern part of the United States where there is very little federal park and recreation land. Local government park and recreation areas are usually of small size. Thus, the states provide a large share of the supply of recreation resources. In the state of New York, for example, Adirondack State Park was established in 1892 and includes 3.4 million acres of state, local government, and private land. As such, it is several times larger than any of the national parks. It includes the 2.0-million-acre, state-owned Adirondack Forest Preserve. In addition, there are 3.7 million acres of private land over which the state maintains land use controls to keep the park attractive while allowing logging, mining, and continued operation of resorts such as Saratoga Springs. Even in the western United States, where federal parks and forests offer extensive opportunities for recreation, state parks are important. They often are located on the plains or in the foothills around small reservoirs or lakes. State parks often provide warm-water fishing, camping, picnicking, and other recreation activities within one or two hours drive from the larger cities in the region.

Historically, expenditures on state park and recreation programs have been second only to city government, according to the Census. Table 14-1 shows that total park and recreation spending by the states was $1.37 billion in 1982. It accounted for only 0.6 percent of the total spending by state government in 1982. It was equivalent to a cost per capita of about $6. The trend in per-capita expenditures is also shown. The data indicate that state recreation expenditures grew moderately during the 1960s. Growth slowed in the 1970s, but was at the same rate as total government expenditures for park and recreation programs. State spending fell sharply in the early 1980s. After removing the effects of inflation, the annual change in spending per capita was:

1967-1972	4.5%
1972-1977	3.5
1977-1982	-3.6

Note that per capita spending for state park and recreation programs decreased by an average of 3.6 per year from 1977 to 1982.

Table 14-4 summarizes information on the number of visits, costs, and user charges for each of the 50 states. The data are not directly comparable to Census data on state park and recreation programs. In some states, the data were only for state parks. Some states omitted expenditures for fixed capital investments. In other states, the agency included forestry, fish and wildlife, and other functions. Total expenditures on state park and recreation programs were reported as nearly $900 million in 1983 (with a few states reporting for 1984). Of this amount, direct operating costs were 71 percent, and capital investments, 29 percent. With 647.5 million visits, operating costs averaged nearly $1.00 per visit and total expenditures, including capital invest-

Table 14-4. User Charges as a Percent of Park and Recreation Expenditures by State Government, United States, 1983

State	Total Visits, Millions	Expenditures, Million Dollars Operating	Capital	Total	Average Total Expenditures per Visit	User Charges Million Dollars	Percentage of Operating Expenditures	Total Expenditures
Total or Average	$647.5	$638.6	$260.9	$899.7	$1.40	$234.9	37%	26%
Alabama	5.2	11.9	—	11.9	2.30	7.9	66	66
Alaska	3.6	5.4	0.2	5.6	1.60	0.0	0	0
Arizona	2.1	3.3	2.4	5.7	2.70	0.9	27	16
Arkansas	6.6	12.5	0.7	13.2	2.00	6.6	53	50
California	61.3	80.9	60.5	141.4	2.30	25.7	32	18
Colorado	6.4	5.8	2.0	7.8	1.20	2.7	47	35
Connecticut	9.1	8.0	1.6	9.6	1.10	2.3	29	24
Delaware	2.9	2.6	1.0	3.6	1.20	2.0	77	56
*Florida	14.8	20.1	18.4	38.4	2.60	7.0	35	18
Georgia	10.2	16.2	1.3	17.5	1.70	6.5	40	37
Hawaii	11.9	3.9	4.6	8.5	0.70	0.7	18	8
Idaho	1.9	1.9	1.5	3.3	1.70	0.6	32	18
Illinois	30.5	21.6	14.2	35.8	1.20	2.0	9	6
*Indiana	8.7	7.2	3.5	10.7	1.20	5.7	79	53
Iowa	14.8	4.8	—	4.8	0.30	1.0	21	21
Kansas	4.4	4.6	1.2	5.8	1.30	1.4	30	24
Kentucky	22.9	42.0	1.5	43.5	1.90	27.2	65	63
*Louisiana	1.1	6.8	1.1	7.9	7.20	0.9	13	11
*Maine	2.8	3.5	0.8	4.3	1.50	0.9	26	21
Maryland	5.6	9.1	3.6	12.7	2.30	3.7	41	29
Massachusetts	11.5	13.7	17.8	31.4	2.70	5.8	42	18
Michigan	20.7	14.7	5.3	20.0	1.00	10.5	71	53
Minnesota	6.1	9.5	2.0	11.5	1.90	3.2	34	28
Mississippi	4.5	10.9	0.8	11.7	2.60	3.7	34	32
Missouri	9.7	7.5	8.3	15.8	1.60	1.8	24	11
Montana	3.6	2.1	2.2	4.2	1.20	0.1	5	2
Nebraska	7.9	4.8	1.0	5.8	0.70	2.2	46	38
Nevada	4.2	2.4	1.3	3.7	0.90	0.4	17	11
New Hampshire	4.2	4.3	3.8	8.2	2.00	4.1	95	50
New Jersey	8.9	13.2	0.5	13.7	1.50	2.7	20	20
New Mexico	5.0	4.6	1.8	6.4	1.30	0.8	17	13
New York	49.4	73.8	15.5	89.4	1.80	21.3	29	24
North Carolina	5.2	4.8	1.9	6.7	1.30	0.5	10	7
North Dakota	0.9	2.1	0.9	3.0	3.30	0.4	19	13
Ohio	62.1	28.1	5.8	33.9	0.50	8.5	30	25
Oklahoma	17.8	17.4	3.1	20.5	1.20	4.7	27	23
Oregon	32.2	13.2	1.3	14.5	0.50	4.1	31	28
*Pennsylvania	35.0	26.0	30.5	56.5	1.60	4.6	18	8
*Rhode Island	6.8	3.8	—	3.8	0.60	1.3	34	34
South Carolina	11.3	8.9	1.4	10.4	0.90	6.2	70	60
South Dakota	4.9	3.7	1.8	5.4	1.10	2.1	57	39
Tennessee	20.0	20.5	8.5	29.0	1.50	11.8	58	41
Texas	18.1	22.6	9.8	32.4	1.80	7.6	34	23
Utah	5.7	6.1	3.3	9.5	1.70	1.5	25	16
Vermont	0.9	2.5	0.4	2.9	3.20	2.3	92	79
Virginia	3.3	4.3	3.0	7.3	2.20	1.1	26	15
Washington	39.6	16.0	4.8	20.7	0.50	3.7	23	18
West Virginia	8.2	14.1	1.4	15.5	1.90	8.6	61	55
Wisconsin	10.8	8.2	2.8	11.0	1.00	3.6	44	33
*Wyoming	2.1	2.3	0.9	3.2	1.50	0.1	4	3

* = 1984.
Source: National Association of State Park Directors.

ment, $1.40 per visit. There was a great deal of difference among the states in average total expenditures per visit. Highest was Louisiana with expenditures of $7.20 per visit. North Dakota was second with $3.30 per visit and Vermont third with $3.20 per visit. Lowest was Iowa with $0.30 per visit. Ohio and Oregon each reported expenditures of $0.50 per visit.

There is evidence to suggest that the proportion of costs recovered by the states from user charges was relatively stable for 25 years. Table 14-4 shows that user charges were 37 percent of direct operating costs in 1983 compared to 39 percent in the 1950s, according to Clawson and Knetsch. User charges were equal to 26 percent of total expenditures in 1983 compared to 23 percent in the 1950s. The small difference in the percentages for the two points in time may be explained by the decline in fixed capital expenditures in the early 1980s.

Many of the state park and recreation agencies have made considerable progress toward the objective of users paying for the costs. Table 14-4 shows that considerable variation among the states remained in 1983. User charges were the highest in the Northeast, where they were 95 percent of operating costs in New Hampshire and 92 percent in Vermont. In the Midwest, user charges were 79 percent of operating costs in Indiana and 71 percent in Michigan. In the South, user charges were 70 percent of operating costs in South Carolina and 66 percent in Alabama. User charges were the lowest in the West, where they were 4 percent of operating costs in Wyoming and 5 percent in Montana. Apparently, states in the highly populated East provided more developed recreation sites where it was appropriate to charge user fees, while states in the sparsely populated West had more sites in natural areas where it was less appropriate to charge. State parks in Michigan and New Hampshire recovered all of their operating costs from user fees. Buechner reported that Michigan state parks charged an average of $0.60 per visit which was equal to 116 percent of operating costs in 1975. In New Hampshire, user charges averaged $0.62 per visit which recovered 109 percent of operating costs in the same year.

Nearly all states reported one or more type of user charge. These included: entrance fee, 37 states; camping fee, 46; camping reservation fee, 26; cabin and lodge room rental, 36; concessioners, 50; beach and pool, 18; golf courses, 17; and revenue for other operations, 43. Entrance fees at state park and recreation sites ranged from $0.50 per vehicle in Florida to $4 in New Hampshire and several other states. Minnesota charged residents $3 per vehicle and nonresidents $4. Annual passes averaged $25 per vehicle, ranging from $8 in Rhode Island to $65 in California and $125 in New Jersey. Camping fees at modern sites averaged $7 per day and ranged from $3 in Kansas to $12 in Delaware. At primitive campsites, fees averaged $5 per day, ranging from $0.25 in South Carolina to $8 in California. States that accepted reservations for camping charged reservation fees averaging $3 and ranging from $1 in Indiana to $5 in West Virginia. Rental rates for cabins, cottages, and lodge rooms averaged about $35 per night, ranging from $4 in North Dakota to $144 in Washington state. These user charges are summarized as follows:

	Average	Range
Entrance Fee	$ 3	$0.50-$4
Campsite, Primitive	5	1-8
Campsite, Modern	7	3-12
Cabin, Lodge Room	35	4-144

There are a number of important points that should be made about the role of states in recreation. The first is that state government has been the lead organization in the national effort to supply recreation resources since passage of the Land and Water Conservation Fund Act of 1965. In most states, a division of planning for recreation has prepared plans and coordinated the distribution of grants to agencies of the state and local government. The Act provided each of the states with matching funds. The states have allocated these financial resources to acquire land, develop facilities, and improve programs. The states have provided technical assistance to local government agencies preparing proposed projects to receive grant money. Eligibility of the proposed projects has been evaluated in terms of their contribution to state comprehensive recreation plans. In addition, the states have received historic preservation funds. State agencies have reviewed federal environmental impact statements, and their comments have affected federal programs within the states.

Second, most states have had tourist promotion divisions to advertise recreation opportunities, both public and private. Budgets for tourism promotion increased dramatically in the 10-year period from 1975 to 1985. Spending increased from about $45 million in 1975 to $120 million in 1982 and to $189 million in 1985. With these revenues, the states produced publications and advertised in newspapers, magazines, radio, television, and at travel exhibitions. They also used direct mail advertising, and replied to requests for information about recreation opportunities in the state. The state agencies coordinate their work with chambers of commerce and private companies in tourist areas. Surveys by tourist promotion organizations show that expenditures by the states for promotion are more than compensated for by increased sales taxes paid by the increased number of visitors, as illustrated in Chapter 12. But problems of coordination between agencies may develop. One agency promoted additional recreation use of state parks, for example, while managers of the parks lacked sufficient revenue to cope with the effects of resulting overuse.

Third, the states have land that is used for recreation although it was acquired for other purposes. In addition to the 9 million acres of state park and recreation areas, the states reported 9 million acres of fish and wildlife areas and over 10 million acres of forests in 1980. In the past, the recreation use of state forests was often considered secondary to the primary purpose of timber production and sale. Access was usually by unimproved fire lanes and logging roads. Campgrounds were primitive with few developed sites. More recently, state forest managers have begun to consider the aesthetic and recreation effects of timber production, especially in the northeast and midwest where public recreation lands are particularly scarce. Some observers have suggested that recreation user fees should be charged at state forests to compensate for the reduced revenue from timber sales. Although acquisition and maintenance of fish and wildlife areas are paid mainly by hunters and anglers, the areas are used less for hunting and fishing than for other recreation activities, such as wildlife study, photography, hiking, picnicking, and camping. Although many of the individuals who engage in these activities are also hunters and anglers, some observers have suggested that user fees should be charged in the interest of fairness. They believe that all recreation users should share in the costs of fish and wildlife areas.

State Fish and Wildlife Programs

According to common law, fish and wildlife are property of the states until they are captured and become the private property of individual anglers and hunters. For this reason, economists refer to wildlife as a fugitive resource. Although some migratory birds and endangered species are controlled by federal law and by international treaty, the states have the principal responsibility for controlling wildlife, hunting, and fishing whether it be on private, state, or federal land. As a result, each state has a wildlife agency responsible for the management of fish and game. The agencies regulate fishing and hunting, conduct research and stocking programs, and manage fish and wildlife populations on public lands. In addition, wildlife agencies assist landowners in the management of habitat and wildlife populations on private land.

The states began issuing licenses and imposing seasons to protect game animals from indiscriminate slaughter in the middle of the 19th Century. Today, a fishing license permits the holder to engage in fishing in the particular state for 1-year. A license usually must be purchased in the state where an individual fishes; however, in a few cases, states have reciprocal agreements that allow the license holder in one state also to fish in an adjoining state. A hunting license may be for an entire year but is usually restricted to a shorter period of time such as a 2-week period of authorized deer hunting, or a 3-month period of pheasant hunting. Usually a separate license is required for big-game hunting (deer, elk, bear, etc.) and for small-game hunting (upland birds, waterfowl, rabbits, squirrels, etc.). The purchase of a federal duck stamp is required for hunting certain migratory waterfowl.

Total revenue from the sale of fishing and hunting licenses was $418.4 million in 1980. Table 14-5 shows that 28 million anglers paid $196.3 million for state fishing licenses and 16.4 million hunters paid $222.1 million for hunting licenses. The average price of a license to fish was $7.00, about half of the $13.66 to hunt. The table shows considerable difference among states in the level of license fees. Fishing licenses ranged from $2.18 in Louisiana to $13.26 in Alaska. Hunting licenses ranged from $5.98 in Connecticut to $54.10 in Colorado. Differences in license fees reflect differences in the costs of fish and wildlife management programs. For example, big-game are usually more costly to manage than small-game and cold-water fishing programs are more costly than warm water. Also, average license fees in some states are affected by the proportion of resident and nonresident licenses since the latter are typically higher priced. Georgia had 12 percent nonresident anglers compared with 41 percent in Alaska. Connecticut had 7 percent nonresident hunters compared to Colorado's 35 percent.

These figures represent average license fees per individual purchaser regardless of the number of licenses purchased. It is important to note that not all individuals who participate in fishing and hunting purchase licenses. There were approximately 42 million anglers in the United States, considerably more than the 28 million purchasing licenses. Exempt were children under 16 years of age, those over 65, and disabled persons. Marine fishing was exempt, except for some states on the East Coast. In addition, there was some illegal fishing and hunting.

Trends in user charges differed for fishing and hunting. The price of fishing licenses after removing the effects of inflation declined, but the price of hunting licenses increased. Table 14-6 shows that the average price of fishing licenses increased 88 percent from 1970 to 1980 or 5 percent less than inflation of 93 percent. However, the average price of hunting licenses increased 107 percent during the same time period, or 14 percent more than inflation. This relative price change for fishing and hunting may have affected quantity demanded. The number of fishing licenses increased by 15 percent compared with a 6 percent increase in hunting licenses during the decade from 1970 to 1980.

License fees and other user charges for fishing and hunting recover a substantial proportion of the costs of state wildlife management programs. Table 14-6 shows the results of a national survey of the sources of funding for state fish and wildlife agencies in 1982. Hunting and

483

Table 14-5. Number of Paid License Holders and License Sales by States for Fishing and Hunting in the United States, 1980

State	Number of Paid Fishing License Holders,[a] 1,000's	Fishing License Sales, $ Millions	Average Cost per Fishing License	Number of Paid Hunting License Holders 1,000's[a]	Hunting License Sales, $ Millions	Average Cost per Hunting License
Alabama	556.4	$ 3.5	$ 6.29	297.6	$ 3.5	$11.76
Alaska	196.1	2.6	13.26	72.1	2.7	37.45
Arizona	457.8	3.7	8.08	198.7	2.9	14.59
Arkansas	638.0	5.2	8.15	348.3	4.4	12.63
California	2,186.2	19.8	9.06	540.4	6.6	12.21
Colorado	707.0	5.3	7.50	312.4	16.9	54.10
Connecticut	199.0	0.8	4.02	83.6	0.5	5.98
Delaware	15.1	0.08	5.30	26.9	0.2	7.43
Florida	704.6	4.7	6.67	253.6	3.7	14.59
Georgia	664.8	2.5	3.76	384.0	3.1	8.07
Hawaii	7.6	0.03	3.95	11.4	0.09	7.89
Idaho	395.1	2.4	6.07	238.0	4.5	18.91
Illinois	751.5	3.9	5.19	353.4	4.7	13.30
Indiana	716.1	3.5	4.89	350.4	2.2	6.28
Iowa	453.1	2.9	5.96	292.9	4.8	16.39
Kansas	337.0	1.8	5.34	248.4	2.5	10.06
Kentucky	614.0	3.8	6.19	309.7	3.1	10.01
Louisiana	458.1	1.0	2.18	384.2	3.0	7.81
Maine	255.6	2.4	9.39	239.4	3.6	15.04
Maryland	140.2	0.7	4.99	170.0	2.3	13.53
Massachusetts	186.4	1.8	9.66	114.6	1.1	9.60
Michigan	1,325.2	10.6	8.00	957.2	12.2	12.75
Minnesota	1,452.0	9.5	6.54	496.0	7.0	14.11
Mississippi	441.3	2.8	6.34	288.5	2.7	9.36
Missouri	874.9	8.4	9.60	473.9	6.2	13.08
Montana	332.1	4.0	12.04	217.4	4.7	21.62
Nebraska	207.8	1.8	8.66	175.1	3.4	19.42
Nevada	171.4	1.3	7.58	52.2	1.0	19.16
New Hampshire	135.5	1.3	9.59	83.5	1.1	13.17
New Jersey	182.1	2.0	10.98	175.3	2.3	13.12
New Mexico	220.5	2.1	9.52	144.3	3.3	22.87
New York	901.9	5.7	6.32	741.4	7.8	10.52
North Carolina	463.5	3.9	8.41	353.1	4.2	11.89
North Dakota	141.1	0.6	4.25	100.1	1.4	13.99
Ohio	1,004.0	7.1	7.07	488.5	5.3	10.85
Oklahoma	620.1	3.5	5.64	301.1	2.8	9.30
Oregon	722.6	6.2	8.58	394.3	6.9	17.50
Pennsylvania	1,005.4	8.7	8.65	1,274.8	15.7	12.32
Rhode Island	29.8	0.2	6.71	13.4	0.1	7.46
South Carolina	422.6	2.1	4.97	222.3	2.2	9.90
South Dakota	137.6	0.7	5.09	142.7	2.3	16.12
Tennessee	701.5	5.2	7.41	515.6	5.9	11.44
Texas	1,745.1	7.1	4.07	939.3	6.2	6.60
Utah	487.0	3.4	6.98	287.6	4.1	14.26
Vermont	159.3	0.8	5.02	137.4	2.1	15.28
Virginia	503.5	2.7	5.36	469.6	4.5	9.58
Washington	907.3	6.3	6.94	360.7	6.0	16.63
West Virginia	277.3	2.1	7.57	314.7	3.2	10.17
Wisconsin	1,515.0	11.4	7.52	713.2	11.2	15.70
Wyoming	268.6	2.5	9.31	193.5	10.0	51.68
Total or Average						
1980	28,094.9	$196.3	$ 7.01	16,357.1	$222.1	$13.66
1970	24,434.7	90.9	3.72	15,370.5	101.6	6.61

[a]A paid license holder is one individual regardless of the number of licenses purchased. Data certified by state fish and game departments. Period covered not identical for all states. Persons who hunted in more than one state are counted in each state where they hunted. Therefore, the total exceeds the total number of license holders in the United States.
Source: U.S. Department of the Interior.

Table 14-6. User Charges and Other Funding Sources for Fish and Wildlife Programs of State Governments, United States, 1982

Source	Number of States Reporting Funds[a]	Total Revenue, Million Dollars	Percent of Total Revenue
Direct User Payments, Total	47	$ 443.4	36.6%
Hunting and Fishing Permits	47	411.0	34.0
Boat Registration Fees	24	16.7	1.4
Camping and Day Use Fees	6	9.0	0.7
Fines, Confiscations	37	6.7	0.6
Federal Transfer Payments, Total	47	$ 238.7	19.7%
Pittman Robertson Act	47	76.9	6.4
Hunter Safety	34	5.3	0.4
Dingell Johnson Act	47	29.8	2.5
Endangered Species (nongame)	28	4.5	0.4
Corps of Engineers	14	7.1	0.6
U.S. Forest Service	17	9.2	0.8
Environmental Protection Agency	8	21.3	1.8
Bureau of Outdoor Recreation (HCRS)	7	40.8	3.4
CETA and YACC	12	10.4	0.9
Other Federal Agencies	—	33.4	2.8
State Taxes, Total	25	$ 419.2	34.6%
Legislative Appropriation	29	279.0	23.1
Excise Taxes	25	45.2	3.7
Severance Taxes	7	35.8	3.0
Property Taxes	8	16.8	1.4
Personal Income Tax Check-Off	26	1.7	0.1
Sales Taxes	22	30.6	2.5
Corporate Taxes	1	10.1	0.8
Other Sources of Revenue, Total	39	$ 108.7	9.0%
Magazine Subscriptions	29	6.2	0.5
Interest on Investments	25	18.2	1.5
Commercial Fishing Permits	24	9.4	0.8
Sale of Products	39	25.3	2.1
Other Miscellaneous Income	—	49.6	4.1
Total Revenue From All Sources	47	$1,210.0	100.0

[a]Arkansas, Connecticut and Indiana did not respond to a survey by Whitehead in 1982.

fishing licenses sales reported by 47 of the 50 states were $411 million, or 34 percent of estimated total funding of $1.2 billion. The estimate of 34 percent probably understates the true proportion attributed to license fees. Whitehead found that some states were not able to separate funding for fish and wildlife programs from some recreation, park, and other natural resource programs. Thus, user fees from boat registration and camping are included along with funds from the Environmental Protection Agency and other federal agencies which may not be directly related to fish and wildlife management. In addition, funds received by the states from the federal government are appropriated by state legislatures in authorizing the budget of state wildlife agencies. Thus, it is not clear that all of the 23.1 percent state legislative appropriation is from the general tax fund of states.

The limited information available suggests that license fees and other user charges may have provided a larger share of the funding of state wildlife programs in the past. Hoover estimated that license fees were 70 to 85 percent of the total costs of most state wildlife agencies in the 1960s and 1970s. For example, license fees accounted for 89 percent of the California wildlife budget in 1969 with nearly all of the rest from federal Dingell-Johnson and Pittman-Robertson excise tax revenues on fishing and hunting equipment, according to Unkel. In 1978, the California legislature indexed increases in fishing and hunting licenses to inflation and began providing state tax revenues to pay the costs of free fishing and hunting, nongame wildlife programs, and other environmental protection programs. By 1983, license sales were $37.3 million and state tax revenues for nongame programs, $9.4 million. This trend was also apparent in Canada. During the 1960s, license fees and other user charges were equal to expenditures on wildlife programs in the province of Alberta, Canada, according to Neave and Goulden. By 1982, the proportion of license fees to the total costs of the wildlife program had declined to 33 percent. This was not unique to Alberta; license fee accounted for about 40 percent of the Manitoba wildlife budget in the same year.

Some state wildlife agencies have been more successful than others in obtaining state tax revenues to pay the costs of free fishing and hunting by children, retired, and disabled persons, nongame wildlife programs, and environmental protection programs. Unlike other state agencies, the wildlife programs of many states have not received revenues from their general tax fund. For example, Spencer et al. reported that license fees accounted for 71 percent of the Alabama wildlife budget in 1982, while 23 percent came from federal excise tax revenues on fishing and hunting equipment, 4 percent from fines, and 2 percent from such miscellaneous sources as rentals and timber sales. License fees accounted for 58 percent of the Washington state wildlife budget in 1982, while 38 percent came from federal funds, and 4 percent from such miscellaneous sources as mitigation damages and private donations. As a result, the state of Washington could support only one wildlife enforcement agent per 230,000 days of fishing and hunting in the state compared with an average of one agent per 75,000 days in eight western states. Contrast this experience with the state of Missouri where license fees accounted for 23 percent of the wildlife budget in 1982, while over half came from a one-eighth of 1 percent sales tax, with the balance from federal excise tax revenues and miscellaneous sources. The broader funding base provided by the special sales tax was passed by vote of the people in 1976. Other state fish and wildlife agencies have been successful in obtaining a broader funding base in numerous ways as illustrated in Table 14-7. Still, in many states when license fee revenues went up, the wildlife agencies were required to reduce expenditures of tax funds.

Table 14-7. User Fee Revenues at Federal Recreation Sites, United States, 1981 and 1983

Federal Agency	Recreation Visitor Days, Millions			Receipts From User Fees	
	Total, Fee and Nonfee Sites	User Fee Sites	Percent Fee Sites	Total, Million	Per Visitor Day at Fee Sites
National Park Service					
1981	100.0	78.8	79%	$16.1	$0.20
1983	106.3	73.8	69	21.1	0.29
Forest Service					
1981	235.7	28.1	12	8.5	0.30
1983	227.7	25.2	11	11.3	0.45
Corps of Engineers					
1981	181.1	9.3	5	6.0	0.65
1983	146.9	10.6	7	8.7	0.82
Other Federal Sites[a]					
1981	83.0	2.3	3	1.6	0.70
1983	85.1	1.2	1	1.7	1.42
Total, Federal					
1981	599.8	118.5	20%	$32.2	$0.27
1983	556.0	110.8	20	42.8	0.39

[a]Includes the Bureau of Land Management, Bureau of Reclamation, Fish and Wildlife Service, and Tennessee Valley Authority.
Source: U.S. Department of the Interior, 1982 and 1984.

The traditional federal sources of funds for state fish and wildlife management provided less than 10 percent of the total revenues in 1982. Pittman-Robertson funds for wildlife management were $76.9 million, Dingell-Johnson funds for fish management, $29.8 million; and hunter safety funds, $5.3 million. These funds represent a user fee in the form of excise taxes on sporting arms, ammunition, and fishing tackle. The federal government has provided grants to the states for wildlife management under the Pittman-Robertson Act since 1938. That program is financed by excise taxes of 11 percent on sporting arms, ammunition, and certain archery equipment, and 10 percent on pistols and revolvers. The industries whose products are taxed and the hunters who ultimately pay the taxes have consistently supported this program. A similar act was passed in 1951 for sport fisheries. The Dingell Johnson Act derived all its funding from a manufacturer and importer excise tax of 10 percent on fishing rods, reels, creels, and lures until 1984, when an amendment extended the tax to additional items of sport fishing tackle, yachts and other pleasure craft, and part of the motorboat fuel tax. The programs provide assistance for managing fish and wildlife species, hunters, and anglers. Nearly 70 million hunters and anglers are served by these programs, as are millions of other Americans who enjoy the same species as they participate in nonconsumptive activities. However, species that can be harvested through hunting and fishing constitute no more than 10 percent of America's vertebrate fauna. The remaining 90 percent are nongame species and receive only peripheral management, even though they are of value to an even larger number of Americans. The Fish and Wildlife Conservation Act of 1980, although not fully funded, provided about $4.5 million in grants to the states for the management of nongame species. Funding of nongame wildlife programs is expected to increase in the 1980s.

Several points should be made about the sale of licenses to fish and hunt. First, the most important recreation economic decision of wildlife managers is how to allocate the limited supply of fish and game when there is excess demand for fishing and hunting. The number of licenses available is determined by estimating the number of hunters, which would result in the target harvest level in each region of a state. Harvest levels are related to biological carrying capacity including reproduction rates and conditions of the habitat. Excess demand refers to a situation where there are more applications for a license to fish and hunt than can be issued because of the limited supply of fish and game. For example, Sandry et al. reported that the excess demand for cow and calf elk licenses was more than double the 15,600 licenses available in Oregon in 1981. In Montana, nearly 36,000 applications were received for 7,360 elk hunting permits, and in the state of Washington, there were about 24,000 applications for 3,300 elk hunting licenses available in 1980. Excess demand is expected to increase in the future.

Increasingly, state wildlife agencies have used a combination of fees, drawings, and waiting lines to allocate big-game hunting permits. The price of nonresident licenses usually has been set closer to market clearing levels than for residents. For example, nonresident licenses to hunt elk in Colorado were $210 in 1984 compared with $25 for residents. Typically, if applications exceed the number of licenses available in a region, a random drawing is conducted to determine which individuals will be allowed to hunt. Often the winners are required to surrender the right to apply for licenses to hunt the species for a number of years. Unfortunately, when permits are allocated by a drawing rather than by market clearing prices of licenses, the benefits from big-game hunting are reduced by about 40 percent. Loomis has shown that the primary losers from higher license prices would be hunters with relatively low willingness to pay who were winners in the drawing but who would refuse to hunt at higher license prices. Those who would benefit from higher license prices would be those with greater demand who were losers in the drawing and denied access to hunt at prices they were more than willing to pay (Sandry et al.). Benefit cost studies need to take into account the distortion in benefit estimates introduced by drawings or lotteries (Mumy and Hanke).

Second, it is important to distinguish between licenses which are usually issued by public agencies and access permits to public or private property which are usually obtained from landowners.

Licenses ordinarily authorize the holders to perform the act of fishing or hunting during a specified period of time, but seldom authorize them to do so at a particular site. More and more states have required individuals to obtain written permission from landowners to fish and hunt on private property. Access fees of $25 or more have been paid to private landowners. Written permission also has been required at some state parks and other public recreation sites. However, entrance fees seldom have been charged for fishing and hunting on public land. Congress has been reluctant to authorize federal agencies to charge for fishing and hunting. Representatives of the states believed that federal entrance fees for fishing and hunting would adversely affect state license sales.

The third and final point is that the experience of wildlife agencies with fee collection has important implications for other recreation programs. The states appear to have developed one of the most efficient user fee collection systems in the United States. Licenses to fish and hunt are sold by sporting goods stores for a small commission, usually 5 percent of the purchase price. For example, retailers receive 50 cents for selling a license costing resident anglers $10. For nonresident deer hunting licenses costing $100, the retailer receives $5. The retail stores purchase bonds to protect the wildlife agency against loss if for some reason a store fails to turn in the money from license sales. In 1984, the state of Colorado had to recover only $50,000 from bonding companies, or about 0.2 percent on license sales of $28 million. With more than 1,000 license agents in the state, the system is convenient for anglers and hunters. Wildlife enforcement agents verify the purchase of licenses by making spot checks of anglers and operating highway check stations for big-game such as deer and elk.

Federal Park and Recreation Programs

Historically, federal expenditures on park and recreation programs have ranked third behind the cities and states. In the early 1980s the federal government moved into second place. Table 14-1 shows that park and recreation spending by the federal government was about $1.38 billion in 1982, according to the Census. This was equivalent to a cost per capita of nearly $6. Park and recreation programs accounted for only about 0.02 percent of total spending by the federal government in 1982. The trend in per-capita expenditures is also shown. The data indicate that federal recreation expenditures grew moderately during the 1960s, and then declined with the advent of the energy crisis during the 1970s. Growth accelerated in the early 1980s with the start of park rehabilitation programs. After removing the effects of inflation, annual growth in spending per capita was estimated as 2.6

percent from 1967 to 1972, -2.2 from 1972 to 1977, and 3.5 percent from 1977 to 1982.

The federal government administers one-third of the land area of the United States and another 2 percent is held in trust for American Indians. This compares with about 5 percent managed by the states and about 1 percent by local government. Although the supply of recreation opportunities on federal land is influenced by more than 100 agencies, seven have been designated the principal land management agencies offering recreation opportunities. The National Park Service and the Fish and Wildlife Service administer lands reserved for these purposes. The Forest Service and Bureau of Land Management have the largest area of multiple-use lands. The Corps of Engineers, Bureau of Reclamation, and Tennessee Valley Authority manage reservoirs and other water projects.

Federal collection of user fees began at Mount Rainier National Park, Washington, in 1908; at Kings Canyon and Sequoia, California, in 1910; at Crater Lake, Oregon, in 1911; at Mesa Verde, Colorado, in 1914; and at Yellowstone and Grand Teton, Wyoming, in 1915. In 1916, the entrance fee at Mount Rainier was $6 per vehicle; Yosemite National Park, $8; and Yellowstone, $10. From this early beginning until the present time, a part of costs has been paid from entrance fees, licenses, permits, and other kinds of user charges.

The recent history of user charges began with passage of the Land and Water Conservation Fund Act (LWCFA) in 1965. The act authorized the Interior Department to manage a coordinated federal recreation fee program. The pay-as-you-go fee collection process was intended to comply with the user fee statute of 1951 under which all federal fee systems were to "be as uniform as practicable and subject to such policies as the President may prescribe." The LWCFA authorized the seven agencies to charge fees at sites where specialized outdoor recreation facilities, equipment, or services were provided at federal expense. The agencies were authorized to collect three types of recreation revenue: entrance fees, user fees, and special permits.

User charges have been a constant subject of controversy since passage of the LWCFA legislation. In 1968, Congress terminated the coordinated federal recreation fee program effective in 1971. In the same year, Congress prohibited the Corps of Engineers from charging entrance fees for access to water recreation at reservoirs administered by the agency. The act was interpreted to prohibit charging a fee for access to water, meaning the recreation use of reservoirs, lakes, and rivers. Other federal agencies interpreted the Act to prohibit them from charging entrance fees for access to any natural resources unless specialized recreation facilities, equipment, or services were provided at federal expense.

As a result, the National Park Service was the only federal agency collecting entrance fees. Six of the seven federal recreation agencies limited their user fee program almost entirely to campgrounds that require personal supervision by agency employees and maintenance expenses in developed facilities. Campgrounds that lacked essential services, in particular drinking water, were exempted from the collection of user fees. Congress even prohibited the National Park Service from initiating entrance fees at nonfee sites or raising entrance fees at existing fee sites. Entrance fees were not raised or initiated for more than 10 years. The General Accounting Office reported that from 1971 to 1981, average costs increased from $0.61 to $1.52 per visitor yet average entrance fees declined from about $0.05 to $0.03. Entrance fees were collected at only 64 of the 330 sites in the national park system, or about 20 percent. Fees ranged from $1 to $3 per vehicle, including all passengers, and from $0.50 to $1.50 per person at walk-in parks.

Beginning in the early 1980s, under a new administration in Washington, a concerted effort was made to increase the proportion of costs recovered from recreation users. The President's Task Force on User Charges (the Grace committee) recommended substantial increases in user fees to recover a greater percentage of the cost of operating the facilities. Although the task force's ideal solution was to achieve complete cost recovery through a user fee system, they concluded that public policy is served by some tax-subsidized programs that protect natural areas for the benefit of present and future society. It seemed reasonable that user fees should reflect the direct costs of the services provided by the public agencies. Congress was less restrictive with respect to user fees for specialized recreation activities within a recreation site, for example, camping, boat launching, etc.

Table 14-7 illustrates the trend in user fee revenues at federal park and recreation sites during the early 1980s. This is based on data from Federal Recreation Fee Reports prepared annually by the U.S. Department of the Interior since 1971. These reports provide annual recreation use and fee information for the seven federal agencies which administer most of the federal outdoor recreation sites in the United States. User fees increased from $32.2 million in 1981 to $42.8 million in 1983, or by one-third in two years when inflation was 11 percent. This was equal to an average of $0.27 per recreation visitor day at fee sites in 1981 and $0.39 in 1983. However, user fees were charged at sites accounting for only 20 percent of the total recreation use of federal sites.

Table 14-8 shows that there was considerable variation among the states in user charges for federal park and recreation programs. Average user fees at federal sites ranged from a low of $0.09 per recreation visitor day in North Carolina and $0.10 in Hawaii, Maine, and Maryland, to $1.09 in South Dakota and $1.16 in Iowa. The proportion of total federal park and recreation at fee sites ranged from lows of 1.5 percent in Mississippi, 2.1 percent in Vermont, 3.6 percent in Nebras-

Table 14-8. User Charges per Recreation Visitor Day at Federal Park and Recreation Facilities in States, 1983

Federal Government in the State of	Recreation Visitory Days (RVD)		Total User Charges, Thousands	User Charge Per RVD
	Million	Percent at Fee Sites		
Total	555.6	19.9%	$41,628.3	$0.38
Alabama	7.4	3.8	153.3	0.55
Alaska	5.8	6.1	169.6	0.48
Arizona	22.6	22.3	2,554.6	0.51
Arkansas	27.9	13.1	1,811.9	0.50
California	108.4	13.3	7,819.0	0.54
Colorado	30.1	15.2	2,324.9	0.51
Connecticut	0.5	N.A.	14.0	N.A.
Delaware	0.1	N.A.	6.5	N.A.
Florida	12.6	22.6	1,192.9	0.42
Georgia	18.8	N.A.	3,109.9	N.A.
Hawaii	1.3	13.1	17.2	0.10
Idaho	16.6	7.0	501.6	0.43
Illinois	6.8	9.1	562.3	0.91
Indiana	4.2	10.7	170.5	0.38
Iowa	4.8	6.1	339.7	1.16
Kansas	11.6	5.6	339.4	0.53
Kentucky	14.3	9.5	1,371.3	1.01
Louisiana	1.6	3.7	54.9	0.93
Maine	2.6	98.3	260.9	0.10
Maryland	4.5	34.9	163.2	0.10
Massachusetts	2.2	31.5	218.3	0.31
Michigan	6.2	14.3	370.3	0.42
Minnesota	5.7	6.4	304.8	0.83
Mississippi	13.3	1.5	102.8	0.50
Missouri	12.3	13.8	960.7	0.56
Montana	18.0	32.9	772.5	0.13
Nebraska	5.1	3.6	90.9	0.49
Nevada	9.5	62.9	1,125.4	0.19
New Hampshire	3.0	27.3	276.3	0.33
New Jersey	0.6	5.8	16.8	0.47
New Mexico	14.2	35.8	1,110.1	0.22
New York	6.1	4.6	223.5	0.79
North Carolina	18.1	63.9	1,049.1	0.09
North Dakota	3.2	N.A.	85.6	N.A.
Ohio	17.1	N.A.	67.7	N.A.
Oklahoma	33.3	4.5	1,072.7	0.71
Oregon	24.7	9.4	949.3	0.41
Pennsylvania	10.1	9.6	593.6	0.61
Rhode Island	0.1	0	0	0
South Carolina	4.3	4.3	114.4	0.62
South Dakota	7.8	8.5	726.0	1.09
Tennessee	20.1	30.1	1,194.5	0.20
Texas	45.0	5.3	253.6	0.11
Utah	21.2	28.5	1,616.3	0.27
Vermont	0.9	2.1	17.8	0.98
Virginia	10.1	29.6	1,573.8	0.52
Washington	24.0	17.3	1,212.4	0.29
West Virginia	5.1	7.3	269.4	0.72
Wisconsin	3.4	11.3	287.1	0.75
Wyoming	19.8	44.3	2,479.6	0.28

N.A. = Not available.
Source: U.S. Department of the Interior.

ka and 3.7 percent in Louisiana to highs of 63.9 percent in North Carolina, 62.9 percent in Nevada, and 98.3 percent in Maine. This variation in federal fee policy reflects the charging of higher user fees at campgrounds and the absence of entrance fees to the national forests and reservoirs.

The increase in user charges during the 1980s was a marked change from the fee policies during the previous decade. The seven federal agencies reported that recreation user fee revenues increased from $20.6 million in 1975 to $26.7 million in 1979, or about the same as the 30 percent increase in inflation. This was accomplished by increasing average user fees from $0.11 per recreation visitor day at fee sites in 1975 to $0.23 in 1979. Average user fees at the sites of the three most important federal recreation agencies were:

	1975	1979	1984
National Park Service	$0.11	$0.20	$0.24
Forest Service	0.18	0.30	0.47
Corps of Engineers	0.08	0.42	0.93
Total Federal	0.11	0.23	0.36

Total fee revenues increased less than average fees because users were charged at fewer and fewer sites. For example, the Corps of Engineers reported that visitors subject to payment of user fees decreased by nearly two-thirds from 1975 to 1979. Table 14-7 shows that this trend was reversed during the early 1980s, when the Corp increased the number of visitors subject to the payment of user fees from 5 percent in 1981 to 7 percent in 1983.

The National Park Service collected nearly one-half of the total user fees of federal agencies in 1983. The agency reported entrance fees of $8.6 million at 62 parks and recreation areas and revenues of $1.2 million from the sale of 123,000 Golden Eagle annual passes. Entrance fees of $1-3 per vehicle were charged at 62 national parks, monuments, recreation areas, seashores, historic sites, and memorial parks. The National Park Service also collected $11.1 million in recreation user fees, primarily for camping. Examples of other user fees include boat launching and parking. Special permit fees were generally considered a type of user fee. Examples include renting a picnic shelter for a group activity, or a site for a special recreation event such as an off-road vehicle race. Special permit fees were charged outfitters and guides for horseback excursions and river rafting. Omitted from the Federal Recreation Fee Report was $5 million of other indirect fees for recreation use such as lease revenues from concession operations at ski sites, resorts, campgrounds, and boat marinas. Also omitted were special use permits such as for summer home sites.

Of the federal agencies, the Forest Service made the most progress in shifting the cost of financing recreation programs from the general tax base to recreation user fees and permits during the early 1980s. Table 14-9 illustrates the trend in receipts from recreation user fees and special use permits of the Forest Service during this period of

Table 14-9. Comparison of User Fee and Special Use Permit Revenues to Expenditures on the Recreation Program, U.S. Forest Service, 1980, 1983, and 1985

Types of Recreation Revenue	Revenue, Million Dollars			
	1980	1983	1985 (Est.)	Under new authority, 1985 (Est.)
Recreation User Fees				
Camping	$ 6.4	$ 10.5	$ 11.9	$19.2
Picnicking	0	0	0	2.0
Swimming	0.1	0.2	0.2	1.2
Boat Launching	0	0	0	1.7
Other (interpretative, playground, caves, etc.)	0.2	0.6	0.7	4.4
Total	6.7	11.3	12.8	28.5
Special Use Permits				
Ski areas	5.5	9.0	11.0	
Summer homes	3.2	5.0	6.5	
Resorts, marinas, etc.	1.0	1.1	1.3	
Outfitters and guides	0.5	1.4	4.6	
Total	10.2	16.5	23.4	
Total Revenues	16.9	27.8	36.2	51.9
Total Appropriations[a]	113.4	117.0	120.0	
Revenues as a Percent of Expenditures	15%	24%	30%	43%

[a]Includes annual costs of construction, management, operation, and maintenance of all recreation resources. Does not include road construction, overhead, fire control, law enforcement, or costs of environmental impact statements.
Source: Adapted from Driver, Bossi, and Cordell.

time. Total receipts from these two sources increased from $16.9 million in 1980 to an estimated $36.2 million in 1985. In 1980, these recreation user fee and permit revenues accounted for only 15 percent of the agency's expenditures of $113.4 million for the recreation program. By 1985, recreation user fee and permit revenues increased to approximately 30 percent of estimated expenditures of $120 million.

The Forest Service estimated that user fee revenues could have been increased another $15.7 million in 1985 with added authority from Congress to charge user fees at developed recreation sites without standard facilities or drinking water. In that event, user fee and permit revenues would have equaled approximately 43 percent of expenditures on the recreation program.

Camping fees accounted for much of the rise in user charges. Fees increased at 1,900 campgrounds from an average of about $2.80 per campsite in 1980 to $5.50 in 1985. The number of fee campsites increased slightly during the same time period. Fees were related to the quality of service provided. Few campgrounds were highly developed with flush toilets and utility hookups. For the most part, camping fees ranged from $1 to $8 per night in the following pattern:

User Fee Per Campsite	1980	1983	1985
$1	8.4%	—	0.9%
2	28.8	0.3%	0.4
3	33.4	8.8	2.5
4	28.5	8.9	10.1
5	0.4	37.7	34.3
6		36.9	36.3
7		6.5	10.9
8		0.9	4.5
Average	$2.82	$5.25	$5.52

In addition, revenues from special use permits for ski areas and summer homes doubled from 1980 to 1985. Permit revenues from outfitters and guides increased from $0.5 million to $4.6 million.

Table 14-10 shows the potential increase in federal recreation fee revenues recommended by the President's Task Force on User Charges. The task force recommended that user charges of $31.2 million in 1982 be increased by $157 million in the first year, rise to $176.3 million in the second year, and to $193.8 million in the third year. More than two-thirds of the increase in user charges would be collected by the Forest Service, nearly 20 percent by the National Park Service, and about 10 percent would come from the initiation of entrance fees at Corps of Engineers reservoirs.

Table 14-10. Potential Increase in Federal Recreation Revenues Recommended by the President's Task Force on User Charges, United States

Federal Agency	Recommended Increase in Recreation Use Fee Revenues, Million		
	First Year	Second Year	Third Year
National Park Service, Total[a]	$ 30	$ 33	$ 36
Increase Entrance Fees	11		
Extend Collection Hours	5		
Initiate Entrance Fees at Nonfee Sites	7		
Increase Price of Golden Eagle Pass	2		
Increase Fees for Special Services	5		
Forest Service, Total[b]	$112	$123.5	$136
Initiate Entrance Fees	100	110	121
Increase Ski Resort Special Use Fees	5	5.5	6
Increase Summer Home Special Use Fees	7	8	9
Corps of Engineers, Total[c]	$ 15	$ 19.8	$ 21.8
Initiate Entrance Fees	15	19.8	21.8
Three Agencies, Total	$157	$176.3	$193.8

[a]National Park Service net revenue is after collection costs of $2.5 million, or 8 percent.
[b]Forest Service net revenue is after collection costs of $25 million or 20 percent.
[c]Corps net revenue is after collection and implementation costs of $13 million during the first year, and $10 million each subsequent year, or about one-third of total fee revenue.
Source: President's Task Force on User Charges.

The task force concluded that user fees should not be expected to recover the total cost of operating the National Park Service. More than any other federal agency, the National Park Service is charged with protecting natural, cultural, and historic resources as well as providing opportunities for recreation use. But receipts should recover more than the 10 percent of operation and maintenance costs of sites where fees were charged in 1982. The committee recommended that recreation receipts be increased by $30 million in the first year, $33 million in the second, and $36 million in the third. They reported that the increase in receipts would enable the agency to recover 27 percent of the cost of operating and maintaining the fee sites. Subsequently, the Secretary of Interior requested that Congress authorize increasing user fees from 7 percent to 25 percent of the costs of maintaining and operating national parks, national monuments, wildlife refuges, and other recreation areas under the department's jurisdiction.

One reason that the task force's recommended increase was not higher is the little known fact that the National Park Service operates large recreation areas in and near the central cities. It manages the oldest urban park system in the United States, the National Capital Parks in Washington, D.C., which, as a courtesy to visitors, does not charge user fees. In 1984, the national parks, monuments, historic sites, and recreation areas in the large cities accounted for 37 percent of total visits to the agency's facilities compared with 29 percent in 1978. The agency's sites that are located in Standard Metropolitan Areas accounted for 68 percent of total visits in 1984 compared with 63 percent in 1978. These urban sites provided recreation opportunities at significantly lower costs per visitor than did large parks in the rural areas of the western states. In 1977, for example, costs per visit at Gateway in New York City were $0.75; Golden Gate in San Francisco, $0.57; and Jefferson National Expansion Memorial in St. Louis, $0.52. This compares with costs per visit of $3.03 at Yellowstone in Wyoming; Yosemite in rural California, $2.14; and Grand Canyon in northern Arizona, $1.92. Part of the difference in costs per visitor may be explained by length of stay. Visitors to Yosemite or Yellowstone stay much longer than do visitors to Gateway or Golden Gate and, in doing so, consume more park service which increases costs. Still, it is fortuitous that sites in metropolitan areas without user fees apparently have substantially lower costs than do sites in rural areas with user fees.

How would the additional revenue be obtained? The Task Force recommended increasing the price of the annual Golden Eagle pass from $10 to $25 to raise an additional $2 million. Increasing entrance fees at 25 sites from an average of $2 ($1-3 range) in 1980 to $5 ($2-7 range) per vehicle would increase revenues by about $11 million. Initiating entrance fees at 23 sites where entry was free (thereby charging fees at all 48 national parks) would increase revenues by $7 million. Extending the hours during the day when fees are collected would increase revenues by approximately $5 million. Finally, the task force recommended increasing other recreation fees by $5 million for such services as camping, boat launching, and indirect recreation fees paid by concessioners from visitor expenditures for food, lodging, swimming, equipment rental, etc.

About 530 concessioners operating in 333 national park areas reported total sales of $266 million in 1981, with profits of $24 million or 9 percent of sales. The government received franchise fees of $5.2 million or 2 percent of sales. Concessioner fees were based on a weighted average percentage of sales with the following rates: food, lodging, and saddle horses, 0.75 percent; groceries, vending machines, snack bars, boat rentals, and campgrounds, 1.5 percent; gasoline, transportation, and photo supplies, 3.0 percent; souvenir and curio sales, except Indian handicrafts, 5.0 percent. The task force recommended that fees be increased from 2 to 4 percent of sales. This would be closer to private franchise fees outside of the parks.

The task force concluded that Forest Service recreation user charges should be increased to recover much more than the 18 percent of total expenditures to operate and maintain recreation sites in 1982. They recommended that recreation use receipts be increased by $112 million in the first year, $124 million in the second, and $136 million in the third. They apparently considered it appropriate for recreation use revenues to cover virtually all of the costs of recreation management. The Forest Service expenditures for recreation management were approximately $119 million at the time. The task force anticipated that the agency's recreation budget, which had been declining in real dollars during the previous three years (MacCleery), would be increased from 1983 through 1985, consistent with increase in recreation user revenues.

The task force recommended that Congress amend the 1965 Land and Water Conservation Fund Act to enable the Forest Service to charge entrance fees for access to all recreation land and water administered by the agency. They estimated that entrance fees of the Forest Service would produce net revenues of $100 million per year based on an annual entrance fee equivalent to $0.50 per 12-hour recreation visitor day. The Task Force concluded that gross entrance fee receipts would be at least $125 million per year, less $25 million collection costs. They noted that collection costs of 20 percent represent the historic level for the Forest Service and should not be considered the most acceptable target level (see the section on collection costs below). The estimate of entrance fee revenues also included increasing the price of the Golden Eagle pass from $10 to $25, which would raise an additional $5.8 million. This assumes that the Forest Service could sell at least twice as many annual passes as the National Park Service as it has twice the recreation use. The task force recommended that the historic basis for setting special recreation use permits be changed to a fixed fee based on percent of appraised land value. This would yield $5 million in increased fees from ski resorts and $7 million from summer home sites.

The task force recommended that the Secretary of Interior appoint a single manager of all federal recreation programs to allow for more efficient planning and management. The task force also provided a general framework for reviewing the federal recreation programs from a managerial economic point of view. This means that the program manager would determine the rates to be charged for federal recreation facilities, which would be based on the six criteria prescribed by law, including the market clearing price for the recreation opportunities provided. The federal recreation agencies would institute comparable cost-accounting procedures and other management information systems and they would account for all costs attributed to provision of recreation facilities. These costs would include: operation and maintenance; capital costs of equipment, buildings, and land acquisition; and personnel costs including payroll overhead, training, and retirement benefits. To this list should be added the opportunity costs of foregone development, external cost such as may be shifted to private firms or other governmental agencies, and costs of environmental protection. A shortcoming of the task force report is its nearly complete orientation toward internal cost accounting to the exclusion of important external costs and benefits.

The task force also recommended that more precise fee-collection cost data be developed. They recommended that all federal recreation user fees be earmarked for payment of the costs of the collecting agency. A marketing program should inform the consuming public that the fee revenues would be used to pay the costs of the recreation services received. Recreation users should be assured that their payment is reasonable in relation to benefits received. Finally, an advisory group should be formed to consider the role of the federal government in the business of managing recreation resources. Where fee revenues historically have been below a level of acceptable cost recovery, the particular site or program should be considered for possible termination or sale. The advisory group would consider existing policies and interests, then issue a new policy concerning what proportion of total costs should be recouped from users and how much the general taxpayers should pay.

Several additional points should be made about the federal recreation fee policy. First, the belief that only highly developed recreation sites incur significant direct costs or provide valuable services to users is contrary to available evidence. A number of studies have found that the costs of providing the opportunity to engage in recreation activities is usually not appreciably lower than the costs of providing camp-grounds and often is higher per recreation visitor day (Gibbs et al.). Studies have shown that the willingness to pay measure of the benefit of recreation activities is usually higher than for camping. In fact, the purpose of camping often is to provide access to related recreation op-portunities such as sightseeing, hiking, fishing, and hunting (Sorg and Loomis).

The mistaken belief that highly developed camping was virtually the only service provided by six of the seven federal recreation agencies has had several unfortunate consequences. For example, because developed recreation facilities are excluded by law from designated wilderness areas, entrance fees are not charged. In addition, activities such as backpacking and camping in undeveloped sites in the backcountry are exempt because it is erroneously believed that no services are provided. However, during the early 1980s, a few wilder-ness areas experimented with backpacking permits for which $3 per party was charged to cover the costs of administering the permit pro-gram, including private sales of the permits at convenient locations in the region. This program demonstrated the feasibility of charging user fees for camping in wilderness areas.

The costs of providing opportunities for wilderness recreation have included significant levels of direct personal services for safety patrol, trash removal, and maintenance of trails and signs within the sites. Wilderness areas also require substantial investments in access roads, parking lots, and toilets at trail heads in the national forests on the border of wilderness areas. In addition, there have been significant costs of protecting environmental quality in wilderness areas, as at all recreation sites. These include forest fire control; air pollution abate-ment; water quality improvement; fish and wildlife management for fishing, hunting, and viewing; wild and scenic river administration; etc. Not all of these environmental quality protection programs are administered by the federal recreation agencies. However, they are the logical choice to collect user fees which would include a part of the costs of natural resource protection programs. One acceptable basis for allocating the costs of recreation use and environmental protection programs would be based on the proportion of benefits received by users compared to the general public. This will be illustrated in a later section of this chapter.

Second, problems arise in estimating the potential revenue from en-trance fees. In the past, the number of users who were subject to the payment of entrance fees was not the same as the total number of users of a park or other recreation facility. Some users arrived at en-trance fee stations at night or early in the morning when the stations were not staffed or for some other reason avoided payment. Some were exempt from payment or paid a reduced rate because of age.

Others arrived during the promotion of facility use on free days. For example, a General Accounting Office report estimated, and park managers agreed, that approximately 14 percent of the families entering national parks were exempt from payment because an occupant of the vehicle was over 61 years of age. Where entrance fees were charged per person, such as Muir Wood National Monument located 17 miles north of San Francisco, only 60 percent of visitors, those between the ages of 16 and 61, were subject to the fee. Similarly, park managers estimated that one-third of the 1.5 million annual users would not be subject to payment of entrance fees at the Jefferson National Expansion Memorial on the Mississippi River in downtown St. Louis.

Federal recreation agencies exempt persons who are blind, disabled, or over 61 years of age and people accompanying them, youths less than 16 years of age, and anyone who has purchased a pass good for a calendar year. State, county, and city recreation agencies offer similar exemptions. Golden Age Passports are free lifetime passes available to persons who are over 61 years of age. Golden Access Passports are free lifetime passes available to persons who were blind or permanently disabled. The passes admit the permit holder and a carload of accompanying people. Where entry is not by private car, the passes admit the permit holder and his or her spouse, children, and parents. Both passes also allow a 50 percent discount on recreation user fees for such services as camping, boat launching, and parking. Information is not available on the total number of free passes that have been issued since they were authorized in 1965. However, more than one-quarter million lifetime free passes were issued each year in the early 1980s. In 1983 alone, 284,000 Golden Age and 14,000 Golden Access passes were issued by federal agencies. It has been estimated that 14 percent of the vehicles entering national parks had an occupant over 61 years of age, blind, or disabled, and are exempt from the payment of entrance fees (General Accounting Office). In addition, at recreation sites where entrance fees were charged per person rather than per vehicle, youths under 16 years of age were admitted free. It was estimated that 24 percent of the persons entering national park facilities were under 16 and therefore exempt from payment of entrance fees.

A Golden Eagle Passport is available to anyone at a cost of $10 and is good for one calender year. It allows free and unlimited entrance by the permit holder and any accompanying passengers in a private non-commercial vehicle to federal parks, monuments, and recreation areas. Where entry is not by private vehicle, the pass allows free entry by the permit holder, spouse, children, and parents. It does not cover the user fees for camping, boat launching, or parking. Only about 120,000 Golden Eagle Passports were issued each year during the early 1980s with total receipts of about $1.2 million per year. Information is not available on the number of visits to federal recreation sites by Golden

Eagle passholders. It is believed that the revenue from the sale of annual Golden Eagle passes roughly offset the entrance fees lost from free entry to recreation sites by passholders (General Accounting Office).

Third, problems may arise when entrance fees are set on a per unit basis, such as per vehicle or per person entering the park. Facilities in the national parks usually were built so that sufficient services were available during the summer months when there was a great deal of seasonal demand by visitors on vacation trips. Yet most entrance fees were set so that the effective rate fell for this extra consumption. The practice was to charge all users the same fee, ignoring the fact that it was more expensive to serve visitors who remained in the park for several days. The practice was equivalent to granting quantity discounts. For example, a uniform fee of $4 per visit would be equal to $1.00 per hour for the typical 4-hour visit, and would fall to 10 cents per hour for the 40-hour visit, or one-tenth as much. Recreation facilities and parks were built to supply peak demand. If it were not for these peaks which occur infrequently, the cost of larger parks could be avoided. Yet it is at times of peak demand, when prices should be the highest, that they are often the lowest.

Fourth, there are problems in measuring the performance of agency fee practices by comparing total annual expenditures with total receipts from user fees. This measure may be of limited reliability because many of the costs are capital investments that provide outputs for 20 years or more. Capital costs, most observers would agree, should properly be amortized over time. Government accounting procedures typically have not adequately addressed this issue. The full costs of facility construction, for example, are often charged against recreation user fees during the year of construction. For example, annual Forest Service budgets include the total expenditures for recreation use management, site operation, maintenance, rehabilitation, and construction of capital facilities. In the era of declining availability of funds for recreation construction, the problem has become less important.

	Total Expenditures, Millions	Construction, Millions
1978	$105.0	$19.3
1980	113.4	9.6
1982	119.0	4.8

The problem was not very important in 1982, when construction of facilities accounted for only 4 percent of the total Forest Service recreation budget, compared with 18 percent in 1978. It will become more important in the future if capital construction budgets increase.

Finally, there are problems in setting fees for recreation use when, unlike most goods and services, there is no standard unit of measurement. Reiling and Anderson pointed out that user fees are usually assessed per car, per party, and per person entering a park or other recreation site. However, the most widely used measure of recreation use is the recreation visitor day (RVD) which is one person for 12 hours, 12 persons for one hour each, or any combination totaling 12 hours. A family of four persons using a campsite for 24 hours accounts for 8 RVDs but the user fee is for one occupied site for one night. In contrast, 96 persons (= 8 RVDs) who arrive at a picnic site at the same time and use it for an hour may have a very different effect on costs than the family of four persons for one overnight stay. Thus, the RVD measure of use may not accurately relate to costs. Reiling and Anderson recommend that user fees be based on a measure of use that accurately reflects costs of service.

MARGINAL COST PRICING

Economists generally recommend that user fees be set where the added costs of producing recreation opportunities equal the added benefits. This means that marginal cost prices would be set at the intersection of the demand (or marginal benefit) curve and the supply (or marginal cost) curve. To understand how the principle of marginal cost pricing applies to the problem of recreation user fees, it is helpful to review the effect of alternative levels of demand on marginal and average total costs of production. Look at the first panel of Figure 14-1. Note that there are only three possible situations. Park and recreation agencies exhibit either:

(1) Minimum Cost Production — with demand equal to supply, marginal cost prices equal average total costs including investment costs, resulting in pay-as-you-go operations (panel 2);

(2) Decreasing Cost of Production — with excess supply relative to demand, marginal cost prices are less than average total costs, resulting in subsidies to cover losses (panel 3); or

(3) Increasing Cost of Production — with excess demand relative to supply, marginal cost prices are greater than average total costs, resulting in surplus revenues to expand operations (panel 4).

Each of these situations will be explained below. But first, it is important to understand the dynamic relationship between marginal cost prices and demand. Krutilla has observed that initially when park and other recreation sites are developed, there is excess capacity of in facilities, justifying a low marginal cost pricing policy in the short run, which does not recover average total costs including investment costs (panel 3). However, as use of capacity increases in a growing economy, marginal cost prices would rise until a point is reached where the revenue from user fees covers average total costs including investment

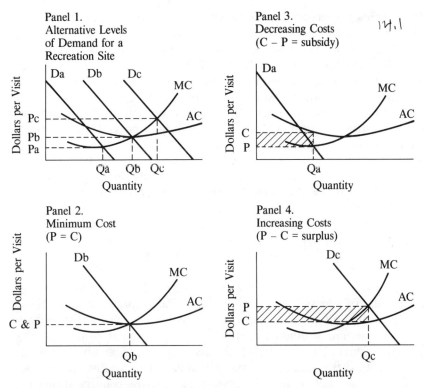

Figure 14-1. Effect of Demand on Marginal Cost Pricing

costs. User fees would be equivalent to the competitive equilibrium price in the long run (panel 2). Where excess demand for use of capacity develops, marginal cost prices would rise still further, demonstrating sufficient willingness to pay to justify an expansion of facilities (panel 4). This illustrates the fact that the problem of efficient pricing is twofold: in the short-run, to encourage the best use of existing facilities; and in the long-run, to find the optimum level of investment in capacity.

Minimum Cost Production

The efficient pricing solution for a government agency is to attempt to provide the competitive industry result, according to the Musgraves in their authoritative textbook on public finance. Effective price competition among private suppliers would drive user fees to minimum-cost levels. However, without the discipline of competitive markets, it may be difficult for managers of government agencies to find the competitive solution. As a result, the efficient operation of recreation programs by public agencies is likely to depend on the ability of managers to adopt the correct least-cost price policy.

The recreation economic decision would be to set user fees at the intersection of the demand curve (Db) with the marginal cost (MC) and average cost (AC) curves, according to Robinson. This is shown in the second panel of Figure 14-1. The Pennsylvania State University economist correctly reasoned that this would be equivalent to the competitive equilibrium result. Public recreation opportunities would be supplied at minimum cost, i.e., at the lowest point on the average total cost curve. Consumers would get the largest possible total supply, user fees would equal marginal cost as well as average total cost, resources would be efficiently used, and no operating deficits or surpluses would occur. If demand at this price turns out to be less than the quantity which would yield minimum average total cost, the losses would be avoided by reducing the capacity of park and recreation programs. Some recreation sites or facilities would be closed. On the other hand, when demand at this price turns out to be in excess of supply, an expansion of capacity would be recommended.

To see that this would be equivalent to the competitive industry result, consider the market for ski lift tickets, which are purchased by individuals for access to downhill skiing. The second panel in Figure 14-1 illustrates a typical demand curve for ski lift tickets (Db) with a series of alternative quantities demanded at different prices moving along the demand curve. If lift tickets are offered at an exorbitant price, the market potential of downhill skiing may decline sharply because skiers are apt to find it cheaper to go cross-country skiing instead. If the price is lowered to more reasonable levels, downhill skiing will attract many skiers who find it much more exciting than cross-country skiing. If the price is lowered still further, even more downhill skiing is likely to be demanded.

Price not only influences quantity demanded; it also affects the quantity that will be supplied. This has always been true for private companies supplying outdoor recreation goods and services. It is increasingly the case for government agencies supplying outdoor recreation opportunities. The second panel in Figure 14-1 displays the supply curve (MC) for our illustrative downhill skiing market. If the price of lift tickets is so low that it does not cover the average total cost (AC) of operating most ski areas, little or no downhill skiing will be provided in the long run. If the price is raised somewhat, we may expect suppliers to provide more skiing opportunities. And at even higher prices, they may be willing to provide still more.

There is one point in the diagram at which the supply curve (MC), average total cost curve (AC), and the demand curve (Db) intersect. At the price corresponding to that point, the quantity supplied is equal to the quantity demanded. Prices should be set at this point if recreation resources are to be managed efficiently in the long run. The quantity demanded will exceed the quantity supplied at a lower price and the quantity supplied will exceed quantity demanded at a higher price. The price at which supply and demand are equal is the competitive long-run equilibrium price. In this market, it is the lift ticket price at which willing sellers exchange skiing opportunities with willing buyers. This is not the whole story, of course, because the demand and supply of downhill skiing are affected by other things, for example, travel costs and other variables that were discussed in Chapters 7 and 13.

Problems may occur when low user fees are raised to put parks and other recreation programs on a pay-as-you-go basis. Increasing user fees can be a costly source of revenue, according to Vickrey. Swimming pools are a case in point. Suppose that a city-owned pool increases the adult daily user fee from $1.50 to $2 per person to equal average total costs under least-cost operation. As a result of this 33 percent increase in user fees, assume that the number of swimmers falls off 10 percent. Then, for every 100 swimmers per day who previously paid $1.50, yielding $150 of total revenue, there will be 90 swimmers per day paying $2 and yielding $180, a net increase of $30. The increase in user fees paid by the 90 persons who continue to swim will be 50 cents each, or a total of $45. The loss in benefits to 10 former swimmers, who chose an alternative form of recreation they considered inferior to the $1.50 swim but preferable to the $2 swim, would range from 0 to 50 cents, or an average of 25 cents. This totals $2.50 per day for all 10 persons excluded from the pool by the price increase. Thus, the burden on recreation users, both continuing and former swimmers combined, totals $47.50 per day (= $45 + $2.50) compared to increased revenue of $30. This is equivalent to a user cost of $1.58 for each $1 of new revenue for pool operations. If costs are not appreciably changed by 10 percent lower use of pool capacity, as seems likely, this is a reasonable approximation of the marginal cost of the added revenue.

Another objection to pricing recreation appropriately is that higher user fees would hurt the poor. This is especially pertinent to city park and recreation programs such as swimming pools because an increase in user fees is regressive, imposing approximately the same dollar burden on adults drawn from a wide range of income levels. The poor, along with everyone else, would pay more if user fees were raised. The challenge is to devise special user fee schedules for those who cannot pay. A study by Economic Research Associates found that in 1975, nearly 25 percent of a sample of city park and recreation departments reported charging low income and welfare families reduced or no user fees. Other groups that were charged reduced or no fees included more than 55 percent of the children and students, over 50 percent of the elderly, and 14 percent of young adults. As a result of these and related programs, only 8 percent of the managers of city park and recreation departments reported that fewer lower income families would participate in outdoor recreation with increased user fees. In addition, there may be more direct and efficient ways of helping the poor than to underprice outdoor recreation for all users. Perhaps an income supplement or subsidized housing, better education, job opportunities, special counseling, and similar programs would serve the targeted groups more effectively without inducing wasteful recreation resource use practices in all of the population.

Decreasing Costs of Production

In the past, studies of most park and recreation programs concluded that average total costs were decreasing. The third panel in Figure 14-1 illustrates this case of decreasing costs. The important difference from the competitive solution illustrated in the second panel is that with excess supply relative to demand, marginal costs are less than average total costs. Marginal costs are always below average total costs when average costs are declining. Thus, the competitive equilibrium solution would not be recommended for public agencies operating under conditions of decreasing costs. Economies of scale can be achieved by setting user fees at a lower level to encourage additional use.

Since the principle of marginal cost pricing was first developed, its advocates generally have held that it is the proper solution to the problem of achieving economic efficiency under conditions of decreasing costs such as occur in public recreation. They would set user fees exactly at marginal cost, or as close to this level as would be feasible given difficulties in estimating marginal cost and in keeping user fees in line with these estimates. Because the intersection of the demand curve and the marginal cost curve would occur at a price (P) where marginal cost is below the average cost of production (C), the result would be a net loss from operating recreation programs (C - P) shown as the shaded rectangle in the third panel. The deficit would be subsidized from taxes or other sources that are not related to participation rates, in order to avoid interfering with efficient pricing.

Under conditions of decreasing costs of production, the most important advantage of marginal cost pricing is that it would result in larger output and lower average total cost per visit than would average cost pricing which recovers all operating and capital costs. You can verify that this is the case by drawing a line in the third panel from the intersection of the demand curve (Da) and the average cost curve (AC) perpendicular to the horizontal axis, and compare that output level to the marginal cost price solution shown in the panel. The inefficiencies resulting from average cost pricing under conditions of decreasing costs of production are readily apparent. The output would be overpriced, underproduced, and underconsumed.

It is often argued that when a recreation site has excess capacity, managers might as well price services very low so that consumers will be encouraged to use capacity more fully. The rationale is that once a recreation facility is in place, the marginal cost of serving additional users may be very low, and to restrict use by causing them to pay the average total costs, including cost of the "sunk" investment, would lead to a misallocation of resources. The argument usually assumes that the price of recreation services then will be raised to recover the cost of new investment as capacity is reached. This position has serious drawbacks.

One possible problem is that recreation users may regard the low price early in the history of recreation sites as the long-term price and make recreation plans accordingly (Howe). If price is kept low during a period of excess capacity, users are likely to make long-lived decisions affecting recreation use based on the low price. These users may then suffer unexpected losses when recreation use fees are later raised. Examples include the purchase of large travel trailers and recreation vehicles. Buyers may over-invest in recreation equipment in anticipation of offsetting this expense by access to the low priced recreation opportunities provided at public recreation sites. In principle, this could be prevented by providing users with estimates of probable future prices. However, once a low price is established, groups who benefit will often be able to bring political pressure to bear on public agencies to maintain the low price for the services of existing facilities and to extend the same low pricing practice to new facilities.

There are other major difficulties in applying this pricing solution. One is that to apply marginal cost pricing only to a selected group of public parks and recreation areas would mean that they would be competing with other public and private sites priced significantly above marginal cost. This could result in a substantial market distortion. The situation illustrates what is sometimes referred to as the principle of second best. This means that whenever there is a general rule that cannot be applied uniformly throughout all parts of an interrelated system, the best adaptation that can be made is to modify or depart from the rule. It is usually best in such cases not to try to follow the rule exactly in one part of the recreation industry, but rather to allow for some appropriate deviation throughout. The application of this second best principle to marginal cost pricing, according to Vickrey, calls for prices of public recreation services to be set above marginal cost by an amount corresponding to the degree that prices of alternative suppliers exceed their marginal cost. It may be efficient for a government agency to charge a price in excess of marginal cost to avoid undue substitution of its output for the overpriced output of other public and private sites. On the other hand, if the competing output is complementary to that sold by the government agency, efficiency may call for a public price below marginal cost so as to encourage consumers to buy a more efficient package of private and public services, according to the Musgraves.

Problems arise in the administration of tax subsidized recreation programs. First, subsidies may encourage users to demand that a service be unduly expanded or improved in quality. This would be the expected result when consumers who expect to benefit would not be called upon to bear the full burden of the added taxes. An agency that relies on user fee revenues may be better able to resist such demands than would an agency able to finance expansion of its programs from an open-ended subsidy. A second point is that an agency may have less incentive to hold costs down when it is able to draw on a subsidy than when it is required to function within the revenues available from user charges. Vickrey suggests that the subsidy be independent of the manner in which the service is supplied, especially that it not take the form of subsidizing a particular category of cost. Otherwise, incentives for distortion can result in the inefficient management of recreation resources. For example, campground expenditures classified as capital outlays could be subsidized from general tax revenues, while an increasing proportion of direct operating expenses could be met from user fees, with fee increases being mandatory if operating expenses were not so covered. As a result, there would be an incentive for levels of service to be drastically cut and maintenance expenditures skimped. At the same time, new construction could proceed with relatively lavish new drinking water and wastewater facilities, which may be furnished without adequate thought as to how the new facilities would be maintained when ready. Also new equipment would be purchased to replace items prematurely retired because of poor maintenance.

A third point is that a change in political administrations and personnel may change the availability of trained persons for maintenance and budgets for construction such as to meet new public health standards relative to environmental quality. A fourth point is that a subsidized agency may spend an excessive proportion of its administrative effort in trying to justify increases in the subsidy to enlarge the scope of its own operations. In each particular case, a decision of whether to eliminate or limit the extent of subsidy should be made on the basis of weighing the above considerations against the loss of economic efficiency entailed by a limitation of the subsidy.

Increasing Costs of Production

By the 1980s, the logic of decreasing costs of production seemed less compelling. Several developments in the preceding decade contributed to the realization that more and more public recreation sites experienced increasing costs. Suitable sites for many kinds of recreation were increasingly scarce and land costs were rising rapidly. The costs of new facility construction rose to prohibitively high levels. Demand continued to increase at a rate in excess of population growth, and shortages of facilities resulted in rising congestion on peak days of use. Managers became more aware of the environmental damages of excess demand for some types of recreation. As a result, emphasis shifted away from the case of decreasing costs with government subsidizing recreation use.

The fourth panel of Figure 14-1 illustrates the effect of these increasing costs on marginal cost prices. The important thing to note when resources are very scarce relative to demand, is that marginal costs are above average total costs. Thus, the recreation economic decision to set user fees (P) at the intersection of the demand curve (Dc) and the marginal cost curve (MC) has two effects. First, it yields surplus revenue (P - C) to expand recreation programs. When users demonstrate they are willing to pay more for recreation opportunities than the average total cost of existing programs, this would be clear evidence of the need for expansion, and the surplus revenue available would enable this expansion to occur without government subsidies. Second, it restricts output to the point where marginal costs intersect the demand curve even though average total costs could be recovered at a lower price and larger output. Thus, it correctly rations the use of existing capacity to the users who value the experience more highly than the added costs of providing the recreation opportunity. A lower price equal to average total cost would violate this principle.

In other words, this solves both problems of efficient pricing by public agencies producing recreation opportunities: in the short-run, to encourage the best use of existing facilities; and in the long-run, to find the optimum level of investment in capacity. Under conditions of increasing costs, the chief advantage of marginal cost pricing is that it serves these two basic purposes: first, to discourage excess demand, i.e., more recreation use than the optimum carrying capacity of existing facilities in the short run; and second, to generate surplus revenue for capital investment to expand recreation programs in the long-run.

In a competitive industry, increasing cost of production would not be a stable situation. In the long-run, new investment would expand capacity which shifts the cost functions for recreation to the right. The objective of managers of public agencies should be to expand recreation opportunities until the demand curve (Dc) equals the new marginal cost curve where it intersects the new average total cost curve. You will recall that in the long-run, the recreation economic decision would be to set user fees at this level. Public recreation opportunities would be supplied at least cost, i.e., at the lowest point on the new average total cost curve. Consumers would get the largest possible supply and resources would be efficiently used without operating deficits or surpluses.

Unfortunately, prices that correctly ration the use of capacity and deal with congestion may or may not provide sufficient revenues for expansion. Expansion decisions should be based on whether the revenues are sufficient to cover the costs of expansion at the time in the future when they are contemplated. In an inflationary era, future replacement or expansion costs may bear little relation to investment costs at an earlier period. Thus, deciding whether the revenues generated by user fees justify an expansion of facilities cannot be determined by covering the historical capital costs, although that may be required for legal purposes. Applying the opportunity cost principle to long-run investment decisions in an inflationary era would shift the long-run marginal cost curve to a higher level than for the cost reimbursement problem of current recreation programs (Reiling, et al.). This distinguishes the case of increasing cost (panel 4) from the least-cost situation (panel 2) in Figure 14-1.

Problems may arise in the definition of increasing marginal cost. If marginal cost pricing is to be effectively applied by government agencies under conditions of increasing costs, more recreation economic research is needed to define and measure marginal cost itself. In the past, much of the discussion of marginal cost pricing under conditions of decreasing internal costs of recreation agencies missed the essential point. That is, the relevant costs should include more than the internal operation and maintenance costs of the public agencies administering recreation programs. In the case of almost every output of a recreation facility, the greatest influences on marginal cost, properly conceived, are two external effects — congestion and opportunity costs. Congestion results when too many users impose external costs on each other. Opportunity costs may result from using natural resources for recreation at the expense of another purpose. An example would be the opportunity cost of foregoing the diversion of water from a reservoir during the recreation season to generate hydroelectric power, which would adversely affect boating and fishing on the reservoir and downstream.

In order to make appropriate recreation economic decisions with respect to prices, they should be related to appropriate measures of cost. The cost concepts used in economics are sufficiently general that it becomes difficult to include the many relevant categories of recreation resource related costs in the analysis. In the usual recreation sup-

510

ply situation, there are: (1) capital costs to acquire land and to develop access roads and facilities, (2) environmental resource protection costs; (3) agency operation, maintenance, and replacement costs; (4) administrative overhead costs; (5) congestion costs of users; (6) other associated costs; and (7) opportunity costs of foregone resource development. The shape of the marginal cost curve depends on the number of these inputs which vary as the level of output is increased. As discussed in Chapter 13, this depends, in part, on the length of the planning period to which the marginal cost refers. While it is apparent that in the very short-run, some internal costs of the agency may decline with increased use of a site owing to the fixed nature of their recreation inputs, costs external to the agency often increase in the long-run.

Sometimes recreation is supplied by a private company with the ability to set prices. Marginal cost pricing of the output of a private monopoly facing an increasing marginal cost curve threatens the possibility that it may enjoy excess profits, i.e., surplus P-C in panel 4 of Figure 14-1. It has long been observed that public recreation sites, particularly those endowed with unique natural, historic, and cultural resources have some characteristics of monopolies. The same is expected to be true for some private recreation sites either with truly unique natural or simulated resources and capital improvements (i.e., theme parks). For this reason, the discussion during the 1980s of monopoly in recreation and other natural resource related industries became more concerned with using high marginal cost pricing to restrain the growth of quantity demanded, while encouraging expansion of capacity on the supply side. Emphasis in public policy shifted to deregulation and stimulating the entry of new competition rather than regulating industry prices or profit margins. The previous concern that marginal cost prices be low to encourage consumption with government subsidies of recreation use seemed less relevant (at ski areas and campgrounds, for example). These insights, which seem plausible, were suggested by Randall, a leading natural resource economist at Ohio State University.

Peak Load Pricing

The application of marginal cost pricing by managers of parks and other recreation sites often results in variable user fees at different times of the day, week, or season of the year. Economists use the term "peak load pricing" when they refer to the practice of charging different prices for the same services demanded at different points in time. It makes sense to charge higher prices during peak periods of demand and lower prices during off-peak periods. Since the demand for most recreation opportunities is higher at some times than others, ca-

511

pacity has to be large enough to accommodate demand during the peak periods. This results in substantial excess capacity during off-peak periods. A large part of the capacity of parks and other recreation facilities stand idle a good bit of the time. The costs of this capacity can be covered by adoption of a marginal cost pricing policy that charges peak users more than off-peak users.

Peak load pricing can be illustrated by referring to the first panel of Figure 14-1. Assume that the demand curve, Dc, represents the weighted average demand curve for all peak days and Da all off-peak days. During the off-peak period, low user fees are set at Pa where marginal cost is equal to the marginal benefit of off-peak users. During the peak period, high user fees are set at Pc where marginal cost is equal to the marginal benefit of peak users. As a result, off-peak users pay only the lower operating costs to provide the recreation opportunities they consume. However, peak users pay both the operating costs and the costs of increased capacity to provide the additional recreation opportunities.

For example, a peak price of $6 and an off-peak price of $2 would cover average total costs of $4 when one-half of the annual use of a site occurs on peak days and one-half on off-peak days. Figure 14-1 illustrates the situation where demand on peak days is double that on off-peak days. But there are roughly twice as many off-peak days in the midweek as peak days on weekends and holidays, so that approximately one-half of the annual recreation use occurs on peak days and one-half on off-peak days. Of course, if annual peak and off-peak use differs, then they must be weighted accordingly. The competitive equilibrium result occurs when the aggregate demand curve, Db, represents the weighted average of the demand curves for peak and off-peak days.

The difference between the $6 peak and $2 off-peak period prices represents two types of costs: (1) increased operating costs incurred to provide the recreation services users consume at higher levels of output; and (2) a capacity charge, representing the annualized value of capital improvements at the site, divided by the number of users in the peak period. This means that a capacity charge is added to operating cost in the peak period so that demand and supply will be in equilibrium.

In the long-run, the value of the capacity charge takes on added significance. As the demand for recreation use increases over time, the capacity charge also increases to maintain the equilibrium between quantity demanded and capacity of the park. If the number of visitors in the peak period is known, then multiplying peak usage by the capacity charge per user represents the total revenue remaining after payment of the cost of operation. If this is greater than the annual capital costs of new construction, expansion of park capacity is justified and should be done. This means that additions to capacity should be made until the daily capacity charge, multiplied by the number of users in the peak period, equals the annual capital costs associated with expansion. Hence, the value of the capacity charge required to clear the market during the peak period indicates whether expansion of park facilities is justified from an economic viewpoint.

Peak load pricing has two additional advantages. First, the approach provides casual users with an economic incentive to visit the facilities during off-peak periods when entrance fees are lower. This would tend to reduce the seasonal variation in the number of daily users and to partially equalize costs over time. Second, when peak period users pay an additional cost to reflect the scarcity of recreation opportunities during peak periods, this guarantees that those users who place the highest value on recreation use of the site are the ones that actually are admitted. This is important because as a result, only those persons whose benefits equal or exceed the added costs of providing the recreation resources will use them. Those for whom the experience is of lower value will conserve their use. They will be discouraged from entering recreation sites and committing them to uses of very low value. In this way, marginal cost pricing will result in the production of recreation opportunities that maximize total user benefits at the lowest possible cost.

Peak load pricing may create problems of equity, particularly with regard to weekend and midweek use of parks and other recreation facilities. Weekend users may tend to be lower-income workers and youth who are prevented from weekday use by fixed work or school schedules. Midweek users are more likely to be higher income vacationers and retired persons whose time is less constrained. Thus, the imposition of peak load pricing may lead to undesirable distribution results. The problem may be less pronounced at private resorts since most users are relatively affluent. In terms of equity, improved resource allocation might require peak load pricing at private resorts and reduced fees at public sites. However, to the extent that the demand for resorts and public sites is inelastic, relatively little misallocation of resources should result from this policy.

When a new park or other recreation facility at first is very lightly used, the marginal cost of additional users is low, and marginal cost pricing would result in a corresponding low user fee. Meanwhile, higher marginal cost at older, crowded recreation sites would call for a correspondingly higher price on the same basis. But this would understandably strike many users of older facilities as piling insult on injury. It may be regarded as a necessary discrimination to single out one particular region for the new facility simply because one must do one thing at a time. Vickrey has warned that to give the users of a new recreation site a lower price than those using the older, crowded site may not only provoke hard feelings but also create a disruptive political climate preventing the construction of new sites in rational sequence. In short, the felt injustices involved and the political tensions generated by peak load prices must be taken into account.

Problems also may arise when peak load pricing is imposed at private recreation facilities, as is frequently the case, without concomitant peak load pricing at publicly provided facilities. This would lead to an excessive utilization of already congested, publicly provided facilities during periods of peak demand. Thus, it would reduce rather than improve overall resource allocation. This would be the expected result for substitute recreation sites such as campgrounds. In the case of complements, however, the absence of peak load pricing for public services may encourage consumers to buy a more efficient package of private and public services.

Implementation of peak period pricing would require information that should not be difficult to obtain. First, the number of users during peak and off-peak days should be readily available from fee receipts. More difficult to obtain is information regarding the number of potential users turned away from the site on peak days. This would be needed to accurately estimate the quantity of use demanded at the given user fees. Peak load pricing would be contrary to many existing pricing practices where unrestricted annual passes result in decreasing prices with increased use, even on peak days. Examples include the Golden Eagle pass at federal recreation areas, and annual passes at state parks and municipal facilities, such as swimming pools and golf courses. Daily user fees should be charged, in addition, to reflect marginal costs.

Despite these problems, Howe concludes that additional thought deserves to be given to both seasonal and daily peak pricing methods. This is based on the observation that the cost of developing new recreation sites and facilities is going up everywhere, quite aside from inflation. The more peak period users, the sooner the agencies will be forced to develop new, higher cost sites. Thus, the only sensible pricing policy is one that increases with the quantity of use on peak days.

COMPARABLE PRICING AND MARKET STRUCTURE

The pricing guidelines of the federal government recommend that recreation agencies compare their own user fees to charges by other federal, non-federal public agencies, and private enterprises which provide similar facilities and services in the region. Differences not explained by the level of development and amount of service should be noted and user fees adjusted accordingly. In practice, comparable pricing represents charging the average of user fees charged by other organizations for equivalent services. Managers of public campgrounds periodically take surveys of public and private camping fees in the region, and attempt to charge the average user fee. When, for example, it was found that campgrounds with comparable facilities and services charged user fees ranging from $4 to $8 per night, public agencies proposed raising camping fees to $6 per night. In 1978, the Forest Service compared the average camping fees at private campgrounds to fees at its own campgrounds and as a result, raised camping fees in subsequent years.

Pricing public recreation opportunities at the going market rate has several advantages. Perhaps the most important observation is that the market establishes the range of prices that are acceptable to users. Thus, it would tend to avoid controversy because the agency's prices would be consistent with those charged by other suppliers. Moreover, the market price represents the collective wisdom of suppliers in the region concerning what is fair and equitable. Thus, the practice would ensure that the public operation of recreation sites such as campgrounds would not impede the success of private campgrounds and reduce the range of camping opportunities available. If public campgrounds charged lower prices, it could be detrimental to commercial campgrounds and result in congestion and turnaways at the public campground. These and related advantages of pricing at the market level were suggested by Crompton. The noted professor of recreation management at Texas A & M University has published several studies of the problem of pricing recreation services.

Problems may arise in applying the comparable pricing standard. First, where public facilities are new or unique, there may be no similar sites in the region from which to draw market prices for comparison. For example, the so-called "crown jewels" of our National Park system, such as Grand Canyon, Yellowstone, and Yosemite, are unique and no similar recreation sites exist. However, the user fees at these parks have been compared to those at other unique recreation sites with a large amount of use. Table 14-11 shows the trend in user fees at 10 unique sites including Disneyland, Marineland, Cypress Gardens, and the Empire State Building. Average entrance fees for adults increased from $2.66 in 1971 to $6.22 in 1981, or by 147 percent. This was 45 percent more than inflation of 102 percent. Average entrance fees for children increased even more, from $1.33 to $3.46 during the same years. A report to Congress considered these prices sufficiently comparable to recommend that the major National Parks raise entrance fees by equivalent percentages from much lower levels.

Where public facilities are not new or unique, comparable prices in the region may not accurately reflect social values. It is a common situation for comparable market prices to under- or over-estimate social values. Either the user fees charged by other public agencies do not

Table 14-11. Comparable Entrance Fees at Other Unique Recreation Sites, United States, 1971 and 1981

| Recreation Site | Number of Visits, 1980 | | Entrance fee | | Percentage Increase in Adult Fee |
			December, 1971	December, 1981	
Hearst Castle[a]	960,262	Adult	$4.00	$7.80	95%
		Child	2.00	3.80	
San Diego Zoo	3,700,262	Adult	1.50	4.25	183
		Child	Free	1.00	
San Diego Wild Animal Park	1,086,890	Adult	1.25	4.50	260
		Child	Free	2.75	
Marineland[b]	1,000,000	Adult	3.50	7.95	127
		Child	2.75	5.95	
		Child	1.25	—	
Mount Vernon	968,646	Adult	1.00	3.00	200
		Child	0.50	1.50	
Disneyland[b]	11,300,000	Adult	3.50	8.00	129
		Child	2.50	6.00	
		Child	0.75	4.00	
Empire State Building	1,823,541	Adult	1.60	2.50	56
		Child	0.80	1.35	
Universal Studios[b]	3,767,558	Adult	4.00	9.50	138
		Child	3.00	7.50	
		Child		2.00	
The Queen Mary	950,000	Adult	2.50	6.75	170
		Child	1.25	4.00	
Cypress Gardens	1,366,000	Adult	3.75	7.95	112
		Child	2.10	4.50	
Average Entrance Fee		Adult	$2.66	$6.22	147
		Child	1.33	3.46	160

[a]Entrance fee includes a guided tour. Entrance fee without tour is not available.
[b]This recreation attraction had two levels of fees for persons under 18, depending on age.
Source: General Accounting Office.

cover the social cost of all inputs used in the production process, or excess user fees are charged by private producers who have a substantial degree of market power. Many recreation sites are unique or at least out-perform all competing sites in some manner. Just as Yellowstone or Grand Canyon are dominant with respect to their attributes nationally, a local boating, fishing or camping site could monopolize its relevant market for weekend visitors. In 1981, the highest camping fee in Massachusetts was at Martha's Vineyard with $14 for two people, plus $6 for each additional person. In Tempe, Arizona, it was $14 for two and $2 extra for each added person. At the same time, the majority of the rates for private campgrounds were within the range of $8-10 for a family of four in moderately developed sites.

Managers should consider the direction and likely magnitude of the divergence from social values in estimating the upper and lower bounds of the comparative price estimate. Comparable prices charged by private suppliers may need to be adjusted when competitive market forces are weak, to ensure effective competition, or to establish minimum standards of performance. The purpose of this section is to discuss some important effects of market structure and behavior on the practice of comparable pricing by government agencies.

Monopoly and Competition

You will remember that the efficient pricing solution for a government agency is to attempt to provide the competitive industry result. The recreation economic decision of a public agency would be to set user fees at the intersection of the demand curve with the marginal cost and average cost curves. Public recreation opportunities would be supplied at efficient minimum cost levels, i.e., at the lowest point on the average total cost curve. Consumers would get the largest possible total supply, resources would be efficiently used, and no operating deficits or surpluses would occur. This means that recreation markets should have a competitive structure if they are to serve as a standard for comparable pricing. Under competitive conditions, markets have so many sellers that no single one has any appreciable say as to the price of their output. All sellers are price takers, not price makers. The price is determined in a competitive market through the impersonal forces of supply and demand. Each operator would be too small a frog in too large a puddle to have any influence on market prices. Individual operators would take price as given, confident that with a very small share of the market, they would be able to sell whatever services they can supply. In competitive markets, private suppliers of recreation opportunities would charge comparable prices.

Sometimes recreation opportunities are provided by private companies that have the ability to exercise a substantial degree of control over their prices. In those recreation markets in which some suppliers are able to affect price, competition tends to give way to the exercise market power. Where one or a few suppliers have control over supply, the market structure is said to be monopolistic. Suppliers have the ability to restrict output, raise price, and earn profits in excess of the opportunity cost of capital employed. In a competitive industry, producers are forced to price their products or services at the lowest point on their average total cost curves (including the opportunity cost of capital). Monopolists will attempt to set prices at a level above these costs. Thus, the market may fail to perform satisfactorily when recreation facilities are provided by one or a few producers, i.e., when monopoly or oligopoly is present.

Economists define the term, "oligopoly," to mean markets with a few dominant sellers in which mutual interdependence is recognized. A competitive fringe of small sellers follows the price leadership of the dominant firms. There are high barriers to the entry of new firms, and products or services are usually highly differentiated. As a result, average revenue is consistently above average cost in the long run. These conditions are present in some regional markets for skiing. The term, "monopolistic competition," refers to markets with a large number of small sellers in which interdependence is not recognized. Products and services are usually highly differentiated. Rivalry involves the periodic introduction of variation in products and services which raise production and marketing costs. With relative ease of entry by new firms, average revenue equals average cost in the long run as excess profits are squeezed out by rising costs. These conditions are typical of restaurants and overnight accommodations in some resort areas and of sellers of some recreation equipment. Under these and related market structures, private market prices would not provide a suitable standard for comparable pricing by public agencies.

Market power may develop for several reasons. Most producers have locational advantages. A single site or perhaps a few sites provide the only opportunity for a particular recreation activity in a local or regional market. Others operate sites that provide a truly different recreation experience; some have been endowed with unique natural, historic, and cultural resources; others have simulated these site characteristics by artistic design and capital improvements, as for example, theme parks. The government awards concessioners an exclusive right to operate recreation businesses in a particular park or other recreation site. These concessioners may gain substantial control over lodging, food service, equipment rental, and related services at the site. In other cases, decreasing costs of producing recreation services may allow a single company or perhaps a few companies, to have lower costs than potential producers who might contemplate entering. Callahan and Knudson studied the structure of the private recreation market in southern Indiana. The authors found considerable seller concentration and product differentiation resulting from location, quality of service, and advertising.

When entry is discouraged, for whatever reasons, then one or a few existing producers may be free to set the prices of recreation opportunities at whatever level they wish and to serve as many users as they can at those prices. The producers are constrained only by the demand for the recreation opportunity at the price they set and not by any threat that competitors will undercut their prices and lure their customers away. The presence of market power can prevent the efficient functioning of the market. Consumers must accept the higher prices on a take-it-or-leave-it basis when there is little or no chance that competitors will move in and provide similar recreation opportunities at a lower price.

A comparison of panels 1 and 2 of Figure 14-2 illustrates the effect of market structure on the prices of private recreation suppliers. Panel

518

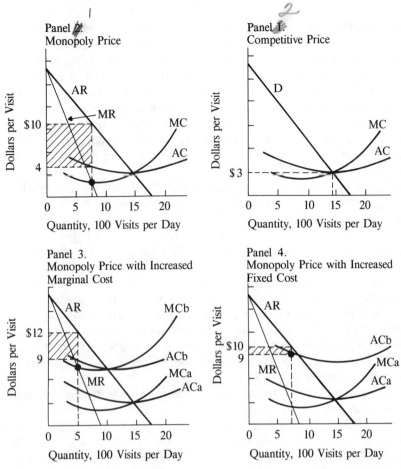

Figure 14-2. Effects of Market Structure and Costs on User Fees of Private Suppliers of Recreation Services

1 represents the case of a monopoly that is of much concern to recreation resource economists. Shown are the usual average total cost (AC) curve, marginal cost (MC) curve, demand (D) curve or average revenue curve, and the marginal revenue (MR) curve for a typical monopoly. Notice that the marginal revenue curve is below the demand curve. When monopolies lower their price to increase sales, then the additional revenue that they take in is the price they collect from their new customers minus the revenue they lose by cutting the price paid by all of their old customers.

Like any other private company, monopolies maximize their profits by setting marginal revenue (MR) equal to marginal cost (MC). They would select the point in the diagram where output is 750 visits. But that point does not tell us the monopoly price because, as we have just seen, price exceeds MR for a monopolist. To learn what price the monopolist charges, we must use the demand curve to find the price at which consumers are willing to make 750 visits. The answer, we see, is that the monopoly price is $10 per unit, which exceeds both MR and MC (which are equal to $2). The monopoly depicted in panel 1 is earning a tidy profit. This profit is shown as the shaded rectangle whose height is the difference between price and average cost, and whose width is the quantity produced (750 visits). In this example, profits are $6 per visit times 750 visits, or $4,500 per day.

Panel 2 represents the case of a competitive market which, you will remember, provides a suitable standard for comparable pricing by public agencies. The average total cost (AC) curve, marginal cost (MC) curve, and demand (D) curve are identical to those shown in panel 1 for monopolies. The competitive equilibrium would occur where price equals $3 per visit and quantity equals 1,500 visits per day. This is the point where the quantity demanded (which we read from the demand curve) and quantity supplied (which we read from the MC = supply curve) are equal. By comparing this competitive result with panel 1, we can see that monopolies would produce fewer recreation opportunities than would a competitive industry with the same demand and cost conditions. The monopoly output at which MC = MR falls from 1,500 to 750 visits per day. Note that the monopoly price of $10 per visit exceeds the $3 price that would result from competition by $7 per visit.

Consumers are willing to pay an amount for an additional visit that exceeds what it costs to produce that visit (its MC). But monopolies refuse to lower prices to increase production, for if they raise output by one unit, the revenue they will collect (MR) will be less than the price that consumers will pay for the additional visit. So monopolies do not increase their production and resources are not allocated efficiently. Because they are protected from entry of competitors, monopolies earn profits in excess of the opportunity cost of capital. At the same time, monopolies bring about inefficient resource allocation by producing too little output and charging too high a price. This illustrates the essence of truth behind the popular view that monopolies "gouge the public."

The comparison between monopoly and competition in the real world is not quite the same as in our example. In practice, price is usually set at a level somewhere between monopoly and competition. With more market power, the price will be closer to the monopoly level. With less market power, price will approach the competitive level. In addition, we have assumed that the cost curves are the same whether the industry is competitive or a monopoly. Consider a real world case where companies above a minimum size are required to pay an environmental quality control charge. Monopolies are subject to the tax but small competitive companies which have little or no effect on environmental quality are exempt. The problem is to determine whether monopolies will merely raise the price of their product, passing the pollution charge on to their customers.

A comparison of panels 1 and 3 of Figure 14-2 illustrates the effect of a $5 per visit pollution charge on monopolies. Panel 1 shows the monopoly equilibrium without a pollution charge where price equals $10 and quantity, 750 visits. In panel 3, a $5 fee is levied on each unit of polluting output. This raises the marginal cost curve and average total cost curve by the amount of the fee. As a result, the output at which MC = MR falls from 750 to 500 visits and price rises from $10 to $12 per visit. Note that this $2 price rise is less than the $5 pollution fee, so monopolies will be stuck with the remaining $3 of the charge. These effects are summarized as follows:

	Output	Price	Cost	Profit
Before	750	$10	$4	$6
After	500	12	9	3
Difference	-250	2	5	-3

This shows that monopolies can usually shift part of the pollution charge to their customers. Economists such as Boumal and Binder argue that this shifting of part of the pollution charge to consumers is a proper part of the effective pollution control program as it encourages consumers to redirect their purchases from goods and services that are highly polluting to those that are not. But more important for our discussion here is the other side of the matter. While some part of a pollution charge is usually paid by consumers, sellers also will be stuck with some part of the charge. Clearly with a negative sloping demand curve, if monopolies raise price, they will lose customers, which will eat into profits. Thus, pollution charges hurt polluters even if they are monopolies, and forces them to cut their polluting outputs. Monopolies will be better off if they absorb some of the charge themselves rather than try to pass all of it on to their customers.

There is an even more important reason why the comparison between monopoly and competition in the real world would not be the same as in our initial example. Most recreation markets include private companies that have purchased the operation from previous owners. Freeman points out that the only individuals who profit from the creation of market power are those who own an enterprise at the time the power is created. The purchase price tends to be inflated by the expectation of future monopoly profits. In this way, the subsequent owners pay the creators of monopoly profits. Thus, subsequent owners may earn little more than normal rates of profit on their own investment. Of course, unexpected growth of the market would lead to subsequent increases in the market value of companies with monopoly power. And, unexpected increases in operation costs would reduce the value of market power.

A comparison of panels 1 and 4 of Figure 14-2 illustrates the effect of a $5 per visit increase in average total cost resulting from the capitalization of monopoly profits. The first panel shows the monopoly equilibrium without an increase in fixed cost, with price equal to $10 and quantity equal to 7,500 visits per day. In the fourth panel, a $5 fixed charge is added to each unit of output. After sale of the facility to new owners, most of the present value of future monopoly profits is capitalized into the sales price. This raises the average total cost curve by the amount of the fixed charge. However, the marginal cost curve does not change because variable costs are not likely to be charged by the sale of the recreation facility. As a result, the price of $10 per visit and the profit maximizing output of 7,500 visits do not change. However, average total costs at this output rise sharply from $4 to $9 per visit or by $5. Thus, excess profits which were equal to $6 per visit initially fall to $1 per visit.

This has an important implication for comparable pricing by public agencies. The accounting records of operators who have acquired the right to monopoly profits through the purchase of existing assets will overestimate the social cost of production. They count as a cost the capital expenditure for the right to the monopoly profit, as well as the expenditures on factors of production. Only the latter represent true opportunity costs to society.

Price Discrimination

Generally, economists assume that sellers of comparable services in the region of a park or other public recreation facility can charge only a single price to all buyers. However, price differences can be found almost everywhere in the recreation industry. Sellers vary prices according to the buyer's age, location, income, when the facilities are used, and for other reasons. The young pay less than adults to enter zoos and parks, attend outdoor theater and concerts, play tennis and other outdoor sports, and buy licenses to fish and hunt. Retired persons either pay lower fees or are exempt from the payment of fees.

State wildlife agencies charge nonresident anglers and hunters higher license fees than residents, who often pay state taxes in support of wildlife programs. Some campgrounds charge more for campsites located on the edge of a lake or stream than for interior sites. Municipal golf courses charge higher green fees per round of golf after 4 P.M. on weekdays and on weekends and holidays. Resort hotels and restaurants charge more during the peak season than off-peak. Lodging establishments often have higher daily rates than for stays of a week or longer. Recreation condominiums located on the side of a building with the most favorable view are higher priced. Airlines have first-class fares for higher income travelers who are willing to pay to avoid the inconvenience of lower discount and standby fares. Quantity discounts are often available for groups of 10 or more persons.

Price discrimination is defined as charging different prices for the same goods and services where the price differences are not proportional to differences in costs. Either different buyers are charged different prices or each buyer is charged different prices for succeeding units purchased. Not all price differences represent price discrimination. When price differences are proportional to cost differences, they represent the competitive market result. Were uniform prices charged under conditions of differences in the costs of serving different buyers or for succeeding units purchased by each buyer, it would be a form of price discrimination. Common usage of the term by economists has no odious connotation, although the antitrust laws make certain kinds of price discrimination illegal.

The purpose of price discrimination is to get as much of the buyer's consumer surplus as possible. If some buyers are ready and willing to pay more than the market price, most sellers wouldn't mind giving them an opportunity to do so. Few sellers are likely to succeed in getting all of the consumer's surplus. But some probably get quite a lot of it. Price discrimination of one kind or another can be found almost everywhere because it is such good business.

Economists refer to three degrees of price discrimination. First, "perfect" price discrimination occurs when a seller extracts all of the potential consumer surplus by charging buyers a price equal to their willingness to pay for each unit purchased. Second, "imperfect" price discrimination occurs when a seller extracts some but not all of the potential consumer surplus with discounts for blocks of units rather than individual units. Third, price discrimination to "maximize profits" involves separating buyers into groups with different elasticities of demand and setting prices so that marginal revenue equals marginal cost in each. These three practices are sometimes referred to as first, second, and third degree price discrimination, respectively.

In first degree price discrimination, all buyers pay the maximum amount that they would be willing to pay rather than do without the recreation activity. Perfectly discriminating monopolists would be aware of these maximum prices and would establish different prices at these levels. In situations without price discrimination, all but the last buyer pay less than they would have been willing to pay, because the last buyer is the only one who is willing to pay the price asked. All other buyers are higher on the demand curve and would have been willing to pay more but were not required to. Without price discrimination, in order to sell a given quantity, all units of output would be sold at the same price. As illustrated in panel 1 of Figure 14-3, 10 units would be sold at a price of $20 each. Total revenue would be $200 (= 10 × $20) as represented by the rectangle determined by these values.

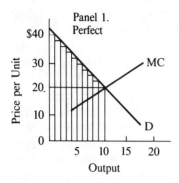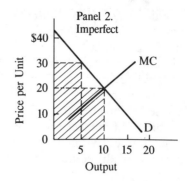

Figure 14-3. Perfect and Imperfect Price Discrimination

With perfect price discrimination, sellers turn the entire area under the demand curve into total revenue. The perfectly discriminating monopolists establish prices so as to extract from each consumer the full value of their consumer surplus. If a ski area, for example, could sell some lift tickets for $40, while also selling others for $39, for $38, for $37, and for $36, etc., the total revenue the seller could collect would be much larger. Total revenue becomes the sum of all the revenue received for all of the prices shown on the vertical axis: $40 + $39 + $38 + ... + $20 = $300. This is $100 or 50 percent more than the $200 the seller can get without price discrimination.

In practice, perfect price discrimination is rare because it is difficult to segment the market and to know the preference structure of potential buyers. It is most likely to occur in markets with a small number of buyers of a specialized product. For example, condominium developers in a resort area conduct a market survey showing that prospective buyers are willing to pay $200,000 to $400,000 for a 3-bedroom, 2-bath unit and vary their prices accordingly. The units may cost virtually identical amounts to construct in the same apartment complex; however, some are located on the top floor with a favorable view, some on the first floor with easy access, and others on the back side of the building with a clear view of the parking lot, etc. On this basis, prices are varied for all buyers who enter the market to capture their consumer surplus.

In the historic Dutch auction for fresh flowers in rural Netherlands, the auctioneer started the asking price at a high level and then slowly reduced it. The first buyer to accept a price bought the produce. Individuals bid as soon as the price fell to their maximum willingness to pay, because they did not know what the second most eager buyer would pay. This differs from the conventional auction in which the asking price starts low and is slowly increased. In the conventional auction, buyers pay only slightly more than the second most eager buyers are willing to pay rather than their maximum willingness to pay.

524

Second degree price discrimination involves the same underlying principle except that sellers take part, but not all, of consumer surplus. With imperfect price discrimination, sellers turn some of the area under the demand curve into total revenue. Different prices are established for two or more blocks of units rather than for each individual unit. The result is a stair-step pricing effect illustrated in panel 2 of Figure 14-3.

For example, a ski area could offer the first 5 days of skiing for sale to each individual at a price of $30 per day. If skiers wish to purchase more than 5 days of skiing, the additional days can be purchased at a lower price, say $20. The total revenue the seller collects from 10 days of individual skiing per year becomes $250 (= 5 × $30 plus 5 × $20). This is $50 or 25 percent more than the $200 the seller can get without this type price discrimination. However, some of the consumer surplus ($50) remains, as indicated by the unshaded triangles above the two price lines.

In this example of less than perfect price discrimination, only two price lines (known as block rates) are set to illustrate the method. In practice, the number of price lines could be increased to approach the results of perfect price discrimination. As the number of price lines is increased, more and more of the consumer surplus would be captured by the seller as additional revenue.

Third degree price discrimination is the maximization of total profits by setting prices of a product or service in two or more different submarkets so that marginal revenue equals marginal cost in each. To practice third degree price discrimination, sellers must have sufficient market power to set their own prices, serve two or more submarkets with different elasticities of demand, and be able to prevent transfers among customers in different submarkets. This can be demonstrated by an example.

Suppose a ski area is selling the same service, downhill skiing, to two separate submarkets of skiers — youth and adult. Youth and adult skiers can be easily identified and segregated at moderate cost. Buyers are unable to transfer the lift tickets easily from youth to adults, as they are two distinct colors. Otherwise it would be possible for skiers to make money by buying the lower price youth lift tickets and selling them at a higher price to adults, thus making it difficult to maintain the price differentials between the two groups of customers.

Figure 14-4 illustrates the separate submarkets for skiing. The elastic demand curve for youths is shown in the first panel, and the inelastic demand curve for adults in the second. The aggregate demand curve for the ski site is shown in the third panel. It represents the horizontal sum of the number of skier days demanded at each price in the two submarkets. The marginal cost curve shown in the third panel is applicable to both submarkets. Costs of serving youth and adult

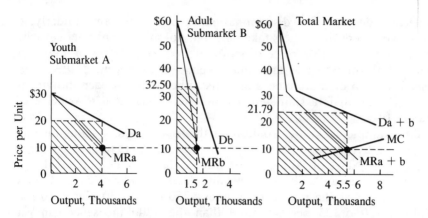

Figure 14-4. Price Discrimination for an Identical Product Sold in Two Submarkets
Source: Adapted from Brigham and Pappas.

skiers are virtually identical. Thus, from a production standpoint, it
does not matter whether a lift ticket is sold in the submarket for youth
or for adults. Of course, if production costs differ between the two
submarkets, this fact would have to be taken into account.

The solution to this pricing problem is a two-part process. First, the
ski site must determine the optimum total output level. Profit maximization occurs at that aggregate output where marginal cost and marginal revenue are equal. As shown in Figure 14-4, the optimum output
is 5,500 skiers per day where marginal cost and marginal revenue are
both equal to $10 per skier. Second, the managers of the ski site must
allocate this output between the two submarkets. Proper allocation of
the total output between the two submarkets can be illustrated graphically by drawing a horizontal line through the first two panels at $10
to indicate that this is the marginal cost in each market at the indicated aggregate output. The intersection of this horizontal line with the
marginal revenue curve in each submarket indicates the optimum distribution of sales of lift tickets to youth and adults and the appropriate discriminating price levels.

According to Figure 14-4, the ski site maximizes total revenue by
selling a total of 5,500 ski lift tickets per day, including 4,000 tickets
to youth at a price of $20 and 1,500 tickets to adults at a price of
$32.50. The profit-maximizing price of lift tickets in the less elastic
adult skier submarket is over 50 percent higher than the price charged
in the youth submarket where demand is relatively elastic. The effects
on total revenue of the ski corporation are summarized as follows:

(1) With Price Discrimination:
Youth, Market A: $ 80,000 (= 4,000 skiers × $20)
Adult, Market B: 48,750 (= 1,500 skiers × $32.50)
Total $128,750

526

(2) Without Price Discrimination:
   Total Market: $119,845   (= 5,500 skiers × $21.79)

Thus, price discrimination increases total revenue by $8,905 per day or 7.0 percent. This could be the difference between making a profit or loss.

One important reason for having public recreation facilities is to protect the consumer from the more damaging effects of price discrimination. For example, when one group of consumers consistently pays higher prices than do other groups, the result can be a redistribution of recreation opportunities from those who would receive more benefits to those with less. The total welfare of society may be reduced accordingly. For this and other reasons, comparable prices charged by private suppliers may need to be adjusted to bring about more effective competition and performance.

FEASIBILITY OF FEE COLLECTION

In the past, most observers considered the economic and administrative feasibility of fee collection to be the most important pricing problem of public agencies supplying recreation opportunities. Economists refer to any cost associated with the sale of permits to users and their purchase by users as "transaction costs". Studies of transaction costs traditionally focused on the investment in collection booths, in building a fence around the site, and the salaries of ticket takers and guards. As a result, it should not be surprising that many managers have concluded they would not be able to collect sufficient revenue to offset collection costs at sites with low annual use and/or a large number of entrances. They have found it less costly to arrange for the payment of most types of recreation programs out of general tax revenues rather than through the collection of user fees.

In the past, the collection of user fees was limited to those activities where transaction costs were low relative to user charges at sites with high annual use and/or a few entrances. More recently, some observers have begun to question whether these conditions are necessary for efficient user fee collection. The people involved are interested in what can be learned from recent experience to help formulate sound user fee policies for the future. Without information on recent technological improvements, too few public agencies would adopt efficient fee collection methods. The purpose of this section is to illustrate the potential of self service user fee collection to reduce transaction costs in parks and other recreation sites.

Consider the findings of a Report to Congress by the General Accounting Office in 1982. The study was based on a 20 percent sample of the 330 recreation areas administered by the National Park Service, 26 sites with entrance fees and 45 without. The authors found that revenues from entrance fees exceeded collection costs at all existing fee sites. The report recommended that congress authorize the Park Service to: increase entrance fees and collection hours at existing fee sites, representing about 20 percent of all sites; begin charging entrance fees at 40 percent of the sites; and that 40 percent remain non-fee sites. The economic and administrative reasons for recommending against entrance fees is especially relevant to this discussion. The report concluded that collecting entrance fees would not be economical at 30 percent of the sites and not administratively feasible at nearly 10 percent.

The most important reason why collection costs would exceed fee revenue was the presence of too many access points to control entry. About 16 percent of the recreation sites administered by the National Park Service cannot meet the primary requirement for a service to be financed by user fees, namely, that nonpayers be restricted from using the service. For example, the report recommended against charging entrance fees of more than 2 million visitors per year to Olympic National Park, located 60 miles northwest of Seattle, Washington. The park has uniquely varied geography, including snow-covered Olympic Mountains, rain forests and Pacific Ocean beaches. The park also has 14 entrances rather than the usual one or two entrances at most recreation sites with a single access road. The report concluded that the cost of constructing and operating 14 entrance fee collection stations would exceed the revenue obtained. Examples of other sites with too many accesses include: Acadia, Biscayne, C&O Canal, Cape Hatteras, Delaware Water Gap, Lake Meredith, North Cascades, and Shiloh.

The second reason collection costs would exceed fee revenue was low annual recreation use. Nine percent of the recreation sites did not have a sufficient number of visitors to allow the revenues from user fees to equal or exceed the cost of constructing and operating entrance fee collection stations. Examples include: Devils Postpile, Fort Caroline, Fort Matanzas, George Rogers Clark, and Saratoga.

The third reason why collection costs would exceed fee revenue was the high cost of capital investment in collection facilities. Five percent of the recreation sites did not have existing entrance stations where park employees provide information to visitors. The costs of road widening and construction of a booth (or kiosk) would exceed the revenue collected as user fees. Examples of such sites include: Fort Clatsop, Nez Perce, and Whitman Mission.

Finally, the report concluded that collecting entrance fees would not be administratively feasible at nearly 10 percent of the sites. In some cases (6 percent), the initial legislation authorizing the recreation site or the covenants of property deeded to the agency required free access. For example, Congress prohibited charging entrance fees at Alaska units of the National Park system. Similar restrictions were made in the case of Acadia, Mount Rushmore, Gateway, Golden Gate and

Lincoln Home. At Great Smoky Mountain, the state of North Carolina deeded land to the federal government with the provision of free access by its citizens. At other sites (4 percent), visitors were already charged user fees for special transportation or a tour to see the main attraction at the site and it was not consider feasible to add an entrance fee. For example, Mammoth Cave charged $3 per person for a guided tour. At the Statue of Liberty, a concessioner charged visitors $1.50 for the boat trip to Liberty Island.

Trend in Collection Costs

The trend in collection costs as a proportion of total revenues from recreation user fees was sharply down with few exceptions. At least, this was the trend indicated by data available from the Federal Recreation Fee Reports prepared by the U.S. Department of the Interior. These trends are illustrated below:

	National Park Service	Forest Service	Corps of Engineers	Average
1976	29%	32%	68%	43%
1980	38	44	41	41
1982	34	19	28	31
1984	28	29	21	26

In 1976, for example, collection costs were reported to be about one-third of the user fee revenues for the National Park Service and Forest Service, and about two-thirds for the Corps of Engineers recreation programs. From 1976 to 1980, collection costs increased for the National Park Service and the Forest Service, while they decreased for the Corps. By 1980, the Forest Service had the highest collection costs among the major federal recreation agencies with 44 percent. Then from 1980 to 1984, collection costs as a percentage of user fee revenues, decreased substantially for all of the federal agencies, particularly the Corps. By 1984, the Corps had the lowest collection costs, accounting for 21 percent of user fee revenues. The Forest Service and the National Park Service had the highest collection costs, nearly 30 percent of user fee revenues.

The most important change in recreation pricing during the early 1980s was the increase in camping fees at public campgrounds. Driver et al., noted that the new administration in Washington D.C. endorsed the idea that recreation users should pay their own way. The National Park Service increased average camping fees from about $3 per campsite in 1981 to $4.75 in 1982, or by two-thirds. As a result, total user fee revenue increased by 50 percent. This suggests that the price elasticity of demand for camping in the national parks was not very responsive to price changes within this range. Each one percent change in price resulted in a 0.15 percent fall in demand, other things remaining equal in the two years. The Forest Service increased average camping fees from about $3 per campsite in 1981 to $4 in 1982, or by one-third. As a result, total revenue from camping also increased by nearly one-third, which suggests that the price elasticity of demand for camping was very inelastic. Each one percent change in price resulted in a 0.06 fall in demand. The Corps of Engineers increased average camping fees from about $3.50 in 1981 to $4.50 in 1982, or by one-third. As a result, total revenue from camping fees also increased by one-third, which suggests that the price elasticity of demand for camping was virtually zero. Thus, it is not surprising that increased user fees resulted in a substantial growth in total revenue from user charges.

Park managers estimate that initiating user fees at nonfee sites would decrease the number of visits for about two years. Once visitors become accustomed to paying a reasonable entrance fee, recreation use is expected to increase above pre-entrance fee levels. At Jefferson National Expansion Memorial in St. Louis a $0.50 per person fee would reduce initial year visits by 15 percent, according to park managers. An entrance fee of $1 at the Charlestown Navy Yard and $0.50 at Bunker Hill Monument in Boston National Historical Park, would reduce initial year visits by 10 percent. A $3 per vehicle fee at Hurricane Ridge in Olympic National Park would reduce initial year visits by 10 percent. At Muir Woods National Monument near San Francisco, a $1 per person fee would reduce initial year visits by 3 percent. At Lake Mead National Recreation Area, a $2 per vehicle fee would reduce initial year visits by 5 percent. At Glen Canyon National Recreation Area in Arizona, a $2 per vehicle fee would have an insignificant effect on number of visits.

For the most part, the decline in costs of collection as a proportion of total revenue collected was the result of sharply increased charges at existing fee collection sites. User fees can be increased at existing fee sites without appreciably affecting the level of collection costs. User fees were substantially increased in 1982 without changing collection costs. For example, the Forest Service and the Corps increased camping fees by about one-third from 1981 to 1982 with little or no additional collection cost other than would have occurred anyway owing to inflation. Collection costs increased by 7.5 percent which was about equal to the inflation rate.

Apparently user fees could be increased to marginal cost levels at existing fee sites without any significant increase in fee collection costs. As user fees are increased, the costs of collection are likely to decline as a proportion of total revenue collected. But what would be the cost of collection when user fee programs are initiated at existing nonfee sites? Indications are that collection costs would rise sharply during the first year and remain at higher levels during subsequent years than at existing fee sites. At least, this was indicated by the data available in the President's Task Force Report on User Charges. For examples, the Corps collection costs were projected to be 46 percent of revenue obtained during the first year, including 11 percent one-time implementation costs. Then collection costs would level off at 36 percent of revenue during subsequent years. This suggests that collection costs would remain at a higher level than the 26 percent of revenues at fee sites in 1984. The costs of collection are expected to rise as charges are introduced at more and more nonfee sites.

The people involved are interested in what can be learned from recent experience to help develop efficient user fee programs for the future. One technological improvement which shows promise to dramatically reduced collection costs is the self service system. Indications are that the costs of collecting campground fees can be reduced to less than one-half the cost of entrance booths manned during daylight hours. The Federal Recreation Fee Report shows that annual collection costs in Forest Service campgrounds were about $50 per campsite in the early 1980s compared to $100 per campsite for Corps and $120 per campsite at National Park Service campgrounds. This reflects the fact that the Forest Service has more self service fee collection stations than either of the other two agencies. Forest Service revenues collected from 12 percent of its visitors at sites where fees were charged increased from 24 cents per RVD in 1980 to 41 cents per RVD in 1982. During the same time period, fee collection costs decreased from 11 cents to 8 cents per RVD. Apparently, the efficiency of fee collection improved with self service.

Costs of Alternative Methods of Collection

Most managers of recreation sites have little or no experience in charging user fees. Until recently, most of them relied on revenues from general taxes and transfer payments from other units of government rather than user fees. Now, managers are interested in information that would help them decide whether or not to initiate user fees. They have begun to ask whether collecting a portion of total revenue from users would enable them to improve the quality of user services and contribute to equity by charging users a portion of the costs of service. The problem is to decide whether or not it is efficient to initiate user fees, and if so, what method of collection would be the most cost effective. The choice is between two alternatives: (1) a self-service collection system at each relevant recreation entrance or (2) a manned collection booth.

In the past, most parks and other recreation sites that charged entrance fees had entrance booths occupied by employees during day-

531

light hours located at each of the primary entrances to the parks. This fee collection system was favored by managers because it allowed employees to provide maps and other information, to observe individuals as they enter the park, and to remind them of park rules concerning alcohol consumption, the leashing of dogs, etc. More recently, some observers have begun to question whether staffed entrance stations are always a cost-effective use of employee time. When vehicles are not entering the park, employees in the entrance booths are idle (see Chapter 10). Managers are interested in learning from the experience with self-service fee collection at the entrance to some state parks and federal campgrounds where it has been tried. This would free employees to patrol the recreation site and to provide both random checks of fee compliance and information on the spot of the recreation activity where it would be most useful to visitors.

Experience with both fee collection systems indicates compliance may be greater with self-service than entrance booths. The term compliance refers to the proportion of the total number of recreation users entering a site who are eligible to pay user fees and actually do pay. It is usually expressed as a percentage of total recreation use. For example, voluntary payment of self service fees has been approximately 70 percent for vehicles entering Forest Service campgrounds in the Rocky Mountains without a resident employee or volunteer. For campgrounds with a voluntary host living on the site, compliance has approached 92 percent. Self-service fee collection has the advantage that it is operative 24 hours every day of the year. It would seem a relatively minor inconvenience to require all vehicles at a recreation site to display a receipt for payment and/or individuals to have a receipt in possession while engaging in recreation activities such as swimming, boating, hunting, and fishing.

The primary deficiency of the system of fee collection by employees at entrance booths is that a substantial proportion of the users of many recreation sites can escape payment by entering at points where there are no entrance stations or at times when they are closed such as during early morning and late evening hours. The General Accounting Office studied proposed entrance fee booths at the Lake Mead National Recreation Area, a 1.5 million acre site located 25 miles east of Las Vegas, Nevada. The study concluded that it would be economical to collect fees at only three entrances (with four collection stations) accounting for about 64 percent of the annual use of the recreation area. The study proposed that the entrance booths be operated only during daylight hours for seven months of the year, April to October, when 80 percent of the 5.2 million annual visitors use the site. In this case, the solution may be to establish self service fee collection stations at convenient locations to provide the remaining 50 percent of the total users an opportunity to pay.

Most recreation sites are small with too little recreation use to enable managers to efficiently operate collection booths. This depends on the level of user charge, of course, and seasonal use. Consider the case where user fees are $3 per vehicle. In this event, the first column of Table 14-12 shows that total revenue would equal collection costs with payment of the fees by an average of 43.8 vehicles per day year around. With an average of three persons per vehicle, this would be equivalent to the payment of fees by 48,000 visitors per year. If, as seems likely, about 20 percent of the vehicles entering the site would be exempt from payment, total annual use would have to approach 60,000 visits per year before a single fee collection booth would become cost effective. Moreover, recreation sites usually have more than one entrance. With two entrances, the minimum recreation use to efficiently install two collection booths would rise 120,000 visits. Most recreation sites in the United States do not have this much use.

Table 14-12. Costs of Alternative Methods of User Fee Collection at Parks and Other Recreation Sites, United States, 1985

Types of Collection Cost	Alternative Methods of User Fee Collection		
	Collection Booth, Operated 7 AM to 9 AM	Self Service Collection Station, 24 Hour	Cost Savings With Self Service, Percent
Capital			
Construction of Facilities, Utilities, Equipment	$23,700	$ 2,000	92
Road Construction, Widening, Signs, Site Vegetation[a]	27,500	21,400	22
Total Capital Investment	51,200	23,400	54
Annual Collection Costs			
Fixed Costs, Annual Depreciation and Interest on Capital Investment[b]	8,300	3,700	55
Variable Costs			
Salaries and Salary Overhead[c]	33,700	1,500	96
Employee Transportation[d]	4,000	900	77
Maintenance, Repairs, Supplies[e]	2,600	1,700	35
Total Variable Costs	40,300	4,100	90
Total Annual Collection Costs	48,600	7,800	84
Collection Costs Per Vehicle			
5 Vehicles Per Day	$26.63	$4.27	
10 Vehicles Per Day	13.32	2.14	
20 Vehicles Per Day	6.66	1.07	
50 Vehicles Per Day	2.66	0.43	
100 Vehicles Per Day	1.33	0.21	
200 Vehicles Per Day	0.67	0.11	
500 Vehicles Per Day	0.27	0.04	

[a]This is for asphalt sites. For gravel sites, reduce the road construction by 58 percent to $8,900 for the self-service fee collection station and to $11,600 for the collection booth.
[b]Total capital investment ammortized at 10 percent interest and 10 years useful life.
[c]Collection booth: GS-3 grade salary $12,500 per year for 2.45 persons with booth manned 14 hours per day 7 days per week. Self Service: GS-5 grade salary $16,000 per year divided by 10 sites. Salary overhead assumed equal to 10 percent of direct salary.
[d]Collection booth: employee vehicles at $333 per month including mileage. Self Service: four-wheel-drive vehicle at $375 per month plus 23 cents per mile for 18,000 miles per year. Total vehicle cost, $8,640 per year, divided by 10 sites.
[e]Maintenance and supplies equal five percent of capital investment. Includes collection envelopes at 5 cents each.
Source: General Accounting Office and Arapaho-Roosevelt National Forest.

	12 Months		6 Months		3 Months	
	Start	Stop	Start	Stop	Start	Stop
Costs Per Day	$131.51	$110.41	$152.61	$110.41	$194.81	$110.41
Vehicles Per Day	43.8	36.8	50.9	36.8	64.9	36.8
Visits Per Day	131.5	110.4	152.4	110.4	194.8	110.4
Total Visits	48,600	40,300	27,800	20,150	17,800	10,100

Fortunately, when the use of a recreation site is concentrated into one or two seasons of the year, the total use to efficiently operate fee collection booths is less than when use is spread over the entire years. For sites operated 6 months per year, total revenue from user fees of $3 per vehicle would equal collection costs with payment of fees by about 28,000 visitors per year. For sites operated 3 months per year, revenues would equal collection costs with payment of fees by nearly 18,000 visitors per year. These seasonal outputs are substantially lower than for year-around operation. Yet, many seasonal recreation sites do not have even this much use. Thus, even when the use of a recreation site is concentrated into a single summer or winter season, the number of users required to efficiently operate fee collection booths exceeds the use of many recreation sites.

A number of recreation sites with fee collection booths have closed them to improve efficiency of overall operations of the recreation facility. The information presented in Table 14-9 can be applied to this question. At what level of use would it become cost effective to close an existing fee collection booth? For year-around operations, the efficient shut down point occurs with 36.8 vehicles per day. With an average of three persons per vehicle, this would be equivalent to payment of fees by 40,300 visitors per year. This is where the variable cost of collection equals the revenue collected, omitting depreciation and interest on the collection facilities. The shut down point for 6-month and 3-month operations is also 36.8 vehicles per day; however, with the shorter seasons, this would be equivalent to the payment of fees by about 20,000 and 10,000 visitors, respectively. It is important to note that these shut down levels of use are equal to one-half and one-fourth, respectively, of the shut down level for year-around recreation sites. Thus, it is efficient to continue operating collection booths at seasonal recreation sites with use levels which would lead to shutting down year-around facilities.

Table 14-12 illustrates why self-service fee collection would be more efficient than collection booths. For example, with 100 vehicles per day, self service fee collection would have average total costs of $0.21 per vehicle compared with $1.33 per vehicle for collection booths, or a cost savings of 84 percent for self-service. Most of the advantage of self service results from savings in facility construction and labor costs. For example, the self-service envelope depository costs about $1,000 and the instruction signs an additional $1,000. Compare this to the collection booth (or kiosk) which costs $23,700 including utilities and equipment. Self-service entrance fee collection costs also are expected to be somewhat lower for road widening, highway signs, and site vegetation or landscaping. Of course, this would vary depending on terrain, soil composition, remoteness, desired parking areas, width and thickness, whether asphalt or gravel, etc. For example, a pull over at a self-service fee collection site would cost $21,400 compared with $6,660 for a similar site on a gravel road. This is illustrated in Figure 14-5.

It is with respect to labor costs that self service would be most efficient. Self-service fee collection appears to represent potential labor saving of about 96 percent. A single fee collection officer can service 10 fee collection stations at least every other workday traveling a round trip of approximately 100 miles at an annual cost of about $1,600 per station. Typically, the fee collection officer would be a GS-5 grade with annual salary of about $16,000. If a fee collection booth is occupied 14 hours a day from 7 A.M. to 9 P.M. 7 days a week, it would require in excess of 2.5 work-years of labor. Fee collec-

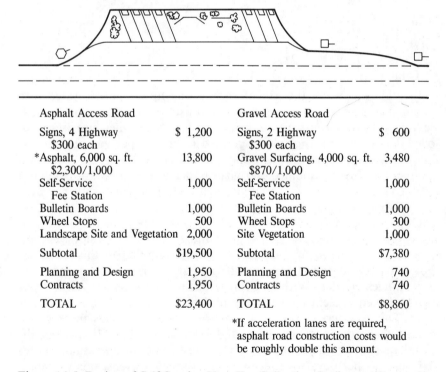

Asphalt Access Road		Gravel Access Road	
Signs, 4 Highway $300 each	$ 1,200	Signs, 2 Highway $300 each	$ 600
*Asphalt, 6,000 sq. ft. $2,300/1,000	13,800	Gravel Surfacing, 4,000 sq. ft. $870/1,000	3,480
Self-Service Fee Station	1,000	Self-Service Fee Station	1,000
Bulletin Boards	1,000	Bulletin Boards	1,000
Wheel Stops	500	Wheel Stops	300
Landscape Site and Vegetation	2,000	Site Vegetation	1,000
Subtotal	$19,500	Subtotal	$7,380
Planning and Design	1,950	Planning and Design	740
Contracts	1,950	Contracts	740
TOTAL	$23,400	TOTAL	$8,860

*If acceleration lanes are required, asphalt road construction costs would be roughly double this amount.

Figure 14-5. Design of Self Service User Fee Collection Stations at Recreation Sites, and Capital Investment Costs With Asphalt and Gravel Access Roads, 1985
Source: Lance Tyler and John Heaton, Arapaho-Roosevelt National Forest.

tors at entrance stations could be GS-3 grade with annual salary of $12,500. Costs would be less for temporary rather than for permanent employees. General administration and supervision expenses are estimated as 10 percent of direct salary costs.

Most recreation sites are large enough with sufficient recreation use to enable managers to efficiently operate self-service collection stations. This depends on the level of user charge and seasonal use. If user fees are $3 per vehicle, the second column of Table 14-12 shows that total revenue would equal collection cost with payment of fees by only 7.1 vehicles per day year around. With an average of three persons per vehicle, this would be equivalent to the payment of fees by only 7,800 visitors per year. If, as seems likely, about 20 percent of the vehicles entering the site would be exempt from payment, total annual use would approach 10,000 visits per year for a single self-service station to be cost effective. For recreation sites with two entrances, the minimum recreation use to efficiently install two stations would rise to 20,000 visits. Most year-around recreation sites in the United States have at least this much use.

	12 Months		6 Months		3 Months	
	Start	Stop	Start	Stop	Start	Stop
Costs Per Day	$21.37	$11.23	$31.50	$11.23	$51.78	$11.23
Vehicles Per Day	7.1	3.7	10.5	3.7	17.3	3.7
Visits Per Day	21.4	11.2	31.5	11.2	51.8	11.2
Total Visits	7,800	4,100	5,750	2,050	4,725	1,025

In addition, when the use of recreation sites is concentrated into one or two seasons of the year, the total use to efficiently operate self-service fee collection stations would be less than when use is spread over the entire year. For sites operated 6 months per year, total revenue from user fees of $3 per vehicle would equal collection costs with payment of fees by about 6,000 visitors per year. For sites operated 3 months per year, revenues would equal collection costs with payment of fees by only about 5,000 visitors per year.

Once self-service collection is started, it is important to consider at what decline in the level of use it would be efficient to stop. The information presented in Table 14-12 can be applied to this question. For year-around operations, the efficient shut down point occurs with 3.7 vehicles per day. With an average of three persons per vehicle, this would be equivalent to payment of fees by only 4,100 visitors per year. This is where the variable cost of collection equals the revenue collected, omitting depreciation and interest on the collection facilities. The shut down point for 6-month and 3-month operations is also 3.7 vehicles per day; however, with the shorter seasons, this would be equivalent to the payment of fees by 2,000 and 1,000 visitors, respectively. It is important to note that these shut down levels of use are equal to one-half and one-fourth, respectively, of the shut down level of year-around recreation sites. Thus, it is efficient to continue operating self-service collection stations at seasonal recreation sites with use level which would lead to shutting down year-around facilities.

Self-service fee collection stations may be cost effective at numerous sites where recreation use is very low. These would include remote access roads and trail heads, very small campgrounds, tennis courts, and where it is efficient to staff an entrance booth only during daylight hours. At such sites the capital investment required to begin self-service fee collection would not exceed $2,000 for the signs and depository. There would be little or no added costs for road construction to allow temporary parking at the site. Also, operator salary and transportation costs could be reduced by half through the pick up of revenues from the depository every 4 days rather than 2. Annual collection costs would become:

Facility, depreciation, and interest	$ 320
Salaries and salary overhead	750
Employee Transportation	450
Maintenance, repairs, supplies	100
Total Annual Costs	$1,620

This condensed version of self-service costs presented in the second column of Table 14-12 indicates that total revenue would equal collection cost with payment of fees by only 1.5 vehicles per day, year around. This would be the case when user fees are $3 per vehicle, as in the precious examples. With an average of three persons per vehicle, this would be equivalent to the payment of fees by only 1,600 visitors per year. If about 20 percent of the vehicles entering the site would be exempt from payment, total annual use would be roughly 2,000 visits per year for a single self-service station to be cost effective. Virtually all year-around recreation sites in the United States have at least this much use.

	12 Months		6 Months		3 Months	
	Start	Stop	Start	Stop	Start	Stop
Costs Per Day	$4.44	$3.56	$5.32	$3.56	$7.08	$3.56
Vehicles Per Day	1.5	1.2	1.8	1.2	2.4	1.2
Visits Per Day	4.5	3.6	5.4	3.6	7.2	3.6
Total Visits	1,643	986	986	657	657	329

When the use of recreation sites is concentrated into one or two seasons of the year, the total use to efficiently operate self-service fee collection stations at very small sites is less than when use is spread over the entire year. For very small sites operated 6 months per year, total revenue from user fees of $3 per vehicle would equal collection costs with payment of fees by about 1,000 visitors per year. For sites operated 3 months per year, revenues would equal collection costs with payment of fees by only about 650 visitors per year.

Managers should also consider at what possible decline in the level of use it would be efficient to shut down self-service fee collection at very small sites. For year-around operations, the efficient shut down point occurs with 1.2 vehicles per day. With an average of three persons per vehicle, this would be equivalent to payment of fees by only 1,000 visitors per year. You will recall that this is the point where the variable costs of collection equal the revenue collected, omitting capital investment costs. The shut down point for 6-month and 3-month operations is also 1.2 vehicles per day; however, with shorter seasons, it would be equivalent to the payment of fees of 650 and 330 visitors per year, respectively.

This suggests that self-service fee collection can be cost effective for sites where recreation use is very low. Practically all recreation sites have this much annual use. The number of users required to efficiently operate self-service fee collection stations is less than the use of nearly all recreation sites in the United States. There are few, if any, recreation sites or access road and trails where use is lower; managers would have found it cost effective to close them rather than to allow free entry and incur the costs of operating sites with so few users.

PAYMENT FOR RECREATION USE AND ENVIRONMENTAL PROTECTION PROGRAMS

The problem of pricing is complicated by the fact that outdoor recreation agencies produce both onsite and offsite benefits. There are benefits that accrue to individuals in addition to the values they receive from visiting a site or to individuals who may never visit the site at all. These offsite (i.e. public or external) benefits have been described as the willingness to pay for: (1) the option of possibly visiting a site in the future; (2) the value from simply knowing a site exists; and (3) the satisfaction from knowing the site will be available to future generations. Our purpose here is to illustrate the proportion of total recreation resource benefits that are attributable separately to recreation use and to protecting the quality of the resource. The pricing guidelines of the federal government recommend that recreation agencies establish user fees consistent with the benefits to users and the general public. The pricing guidelines contain the related point that recreation agencies must consider the public policy or purpose of the agency as spelled out in its enabling legislation.

History of the Concept

Most parks and other recreation sites were established for two reasons: first, to preserve their unique historic, scenic, natural, and wildlife resources; and second, to make them available for the enjoyment of people. Historically, the federal government became involved with recreation as a result of policies designed to achieve other objectives, notably the protection of unique environmental resources. For example, Congress created Yellowstone National Park in 1872 "to conserve the scenery and the natural and historic objects and the wildlife, and to provide for the enjoyment of the same by such means as will leave them unimpaired for the enjoyment of future generations." Similar language appears in legislation to establish other national parks, separating the recreation use management contribution from natural resource protection. National Forests were established in 1891 as federal forest reserves to preserve valuable forest lands and watersheds. Recreation use programs were introduced more recently under the multiple-use concept. Also, the Soil Conservation Service, Corps of Engineers, and Bureau of Reclamation undertook water resource development projects to supply electricity, flood control, navigation, and irrigation water. Prior to 1965, the recreational potential of their reservoirs was not recognized in project planning or evaluation. The multiple-use resource management objectives of these agencies require careful judgments in allocating costs to specific recreation user groups and the public at large. This problem was discussed in Chapter 13.

Based on this experience, John Ise concludes in a critical history of *Our National Park Policy* that visitors to the parks should not pay the entire cost of their operation. Some of the agency's output benefits the general public, and not just visitors to the parks alone. Clawson and Knetsch note that if there are broad social benefits to the general population, then it is appropriate that much of the costs be met by taxes imposed upon all of the citizens. On the other hand, if most of the benefits of recreation resource management are received directly by users engaged in recreation activities at the site, it is appropriate that more of the costs be paid directly by user fees. Clawson and Knetsch suggest that research is needed to provide a basis for allocating the costs of recreation resource management between recreation and other outputs. Max Peterson, Chief of the U.S. Forest Service, believes that: "First, we must establish the true value of outdoor recreation to the American people, and then recognize that value in our planning and our politics."

Table 14-13 shows the distinctions that economists make between the outputs of recreation use and environmental programs. Economists consider the output of recreation resource management as a private good or service that has some public good characteristics. This means that part of the benefits are private in that they are received by individual users and part by the general public. The most important characteristic of recreation use, whether privately or publicly supplied,

Table 14-13. Payment for Recreation Use and Environmental Protection Programs

| Variable | Output of Recreation and Environmental Programs | | | |
	Privately Supplied Recreation Use	Publicly Supplied Recreation Use	Partial Public Goods, With External Effects	Public Goods, With Jointness in Supply
Distinguishing Characteristic	Exclusive and divisible output	Predominantly exclusive and divisible output	Not exclusive, external costs and benefits to others are present	Not divisible, equally available to all persons, collective goods, merit goods
Production Process	Usually services are intangible, nonstorable, with simultaneous production and consumption	Same as privately supplied recreation use	Spillovers, site congestion, associated costs	Often nonreproducible, gifts of nature, available at zero marginal cost
Role of Government	Protect private property rights, administer private concessioner contracts on public land	Multiple-use management, e.g., recreation, wildlife, water, forest	Requires government intervention	Must be provided by government agencies
Examples	Resort lodges, campgrounds, amusement parks, swimming pools and beaches, private hunting reserves, charter boat fishing, ski areas, etc.	Parks, trails, playgrounds, campgrounds, fishing, hunting, swimming pools, beaches	Environmental damages, wildlife on private land, site carrying capacity, location advantages	Protection of the quality of air, water, natural scenery, wilderness areas, wild and scenic rivers, endangered species of wildlife
Payment Policy	User fees	User fees, taxes	User fees, taxes, subsidies	General tax revenues

Source: Adapted from Randall.

is that it can be divided among individuals who purchase the amount desired for their individual exclusive use. The distinguishing characteristic of public benefits is that generally they are not divisible or exclusive. This means that once they are supplied, they are equally available to all individuals. Also, some individuals can obtain greater satisfaction from the knowledge of programs to protect environmental quality without reducing that obtained by others. Such public benefits usually are provided by government from general tax revenues since there is no way that user fees can be charged for output that cannot be divided among individuals.

The "benefits received" principle of taxation states that the payment by individuals for government services should correspond to the benefits that individuals receive. Consider first, those who participate in recreation activities and benefit directly from improvements in recreation facilities and environmental quality at recreation sites. According to this principle, the proportion of total costs recovered as user fees would equal the proportion of total benefits received by individuals who participate in recreation activities. Second, consider the population as a whole which benefits indirectly from resource protection programs. A number of studies have shown that most people receive satisfaction from option, existence, or bequest demands for recreation facilities and environmental quality. In this case, the individual citizens who benefit from government expenditures cannot be charged a user fee. Rather, total cost would be subsidized to the extent that preservation benefits are perceived by all or a great majority of the citizens. The extra output justified by the public benefits would be subsidized by general taxes. This means that the proportion of total costs covered by general tax revenues would equal the proportion of total benefits received by the general public. When recreation resources are supplied by a federal tax on the general public, it could perhaps be thought of as the most general form of collective benefit tax. Of course, there is no precise relation between the taxes individuals pay and the public benefits they receive. Tax payments to federal, state, and local units of government go toward the payment for a variety of government programs including parks and recreation, and environmental protection.

Empirical Estimate of Public Benefit

Recreation economics has traditionally focused on the benefits of recreation use. Although we are interested in such benefits, our concern here is to introduce a measure of the preservation benefits to the general public. Data were obtained from a household survey designed to represent the population of the state of Colorado. Personal interviews were conducted in the homes of a subsample of 198 households in 1983. The results illustrate a practical way to measure the benefits of recreation and resource protection programs to users and to the general public. The survey design was based on the federal guidelines, discussed in Chapter 8. The interagency committee recommended use of the contingent valuation method in recreation and environmental benefit studies. Thus, the research method should be acceptable and the results of this pilot study useful in future research designed to assist actual policy making by public decision makers.

Figure 14-6 provides some tentative evidence as to the allocation of total benefits between recreation use and resource protection. For example, the pilot study suggests that recreation use benefits account for only about one-third of the total benefits from the construction and maintenance of recreation facilities. This suggests that user fees should recover only about one-third of the costs of their construction and maintenance. The general public, including both users and nonusers, apparently is willing to pay about two-thirds of the costs of recreation facilities from general taxes. Most people receive satisfaction from knowing that public recreation facilities are available and in good con-

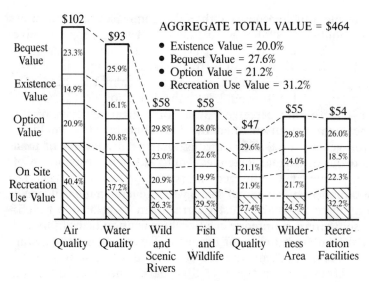

Figure 14-6. Average Annual Willingness to Pay per Household for Recreation Use and Environmental Protection Programs in the State of Colorado

dition. Their motivations for payment include the option of possibly using the facilities in the future, the knowledge that they exist, and that they will be available to future generations.

The essential point is that presence of preservation benefits could justify user prices at less than marginal costs of the resource management program. This would not necessarily mean that recreation resources would be supplied free of charge to individual consumers. It is both possible and desirable to levy user charges. A proper user charge would equate marginal user benefits to marginal user cost. For example, one possibility would be to charge individual users all of the variable costs for which they are directly responsible. The proportion of the capital investment costs that should be subsidized depends on the extent to which the nonusing public benefits, according to Crompton. The recreation resource management specialist at Texas A & M University has recommended that if the offsite benefits to the general public increase, the proportion of fixed costs met by the subsidy should also increase.

In the past, managers of parks and other recreation sites often have established user fees that covered direct variable costs and some proportion of fixed costs. The proportion of fixed costs subsidized by general tax revenues was decided in some arbitrary way, frequently based on prevailing political pressures. The remaining fixed costs were paid from general tax revenues, as a subsidy of the recreation program. For example, Crompton has shown that partial overhead prices (POP) would equal:

POP = AVC + AFC − G

Where AVC = average variable costs of $1; AFC = average fixed costs of $3; and G = average government subsidy of $2; then the partial overhead price would equal:

$2 = $1 + $3 − $2

The user fee would be $2 when the subsidy from general tax funds equals two thirds of average fixed costs, as in the pilot study.

In practice, recreation and park managers usually have considered only the internal costs incurred by the agency. They have included the direct variable costs associated with operating a recreation site or facility, and sometimes a proportion of the agency's fixed costs including a share of the capital costs of the facility, equipment, and the administrative overhead of the agency when the contribution of administrative personnel was essential to these programs. Few recreation and park agencies considered the external costs incurred by other agencies whose services were also essential to recreation and park programs. For example, the total social costs of recreation may include part of the fish and wildlife department's costs as it provides consumptive and nonconsumptive wildlife recreation opportunities.

Clearly, the quality of environmental resources contributes to the benefits of recreation. Figure 14-6 shows for one state the recreation use portion of the total benefits of resource protection programs. Direct recreation benefits accounted for slightly more than 30 percent of total willingness to pay for six important environmental resource programs. The lowest recreation use benefits, as a proportion of total benefits, was reported for wilderness areas (25 percent). They also had the largest proportion of existence value and bequest value, reflecting the benefits to the general public of protecting unique natural environments. The highest recreation use benefits, as a proportion of total benefits, was reported for air quality (40 percent) which also had the lowest proportion of existence value and bequest value. This may be related to the importance of sightseeing recreation activity and appreciation of the scenic vista with good air quality. Also, air quality contributes to user satisfactions from all recreation activities, especially the physically active outdoor sports.

The pilot study suggests that households were willing to pay, on average, a total of $145 per year for the recreation use value of the seven resources. This includes $18 per year to construct and maintain facilities in parks and other recreation sites located in the states where they live. However, the largest proportion of total recreation use benefit was attributed to programs that protect the quality of environmental resources such as the air, water, forest, fish, and wildlife. These annual household values are summarized as the following:

543

	Recreation Use Value	Public Preser- vation Value	Total
Park and Recreation Facilities	$18	$36	$54
Environmental Protection Programs	$127	$283	$410
Total	$145	$319	$464

With approximately 85 million households in the United States, the pilot study suggests a willingness to pay $12.3 billion per year for the recreation use value of the seven resources. Of this amount, $1.5 billion would be for park and other recreation facilities and $10.8 billion for protection of environmental quality in the states where they reside. These total U.S. values, in billion dollars per year, are summarized below:

	Recreation Use Value	Public Preser- vation Value	Total
Park and Recreation Facilities	$1.5	$3.1	$4.6
Environmental Protection Programs	$10.8	$24.0	$34.8
Total	$12.3	$27.1	$39.4

Elsewhere in this book, it was reported that the total use of public recreation sites was approximately 3.1 billion recreation visitor days in 1982. On this basis, the recreation use value of the construction and maintenance of recreation facilities would equal about $0.50 (=$1.5/3.1) per recreation visitor day and public benefits, $1.00 (=$3.1/3.1). By comparison, the recreation use value of environmental protection programs at recreation sites would equal $3.50 (=$10.8/3.1) per recreation visitor day, or six times more than recreation facilities ($0.50). This comparison leaves out the benefits of the operation of park and other recreation programs to users and the general public. Even so, it illustrates the need to distinguish the recreation user benefits of facility management from the user benefits of the natural characteristics of recreation sites and other areas in the surrounding forest that are managed under other environmental protection or multiple-use programs. Examples of the former include campgrounds, swimming beaches, boating sites, and a portion of access roads and trails. Examples of the latter include reforestation, fire protection, insect control, soil conservation, water quality and wildlife habitat management.

Several points should be made about the implications of this information for pricing policy by public agencies. First, it is important to determine whether recreation use of the resource causes external benefits to the general public. In some cases, external or public benefits are produced by protection of the resource, and the amount of external benefit does not vary with the amount of recreation use of the resource. In other cases, the external benefits may be proportional to recreation use of the resource, i.e. declining benefits to society with reduced recreation use. Economists refer to these two cases as "public good" and "merit good" external effects, respectively. The distinction has important implications for the pricing policy of government agencies, as developed by Due and Friedlaender.

To the extent that protection of resources is a public good, recreation users could be charged entrance fees high enough to cover the total costs of recreation use. Society, for example, may regard the existence of wild and scenic rivers as of vital importance, the external benefit relating only to their existence, not their actual use. Accordingly, the recreation boaters could be charged user fees high enough to cover the total costs of recreation use, since reduction in use would have little effect on the total benefit to society from wild and scenic river protection.

Whenever public benefits depend upon the recreation use of the resource, the level of user charges affects external gains. If, for example, charges for a merit good such as the recreation use of city parks were set at levels to cover total fixed and variable costs, the total output would be substantially less than current recreation use, and society would lose the advantages of the external benefits from the larger output. Also, if city parks provide significant external benefits in the form of reduced congestion and cost at state and federal parks and other recreation sites, fees set to cover total costs of city parks would sacrifice advantages of the external effect. Moreover, public subsidy to increase use of city parks, which are closer to home relative to state and federal parks, benefits recreation users as a group because it tends to reduce the associated costs of travel for access to recreation opportunities.

In some cases, the external or public benefits are satisfied by the maintenance of a safe minimum standard. Society, for example, may regard the protection of fish and wildlife as of vital importance, with the external benefits relating only to protection, not to the actual use for fishing and hunting. Accordingly, the anglers and hunters could, in terms of resource allocation, be charged license fees high enough to cover the total costs of fish and wildlife management programs. Reduction in fishing and hunting in response to the fees would not lessen the total benefits to society from fish and wildlife protection. On the other hand, higher user fees may stimulate a reduction in fishing and hunting to allow the stock to recover to levels that would enhance external benefits to the general public. The point is that recreation use beyond a certain level may have an external cost to society. In this case, public benefits depend upon use of the resource, with a decline in the benefits to society as more is used, i.e., when the stock of fish and wildlife is depleted below optimum carrying capacity levels. Once fishing or hunting is reduced to the point that pressure on the species is eliminated, there may be no gain from user fees and restrictions on license sales that further reduce fishing and hunting.

SUMMARY

In this chapter, we introduced the problem of charging users for the cost of recreation services and protection of recreation resources. We illustrated how to evaluate pricing practices in terms of agency policy, costs, benefits, comparable prices, feasibility of fee collection, and other effects. Economists generally recommend that user fees be set where the added costs of producing recreation opportunities equal the added benefits. This means that prices would be set at the intersection of the demand (or marginal benefit) curve and the supply (or marginal cost) curve. In other words, the efficient pricing solution for a government agency is to attempt to provide the competitive industry result. Public recreation opportunities would be supplied at efficient minimum cost levels, i.e., at the lowest point on the average total cost curve. Consumers would get the largest possible total supply, resources would be efficiently used, and operating deficits or surpluses would not occur.

The problem of efficient pricing by public agencies producing recreation opportunities is twofold: in the short-run, to recover the cost of operating existing facilities; and in the long-run, to pay for the optimum level of investment in capacity. Initially when parks and other recreation sites are developed, there is excess capacity of facilities, justifying a low marginal cost pricing policy in the short-run, which does not recover average total costs including investment costs. However, as use of capacity increases in a growing economy, marginal cost prices would rise until a point is reached where the revenue from user fees covers average total costs including investment costs. User fees would be equivalent to the competitive equilibrium price in the long-run. Where excess demand for use of capacity develops, marginal cost prices would rise still further, demonstrating sufficient willingness to pay to justify an expansion of facilities. Expansion decisions should be based on whether the revenues are sufficient to cover the costs of expansion at the time in the future when they are contemplated.

In order to make appropriate recreation economic decisions with respect to prices, they should be related to appropriate measures of cost. In the past, much of the discussion of marginal cost pricing under conditions of decreasing internal costs of recreation agencies missed the essential point. That is, the relevant costs should include more than the internal operation and maintenance costs of the public agencies administering recreation programs. In the case of almost every output of a recreation facility, the greatest influences on marginal cost, properly conceived, are two external effects — congestion and opportunity costs. Congestion results when too many users impose external costs on each other. Opportunity costs may result when resources are used for recreation at the expense of another purpose.

We introduced the problem of external benefits and costs. The problem of pricing has been complicated by the fact that parks and other recreation sites were established for two reasons: first, to preserve their unique historic, scenic, natural, and wildlife resources and second, to make them available for the enjoyment of people. This means that recreation agencies produce both onsite and offsite benefits. There are benefits which accrue to individuals in addition to the values they receive from visiting sites or to individuals who may never visit sites at all. These offsite benefits have been described as the willingness to pay for: (1) the option of possibly visiting a site in the future; (2) the value from just knowing it exists; and (3) the satisfaction from knowing it will be available to future generations. In this chapter, we illustrated from a pilot study the tentative proportion of total recreation resource benefits attributable separately to recreation use and to protecting the quality of the resource.

The "benefits received" principle of taxation states that the payment by individuals for government services should correspond to the benefits that individuals receive. If most of the benefits of recreation resource management are received directly by users engaged in recreation activities at the site, it is appropriate that more of the costs be paid directly by user fees. Those who participate in recreation activities benefit directly from improvements in recreation facilities and environmental quality at recreation sites. Thus, according to this principle, the proportion of total costs recovered as user fees would equal the proportion of total benefits received by individuals who participate in recreation activities. On the other hand, if there are broad social benefits to the general population, then it is appropriate that much of the costs be met by taxes imposed upon all of the citizens. The population as a whole may benefit indirectly from resource protection programs. A number of studies have shown that most people receive satisfaction from option, existence, or bequest demands for recreation facilities and environmental quality. In this case, the individual citizens who benefit from government expenditures cannot be charged a user fee. Rather, total cost would be subsidized to the extent that preservation benefits are perceived by all or a great majority of the citizens. The extra output justified by the public benefits would be supported by general taxes. This means that the proportion of total costs covered by general tax revenues would equal the proportion of total benefits received by the general public.

We discussed the effects of market structure and behavior on the practice of comparable pricing by government agencies. Pricing public recreation opportunities at the going market rate has several advantages, most notably that it tends to avoid controversy. However, comparable prices in the region may not accurately reflect social values. Market prices often under- or over-estimate social values. Either the user fees charged by comparable public agencies do not cover the social cost of all inputs used in the production process, or excess user fees are charged by private producers with some market power. Managers should consider the direction and likely magnitude of the divergence from social values in estimating the upper and lower bounds of comparative price estimates. Comparable prices charged by private suppliers may need to be adjusted when competitive market forces are weak, to ensure effective competition or to establish minimum standards of performance.

Next, we distinguished between several types of price discrimination and the related practice of peak load pricing. Price discrimination was defined as charging different prices for the same goods and services where the price differences are not proportional to differences in costs. Either different buyers are charged different prices or each buyer is charged different prices for succeeding units purchased. The purpose of price discrimination is to get as much of the buyer's consumer surplus as possible. If some buyers are ready and willing to pay more than the market price, most sellers wouldn't mind giving them an opportunity to do so. Few sellers are likely to succeed in getting all of the consumer's surplus. But some probably get quite a lot of it. The reason that price discrimination of one kind or another can be found almost everywhere is because it is such good business. One important reason for having public recreation facilities is to protect the consumer from the more damaging effects of price discrimination. But not all price differences represent price discrimination. When peak load price differences are proportional to cost differences, they represent the competitive market result. Were uniform prices charged under conditions of differences in the costs of serving different buyers or for succeeding units purchased by each buyer, it would be a form of price discrimination.

We considered the economic and administrative feasibility of fee collection. In the past, the collection of user fees was limited to those activities where transaction costs were low relative to user charges at sites with high annual use and/or a few entrances. Recently, some observers have begun to question whether these conditions are necessary for efficient user fee collection. The people involved are interested in what can be learned from recent experience to help formulate sound user fee policies for the future. Without information on recent technological improvements, too few public agencies would adopt efficient fee collection methods. We illustrated the potential of self-service user fee collection to reduce transaction costs in parks and other recreation sites. This was based on the experience with self-service fee collection at the entrance to some state parks and federal campgrounds where it has been tried. This suggests that self-service fee collection can be cost effective for sites where recreation use is very low. The shut down point would be 1.2 vehicles per day, equivalent to the payment of fees by 330 visitors per year with a season of 3 months. The self-service system would free employees to patrol the recreation site and to provide both random checks of fee compliance and information on the spot of the recreation activity where it would be most useful to visitors. Experience indicates compliance may be greater with self service than with entrance booths.

This chapter also discussed the results of recent studies of cost recovery by user charges for local, state, and federal government park and recreation programs. The park and recreation programs of local government provide the most important public supply of outdoor recreation opportunities in the United States. Local recreation expenditures grew rapidly during the 1960s and continued moderate growth in the 1970s. But there was little or no growth in the early 1980s. The slow down has been of major concern to recreation managers and consumers. In a period of inflating costs and growing scarcity of tax revenues to support local park and recreation programs, the increase in user charges by the cities was less than expected. Overall, city park and recreation departments recovered 17.8 percent of total expenditures in 1982, compared with 16.2 percent in 1977. The balance was subsidized from general tax revenue and grants from federal and state government. In California cities where Proposition 13 sharply curtailed property tax revenues for local government programs, user fees increased less than for cities in the rest of the nation. Suburbs with more medium- to high-income residents were more able to pay for recreation services from user charges. Older neighborhoods in the central cities have had immigration of poorer people and loss of medium- and high-income residents. From an income distribution viewpoint, it may be desirable that large cities continue to recover less of cost from user fees than other levels of government. Historically, cities have subsidized childrens' recreation activities from general tax revenues on the principle that recreation activities were wholesome and character building. Also, several of the programs for senior citizens and the handicapped were fully supported through general tax revenues.

State government has been the lead organization in the national effort to supply recreation resource since passage of the Land and Water Conservation Fund Act of 1965. Most states prepare plans and coordinated the distribution of grants to agencies of the state and local government to acquire land, develop facilities, and improve programs.

States are especially important in the eastern part of the United States where there is very little federal park and recreation land. Local government park and recreation areas are usually of small size. The states provide a large share of the supply of recreation resources. Expenditures on state park and recreation programs were second only to city government. State recreation expenditures grew moderately during the 1960s. Growth slowed in the 1970s, but grew at the same rate as total government expenditures for park and recreation programs. State spending fell sharply in the early 1980s. In a period of inflating costs and growing scarcity of tax revenues to support recreation programs, the states did not increase user charges sufficiently to maintain their programs at former levels. The reasons may be related to the fact that the states already recovered more of their costs from user charges than did either local or federal government. User charges may have approached the upper limit of acceptability to state legislatures. The evidence suggests that cost recovery has not increased since the 1950s. User charges were 37 percent of direct operating costs in 1983 compared with 39 percent in the 1950s. State license fees for fishing and hunting recovered 34 percent of the costs of state wildlife management programs in 1980. License fees may have provided a larger share of the funding of state wildlife programs in the past.

Historically, federal expenditures on park and recreation programs have ranked third behind the cities and states. Federal recreation expenditures grew moderately during the 1960s, and then declined with the advent of the energy crisis during the 1970s. Growth accelerated with the start of a park rehabilitation program in the early 1980s. Also, the new administration in Washington made a concerted effort to increase the proportion of costs recovered from recreation users. Of the federal agencies, the Forest Service made the most progress in shifting the cost of financing recreation programs from the general taxpayer to recreation users. Fee and permit revenues increased from 15 percent of expenditures in 1980 to nearly 30 percent in 1985. However, in the National Park Service, user charges recovered less than 5 percent of the operating costs. Overall, the federal government recovered less than 10 percent of costs from users of recreation facilities. This situation prompted the President's Task Force on User Charges (the Grace committee) to recommend substantial increases in user fees to recover a greater percentage of the cost. While their ideal solution would be to achieve complete cost recovery through a user fee system, they concluded that public policy would be served by some tax-subsidized programs that protect natural areas for the benefit of present and future society.

READINGS

Aiken, Richard A. "Public Benefits of Environmental Protection in Colorado." Masters Thesis, Colorado State University, Fort Collins. 1985.

Baumol, William J., and Alan S. Blinder. *Economics: Principles and Policy.* 2nd Edition. Harcourt Brace Jovanovich, New York. 1982.

Baumol, W. J., and D. F. Bradford. "Optimal Departures from Marginal Cost-Pricing." *American Economic Review* 60(June 1970):265-83.

Becker, Boris W. "The Pricing of Educational-Recreational Facilities: An Administrative Dilemma." *Journal of Leisure Research* 7(No. 2, 1975):86-94.

Brazer, Harvey E. "Outdoor Recreation as a Public Good and Some Problems of Financing." In *Elements of Outdoor Recreation Planning.* B. L. Driver (ed.) University of Michigan Press, Ann Arbor. 1970.

Brigham, Eugene F., and James L. Pappas. *Fundamentals of Managerial Economics* The Dryden Press, New York. 1981.

Buechner, Robert D. "State Park Systems." *Parks and Recreation* 11(No. 7, 1976):35-37,98.

Callahan, John C., and Douglas M. Knudson. "Economic Aspects of Commercial Outdoor Recreation Enterprises in Southern Indiana." Research Bulletin No. 814, Agricultural Experiment Station, Purdue University, Lafayette, Ind. 1966.

Crompton, John L. "How to Find the Price That's Right." *Parks and Recreation* 16(No. 3, 1981):32-39, 64.

Crompton, John L. "Psychological Dimensions of Pricing Leisure Services." *Recreation Research Review* 9(Oct. 1982):12-20.

Crompton, John L., and Charles W. Lamb. *Marketing Government and Social Services.* John Wiley and Sons, New York. 1986.

Downing, Paul B. (ed.). *Local Service Pricing Policies and Their Effect on Urban Spatial Structure.* University of British Columbia Press, Vancouver, Canada. 1977.

Downing, Paul B., and James E. Frank. "Recreational Impact Fees: Characteristic and Current Usage." *National Tax Journal* 36(Dec. 1984):477-89.

Driver, B. L. "Recreation on Public Lands: Should the User Pay?" *American Forests* 90(No. 3, 1984):11, 51-53.

Driver, B. L., James E. Bossi, and H. Kenneth Cordell. "Trends in User Fees at Federal Outdoor Recreation Areas." 1985 National Outdoor Recreation Trends Symposium II, Volume I. General Technical Report NE-137, Northeastern Agricultural Experiment Station, U.S. Dept. of Agriculture, Broomall, Pa. 1985. 222-42.

Due, John F., and Ann F. Friedlaender. *Government Finance.* 7th Edition, Richard D. Irwin, Inc., Homewood, Ill. 1981.

Economic Research Associates. "Evaluation of Public Willingness to Pay User Charges." Report to the U.S. Department of the Interior, Washington, D.C. 1975.

Freeman, A. Myrick III. *Intermediate Microeconomic Analysis.* Harper and Row, Publishers, New York. 1983.

Gittinger, J. Price (ed.). *Compounding and Discounting Tables for Project Evaluation.* Johns Hopkins University Press, Baltimore. 1973.

Hendon, William S., James L. Shanahan, and Alice J. MacDonald (eds.). *Economic Policy for the Arts.* Art Associates, Inc., Cambridge, Mass. 1980.

Hines, Thomas L. "Revenue Sources Management in Parks and Recreation." National Recreation and Parks Association, Arlington, Virginia. 1974.

Hoover, Robert L. "User Fees for Hunting and Fishing on Public Lands." Colorado Division of Wildlife, Denver. 1978.

Howard, Dennis R., and John L. Crompton. *Financing, Managing and Marketing Recreation and Park Resources.* W. C. Brown Co., Dubuque, Ia. 1980.

Ise, John. *Our National Park Policy: A Critical History.* Johns Hopkins University Press, Baltimore, Md. 1961.

Kotler, Philip. *Marketing for Nonprofit Organizations.* 2nd Edition. Prentice Hall, Englewood Cliffs, N.J. 1982.

Knudson, Douglas M. *Outdoor Recreation.* MacMillan Publishing Co. New York. 1980.

LaPage, Wilbur F., Paula L. Cormier, George T. Hamilton, and Alan D. Cormier. "Differential Campsite Pricing and Campground Attendance." Research Paper NE-330, Northeast Forest Experiment Station, Forest Service, U.S. Department of Agriculture, Darby, Pa. 1975.

Loomis, John B. "Use of Travel Cost Models for Evaluating Lottery Rationed Recreation: Application to Big Game Hunting." *Journal of Leisure Research* 14(No. 2, 1982):117-24.

Loomis, John B. "Effects of Nonprice Rationing on Benefit Estimates from Publicly Provided Recreation." *Journal of Environmental Management* 14(Apr. 1982):283-89.

Loomis, John B., and Richard G. Walsh. "Assessing Wildlife and Environmental Values: State of the Art." *Journal of Environmental Management* 18(No. 2, 1986): In press.

MacCleery, Douglas W. "Adjusting Federal Outdoor Recreation Programs to a Tight Budget Situation." Presented at the National Energy and Tourism Conference II, Washington, D.C. 1981.

McCallum, J. D., and J. G. L. Adams. "Charging for Countryside Recreation: A Review with Implications for Scotland." *Transactions, New Series, Institute of British Geographers* 5(No. 3, 1980):350-68.

Moss, Philip I. "Pricing Recreation Services." in *Public Prices for Public Products.* Selma Mushkin (ed.). The Urban Institute, Washington, D.C. 1972. 335-50.

Mumy, Gene E., and Steve H. Hanke. "Public Investment Criteria for Underpriced Public Products." *American Economic Review* 65(Sept. 1975):712-19.

Munger, James A. "Public Access to Public Domain Lands, Two Case Studies of Landowner Sportsman Conflict." Miscellaneous Publication No. 1122. Economic Research Service, U.S. Dept. of Agriculture, Washington, D.C. 1968.

Musgrave, Richard A., and Peggy B. Musgrave. *Public Finance in Theory and Practice.* 4th Edition. McGraw-Hill Book Co., New York. 1984.

National Association of State Park Directors. "Annual Information Exchange." Division of State Parks, State of Indiana, Indianapolis. 1986.

Nautiyal, J. C., and R. L. Chowdhary. "A Suggested Basis for Pricing Campsites: Demand Estimation in an Ontario Park." *Journal of Leisure Research* 7(No. 2, 1975):95-107.

Neave, David, and Richard Goulden. "Provincial Wildlife Revenue Sources and Commitments." *Transactions.* 48th North American Wildlife and Natural Resources Conference. Wildlife Management Institute, Washington, D.C. 1983.

Odell, Robert M., Jr. "Use of Recreation Service Charges." *Government Finance* 1(Febr. 1972):19.

Owen, Robert. *The Price of Leisure.* McGill-Queen's University Press, Montreal, Canada. 1970.

Peterson, R. Max. "Looking at Recreation Through Forest Service Eyes." *Parks and Recreation* 16(No. 3, 1981):42-47.

President's Private Sector Survey on Cost Control. "Task Force on User Charges." U.S. Government Printing Office, Washington, D.C. 1983.

Randall, Alan. *Resource Economics: An Economic Approach to Natural Resource and Environmental Policy.* Grid Publishing, Inc., Columbus, Ohio. 1981.

Randall, Alan, John P. Hoehn, and George S. Tolley. "The Structure of Contingent Markets: Some Results of a Recent Experiment." Paper presented at the Annual Meeting of the American Economic Association, Washington, D.C. 1981.

Reiling, Stephen D., and Mark W. Anderson. "Equity and Efficiency in Public Provision of Forest-based Recreation Opportunities." *Journal of Environmental Management* 20(No. 1, 1985):149-61.

Robinson, Warren. "The Simple Economics of Outdoor Recreation." *Land Economics* 43(Febr. 1967):71-83.

Rosenthal, Donald H., John B. Loomis, and George L. Peterson. "Pricing for Efficiency and Revenue in Public Recreation Areas." *Journal of Leisure Research* 16(No. 3, 1984):195-208.

Sandrey, Ronald A., Steven T. Buccola, and William G. Brown. "Pricing Policies for Anterless Elk Hunting Permits." *Land Economics* 59(Nov. 1983):432-43.

Sorg, Cindy F., and John B. Loomis. "Empirical Estimates of Amenity Forest Values: A Comparative Review." General Tech. Report RM-107. Rocky Mountain Forest and Range Experiment Station, U.S. Forest Service, Fort Collins, Colo. 1984.

Spencer, Sam, Edwin H. Glaser, and Larry Lennox. "State Wildlife Revenue Sources and Commitments, Alabama, Missouri and Washington." *Transactions.* 48th North American Wildlife and Natural Resource Conference. Wildlife Management Institute, Washington, D.C. 1983.

Unkel, William C. "Public Financing of Fish and Wildlife Conservation: The California Experience." *Transactions.* 48th North American Wildlife and Natural Resources Conference. Wildlife Management Institute, Washington, D.C. 1983.

U.S. Dept. of the Interior. "Federal Aid in Fish and Wildlife Restoration, 1980." U.S. Fish and Wildlife Service, Washington, D.C. 1981.

U.S. Dept. of the Interior. "User Fee Handbook." Heritage Conservation and Recreation Service, Washington, D.C. 1981.

U.S. Dept. of the Interior. "1980 National Survey of Fishing, Hunting and Wildlife Associated Recreation." Fish and Wildlife Service. U.S. Govt. Printing Office, Washington, D.C. 1982.

U.S. Dept. of the Interior. "Construction Cost." National Park Service, Washington, D.C. 1984.

U.S. Dept. of the Interior. "Federal Recreation Fee Report, 1984." National Park Service, Washington, D.C. 1985.

U.S. Dept. of Commerce. "1982 Census of Governments." U.S. Govt. Printing Office. Washington, D.C. 1985.

U.S. General Accounting Office. "Increasing Entrance Fees — National Park Service." Report to the Congress of the United States by the Comptroller General. GAO/CED-82-84. Washington, D.C. 1982.

U.S. Senate. "Recreation Fees Authorized in the Land and Water Conservation Fund Act of 1965, As Amended." Hearings before the Subcommittee on Public Lands, Reserved Water and Resource Conservation of the Committee on Energy and Natural Resources. 99th Cong., 1st Sess., Washington, D.C. June 7, 1985.

Verhoven, Peter J., and Roger A. Lancaster. "Municipal Recreation and Park Services." *The Municipal Year Book* 43(1976):203-15.

Vickerman, R. W. *The Economics of Leisure and Recreation*. MacMillan Press, London. 1975.

Vickrey, William S. "Economic Efficiency and Pricing." in *Public Prices and Public Products*. Selma Mushkin (ed.). The Urban Institute, Washington, D.C. 1972.

Walsh, Richard G., Derek R. Bjonback, Donald H. Rosenthal, and Richard A. Aiken. "Public Benefits of Programs to Protect Endangered Wildlife in Colorado." Issues and Technology in the Management of Impacted Western Wildlife. Thorne Ecological Institute, Boulder, Colo. 1985.

Wettstone, Jerry R. "User Fees." National Recreation and Park Assn., Arlington, Virginia. 1963.

Whitehead, Clifton J. "State Fish and Wildlife Agency Responses to Funding Challenges." *Transactions*. 48th North American Wildlife and Natural Resources Conference. Wildlife Management Institute, Washington, D.C. 1983. 139-48.

Willis, C. E., J. J. Canavan, and R. S. Bond. "Optimal Short-run Pricing Policies for a Public Campground." *Journal of Leisure Research* 7(No. 2, 1975):108-13.

Chapter Fifteen

Comparing Benefits and Costs

This chapter introduces the concept of discounting and net present value; shows how comparing benefits and costs can help public decision makers choose among alternative recreation projects which vary in size, design, and purpose; discusses several problems in comparing benefits and costs; summarizes the results of recent benefit cost studies, and shows how to improve future applications of the approach to recreation economic decisions

In principle, the managerial approach to evaluation of recreation and park programs is the same as when individual consumers compare the benefits and costs of alternative recreation activities described in Chapter 5. It differs from the individual approach to decision making in two ways. First, if managers are to make difficult choices among alternatives that yield streams of benefits and costs stretching into future years, we must use discounting and net present value to compare those occurring at different times. Second, the values that count are not those of the individual manager or planner, but rather the values held by the people, that is, the citizens of the nation. Two managers with different personal values should generate very similar estimates of the worth of a project.

PUBLIC AND PRIVATE DECISIONS

Benefit cost studies of public proposals ask the question: "Do the net benefits to the people exceed the costs required of them?" If the answer is "yes," the proposal is an efficient one. If it is "no," the proposal would waste resources and would not be in the public interest. Benefit cost studies are concerned with social gains and losses. For the evaluation of public recreation programs, the denominator in 'the benefit cost ratio is the present value of agency operations and opportunity costs, and the numerator is the present value of net benefits (consumer surplus) to the citizens.

Benefit cost studies of public recreation programs ask the same question as do managers and accountants in private business. Although economic analysis asks the same question as financial analysis, it is asked about a wider group of people, those who comprise society. Instead of asking whether the private business will become better off by engaging in one project rather than another, benefit cost studies ask whether society as a whole will be better off. For private recreation sites, the benefit cost ratio would be defined as total revenue or sales divided by the total costs incurred by the company. Benefit cost studies substitute the concept of benefits to society for the concept of total revenue or sales of the private business. For the total operating costs of the private business, benefit cost studies substitute the concept of opportunity cost — the social value foregone when resources are moved from alternative economic activities into the proposed project. For the net profits of the firm, benefit cost studies substitute the concept of net benefits to the people ($B - C$), or some related concept.

Schultze, former chief economic advisor to the President of the United States, sees the need to compare benefits and cost as resulting from the scarcity of public resources and the nonmarket context of public decisions. The resources of the government are always less than needed to accomplish all of the useful things that we would like to do. Therefore, from among the competing claims on resources, decision makers must choose those that contribute most to our national objectives, and choose efficiently in order to free scarce resources for other useful programs. Second, government programs rarely have an automatic regulator that indicates when a program has ceased to be productive, could be made more efficient, or should be replaced by another program. In private business, society relies upon profits and competition to furnish the necessary incentives and discipline and to provide a feedback on the quality of decisions. While this self-regulatory mechanism is basically sound in the private sector, it is virtually nonexistent in the public sector. In government, we must find another tool for making choices which resource scarcity forces upon us.

In the United States, the benefit cost approach (synonymous with cost benefit analysis in Europe) was first authorized by the Rivers and Harbors Act of 1902 and the Flood Control Act of 1936 which provided for the comparison of benefits "to whomsoever they may accrue" with costs. Until 1965, the method was limited primarily to the Corps of Engineers and Bureau of Reclamation study of water resource development projects. Since then, with a new emphasis on accountability in government, benefit cost studies of all social programs has flourished. Now the approach is routinely applied in such program areas as parks and recreation, environmental quality, education, criminal justice, foreign assistance, personnel training, transportation, urban renewal, health, and welfare.

The impact of government on the allocation of resources is pervasive in the United States. Over 20 percent of the nation's land, labor, and capital produce goods and services distributed to the people by some level of government. In the case of recreation, for example, with less than three-tenths of 1 percent of the nation's resources, government provides nearly one-half of total park and recreation opportunities (3.1 of 6.6 billion recreation visitor days in 1982). Yet in the 1970s and 1980s, there was a steady decline in budgets for managing recreation resources. As a result, the level of public service declined. For example, government campgrounds provided 30 percent of the total camping in 1979, down from 35 percent in 1969. Recreation planners and managers are faced with the problem of allocating increasingly scarce resources among competing uses. The people involved are interested in improving the application of economics to assist in the decision-making process.

Much has been written about benefit cost studies, both pro and con. Some have attacked them, either as an attempt to quantify what cannot be measured, or as an effort on the part of economists to usurp the decision making function of managers and political leaders. Most observers, however, have recognized benefit cost studies for what they are, a means of helping responsible public officials make decisions. In Schultze's view, they are not a mechanical substitute for good judgment, political wisdom, and leadership of public officials. Wise choice ultimately depends on good judgment. However, this is not the same as saying that good judgment alone makes for wise choices. Consider a decision maker forced to choose among irrelevant alternatives on the basis of misleading evidence. Without access to a comparison of benefits and costs, even the best judgment can do little but grope intuitively in the dark. Benefit cost studies are a means to improve the decision making process in order to assist the final judgment, not to supplant it.

The comparison of recreation benefits and costs is as yet in its infancy. Still, research efforts to obtain benefit estimates, for example, have produced results significantly different from zero which are more helpful to the decision maker than unstudied assertions or ad hoc judgments. The continuing efforts to estimate the benefits and costs of recreation programs need result in only a small increase in the efficiency of a recreation program to justify their cost.

OPTIMUM SOCIAL BENEFITS AND COSTS

Benefit cost studies ask whether society is better off because of expenditures on government programs. Are the social gains greater than the social losses or less? This problem has been clearly described by Haveman in his excellent book, *The Economics of the Public Sector.* He begins by showing that the operations of public agencies represent a series of transfers of resources from private individuals to public authorities, and then a series of transfers of outputs back to individuals. The control over some resources is shifted to the government when it levies taxes and fees on private individuals. In turn, the government either allocates this revenue to income transfer programs supporting some groups in the private sector, or it uses the revenues to purchase goods and services from the private sector and transforms them into public output, such as recreation opportunities which benefit people in the private sector.

In benefit cost studies, then, the comparison is between the value to the private sector of what it gives up to support a government recreation program (represented by taxes, user fees, and opportunity costs) and the value of the output that the government provides with the resources (represented by the willingness of citizens to pay for the government-produced opportunities, if they had to). A public recreation program can increase the welfare of society if the resources given up by the private sector are used to produce greater benefits than they would produce in the absence of the government programs. Benefit cost studies help public decision makers choose among alternative recreation programs and projects which vary in size, design, and purpose. It assists decision makers in: (1) developing the optimum size program or project; (2) designing the program to be of maximum efficiency; and (3) choosing from the available alternative projects those that are most productive. We will discuss each of these functions.

Optimum Program Size

Consider, first, a fundamental recreation economic problem of governments throughout the world: How large should the program be? How much should government tax and spend for recreation? The question of the size of the public program is a problem of resource allocation. How many of society's resources should be allocated to the production of recreation opportunities? Benefit cost studies can assist decision makers in thinking meaningfully about this question. To achieve efficiency in government, spending on recreation programs should be increased in each area and in total until the marginal social benefits of the last recreation visitor days equal their marginal social costs. This will ensure that the net benefits of recreation programs to society are as large as possible.

In Figure 15-1, for example, panel 1 shows the total social benefits of public recreation in the United States compared to the total social costs of producing these recreation opportunities. Panel 1 also shows the marginal social benefits and costs derived from the totals. The marginal curves are simply the changes in value of the total curves resulting from changes in the amount of recreation opportunities provided. They may be more familiar to you as demand and supply curves, with optimum output occurring where the two intersect, i.e., where supply equals demand. If the relationship between total and

558

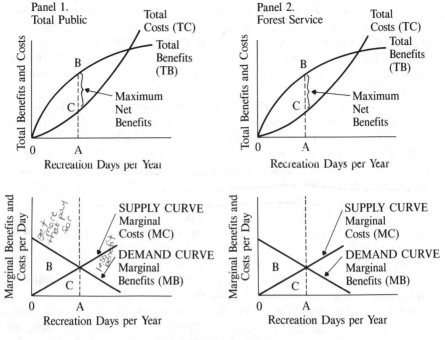

Figure 15-1. Optimum Size of Public Recreation Programs, United States

marginal benefits and costs is not clear to you, review the first section of Chapter 5 on the individual demand curve and travel costs of recreation trips.

Assume that the government has detailed information on citizens' willingness to pay for the relevant expenditure categories of the recreation program, from which we are able to derive the total social benefits for output over the full range of alternative recreation expenditure levels. The result is the total social benefits curve (TB) for the entire recreation program shown in panel 1 of Figure 15-1. The total social cost curve (TC) is also drawn. Land must be acquired or set aside for recreation sites, and personnel must be hired for planning, supervision, and operation. In addition, some recreation programs have social opportunity costs, such as foregone production of timber, minerals, energy, and the like. All of the social costs of providing recreation opportunities are summed in the total social cost (TC) curve in panel 1 of Figure 15-1.

The total social benefits (TB) curve shows that for the first dollars the government spends on recreation programs, citizens are willing to pay a great deal because of the scarcity of recreation opportunities; there are very large social benefits. However, as more dollars are spent, the value generated by each additional dollar becomes smaller, i.e., diminishing marginal benefits. As individual demand for recreation activities is fully satisfied, the shape of the TB curve becomes flatter as more and more dollars are spent on public recreation. The total social costs (TC) curve shows that the first dollars the government spends on recreation programs produce a large output of recreation opportunities. However, as more dollars are spent, less additional output is produced by each additional dollar, i.e., increasing marginal costs. The reason is that the efficiency of additional government expenditure falls as less suitable sites are developed and the opportunity costs of alternative uses rise. As a result, the shape of the TC curve rises as more and more dollars are spent on public recreation.

As you will recall, economics suggest that the recreation economic decision maker continue increasing the size of the program until the excess of its benefits over its costs is as large as possible. In the upper panel 1 of Figure 15-1, we see that from an economic viewpoint, the government budget for recreation programs should be at output ●A. At an output of OA, the government budget would be AC and total benefits, AB. The benefit cost ratio is AB/AC and the excess of benefits over costs (net benefits) is BC, which is the greatest vertical distance that exists between these two curves. If government recreation output were less than OA, there would be some potential net benefits which were not being realized. If the output were larger than ●A, all dollars spent in excess of AC would entail social costs in excess of the benefits that they produced. The same result is shown in the lower panel 1 of Figure 15-1 for the marginal curves — marginal social benefit (MB) and marginal social cost (MC) — associated with the total curves of the upper panel. There, the familiar economic proposition is applied to the public sector; net benefits (area B) are maximized where marginal social benefits (MB) equal marginal social costs (MC).

Debate over public recreation budgets may be characterized as addressing the question of whether the agencies involved produce outputs that are less than optimum or greater than optimum. Managers of public recreation programs, in effect, argue that existing budgets are insufficient and should be increased to point OA, but opponents argue that the proposed budgets are excessive and should be decreased to point OA. No one knows for sure which view is correct, and citizens have various opinions on the matter. However, the issue could be better resolved with more accurate benefit cost studies of the question.

Expenditures on recreation programs by federal, state, and local government in the United States were estimated at approximately $8 billion in 1982. These dollar amounts have changed substantially to the present, based in part on changes in the general price level. In 1982, government output was estimated at 3.1 billion recreation visitor days. On this basis, government expenditures were equal to about $2.50 per recreation visitor day. It seems likely that total benefits substantially exceeded government costs. If benefits in the same year averaged $5 to $10 per recreation visitor day, the total benefits of 3.1 billion recreation visitor days would have amounted to $15-30 billion. Assuming this represents an approximation of the annual equivalent of the present value of social costs and benefits, it would equal an excess of benefits over costs (net benefits) of roughly $7-23 billion and a benefit cost ratio of approximately 2.0 to 4.0. Panel 1 of Figure 15-1 indicates that when benefits exceed costs by these amounts, output is likely to be less than optimum. All budgets to the left of AC have higher benefit cost ratios than budgets to the right.

Benefit cost analysis of the recreation program of a single government agency is identical to that of the total recreation program. Consider the U.S. Forest Service, which supplied 233 million recreation visitor days or 7.5 percent of total public recreation opportunities in 1982. Expenditures on the recreation program of the agency were reported at $116 million in the same year or only $0.50 per recreation visitor day. If benefits averaged $5 to $10 per recreation visitor day, the total benefits of 233 million recreation visitor days would have amounted to approximately $1.2 to $2.3 billion. This would represent an excess of benefits over costs (net benefits) of roughly $1.0 to $2.2 billion and a benefit cost ratio of approximately 10.0 to 20.0. Panel 2 of Figure 15-1 indicates that when benefits exceed costs by such large amounts, output is likely to be much less than optimum. On this basis, the Forest Service recreation budget appears certain to have been to the left of OA, with potential output of recreation opportunities and net benefits not being realized. Apparently, the government could have increased the welfare of society by allocating more resources to the Forest Service recreation program in the early 1980s.

For efficiency in government when undertaking specific projects, public agencies should choose the alternative for which the benefits to society exceed the costs by the greatest amount and should reject any project if its benefits do not exceed the costs (Haveman). Note, first, this principle states a "minimum test" that any public recreation project should meet if it is to be in the public interest. This test requires that a proposed project demonstrate that expected benefits will exceed anticipated costs before it is approved. If the government undertakes projects failing this test, it would be extracting higher valued resources from private citizens and devoting them to lower valued public uses, and the social costs of the undertaking would exceed the gains. Consider, for example, panel 1 of Figure 15-2, where the total social costs and benefits are shown for an efficiently designed forest campground of each possible size. Assume that outputs A, D, G, and K represent the only possible sizes. From the diagram, we can clearly see that size K can be ruled out because its costs exceed benefits. Similarly, size G can be excluded because benefits just equal costs; the program would

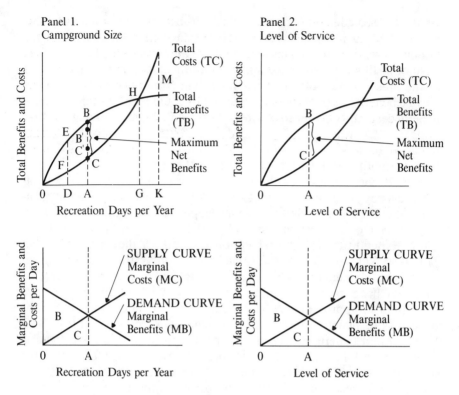

Figure 15-2. Efficient Campground Size and Level of Service

have no net gain and society would be just as well off without the program as with it.

Second, for those campgrounds that pass the minimum justification
test, the principle imposes a "maximum test." To obtain maximum
social benefits, the public decision maker should make a reasonably
complete search of alternative ways to accomplish the objective, then
choose the one that maximizes the excess of social benefits over social
costs (net benefits). Thus, if decision makers face two alternatives, A
and D, with benefits and costs as shown in panel 1 of Figure 15-2,
they should choose alternative A, which yields the greater excess of
benefits over costs. Note that both sizes A and D are worthwhile because benefits exceed costs in each case. But the lower panel resolves
the choice. At output D, the last dollar of cost generates more than a
dollar of benefits, indicating that campground size should be increased
until the marginal benefits equal marginal costs at size A. As you can
see on the upper panel, this is the optimum project size where net
benefits (total benefits minus total costs) are the greatest.

Finally, it is important to note that although project A is the optimum size campground, project D has a greater benefit cost ratio,
DE/DF. As you can clearly see, this exceeds project A's ratio AB/AC.

562

In fact, all campgrounds to the left of A would have a more favorable benefit cost ratio than project A. The lesson, then, is that choosing the project size with the highest benefit cost ratio may lead to the wrong choice. For finding the optimum project size, the appropriate rule is to maximize net benefits (total benefits minus total costs) where marginal benefits equal marginal costs (MB = MC) and not to maximize the benefit cost ratio. In a later section of this chapter, we will see that once the optimum size project has been determined for each alternative purpose or site, then benefit cost ratios are often useful in choosing among projects (all of which are of optimum size).

Efficient Project Design

The problem of developing a particular project involves questions of design as well as size. In economics, "design" of a project means combining the available inputs of land, labor, and capital in the most efficient way, so that they yield the most benefits for the costs. This aspect of the problem is presented in panel 2 of Figure 15-2. The level of service designed into a project is plotted on the horizontal axis. The vertical axis shows the value of both inputs and outputs of service, expressed in dollars. The total benefits and costs for a project with each possible service level are shown by the curves TB and TC. The question that comparisons of benefits and costs can assist in answering is the following: Which of the possible designs for any given project size is the optimum (i.e., yields the greatest net benefits)?

Assume that optimum project size has been selected (from the previous panel 1 of Figure 15-2), representing a campground with 35 campsites. Given this project size, economic efficiency considerations attempt to maximize the net benefits (total benefits minus total costs) of its design. The rule is to expand the services provided in the design of the campground to the point at which their marginal benefits equal marginal costs. In Figure 15-2, the optimum service level is shown on the lower panel 2 where, up to point A, expanding the campground service yields more benefits than it costs. Net benefits are maximized at the point where it stops paying to expand services. The upper panel shows that this optimum service level is at point A, where net benefits, BC, are maximized. Economists will be familiar with the total benefit curve presented in Figure 15-2 as the aggregate benefit function proposed by Bradford in the analysis of willingness to pay for public goods. Brookshire, Randall, and Stoll extended this concept to the valuation of all natural resource service flows, including those resulting from recreation project design.

The subject of project design is an important part of the more general problem of appropriate technology and size (Schumacher). Most forest campgrounds are located beside rivers and lakes in narrow mountain valleys with fragile ecosystems. Proper design of forest campgrounds involves the management of environmental resources, such as forests, water, fish and wildlife, and scenery. Recent studies suggest that environmental quality may contribute more to the total benefits of camping than do congestion levels, access roads, and provision of facilities, such as tables, drinking water, toilets, and trash barrels. For example, users of developed campgrounds in the Rocky Mountains were willing to pay $5 per recreation visitor day for standard campground services compared with $6 per day for an optimum number of trees, which provide shade, seclusion, and scenic quality of the site both in 1980 dollars. Project design involves using all of the available resources to best advantage.

From this discussion, it should be clear that benefit cost studies are important in both the design of projects and the choice of project size. In fact, the two decisions are interdependent. The most efficient design for each project size has to be determined before either the total benefit or the total cost curve can be estimated. The optimum size and design combination can be determined only after rather comprehensive benefit cost calculations. Imagine a family of total benefit and total cost curves in panel 1 of Figure 15-2, one for each design or service level. One of these alternative designs might generate net benefits of B'C' and another, net benefits of BC. Clearly, the decision maker would attempt to choose the design that is on the TB curve, as this curve is derived from the optimum designs for each project size. In our example, this is the design yielding BC of net benefits. No matter what size project is chosen, an efficient design requires that the most benefits are produced for the costs incurred.

Choosing Among Alternative Projects

Finally, benefit cost analysis can help decision makers choose among worthwhile alternative projects with different purposes or at different sites, when all of them cannot be undertaken at once. For example, assume that in the National Park Service the director, who has $1 million to allocate to campground improvement projects in California this year, is presented with the 16 alternatives shown in Table 15-1. All of these projects are of optimum size and, it will be noted, have benefit cost ratios greater than 1.0. The costs of the projects vary from $250,000 to $1 million. Which of the 16 projects should be undertaken this year? The decision rule is to choose the combination of projects that provides the most net benefits (total benefits minus total costs). As will be shown, this cannot be achieved by simply ranking all projects by either their net present values (net benefits) or their benefit cost ratios.

Table 15-1. Benefits and Costs of Alternative Campground Improvement Projects, National Park Service, California

Project	Present Value of Benefits, $1,000	Present Value of Costs, $1,000	Net Present Value of Net Benefits, $1,000	Benefit Cost Ratio
A	$ 400	$ 250	$ 150	1.6
B	800	250	550	3.2
C	500	250	250	2.0
D	350	250	100	1.4
E	360	250	110	1.44
F	1,100	500	600	2.2
G	800	500	300	1.6
H	600	500	100	1.2
I	1,000	500	500	2.0
J	1,250	500	750	2.5
K	800	750	50	1.07
L	1,000	750	250	1.33
M	1,500	750	750	2.0
N	900	750	150	1.2
O	1,100	750	350	1.47
P	2,300	1,000	1,300	2.3

The decision maker should carefully search through the list of alternatives to select the few that together maximize net benefits of the $1 million budget. This is obviously superior to applying the rule of first-proposed, first-built and choosing the first four proposed projects, A, B, C, and D, exhausting the budget to obtain $1.1 million net benefits. Or, the decision maker could do even better by ranking the projects according to amount of net present value (net benefits), with project P the highest. With costs of $1 million, project P exhausts the total budget, but it does provide the highest net benefits of $1.3 million. Could the decision maker do even better? Or is $1.3 million the maximum net benefits that can be achieved? Sassone and Schaffer recommend that to maximize the total (or sum of) net benefits over several independent projects subject to a capital budget constraint, the rule is to adopt projects based on their benefit cost ratios, implementing successively lower projects until the capital budget is exhausted or until the benefit cost ratio reaches unity. In this case, ranking by benefit cost ratios is equivalent to maximizing the sum of net benefits over all feasible sets of projects.

By a search and elimination process using benefit cost ratios as a guide, a few projects with more than $1.3 million net benefits can be found. This yields a combination of projects B, J, and C, which, taken together, exhaust the budget and provide net benefits of $1.55 million. Projects B and J are selected because they have the highest and second highest benefit cost ratios of 3.2 and 2.5, respectively. Note that their costs are $500,000 and $250,000, respectively, totaling $750,000. Project C is also selected because it has the highest benefit cost ratio (2.0) of the few projects that could be built with the remaining budget of $250,000. By choosing these three projects, net benefits are maximized. Spending $1 million generates $2.55 million of total benefits. The advantages of this procedure are:

	Choices	Net Benefits
First-proposed, first-built	A,B,C,D	$1.1 million
Net present value (net benefits)	P	$1.3 million
Benefit cost ratios to maximize net benefits	B,J,C	$1.55 million

It should be noted that there is considerable controversy among economists concerning the proper procedure to use in recommending alternative projects for funding. If you are interested in exploring the issue, consult a more detailed treatment of the subject such as contained in Randall, Gittinger, or Sassone and Schaffer.

In this illustration, we assumed that the 16 proposed projects were independent of one another. A project is independent of other projects when net benefits and costs would not change if any of the other projects were implemented. In comparing campground improvements in a single state such as California, possible interdependence may exist between project benefits. In this event, the net benefits of several projects located in the same market may not equal the sum of net benefits for the individual projects. When projects are interdependent, the proper way to proceed is to assume that all possible combinations of projects are built, then to evaluate the net benefits of each such combination. For example, Sassone and Schaffer demonstrated the interdependence of three public beaches proposed to be located within 40 miles of each other. Beach A would have net benefits of $120 million when considered alone. But its net benefits would fall to $40 million if sites A and B were constructed, and to $75 million if site C were built in combination with site A.

DISCOUNTING AND NET PRESENT VALUE

Discounting is essential to the comparison of benefits and costs. Its function is to convert future benefits and costs of a project into present value (today's dollars) at the time of decision. Quite simply, it telescopes to the present all the benefits and costs during the life of the project. It makes sense to measure future benefits and costs in terms of today's dollar values, because decision makers choose between short-run recreation projects, which have no future benefits and costs, and long-run projects, which do. To compare the various streams of benefits and costs over time, the usual procedure is to discount them to present values. The sum of the discounted benefits less the sum of the discounted costs over the life of the project measures the economic value of recreation investments. In economics, this net present value is defined as the amount of investment now that would yield the expected annual benefits minus the costs of the project. Remember, the rule for selecting among alternative projects is to maximize net benefits (B - C) at the time of decision.

Public recreation investments produce benefits and costs for various numbers of years into the future. Figure 15-3 illustrates the typical recreation project that involves a large initial capital investment, low annual costs of operation and maintenance, and annual benefits that increase over the life of the project. A good example is a major downhill ski area where an expansion in facilities was planned (initial capital investment costs were incurred) in 1984, but the first skiing on the new slopes would not occur until 1987. In an example such as this, the time profile of costs in Figure 15-3 shows very high costs in the construction stages (years 1, 2, and 3) but quite modest annual costs of operation, maintenance, and repair once the facility is developed. In this case, the benefits may not start until year 3, but then they grow significantly until the investment matures in about 15 years.

Most of the total costs of a project occur early in the planning period and most of the total benefits, in later years. As a result, the discount rate is critical in determining the scope of recreation programs. The higher the discount rate, the lower the value of future benefits as compared to initial costs. Figure 15-4 shows, for example, that the present value of $100 in benefits expected 25 years in the future is about $38 discounted at 4 percent, $23 discounted at 6 percent, but only about $9 discounted at 10 percent. Thus, present values of benefits 25 years in the future can be changed by more than a factor of 4 depending on the discount rate. The discount rates used in the evaluation of recreation projects will be discussed in a later section of this chapter.

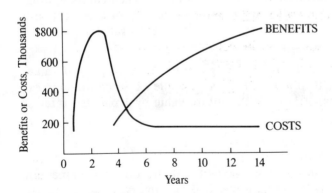

Figure 15-3. Time Paths of Benefits and Costs
Source: Barkley and Seckler.

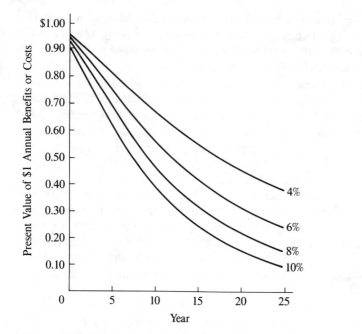

Figure 15-4. Present Value of $1 Received or Paid in Future Years Discounted at 4, 6, 8, and 10 Percent

Most people find compound interest and future value easier to understand than discounting and present value. We are all familiar with the idea of compound interest. For example, if you invest money in a bank or savings institution, you can either take the interest earned on the investment each year or leave it in the account to earn more interest. If you leave the interest in the account to be added to the principal, you can calculate what the investment will be worth each year by using a compound interest formula. When compounding, to find the future value (FV) in some future year (t) of a present sum (PV), multiply the present sum by 1 plus the interest rate (r):

$$FV_t = PV(1 + r)^t$$

The formula can be easily revised to go from future to present value. When discounting, to obtain the present value of some amount expected in future year (t), divide the future value by 1 plus the interest rate:

$$PV = \frac{FV_t}{(1 + r)^t}$$

Thus, the interest rate and the discount rate are different names for what is arithmetically the same thing. It is customary, however, to use the two terms in different contexts. When we start with a sum of money and calculate the earnings on it into the future, we speak of the interest rate. When we start with the expected payment of a sum of money at some time in the future and calculate back in time to the present to determine the present value, we speak of the discount rate.

Remember that compound interest is the amount paid on the principal and the interest earned in previous time periods. This means that $100 invested now will accumulate, at 10 percent interest, to $110 in a year:

$110 = $100 × (1 + 0.10)

After another year of compounding at 10 percent interest, the investment will become $121, and so on:

$121 = $100 × (1 + 0.10)(1 + 0.10)

Note that if we keep the $100 invested at 10 percent interest for 2 years, it is turned into $121 by going through the same calculation two times. With a hand calculator, it would be a simple matter to construct Table 15-2. At 10 percent interest, the table shows the compounding factor for 2 years as 1.21, the same value calculated above.

We could conclude that individuals who invest at 10 percent interest consider having $100 now, $110 in 1 year, or $121 in 2 years as equivalent amounts. Because discounting corresponds to compounding, we can say that $110 in 1 year or $121 in 2 years has a present value of $100 at a discount rate of 10 percent. The $110 received in 1 year divided by 1.10 has a present value of $100:

$$\$100 = \frac{\$110}{(1 + 0.10)}$$

Similarly, $121 2 years from now divided by 1.21 has a present value of $100:

$$\$100 = \frac{\$121}{(1 + 0.10)(1 + 0.10)}$$

You can check the complete correspondence of compounding and discounting by comparing Tables 15-2 and 15-3. As noted above, Table 15-2 shows the compound factor for $1 invested for 2 years is 1.21, at a 10 percent interest rate. Table 15-3 shows that at a discount rate of 10 percent, the present value of $1 received 2 years from now is 0.83:

$$0.83 = \frac{1}{1.21}$$

The factor for present value (0.83) is equal to 1 divided by the factor for compound value (1.21). Based on this mathematical rule, discount factor tables have been worked out for various discount rates and number of years, as shown in Table 15-3. For the case considered above, look down the years column to the row for year 2, discounting at 10 percent. The figure shown there, 0.826, is the discount factor

Table 15-2. Future Value of $1 with Compound Interest of 4, 6, 8, and 10 Percent

Year	Future Value of $1 with Compound Interest of[a]			
	4%	6%	8%	10%
1	1.040	1.060	1.080	1.100
2	1.082	1.124	1.166	1.210
3	1.125	1.191	1.269	1.331
4	1.170	1.262	1.360	1.464
5	1.217	1.338	1.469	1.611
6	1.265	1.419	1.587	1.777
7	1.316	1.504	1.714	1.948
8	1.369	1.594	1.851	2.144
9	1.423	1.689	1.999	2.358
10	1.480	1.791	2.159	2.594
11	1.539	1.898	2.332	2.853
12	1.601	2.012	2.518	3.138
13	1.665	2.133	2.719	3.452
14	1.731	2.261	2.937	3.797
15	1.801	2.397	3.172	4.177
16	1.873	2.540	3.425	4.595
17	1.948	2.693	3.700	5.054
18	2.026	2.854	3.996	5.560
19	2.107	3.026	4.316	6.116
20	2.191	3.207	4.661	6.728
21	2.279	3.399	5.034	7.400
22	2.370	3.604	5.437	8.140
23	2.465	3.820	5.871	8.954
24	2.563	4.049	6.341	9.850
25	2.666	4.297	6.848	10.835
26	2.772	4.549	7.396	11.918
27	2.883	4.822	6.988	13.110
28	2.999	5.117	8.627	14.421
29	3.119	5.418	9.317	15.863
30	3.243	5.743	10.063	17.449
31	3.373	6.088	10.868	19.194
32	3.508	6.453	11.737	21.114
33	3.648	6.841	12.676	23.225
34	3.794	6.251	13.690	25.548
35	3.946	7.686	14.785	28.102
36	4.104	8.147	15.968	30.912
37	4.268	8.636	17.246	34.004
38	4.439	9.154	18.625	37.404
39	4.617	9.704	20.115	41.145
40	4.801	10.286	21.724	45.259
41	4.993	10.903	23.462	49.785
42	5.193	11.557	25.339	54.764
43	5.400	12.250	27.367	60.240
44	5.617	12.985	29.556	66.264
45	5.841	13.765	31.920	72.890
46	6.075	14.590	34.474	80.180
47	6.318	15.466	37.232	88.197
48	6.570	16.394	40.211	97.017
49	6.833	17.378	43.427	106.719
50	7.107	18.420	46.902	117.391

[a]The compound factor shows how much $1 becomes at a future date.
Source: Gittinger.

Table 15-3. Present Value of $1 Received or Paid in Future Years Discounted at 4, 6, 8, and 10 Percent

Year	Present Value of $1 with Discount Rate of[a]			
	4%	6%	8%	10%
1	0.962	0.943	0.926	0.909
2	0.925	0.890	0.857	0.826
3	0.889	0.840	0.794	0.751
4	0.855	0.792	0.735	0.683
5	0.822	0.747	0.681	0.621
6	0.790	0.705	0.630	0.564
7	0.760	0.665	0.583	0.513
8	0.731	0.627	0.540	0.467
9	0.703	0.592	0.500	0.424
10	0.676	0.558	0.463	0.386
11	0.680	0.527	0.429	0.350
12	0.625	0.497	0.397	0.319
13	0.601	0.469	0.368	0.290
14	0.577	0.442	0.340	0.263
15	0.555	0.417	0.315	0.239
16	0.534	0.394	0.291	0.218
17	0.513	0.371	0.270	0.198
18	0.494	0.350	0.250	0.180
19	0.475	0.331	0.232	0.164
20	0.456	0.312	0.215	0.149
21	0.439	0.294	0.199	0.135
22	0.428	0.278	0.184	0.123
23	0.406	0.262	0.170	0.112
24	0.390	0.247	0.158	0.102
25	0.375	0.233	0.146	0.092
26	0.361	0.220	0.135	0.084
27	0.347	0.207	0.125	0.076
28	0.333	0.196	0.116	0.069
29	0.321	0.185	0.107	0.063
30	0.308	0.174	0.099	0.057
31	0.296	0.164	0.092	0.052
32	0.285	0.155	0.085	0.047
33	0.274	0.146	0.079	0.043
34	0.264	0.138	0.073	0.039
35	0.253	0.130	0.068	0.036
36	0.244	0.123	0.067	0.032
37	0.234	0.116	0.058	0.029
38	0.225	0.109	0.054	0.027
39	0.271	0.103	0.050	0.024
40	0.208	0.097	0.046	0.022
41	0.200	0.092	0.043	0.020
42	0.193	0.087	0.039	0.018
43	0.185	0.082	0.037	0.017
44	0.178	0.077	0.034	0.015
45	0.171	0.073	0.031	0.012
46	0.165	0.069	0.029	0.012
47	0.158	0.065	0.026	0.011
48	0.152	0.061	0.024	0.010
49	0.146	0.058	0.023	0.009
50	0.141	0.054	0.021	0.009

[a]The discount factor shows how much $1 in a future year is worth today.
Source: Gittinger.

which, when multiplied by the expected $100 benefit in 2 years, yields its present value (rounded to the nearest dollar):

$83 = $100 × 0.83

The essential idea is that waiting involves an opportunity cost. Freeman reminds us that everyone, under almost any circumstance, would prefer $100 now to $100 a year or two from now. A sum of money in hand is worth more than a promise of the same sum at a specified time in the future, because the money may be invested and produce earnings in the intervening time. This is true whether the money is to be invested by an individual, business, or government, which must raise the necessary funds through taxation or borrowing. Take the case of an individual who is to be paid a sum of money a year from now. There is a lesser sum that he or she can invest today, for instance by depositing it in a savings bank, that will accumulate to that amount by the time the year has passed. This lesser sum is the present value of receiving the payment 1 year hence.

Notice that we have not said anything about risk. We assume no risk is involved here and that the individual $100 of benefits is as certain as anything can be. Rather, we are saying that having to wait for payment means foregoing the income that could be earned on the money in the meantime. In other words, waiting carries a cost in the form of a lost opportunity. This is not to suggest that risk should be ignored in studying a project, but merely that this is not where it should enter. In the real world, uncertainty and waiting are often entangled; it is important that we understand they are separate phenomena. The effects of risk and uncertainty were considered in Chapter 10.

Finally, although the calculation of present value ordinarily involves flows of dollar amounts, the method is applicable to any future effects that are measured in the same units. Thus, we could discount recreation visitor days for alternative recreation projects rather than dollars. Davidson et al. used a demand function to forecast the participation in boating and fishing in the Delaware River, which passes through Philadelphia. Then they discounted the increase in annual days of participation with improved water quality for 35 years from 1965 to 1990. Once recreation use was forecast and discounted to present value, it became a relatively simple matter to illustrate the effect of alternative estimates of benefits per recreation day on total benefits of improved water quality.

BENEFIT COST RATIO

Benefit cost studies usually result in the calculation of a benefit cost ratio (B/C), in which the benefits of a project are divided by its costs:

$$\text{B/C} = \frac{\text{Present value of total benefits (B)}}{\text{Present value of total costs (C)}}$$

If the ratio is greater than 1.0, public expenditures for the project are judged to be economically worthwhile. If it is equal to 1.0, the public expenditure adds nothing, on balance, to the nation's economic welfare. If it is below 1.0, it detracts from the economic welfare of the nation. The reason is that the ratio measures the comparative benefits of alternative projects using the same resources. If the ratio for a particular project is more than 1.0, it is better than other projects; if the ratio is less than 1.0, that project is worse. If the ratio is 1.0, the particular project is no better or worse than other projects.

The numerator of this ratio is defined as the present value, expressed in dollars, of all of the expected economic benefits of the proposed project. The monetary values that are attached to these benefits are those which society has placed on them, as observed in competitive markets or inferred from willingness to pay studies. In symbolic terms, the numerator of the benefit cost ratio, the present value of total benefits, is:

$$\text{Total benefits} = \Sigma \frac{B_t}{(1 + r)^t}$$

in which Σ means "summation over all the years," B_t stands for the benefits expected in the t th year, and $(1 + r)$ is the discounting factor by which values expected in the future are turned into today's values.

The denominator of the benefit cost ratio is defined as the present value of all of the expected economic costs of undertaking and operating the project. If the project involves capital investment (a new park, campground, access highway, or a trail, for example), costs are of two types: (1) initial construction costs, and (2) operation, maintenance, and repair costs. Capital construction costs usually occur before the project begins producing output of recreation opportunity. The remaining costs — operating, maintenance, and repair — are future ongoing expenses, which occur after the project is operating. In symbolic terms, the denominator of the benefit cost ratio, the present value of total capital and future operation costs, is:

$$\text{Total costs} = K + \Sigma \frac{C_t}{(1 + r)^t}$$

in which K is the capital or construction costs (assumed to occur in the current year) and C_t are the operation, maintenance, and repair costs expected in the t th year.

The full benefit cost ratio (B/C), expressed in symbolic terms, is:

$$\text{B/C} = \frac{\Sigma \dfrac{B_t}{(1 + r)^t}}{K + \Sigma \dfrac{C_t}{(1 + r)^t}}$$

573

or the ratio of the present value of the benefits over the present value of capital investment and future operation costs. It should be noted that these present value formulas are very close to the ones in the previous section on discounting. The main difference is that the formulas for the benefit cost ratio have a summation sign (Σ) in them. This must be included because the formula in the previous section gives the present value (PV) for some benefit or cost expected in future year t (FV_t). Most government recreation projects have benefits that occur in each of a number of future years. The formula for the benefit cost ratio states that the present value of these future benefits must be added together to get the total present value of the entire stream of benefits during the expected life of the project.

Assume, for example, that a park superintendent has asked you to evaluate the benefits and costs of a proposed investment in automatic entrance fee equipment to improve the productivity of labor in park operations. The initial capital investment would be $20,000. The acquisition would commit the government to annual operation, maintenance, and repair costs of $1,000 per year during the expected life of the equipment. The project would result in annual benefits of $10,000 representing the labor savings at entrance stations to the park. Assume that the equipment has a useful life of 3 years and no salvage value. The discount rate is 10 percent.

Calculate the present value of total benefits, as illustrated in the previous section:

$$\begin{aligned} \text{Total Benefits} &= \frac{10,000}{1 + 0.10} + \frac{10,000_2}{1 + 0.10^2} + \frac{10,000_3}{1 + 0.10^3} \\ &= 9,091 + 8,264 + 7,513 \\ &= 24,868 \end{aligned}$$

The annual benefits of $10,000 in labor savings at entrance stations to the parks have a present value of $24,868.

Next, calculate the present value of total costs of the project:

$$\begin{aligned} \text{Total} &= 20,000 + \frac{1,000}{1 + 0.10} + \frac{1,000_2}{1 + 0.10^2} + \frac{1,000_3}{1 + 0.10^3} \\ &= 20,000 + 909 + 826 + 751 \\ &= 22,487 \end{aligned}$$

The $20,000 capital investment costs of the automatic equipment occur before the project begins producing output and are not discounted. The remaining costs of $1,000 per year (for operating, maintenance, and repair) are discounted in the same way as annual benefits. The total costs of capital investment and future operation have a present value of $22,487.

The ratio of the present value of total benefits over the present value of total costs of the capital investment and future operation is:

$$\frac{\text{Benefit}}{\text{Cost Ratio}} = \frac{\$24,868}{\$20,000 + \$2,487}$$
$$= 1.1$$

The benefit cost ratio of 1.1 indicates that the public expenditures for the parks project are judged to be economically worthwhile. Each $1 of social costs generates $1.10 of social benefits, or 10 cents more. The public recreation expenditure contributes 10 percent more to the nation's economic welfare than an equivalent expenditure elsewhere in the economy.

Most recreation projects and programs have long-run consequences with annual benefits and costs extending for 10 to 50 years (or more) into the future. Calculating the present value of long-run benefits and costs by hand, as in the previous example, would be cumbersome. So discount factor tables have been worked out for various discount rates and numbers of years as, for example, in Table 15-3. For the case considered above, look down the years column to the row for the year 3, discounting at 10 percent. The figure shown there, 0.751, is the discount factor which, when multiplied by the expected benefits and costs in 3 years, yields their present value. This is the same result we obtained in working out the present value by hand. Using a discount factor table greatly simplifies application of the present value concept, as illustrated in Table 15-4.

In recent years, recreation planners and managers have compared benefits and costs of both construction and nonconstruction programs. For example, consider a proposed 10-year program to provide park visitors with interpretive services. Although the information program has no initial capital investment, it will commit the government to annual expenditures for personnel training, supervision, and operation of the program (column 2 of Table 15-4). Costs rise during the first few years as effective procedures are being learned, then decline as the

Table 15-4. Present Value of Long-run Benefits and Costs for a Recreation Program with No Capital Investment

(1) Year Since Initiation	(2) Expected Annual Costs[a]	(3) Expected Annual Benefits[a]	(4) Discount Factor for 10 Percent	(5) Present Value of Costs[a] (Col. 2 × Col. 4)	(6) Present Value of Benefits[a] (Col. 3 × Col. 4)	(7) Net Present Value[a] (Col. 6 - Col. 5)
1	$ 10	$ 0	0.909	$ 9.1	$ 0.0	-$ 9.1
2	20	0	0.826	16.5	0.0	-16.5
3	30	5	0.751	22.5	3.8	-18.7
4	30	10	0.683	20.5	6.8	-13.7
5	20	30	0.621	12.4	18.6	6.2
6	10	40	0.564	5.6	22.6	17.1
7	5	40	0.513	2.6	20.5	17.9
8	5	40	0.467	2.3	18.7	16.4
9	5	40	0.424	2.1	17.0	14.9
10	5	25	0.386	1.9	9.7	7.8
Total	140	230		95.5	117.7	22.2

[a]All benefits and costs in thousand dollars.
Source: President's Office of Management and Budget.

program becomes a routine part of park operations. Annual benefits of the interpretive program to park visitors are shown in column 3. Benefits are low during the first few years of most new programs, then rise as they become a popular activity of visitors to the park. The discount factor for 10 percent from Table 15-3 is reproduced as column 4. Note that the present value of costs (column 5) for each of the 10 years is calculated by multiplying expected annual costs (column 2) by the discount factor (column 4). In the same way, the present value of benefits (column 6) for each of the 10 years is calculated by multiplying expected annual benefits (column 3) by the discount factor (column 4). All benefits and costs are in thousands of dollars.

The present value of total benefits, $117.7, and the present value of total costs, $95.5, are obtained by summing the present value of benefits and costs for each of the 10 years (columns 5 and 6). The ratio of the total benefits over total costs is

$$\frac{\text{Benefit}}{\text{Cost Ratio}} = \frac{\$117.7}{\$95.5} = 1.23$$

The benefit cost ratio of 1.23 shows that the public expenditures for the interpretation program are judged to be economically worthwhile. Each $1 of social costs generates $1.23 of social benefits, or 23 cents more. The public recreation expenditure contributes 23 percent more to the nation's economic welfare than an equivalent expenditure elsewhere in the economy.

The problem illustrates an important principle in evaluating long-run nonconstruction programs. The planning period should be relevant to the nature of the program. In this case, if the interpretive program had been evaluated before it became effective, say, at the end of 3 years, it would not have been judged to be economically worthwhile, as total benefits would be insignificant compared to total costs at that time. The program should be re-evaluated after 10 years because annual benefits are expected to decline as most park visitors become informed of the historic and natural features of the park. After 10 years, it would be continued from year to year if the incremental benefits to new park users are expected to exceed incremental costs.

SOCIAL DISCOUNT RATE

In the past, the federal government used three different discount rates in benefit cost studies of recreation programs: (1) a low discount rate of 4 percent based on social time preference was authorized for evaluation of forest recreation projects; (2) a discount rate of approximately 8 percent, based on the average cost of federal borrowing, was used for evaluation of water-based recreation projects; and (3) a high, 10 percent market discount rate was applied uniformly by nearly all agencies of the federal government to the evaluation of recreation projects. Those agencies authorized to use lower discount rates were requested, in addition, to display the effects of the higher rate. Table 15-5 provides a brief summary of the basis for each of these three federal discount rates and a fourth rate of 6 percent based on the opportunity cost of capital. The following discussion will compare these four distinct approaches to social discounting and show how the choice of discount rate can affect the results of benefit cost studies.

Social Time Preference

For many years, the U.S. Forest Service was authorized to use a social discount rate of 4 percent. The President's Office of Management and Budget approved the use of a low discount rate when prescribed by law or authorized by executive order. The low rate, in this case, was based on the fact that the benefits of most current investments in forest management occur in the very distant future (50-150 years), and the belief that a high discount rate would interfere with the attainment of goals other than economic efficiency, such as environmental

(Reservation oriented)

Table 15-5. Social Discount Rates Used for Public Outdoor Recreation Projects

Social Discount Rate	Type	Application	Basis
4 percent	Social time preference	Forest Service	Low discount rate for very long-run forest management programs; to bequest forest resources to future generations
6 percent	Opportunity cost of capital	Recommended rate (Randall)	Marginal rate of profit on private investment; assumed equal to the long-run prime lending rate by large banks to favored corporations after inflation, plus corporate income tax
8 percent (varies)	Cost of government borrowing	Bureau of Reclamation, Corps of Engineers, etc. (Water Resources Council)	Average yield on U.S. government securities outstanding with 15 years or more remaining to maturity, providing the rate cannot increase or decrease by more than ¼ percent per year
10 percent	Market interest rate	All federal agencies (Office of Management and Budget)	High discount rate to facilitate comparison of projects among agencies; assumed equal to the average rate of profit on private investment after inflation, before corporate income tax

preservation and national security associated with domestic timber supply. Recreation projects such as campgrounds with a much lower expected life (20 years), also were evaluated using a discount rate of 4 percent in order not to place them at a disadvantage compared to the timber management projects of the agency. The effect of the low discount rate would be to favor forest recreation projects over recreation projects in other federal agencies using a higher discount rate.

The idea of a social rate of discount is based on the distinction between the private time preference of individuals acting on their own, and the social time preference of individuals acting collectively. When we say that individuals acting on their own have a high time preference, we mean that they want to consume now rather than defer consumption in order to provide resources for future generations. Also, future generations are unrepresented now so their interests are not adequately considered. Government as a collection of individuals should use a low social discount rate because a lower rate gives greater weight to the future than does a higher rate. This is based on the belief that society, in its role as trustee for the future, has a longer time horizon than do individuals; therefore society's discount rate should be lower.

There is convincing evidence that individuals have more concern for the future than their savings and investment behavior as individuals indicates. Their individual behavior suggests they would choose to invest less for the future. However, when collective action is possible through forest management programs, most individuals would invest as part of society as a whole and be better off for having done so. Recent studies have shown that individuals get satisfaction from knowing that future generations will inherit the forest resources that present society has provided through forest mangement programs. Individuals would devote current funds to projects that will pay benefits to future generations, even though living in the present, they forego some consumption opportunities. Thus, individuals would be better off by having forest management decisions made on the basis of the social discount rate rather than the individual discount rate.

Unfortunately, this means that the social discount rate cannot be derived from data on individual investment decisions, because the social discount rate is based on the social time preference of individuals acting collectively. Time preference for individuals acting on their own is most clearly seen when they have a choice between income now and income some time in the future. If we have information about past consumer investment decisions which the individuals consider satisfactory, we can calculate a time preference rate of discount. If individuals were satisfied with an additional investment of $100 at 12 percent interest, they apparently valued income in the future by the difference between $100 and $112, which includes the $12 interest received 1 year hence. Individuals estimate their real personal discount rate after inflation and personal taxes. Thus, if the inflation rate was 4 percent and the personal tax rate 25 percent, the real personal discount rate was

= 12 − (12 × 0.25) − (100 ×0.04)
= 12 − 3 − 4
= 5

This indicates that these individuals acting on their own discounted future earnings at a rate no higher than 5 percent. The difference between their own personal discount rate of 5 percent and the implied 4 percent social discount rate for individuals acting collectively to provide long-run forest projects equals 1 percent. Of course, there are other individuals who, at any available interest rate, prefer current to future consumption depending on expected income and the general state of the economy.

In theory, capital markets determine the interest rate where the supply of loanable funds and demand for investment opportunities intersect. Figure 15-5 shows the supply curve rising with successively higher interest rates, that is, as the marginal rate of time preference increases. This means that increases in the interest rate encourage individuals to forego larger amounts of present consumption in favor of increased savings, which increases the supply of loanable funds. The demand curve for investment capital falls with successively lower interest rates; that is, the marginal efficiency of investment falls as total investment becomes larger. This means that as investment increases, successive additional investment opportunities generate successively lower rates of return on investment. The distinction between private and social time preference represents a shift to the right in the marginal time preference or supply curve. In other words individuals are

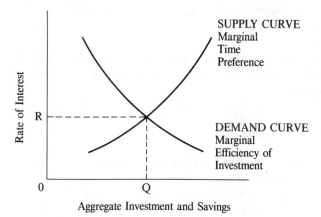

Figure 15-5. Demand and Supply Curves for Capital
Source: Randall.

willing to accept a lower interest rate to forego consumption in favor of saving for investment in long-run forest projects.

Most economists object to use of low social discount rates because of the belief that they often are lower than marginal time preference and opportunity cost of capital. They believe that diverting funds from private to public investment with a low rate of return would be an inefficient undertaking, and benefit cost studies should identify it as such. There may be good reasons to undertake an inefficient public investment, but its inefficiency should be recognized. Use of a low social discount rate in order to make the inefficient appear efficient serves no useful purpose. Recognizing this problem, the Office of Management and Budget asked that agencies compute two different estimates of project benefits and costs, one with the low social discount rate and the other with the high, 10 percent rate to show the sensitivity of the comparison of benefits and costs to use of the low social discount rate.

Still the basic problem of benefit cost studies remains. The method is dependent on discount rates which, as currently applied, discourage projects with very long-term consequences. An alternative solution, presented in Chapters 4, 8, and 14, would be to develop effective methods of quantifying preservation (option, existence, and bequest) values held by the general population so that they may be included as benefits of very long-run forest quality programs. This would provide a direct measure of the social time preference of individuals acting collectively. For example, a sample of households in the state of Colorado reported they would be willing to pay an average of $14 per year to provide forest resources for future generations, and an additional $14 per year to provide forest recreation facilities (see Chapter 14). These first approximations should be considered tentative and subject to change with further research. However, the fact that the measured values are significantly different from zero suggests that bequest values could be added to the recreation use benefits of very long-run forest projects. This may become a practical alternative to the difficult empirical problem of estimating social time preference of individuals acting collectively to provide very long-run investments in environmental resources.

Opportunity Cost of Capital

A discount rate of about 6 percent has been recommended by Randall, a distinguished economist at Ohio State University. This is considered a reasonable approximation of the opportunity cost of capital in the United States. The prime rate of interest on loans by large banks to favored corporations is taken as the best available proxy for the marginal efficiency of investment, when adjusted for the rate of inflation and the corporate income tax. The prime rate of interest includes a premium for anticipated inflation during the period of the loan, removal of which is consistent with the practice of valuing future benefits and costs in constant (or current) dollars at the time of decision. Where corporate income taxes approach 50 percent, a private corporation undertaking an investment needs to earn approximately twice the prime interest rate. Studies have shown that with the inflation rate removed, the prime lending rate has been about 2.5 to 3.0 percent in the long run, i.e., in a period of time sufficiently long that short-run business cycles do not appreciably influence the results. This suggests that the marginal productivity of investment has been about 6 percent in real terms (constant dollars).

$$6 = 3.0 \times [1/(1 - 0.5)]$$

Notice that no adjustment for the risk premium included in the bank prime lending rate was made on the assumption that loans by large banks to large and diversified corporations are about as low risk as investment by the federal government.

The opportunity cost approach is fundamental to public finance. When the government imposes taxes to pay for recreation resource development, it leads to a reduction of private consumption and investment, releasing the private resources for the public project. The opportunity cost of the taxes raised from foregone private investment is equal to the marginal rate of return. This represents the future flow of national income foregone to pay for the recreation project. The marginal productivity of investments would equal the profitability of using the last available capital. The prime rate of interest on loans by large banks to favored corporations is considered a suitable proxy for the profit rate on the marginal investment, when adjusted as above. Row and Kaiser discuss the opportunity cost approach to the discount rate of the U.S. Forest Service.

Cost of Government Borrowing

Water-based recreation projects were evaluated using a social discount rate of approximately 8 percent in 1984. The federal guidelines provide that the rate be recalculated each year based on the average yield of U.S. government securities with 15 years or more remaining to maturity. The rate has been referred to as the "risk free" social discount rate because it was based on the yield of securities that are nearly without risk to the investor. The rate was expected to vary from year to year with the business cycle. However, it has increased each year since the policy was initiated during the latter half of the

1960s. Still the rate has been lower than the yield on long-term government securities because of a legal restriction on the amount of increase each year. In order to dampen short-run changes in the discount rate, it could not be raised or lowered by more than 1/4 percent in any single year. When the average yield in the preceding year exceeded the established discount rate by more than 1/4 percent, the rate was raised. Whenever the average yield becomes less than the established discount rate by more than 1/4 percent, the rate will be lowered.

In the past, the federal water resource agencies used rates of discount that most economists regarded as low. Figure 15-6 shows that during the 1950s and into the 1960s, the discount rate was only 2-5/8 percent for the multipurpose water projects of the Corps of Engineers, Bureau of Reclamation, and Soil Conservation Service. The reason was that, in the early post-war years, Federal Reserve policy allowed the U.S. Treasury to borrow at artificially low rates of interest, by purchasing government bonds that could not be sold to private investors at the low level. As a result, the cost of government borrowing represented by the "coupon rate" on long-term government securities was only 2-4/8 percent during the 1950s, rising gradually to 3-2/8 percent in 1968. The cost of funds was approximately equal to the discount rate in the 1950s and about 1/2 percent higher in 1968. However, with relaxation of the Federal Reserve policy, the average "yield" on long-term government securities rose to 4 percent in 1960 and to 4-2/8 percent in 1968, or 1-4/8 percent more than the discount rate.

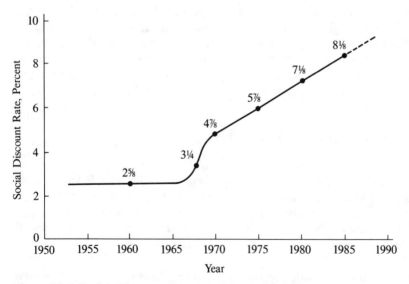

Figure 15-6. Social Discount Rate Used by Federal Water Resource Agencies Based on the Cost of Government Borrowing

Economists define "yield" as the effective rate of interest on long-term government securities, or the annual interest payment divided by the current market price of the securities. The "coupon rate" is of little significance as it is only the annual interest payment divided by the redemption price of the securities. In an inflationary era, the market prices of long-term government securities with low coupon rates are discounted so that yields are approximately equal among outstanding securities with the same redemption date.

For many years, federal agencies and their clientele groups resisted increases in the discount rate because of its effect on the present value of benefits of water resource projects. For example, Fox and Herfindahl evaluated federal water projects authorized by Congress in 1962, which generally used a discount rate of 2-5/8 percent. At higher discount rates, fewer projects had benefits in excess of costs.

Discount rate	2-5/8%	4%	6%	8%
Proportion of projects with benefits in excess of costs	100%	92%	36%	20%

The effect of the low discount rate was to favor water-based recreation projects over other public and private investments using a higher discount rate. Thus, the supply of resources providing opportunities for boating, fishing, swimming, and camping increased dramatically during the 1950s and 1960s.

The low discount rate was considered a subsidy to water interests, and a change in policy became a national issue. In 1962, Senate Document 97 recommended basing the discount rate on the coupon rate of interest for government securities outstanding that were issued with terms of 15 years or more. This interim solution was designed to ease the transition to a higher discount rate. Implementation was delayed until the fiscal year 1968 when the discount rate was raised to 3-2/8 percent, equaling the coupon rate at the time. Early in fiscal year 1969, the federal guidelines changed the basis for the discount rate to the average yield on long-term government securities rather than the coupon rate. This increased the discount rate to 4-7/8 percent in 1970. As a result of these changes in policy the discount rate nearly doubled during the decade. However, the average yield on long-term government securities had increased to 7-6/8 percent in 1970, nearly 2 percent more than the discount rate in the same year. Thus, most economists considered the discount rate still much too low.

In the inflationary era from 1970 to 1984, the effect of basing the discount rate on the cost of government borrowing was to steadily increase its level. From 1970 to 1980, the authorized rate of discount increased by nearly one-half from 4-7/8 to 7-1/8 percent, and in 1984, it was 8-1/8 percent. Changes of this magnitude substantially reduced the present value of benefits relative to costs of federal water resource projects. As a result, during the latter half of the 1970s and the early 1980s, very few new multipurpose water resource projects were approved by Congress. Thus, the rapid increase in opportunities for water-based recreation activities on federal reservoirs ended. Fortunately, during the same time, the states and municipalities became increasingly active in water resource development, primarily for domestic and industrial water supply. This has been part of a national program to decentralize government decision making in the United States. Many states used a social discount rate of 4 to 6 percent, which substantially increased the present value of benefits for state water resource projects compared with the federal rate of 8 percent. As a result, states and municipalities provided increased opportunities for water-based recreation activities during the latter half of the 1970s and the 1980s.

So long as the discount rate policy of federal water resource agencies remains unchanged, we can expect continued increases in the discount rate. If the yield on long-term government securities continues to be above 10 percent, the authorized discount rate is expected to steadily increase at a rate of 1/4 percent per year to a level of 10-1/8 percent in 1992. If the average yield on long-term government securities exceeds 12 percent during the 1990s, the discount rate will increase to 12-1/8 percent in the year 2000.

There are several problems with this policy, the most important of which is that governments should use the "real" social discount rate, excluding inflation, in making capital expenditure decisions. The discount rate policy was authorized in the 1960s when inflation had less effect on the cost of government borrowing than in the 1970s and 1980s. At that point in the business cycle, it was reasonable to ignore inflation. However, for the policy to endure in the long-run, it should be modified to include an adjustment for inflation. For example, when inflation averages 6 percent per year in the long-run, the real cost of government borrowing is only 4 to 6 percent when the average yield on long-term government securities is 10 to 12 percent. In this case, the inflation-adjusted discount rate used by water resource agencies would range between 4 and 6 percent.

Governments should not ignore the costs of borrowing in making capital investment decisions. The expected cost of long-term government securities over the life of the project is relevant to the potential repayment of the costs of water resource projects from marketable output (such as electricity, irrigation water, and recreation), but this is a separate question from evaluation of projects with social benefits and costs in constant dollars, which requires that the social discount rate exclude the effects of inflation.

584

Market Interest Rate

A standard discount rate of 10 percent has been used by all agencies of the federal government for the evaluation of projects for which benefits or costs extend 3 or more years beyond the project startup. The Office of Management and Budget, Circular A-94 (1972), suggested that this uniform high rate be used for evaluation of alternative projects within agencies and required that it be used for projects and programs submitted to the President and Congress. Water resource projects and those of a few other agencies were specifically exempted from use of the 10 percent rate. But the agencies authorized to use a lower discount rate were requested also to display the effects of the higher rate in order to facilitate the comparison of all recreation projects on a uniform basis.

This so-called "market" discount rate has been widely used for the evaluation of public and private recreation projects in the United States and throughout the world. It was authorized by many recreation resource planning agencies at all levels of government. It was considered the risk-free discount rate in the evaluation of economic development projects in India and other Third World countries. Many private banks have routinely evaluated recreation investment proposals using a 10 percent discount rate. As a result, whatever empirical basis exists today for this uniform high discount rate has been all but lost in its popularity among the financial community.

At the time the 10 percent rate was established, it was an approximation of the average rate of return on private investment before taxes and after inflation. Three points should be made concerning this approach. First, no one knows what the average rate of return on private investment really is. Rates of return have ranged from very high to very low, depending on wide variations in the productivity of investment, the anticipated rate of inflation, and the investor's risk. Estimating the average rate of return in private investment throughout the economy involves measuring the average returns in various investment categories and deciding how much weight to place on each category. At any given time, average rates of return can vary from less than 2 percent for agriculture to more than 40 percent for some particularly favored manufacture, construction, or trade.

Economists have estimated that the average pretax rate of return on private investment in the long-run ranged from 8 to 15 percent and averaged about 12 percent. On this basis, the standard discount rate of 10 percent was justified when inflation averaged 2 percent per year:

$$10 = 12 - 2$$

However, in the 10-year period after the rate was established (1973-83), inflation averaged 7 percent per year. Thus, the average rate of return would have to increase to 17 percent for the standard discount rate to be justified.

$$10 = 17 - 7$$

If the long-run average rate of return (12 percent) had prevailed during this period, the inflation adjusted discount rate would have been much less than 10 percent. In this case, it would have been one-half of the standard rate:

$$5 = 12 - 7$$

The point is that changes in the average rate of return and the rate of inflation over the life of a project may justify a higher or lower rate of discount than 10 percent.

Finally, the approach appears to assume that the average rate of return on private investment is a satisfactory proxy for the marginal social cost of transferring funds from private to public investments. This would be equivalent to withdrawing private funds from all investment opportunities in equal proportions, including those with high as well as low rates of return. In effective capital markets, the transfer of funds to public investments would reduce private investments in projects with low rates of return but those with high rates of return would not be affected. Projects with high rates of return bid investment funds away from projects with low rates of return. As a result, the rate of return foregone on the marginal decrease in total private investment may be well below the average rate of return on the total.

We can see this in Figure 15-5 where the demand curve for loanable funds slopes downward and to the right as successive additional investment opportunities generate successively lower rates of return on investment. The average rate of return is equal to the total area under the demand curve to the left of its intersection with the supply curve, divided by the quantity of capital at that point. Visual inspection indicates that this would be higher than the marginal rate of return on investment where demand and supply intersect.

Effects of the Discount Rate

Selecting the rate of discount to use in valuation of the future consequences of projects is probably the most important problem in comparing benefits and costs. Several points should be made about its effects. First, the higher the discount rate, the lower the present value of benefits. Table 15-6 and Figure 15-7 illustrate the effect of changes in the discount rate on the present value of uniform annual benefits of $1 discounted each year of a 25-year planning period. If benefits were not discounted to account for the passage of time, total benefits in the numerator of the benefit cost ratio would be $25 (= 25 years × $1). Using discount rates of 4 to 10 percent, the present value of $1 annual benefits for 25 years would range from $9.08 to $15.62. Note that the present value of benefits for agencies using a low social discount is two-thirds more than for those using a high, 10 percent rate.

The second point is that annual benefits received late in the planning period have very little present value. Table 15-6 and Figure 15-8

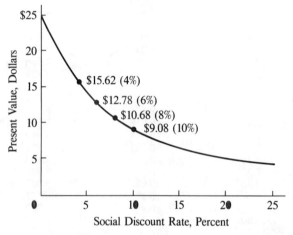

Figure 15-7. Effect of the Discount Rate on the Present Value of $1 Annual Benefits for 25 Years

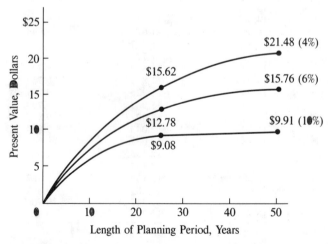

Figure 15-8. Effect of Length of the Planning Period on the Present Value of $1 Annual Benefits

Table 15-6. Present Value of $1 Received or Paid Annually for 1-50 Years Discounted at 4, 6, 8, and 10 Percent Interest

Year	Present Value of $1 with Discount Rate of[a]			
	4%	6%	8%	10%
1	$0.962	$0.943	$0.926	$0.909
2	1.886	1.833	1.783	1.736
3	2.775	2.673	2.577	2.487
4	3.630	3.465	3.312	3.170
5	4.452	4.212	3.993	3.791
6	5.242	4.917	4.623	4.355
7	6.002	5.582	5.206	4.868
8	6.733	6.230	5.747	5.335
9	7.435	6.802	6.247	5.759
10	8.111	7.360	6.710	6.145
11	8.760	7.887	6.139	6.495
12	9.385	8.384	6.536	6.814
13	9.986	8.853	7.904	7.103
14	10.563	9.295	8.244	7.367
15	11.118	9.712	8.559	7.606
16	11.652	10.106	8.851	7.824
17	12.166	10.477	9.122	8.022
18	12.659	10.828	9.372	8.201
19	13.134	11.158	9.604	8.365
20	13.590	11.469	9.818	8.514
21	14.029	11.764	10.016	8.649
22	14.451	12.042	10.201	8.772
23	14.857	12.303	10.371	8.883
24	15.247	12.550	10.529	8.985
25	16.622	12.783	10.675	9.077
26	15.983	13.003	10.810	9.161
27	16.330	13.211	10.935	9.237
28	16.663	13.406	11.051	9.307
29	16.984	13.591	11.158	9.370
30	17.292	13.765	11.258	9.427
31	17.588	13.929	11.350	9.479
32	17.874	14.084	11.435	9.526
33	18.148	14.230	11.514	9.569
34	18.411	14.368	11.587	9.609
35	18.665	14.498	11.655	9.644
36	18.909	14.621	11.717	9.677
37	19.143	14.737	11.775	9.706
38	19.368	14.846	11.829	9.733
39	19.584	14.949	11.879	9.757
40	19.793	15.046	11.925	9.779
41	19.993	15.138	11.967	9.799
42	20.186	15.225	12.007	9.817
43	20.371	15.306	12.043	9.834
44	20.549	15.383	12.077	9.849
45	20.720	15.456	12.108	9.863
46	20.885	15.524	12.137	9.875
47	21.043	15.589	12.164	9.887
48	21.195	15.650	12.189	9.897
49	21.341	15.708	12.212	9.906
50	21.482	15.762	12.233	9.915

[a]The annuity factor shows how much $1 received or paid annually for X years is worth today.
Source: Gittinger.

illustrate the effect of increasing the length of the planning period from 25 to 50 years on the present value of benefits. Recall that without discounting, total benefits would be $25 for the first 25 years and an additional $25 for the second 25 years, or $50 over the total 50 years. However, with discounting, benefits accruing only 25-50 years hence are reduced substantially. For example, using a discount rate of 6 percent, the present value of $1 annual benefits for the second 25 years is only $2.98. Note that the present value of benefits for the second 25 years averages about one-fourth as much as for the first 25 years.

The third point is that when projects have consequences extending beyond 50 years, the discounted benefits of future generations are reduced to trivial amounts. For example, using a discount rate of 6 percent, the present value of $1 annual benefits for the second 50 years is about $0.86. Note that the present value of benefits for the second 50 years averages about one-twentieth as much as for the first 50 years.

Discount rate	4%	6%	8%	10%
First generation, 1-50 years	$21.48	$15.76	$12.23	$9.91
Second generation, 51-100 years	$ 3.02	$ 0.86	$ 0.26	$0.08
Total, 100 years	$24.50	$16.62	$12.49	$9.99

Thus far, no completely satisfactory remedy has been found for the intergeneration problem associated with very long-run projects and programs. A tentative solution has been suggested by Mishan, a contemporary British economist who has written several books on comparing benefits and costs. He assumed generations of successive 50-year lifespans, 1-50, 51-100, etc. In the real world, generations obviously overlap in time; to assume that generations are completely separate simplifies the arithmetic without changing the nature of the problem. In practice, the assumption would mean that the useful life of very long-run projects would be divided into 50-year segments, one for each generation affected. The annual benefits for years 1-50 would be discounted in the conventional way.

For example, using a discount rate of 6 percent, the present value of $1 annual benefits for 50 years would be $15.76. The Mishan proposal is to simply restart the discounting process at the 51st, 101st, 151st years, and so on throughout the useful life of the project. For each generation adopting a 6 percent discount rate and receiving $1 annual benefits, present value would be $15.76, rather than $0.86 for the second generation, and even less for each succeeding generation, under the conventional procedure. The present value of benefits for a 100-year project would be $31.52 for two generations, nearly double the $16.62 present value of benefits without the proposed procedure.

This proposal is based on the economic principle that individuals are the best judges of their own benefits and costs at a given time. Clearly, individuals born into the second generation will discount benefits to year 1 of the second generation's planning period, not to year 1 of the first generation. The procedure also is consistent with the principle of equality between generations. It seems reasonable to assume that the benefits of a park or recreation area will be just as valuable to the second generation of users as to the first. Of course, the preferences of individuals in future generations may differ from those of the current generation, and the per-capita income of future generations is expected to be much greater. Thus, future patterns of demand may vary, and future benefits from current investment decisions may be more or less than for the current generation. Despite these limitations, the procedure would avoid the problem in which projects having large benefits to later generations and small cost to the present generation may be rejected on the basis of the conventional present value approach. Or even more tragically, projects that inflict large costs on later generations may be accepted on the basis of small benefits to the present generation. There are many choices today that can be reversed only at extremely high cost to future generations, or not at all.

The fourth point is that it would not be correct to use a zero discount rate to solve the intergeneration problem. The concepts of present value and discounting are fundamental to the evaluation of investment decisions. Because conservation decisions are basically investment decisions, it would not be correct to use a zero discount rate to achieve the protection of unique environmental resources. For the same reason, it would not be correct for water development projects in arid regions of the world to use a zero discount rate to provide water that would enable the deserts to produce essential foods and fiber, as well as recreation opportunities. For many years, the Soviet Union used a zero discount rate to evaluate large-scale capital investment. Under Marxist doctrine it was not considered proper to pay a return to capital because, in theory, all value was created by labor. As a result, long-run projects had very favorable benefits relative to costs and were undertaken despite a serious shortage of capital. When the serious problems of resource allocation associated with a zero discount rate were recognized, the Soviet government required that projects pay back their initial cost within a specified period of time. This allowed more resources to be allocated to consumer goods and services.

The fifth point is that the level of the interest rate used in project evaluation affects the choice of methods of production. High interest rates restrain investment by making long-run government projects more difficult to justify economically. The higher the discount rate, the lower the present value of annual labor costs relative to the initial capital investment. As a result, more labor and less capital will be used in the production of recreation opportunities. Higher discount rates, for example, favor hiring interpretive specialists rather than constructing elaborate visitor centers and acquiring mechanical displays (with the same amount spent on interpretive services). Higher discount rates favor less durable government investments and related expenditures. They also favor natural river preservation over reservoir construction, hunting and other backcountry recreation over downhill ski resorts, beach swimming over pool swimming, and scenic easements over public land acquisition. In addition, higher discount rates affect international tourism. With higher interest rates in the United States, currency exchange rates encourage U.S. citizens to travel abroad and discourage foreign tourist travel in the United States.

The final point is economists have not been successful thus far in discovering the "correct" rate of discount; thus, rational observers will continue to disagree for legitimate reasons. Traditionally, lower discount rates have been favored by managers of private business and public agencies who are growth oriented and by consumers of their outputs. Higher discount rates have been favored by the Office of Management and Budget, taxpayer groups, lenders, and stockholders. Because there is no consensus on the discount rate problem, benefit cost studies should display the effects of several relevant discount rates. Typically, three discount rates should be used — high, medium, and low. It is not difficult to calculate present value at various rates of discount once the benefits and costs have been forecast for each year in the planning period.

PROBLEMS IN APPLICATION

The purpose of this section is to discuss several additional problems in the comparison of benefits and costs, to summarize the results of recent benefit cost studies, and to suggest ways of improving future applications of the approach to recreation economic decisions. Previously, we discussed the distinction between financial and economic analysis, optimum project design and size, and choice of the discount rate. In previous chapters, we discussed the treatment of inflation, recreation use and preservation benefits to the general public, forecasting benefits and costs, the separate account for regional economic impacts, and when to use cost-effectiveness analysis. Now we turn to a brief discussion of several additional problems in benefit cost studies, including the multiobjectives of natural resource planning, choice of alternatives, the planning period, time phasing of investments, risk and uncertainty, income distribution, nonmonetary effects, and sensitivity of the results to changes in the variables.

591

Search for Alternatives

The first and perhaps most important problem in applying the benefit cost approach is to choose relevant alternatives to be evaluated. Recreation economic decisions nearly always involve the comparison of two or more distinct possibilities. Whenever an individual consumer, private company, or government agency contemplates doing something, the alternatives of doing nothing and doing something else should be considered. The selection of alternative plans should be approached in a systematic manner to insure that all reasonable alternatives are evaluated. In practice, a number of alternative plans will usually be identified early in the planning process. Then they will be refined as more information is developed during the study. Additional alternatives can be introduced at any time.

The federal guidelines define an alternative plan as a combination of structural and/or nonstructural measures to solve a problem or take advantage of an opportunity. Structural aspects include the capital investment costs of land, roads, facilities and equipment to maintain or increase the flow of output in the future. Nonstructural aspects include the costs of changes in existing management practices, laws, and regulations. When institutional barriers would prevent the initiation of an economically attractive alternative, possible changes in existing laws and regulations should be identified. Alternatives are not limited to those that the planning agency could implement directly under current authority. Alternative plans could be implemented by other public agencies of federal, state, and local governments, or by private companies and nonprofit organizations.

A reasonable number of alternatives should be evaluated. A "no action" alternative is included to show the benefits and costs of continuing the current program without change. An alternative is formulated which reasonably maximizes the contribution to national economic development defined as the net present value of benefits to society. Subsequent alternatives may reduce net economic benefits in order to achieve other objectives. The purpose of the other alternatives is to provide decision makers the opportunity to judge whether their beneficial effects outweigh the loss in net economic benefits. Another alternative is formulated to maximize the protection of environmental quality. Finally, there should be one or more significantly different alternatives in between the economic and environmental alternatives that are designed to enhance the best features of both. The alternative selected for implementation should have the most net economic benefits consistent with protecting the natural environment. Exceptions may be made when there are overriding reasons for recommending an alternative based on other objectives such as regional development or other social effects.

There are a number of tests that have been used to evaluate possible alternatives. They should be complete plans that cover all of the necessary investments and operating programs. This includes appropriate mitigation of adverse environmental effects as required by law. They should be effective plans, which means they can be expected to achieve their objectives. This includes considering the capability of cooperating agencies and businesses to finance their proportionate share of the programs. They should be efficient plans representing the most cost-effective (lowest cost) combination of resources to meet the objectives. This means the alternatives that combine features of other alternatives should produce enough output of each to support an economically viable program (Hof, Marose, and King). They should encompass a broad range of output and expenditure levels. Within historical budget trends, specific programs can differ in rate of increase or decrease. They should be acceptable plans which represent politically viable, workable programs compatible with existing laws, regulations, and public policies. When managers are limited in the consideration of alternatives by regulation or legal constraint, some alternatives may be investigated by other interest groups.

In the past, alternatives were often formulated in relation to the previous year's budget. This was the apparent procedure under a Zero Based Budgeting directive of President Carter's Office of Management and Budget in 1977. Alternative programs were broadly defined as: (1) a minimum level below which it would not be feasible to continue the program; (2) the current level equal to last year's budget plus supplemental funding for pay raises; (3) at 105 percent of the current level; (4) at 110 percent of the current level; and (5) at an unconstrained increase in budget, somewhat higher than the 110 percent increase. Merewitz and Sosnick evaluated the zero based budgeting approach and suggested that three alternatives would be sufficient: reduction, stability, and expansion of programs. The first could be the same dollar amount as the previous year, the second would provide sufficient dollars to maintain the same performance as the previous year, and the third would improve services. This seems overly restrictive. At a minimum, a fourth alternative should be included to allow decision makers to evaluate at least two levels of expansion of output.

More recently, alternative plans have been based on the objectives of the agency. Specific objectives are usually described in terms of the desired output of goods and services expected to alleviate a problem or realize an opportunity to increase the welfare of society. The output of multiobjective agencies such as the U.S. Forest Service includes increasing the net value of goods and services that are marketed and those that may not be marketed. Nonmarket output includes recreation, fish, wildlife, wilderness, environmental protection, and the like. Market output includes timber, range, minerals, and energy. Table 15-7 illustrates the low, moderate, and high output goals for these

Table 15-7. Effect of Alternative Programs on the Net Present Value of Market and Nonmarket Output, U.S. Forest Service, 1985-2030

Output and Net Present Value	Alternative Plans								
	Constant Outputs ALT 1	High Market ALT 2	High Non-Market ALT 3	High All Resources ALT 4	Reduced ALT 5	Implement Plans ALT 6	High Present Net Value ALT 7	1980 RPA ALT 8	High Productivity ALT 9
Timber	◔	●	◔	◕	○	◑	◑	◑	●
Range	◑	●	◔	◕	○	◕	◑	◑	●
Recreation	◔	◕	●	●	○	◕	●	●	◕
Wilderness	◔	◔	●	◕	○	◕	◕	●	◔
Wildlife and Fish	◔	◔	●	◕	○	●	◕	◑	○
Minerals and Energy	◔	●	◕	●	○	◕	◕	◑	●
Water	◔	●	◔	◕	○	◑	◑	◑	●
International Forestry	◔	◑	◑	◑	○	●	●	●	◑
Protection and Support	◔	●	◑	●	○	●	◕	◕	●
Net Present Value, Billion Dollars	58.4	73.2	89.6	82.7	50.3	79.2	90.5	79.2	70.0

Output of Goods and Services:	○ Low	◔	◑ Moderate	◕	● High

aSource: Draft Environmental Impact Statement, 1985-2030. Resources Planning Act Program. Forest Service, U.S. Dept. of Agriculture, Washington, D.C. 1984.

goods and services during the planning period, 1985-2030. The table is based on agency evaluation of nine alternatives, including high present net value, constant output at the 1982 program level, a reduced program, high market output, high nonmarket output, and others in between.

It is interesting to note that the net benefits of the high nonmarket alternative ($89.6 billion) are expected to be nearly as great as the national economic development alternative, high present net value ($90.5 billion). By comparison, the high market output alternative had present net value of $73.2 billion or 22 percent less. Apparently, the agency should produce more recreation, fish, and wildlife with less emphasis on traditional output such as timber and range if it is to increase the welfare of society in the long run.

There are two additional points that should be made to illustrate the importance of including each national objective as a prominent feature of an alternative. Omitting an important alternative can be serious. In a study to evaluate potential wilderness areas in California (RARE II), the U.S. Forest Service did not include an alternative designed to maximize environmental protection. A Federal District Court ruled that the agency should restudy the problem and include the omitted alternative.

The largest single planning effort in the history of the National Park Service was to develop the General Management Plan and Environmental Impact Statement for Yosemite National Park in California. It took about 5 years to prepare, at a cost of nearly $1 million. The four alternatives for management of the park were based on a cluster analysis of 5,000 of the 20,000 public responses to detailed opinion questions. One alternative would presumably maximize the profits of the large concessioner operating in the park, as it was based on the concessioner reply to this survey. A second alternative would maximize environmental protection. The other two alternatives in between the commercial development and environmental quality alternatives were not significantly different from each other. As a result, the study appears not to have included an alternative designed to maximize net economic benefits to society.

Four Objectives of Natural Resource Planning

The limitations of benefit cost studies are readily apparent when recreation economic decisions involve more than one objective. The federal guidelines, for example, have established four objectives in evaluating the effects of alternative plans. They are: national economic development (NED), environmental quality (EQ), regional economic development (RED), and other social effects (OSE). These four subjects are intended to include all of the significant effects of a recreation program on the human environment as required by the National Environmental Policy Act of 1969 (NEPA). Throughout this book, we have focused on the national economic development objective. A single chapter dealt with regional economic development. This is consistent with the division of labor between economists and others. The environmental quality objective introduces the study of biology, geology, natural history, archeology, and related subjects. The study of other social effects brings in sociology, psychology, and philosophy. The best source of information on the application of these four objectives in decision making is contained in the federal guidelines and related literature on the benefit cost approach. Federal agencies attempt to identify the beneficial and adverse effects under each of the four accounts.

The national economic development objective has been defined as maximizing the effect of alternatives on the net present value of the output of goods and services no matter who receives them. Although economists may refer to this as the economic efficiency objective, you should keep in mind that what they mean is maximizing the net benefits or welfare of all of the citizens as expressed by individual willingness to pay. We learned in Chapter 5 that net willingness to pay for the output of recreation goods and services is the recommended measure of the benefits of recreation programs. The value of public recreation programs is defined as the net willingness to pay by all of the citizens less the sum of the public agency's operating and opportunity costs. Economists intend this to be total or social net benefits referring to the fact that both internal and external benefits and costs should be included in the calculation. You will recall from the last section of Chapter 14, we learned that the output of recreation agencies includes both recreation use benefits and environmental protection benefits to the general public. Recreation use may be classified as an internal or on-site benefit, and much of environmental protection represents an external or offsite preservation benefit to the general population including users and nonusers.

Understanding the recreation economic decisions of individual consumers provides the foundation for benefit cost analysis. The net benefits of individual users represent the total or social benefits of public recreation programs. You will recall from Chapter 1 that the purpose of economics is to increase the well being of all individuals in society, and that each individual is the best judge of how well off he or she is in a given situation. Both of these propositions follow the predominant Western moral tradition of recent centuries, which regards individual welfare as the ultimate objective of public policy.

This is not the same thing as financial or commercial development (a distinction drawn earlier in this chapter). For private recreation sites, the owner's net benefits are defined as profits, representing the difference between total revenue or sales and total costs incurred by the corporation. Costs include the opportunity costs of foregone earnings and the operating costs of the corporation. Often excluded by private corporations are such external costs as environmental damages, which can be shifted to other individuals, companies, or agencies.

The environmental quality objective has been defined as maximizing the beneficial effects of alternatives on the ecological and aesthetic attributes of natural and cultural resources. Although environmental quality sustains and enriches human life, it is not usually measured in monetary terms. An ecosystem is a complete interacting system of organisms considered together with their environment. Ecology refers to the study of the dynamic and diverse interaction among all living and nonliving things, such as plants, animals, land, water, and atmosphere. Ecological effects include the quality of water, land, and air; the biology and geology of open and green space; wild and scenic rivers; lakes and shorelines; mountains and forests; prairie, wetlands, and estuaries; and other natural systems.

Cultural resources are the historical or archaeological remains of sites, structures, and objects used by people. This is the physical evidence of past and present habitation by humans. Archaeological and historic studies of artifacts, structures, and sites provide information to understand, reconstruct, and preserve physical evidence of the diversity of human cultures. Aesthetic effects are the human perceptions, enjoyment, and appreciation of pleasant surroundings. Included are the sensations of sight, sound, scent, and other human impressions of the natural and cultural resources.

All of these aspects of environmental quality may be described in terms of location, magnitude, duration, or frequency. Thus, ecological and cultural effects are not measured in the same units. Where tradeoffs between objectives are based on values that are not measured in the same units (economists say noncommensurable), choices must be made through the political system. Thus, Congress has passed legislation requiring the protection of the natural environment and that mitigation of adverse effects must be included in each alternative plan. Mitigation usually refers to programs that rectify, repair, rehabilitate, or restore the damaged environment. Mitigation also may refer to the replacement in kind of damaged habitat for fish and wildlife. For example, when a city constructs a reservoir for use as a domestic and industrial water supply, it may have to provide public access to a stretch of river equivalent to that inundated by the reservoir.

The regional economic development objective is to consider changes in the distribution of regional economic activity, income, and employment resulting from each alternative plan. The federal guidelines recommend that regional economic development be treated as income transfer in a separate account to distinguish it from national economic development represented by the net benefits to individual consumers which contribute to general welfare. The region is usually defined as the two to six county area where the recreation project or program will have particularly significant income and employment effects. When these effects are outside of the region, they should be placed in a "rest of nation" category.

Regional income effects are equal to the sum of net economic benefits that remain in the region plus transfers of income to the region from the rest of the nation. Transfers of income include income from outlays to implement the plan and expenditures in the region by recreation users from outside the region, along with their indirect effects and induced effects discussed in Chapter 12. Employment effects parallel those on regional income and can be derived from the same calculation. Changes in employment should be divided into relevant service, trade, agriculture, and industrial sectors of the regional economy. Also, employment effects should be classified as to level of skill required — unskilled, semiskilled, and highly skilled.

Finally, other social effects of alternative plans should be displayed for the information of decision makers. There may be effects on the quality of human life, health, and safety; on distribution of income, employment, and population; the fiscal condition of local government; energy conservation; long-term productivity of resources; and other significant effects of the alternative plans not measured in monetary terms. Effects are usually evaluated in terms of their impacts on community development in the region of the proposed recreation site.

Effects in the category of life, health, and safety include the risk of disasters — such as flood, avalanche, rock or mud slide — with potential loss of property and essential public services. There may be adverse effects of clearing the forest for roads and recreation facilities. The long-term productivity of resources may be affected including the sustained yield of fish and wildlife, forest, forage, water, and other resources. Periodic breakdown of the drinking water and wastewater systems operated under adverse weather conditions is inevitable in some recreation areas and may result in the outbreak of epidemics such as giardia and other human ailments.

Alternative plans may affect the population of the region where the park or other recreation site is located through the displacement of people, businesses, and farms. This, in turn, may affect the fiscal condition of state and local government. Lifestyles may be altered, meaning the way people live, their consumption patterns, work, leisure, and other activities. Social well-being is indicated by the opportunity of all of the people, particularly minorities, to share in the good life — health, education, culture, and leisure pursuits such as recreation.

Interest in particular social effects changes from time to time. In the 1950s, there was concern about the effects on national security. In the

1960s, we were interested in social well-being, opportunities for racial minorities, and prospects for the long-term productivity of resources. By the 1970s, emphasis had shifted to energy requirements and conservation. The 1980s saw renewed interest in the opportunities for the disadvantaged, particularly women. The future is likely to see continued shifts in emphasis among these and other social effects.

Managers have been interested in the effect of alternative plans on income distribution and equity. Income distribution represents an index of the ability of individuals and households to enjoy the full range of output of the public and private sectors of the economy. Income is a useful measure of the goods and services — food, clothing, recreation, etc. — available to individuals and families. The relation between income levels and access to public services, such as campgrounds with substantial user fees, remains a continuing social concern. For example, in California, campers tend to be people with lower income than those who stay in motels and resort lodges (Drake, et al.). The rapid increase in camping fees during the early 1980s was not only inflationary but it also excluded some low and middle income people from the opportunity to use other recreation resources in conjunction with campgrounds.

Finally, energy conservation has been an important problem in the past and is likely to be so again. The energy requirement of alternative plans may differ significantly. For example, consider alternative ways to provide downhill skiing. One is to have a few large vacation ski resorts with most users traveling by commercial airline. Another is to develop many small ski slopes throughout the country with most users traveling by private auto. In other words, what if air travel replaces auto travel so that skiers fly rather than drive? What are the energy requirements of the two alternatives?

Energy consumption is measured in British thermal units (BTU) rather than monetary units. Although energy efficiency (BTUs per person mile) continues to improve the following historic data are sufficient to illustrate the relationship between the energy efficiency of autos and planes:

	BTUs per Person Mile	Skier Days Per Trip	Round Trip Miles Traveled	BTUs per Skier Day
Auto	3,400	2	300	510,000
Airline	8,400	6	2,000	2,800,000

About 50 percent of the seats are occupied in both autos and planes.

This example suggests that typical airline travelers to large vacation ski resorts would consume about 4.5 times more energy than do auto travelers to smaller ski sites. Air travel would become more efficient than auto only if both large and small ski sites were located equal distance from users and if air travelers stayed an average of 6 days compared with 2 days by auto travelers. Skiers are not likely to change their travel patterns to this extent. Thus, it appears that auto travel to small ski sites would contribute more to the conservation of energy.

Choosing When To Start and End the Planning Period

Two other important problems are when to begin and how long to continue recreation programs. When to start up is important because it defines the "present" for calculation of the present value of net benefits. A reasonable definition is the earliest date when the project is likely to receive final approval by decision makers. In this case, the present value of benefit and cost would mean the at-approval value. How long to continue a project also is important because it defines the relevant planning period. A reasonable time horizon from beginning to end of expenditures on programs is the useful life of the most durable assets. The federal guidelines recommend that alternatives should have uniform planning periods, meaning that they begin and end in the same years. Otherwise, the alternatives would not receive a fair comparison.

Economists recommend that recreation programs should begin in the year that maximizes the present value of net benefits. Before then, postponing programs would increase their value to society. Postponing beyond that time would reduce their net benefits. Postponing the start of a program can be beneficial to society only if doing so would increase the present value of net benefits. For example, when a new campground is planned in anticipation of expanding demand for camping in future years, capacity of the facility will exceed demand during the early years after construction and become fully utilized during years 10 to 20, late in the life of the facility. In this case, delaying construction of the entire campground would increase net benefits. Perhaps construction should be phased with the first loop built in year 1, the second loop in year 5, and the third loop in year 10 consistent with the expanding demand. Herfindahl and Kneese discuss this issue and Gittinger describes some simple tests for determining when to start.

Most government agencies specify the length of the planning period. For example, the National Park Service develops 5- and 10-year general management plans for each park. Recreation facilities located at reservoirs of the Corps of Engineers and Bureau of Reclamation are assumed to have a life of 50 years. In the past, the planning period for these two agencies was 100 years. More recently, this was lowered because discount rates increased. The present value of a dollar received or paid 50 years hence, discounted at 8 percent, is only 2 cents. Discounted at 4 percent, it is 14 cents, or seven times more. Another consideration is that reservoirs usually last longer than 50 years. A question may be raised as to how long will the need for a particular facility last? Earlier in this chapter, the conditions for planning very long run programs were shown. For example, a wilderness area may be assumed to have a perpetual life, in which case, the relevant planning period may be a continuous series of 50-year plans.

The U.S. Forest Service prepares 45-year plans under authorization of the Forest and Rangeland Renewable Resources Planning Act (RPA) of 1974. Long run programs were initially developed in 1975 and updated in 1980 and 1985 with projections from 1982 to the year 2030 (Table 15-7). They will be updated again in 1990. The agency's planning horizon varies for specific outputs. The growth cycle for commercial timber can range from 40 to 150 years. The planning period for campgrounds is usually 20 years, based on the longest useful life of the fixed assets — access roads within the site.

Table 15-8 shows that picnic tables have a shorter life span as do most investments in campgrounds. Many public and private campgrounds also have an office and store with a useful life of 20 years. But the furniture and equipment in these facilities often have a shorter useful life as shown in the table. When campgrounds are located on a lake or reservoir, they often have a diving board and raft with a shorter life span. Resort lodges and restaurants usually have a useful

Table 15-8. Average Useful Life of Durable Recreation Equipment for Campgrounds, Resorts, and Consumers

Campground	Years	Furniture	Years
Road	20	Beds	20
Drinking water system	15	Mirrors	20
Storage shed	15	Wood furniture	15
Diving board and raft	10	Lamps	15
Pit toilet	10	Card tables	10
Fireplace grills	10	Upholstered furniture	10
Picnic tables	5	Carpets	
Signs	5	under $5/yd	5
Vehicles	3-5	$5-10/yd	10
Garbage cans	3	Over $10/yd	20
		Children's furniture	5
Office Equipment	**Years**	**Major Appliances**	**Years**
Building, office and store	20	Freezers	20
Furniture	20	Stoves, ranges	15
File cabinets	20	Dryers	12
Typewriters	10	Dehumidifiers	10
Mimeograph machines	10	Dishwashers	10
		Air conditioners	10
Consumer Equipment	**Years**	Stereos	10
Hunting firearms	25	Tape recorders	10
Luggage	20	TV sets	10
Knives	20	Vacuum cleaners	10
Golf clubs	10	Clothes washer	8
Tents	10		
Fishing gear	10		
Wallets, key holders	5		

[a]Source: Allentuck and Bivens; Alden.

life of at least 20 years, with furniture and appliances having a shorter life span. Consumer recreation equipment shows a similar variation in useful life.

One problem in benefit cost studies that is often overlooked is the fact that some of the initial capital investment in durable assets will be replaced periodically throughout the planning period for the recreation site. In the past, there were two ways to treat the costs of replacing worn out assets. The federal guidelines recommend that as durable assets are replaced or rehabilitated periodically throughout the 20-year planning period, the expenditure be counted as a maintenance cost in the year of replacement and discounted back to the present from that year. A less satisfactory solution would be to calculate a weighted average of the useful lives of all durable assets and consider that as the planning period. For example, the weighted average useful life of durable assets in Forest Service campgrounds has been estimated as 17 years. This method tends to bias the results somewhat because of the nature of discounting. Equal expenditures for replacement of short-lived assets have a much higher present value than replacement of long-lived assets, because of the rapidly declining present value with the passage of time.

Another problem in an era of increasing concern about efficiency in government results from the fact that more and more parks and other recreation sites are being treated as separate units for accounting purposes and operated on a pay-as-you-go basis. This means that capital investment is converted to annual cost by amortization or some other basis of capital recovery. In this case, length of the planning period has a significant effect. Fixed assets of equal value but different useful lives will have significantly different annual cost. For example, employee vehicles are durable assets that routinely have been amortized on an annual basis. Table 15-9 shows that the annual cost of a capital investment of $10,000 at 10 percent interest varies with useful life:

Three years $4,020
Five years $2,640

The appropriate method of converting capital investment to annual cost depends on whether investments are financed by taxes, the sale of revenue bonds, or by user fees. Amortization is recommended to estimate the full social cost of investments from tax revenues. Amortization also is an appropriate measure of the annual obligation to repay the principle plus interest on revenue bonds. However, a sinking fund would be appropriate when users are charged fees sufficient to replace recreation facilities as they wear out. These two methods are illustrated in Tables 15-9 and 15-10.

Amortization is defined as the annual payment to recover an investment plus the payment of compound interest on the unpaid balance at the end of each year. The sinking fund method is defined as the annu-

Table 15-9. Ammortizing a $1 Investment in 1-50 Years With Payment of Compound Interest of 4, 6, 8, and 10 Percent

Year	Annual Payment to Recover $1 With Compound Interest of[a]			
	4%	6%	8%	10%
1	1.040	1.060	1.080	1.100
2	.530	.545	.561	.576
3	.360	.374	.388	.402
4	.275	.289	.302	.315
5	.226	.237	.250	.264
6	.191	.203	.216	.230
7	.166	.179	.192	.205
8	.149	.161	.174	.187
9	.134	.147	.160	.174
10	.123	.136	.149	.163
11	.114	.127	.140	.154
12	.107	.119	.133	.147
13	.100	.113	.127	.141
14	.095	.106	.121	.136
15	.090	.103	.117	.131
16	.086	.099	.113	.128
17	.082	.095	.110	.125
18	.079	.092	.107	.122
19	.076	.090	.104	.120
20	.074	.087	.102	.118
21	.071	.085	.100	.116
22	.069	.083	.098	.115
23	.067	.081	.096	.113
24	.066	.080	.095	.111
25	.064	.078	.094	.110
26	.063	.077	.093	.109
27	.061	.076	.091	.108
28	.060	.075	.090	.107
29	.059	.074	.090	.107
30	.058	.073	.089	.106
31	.057	.072	.088	.105
32	.060	.071	.087	.105
33	.055	.070	.087	.104
34	.054	.070	.086	.104
35	.054	.069	.086	.104
36	.053	.068	.085	.103
37	.052	.068	.085	.103
38	.052	.067	.085	.103
39	.051	.067	.084	.102
40	.050	.066	.084	.102
41	.050	.066	.084	.102
42	.050	.066	.083	.102
43	.049	.065	.083	.101
44	.049	.065	.083	.101
45	.048	.065	.083	.101
46	.048	.064	.082	.101
47	.048	.064	.082	.101
48	.047	.064	.082	.101
49	.047	.064	.082	.101
50	.046	.063	.082	.101

[a]The capital recovery factor shows the annual payment that will repay a $1 loan in X years with payment of compound interest on the unpaid balance.
Source: Gittinger.

Table 15-10. Sinking Fund Method of Recovering A $1 Investment in 1-50 Years With Compound Interest of 4, 6, 8, and 10 Percent

	Annual Payment to Recover $1 With Compound Interest of[a]			
Year	4%	6%	8%	10%
1	1.0000	1.0000	1.0000	1.0000
2	.4902	.4854	.4808	.4762
3	.3203	.3141	.3080	.3021
4	.2355	.2286	.2219	.2155
5	.1846	.1774	.1705	.1638
6	.1508	.1434	.1363	.1296
7	.1266	.1191	.1121	.1054
8	.1085	.1010	.0940	.0874
9	.0945	.0870	.0801	.0736
10	.0833	.0759	.0690	.0627
11	.0741	.0668	.0600	.0540
12	.0666	.0593	.0527	.0468
13	.0601	.0530	.0465	.0408
14	.0547	.0476	.0413	.0357
15	.0499	.0430	.0368	.0315
16	.0458	.0390	.0330	.0278
17	.0422	.0354	.0296	.0247
18	.0390	.0324	.0267	.0219
19	.0361	.0296	.0241	.0195
20	.0336	.0272	.0219	.0175
21	.0313	.0250	.0198	.0156
22	.0292	.0230	.0180	.0140
23	.0273	.0213	.0164	.0126
24	.0256	.0197	.0150	.0113
25	.0240	.0182	.0137	.0102
26	.0226	.0169	.0125	.0092
27	.0212	.0157	.0114	.0083
28	.0200	.0146	.0105	.0075
29	.0189	.0136	.0096	.0067
30	.0178	.0126	.0088	.0061
31	.0169	.0118	.0081	.0055
32	.0159	.0110	.0075	.0050
33	.0151	.0103	.0069	.0045
34	.0143	.0096	.0063	.0040
35	.0136	.0090	.0058	.0037
36	.0129	.0084	.0053	.0033
37	.0122	.0079	.0049	.0030
38	.0116	.0074	.0045	.0027
39	.0111	.0069	.0042	.0025
40	.0105	.0065	.0039	.0023
41	.0100	.0061	.0036	.0020
42	.0095	.0057	.0033	.0019
43	.0091	.0053	.0030	.0017
44	.0087	.0050	.0028	.0015
45	.0083	.0047	.0026	.0014
46	.0079	.0044	.0024	.0013
47	.0075	.0041	.0022	.0011
48	.0072	.0039	.0020	.0010
49	.0069	.0037	.0019	.0009
50	.0066	.0034	.0017	.0009

[a]The sinking fund factor shows the annual payment that will repay a $1 loan in X years with receipt of compound interest on investment of the accumulating fund.
Source: Gittinger.

604

al payment that must be set aside each year to be invested at compound interest, in order to recover the original investment at the end of its useful life. The key difference is in the treatment of interest. Amortizing involves the payment of compound interest, and a sinking fund receives compound interest. For example, the annual payment into the fund could be invested in government bonds paying 10 percent interest. The importance of this distinction is the difference in the annual cost of investment under the two methods which increases for higher interest rates and longer planning periods.

The social cost of investment could be much lower with annual payments deposited in a sinking fund and invested in interest-bearing bonds. For example, consider a capital investment of $10,000 with a useful life of 20 years and an interest rate of 10 percent. The annual cost of the investment would be:

Amortization	$1,175
Sinking Fund	$175
Saving	$1,000

This means that annual payment of $175 per year and the interest that accumulates on the payments over the 20 years will result in a balance of $10,000. With 1,000 RVDs per year, amortized investment cost would equal about $1.18 per RVD compared with only about $0.18 per RVD payment into a sinking fund. The payment of only $0.18 per RVD would be sufficient to replace existing facilities with revenues generated from user fees. As a result, the agency would be self-supporting in the provision of the existing capacity of facilities which otherwise would require a tax subsidy of $1.18 per RVD, or $1.00 per RVD more. This potential saving represents a strong case for sinking fund financing of recreation investments out of user fees.

Other Problems in Application

Several additional points should be made about the comparison of benefits and costs. Here we will discuss four, having to do with uncertainty, sensitivity analysis, income distribution, and noneconomic effects.

After a study presents the best estimates of benefits and costs, it is important to include information on the effects of uncertainty. This refers to the absence of accurate information, or to that which is unknown. Uncertainty is an important problem when comparing benefits and costs because there is always some degree of error in the measurements. The federal guidelines recommend that studies include comparisons of the sensitivity of the results to uncertainty in the data and assumptions of future conditions. The objective is to help decision makers understand the effects of possible variation in conditions.

Sensitivity studies: (1) vary the data and assumptions as to economic, demographic, environmental, and other important conditions; and (2) report the effects on benefits and costs. Typically, benefits and costs are calculated for high, low, and medium levels of each important variable. This is an attempt to account for the variance (or degree of error) in the estimates of benefits and costs. Sassone and Schaffer discuss three possible mathematical approaches to limit sensitivity studies to the most important variables.

Also, studies should show the effects on income distribution and equity. In the basic comparison of benefits and costs, it does not matter who benefits and who pays the costs. Benefit cost studies are primarily concerned with the objective of economic efficiency, and less with other possible objectives such as income distribution. This means that we measure the net benefits to all of the people rather than to special interest groups. But after the basic comparison, studies should show decision makers how costs and benefits are distributed to different populations. With this information, they can decide whether, on equity grounds, the cost to one population is worth the benefits to another population.

Whenever government investment and operating costs are not fully reimbursed by users, they result in an income distribution effect. Many of the services of park and recreation programs are not regarded as suitable for sale on a pay-as-you-go basis. For example, it has been public policy that the youth and the aged should be entitled to the services of most park and recreation programs whether they can pay or not. Society desires that all persons have the opportunity to receive the services as a matter of principle because of distributional considerations. This results in a transfer of income in kind to those who do not pay from those who do.

When society attaches a different value to a dollar of cost or benefit for different groups of users, our unadjusted measures would need to be changed. For example, when benefits are adjusted on the basis of federal income tax weighting, those attributed to low income users of recreation sites in Massachusetts increase by 7 percent, according to a study by Harou. In New York state, the benefits of low income users of water-based recreation sites increase by 14 percent, based on a similar adjustment by Shabman and Kalter. The effect of adjusting the value of benefits and costs for different income groups should be shown after the basic comparison without the adjustment.

It is important that all of the potentially significant costs and benefits be measured or at least discussed. Studies should describe any beneficial or adverse effects that cannot be quantified in monetary terms. There are two important reasons: (1) the description provides decision makers the opportunity to make their own estimates of the possible effects of the missing data on net benefits of the alternatives;

and (2) it identifies the areas where research is most needed for future decision making. Gaps in scientific data prevent our measuring some costs and benefits. This is evidently a limiting factor in the case of physical and biological conditions that affect the quality of recreation experiences (Jubenville, Matulich, and Workman). For example, the relation between fish stocking programs and fishing success is not fully known. Because of limited knowledge, the term, benefit cost analysis may suggest a degree of precision that is seldom attainable.

Still, methods are available to achieve levels of accuracy in measuring benefits and costs that are reasonable and consistent with levels obtained in other areas of economics and in other disciplines. Readers interested in a detailed discussion of the issue of reliability in the comparison of benefits and costs are referred to the work edited by Peterson, Driver, and Gregory. The authors caution us to remember that the comparison of benefits and costs, like any other approach, cannot be applied blindly. It is important to check whether the assumptions underlying the approach are at least approximately correct, and to be aware of the problems that may arise in applications to recreation economic decisions. Although the assumptions underlying the comparison of benefits and costs are unlikely to be met completely, they are close enough in a sufficiently large number of cases that it is a powerful approach.

SUMMARY

In this chapter, we were introduced to the concept of discounting and net present value. This can be useful when making difficult choices among alternatives that yield streams of benefits and costs stretching into future years. The function of discounting is to convert future benefits and costs of a project into present value (today's dollars) at the time of decision. Quite simply, it telescopes to the present all the benefits and costs during the life of the project. It makes sense to measure future benefits and costs in terms of today's dollar values because decision makers choose between short-run recreation projects, which have no future benefits and costs, and long-run projects, which do. To compare the various streams of benefits and costs over time, the recommended procedure is to discount them to present values. The sum of the discounted benefits less the sum of the discounted costs over the life of the project measures the economic value of recreation investments. In economics, this net present value is defined as the amount of investment now that would yield the expected annual benefits minus the costs of the project. Remember, the rule for selecting among alternative projects is to maximize net benefits (B-C) at the time of decision.

We considered the fundamental recreation economic problem of governments throughout the world: How large should the recreation program be? How much should government tax and spend for park recreation programs? Questions about the optimum size, design, and purpose of recreation programs are problems of resource allocation. How many of society's resources should be allocated to the production of recreation opportunities? Benefit cost studies can assist managers in thinking meaningfully about this question. We saw how benefit cost studies help decision makers choose among alternative recreation programs which vary in size, design, and purpose. They assist decision makers to improve operations toward the objectives of developing the optimum size program, designing the program to be of maximum efficiency, and choosing from the available alternatives those that are most productive. To achieve efficiency in government, spending on recreation programs should be increased in each area and in total until the marginal social benefits of the last recreation visitor days equal their marginal social costs. This would help managers produce the most benefits of public recreation programs for society.

In benefit cost studies, then, the comparison is between the value to the private sector of what it gives up to support a government recreation program (represented by taxes, user fees, and opportunity costs) and the value of the output (represented by the willingness of citizens to pay for the government-produced opportunities, if they had to).

A public recreation program can increase the welfare of society if the resources given up by the private sector are used to produce greater benefits than they would produce in the absence of the program. Benefit cost studies of proposals ask the question: "Do the net benefits to the people exceed the costs required of them?" If the answer is "yes," the proposal is an efficient one. If it is "no," the proposal would waste resources and would not be in the public interest. Benefit cost studies are concerned with social gains and losses. For the evaluation of public recreation programs, the denominator in the benefit cost ratio is the present value of agency operations and opportunity costs, and the numerator is the present value of consumer surplus (net benefits) to the citizens.

Selecting the rate of discount to use in valuation of the future consequences of projects is probably the most important problem in benefit cost studies. In the past, the federal government has used three different discount rates for benefit cost studies of recreation projects and programs: (1) a low discount rate of 4 percent based on social time preference was authorized for evaluation of forest recreation projects, (2) a discount rate of approximately 8 percent, based on the average cost of federal borrowing, was used for evaluation of water-based recreation projects; and (3) a high, 10 percent market discount rate was applied uniformly by nearly all agencies of the federal government, including the evaluation of recreation projects. Those agencies authorized to use lower discount rates were requested, in addition, to display the effects of the higher rate. We discussed the basis for each of these three federal discount rates and a fourth rate of 6 percent based on the opportunity cost of capital. Then we compared these four distinct approaches to social discounting and saw how the choice of discount rate can affect the results of benefit cost studies.

Finally, we discussed several problems in applying the benefit cost approach, summarized the results of recent benefit cost studies, and suggested ways of improving future applications of the approach to recreation economic decisions.

READINGS

Alden, Howard R. "So You're Planning an Outdoor Recreation Enterprise." Agricultural Extension Service Bulletin 493. University of Idaho, Moscow. 1968.

Allentuck, Andrew J., and Gordon E. Bivens. *Consumer Choice, The Economics of Personal Living.* Harcourt Brace Jovanovich, Inc., New York. 1977.

Barkley, Paul W., and David W. Seckler. *Economic Growth and Environmental Decay.* Harcourt Brace Jovanovich, Inc., New York. 1972.

Baumol, William J. (ed.). *Public and Private Enterprise in a Mixed Economy.* The MacMillan Press Ltd., London. 1980.

Baumol, William J. "On the Social Rate of Discount." *American Economic Review* 58(Sept. 1968):788-802.

Bradford, David F. "Benefit-Cost Analysis and Demand Curves for Public Goods." *Kyklos* 23(No. 4, 1970):775-91.

Bronfenbrenner, Martin., Werner Sichel, and Wayland Gardner. *Microeconomics.* Houghton Mifflin Co., Boston. 1984.

Brookshire, David S., Alan Randall, and John R. Stoll. "Valuing Increments and Decrements in Natural Resource Service Flows." *American Journal of Agricultural Economics* 62(Aug. 1980):478-88.

Brown, R. E., and W. J. Hansen. "Condition and Operation Studies — Recreation." U.S. Army Engineer Institute for Water Resources, IWR Research Report 78-R3, Washington, D.C. November, 1978.

Caulfield, Henry. "Federal Guidelines for Water Resource Project Evaluation." in *Environmental Impact on Rivers.* Hsieh Wen Shen (ed.). Colorado State University, Fort Collins. 1971.

Drake, Ronald, L. T. Wallace, Oliver R. Stanton, and Harry S. Hinkley. "Selected Economic Consequences of Recreation Development: Tuolumne County, Case Study." Information Series in Agricultural Economics No. 68-4, Agricultural Extension Service, University of California, Davis. 1968.

Fox, Irving, and O. C. Herfindahl. "Attainment of Efficiency in Satisfying Demands for Water Resources." *American Economic Review* 54(May 1964):198-206.

Freeman, A. Myrick III. *Intermediate Microeconomic Analysis.* Harper and Row, Publishers, New York. 1983.

Gibbs, Kenneth C., and Frederick L. Reed. "Estimation and Analysis of Costs for Developed Recreation Sites in U.S. Forest Service Region One." Forest Research Laboratory, Research Bulletin 42, Oregon State University, Corvallis. 1983.

Gittinger, J. Price. *Economic Analysis of Agricultural Projects.* 2nd Edition. Johns Hopkins University Press, Baltimore. 1982.

Grant, Eugene L., and W. Grant Ireson. "The Comparison of Alternatives." *Managerial Economics and Operations Research.* Edwin Mansfield (ed.). Revised Edition. W. W. Norton, New York. 1970.

Grubb, Herbert W., and James T. Goodwin. "Economic Evaluation of Water-oriented Recreation in the Preliminary Texas Water Plan." Report 84. Texas Water Development Board, Austin. 1968.

Hanke, Steve H., and James M. Anuyll. "On the Discount Rate Controversy." *Public Choice* 28(Spring 1980):171-83.

Hanke, Steve H., Philip H. Carver, and Paul Bugg. "Project Evaluation During Inflation." *Water Resources Research* 11(Aug. 1975):511-14.

Harou, P. A. "Including Equity in the Evaluation of Outdoor Recreation Benefits." *Canadian Journal of Forest Research* 12(No. 2, 1982):337-41.

Haveman, Robert H. *The Economics of the Public Sector.* 2nd Ed. John Wiley & Sons, New York. 1976.

Herfindahl, Orris C., and Allen V. Kneese. *Economic Theory of Natural Resources.* Charles E. Merrill Publishing Co., Columbus, Ohio. 1974.

Hof, John G., Robin K. Marose, and David A. King. "Potential Pitfalls in Renewable Resource Decision Making that Utilizes Convex Combinations of Discrete Alternatives." *Western Journal of Agricultural Economics* 10(Dec. 1985):391-400.

Howe, Charles W. *Benefit-cost Analysis for Water System Planning.* Water Resources Monograph No. 2, American Geophysical Union, Washington, D.C. 1971.

James, L. Douglas, and Robert R. Lee. *Economics of Water Resources Planning.* McGraw-Hill Book Co., New York. 1971.

Jubenville, Allan, Scott C. Matulich and William G. Workman. "Toward Integration of Economics and Outdoor Recreation Management." Bulletin 68, Agricultural and Forestry Experiment Station, University of Alaska, Fairbanks. 1986.

Kalter, Robert J. "The Economics of Water-Based Outdoor Recreation: A Survey and Critique of Recent Developments." Institute of Water Resources Report 71-8, U.S. Army Corps of Engineers, Washington, D.C. 1971.

Klemperer, W. D. "Economic Analysis Applied to Forestry: Does it Shortchange Future Generations?" *Journal of Forestry* 74(Sept. 1976):609-11.

Krutilla, John V. (ed.). *Natural Environments: Studies in Theoretical and Applied Analysis.* Johns Hopkins University Press, Baltimore. 1972.

Marglin, Stephen A. *Approaches to Dynamic Investment Planning.* North-Holland Publishing Co., Amsterdam. 1963.

Martin, William E., J. Craig Tinney, and Russell L. Gum. "A Welfare Economic Analysis of the Potential Competition Between Hunting and Cattle Ranching." *Western Journal of Agricultural Economics* 3(Dec. 1978):87-97.

Merewitz, Leonard, and Stephen H. Sosnick. *The Budget's New Clothes: A Critique of Planning-Programming-Budgeting and Benefit-Cost Analysis.* Markham, Chicago. 1971.

Mills, Allan S., Joseph G. Massey, and Hans M. Gregersen. "Benefit-cost Analysis of Voyageurs National Park." *Evaluation Review* 4(Dec. 1980):715-38.

Mishan, E. J. *Economics for Social Decisions: Elements of Cost-Benefit Analysis.* Praeger Publishers, Inc., New York. 1973.

Mishan, E. J. *Introduction to Normative Economics.* Oxford University Press, New York. 1981.

Mishan, E. J. *Cost-Benefit Analysis.* 3rd Edition. George Allen and Unwin, London. 1982.

Perkins, J. Robert, Herbert L. Underwood, and Isaac A. Withers. "Swimming Opportunities in the Model Neighborhood." Program Analysis Seminar, Dade County, Fla. 1968.

Peskin, Henry M., and Eugene P. Seskin. *Cost Benefit Analysis and Water Pollution Policy.* The Urban Institute, Washington, D.C. 1975.

Peterson, George L. B C. Driver, and Robin Gregory (eds.). "Toward the Integration of Economics and Psychology in the Measurement of Non-Priced Values." Conference Proceedings, Rocky Mountain Forest and Range Experiment Station, Forest Service, U.S. Dept. of Agriculture, Fort Collins, Colo. 1986.

Prest, A. R., and Ralph Turvey. "Cost-Benefit Analysis: A Survey." *Economic Journal* 75(Dec. 1965):683-735.

Recht, J. Richard, and Robert J. Harmon. "Open Space and the Urban Growth Process." Research Report 31, Center of Real Estate and Urban Economics, University of California, Berkeley. 1969.

Reiling, Stephen D., and Mark W. Anderson. "Estimation of the Cost of Providing Publicly-Supported Outdoor Recreation Facilities in Maine." Bulletin 793, Maine Agricultural Experiment Station, University of Maine, Orono. 1983.

Row, Clark, H. Fred Kaiser, and John Sessions. "Discount Rate for Long-term Forest Service Investments." *Journal of Forestry* 79(June 1981):367-69,376.

Samuelson, Paul A. "The Pure Theory of Public Expenditure." *Review of Economics and Statistics* 36(Nov. 1954):387-89.

Sassone, Peter G., and William A. Schaffer. *Cost-Benefit Analysis: A Handbook.* Academic Press, New York. 1978.

Schultze, Charles L. "Why Benefit-Cost Analysis?" *Program Budgeting and Benefit-Cost Analysis: Cases, Text, and Readings.* Harley H. Hinrichs and Graeme M. Taylor (eds.). Goodyear Publishing Co., Pacific Palisades, Calif. 1969.

U.S. Department of Agriculture. "Long Range Multiple Use Planning of the Kootenai National Forest, Montana." Forest Service, Washington, D.C. 1976.

610

U.S. Department of Agriculture. "Economic and Social Analysis." Forest Service Manual, Chapter 1970. Forest Service, Washington, D.C. 1980.

U.S. Department of Agriculture. "Draft Environmental Impact Statement, 1985-2030 Resources Planning Act Program." Forest Service, Washington, D.C. 1984.

U.S. Dept. of the Interior. "Analysis of Federal Recreation and Recreation-Related Programs." National Urban Recreation Study. Volume II, Technical Reports. Heritage Conservation and Recreation Service, Washington, D.C. 1978.

U.S. Office of Management and Budget. "Discount Rates to be Used in Evaluating Time-distributed Costs and Benefits." Circular A-94 (revised), Washington, D.C. 1972.

Walsh, Richard G. "Relationship Between Price and Costs of Ski Area Operation." Outdoor Recreation and Ski Permits on National Forest Lands. Hearings, U.S. Senate, Washington, D.C. 1976. 224-38.

Walsh, Richard G. "An Economic Evaluation of the General Management Plan for Yosemite National Park." Technical Report No. 19, Colorado Water Resources Research Institute, Colorado State University, Fort Collins. 1980.

Walsh, Richard G., and Gordon J. Davitt. "A Demand Function for Length of Stay on Ski Trips to Aspen." *Journal of Travel Research* 22(Spring 1983):23-29.

Walsh, Richard G., John B. Loomis, and Richard S. Gillman. "Valuing Option, Existence and Bequest Demand for Wilderness." *Land Economics* 60(Febr. 1984):14-29.

Wetztein, Michael E. "An Economic Evaluation of a Multi-Area Recreation System." *Southern Journal of Agricultural Economics* 14(Dec. 1982):51-55.

Young, Robert A., and Robert H. Haveman. "Economics of Water Resources," *Handbook of Natural Resource and Energy Economics,* Allen V. Kneese and James L. Sweeney (eds.). Volume 2. Elsevier Science Publishers (North-Holland), Amsterdam. 1985. 465-529.

611

Problems

CHAPTER ONE

1. How has the subject of recreation economics changed since 1960? What is the basis for this new emphasis?
2. What is the impact of recreation on the U.S. economy and on the economies of individual states?
3. Discuss the effect of the 20th century industrial revolution on the demand and supply of recreation resources.
4. What is the purpose of this book and for whom is it written? How does this relate to the objective of economics and the predominant Western moral tradition of recent centuries?
5. Illustrate the three levels of subject matter treated in this book.
6. Freeman classifies recreation as a part of environmental economics. What does this mean for recreation economic decisions? Why, for example, is wilderness protection a controversial subject?
7. What is the basic decision making framework used throughout this book? Apply the five-part framework to a recreation economic problem with which you are familiar.

CHAPTER TWO

1. Define the terms: household production, comprehensive income, regular income, self-sufficiency time, leisure time, net benefit, isoquant curve, budget line, and the optimum combination of inputs to produce a recreation day.
2. Discuss the evidence presented in this chapter on the effect of income distribution on leisure time, participation in recreation, expenditures on trips and recreation equipment, and happiness.
3. A number of observers have suggested that the expenditure of tax revenues to provide use of public recreation resources free or for nominal entrance fees constitutes a subsidy to middle and high income households at the expense of those with low income. Compare the consumption of recreation by income groups to their tax payment. By this measure, which, if any, income groups receive subsidy? Discuss.
4. The opportunity cost of wages foregone becomes a direct cost of recreation whenever employers deduct wage payments or when earnings are otherwise reduced while an individual is engaged in recreation. Assume that an individual's regular income would be reduced by $50 on each weekday and zero on weekends and holidays. Total benefits for the typical individual are $60 each weekday and $40 per day during the weekend (owing to increased crowding). Travel and other direct costs are $25 per day. What would be the recreation economic decision of this individual? Would he or she choose to participate in weekday or weekend recreation? Explain.
5. Several approaches have been used to estimate the opportunity cost of self-sufficiency time. These include: market prices of outputs, opportunity costs of input time, and willingness to pay for the outputs less purchased inputs. Define each and illustrate using examples from recreation. Which approach is preferred and why?
6. Some observers have noted that there is often a wide variation in the direct out-of-pocket costs of participating in recreation which is unexplained by the usual socioeconomic variables. Define the concept of producer surplus and apply it to participation in recreation. Can you think of any circumstances in which variation in the producer surplus of participants may explain a significant part of the variation in direct costs?
7. An interagency committee of the U.S. government has recommended willingness to pay as the appropriate economic measure of the benefits of recreation. Explain why willingness to pay may be a better measure of benefits than nonmonetary alternatives, such as consumer preference studies. Why are consumer preference studies useful, nonetheless, to economists and to managers of outdoor recreation resources?
8. Lancaster has proposed that consumer demand is related to the characteristics of what we consume. Recreation activities with different characteristics vary in their capacity to satisfy our basic psychological needs and desires. List the recreation activities classified as having primarily active, passive, extractive, appreciative, social, and learning motivations. Discuss the implications of this psychological approach for estimating benefits and costs of recreation.
9. If consumers of recreation services are to make good decisions, they have to know two things: what they want, determined by total benefits, and what they can get, determined by prices constrained by income levels, leisure time, and self-sufficiency. The best buy is what they are willing to pay the most for relative to

what they must pay to get it. The difference is defined as net benefits or consumer surplus.

Assume that downhill skiing has a total annual price of $500, cross country skiing $300, a trip to Europe $1,500, a season of boating $2,000. Assign your individual willingness to pay to each recreation activity. Calculate your consumer surplus and your benefit cost ratio. Which activity is the best buy for you and why?

CHAPTER THREE

1. The output of recreation is defined as visits by the National Park Service, as recreation days by the federal guidelines, and as recreation visitor days by the Forest Service. Define each of these measures and discuss the problem of comparability.
2. The National Park Service estimated that there were 2.7 million visits to Yosemite National Park in a recent year, based on number of persons counted at highway entrance stations. There were an estimated 1.7 million overnight stays in campgrounds and resort lodges, and for those staying overnight, length of stay averaged 2.5 days. How many visitors stayed overnight and how many were single day users? Convert total park visits to recreation days.
3. The Forest Service estimated that there were 100,000 recreation visitor days at a wilderness area in a recent year. A sample survey showed that hiking represented approximately 75 percent of total use and backpacking, 25 percent. Individuals reported an average 4.0 hours per day hiking and 12.0 hours per day backpacking. Convert the total recreation visitor days reported for the wilderness to recreation days, as perceived by individual consumers.
4. A recent national survey showed that the average participant reported 100 days of recreation per year. Sample surveys have shown that approximately 10 percent of the total time away from home on recreation trips is necessary travel time, and 90 percent is devoted to recreation activities, including sightseeing. Assume that roughly 180 million persons participated in recreation in the United States and that recreation days averaged 5.0 hours. The problem is to adjust the results of this national survey and to convert the recreation days to standard recreation visitor days. With this information, Congress could estimate the proportion of total recreation provided by federal agencies. The Forest Service had 230 million recreation visitor days and the National Park Service 300 million visits averaging 4 hours each.
5. A state Wildlife Division reported 200,000 big game hunters in a recent year. The estimate was based on the number of licenses sold. Information obtained by game check stations revealed that hunters averaged 6.0 days per year and 5.0 hours per day hunting big game. In addition, a recent study estimated that poaching represented as much as 20 percent of the big game harvest in the state. Assume that poachers and legal big game hunters had the same success ratio, number of annual days, and number of hours per day. What is the estimated total number of big game hunters, recreation days, and recreation visitor days?
6. A national survey by the U.S. Fish and Wildlife Service estimated that there were 700 million recreation days of fishing in a recent year, excluding children under 12 years of age. Other than a few studies that suggest that children are as likely to fish as their parents, little is known about fishing by children. The national survey estimated that including children 9-12 years of age would increase recreation fishing days by 9.0 per cent. On this basis, it is reasonable to assume that including all children under 12 years of age would increase recreation fishing days by roughly 25 percent. Fishing recreation days average 4.0 hours in length. The problem is to convert the recreation days of fishing by all ages of the population to recreation visitor days. With this information, the Forest Service could estimate the proportion of total fishing provided by the agency. Note that the agency's recreation information system shows 18 million visitor days by fishermen of all ages.
7. One of the two largest ski areas in North America reported 1.3 million recreation days of skiing in a recent year. The estimate was based on daily tallies of the number of lift tickets issued during the 140 day season. Approximately 40 percent were multi-day ticket holders who actually skied 90 percent of the days to which they were entitled. Individuals reported an average of 5.0 hours skiing per day. First, correct the total number of recreation days of skiing reported. Then, convert recreation days to recreation visitor days.
8. Calculate the number of visits, recreation days and visitor days for two individuals: (1) arrives at the park at 6:30 PM Friday evening and departs at 6:30 PM Sunday; (2) arrives 9 AM on Saturday morning and departs at 9 PM Sunday evening. Discuss.
9. In the past, managers of parks and other recreation sites were primarily concerned with measuring the output of onsite recreation activities. More recently, several observers have suggested that the total recreation experience includes two types of indirect consumption which are only beginning to be measured. What are they?

10. Describe four characteristics of the services of a park or other recreation site that distinguish the production of recreation services from the manufacture of recreation equipment. How can consumer perception of the quality of recreation services be improved?

11. Managers define the physical capacity of recreation sites as the maximum number of persons who can occupy a site at one time. This physical measure of carrying capacity varies from the practical capacity of recreation sites. Define the concept of practical capacity and illustrate the implications for management.

CHAPTER FOUR

1. Define these terms: entrance fee, direct travel cost, travel time cost, opportunity cost of recreation time, and transfer cost.

2. The basic premise of the travel cost approach to demand for a recreation site is that per capita use will decrease as the roundtrip costs of travel increase, other things remaining the same. Assume the following: direct costs of automobile travel average 20 cents per mile, no entrance fees, single day trips, with three persons per household or vehicle, 40 miles per hour, and household travel time valued at $4 per hour. Estimate the effect of a 10-mile increase in one-way distance on the price per recreation day at the site. What proportion of this is time cost?

3. Assume conditions are identical to those in question 2 above, except that one-third of the users travel 120 miles one-way and stay two days. Their overnight lodging costs average $40 per household or vehicle. Re-estimate the effect of a 10 mile increase in one-way distance on the price per recreation day at the site: (1) to those who stay overnight, and (2) to the average or representative user of the site.

4. Consider the alternatives available to a Dallas, Texas, family of three persons planning a ski trip to Colorado. Their problem is to decide whether to ski at Vail, Winter Park, or Hidden Valley (located in Rocky Mountain National Park near the town of Estes Park). Travel costs would not change and can be ignored. Assume that the only costs that do change are food, lodging, and lift tickets. Daily food costs of $4 per person at home increase by 10 percent at Hidden Valley, 20 percent at Winter Park, and 40 percent at Vail. Assume that lift tickets are $25 per person at Vail, $20 at Winter Park, and $10 at Hidden Valley. Consult Table 4-6 for the lowest cost lodging in each area during the ski season. Sum the relevant prices per recreation day at the three ski areas. By how much would benefits from skiing at Vail and Winter Park have to exceed benefits from skiing at Hidden Valley to make their choice an efficient recreation economic decision?

5. A friend has asked you to help him make a decision whether to purchase backpacking equipment. The backpack, tent, sleeping bag, boots, cooking gear, and other necessary equipment he prefers cost $550. Your best estimate of average useful life is 10 years and salvage value, $50. Interest is 20 percent and annual maintenance is expected to average 5 percent of purchase price. The problem is that he is a freshman in college and if he works during in the summer, he will use the equipment only 10 days a year. If he does not find summer employment, he will use the equipment 30 days per year. Last summer he rented equipment for $5 per day. You check the want ads and find that suitable used equipment is available for $250, but at the end of five years of use, it would have no salvage value. Set up the structure of a decision. Advise your friend.

6. What is the distinction between short-run and long-run price? Define and explain when each concept is relevant to consumer decision making in recreation.

7. What three things must be decided before calculating depreciation costs on recreation equipment? How sensitive are the results to changes in the variables? Illustrate.

8. Distinguish between the gross expenditure measure of the price of recreation and the concept of total direct cost as price.

9. This is a thought question. You are asked to speculate about differences in the level and type of expenses that individual consumers would be expected to pay on day outings, overnight trips, and vacations.

CHAPTER FIVE

1. Define these terms: total benefit, marginal benefit, diminishing marginal benefit, economic decision rule, demand curve, ordinary demand curve, inverse demand curve, consumer surplus, and benefit cost ratios for individual consumers and for government recreation programs.

2. In the recent past, recreation has been a nonmarket service, provided free of any entrance fee or price in the usual sense. However, this does not mean that recreation does not have a price. Users incur expenses in the form of travel costs, added food, lodging, fishing and hunting licenses, etc. The sum of these direct expenses plus the value of the individual's time and effort are a surrogate for the price of

recreation. For rational consumers, price is equal to the marginal benefits of the last annual trip, but price is not a measure of the benefits of recreation. Consumer surplus is the recommended measure of the net benefits of public recreation; it is defined as the difference between total benefits and price. Estimate the representative individual's total annual consumer surplus from a recreation activity. What is the average consumer surplus per trip? Use the demand curve presented in Figure 5-1. Discuss.

3. Marginal benefits may diminish either rapidly or slowly as more trips are taken, depending on the nature of the recreation activity and consumer attitudes. Assume that it has been determined that the slope of an ordinary demand curve for individual anglers is -0.4 compared with -0.1 for hikers.

   ⬤therwise, conditions remain the same as in Figure 5-1. Average price is $20 per trip for five trips per year for both anglers and hikers. Diagram the two ordinary demand curves and discuss the effects of slope.

4. Assume that you are employed by a parks and recreation agency which receives the following letter, asking for information and advice:

   "My husband and I are typical campers in the Rocky Mountains and like a little comfort when we go. A salesman for camper trailers approached us last week with an offer that is hard to refuse. For $60 per month ($720 per year) we can lease a nice little trailer year around. Our old camping equipment is worn out and should be replaced. We don't know what camping costs us; we just enjoy it. You are experts on camping. Please advise us. Is this a good buy? What is the maximum we should pay for additional camping equipment? If we go ahead and buy the new unit, how many days a year should we plan to use it?"

   Your supervisor has asked you to prepare a reply to this request. The first thing you do is look up the literature on demand for camping. A national survey shows that the average user of developed campgrounds in the western United States camps 8.3 days per year, and the slope of an ordinary demand curve is -0.15. That's all the economic information you can find. Do your analysis on a 12 month basis for each of two people.

5. A backpacking enthusiast reported the following total benefits for additional days per trip. Assume that once travel costs for the trip are paid, additional days on the trail are free; i.e., no additional costs are incurred. Diagram the marginal benefit function per day. How many days per trip should this individual spend in the wilderness? Explain.

Days on Wilderness Trail per Trip	Total Benefits per Trip
0	$ 0
1	30
2	50
3	60
4	60
5	50

6. What is the price intercept and the slope of an inverse demand curve for cross-country skiing? A sample survey has revealed that consumer surplus averages $20 per trip and the representative individual takes 10 trips per year. If the direct cost or price is $20 per trip, what is the total benefit of cross-country skiing per year? What is the horizontal intercept for number of trips annually at zero price? If the slope of the inverse demand curve doubles, what is the effect on the average consumer surplus per trip?

7. The superintendent of a state park has asked you to estimate the effect of an increase in the price of gasoline on the number of recreation trips to the park. The slope of an ordinary demand curve for individuals visiting the park is -0.2 with an average of 5 trips per year. Price is expected to increase by $5 per trip. Last year there were 1 million visits (trips) to the park. Diagram the demand curve for the individual user and the aggregate demand curve for the recreation site. Discuss your results.

8. A representative sample of 1,500 households were interviewed as they left Yosemite National Park, California, in the summer of 1975. They reported direct cost or price per day in the park and maximum willingness to pay per household with improved management practices. Estimate the consumer surplus and consumer benefit cost ratio today with improved management practices and 50 percent inflation in the consumer price index. Assume the total number of household days remains the same.

616

Type of Use	Household Days, Thousands	Willingness to Pay per Day	Direct Cost or Price per Day, Dollars
Day Users	574	$51	$24
Back-country Camping	47	47	18
Developed Campgrounds	242	39	24
Low Cost Lodging	202	56	39
High Cost Lodging	109	76	71
Total House-hold Days	1,174	51	30

Discuss and illustrate the effects of a shift in consumer preference, reducing high cost lodging use by 50,000 household days and increasing back country camping by the same amount.

CHAPTER SIX

1. Define these terms: least squares regression, regression coefficient, mean of the variables, categorical (dummy) variable, standard errors of the coefficients, coefficient of determination, correlation coefficients, standard error of the estimate for the regression, heteroscedasticity, and multicollinearity.
2. What is the relationship between a demand function and a demand curve? What is a demand shift? What is a movement along a demand curve? Illustrate and explain.
3. Assume that the director of recreation programs for a government agency is not trained in applied economics, and has asked you to explain the following recreation demand function to him. Interpret the demand function and explain the use of the regression statistics provided. To what possible difficulties or shortcomings would you alert the director?

$$Q = 3.5 - 0.15P + 0.4Y + 0.06S + 0.6A$$
$$\quad\quad (-0.10)\quad (0.3)\quad (0.10)\quad (0.4)$$

where Q = trips per year; P = direct cost or price ($); Y = income ($1,000); S = price of substitutes and A = quality of the site.

$R^2 = 0.15 \quad F = 3.25$

Standard error of the estimate = 10.0

Mean price = $20 per trip; income = $25,000; substitute price = $30; and site quality index = 2.0.

4. A recent study of the individual demand for recreation use (Q) of a site reported the following individual demand function:

$$Q = 3.7 - .1P + .1Y + .054S$$

Where P = direct cost or price per trip, Y = household income ($1,000), and S = the direct cost or price of trips to substitute sites. Average income of the population of users is $20,000 per year and the average price of trips to substitute sites is $24.

Condense the demand function and derive a demand curve. Illustrate. Then, estimate total and average consumer surplus per trip when direct cost or price is $20 per trip. If there are 10,000 users per year, what is the annual benefit (consumer surplus)?

5. Managers of a National Park have prepared plans for next year that result in a $250,000 increase in the cost of operations. You have been asked if the expected increase in benefits will justify this increased cost?
   (a) How much will demand for recreation visits to the park increase next year? Assume that it is located in energy rich Wyoming where real income (after inflation) is expected to increase by $1,500 next year. The regression coefficient for each $1,000 increase in income is approximately 0.05 in an individual demand function. Last year the park had 3 million recreation days with an average of 5 days per individual user. Assume no other conditions change.
   (b) What are the average benefits per day of the added park use next year? Average individual use is 5 days per year and the regression coefficient for direct cost or price is -0.1 for the representative individual.
   (c) What is the benefit cost ratio for the increased cost of park operation? Is the added expenditure an efficient use of public revenues?
6. You are employed by a National Forest District that has two types of recreation use: dispersed roadless and developed campground. The daily demand for the site is:

Dispersed: $Q = 20 - .4P$
Developed: $Q = 100 - 5P$
Where $Q =$ visits per day and $P =$ direct cost or price per visit. What is the net value (consumer surplus) to each group if direct cost or price is $20 per visit? What is the average consumer surplus per visit of each type?
7. Regression analysis of observations for the past 30 years provides the following demand function for the recreation use of parks in a large metropolitan city. Estimate the total number of visits expected next year when the independent variables are predicted to have the following mean values.

Independent Variables	Mean Values	Regression Coefficients
Constant		50,000
Price (cents per visit)	300	-2,000
Income (dollars)	$25,000	15
Price of substitutes (cents)	650	1,000
Attractiveness (acres)	1,000	500
Population in market (persons)	1.5 mil.	.15

CHAPTER SEVEN

1. What determinants of demand should be included as independent variables in statistical demand functions for recreation? Why?
2. What is an inferior good? Illustrate and explain why some recreation activities appear to be inferior goods?
3. How does occupation affect participation in recreation?
4. The value of travel time and on-site recreation time represent important determinants of demand for recreation sites, at least for some individuals. Discuss the effects of time costs on recreation demand curves and consumer surplus estimates. Explain.
5. Define the concepts "substitute" and "complement" with respect to demand for recreation goods, services and activities. Illustrate. Why are these concepts are important to managers of recreation sites?
6. Studies of the demand for recreation sites should include measures of the physical characteristics of the sites that are relevant to individual users. Explain for downhill skiing.
7. Studies of crowding on peak days of recreation use have shown that the economic optimum number of users per day almost never equals the number that some managers or individual users would prefer. The superintendent of a state park has asked you to explain why efficient management would neither serve the most people nor provide the highest quality experience to individual users? Start by drawing a diagram showing why the economic optimum capacity represents a compromise solution in between these two objectives. Discuss.
8. Most empirical demand studies of recreation in the past have not included an effective taste and preference variable. The omission is due to the lack of an accurate general measure of preferences, rather than any conscious decision by economists that the variable is unimportant as a determinant of demand. What variables have economists used as a proxy for preferences? What direct measures of preferences have been tried? Discuss.

CHAPTER EIGHT

1. Define and illustrate the zonal travel cost method of estimating an ordinary demand curve for a recreation site. Under what conditions should it be used?
2. Davis originated the contingent valuation method (then called bidding game) in a study of household willingness to pay for fishing, hunting, and camping in the Maine woods. What did Davis find with regard to the effectiveness of alternative methods of payment? Compare it to the recommendations of the federal guidelines with respect to methods of payment. What did the first contingent valuation study of environmental quality (by Randall, Ives, and Eastman) find with respect to willingness to pay using alternative methods of payment?
3. Why are iterative questions recommended over open-ended questions when interviewing individuals about their willingness to pay for recreation opportunities and resources?
4. Income has attracted more attention than any of the other socioeconomic variables included in demand functions for recreation. Discuss the significance of the slope of demand curves for low and high income groups. Illustrate.
5. When the travel cost method is used to estimate a demand curve for recreation,

what direct costs should be included in the definition of price? What direct costs may be omitted without affecting the slope or area under the demand curve?

6. Define the terms: option value, existence value, and bequest value. What is the relation between these preservation values of the general population to actual recreation use value? Illustrate for wilderness protection.

7. Derive an ordinary demand curve for a recreation site from a unit-day value of $10 for individuals who take five trips per year to the recreation site. What is its slope?

8. How is a demand curve derived from contingent valuation questions that ask individuals to report their maximum willingness to pay per trip (on the average) for their current number of trips? Illustrate.

CHAPTER NINE

1. Define each of the following terms, giving both a written explanation and the equation: price elasticity, income elasticity, cross elasticity, point elasticity, and average arc elasticity.

2. A ski corporation is convinced that an increase in its price of lift tickets will not reduce its total annual sales. Can you tell from this whether the demand for its lift tickets is price elastic or price inelastic? Explain.

3. Suppose that the relationship between the direct cost or price and the number of visits demanded to a city park is as follows:

Direct Cost or Price (Dollars)	Quantity
1	8
2	7
3	6
4	5
5	4

What is the average arc elasticity of demand when price is between $1 and $2? Between $4 and $5?

4. It has been estimated that an increase in water pollution at Pine Lake, Wisconsin, from an index of 23 to 3 would cause individual recreation demand to fall from an average of 13.9 to about 10.1 days per year. What is the estimated "average" arc elasticity of demand with respect to water quality?

5. The National Park Service has asked you to serve on a study team to estimate the effect on demand of damages to visibility from the proposed construction of a large coal-fired power plant on the Kaiparowits plateau near Glen Canyon National Recreation Area in southern Utah. The resulting air pollution is expected to adversely affect visitors to the Grand Canyon National Park and six other sites within a radius of 60 miles. Assume visibility damages represent 6.6 percent of direct cost or price, and price elasticity of demand is estimated as -0.22. There are 2.9 million visits to the national recreation areas. What is the expected effect of damages to visibility on demand for recreation use?

6. According to the U.S. Department of the Interior, the income elasticity of demand for fishing is about 0.47. If real consumer incomes rise by 1 percent, what effect would this have on the quantity demanded of fishing?

7. London's West End is arguably the greatest live theater district in the world, housing 45 professional theaters. Yet, during the 1980-83 recession, 16 of these were closed and it is estimated only 6 of the remaining 29 had shows turning a profit during the 1980-1983 recession. A study concluded that one of the world's most cherished cultural assets and London's biggest nighttime tourist activity is dying because of rising operating costs, lower government funding, and rising taxation. In short, the necessity to increase ticket prices has resulted in dwindling attendance, according to this study.

You have been asked to evaluate the prospects for live theater in London. Assume that the price elasticity of demand is unitary -1.0, and the average price of theatre tickets is expected to increase 20 percent, in real terms (after inflation). At the same time, real income per capita is expected to rise by 20 percent, and studies have estimated income elasticity of demand as 2.0. Assume these are the only variables that change from 1983 to 1990. If these assumptions are realistic, can some independent theaters survive without government subsidies from the British Arts Council?

The British Sports Council has estimated that the income elasticity of demand for particular recreation activities as 0.5. Assume other conditions are identical to live theater. Can private recreation operators survive without government subsidies from the British Sports Council?

8. What do you think is the sign of the cross elasticity of demand for each of the following pairs of products: (a) fishing licenses and fishing poles, (b) downhill skis and

cross-country skis, (c) tea and coffee, (d) ski and ski boots, (e) tents and mobile homes? Why?

9. The U.S. Forest Service currently operates a developed campground charging a camping fee of $6 per night. Last year its occupancy averaged 100 sites per night. This year, an independent campground manager nearby cut the price of its camp-sites from $6.50 to $5.50 per night. As a result, occupancy of the Forest Service campground declined to only 80 sites per night. Estimate the cross elasticity of de-mand between the Forest Service campground and the independent campground.

10. A park superintendent has prepared a budget resulting in a $250,000 increase in costs of operation. Will expected benefits justify the increased costs?
   (a) By how much will recreation use of the park increase? Real income (after infla-tion) per capita is expected to increase by 3 percent. The income elasticity of demand for recreation days in the park is approximately 0.23. Last year, the park had 3 million recreation days. Assume no other conditions change.
   (b) What are the average benefits per day of the added park use? The typical park user is sightseeing on vacation. Average number of recreation days per partici-pant is 5.4 per year and the regression coefficient for price is -0.2.
   (c) What is the benefit cost ratio of the increase in cost of park operation? Is the added expenditure justified?

11. What is the distinction between short-run and long-run demand elasticities? Define each and illustrate the importance of the distinction.

12. What is the distinction between direct versus derived demand elasticities? Why is this important for recreation economic decisions?

CHAPTER TEN

1. Define the following terms: expected value, probability, state of nature, risk, uncer-tainty, queueing, option value, and individual risk neutral, risk averse, or risk seek-ing attitudes.

2. Discuss the evidence presented on the consumer's perceptions of risk in recreation. How do physical, psychological, and the other types of risk relate to economic measures of risk in recreation? Evaluate results of the empirical research from the viewpoint of your own experience and your impressions as to the experience of oth-ers.

3. Why does Randall conclude that it makes sense to measure option value in public benefit cost analysis? Define and illustrate the concept using a diagram of risk aver-sion. How do private decision makers use the concept of option value?

4. A fisherman is making plans for a trip next weekend to a national forest. The prob-lem is to decide between lake and river fishing, under conditions of risky water quality. Benefits (consumer surplus) for river fishing are $20 with clear water and minus $10 with dirty water during spring peak flow. Benefits of lake fishing are $12 with clear water and $5 with ice covering the lake. The fisherman estimates that there is an 80 percent chance of clear water in both cases. What is the expected value of consumer surplus for lake and for river fishing with (1) certainty of clear water, (2) uncertainty, and (3) risk as subjectively defined by the fisherman? Inter-pret your results.

5. A family is planning to leave this afternoon on a weekend trip to a state park and the problem is whether to take camping equipment and stay at a campground in the park or to stay at a private resort lodge nearby. It is too late to make reserva-tions. They estimate that there is .33 chance that the campground will be full when they arrive, in which case a standby campground may be used which lacks standard services. There is a .67 chance that the resort lodge will be full and they will have to stay in a rundown cabin resort which lacks standard services. What is the expect-ed value of benefits for each alternative with risk as subjectively defined by the household? Interpret your results.

Alternative	Possible Outcomes	
Accommodations	First Choice	Second Choice
Resort benefits	$30	$15
Campground benefits	$30	$15

6. Two tourists are searching for a campground in a recreation area. The first has time costs of $1.25 per additional campground searched, i.e., $1.25 for two camp-grounds, $2.50 for three campgrounds etc. Additional benefit from reduced camp-ing fees are $1.70 for searching for a second campground, $0.80 for a third, $0.50 for a fourth, $0.33 for a fifth, and $0.24 for a sixth. How many campgrounds would it pay this tourist to search for if he or she intends to stay (1) one night, and (2) two nights? A second tourist in a motor home has the same problem, except that his or her income is twice as high which results in the doubling of shopping time

cost from \$1.25 to \$2.50 per additional campground searched. How many campgrounds would it pay this tourist to shop if he or she intends to stay (1) one night, and (2) two nights?

7. The supervisor of interpretive programs at a park asks you to recommend at what rate of capacity utilization the visitor information centers should operate in the park. Consider the problem from the viewpoint of the visitor, park manager, and the public interest in maximizing social benefits relative to social costs. Identify the rate of capacity utilization preferred from each of these three viewpoints. Discuss.

Rate of Capacity Utilization	Average Waiting and Service Time Cost per Customer	
	Visitor	Agency
50 percent	\$0.40	\$1.80
60 percent	0.50	1.50
70 percent	0.66	1.29
80 percent	1.00	1.13
90 percent	2.00	1.00
95 percent	4.00	.95

Benefits equal \$2 per customer receiving information.

8. Managers in the wildlife division of a state seek to increase public use and benefits from game management programs. The division has limited resources and has asked you to prepare a risk analysis of its big-game management program. Suppose the managers are considering three alternative projects which would result in increased big-game hunting opportunities for (1) antelope, (2) elk, or (3) deer. The wildlife biologists would like to know the hunter benefits from each alternative and how benefits would vary with three levels of hunter success — (1) bag an animal, (2) shoot, but miss, and (3) do not see an animal.

(a) A recent study estimated hunter benefits under risk-free conditions. Select the alternative hunting activity which maximizes public benefit under risk-free conditions, that is, under certainty that hunters will be successful. Discuss.

	Possible Level of Hunter Success		
Alternative Project	Bag An Animal	Shoot, But Miss	Do Not See An Animal
		(Benefit per Hunter Day)	
Antelope Hunting	\$140	\$50	\$10
Elk Hunting	200	10	- 5
Deer Hunting	125	60	-10

(b) Suppose you are uncertain about the variability in hunter success. Calculate the expected value of each alternative based on the assumption that each state of nature (success) has an equal chance. Select the alternative hunting activity which maximizes public benefit under uncertainty. Discuss.

(c) It is possible to convert uncertainty to risk, the probability of which can be calculated from variability in past hunter success in the state. Suppose that the odds of shooting, but missing are .6, of bagging a big-game animal .3, and of not seeing a big-game animal, .1. Calculate the expected value of each alternative. Choose the alternative hunting activity which maximizes public benefit. Discuss.

(d) Suppose that the probability of hunter success varies among types of big-game animals. Recalculate the expected value of each alternative. Choose the alternative hunting activity that maximizes public benefit. Discuss.

	Probability of Hunter Success		
Alternative Project	Bag An Animal	Shoot, But Miss	Do Not See An Animal
Antelope Hunting	.8	.1	.1
Elk Hunting	.2	.2	.6
Deer Hunting	.4	.3	.3

(e) Suppose that the composite benefit function for game managers looks like that below for a risk-averse individual. Recalculate the above payoff matrix for risk into expected value adjusted for risk aversion. Select the alternative hunting activity that maximizes the expected value to risk averse game managers. Discuss. Note: The curve is intended to be a 45 degree angle for expected benefits of 0 to \$20. Assume that beyond expected benefits of \$60, the curve is flat.

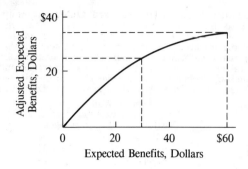

Adjusted Expected Benefits, Dollars (y-axis)

Expected Benefits, Dollars (x-axis)

CHAPTER ELEVEN

1. Define the following terms: time-series, explanatory variables, delphi technique, with and without comparison, market survey approach, simple regression method, multiple regression method, resource capacity method, and the two-step process of forecasting.

2. How has the demand for recreation in the United States changed since World War II? What are the prospects for future growth?

3. A report was summarized on the expected growth in recreation to the year 2030. Discuss its implications for the management of public recreation resources.

4. Explain three methods that have been used to forecast the future demand for recreation. Which method does the federal guidelines recommend, and why?

5. Forecast the future demand for a recreation site using linear and exponential growth curves. Assume that you are forecasting 5 years into the future. Historic information shows that annual consumption in the base year was 2 million visits, with annual growth of 100,000 visits or 5 percent per year. Discuss your results.

6. Another method of forecasting is from a multiple regression. Assume that inflation is under control so that the price level remains constant for the next five years. Also, assume that average income and total population does not change owing to a slow-down in economic growth. What would be your forecast of demand for city park recreation in 5 years if the only change between now and then is to add 2,000 acres of park land? Assume that the regression coefficient for acres in city parks is 500. There are 1 million visits to city parks now. What is the forecast number of visits in 5 years? Discuss your results.

7. The manager of a recreation site has read in the paper that expected increases in the price of gasoline will increase the direct cost or price of recreation days next year by 20 percent. Last year there were 1,000,000 recreation days at the site. The price elasticity of demand is approximately -0.2.
   (a) You are asked to forecast how many fewer recreation activity days will be demanded.
   (b) After you submit your results, the manager objects to your findings. He suggests that the price of substitute sites will also increase by 20 percent, with the result that more use will be made of the study site. The cross-elasticity of demand is approximately 0.3. How many more days will be demanded?
   (c) If these are the only two variables that change next year, what would be the net effect on study site use? Diagram your results.

8. Recently, a state legislature considered the possibility of increasing the speed limit on the state's major highways. The superintendent of a National Park in the state immediately asked for a supplemental budget allocation of $0.75 million to handle the expected increase in tourists traveling to the park next summer. You have been asked to estimate whether the expected benefits will justify the increased costs?
   (a) By how much will recreation use of the park increase if travel time decreases by 30 percent? The elasticity of demand with respect to travel time is estimated as -0.24 percent. Last year the park had 2 million visits. Assume no other conditions change.
   (b) The average consumer surplus per visit to the park is $12. What is the benefit cost ratio? Is the added expenditure justified?

CHAPTER TWELVE

1. Define the following terms: primary and secondary, direct and indirect, multiplier, input-output method, income transfer, and functional economic area.

2. Discuss the evidence presented in this chapter on the multiplier for recreation. How

does size of the region affect the multiplier and why? Discuss the other reasons why multipliers vary for recreation areas.
3. Why did Beardsley and other observers conclude that, in general, it does not make sense to include regional economic impacts of recreation in benefit cost analysis? What do the federal guidelines recommend with respect to regional economic impacts on employment?
4. Describe three basic steps in the application of the input-output method to the study of regional economic impacts. Why does this approach provide a more precise estimate of the multiplier than short-cut methods?
5. Millard and Fischer observed that the regional economic impact of an recreation facility is the net secondary effect of the development. This means that the costs imposed upon the region by the development should be subtracted from the secondary gains in regional income and employment. Discuss the significance of the costs of regional development.
6. Why are the expenditures for regional fishing and hunting trips by the residents of a region excluded from estimates of the economic impact of fishing and hunting on the regional economy?
7. The director of a government agency has asked you to estimate the regional economic impact of tourist visits to recreation sites in a state. The legislature has proposed that the agency's recreation budget for operations of a recreation program in the state be reduced from $1.5 million to $0.2 million, on grounds of financial efficiency in government. The director would like to know the regional economic impact of such a large reduction in the program. A demand study shows that tourist expenditures in the state would fall by 5 percent with the reduced program, which is equivalent to a loss of $50 million of tourist spending. The tourist spending multiplier is approximately 2.0. Net income is 30 percent of direct and indirect output or sales. State taxes are 5 percent of net income. Calculate the gain-loss ratio for the change in the recreation budget and change in tax revenues. Is the budget cut financially efficient? Advise the director and legislature.
8. Until recently, another state ranked 39th among the 50 states in the amount of money the state spent for tourist promotion, about $500,000. This year, the legislature appropriated $2.6 million to be used to advertise tourist attractions in the state. Tourists are expected to spend $150 million more as a result of the additional $2.1 million promotional program. The tourist spending multiplier is approximately 2.0. Net income is about 33 percent of direct and indirect sales, and state taxes are 3 percent of net income. Calculate the state government's gain-loss ratio for the added tourist promotion. Should the governor sign the tourist promotion bill, from the viewpoint of financial efficiency in government?

CHAPTER THIRTEEN

1. Define the following terms: fixed and variable costs, financial and economic analysis, short-run and long-run costs, internal and external costs, opportunity costs, and associated costs.
2. Describe the three methods of measuring costs — engineering economic, cross-sectional, and time-series. Which approach comes closest to the least-cost combination of inputs expressed in economic cost functions? Why?
3. Discuss the evidence presented in this chapter on the average costs of state parks and federal recreation sites. How does this information differ from the study of boat marina costs in Maryland? What are some implications for improving future cost studies for use in recreation economic decisions?
4. Define the cost-effectiveness approach to decision making and discuss when it should be used. What is the most important principle when experts assign effectiveness scores on a scale of value? What are the three basic types of cost-effectiveness studies?
5. Technological change shifts the long-run cost curves for park and recreation programs. Compare your own experience to that of your parents and grandparents with respect to available technology for recreational activity of your choice.
6. Economists distinguish between current inflating dollar values and real or constant dollar values. What is the relation between inflation and the interest rate? How do the federal guidelines recommend we treat inflation in benefit cost studies? Explain.
7. Describe the differences in the nature of fixed and variable costs for private and public recreation sites. What effect does this difference have on management decision making, both private and public, with respect to output and environmental quality?
8. Draw a breakeven chart for small and medium size ski areas based on information presented. Compare them to the breakeven chart for large ski areas. Discuss whether the increase in cash flow with increased size is explained by changes in cost and efficiency or price and revenue.

CHAPTER FOURTEEN

1. Define the following terms: competition, monopoly, monopolistic competition, oligopoly, price discrimination, and peak load pricing.
2. Discuss the history of pricing practices by local, state, and federal government for the 15-year period from 1967 to 1982. Why do you think user charges did not increase very much during this time?
3. The Land and Water Conservation Fund Act (1965) authorized charging user fees at federal recreation sites provided that they are consistent with six criteria. List and discuss four of them.
4. In the past, most studies of park and recreation programs concluded that average total costs were decreasing. More recently, as resources have become increasingly scarce relative to demand, emphasis has shifted to the case of increasing costs. What are the implications of decreasing and increasing costs for user fees and subsidies from general taxes?
5. Describe the reasons why the comparable prices charged by private and public agencies may need to be adjusted before they can serve as an effective standard for pricing policy.
6. Define the three degrees of price discrimination and illustrate the application of each in a recreation related industry. Which is most common today, and which would provide the most advantage to buyers and sellers? Why?
7. Evaluate the basic evidence presented in this chapter on the technological breakthrough, self service fee collection, and discuss its implications for user fee policy in the future.
8. What is the "benefits received" principle of taxation, and what are its implications for marginal cost pricing of parks and other outdoor recreation programs?
9. Assume that you have been employed by the Fish and Wildlife department of a state government. You are asked to estimate the damages to fish and wildlife resulting from a large water development project that would eliminate 5 percent of the wildlife in a region of 100,000 resident households. How much do you think the developer should be asked to pay in mitigation of the damages? Show your calculations and explain the basis for your estimate.

CHAPTER FIFTEEN

1. Define the following terms: discount rate, present value, planning period, and economic optimum size programs. Distinguish between the application of benefits and costs to decision making by individual consumers, managers of private business, and managers of public recreation programs.
2. Describe the benefit cost approach to decision making. Give the benefit cost formula and explain what it shows. What are benefits? What are costs?
3. Net present value is the best measure of what a prudent private investor could afford to pay for an asset. Explain. Is net present value the best measure of what a prudent government could afford to invest in a park or other recreation site? Why or why not?
4. In the past, U.S. government agencies used discount rates of 4, 6, 8, and 10 percent in the planning of recreation projects and programs. Describe the basis for each of these discount rates. Which do you prefer? Why?
5. A noted British natural resource economist, Mishan, suggested a way to treat future generations equitably when programs have very long-run consequences. Explain the problem and the solution. What is the effect of his adjustment on the magnitude of benefits?
6. It is generally true that the lower the discount rate, other things being equal, the higher the present value of benefits. Then why would a high discount rate encourage the preservation of wilderness areas and natural rivers, hunting, beach swimming, and the labor-intensive management of parks and other recreation areas (including interpretive programs and the like)?
7. Calculate the benefit cost ratio for the present value of benefits and costs from the purchase of park equipment with an initial investment cost of $200,000 operation and maintenance costs of $10,000 per year and benefits of $100,000 per year. Assume that the equipment has a useful life of 3 years and no salvage value. The discount rates are 4 percent and 10 percent.
8. A recent study of the demand for recreation visits (Q) to a state park reported the following individual demand function:

$$Q = 3.7 - 0.2P + 0.1Y + 0.108S$$

where P = direct cost or price per trip, Y = household income in thousands, and S = the direct cost or price of trips to substitute sites. Average income of the population of users is $20,000 per year and the average price of trips to substitute sites is $12.

624

Condense the demand function and derive a demand curve for the park. Illustrate. Then, estimate total and average consumer surplus per trip when direct cost or price is $10 per trip. If there are 10,000 visits per year, what is the present value of benefits for a 10-year program? Assume a discount rate of 6 percent.

Index

629

631

635

ABOUT THE AUTHOR

Richard G. Walsh teaches recreation economics at Colorado State University. He was educated at the University of Wisconsin where his Ph.D. dissertation dealt with the private development and management of recreation resources in the Lake States. He has been a professor at the University of Nebraska, visiting professor at the University of Maryland, intergovernmental exchange scholar at the Environmental Protection Agency, and consultant to the National Park Service, Forest Service, Bureau of Land Management, Federal Trade Commission, Department of Justice, and Office of Policy Analysis of the Department of the Interior. He has been an advisor to the Environmental Defense Fund, Sierra Club, American Wilderness Alliance, and other groups. He has testified before committees of the U.S. Congress and helped revise the Water Resources Council guidelines for measuring the benefits of recreation and environmental resources. He is author or co-author of four books and over 100 scientific papers and reports. He was awarded the American Agricultural Economics Association prize for outstanding published research. His biography is listed in Marquis, Who's Who in America, and Who's Who in the World.

Dr. Walsh is best known for his work comparing the benefits and costs of recreation and environmental quality programs. He completed empirical studies of the option, existence, and bequest values to the general population from preservation of air and water quality, wilderness areas, natural rivers, fish and wildlife, forest quality, and developed recreation facilities in the Rocky Mountains. He has studied the effects of water quality, water level, forest quality, and congestion on demand for recreation. He measured the potential benefits of reduced crowding during peak days of recreation use of rivers, lakes, trails, campgrounds, and ski areas. His latest work is a statistical forecast of the demand for fishing and hunting into the 21st century. These studies emphasize the importance of economics in managing recreation, wildlife, and related environmental resources for the future.